THIRD EDITION

INTRODUCTION TO
GLOBAL
POLITICS

Steven L. Lamy
University of Southern California

John Baylis
Swansea University

Steve Smith
University of Exeter

Patricia Owens
University of Sussex

New York   Oxford
OXFORD UNIVERSITY PRESS

Oxford University Press is a department of the University of Oxford.
It furthers the University's objective of excellence in research,
scholarship, and education by publishing worldwide.

Oxford   New York
Auckland   Cape Town   Dar es Salaam   Hong Kong   Karachi
Kuala Lumpur   Madrid   Melbourne   Mexico City   Nairobi
New Delhi   Shanghai   Taipei   Toronto

With offices in
Argentina   Austria   Brazil   Chile   Czech Republic   France   Greece
Guatemala   Hungary   Italy   Japan   Poland   Portugal   Singapore
South Korea   Switzerland   Thailand   Turkey   Ukraine   Vietnam

For titles covered by Section 112 of the U.S. Higher Education Opportunity
Act, please visit www.oup.com/us/he for the latest information about
pricing and alternate formats.

Published by Oxford University Press
198 Madison Avenue, New York, New York 10016
http://www.oup.com

Oxford is a registered trademark of Oxford University Press.

Library of Congress Cataloging-in-Publication Data
Lamy, Steven L.
   Introduction to global politics / Steven L. Lamy, University of Southern California;
John Baylis, Swansea University; Steve Smith, University of Exeter; Patricia Owens,
University of Sussex. -- Third Edition.
      pages cm
   Revised edition of: Introduction to global politics / Steven L. Lamy . . . [et al.].
   2012.
   ISBN 978-0-19-939388-6
1. Geopolitics. 2. World politics. 3. International relations. I. Title.
   JC319.L248 2014
   327--dc23
                                                             2014017046

9 8 7 6 5 4 3 2 1

Printed in the United States of America
on acid-free paper

To all our students—past and present—
who make this all possible.

Brief Contents

Contents

Preface xi
About the Authors xxi
Maps of the World xxv

CHAPTER 4: Critical Approaches 102

Stephen Hobden, Richard Wyn Jones, Patricia Owens,
Steve Smith, and Steven L. Lamy

PART III: GLOBAL ACTORS

CHAPTER 5: Making Foreign Policy 132

Steven L. Lamy

CHAPTER 6: Global and Regional Governance 170

Devon Curtis, Christian Reus-Smit, Paul Taylor,
and Steven L. Lamy

PART IV: GLOBAL ISSUES: SECURITY

CHAPTER 8: Security and Military Power 244
John Baylis, Darryl Howlett, and Steven L. Lamy

**PART V: GLOBAL ISSUES: POLITICAL
ECONOMY AND THE ENVIRONMENT**

Preface

WE HAVE WRITTEN THIS EDITION of *Introduction to Global Politics* with an increasingly interdependent world in mind. Perhaps the word "globalization" has become so overplayed that it has not retained much of its original force. And yet there is no unifying topic more important than globalization, no political trend of the same magnitude. Even our everyday decisions—those as seemingly trivial and isolated as what food to eat, what clothes to wear, what books to read, or what movies to see—affect the quality of life of everyone around us and of billions of people in distant countries. Meanwhile, decisions made around the world affect our daily life.

Not only is the world changing, becoming more complex and interconnected than ever before, but the nature of this course is also evolving. No matter what it's called—international relations, world politics, or global politics—the course has transformed in recent years, asking us to examine not only relations among countries but a broader context of global events and issues. In this book, we therefore take a global approach that fosters an awareness of and appreciation for a variety of worldviews. To quote the French writer Marcel Proust, we believe that "the real voyage of discovery consists not in seeking new landscapes but in having new eyes."

Our Approach

So what does it mean to take a "global" view of world politics? By this, we mean two things: First, this textbook brings together **academics from around the world**, drawing from a diversity of thought unmatched by other textbooks. Despite the range of views represented here, all of the contributors teach international relations courses, and we agree on emphasizing the challenges we all face as members of a global community. This book thus introduces students not only to the diversity of thinking in our field but to its common elements.

Second, we discuss in some detail the various **critical actors in global politics**. We explore the role of individual nation-states as well as international institutions such as the United Nations, the European Union, and critically important economic institutions, including the World Bank Group and the World Trade Organization. We carefully assess how different groups and individuals have shaped these global institutions, holding different views on how best to govern this world of nearly two hundred independent nation-states. We also explore the growing number and significance of **nongovernmental actors**, both multinational corporations such as Nike and McDonald's and nongovernmental organizations such as Oxfam and Doctors Without Borders. The entire world saw how important these actors are as we experienced several significant events early in the twenty-first century, including the global economic crisis that began in 2008; the 2010 earthquake that resulted in the devastation of Haiti and was one of the deadliest earthquakes of all time; and the 2011 earthquake, tsunami, and nuclear crisis in Japan, estimated to be the most expensive disaster in history. The field is changing as the world changes. With this new edition of *Introduction to Global Politics*, we hope to improve on the standard conversation; to bring the introductory course more in line with today's research; to ask (and try to answer) the kind of questions most relevant for students of world politics today.

This textbook will introduce students to the mainstream theoretical traditions of realism and liberalism (Chapter 3) and to critical approaches that are often left out of other texts, including constructivism, Marxism, feminism, and utopianism (Chapter 4). Our goal is to introduce students to all relevant voices so they can make an informed choice about how best to both explain and understand our world. We clearly lay out important theories so that they illuminate the actors and issues we discuss, rather than cloud them in further mystery. In short, we hope these pages will help each student develop a more informed worldview.

Learning Goals

An important assumption of this text is that *theory matters*. Every individual sees the world through theories and uses them to organize, evaluate, and critically review contending positions in controversial policy areas. Unfortunately, many people take positions that lack supporting evidence; they accept a statement or position as true or valid because it fits with their beliefs or reinforces what they believe to be true.

After completing a course using this text, students will know more about the global system, the most important global actors, and the issues that shape the priorities and behavior of states and other actors in that system. This text encourages students to approach global politics in an informed, well-reasoned, and theoretically grounded manner. Overall, the chapters in this edition focus on four core learning goals:

- **Goal One: To develop a comprehensive understanding of the various theoretical traditions in global politics and the roles they play.**
  After taking a course using this text, students should be able to
  - describe the core assumptions of mainstream positions held by realists and liberals, as well as critical approaches taken by constructivists, Marxists, feminists, and utopians.
  - identify the similarities and differences between these theories or approaches.
  - identify how someone with a particular worldview constructs the world in terms of policy priorities and responses to these problems.
- **Goal Two: To understand the relationship between theory and policy making or problem solving in global politics.** Students will come to see how realists, liberals, and critical theorists describe global policy challenges and will review their positions on how we should respond to these challenges.
- **Goal Three: To appreciate the diversity of worldviews and theoretical assumptions that may inform political situations.** Students will explore their own worldview as well as others and will come to understand how these views both limit and liberate.
- **Goal Four: To develop an understanding of the global system and thereby increase the capacity to act or participate at various levels within it.** Students will be able to
  - identify how power is organized, who the key players in the system are, and what role they play.
  - identify opportunities for civic engagement and participation in the policy processes at local and global levels.

In this edition, at the beginning of each chapter we identify specific learning objectives that stem from these overarching goals. The review questions at the end of the chapter check that students have met the learning objectives.

REVIEW QUESTIONS

1. Why do various groups decide to use terrorist tactics? Critical theorists might say it is because they are denied access to public resources and opportunities or because government fails to represent their interests. Do you agree? Would realists and liberals agree?
2. When did terrorism become a truly global phenomenon, and what enabled it to do so?
3. In what ways are the technologies and processes associated with globalization more beneficial to states attempting to stop violence or groups attempting to engage in terrorist attacks?
4. Given that terrorism has been both a transnational and a global phenomenon, why has it not been more successful in effecting change within target states?
5. Of all the factors that motivate terrorists, is any one more important than others, and if so, why?
6. What has changed in terrorism over the past half-century, and have any factors remained the same? If so, what are they and why have they remained constant?
7. What role does technology play in terrorism, and will it change how terrorists operate in the future? If so, how?
8. Are we exaggerating the problems presented by terrorists? Is the issue overblown? Explain.
9. What is the primary challenge that individual states and the international community as a whole face in confronting terrorism?
10. How can globalization be useful in diminishing the underlying causes of terrorism?

Organization

Introduction to Global Politics is divided into five parts. The first two parts are foundational, covering the basic **histories and theories** every student should know to be an informed and engaged citizen in this global society. The third part introduces the main **actors** on the world stage—from states, to intergovernmental organizations, to transnational actors and nongovernmental agencies. The final two parts focus on issues of crucial importance to the **security** and prosperity of the people in the world. We discuss war, terrorism, and human rights, and human security in our section on global security. In the last section of the book we focus on **political economy and the environment**, with an emphasis on trade, development, and environmental sustainability. Each chapter provides essential information about the issue area and presents case studies and worldview questions that encourage students to think about these issues from contending perspectives.

Pedagogical Features

To aid students with the development of their own, more well-informed worldview, we have supplied several **active-learning** features, outside of the main text, within every chapter. These boxed essays and other elements provide **discussion questions** and bring into sharp relief some of the unique themes of this book:

- **Global Perspectives**—Each one of these feature essays opens a window onto another part of the world, showing how other countries and world organizations perceive and manage global politics.
- **Theory in Practice**—These features examine real-world scenarios using a variety of theoretical lenses, demonstrating the explanatory power of theories in global politics.
- **Case Studies**—For a more in-depth analysis of a subject, students can turn to these boxed essays that delve into world events.
- **What's Your Worldview?**—These short, critical-thinking questions in every chapter challenge students to develop their own, more well-informed ideas about global actors and issues.
- **Thinking About Global Politics**—This feature at the end of each chapter presents in-class activities dealing with real-world political issues. These activities give students the opportunity to develop their critical-thinking skills and apply what they have learned. Each activity includes follow-up questions or writing prompts.
- **Engaging with the World**—These short boxes in the margin highlight opportunities to get involved with organizations and individuals working for positive change in the world.

Every part of this textbook has been developed with today's college student in mind. The book includes a number of integrated study aids—such as a **running glossary**, **review questions**, and **annotated lists of further readings** and **online resources**—all of which help students read and retain important information while extending their learning experience. Two opposing quotations open every chapter, setting up two sides of one possible debate for students to consider while reading. At the end of every chapter, rather than simply summarizing the contents for students, we provide a conclusion that requires

Engaging with the
WORLD
Reliefweb

This is a database of jobs, workshops, conferences, and courses in development, international policy, and assistance. It is a particularly useful resource for people who want to travel and to engage with the world. The majority of listings are conferences outside the United States, but there are over 400 listings most days. Check out reliefweb.int.

students to analyze the various topics and themes of the chapter a bit more critically, placing everything they have learned into a broader context across chapters. Students need to acquire strong critical-thinking skills; they need to learn how to make connections among real-world events they hear about in the news and the ideas they learn about in class—and so it is with these goals in mind that the authors and editors have developed this edition.

One last point with regard to pedagogical features: the art program has been carefully selected to support critical thinking as well; not only do we present a number of maps that offer unique global perspectives on historic events and modern world trends, but we have also incorporated data graphics and compelling photographs to engage students visually. The captions of many of these images include questions for further thought—once again connecting the reader back to the core content of the course, with an interesting prompt or relevant point.

New to This Edition

We have thoroughly updated this edition of *Introduction to Global Politics* in light of recent trends and events that are shaping our world, such as the ongoing Arab Spring, the rise of China, and the continuing effects of the global economic crisis. In addition, we have revised for more balanced coverage, and we have strengthened our focus on active learning. In making these revisions, we have taken into account the helpful comments from reviewers as well as our own experience using the first and second editions in our classes.

Revision Highlights

- We have threaded critical IR theories throughout the text more evenly and provided tables summarizing these perspectives alongside traditional IR theories.
- Revised Case Studies offer updated and further analysis on topics such as sexual violence and cyberterrorism.
- Specific learning objectives—which flow from the larger goals laid out in this preface—have been further supported in each chapter introduction and reflected in the review questions at the end of the chapter.
- Throughout the textbook, figures, tables, maps, timelines, and graphs, have been added, replaced, or updated with the latest and most accurate statistics, events, and information.
- We have significantly updated our photo program, replacing nearly half of the photos in the text to coincide with textual updates and keep pace with current events.

Chapter-by-Chapter Improvements

Chapter 1: Introduction to Global Politics

- New emphasis on the role social media and globalization of political activism plays in the outcry for human rights and democratic elections worldwide.
- A brief background and introduction into rational decision-making (as it pertains to politics and political decision making).

Chapter 2: The Evolution of Global Politics

- A brief list of 2013 world events including: the current depth and status of extreme poverty, the latest in climate politics and its relationship with rich and poor states, the aftermath of the Arab Spring (i.e. Egypt and Syria), the aftermath of the War in Afghanistan, the latest activity from religious extremist movements (i.e. Pakistan, Yemen, and Africa), and the attention or lack thereof paid to Nuclear Weapon Programs in Iran and North Korea.
- Further examination into the growing dynamics of international relations between nation-states such as India and China, and Germany and Russia.

Chapter 3: Realism and Liberalism
- The latest on the most pertinent international relations matters including North Korean political and military action and the foreshadowing consequences to Ukraine signing a free trade agreement with the European Union.
- Results from the 2012 NATO Summit (i.e. exit strategy for Afghanistan, establishment of a new "Smart Defense" initiative, and joint management of weapons, ammunitions, and other security resources.

Chapter 4: Critical Approaches
- Inclusion/Introduction to Kant and his Categorical Imperative as it pertains to Foreign Policy.
- Added examples of global social movements based on normative ideas like peace, justice, and ecological balance—i.e. Greenpeace's Arctic 30, the World Social Forum, the Global Fund for Women, and a global campaign to end Indian rape culture.

Chapter 5: Making Foreign Policy
- Further coverage and analysis on the UN Framework Convention on Climate Change.
- Added examples of NGO influence on humanitarian activities—i.e. Action Against Hunger, Doctors Without Borders, and UN resolution sponsored by the French government to prevent further conflict between Christian and Muslim rebel groups.

Chapter 6: Global and Regional Governance
- Revised *What's Your Worldview?* question boxes that address the complications to international/regional organization as well as the inability to address humanitarian challenges and disintegrating states without this organization.
- Inclusion and analysis of major global political events including, the Rio+20 Summit on Environmental Sustainability, and the joint agreement between the UN and the Organization for Prohibition of Chemical Weapons to transport chemical weapons out of Syria and destroy them.

Chapter 7: Nongovernmental Actors
- Added facts about the Occupy Movement and its lasting effects/legacy.
- Updated information to the Forms of INGO Power section, including new information on Information Politics, Symbolic Politics, Leverage Politics, and Accountability Politics.

Chapter 8: Security and Military Power
- Updated information on conflicts taken place in Africa, including: the war in the Democratic Republic of Congo where a ceasefire was agreed upon in late 2013; and, the new UN peacekeeping mission in the Central African Republic to prevent civil wars and sectarian conflicts that create what the UN calls "pre-genocidal" conditions.
- Added examples of the importance of collective action and reliance on international/regional organization—i.e. NATO-led peacekeeping forcing in Kosovo preventing ethnic violence before a 2012 election, NATO preventing piracy activity off the coast of Somalia, and the Peace and Civil Rights Movement offering alternative strategies and actions to the U.S. and NATO for ending wars like the one in Afghanistan.

Chapter 9: Terrorism
- Updated information on the spread of jihadists and Al Qaeda and the geographical extent to which the Obama Administration (and future administrations) will have to go to find them.
- Inclusion of the latest terrorist attacks (i.e. the Boston Marathon Attack) and the controversially expanded role given to American security agencies like the TSA and the NSA.

Chapter 10: Human Rights and Human Security

- Added information on latest human rights crises—i.e. Syria and South Sudan, as well as China who is enforcing regulation and censorship against freedom of press and speech.
- Updated information and analysis relating to the yearly Human Security Report and 2013 UN reports.

Chapter 11: International Political Economy

- Added analysis about government control over their nation's economy, free markets included.
- Updated statistics to charts and graphs including, the Real GDP Growth Chart, and the Volume of World Merchandise Exports graph.

Chapter 12: Global Trade and Finance

- Added analysis on the global economic interconnection—i.e. stocks in Japan dropping as a result to American stock activity in January 2014, and a November 2013 report by the OECD that predicts the Greek economy to shrink further, anticipating European Union intervention once again.
- Added concluding thoughts and analysis.

Chapter 13: Poverty, Development, and Hunger

- Inclusion of the latest global and anti-globalization movements including, the 39th G-8 Summit, the launching of the Big IF campaign to pressure the G-8 countries to increase funding for development and hunger projects, and the movement in Europe known as "Blockupy," which is critical of globalization and institutions that support and promote economic globalization.
- Updated information and analysis in regards to the status of Zimbabwe and their President Robert Mugabe.

Chapter 14: Environmental Issues

- Inclusion of the latest environmental issues including, the Shell oil company drilling in to the Arctic, the rising number of Carbon Emissions emitted on the planet, and the effect climate change is having on living organisms like bees (which are important for sustaining the balance of ecosystems).
- Added information and analysis of the Kyoto Protocol and the results that came from it, and new concluding thoughts and analysis.

Supplements

Oxford University Press offers instructors and students a comprehensive ancillary package for qualified adopters of *Introduction to Global Politics*.

Companion Website at www.oup.com/he/lamy

This open access companion website includes a number of learning tools to help students study and review key concepts presented in the text including learning objectives, key-concept summaries, quizzes, essay questions, web activities, and web links.

Ancillary Resource Center (ARC)

This convenient, instructor-focused website provides access to all of the up-to-date teaching resources for this text—at any time—while guaranteeing the security of grade-significant resources. In addition, it allows OUP to keep instructors informed when new content becomes available. Register for access and create your individual user account by clicking on the Instructor's Resources link at www.oup.com/he/lamy. Available on the ARC:

- **Instructor's Manual:** The Instructor's Resource Manual includes chapter objectives, a detailed chapter outline, lecture suggestions and activities, discussion questions, video resources, and web resources.
- **Test Item File:** This resource includes nearly 1,400 test items, including multiple-choice, short answer, and essay questions. Questions are identified as factual, conceptual, or applied, and correct answers are keyed to the text pages where the concepts are presented.
- **Computerized Test Bank:** Using the test authoring and management tool Diploma, the computerized test bank that accompanies this text is designed for both novice and advanced users. Diploma enables instructors to create and edit questions, create randomized quizzes and tests with an easy-to-use drag-and-drop tool, publish quizzes and tests to online courses, and print quizzes and tests for paper-based assessments.
- **PowerPoint Presentations:** Each chapter's slide deck includes a succinct chapter outline and incorporates relevant chapter graphics.

Course Cartridges

For qualified adopters, OUP will supply the teaching resources in a course cartridges designed to work with your preferred Online Learning Platform. Please contact your Oxford University Press sales representative at (800) 280-0208.

E-Book

Available through CourseSmart at www.coursesmart.com. CourseSmart's eTextbooks can be read on any browser-enabled computer or mobile device and come with the ability to transfer individual chapters or the entire book offline. Furthermore, CourseSmart was the first to introduce free eTextbook apps for the Android and Apple devices for an even better reading experience.

CNN Videos

Offering recent clips on timely topics, this DVD provides up to 15 films tied to the chapter topics in the text. Each clip is approximately 5–10 minutes in length, offering a great way to launch your lectures. Contact your local OUP sales representative for details.

Now Playing Video Guide

Through documentaries, feature films, and YouTube videos, *Now Playing: Learning Global Politics Through Film* provides video examples of course concepts to demonstrate real-world relevance. Each video is accompanied by a brief summary and 3–5 discussion questions.

Now Playing can be purchased separately or packaged for free with a new copy of this text. Qualified adopters Will also receive a Netflix subscription that enables them to show students the films discussed in the book.

The Student Research and Writing Guide for Political Science

This guide provides students with the information and tools necessary to conduct research and write a research paper. This brief guide gives students the basics on how to get started writing a research paper, explains the parts of a research paper, and presents the citation formats found in academic writing. *The Student Research and Writing Guide for Political Science* can be packaged for free with a new copy of this text or purchased separately.

Packaging Options

Adopters of Introduction to Global Politics can package **ANY** Oxford University Press book with the text for a 20 percent savings off the total package price. See our many trade and scholarly offerings at www.oup.com, then contact your local Oxford University Press sales representative to request a package ISBN.

- *Introduction to Global Politics*: *A Reader*, edited by John Masker, offers the best variety of readings, the best coverage of alternative theories, and the best price. Package it with this text and save your students 20 percent!

In addition, the following items can be packaged with the text for FREE:

- *Oxford Pocket World Atlas*, **Sixth Edition:** This full-color atlas is a handy reference for international relations and global politics students.
- **Very Short Introduction Series:** These very brief texts offer succinct introductions to a variety of topics. Titles include *Terrorism* by Townshend, *Globalization*, Second Edition, by Steger, and *Global Warming* by Maslin, among others.
- *Now Playing* **Video Guide:** Through documentaries, feature films, and YouTube videos, *Now Playing: Learning Global Politics Through Film* provides video examples of course concepts to demonstrate real-world relevance. Each video is accompanied by a brief summary and three to five discussion questions. *Now Playing* can be packaged for free with every new copy of this text. Qualified adopters will also receive a Netflix subscription that enables them to show students the films discussed in the book.
- *The Student Research and Writing Guide for Political Science:* This brief guide provides students with the information and tools necessary to conduct research and write research paper. The guide explains how to get started writing a research paper, describes the parts of a research paper, and presents the citation formats found in academic writing.

Please contact your Oxford University Press Sales Representative at (800) 280–0280 for more information on supplements or packaging options.

Acknowledgments

The authors wish to thank all members of Oxford University Press, in particular Jennifer Carpenter, executive editor, for her tireless sponsorship of this complex project, for her guidance, enthusiasm, and insights; Matt Rohal, editorial assistant, who worked efficiently to research art, prepare manuscripts, write copy, and secure permissions; senior production editor Theresa Stockton, who managed the project with skill and grace; Teresa Nemeth, copyeditor, provided the right amount of polish; and last but not least, art director Michele Laseau, who updated the book's inviting design for this edition. Beyond the individual authors and editors of this edition, Steve Lamy would like to thank his research assistants Katelyn Masket and Danika Newlee and his students in the School of International Relations at USC.

Likewise, there are many others who are unaffiliated with the authors and editors, who contributed to this new edition's shape and success as well.

We owe a debt of gratitude to the following people, who reviewed the previous two editions and have provided invaluable insight into putting together the past and future editions of this book:

Expert Reviewer and Supplements Author

John Masker, Temple University

Reviewers for the First Edition

Ali R. Abootalebi
University of Wisconsin, Eau Claire

Linda S. Adams
Baylor University

Klint Alexander
Vanderbilt University

Youngshik D. Bong
American University

Marijke Breuning
University of North Texas

Alsion Brysk
University of California, Irvine

Jeanie Bukowski
Bradley University

Manochehr Dorraj
Texas Christian University

John S. Duffield
Georgia State University

Michelle Frasher-Rae
Ohio University

Brian Frederking
McKendree University

Matthew Fuhrmann
University of South Carolina

David M. Goldberg
College of DuPage

Jeannie Grussendorf
Georgia State University

James R. Hedtke
Cabrini College

Jeanne Hey
Miami University

Jeneen Hobby
Cleveland State University

Arend A. Holtslag
University of Massachusetts, Lowell

Christopher Housenick
American University

Aida A. Hozic
University of Florida

Maorong Jiang
Creighton University

Michael D. Kanner
University of Colorado at Boulder

Aaron Karp
Old Dominion University

Joyce P. Kaufman
Whittier College

Bernd Kaussler
James Madison University

Howard Lehman
University of Utah

Steven Lobell
University of Utah

Domenic Maffei
Caldwell College

Mary K. Meyer McAleese
Eckerd College

Mark J. Mullenbach
University of Central Arkansas

William W. Newmann
Virginia Commonwealth University

Miroslav Nincic
University of California, Davis

Michael Nojeim
Prairie View A&M University

Richard Nolan
University of Florida

Asli Peker
New York University

Meg Rincker
Purdue University Calumet

Brigitte H. Schulz
Trinity College

Shalendra D. Sharma
University of San Francisco

David Skidmore
Drake University

Michael Struett
North Carolina State University

James Larry Taulbee
Emory University

Faedah Totah
Virginia Commonwealth University

John Tuman
University of Nevada, Las Vegas

Brian R. Urlacher
University of North Dakota

Thomas J. Vogly
University of Arizona

Kimberly Weir
Northern Kentucky University

Yi Yang
James Madison University

Reviewers for the Second Edition

Michael R. Baysdell
Saginaw Valley State University

Pamela Blackmon
Pennsylvania State University

Richard P. Farkas
DePaul University

Stefan Fritsch
Bowling Green State University

Robert F. Gorman
Texas State University, San Marcos

Jeannie Grussendorf
Georgia State University

Clinton G. Hewan
Northern Kentucky University

Carrie Humphreys
The University of Utah

Michael G. Jackson
Stonehill College

Michael D. Kanner
University of Colorado at Boulder

Greg Knehans
University of North Carolina at Greensboro

Lisa Kissopoulos
Northern Kentucky University

Cecelia Lynch
University of California, Irvine

Domenic Maffei
Caldwell College

Eduardo Magalhães III
Simpson College

Lawrence P. Markowitz
Rowan University

Emily Rodio
Saint Joseph's University

Anna M. Rulska
North Georgia College & State University

Maria Sampanis
California State University, Sacramento

Edwin A. Taylor III
Missouri Western State University

Alana Tiemessen
University of Massachusetts Amherst

Robert E. Williams
Pepperdine University

Reviewers for the Third Edition

We also owe a debt of gratitude to the following people who reviewed, and gave special attention to, this edition of the book:

Jennifer Bloxom
Colorado State University

Kevin J.S. Duska Jr.
The Ohio State University

John J. Jablowski Jr.
Penn State University

Paul A. Mego
University of Memphis, Lambuth

Alexei Shevchenko
California State University Fullerton

Veronica Ward
University State University

Winn W. Wasson
University of Wisconsin, Washington County

Expert Reviewer and Supplement Author

John Masker
Temple University

The book would not have been the same without the assistance and insight from these outstanding scholars and teachers. Meanwhile, any errors you may find in the book remain our own. We welcome your feedback and thank you for your support.

Steven L. Lamy
John Baylis
Steve Smith
Patricia Owens

About the Authors

Amitav Acharya is the UNESCO Chair in Transnational Challenges and Governance and Professor of International Relations at American University, Washington DC. He has been Professor of Global Governance at the University of Bristol, UK; Professor, Deputy Director, and Head of Research at the Institute of Defence and Strategic Studies (now S. Rajaratnam School of International Studies), Singapore; Professor of Political Science at York University, Toronto; and a Fellow of the Asia Center and the John F. Kennedy School of Government at Harvard University. He is author of *Whose Ideas Matter? Agency and Power in Asian Regionalism* (Cornell 2009) and *Human Security: The Concept and Its Implication* (Zhejiang University Press 2010, in Chinese), and recent articles dealing with international relations theory, norm diffusion, comparative regionalism, and Asian security in International Organization, World Politics, International Security, and International Studies Quarterly. He is co-editor of *Human Security: From Concept to Practice* (World Scientific 2011).

David Armstrong is Emeritus Professor of International Relations at the University of Exeter. His books include *Revolutionary Diplomacy* (California University Press 1977), *The Rise of the International Organization* (Macmillan 1981), *Revolution and World Order* (Clarendon Press 1993), *International Law and International Relations* (co-authored with Theo Farrell and Hélène Lambert; Cambridge University Press 2007), and *Routledge Handbook of International Law* (editor; Routledge 2009).

John Baylis is Emeritus Professor at Swansea University. Until his retirement in 2008 he was Professor of Politics and International Relations and Pro-Vice-Chancellor at the university. His PhD and DLitt are from the University of Wales. He is the author of more than twenty books, the most recent of which are *The Globalization of World Politics: An Introduction to International Relations* (5th ed. with Steve Smith and Patricia Owens; OUP 2010), *Strategy in the Contemporary World: An Introduction to Strategic Studies* (3rd ed. with James Wirtz and Colin S. Gray; OUP 2010), and *The United States and Europe: Beyond the Neo-Conservative Divide?* (edited with John Roper; Routledge 2006).

Alex J. Bellamy is Professor of International Relations and Executive Director of the Asia-Pacific Centre for the Responsibility to Protect at The University of Queensland, Australia. His books include *Understanding Peacekeeping* (with Paul D. Williams, 2nd ed. 2010), *The Responsibility to Protect: The Global Effort to End Mass Atrocities* (Polity 2009), and *Just Wars: From Cicero to Iraq* (Polity 2007). He is currently writing *Massacres and Morality: Mass Atrocities in an Age of Non-Combatant Immunity* (Oxford) and a book on implementing the Responsibility to Protect (with Sara E. Davies; Routledge).

Chris Brown is Professor of International Relations at the London School of Economics and Political Science and the author of *International Relations Theory: New Normative Approaches* (Columbia 1992), *Understanding International Relations* (Palgrave Macmillan 1997; 4th ed. 2009), *Sovereignty, Rights and Justice* (Polity 2002), and *Practical Judgement in International Political Theory* (Routledge 2010), as well as numerous book chapters and journal articles in the field of international political theory. He edited *Political Restructuring in Europe: Ethical Perspectives* (Routledge 1994) and co-edited (with Terry Nardin and N. J. Rengger) *International Relations in Political Thought: Texts from the Greeks to the First World War* (Cambridge 2002). A former Chair of the British International Studies Association (1998/99), he was Head of the Department of International Relations at LSE from 2004 to 2007.

Professor **Michael Cox** holds a Chair in International Relations at the London School of Economics and Political Science. He is the author, editor, and co-editor of over twenty books, including *Soft Power and US Foreign Policy* (Routledge 2010), *The Global 1989* (Cambridge University Press 2010), *US Foreign Policy* (Oxford University Press 2008), *Twentieth Century International Relations* (eight volumes; Sage 2006), *E. H. Carr: A Critical Appraisal* (Palgrave 2000), *A Farewell to Arms: Beyond the Good Friday Agreement* (2nd ed., Manchester University Press 2006), *American Democracy Promotion* (Oxford University Press 2000), *US Foreign Policy after the Cold War: Superpower Without a Mission?* (Pinter 1995), and *The Interregnum: Controversies in World Politics, 1989–1999* (Cambridge University Press 1999). His work has been translated into several languages, including Japanese, Chinese, Russian, Ukrainian, German, Italian, French, and Spanish. Formerly Chair of the European Consortium for Political Research (2006–2009) and Research Fellow at the Norwegian Nobel Institute in 2002 and 2007, he is currently Chair of the United States Discussion Group at Chatham House, London, and Co-Director of IDEAS, a Centre for the Study of Strategy and Diplomacy at the LSE.

Devon E. A. Curtis is Lecturer in the Department of Politics and International Studies at the University of Cambridge and a Fellow of Emmanuel College. Her main research interests and publications deal with power-sharing and governance arrangements following conflict, UN peacebuilding, the "transformation" of rebel movements to political parties in Africa, and critical perspectives on conflict, peacebuilding, and development.

Tim Dunne is Professor of International Relations in the School of Political Science and International Studies and is Research Director of the Asia-Pacific Centre for the Responsibility to Protect, University of Queensland. Previously he spent seven years at the University of Exeter, where he was Head of Politics and then Head of Humanities and Social Sciences. He has written and edited nine books. His most recent is the second edition of *International Relations Theories: Discipline and Diversity* (co-edited with Steve Smith and Milja Kurki; Oxford University Press 2010). He is an editor of the *European Journal of International Relations*, which is in the top five of its kind in the world.

Stephen Hobden is Senior Lecturer in International Politics at the University of East London, where he teaches courses on international relations theory and China's changing international role. He is currently working on a research project, together with his colleague Erika Cudworth, on complexity theory and international relations. This has resulted in the publication of a number of articles, together with the book *Posthuman International Relations: Complexity, Ecology and Global Politics* (Zed, 2011).

Darryl Howlett is Senior Lecturer in the Division of Politics and International Relations at the University of Southampton. His most recent publications include (with Jeffrey S. Lantis) "Strategic Culture," in *Strategy in the Contemporary World* (John Baylis, James Wirtz, Colin S. Gray, editors; 3rd ed., Oxford University Press 2010) and "Cyber Security and the Critical National Infrastructure,"

in *Homeland Security in the UK* (Paul Wilkinson, editor; Routledge 2007).

Richard Wyn Jones is Professor of Welsh Politics and Director of the Wales Governance Centre at Cardiff University. He has written extensively on Welsh politics, devolution, nationalism, and security studies. His book *Security, Strategy and Critical Theory* (Rienner 1999) is regarded as an important work in the area of critical theory. His most recent books are *Wales Says Yes: The 2011 Referendum and Welsh Devolution* (University of Wales Press 2012—with Roger Scully); (in Welsh) "Y Blaid Ffasgaidd yng Nghymru": Plaid Cymru a'r Cyhuddiad o Ffasgaeth (University of Wales Press 2013), and *The Fascist Party in Wales? Plaid Cymru, Welsh Nationalism and the Accusation of Fascism* (University of Wales Press 2014).

James D. Kiras is Associate Professor at the School of Advanced Air and Space Studies, Maxwell Air Force Base, Alabama, where he has directed the School's course of instruction on irregular warfare for almost a decade. He is also Senior Fellow of the Strategic Studies Division at the Joint Special Operations University, Tampa, Florida, and worked for a number of years in the defense policy, counterterrorism, special operations, and consulting world. Dr. Kiras publishes and lectures on subjects including special operations, irregular warfare, and suicide bombing. His most recent book, co-authored with other contributors, is *Understanding Modern Warfare* (Cambridge University Press 2008). Dr. Kiras's first book was entitled *Special Operations and Strategy: From World War II to the War on Terrorism* (Routledge 2006).

Steven L. Lamy is Professor of International Relations in the School of International Relations at the University of Southern California. He is also the Vice Dean for Academic Programs in the College of Letters, Arts and Sciences. His latest research focuses on religion and international relations and is funded by a grant from the Luce Foundation. A book of foreign policy case studies will be published next year.

Anthony McGrew is Professor and Dean of Humanities and Social Sciences at Strathclyde University, Glasgow. He has written extensively on globalization and global governance and is currently working on a project on China and global governance.

Patricia Owens is Reader in the Department of International Relations at the University of Sussex. She was a

Visiting Professor at UCLA and has held research fellowships at Oxford, Princeton, UC–Berkeley, and the University of Southern California. She is author of *Between War and Politics: International Relations and the Thought of Hannah Arendt* (Oxford 2007).

Christian Reus-Smit is Professor of International Relations at the European University Institute, Florence. He is author of *American Power and World Order* (Polity Press 2004) and *The Moral Purpose of the State* (Princeton University Press 1999), co-author of *Special Responsibilities: Global Problems and American Power* (Cambridge University Press, 2012), editor of *The Politics of International Law* (Cambridge University Press 2004), and co-editor of *The Oxford Handbook of International Relations* (Oxford University Press 2008), *Resolving International Crises of Legitimacy* (special issue, *International Politics* 2007), and *Between Sovereignty and Global Governance* (Macmillan 1998).

Brian C. Schmidt is Associate Professor of Political Science at Carleton University, Ottawa, Canada. He is the author of *The Political Discourse of Anarchy: A Disciplinary History of International Relations* (SUNY 1998), *Imperialism and Internationalism in the Discipline of International Relations*, co-edited with David Long (SUNY 2005), and *International Relations and the First Great Debate* (Routledge 2012).

Len Scott is Professor of International History and Intelligence Studies at Aberystwyth University. His recent publications include: An International History of the Cuban Missile Crisis: A 50-year Retrospective (London: Routledge, 2014), co-edited with David Gioe and Christopher Andrew; The Cuban Missile Crisis and the Threat of Nuclear War: Lessons from History (London: Continuum Books, 2007); and Intelligence and International Security: New Perspectives and Agendas (London: Routledge, 2011), co-edited with R. Gerald Hughes and Martin Alexander.

Sir Steve Smith is Vice Chancellor, and Professor of International Relations, at the University of Exeter. He has held Professorships of International Relations at the University of Wales, Aberystwyth, and the University of East Anglia and has also taught at the State University of New York (Albany) and Huddersfield Polytechnic. He was President of the International Studies Association for 2003–2004 and was elected to be an Academician of the Social Sciences (AcSS) in 2000. He was the editor of the prestigious Cambridge University Press / British International

Studies Association series from 1986 to 2005. In 1999 he received the Susan Strange Award of the International Studies Association for the person who has most challenged the received wisdom in the profession. He is the author or editor of fifteen books, including (with the late Professor Martin Hollis) *Explaining and Understanding International Relations* (Oxford University Press 1989) and (co-edited with Ken Booth and Marysia Zalewski) *International Theory: Positivism and Beyond* (Cambridge University Press 1995), and some one hundred academic papers and chapters in major journals and edited collections. From 2009 to 2011 he was President of Universities UK.

Paul Taylor is Emeritus Professor of International Relations and, until July 2004, was the Director of the European Institute at the London School of Economics, where he specialized in international organization within the European Union and the United Nations system. Most recently he has published *The End of European Integration: Anti-Europeanism Examined* (Routledge 2008), *International Organization in the Age of Globalization* (Continuum 2003; paperback version June 2005), and *The Careless State* (Bloomsbury 2010). He is a graduate of the University College of Wales, Aberystwyth, and the London School of Economics.

The late **Caroline Thomas** was Deputy Vice-Chancellor and Professor of Global Politics at the University of Southampton. She specialized in North-South relations and published widely on the global politics of security, development, environment, and health.

John Vogler is Professor of International Relations in the School of Politics, International Relations and Environment (SPIRE) at Keele University, UK. He is a member of the ESRC Centre for Climate Change Economics and Policy. His books include *The Global Commons: Environmental and Technological Governance* (John Wiley 2000) and, with Charlotte Bretherton, *The European Union as a Global Actor* (Routledge 2006). He has also edited, with Mark Imber, *The Environment and International Relations* (Routledge 1996) and, with Alan Russell, *The International Politics of Biotechnology* (Manchester University Press 2000).

Nicholas J. Wheeler is Professor of International Relations and Director of the Institute for Conflict, Cooperation, and Security at the University of Birmingham. His publications include (with Ken Booth) *The Security Dilemma: Fear, Cooperation, and Trust in World Politics*

(Basingstoke: Palgrave Macmillan 2008); (edited with Jean-Marc Coicaud) *National Interest versus Solidarity: Particular and Universal Ethics in International Life* (Tokyo: United Nations University Press 2008); (with Ian Clark) *The British Origins of Nuclear Strategy 1945–55* (Oxford: Oxford University Press). He has also written widely on humanitarian intervention and is the author of *Saving Strangers: Humanitarian Intervention in International Society* (Oxford: Oxford University Press, 2000). He is currently researching a book provisionally entitled *Trusting Rivals: Alternative Paths to Security in the Nuclear Age* as part of a 3-year ESRC/AHRC Fellowship on 'The Challenges to Trust-Building in Nuclear Worlds" through RCUK's "Global Uncertainties: Security For All in a Changing World" program. He is co-editor with Professor Christian Reus-Smit of the prestigious Cambridge Series in International Relations.

Ngaire Woods is Professor of International Political Economy and Director of the Global Economic Governance Programme at Oxford University. Her recent books include *Networks of Influence: Developing Countries in a Networked Global Order*, with Leonardo Martinez-Diaz (Oxford University Press 2009); *The Politics of Global Regulation*, with Walter Mattli (Oxford University Press 2009); *The Globalizers: the IMF, the World Bank and Their Borrowers* (Cornell University Press 2006); *Exporting Good Governance: Temptations and Challenges in Canada's Aid Program*, with Jennifer Welsh (Laurier University Press 2007); and *Making Self-Regulation Effective in Developing Countries*, with Dana Brown (Oxford University Press 2007). She has previously published *The Political Economy of Globalization* (Macmillan 2000); *Inequality, Globalization and World Politics*, with Andrew Hurrell (Oxford University Press 1999); *Explaining International Relations since 1945* (Oxford University Press 1986); and numerous articles on international institutions, globalization, and governance. Ngaire Woods has served as an adviser to the IMF Board, the UNDP's Human Development Report, and the Commonwealth Heads of Government.

MAPS

OF THE WORLD

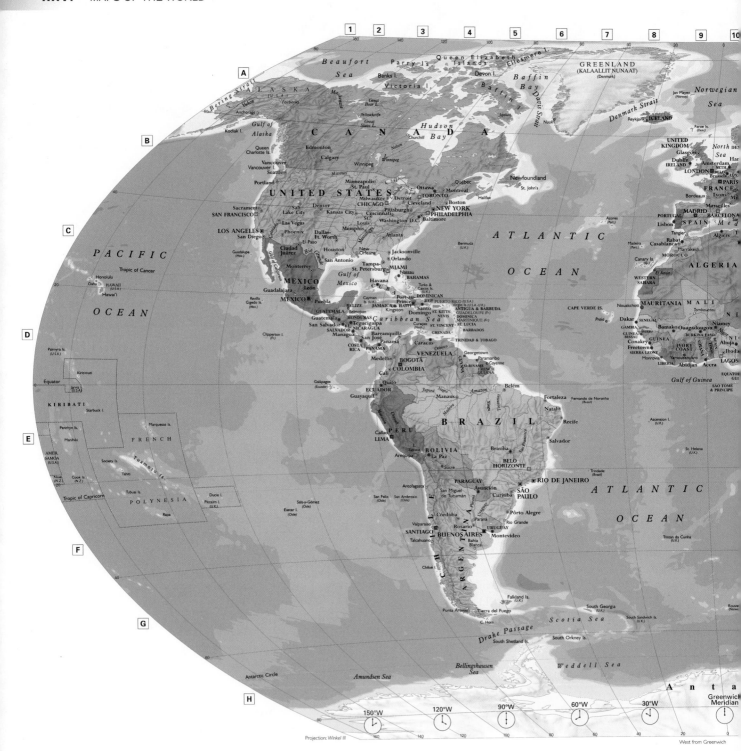

Projection: Winkel III

West from Greenwich

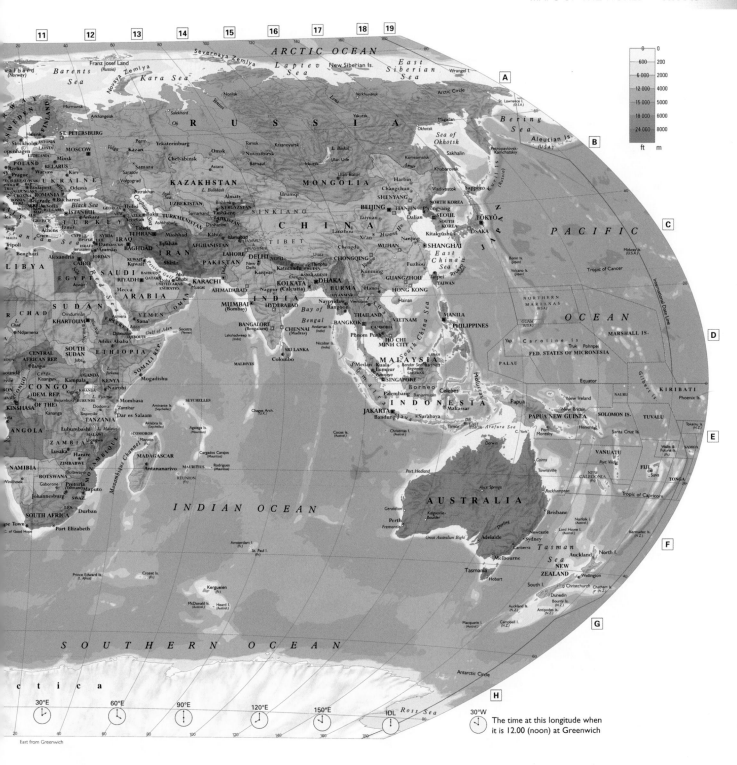

ARCTIC OCEAN

Barents Sea — Franz Josef Land (Russia) — Severnaya Zemlya — Laptev Sea — New Siberian Is. — East Siberian Sea — Wrangel I. — Arctic Circle

Kara Sea — Novaya Zemlya — Norilsk — Yenisey — Lena — Yakutsk — Verkhoyansk — St. Lawrence I. (U.S.A.)

Svalbard (Norway) — NORWAY — SWEDEN — FINLAND — Murmansk — Arkhangelsk — Ob — Salekhard — Magadan — Okhotsk — Bering Sea — Aleutian Is. (U.S.A.)

Helsinki — ST. PETERSBURG — Perm — Yekaterinburg — Omsk — Tomsk — Krasnoyarsk — Sea of Okhotsk — Sakhalin — Petropavlovsk-Kamchatskiy

Stockholm — ESTONIA — LATVIA — MOSCOW — Volga — Kazan — Novosibirsk — Barnaul — Irkutsk — Ulan Ude — Komsomolsk — Kuriles (Russia)

Copenhagen — LITHUANIA — Minsk — RUSSIA — Samara — L. Baikal — Amur — Khabarovsk — Sapporo

POLAND — BELARUS — Kiev — Saratov — Chelyabinsk — Astana — MONGOLIA — Ulan-Bator — Harbin — Vladivostok

Berlin — Warsaw — UKRAINE — Volgograd — Astrakhan — KAZAKHSTAN — L. Balkhash — Almaty — Ürümqi — Changchun — SHENYANG — NORTH KOREA — Pyongyang — PACIFIC

Prague — Odessa — Aral Sea — Bishkek — Tashkent — SINKIANG — BEIJING — TIANJIN — Dalian — SOUTH KOREA — SEOUL — TŌKYŌ

Budapest — Bucharest — Black Sea — GEORGIA — Tbilisi — UZBEKISTAN — Bukhara — KYRGYZSTAN — Taiyuan — Hwang — Kitakyūshū — ŌSAKA

Belgrade — Sofia — BULGARIA — Baku — Samarkand — Dushanbe — CHINA — Lanzhou — Xi'an — Nanjing — SHANGHAI — OCEAN

GREECE — ISTANBUL — Ankara — ARM. — Yerevan — TURKMENISTAN — Ashkhabad — TIBET — Chengdu — WUHAN — East China Sea — Bonin Is. (Japan)

Athens — Izmir — TURKEY — Mashhad — AFGHANISTAN — Kābul — Islamabad — NEPAL — CHONGQING — Fuzhou — Volcano Is. (Japan)

Tripoli — CYPRUS — SYRIA — TEHRAN — DELHI — Kathmandu — BHUTAN — Kunming — GUANGZHOU — TAIPEI — Tropic of Cancer

Benghazi — Beirut — Damascus — IRAQ — Eşfahān — PAKISTAN — New Delhi — Kanpur — Ganges — BANGLADESH — HONG KONG — TAIWAN

Alexandria — ISRAEL — Amman — BAGHDAD — IRAN — Shīrāz — LAHORE — JAMMU — KASHMIR — Lhasa — Hainan — NORTHERN MARIANAS (USA)

CAIRO — JORDAN — KUWAIT — Kuwait — BAHRAIN — Qatar — AHMADABAD — Nagpur (Calcutta) — KOLKATA — BURMA — Hanoi — MANILA

LIBYA — EGYPT — SAUDI — RIYADH — QATAR — UNITED ARAB EMIRATES — Doha — Abu Dhabi — KARACHI — INDIA — DHAKA — MYANMAR — Rangoon — PHILIPPINES — MARSHALL IS.

Aswân — Red Sea — Mecca — ARABIA — Muscat — OMAN — MUMBAI (Bombay) — HYDERABAD — Naypyidaw — THAILAND — VIETNAM — GUAM (USA) — Caroline Is. — Truk — Pohnpei

CHAD — SUDAN — Omdurman — KHARTOUM — YEMEN — Sana'a — Socotra (Yemen) — BANGALORE (Bengaluru) — Bay of Bengal — BANGKOK — CAMBODIA — Yap — FED. STATES OF MICRONESIA

N'Djamena — ERITREA — Aden — Gulf of Aden — Djibouti — Asmara — BANGALORE — CHENNAI (Madras) — Andaman Is. (India) — Phnom Penh — HO CHI MINH CITY — South China Sea — PALAU

CENTRAL AFRICAN REP. — SOUTH SUDAN — ETHIOPIA — Addis Ababa — SOMALIA — Lakshadweep (India) — SRI LANKA — Nicobar Is. (India) — MALAYSIA — Medan — Kuala Lumpur — NAURU — KIRIBATI

Bangui — CONGO — UGANDA — KENYA — Nairobi — Mogadishu — MALDIVES — Colombo — Sumatra — Kuala — SINGAPORE — Borneo — Celebes — Equator — Phoenix Is.

CONGO (DEM. REP. OF THE) — RWANDA — BURUNDI — Victoria — Mombasa — SEYCHELLES — Amirante Is. (Seychelles) — Palembang — Banjarmasin — Makassar — New Ireland — Gilbert Is.

KINSHASA — Kampala — L. Victoria — Dodoma — Dar es Salaam — Aldabra Is. (Seychelles) — Chagos Arch. (U.K.) — INDONESIA — JAKARTA — Bandung — Surabaya — Papua — PAPUA NEW GUINEA — SOLOMON IS. — New Britain — TUVALU

ANGOLA — ZAMBIA — TANZANIA — L. Malawi — Agalega Is. (Mauritius) — Cocos Is. (Austral.) — Java — Timor — Arafura Sea — Port Moresby — Santa Cruz Is. — Tokelau (N.Z.)

Lubumbashi — Lusaka — MALAWI — Lilongwe — COMOROS — Mayotte — Cargados Carajos (Mauritius) — Christmas I. (Austral.) — TIMOR-LESTE — C. York — Darwin — SAMOA

NAMIBIA — Harare — ZIMBABWE — Bulawayo — MOZAMBIQUE — MADAGASCAR — Antananarivo — MAURITIUS — Rodrigues (Mauritius) — VANUATU — Wallis & Futuna Is. (Fr.)

BOTSWANA — Pretoria (Tshwane) — Maputo — SWAZ. — REUNION (Fr.) — Cairns — NEW CALEDONIA — FIJI — Port Vila — Suva — TONGA

Windhoek — Gaborone — Johannesburg — LES. — AUSTRALIA — Townsville — Port Hedland — Rockhampton — Tropic of Capricorn — Norfolk I. (Austral.)

SOUTH AFRICA — Durban — Alice Springs — Brisbane — Lord Howe I. (Austral.)

Cape Town — Port Elizabeth — of Good Hope — Prince Edward Is. (S. Africa) — Crozet Is. (Fr.) — Amsterdam I. (Fr.) — St. Paul I. (Fr.) — Geraldton — Kalgoorlie-Boulder — Great Australian Bight — Perth — Fremantle — Adelaide — Darling — Newcastle — Sydney — Canberra — Tasman Sea — Auckland — North I. — Kermadec Is. (N.Z.)

INDIAN OCEAN — Kerguelen (Fr.) — McDonald Is. (Austral.) — Heard I. (Austral.) — Melbourne — Tasmania — Hobart — NEW ZEALAND — South I. — Christchurch — Dunedin — Chatham Is. (N.Z.) — Bounty Is. (N.Z.) — Antipodes Is. (N.Z.)

SOUTHERN OCEAN — Macquarie I. (Austral.) — Campbell I. (N.Z.) — Auckland Is. (N.Z.) — Ross Sea

Antarctica — Antarctic Circle

30°E — 60°E — 90°E — 120°E — 150°E — IDL — 30°W

East from Greenwich

The time at this longitude when it is 12.00 (noon) at Greenwich

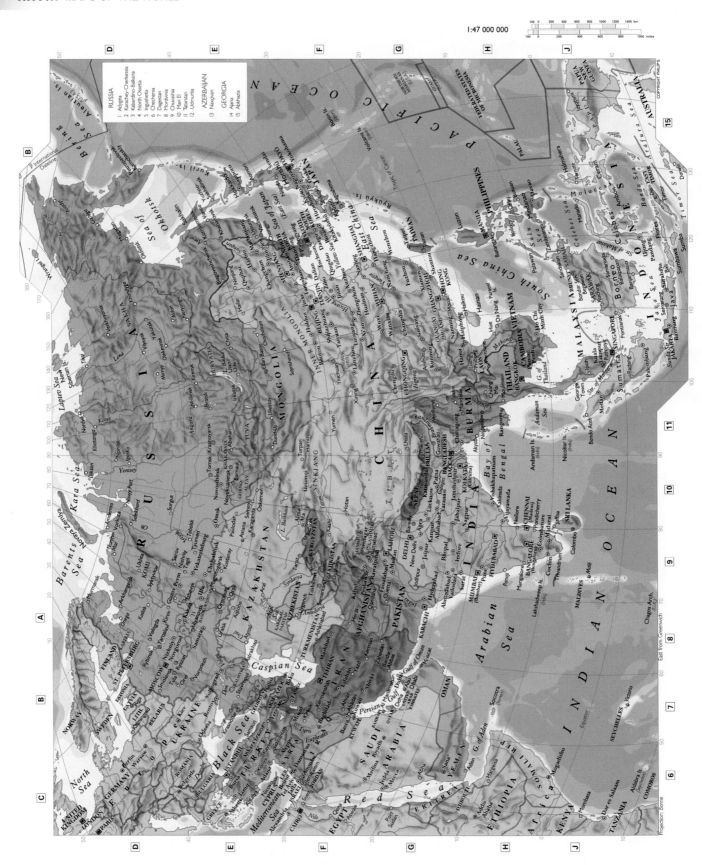

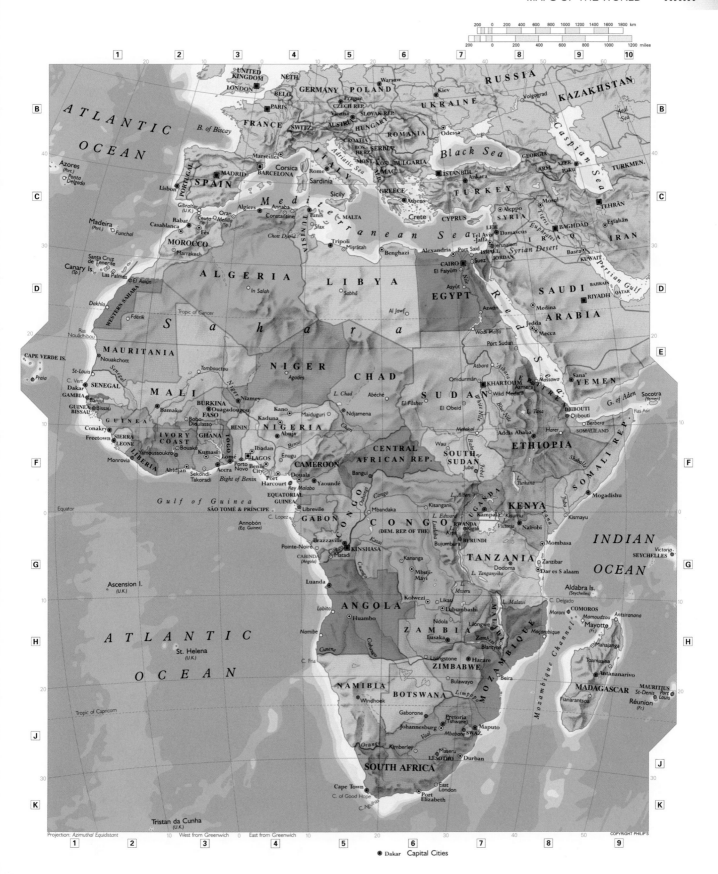

Projection: Azimuthal Equidistant

West from Greenwich | East from Greenwich

COPYRIGHT PHILIP'S

● Dakar Capital Cities

1:35 000 000

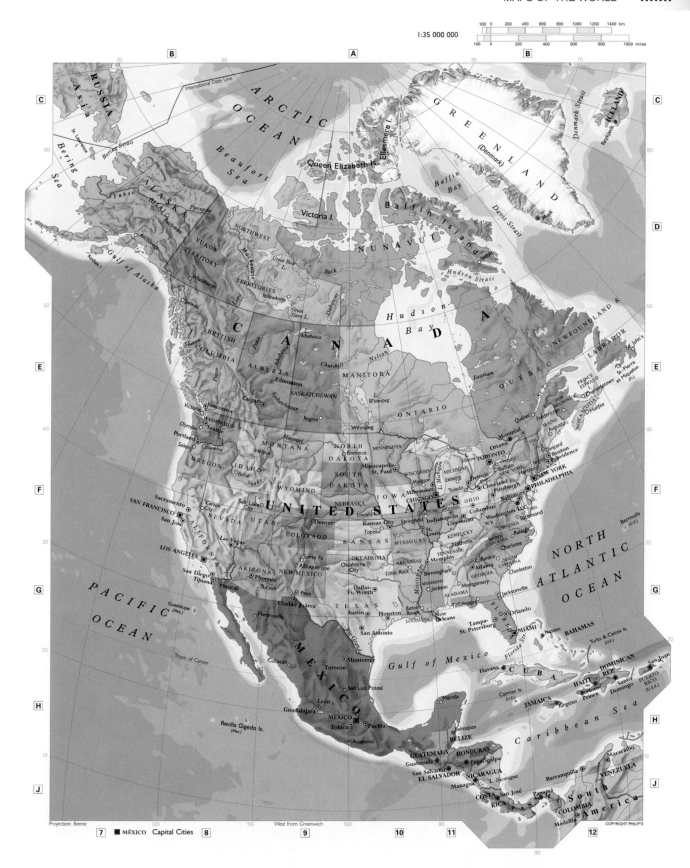

Projection: *Bonne*

■ MÉXICO Capital Cities

West from Greenwich

COPYRIGHT PHILIP'S

1:35 000 000

Projection: Lambert's Azimuthal Equal Area

COPYRIGHT PHILIP'S

■ LIMA   Capital Cities

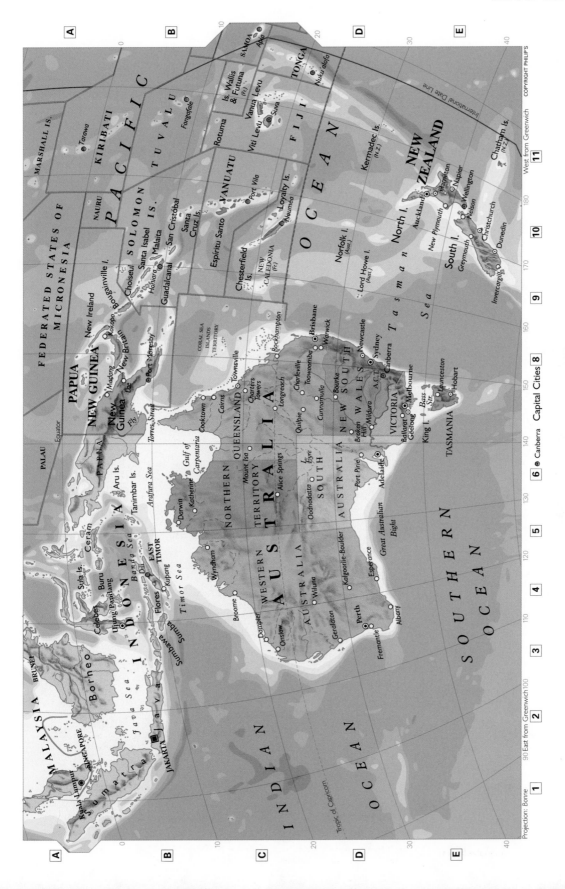

Projection: Bonne

Foundations

In this part of the book, we provide foundational context to help you make sense of globalization. We have two main aims: first, we want to introduce you to *the main aspects of globalization*, which we do beginning in Chapter 1. Then, in Chapter 2, we give you *an overview of the evolution of global politics* from the Peace of Westphalia in 1648 through the beginning of the twenty-first century. Before delving into the study of global politics, it's important to have some basic understanding of these main historical developments as well as some context for thinking about the contemporary period of world history. Chapter 2 covers historical information that's interesting in its own right, but our second aim in both of these introductory chapters is to highlight the *main themes of international history*. You will begin to develop a deeper understanding of the issues, both theoretical and empirical, that the remaining three parts of this book address. The context we provide here lays the groundwork for thinking about globalization: Is it a new phenomenon that fundamentally changes the main patterns of international history, or are there precedents for it that make it seem less revolutionary?

When you finish reading and discussing this first part of the book, you should have a better understanding of globalization and its potential impact on your life and the lives of those in distant lands. For example, you should be able to describe in some detail how globalization shapes economic, political, cultural, and social relations within and among nation-states. You should also have a better understanding of how critical historical events and the actions of individuals, nonstate actors (e.g., Apple Computers and Amnesty International), and nation-states have shaped current global politics.

Antigovernment demonstrators march in Moscow, Russia, in February 2012. Clearly, these demonstrations are influenced by social media and the globalization of political activism. What role do these two elements play?

1 | Introduction to Global Politics

I am a citizen of the world.

—Diogenes

I am not a citizen of the world . . . I am not even aware that there is a world such that one could be a citizen of it. No one has ever offered me citizenship, or described the naturalization process, or enlisted me in the world's institutional structures, or given me an account of its decision procedures . . . or provided me with a list of the benefits and obligations of citizenship, or shown me the world's calendar and the common celebrations and commemorations of its citizens.

—Michael Walzer

Who will lead the world in this century, in this era of globalization? Will the American empire come to an end because of its internal economic problems? Will China or India assume the mantle of leadership, and will this new global leader be willing to set aside national interests for the good of the global system? Although both India and China are emerging as major economic players, both have millions of citizens mired in poverty, and each country has significant domestic challenges that may preclude an activist role in global politics. We need to remember that the United States and its alliances have created a global system that has provided opportunities for most countries to prosper. This is not to say, however, that the current system does not struggle with significant global challenges, such as how to help the "bottom billion," the poorest billion people in the world. But will the new superpowers take responsibility for providing the material and resources needed to manage global problems?

The world is changing, and that change is not only about terrorist networks or the end of the Cold War. Globalization—especially economic globalization—has dramatically reshuffled global power arrangements and created new alliances and coalitions with the power to shape our well-being. This is still a world without a central government, but we all depend on the willingness of some states to lead and manage the institutions essential to controlling the processes of globalization. At the same time, we expect our governments to provide security and opportunities for economic growth, and that is not easily done in this era. Who will lead is one question, and who can afford to lead is maybe an even more

Prime Minister Singh and Premier Li sign an agreement in October 2013 aimed at containing border disputes between their armies. Both countries have aspirations for regional and global leadership.

important question. Still, the global war on terrorism, with tremendous costs in terms of blood and treasure, continues to shape foreign policies of most states. And we know that all nation-states are being dramatically affected by the global economic crisis, which is pinching the wealthy and crushing those without the natural and human resources necessary to compete.

How many of us can remember where we were when we first heard of the subprime mortgage crisis? Was it the summer of 2007, when analysts warned of the impending collapse? Maybe it was in the autumn of 2008, as major banks around the world vanished overnight and the Bush administration struggled to stem the hemorrhage of money in the United States. Perhaps you know people who lost their homes to foreclosure. This persistent global economic crisis threatens to do more damage to the world's financial system than the terrorist events of 2001, 2004, and 2005, yet few of us can explain what is occurring.

Currently, Europe is battling its own debt crisis, which threatens the entire global financial system. This crisis started in 2009 with Greece's inability to stabilize its finances. The euro area, made up of seventeen nation-states, agreed to give the Greek government a bailout of some 110 billion euros ($145 billion) in May 2010, and additional rounds of bailouts in October 2011 and March 2012 followed. Despite these bailout efforts, the debt crisis spread rapidly to Italy, Spain, Portugal, and Ireland. Germany is taking the lead to stabilize the euro, prevent the collapse of Greece, and contain the crisis. Many of the world's leading economies, like the United States and China, have been asked to help, but they are not willing to commit resources or to assume risks if changes are not made in the fiscal policies of the struggling countries. The financial crisis that erupted in 2008 and resurfaced in 2010 in Europe was driven by two false beliefs: that housing prices would never fall and that sovereign governments would never default on their debts.

How we react to momentous events like terrorist attacks and the global financial collapse of 2008–2012 is linked to how we identify ourselves. Are you a citizen of the world, like Diogenes, or a citizen of a specific place, like Michael Walzer? You might be surprised to know how connected you are to the world. Look at the labels in your clothing. The tag says "Made in someplace," but have you ever wondered how the pieces of your sneakers, for example, got to the factory where they were assembled? Or how the shoes traveled from that factory in Asia to the store in California, Kansas, Texas, or Vermont where you purchased them? Have you ever asked yourself who made your sneakers? How does that person live? How do others in the world view the United States or other wealthy and powerful states? How you are connected goes beyond looking at the goods and services you purchase in a given day. Do you have a passport and have you traveled internationally? Do you have a web-capable cell phone and are you constantly plugged into Internet applications like Facebook? Are you on Skype talking to friends you met while on a study abroad program? Have you signed up for news alerts from news agencies? Do you also read the international news from foreign sources such as the BBC or Al Jazeera? Do you belong to a global nongovernmental organization (NGO) like Human Rights Watch, Oxfam, or Greenpeace?

All of us have connections to the world that we are not aware of. Other connections we make, like joining a political group or student club on campus, are more personal and immediate. Yet both types of connections—known and unknown—help shape our identities as individuals in the wider world. The purpose of this book is to help you understand the world of politics that provides those connections. Along the way, you will see how interdependent we all are and how our way of life is shaped by forces of globalization.

We need to remember that globalization is a multidimensional process. Economic or market globalization involves processes of trade, production, and finance that are pushed by communications, technology, and the networking of national markets into a global economy (Stack and Hebron 2011). Political globalization is the spread of political ideas, values, norms, practices, and policies. Those who study globalization also look at its impact on the state and the ability of the state to do what is expected by its citizens. There are two positions here: (1) *hyperglobalists,* who see the state losing sovereignty and sharing power with other actors, and (2) *skeptics,* who believe that states can use globalization to enhance their power and authority.

Perhaps as important as economic globalization is cultural globalization. This involves the spread of popular culture, in areas such as music, film, literature, and consumerism, and the global diffusion of more traditional cultural ideas found in religious and ethnic communities. Globalization is a powerful force that will challenge the authority of both state and nonstate actors in a variety of policy sectors.

This chapter presents an overview of the textbook—the main actors and topics that we will examine. It also introduces the theories that will guide us in our study of global politics. You will learn more about globalization, and you will begin that important journey of discovery by developing new eyes. You will begin to see how different theories construct our world.

Introduction

Probably more than any other series of events, the ongoing economic crisis and the terrorist events of **September 11, 2001** (hereafter 9/11), in the United States, as well as those of March 11, 2004, in Madrid and July 7 and 21, 2005, in London, brought home just how globalized the contemporary world is. The subsequent war in Afghanistan and the particularly controversial invasion of Iraq in 2003, followed by insurgency and civil war, are further clear examples of what it means to call the current era globalized; they involved international coalitions and transnational violent networks in conflicts that linked events in seemingly unrelated parts of the world. Let us look at how aspects of these terrorist attacks illustrate the impact of globalization.

First, 9/11 was an event taking place in one country, the United States, but immediately observed throughout the world; the television pictures of the second plane crashing into the World Trade Center are probably the most widely seen images in television history. Thus, 9/11 was a world event, which had far more of an effect than represented by the number of deaths involved (about 3,000 died in the four attacks that day; on an average day, 30,000 children throughout the world die of malnutrition and preventable diseases, though not often, of course, in the gaze of television cameras). The Madrid and London attacks

September 11, 2001 The day Islamic terrorists in the United States hijacked four passenger jets, crashing two into the World Trade Center in New York, one into the Pentagon, and one into a field in Pennsylvania; also known as 9/11.

People in New York City gather near Ground Zero, the site of the 9/11 terrorist attacks, to celebrate the news of Osama bin Laden's assassination by US Navy Seals in May 2011.

seemed to underscore the seriousness of those who wanted a war against Western culture and its political and economic dominance.

Second, the attacks in the United States were carried out by nineteen individuals in the name of a previously shadowy organization known as Al Qaeda. This organization was not a state or formal international body but a loose coalition of committed men based, it was claimed, in more than fifty countries. This was a truly globalized network and not a traditional organization. The London and Madrid attacks were also directed or inspired by Al Qaeda.

Third, the attacks were coordinated by using some of the most powerful technologies of the globalized world—namely, mobile phones, international bank accounts, and the Internet. Moreover, the key personnel traveled regularly among continents, using yet another symbol of globalization, mass air travel.

Fourth, the reactions to the events throughout the world were intense, instantaneous, and very mixed: in some Arab and Muslim countries, there was jubilation that the West generally, and the United States specifically, had been hit; in many other countries, there was profound shock and an immediate empathy with the attacked countries.

Fifth, with respect to the 9/11 attacks, they were not on ordinary buildings; the Pentagon is the symbol of US military power and hegemony, and the World Trade Center was (as the name implies) an icon of the world financial network and the triumph of capitalism led by the United States and other Western countries.

Sixth, it is worth noting that although the 9/11 attacks targeted the United States, many individuals of other nationalities were killed; it is estimated that citizens from about ninety countries were killed in the attacks on the World Trade Center.

Finally, though there is a lot of disagreement over why Osama bin Laden ordered the attacks, the main reasons seem to have concerned events in yet other parts of the world; bin Laden himself cited the plight of the Palestinians, as well as the continued support of the United States and its allies for the current Saudi regime and the presence of US advisers on that country's "holy" soil. Therefore, although there are many indicators that the world has become increasingly globalized over the last thirty-five years, in many ways, 9/11 and the European attacks are the clearest symbol.

Still, globalization can also be seen as one of the causes of these attacks. In many parts of the world dominated by traditional cultures and religious communities, fundamentalists see globalization as a Western process bringing popular culture and Western ideas that undermine their core values and beliefs. This "Westoxification" pushed and promoted by globalization is the enemy, and the United States is the leader of this noxious process. Many fundamentalist communities are trying to control, manage, and, if possible, stop the process of globalization. This is possible in totalitarian societies, but it is becoming more difficult as the Internet and global communications spread around the world. The recent upheavals in North Africa and the Middle East—the so-called Arab Spring—were organized using social networks like Facebook and messaging services like Twitter. Change agents across the globe are certainly aided by new communication technologies, and these are transboundary tools that states cannot effectively contain.

Generally, people care most about what is going on at home or in their local communities. We usually elect people to office who promise to provide jobs, fix roads, offer loans for housing, build good schools, and provide quality healthcare. These promises may get candidates votes, but people in office soon learn that many of the promises cannot be fulfilled without considering the dynamics of the global economy.

Leaders are now realizing that to provide for their citizens they must manage the processes of globalization, and this is not a task one country can do alone. Not since the energy crisis of the early 1970s has the world experienced the costs of global interdependence and the vulnerabilities created by globalization. We all became aware of the breadth and depth of globalization with the economic crisis that began in 2008 and has continuing effects in 2014. The costs of this global financial crisis are unemployment, home foreclosures, bank failures, a collapse in the stock markets around the world, and a general anger and dissatisfaction with political leaders for failing to anticipate these problems and respond before the near collapse.

Presently, fears of a European recession could grow worse if a rescue plan for Greece does not work. The potential failure of the plan threatens to derail any stock market rally in the United States and to hinder global economic growth and recovery. Governments and regional organizations like the European Union must prove they can regulate global finance and manage the processes of globalization. World leaders have met in a number of settings, including G-20 meetings in Washington, D.C., and Pittsburgh; London, England; Toronto, Canada; Seoul, South Korea; and Cannes, France. These leaders are now hoping that government spending might stimulate demand and that they can work together to regulate global finance. Further, they hope to direct more funds to countries in the developing world and reform the global institutions that must monitor and manage the forces of globalization. Slowly, people throughout the world are realizing that their own well-being or quality of life is directly tied to the well-being of others in distant lands.

Again, the aim of this book is to provide an overview of global politics in this globalized world. Let us start, though, with a few words about the title. It is not accidental. First, we want to introduce you to global politics as distinct from international politics or international relations (a distinction we will explain shortly). Second, many think the contemporary, post–Cold War world is markedly different from previous periods because of the effects of globalization. We think it is especially difficult to explain global politics in such an era because globalization is a particularly controversial term. There is considerable dispute over just what it means to talk of this being an era of globalization and whether it means the main features of global politics are any different from those of previous eras. In this introduction, we explain how we propose to deal with the concept of globalization, and we offer you some arguments for and against seeing it as an important new development in global politics.

Before turning to look at globalization, we want to cover two areas to set the scene for the chapters that follow. We will first say something about the various terms used to describe international relations, world politics, and global politics, and then we will spend some time looking at the main ways global politics has been explained.

Russian President Putin and German Chancellor Merkel meet in Moscow. Although they have strong economic ties, Chancellor Merkel was not afraid to criticize the Russian human rights record and now Germany has voiced its opposition to Russia's annexation of Crimea.

global politics The politics of global social relations in which the pursuit of power, interests, order, and justice transcends regions and continents.

international relations The study of the interactions of states (countries) and other actors in the international system.

nongovernmental organization (NGO) An organization, usually a grass-roots one, with policy goals but not governmental in makeup.

transnational actor Any nongovernmental actor, such as a multinational corporation or one country's religious humanitarian organization, that has dealings with any actor from another country or with an international organization.

government The people and agencies that have the power and legitimate authority to determine who gets what, when, where, and how within a given territory.

nonstate actor Any participant in global politics that is neither acting in the name of government nor created and served by government. Nongovernmental organizations, terrorist networks, global crime syndicates, and multinational corporations are examples.

multinational corporation or enterprise (MNC/MNE) A business or firm with administration, production, distribution, and marketing located in countries around the world. Such a business moves money, goods, services, and technology around the world depending on where the firm can make the most profit.

International Relations and Global Politics

Why does the title of this book refer to **global politics** rather than to international politics or **international relations**? These are the traditional names used to describe the kinds of interactions and processes that are the concern of this text. You could look at the table of contents of many other introductory books and find a similar listing of main topics, yet, often, these books would have either "international relations" or "international politics" in their main title. Furthermore, the discipline that studies these issues is nearly always called international relations or international politics.

Our reason for choosing the phrase *global politics* is that it is more inclusive than either of the alternative terms. With this phrase, we mean to highlight our interest in the politics and political patterns in the world, and not only those among nation-states (as the term *international politics* implies). We are interested in relations among organizations that may or may not be states—such as, for example, multinational companies, terrorist groups, or **nongovernmental organizations (NGOs)**; these are all known as **transnational actors**. Although the term *international relations* does represent a widening of concern from simply the political relations among nation-states, it still restricts focus to *inter-national* relations. We think relations among, say, cities or provinces and other **governments** or international organizations can be equally important. So we prefer to characterize the relations we are interested in as those of world politics—or more specifically, given the powerful influences of globalization, global politics.

However, we do not want such fine distinctions regarding word choice to force you to define politics too narrowly. You will see this issue arising time and time again in the chapters that follow because many academics want to define politics very widely. One obvious example concerns the relationship between politics and economics; there is clearly an overlap, and a lot of bargaining power goes to the person who can persuade others that the existing distribution of resources is simply economic rather than political. So we want you to think about politics very broadly for the time being. Several features of the contemporary world that you may not have previously thought of as political will be described as such in the chapters that follow. Our focus is on the patterns of political relations, defined broadly, that characterize the contemporary world.

Global Actors

After reviewing the foundational and theoretical aspects of global politics in Parts One and Two, we will take a close look in Part Three at a number of important actors on the world stage. Because nation-states (countries) are the most important actors in global politics, we begin our discussion with them in Chapter 5. These are the actors that engage in diplomatic relations, sign the treaties that create the legal foundation for world politics, and go to war.

Increasingly, however, **nonstate actors** are playing important roles in global politics. These can be international or regional organizations that are composed of states. The United Nations (Chapter 6) is the most famous actor in this category; others include the European Union, the Organization of American States (OAS), the Shanghai Cooperation Organization, and the African Union. **Multinational corporations (MNCs)** have also become important players in world politics. These large business organizations can have their headquarters in one country, their design staff in another, and their production facilities in several other countries. Multinational corporations are important in many ways but perhaps most significantly because a factory can provide vital jobs in a developing country.

Starting in Chapter 7, we'll provide an in-depth look at these and other nonstate actors, including a discussion of nongovernmental organizations, which have increased in numbers and influence in global politics. Nongovernmental organizations like Oxfam or World Vision provide expertise for policy makers and provide programs and resources to address global problems like poverty and global health issues. To clarify the difference, some authors call MNCs for-profit nonstate actors and NGOs not-for-profit nonstate actors. We will also look at foundations and research think tanks that are playing more important roles in global politics. Finally, we will explore the role played by individuals, including celebrities who become involved in diplomacy. To lay the groundwork for that future discussion, let's take a moment now to look more closely at the definitions—and debates—involving states and nation-states, as well as consider the problems of the traditional state-centered approach to studying global politics.

Like many of the terms used in the study of global politics, the terms *state* and *nation-state* can be somewhat confusing to newcomers to the field. The two parts of the term nation-state derive from different sources. **Nation** derives from the idea that a group of people sharing the same geographic space, the same language, the same culture, and the same history also share a common identity. As most political scientists use the term, nation conveys a group identity that is bigger than a family group or tribal unit. **State** has its origins in Latin and in the legal system of the Roman Empire. In political science, state is a particularly divisive term because, as we will see in Chapters 3 and 4, academics disagree about what the term means. At a minimum, political scientists agree that the state is the highest-level political structure that makes authoritative decisions within a territorially based political unit. What makes the term confusing for many students in the United States is that the country comprises subunits that are called "states." When

nation A community of people who share a common sense of identity, which may be derived from language, culture, or ethnicity; this community may be a minority within a single country or live in more than one country.

state A legal territorial entity composed of a stable population and a government; it possesses a monopoly over the legitimate use of force; its sovereignty is recognized by other states in the international system.

Wal-Mart, a global corporation, sells manufactured goods made in China in every store in America and now has several supercenters in China. Do you think they are selling American-made goods in these stores?

nation and state are combined in the pair nation-state, we have a term that describes a political unit within which people share an identity. It is important to note that *the state is not always coincidental with a nation.* While the state for many political scientists is a set of governing institutions, *nation* refers to the people who share a history, language, religion, or other cultural attributes. The Flemish in Belgium, the Welsh in the United Kingdom, and the Iroquois of the United States and Canada are examples of nations found within states. Most states, even when called nation-states, actually comprise several nations. As we will see in this book, many problems in the modern international system result from nations with historical rivalry that are forced to live within the borders of one state.

The concepts of state and sovereignty are critical to understand if you are a student of international relations, a diplomat, or a political leader. The **nation-state**—sometimes called "country" or simply "state"—is the primary unit of analysis in the study of international relations. As we will discuss in Chapter 2, the Peace of Westphalia (which ended the Thirty Years' War in 1648) recognized the state as supreme and the sovereign power within its boundaries. The Westphalian ideal of sovereignty emphasizes the principle of the inviolability of the borders of a state. Furthermore, all states agreed with the idea that it was not acceptable to intervene in the internal affairs of other states. **Sovereignty** is a complex and contested concept in international relations; essentially, it suggests that within a given territory the leaders of a state have absolute and final political authority. However, international relations scholar Manuel Castells (2005) has suggested that the modern nation-state might be adversely affected by globalization in four ways; indeed, all our political institutions are facing the same four crises.

1. States cannot effectively manage global problems unilaterally and thus suffer a *crisis of efficiency.*
2. Policy makers are not always representative of their citizens' interests, and as policy making becomes more global, decisions are made further away from citizens. This is a *crisis of legitimacy.*
3. Citizens are being pulled toward their cultural identity and toward identity and affiliation with NGOs and other civil-society actors. A variety of forces pull them away from citizen identity and have created a *crisis of identity.*
4. Globalization has increased inequality in many states and created a *crisis of equity.*

Castells argues that nation-states must create collaborative networks with NGOs and other nonstate actors to respond effectively to these crises. The nation-state will survive, but states might be forced to share sovereignty with other global actors to provide for their citizens, meet their obligations, and face the issues in the world today.

Global Issues

In Part Four, we will turn to global issues, demonstrating the connections among state and nonstate actors in the international system and considering how these global issues are inextricably linked. First, we consider international security and military power—that is, the traditional responsibility of countries to provide for the physical security of the state's territory. Second, we examine terrorism, including the various groups that use this method and the ways that countries have responded to both global and domestic threats. Chapter 10 discusses an emerging issue area of global politics: human rights and human security. The last four chapters

---

nation-state A political community in which the state claims legitimacy on the grounds that it represents all citizens, including those who may identify as a separate community or nation.

sovereignty The condition of a state having control and authority over its own territory and being free from any higher legal authority. It is related to, but distinct from, the condition of a government being free from any external political constraints.

WHAT'S YOUR WORLDVIEW

Are you a member of a nation? Do you identify with a particular ethnic community? Are you a member of an NGO, like Amnesty International or Greenpeace International? How do these identities affect your responsibilities as a citizen of a nation-state?

examine the intersections of trade, finance, poverty, development, and environmental issues. Each of the topics in Part Four overlaps with the others, and it's important not to read these chapters merely in a straightforward fashion but also to review the information from previous chapters as you progress through your coursework.

Libyan citizens attending Muslim prayers show their gratitude to the United States, France, and NATO allies who provided valuable air support and intelligence for the fight that ended the authoritarian rule of Muammar Qaddafi in 2011.

Aid from international agencies like the World Food Program can help provide immediate relief for starving people. Food aid should be a temporary solution. Ultimately, the world economic system must promote agricultural production in developing states.

Engaging with the
W✱RLD
Kiva

So you want to do something about the bottom billion? You want to know more about those who are struggling in our global community and find ways to help them?

Get involved with Kiva by becoming a fellow or starting a campus club.

Kiva is a nonprofit organization that lends money to help people around the world start a business and pull themselves out of poverty. More than 600,000 Kiva members have loaned over $240 million to people without access to traditional banking systems. More than 98 percent of those who received the loans have repaid them! Check out www.kiva.org.

Theories of Global Politics

The basic problem facing anyone who tries to understand contemporary global politics is that there is so much material to look at; it is difficult to know which things matter and which do not. Where on earth would you start if you wanted to explain the most important political processes? How, for example, would you explain the 9/11 attacks on the United States or the 2003 war in Iraq? Why did Al Qaeda attack the United States? Why did President Bush and Prime Minister Tony Blair authorize the attack on Saddam Hussein's Iraq? Why did President Obama change the military strategy for Afghanistan? With the death of Osama bin Laden, why are the United States and its allies still fighting in Afghanistan? Where in the world did the current economic crisis originate? Where will it end—and when? What policies will global leaders develop to respond to this economic crisis? Questions such as these seem impossible to answer definitively. Was the invasion of Iraq motivated by human rights concerns, our dependency on oil, unfinished business from the first Gulf War in 1991, **imperialism**, or the "war against terrorism"? Whether we are aware of it or not, whenever we are faced with such questions, we have to resort to **theories** to understand them and to develop effective responses.

imperialism The practice of foreign conquest and rule in the context of global relations of hierarchy and subordination. It can lead to the establishment of an empire.

theory A proposed explanation of an event or behavior.

What Are Theories?

A theory is not simply some grand formal model with hypotheses and assumptions. Rather, *a theory is a kind of simplifying device that allows you to decide which facts matter and which do not.* A good analogy is sunglasses with different colored lenses. Put on the red pair and the world looks red; put on the yellow pair and it looks yellow. The world is not any different; it just looks different. So it is with theories. Below we will briefly mention the main theoretical views that have dominated the study of global politics to give you an idea of the colors they paint the world. But before we do, please note that we do not think of theory as merely an option. It is not as if you can avoid theory and instead look directly at the facts. This is impossible because the only way you can decide which of the millions of possible facts to look at is by adhering to some simplifying device that tells you which ones matter the most. We think of theory as such a device.

You may not even be aware of your theory. It may just be the view of the world you have inherited from family, a group of friends, or the media. It may just seem to be common sense to you and not anything complicated like a theory. But your theoretical assumptions are implicit (implied though not plainly expressed) rather than explicit (stated clearly and in detail), and we prefer to be as explicit as possible when it comes to thinking about global politics.

The banner reads "Peace and justice, the people's will" as Sudanese citizens protest outside the Sudanese embassy in Cairo, Egypt, in 2013. Security forces representing the government of Omar al-Bashir had fired on mourners at a funeral for a protester killed during a week of demonstrations.

The Rise of Realism

People have tried to make sense of world politics for centuries, especially since the separate academic discipline of international politics was formed in 1919, when the Department of International Politics was set up at the University of Wales, Aberystwyth. The man who established that department, a Welsh industrialist named David Davies, saw its purpose as to help prevent war. By studying international politics scientifically, many scholars believed they could find the causes of the world's main political problems and put forward solutions to help politicians solve them. After the end of World War I, the discipline was marked by this commitment to changing the world, and a number of antiwar organizations embraced this **idealism**. We call such a position **normative**, as its proponents concerned themselves with what *ought to be*.

Opponents of this normative position characterized it as overly idealistic in that it focused on means of preventing war and even making war and violence obsolete. They adopted a theory they called **realism**, which emphasized seeing the world as it really is rather than how we would like it to be. And the world as seen by realists is not a very pleasant place; human beings are at best self-interest oriented and probably much worse. To them, notions such as the perfectibility of human beings and the possibility of an improvement of world politics seem far-fetched. This debate between idealism and realism has continued to the present day, but it is fair to say that realism has tended to have the upper hand. It appears to accord more with common sense than does idealism, especially when the media bombard us daily with images of how awful humans can be to one another.

Having said this, we would like you to think about whether such a realist view is as neutral as it may seem commonsensical. After all, if we teach global politics to generations of students and tell them that people are selfish, then doesn't that become common sense? And don't they, when they go off into the media or to work for government departments, or the military, or even when they talk to their children over the dinner table, simply repeat what they have been taught and, if in positions of power, act accordingly? We will leave you to think about this. For now, we would like to keep the issue open and point out that we are not convinced that realism is as objective or nonnormative as it is often portrayed.

idealism Referred to by realists as *utopianism* since it underestimates the logic of power politics and the constraints this imposes on political action. Idealism as a substantive theory of international relations is generally associated with the claim that it is possible to create a world of peace based on the rule of law.

normative theory The systematic analyses of the ethical, moral, and political principles that either govern or ought to govern the organization or conduct of global politics. The belief that theories should be concerned with what ought to be rather than merely diagnosing what is.

realism A theory that analyzes all international relations as the relation of states engaged in the pursuit of power. Realists see the international system as anarchic or without a common power, and they believe conflict is endemic in the international system.

North Korean troops march in a military parade in Kim Il Sung Square in Pyongyang, North Korea. World leaders have not been able to end North Korea's nuclear weapons program and its aggressive behavior in East Asia.

Rival Theories

Although realism has been the dominant way of explaining global politics in the last nearly 100 years, it is not the only way. In Chapters 3 and 4, we will examine not only realism but its main rival, **liberalism** (which essentially holds that states and nonstate actors want peace and prosperity), and critical approaches such as **Marxism, constructivism, feminist theory**, and utopian views. Both realism and liberalism are considered mainstream or traditional theories. We use the word *critical* to identify theories or approaches that critique traditional theories—that advocate transforming the present global system and creating an alternative system.

In the 1980s, it became common to talk of an **interparadigm debate** among realism, liberalism, and Marxism; that is, these three major theories (designated **paradigms** by influential philosopher of natural science Thomas Kuhn) were in competition, and the truth about global politics lay in the debate among them. At first glance, each seems to be particularly good at explaining certain aspects of global politics, and an obvious temptation is to try to combine them into some overall account. But this is not the easy option it may seem. These three theories, along with the more recently influential constructivism, are not so much different views of the same world as *four views of different worlds*.

Let us examine this claim more closely. It is clear that each of these four broad theoretical traditions focuses on different aspects of global politics (realism on the power relations among states, liberalism on a much wider set of interactions among states and nonstate actors, Marxist theory on the patterns of the world economy, and constructivism on the ways ideas and values shape our image of the world). However, each is saying more than this. Each view claims that it is picking out the most important features of global politics and that it offers a better account than the rival theories. Thus, the four approaches are really in competition with one another, and while you can certainly choose among them, it is not so easy to add bits from one to the others. For example, if you are a Marxist theorist, you think state behavior is ultimately determined by class forces—forces that the realist does not think affect state behavior. Similarly, constructivism suggests that actors do not face a world that is fixed but rather one that they can in principle change—in direct contrast to the core beliefs of realists and Marxists alike. That is, these four theories are really versions of what global politics is like rather than partial pictures of it. They do not agree on what global politics is fundamentally all about.

We should note that most scholars view constructivism, which has become increasingly influential since the 1990s, as a critical *approach* to studying international relations rather than a *theory*. Nick Onuf, a key constructivist scholar, has stated that constructivism is not a theory but a way of studying social relations. We like the way Michael Barnett (2011) compares constructivism with rational choice theory. Rational choice theory is a social theory suggesting that all actors act with fixed preferences, which are to always maximize benefits and minimize costs. Constructivism is also a social theory that is concerned with the relationship between agents and structures and the importance of ideas. From Barnett's view, constructivism is not a substantive theory; that is, it does not have common views about states, the international system, and human behavior, as realism and liberalism do.

We do not think any one of these theoretical perspectives has all the answers when it comes to explaining world politics in an era of globalization. In fact, each sees globalization differently. We do not want to tell you which theory seems best, since the purpose

liberalism A theory that argues for human rights, parliamentary democracy, and free trade—while also maintaining that all such goals must begin *within a state*.

Marxist theory A theory critical of the status quo, or dominant capitalist paradigm. It is a critique of the capitalist political economy from the view of the revolutionary proletariat, or workers. Marxists' ideal is a stateless and classless society.

constructivism An approach asserting that ideas construct or shape how we view the world; concerned with the relationship between agents and structures and the notion that ideas define and can transform global politics.

feminist theory A theory critical of the biases of the discipline. Many feminists focus on the areas where women are excluded from the analysis of major international issues and concerns.

interparadigm debate The debate between the main theoretical approaches in the field of global politics.

paradigm A model or example. In the case of international relations theory, the term is a rough synonym for "academic perspective." A paradigm provides the basis for a theory, describing what is real and significant in a given area so that we can select appropriate research questions.

of this book is to give you a variety of conceptual lenses. By the end of the book, we hope you will work out which of these theories (if any) best explains globalization and other elements of global politics. Part Two outlines the theories in more detail. We also introduce you to a set of other theories, such as feminist theory, that many believe are crucial in explaining globalization but that have not yet been dominant in the discipline of international relations. However, we want to reinforce here our earlier comment that theories do not portray "the" truth. The theories we have mentioned will see globalization differently because they have an a priori view of what is most important in global politics. Therefore, the option is not available of simply answering the tempting question of which theory has the "truest" or "most correct" view of globalization.

Foxconn, a Taiwanese technology company, makes many Apple products. Here some Chinese university students holding mock iPads protest the poor safety record of the company. Have you thought about how the person who made your computer, phone, or television is treated as an employee?

Research Approaches and Levels of Analysis

As curious individuals, we are all interested in understanding the nature of global politics and the behavior of different actors in this global society. Two of the more traditional ways of doing research are the historical and social scientific approaches. A less traditional method of understanding the world is the constructivist approach. These three research approaches, in combination with theories, help us explain and understand decisions and events in global politics.

The Historical Approach

Historians arrive at an understanding of why states take certain actions, or why events happen, after careful review of public documents, memoirs, and interviews with key actors. Their goal is to understand a particular decision or event and create a thorough description or narrative that helps us understand decisions that key actors made. The goal is not to understand all wars or all actions by states but to create a history of a particular war or a very thorough description of a country's decision to take a certain policy position.

The Social Scientific Approach: Levels of Analysis

The intellectual interests of social scientists are slightly different. Social scientists want to bring the precision and certainty of the natural sciences to the social world. Uncomfortable with the subjectivity and ambiguity of many historical accounts, social scientists develop hypotheses based on dependent (Y) and independent (X) variables (e.g., "if X, then Y"); they then test and confirm these hypotheses or revise and refine them until they are accurate. They seek to explain international relations behavior, predict what others may do in similar situations, and develop a list of policy options or prescriptions for relevant policy makers. Research, then, is the search for the independent variable. For example, how do we explain a nation-state's allocation of development assistance or foreign aid? We know the amount of development assistance (dependent variable), but we now must find the independent variable that might explain this allocation.

levels of analysis Analysts of global politics may examine factors at various levels—such as individual, domestic, systemic, and global—to explain actions and events. Each level provides possible explanations on a different scale.

Independent variables reside in one of four **levels of analysis** (which we will discuss in greater depth in Chapter 5):

- *Individual/Human Dimension:* This level explores the range of variables that can affect leaders' policy choices and implementation strategies. Current research reveals that individuals matter, particularly in the midst of crises, when decisions require secrecy and/or involve only a few actors, or when time is of the essence. The influence of individuals increases when they have a great deal of latitude to make decisions and when they have expertise and a keen interest in foreign policy.

- *Domestic Sources or National Attributes:* Factors at this level include a state's history, traditions, and political, economic, cultural, and social structures, as well as military power, economic wealth, and demographics, and more permanent elements like geographic location and resource base.

- *Systemic Factors:* To most realists, the anarchic nature of international relations may be the most important factor at this level. However, the individual and collective actions states have taken to cope with anarchy via treaties, alliances, and trade conventions—formal contracts created by states in an attempt to provide order—also constitute significant systemic factors. More informal constraints based on traditions, common goals, and shared norms shape state behavior as well. For example, most states respect the sovereignty of all states and follow the rule of international law because they expect others to do the same. This notion of reciprocity is the primary incentive for states to support a rule-based international system. Finally, distribution of power in the system (e.g., bipolar, multipolar) and the nature of order (e.g., balance of power, collective security) are also important systemic factors. Remember, the international system is created by the interaction of states and other powerful actors like international and regional organizations.

- *Global Factors:* Often confused with system-level factors, global-level variables challenge notions of boundaries and sovereignty. The processes that define globalization are multidimensional and originate from multiple levels. Globalization and its economic, political, cultural, and social dimensions derive from decisions made or actions taken by individuals, states, and international and regional organizations or other non-state actors, but they are seldom traceable to the actions of any one state or even a group of states. A technological innovation (e.g., the Internet and the information revolution) that diffuses through the system affecting all but does not belong to any single actor is an obvious example. The movement of capital by multinational banks, the broadcasts of CNN, and the revolutionary ideas of religious fundamentalists all represent global factors that shape policy behavior. Natural conditions such as environmental degradation, pandemics (AIDS, SARS, and the flu), and weather patterns also affect foreign policy. Consider, for example, how global climate change and resulting changes in weather patterns might result in excessive rain or the opposite, a drought. Might these conditions influence a country's trade policies? Will a country now need to import food and establish trade relations with other food-producing states? Climate is a global factor that may have an impact on the globalization process.

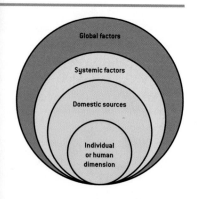

LEVELS OF ANALYSIS.
In the study of global politics, there are four levels of analysis. Some scholars would say there are only three levels, but the authors of this book make a distinction between *systemic* (or international) factors and *global* factors. What is the argument for this distinction?

What is exciting about research in our field is that there is always disagreement about which variables explain the most. The strength of any one argument is based on the quality of the empirical evidence collected to support the hypothesis being tested. Since we are not lab scientists, we cannot conduct experiments with control groups to test our propositions. Instead, we look to the work of historians, public-policy records, government documents, interviews, budgets, and journalist accounts to gather evidence to confirm or reject hypotheses.

The level chosen as a source for an independent variable depends on the situation you wish to examine, the availability of data or evidence, your research skills and interests, and, finally, your creativity and imagination. Each level is like a drawer in a toolbox; the analytic approaches or variables at each level are the tools that the researcher uses to develop and explore the explanatory power of three kinds of hypotheses: (1) causal hypotheses: if it rains, it will flood; (2) relational hypotheses: if it rains, flooding in certain geologic and geographic areas will worsen; and (3) impact hypotheses: if it rains more than n amount, the flooding will be particularly severe.

None of this is new. Both the ancient Greek historian Thucydides and the Enlightenment philosopher Immanuel Kant indirectly discussed levels of analysis in their efforts to explain state behavior. Thucydides focused on the explanatory potential of power capabilities and even suggested that the distribution of power in the international system influenced a state's behavior. Kant referred to the first three levels of analysis when he suggested that nation-states could avoid war by eliminating standing armies, managing the self-interests of rival leaders, and finding ways to provide order in the international system.

The Constructivist Approach

Constructivists question the underlying assumptions supporting historical and social scientific approaches to understanding international relations. Instead, these scholars postulate that there is no single historical narrative. Rather, the interests of specific actors shape the story, and it is their control of that story that gives them power. No perspective offers the truth because words, meanings, symbols, and identities are subjective and are used by individuals, groups, and society to gain and maintain power.

Further, constructivists argue that all of us interpret events and global conditions according to our beliefs, interests, values, and goals. We are not free to do anything we want in any given situation; instead, we are handed a menu reflective of the dominant interests and goals of powerful groups within a state or in the international system.

Decision-Makers: Rationality and Politics

Rational choice: An economic principle that assumes that individuals always make prudent and logical decisions that provide them with the greatest benefit or satisfaction and that are in their highest self-interest.

Bounded rationality: Decision-makers do not always have the ability and information to make a rational decision or one that is optimal. Instead, they first simplify the list of choices available and then apply rationality. Thus, instead of value maximizing, the decision-maker is value satisficing. Herbert Simon who proposed this model suggested that people are only partly rational and emotions, values, and previous experiences may help shape the decision.

Prospect theory: Involves risk aversion and risk acceptance. Decision makers in an environment of gain will avoid risky options and those in an environment of losses will accept risky options.

Poliheuristic theory: A two-stage analysis in which decision makers first eliminate choices based on cognitive shortcuts and then subject the remaining choices to rational processing.

Dimensions of Globalization

globalization A historical process involving a fundamental shift or transformation in the spatial scale of human social organization that links distant communities and expands the reach of power relations across regions and continents.

As we have said, our goal in this book is to offer an overview of world politics in a globalized era, and we must therefore focus on globalization. By **globalization**, we mean *the process of increasing interconnectedness among societies such that events in one part of the world more and more have effects on peoples and societies far away.*

A globalized world is one in which political, economic, cultural, and social events become more and more interconnected and also one in which they have more impact. That is, societies are affected more extensively and more deeply by events of other societies. These events can conveniently be divided into three types: social, economic, and political. In each case, the world seems to be shrinking, and people are increasingly aware of this. The World Wide Web is the most graphic example, since it allows you to sit at home and have instant communication with websites around the world. Electronic mail has also transformed communications in a way that the authors of this book would not have envisaged fifteen years ago.

But these are only the most obvious examples. Others include worldwide television communications, global newspapers, global production of goods (see the case studies in this chapter), international NGOs such as Amnesty International or Greenpeace, global social movements like the International Campaign Against Landmines or the One Campaign aimed at eliminating global poverty, global franchises such as McDonald's and IKEA, the global economy (go and look in your nearest supermarket and work out the number of countries' products represented there), and global risks such as pollution, global warming, and the AIDS epidemic. There are, of course, many other examples, but you get the picture. It is this pattern of events that seems to have changed the nature of world politics from what it was just a few years ago. The important point is not only that the world has changed but that the changes are qualitative and not merely quantitative; a strong case can be made that a new world political system has emerged as a result of globalization.

Having noted this, we want to point out that globalization is not some entirely new phenomenon in world history. Indeed, as we will examine later on, many argue that it is merely a new name for a long-term feature. We leave it to you to judge whether in its current manifestation it represents a new phase in world history or merely a continuation of processes that have been around for a long time, but we do want to note that there have been several precursors to globalization. Hence, looking beyond this quick history of globalization that follows, in Chapter 2 we will also present more detailed examples of previous international orders.

Our final task in this introductory chapter is to offer a summary of the main arguments for and against globalization as a distinct new phase in world politics. We do not expect you to decide where you stand on the issue at this stage, but we give you some of the main arguments here to keep in mind as you read the rest of this book. The main arguments in favor of globalization comprising a new era of world politics are the following:

1. *The pace of economic transformation is so great that it has created a new world politics.* States are no longer closed units; they cannot fully control their own economies. The world economy is more interdependent than ever, with trade and finances ever expanding.

Children teach themselves at a Hole-in-the-Wall learning station. These stations foster collaborative learning among groups of children in Thimphu, Bhutan, including girls, who are often not sent to schools.

CASE STUDY : Global Production and the iPod   **1.1**

Take just one component of Apple's iPod Nano: the central microchip provided by the US company PortalPlayer. The core technology of the chip is licensed from the British firm ARM and is modified by Portal-Player's programmers in California, Washington State, and Hyderabad in India. PortalPlayer then works with microchip design companies in California that send the finished design to a foundry in Taiwan (China) that produces wafers (thin metal disks) imprinted with thousands of chips. The capital costs of these foundries can be more than $2.5 million. These wafers are cut up into individual disks and sent elsewhere in Taiwan to be tested. The chips are then encased in plastic and readied for assembly by Siliconware in Taiwan and Amkor in the Republic of Korea. The finished microchip is warehoused in Hong Kong (China) before being transported to mainland China where the iPod is assembled.

Working conditions and wages in China are low relative to Western standards. Many workers live in dormitories and work long hours. It is suggested that overtime is compulsory. Nevertheless, wages are higher than the average of the region where the assembly plants are located and allow for substantial transfers to rural areas, helping to reduce rural poverty. PortalPlayer was only established in 1999 but had revenues in excess of $225 million in 2005. In 2007 PortalPlayer was bought by Nvidia Corporation. Their chief executive officer has argued that the outsourcing to countries such as India and Taiwan of "non-critical aspects of your business" has been crucial to the development of the firm and its innovation: "It allows you to become nimbler and spend R&D dollars on core strengths."

Since the first iPod was launched in 2001, Apple's share price has risen from just over $7 to more than $518. Those who own shares in Apple have benefited immensely from the globalization of the iPod.

For Discussion

1. Many people are what we call economic nationalists—they support policies and practices that help keep jobs in their home country. How much more would you be willing to pay for your iPod if it were made in your country? Is where it's manufactured at all important to you? Why or why not?
2. Some critics of globalization suggest that it allows companies to search for the lowest common denominator, meaning low wages, no labor or safety laws, and no environmental standards. Without these constraints, profits can be quite high. Should consumers consider these factors before buying products? Should there be global standards for wages, worker safety, and protection of the environment? Why or why not?
3. Most global production takes advantage of each country's comparative strengths or assets, and the result is a great product at a good price. Is this not how capitalism should work? Explain.

Sources: C. Joseph, "The iPod's Incredible Journey," Mail on Sunday *(July 15, 2006);* "Meet the iPod's 'Intel,'" Business Trends *32 (April 2006); World Bank (2006),* Global Economic Prospects 2007: Managing the Next Wave of Globalization *(Washington, D.C.: World Bank), p. 118.*

   2. *Communications have fundamentally revolutionized the way we deal with the rest of the world.* Now events on one side of the world can be immediately observed on the other side. Electronic communications are also converging and thus altering our notions of the social groups we work with and live in. For example, consider how the Arab Spring events in Tunisia and Egypt and the revolution in Libya were influenced by social networking tools.

   3. *There is now, more than ever before, a global culture* so that most urban areas resemble one another. The urban world shares a common culture, much of it emanating from Hollywood and shaped by a global consumer culture.

   4. *The world is becoming more homogeneous in some material and ideational areas.* Differences in political and economic thinking among peoples are diminishing. The desire for democracy is universal, and many want a car, a house, and a television.

   5. *Time and space seem to be collapsing.* Our old ideas of geography and chronology are undermined by the speed of modern communications and media.

   6. *A* **global polity** *is emerging,* with transnational social and political movements and the beginnings of a transfer of allegiance from the state to substate, transnational,

global polity The collective structures and processes by which "interests are articulated and aggregated, decisions are made, values allocated and policies conducted through international or transnational political processes" (Ougaard 2004, 5).

and international bodies. Global governance has become an important part of managing globalization.

cosmopolitan culture A pattern of relations within which people share the same goals and aspirations, generally to improve that culture for all members.

risk culture A pattern of relations within which people share the same perils.

7. *A cosmopolitan culture is developing.* People are beginning to "think globally and act locally."

8. *A risk culture is emerging.* People realize both that the main risks that face them are global (e.g., climate change and pandemics) and that states are unable to deal with the problems without some form of cooperation.

However, just as there are powerful reasons for seeing globalization as a new stage in world politics, often allied to the view that globalization is progressive—that is, it improves the lives of people—there are also arguments that suggest the opposite. Some of the main ones are as follows:

1. One obvious objection to the globalization thesis is that it is *merely a buzzword to denote the latest phase of capitalism.* In a very powerful critique of globalization theory, Hirst and Thompson (1996) argue that one effect of the globalization thesis is that it makes it appear as if national governments are powerless in the face of global trends. This ends up paralyzing governmental attempts to subject global economic forces to control and regulation. Believing that most globalization theory lacks historical depth, they point out that it paints the current situation as *more special than it is* and also as more firmly entrenched than it might in fact be. Current trends may be reversible. They conclude that the more extreme versions of globalization are "a myth," and

Globalization has not ended famine and poverty. Do prosperous countries have an obligation to help people in other lands?

they support this claim with five main conclusions from their study of the contemporary world economy (1996, 2–3): First, the present internationalized economy is not unique in history. In some respects, they say, it is less open than the international economy was between 1870 and 1914. Second, they find that genuinely transnational companies are relatively rare; most are national companies trading internationally. There is no trend toward the development of international companies. Third, there is no shift of finance and capital from the developed to the underdeveloped worlds. Direct investment is highly concentrated among the countries of the developed world. Fourth, the world economy is not global; rather, trade, investment, and financial flows are concentrated in and among three blocs—Europe, North America, and Asia. Finally, they argue that this group of three blocs could, if they coordinated policies, regulate global economic markets and forces. Note that Hirst and Thompson are looking only at economic theories of globalization, and many of the main accounts deal with factors such as communications and culture more than economics. Nonetheless, theirs is a very powerful critique of one of the main planks of the more extreme globalization thesis, with their central criticism that seeing the global economy as something beyond our control both misleads us and prevents us from developing policies to control the national economy.

2. Another obvious objection is that globalization is very *uneven in its effects.* At times, it sounds very much like a Western theory applicable only to a small part of humankind. To pretend that even a small minority of the world's population can connect to the

World Wide Web is clearly an exaggeration, when in reality most people on the planet have probably never made a telephone call in their lives. Thus, globalization only applies to the developed world. We are in danger of overestimating globalization's extent and depth.

3. A related objection is that globalization may be *the latest stage of Western imperialism*. It is the old modernization theory (a controversial theory that suggests nation-states move naturally from traditional societies that are rural and agricultural to modern societies that are complex, urban, and industrial) in a new guise. The forces that are being globalized are conveniently those found in the Western world. What about non-Western values? Where do they fit into this emerging global world? The worry is that they do not fit in at all, and what is celebrated in globalization is the triumph of a Western worldview at the expense of the worldviews of other cultures.

4. Critics have also noted that there are *people who have much to lose* as the world becomes more globalized. This is because it represents the success of liberal capitalism in an economically divided world. Perhaps one outcome is that globalization allows the more efficient exploitation of less well-off states, and all in the name of openness. The technologies accompanying globalization are technologies that automatically benefit the richest economies in the world and allow their interests to override local economies. So not only is globalization imperialist, but it is also exploitative.

5. We also need to make the straightforward point that *not all globalized forces are necessarily good ones*. Globalization makes it easier for drug cartels and terrorists to operate, and the World Wide Web's anarchy raises crucial questions of censorship and preventing access to certain kinds of material.

6. Turning to the so-called **global governance** aspects of globalization, the main worry here is about *responsibility*. To whom are the transnational social movements responsible and democratically accountable? If Microsoft or Shell becomes more and more powerful in the world, does this not raise the issue of how accountable it is to democratic control? David Held has made a strong case for the development of what he calls **cosmopolitan democracy** (1995), but this cosmopolitan democracy has clearly defined legal and democratic features. The concern is precisely that most of the emerging powerful actors in a globalized world are not accountable. This argument also applies to seemingly good global actors such as Oxfam and the World Wildlife Fund.

7. Finally, *there seems to be a* **paradox** *at the heart of the globalization thesis*. On the one hand, globalization is usually portrayed as the triumph of Western, market-led values. But how do we then explain the tremendous economic success that some national economies have had in the globalized world? Consider the economic success of China and India and the so-called Tigers of Asia, countries such as Singapore, Taiwan, Malaysia, and South Korea, which have enjoyed some of the highest growth rates in the international economy but subscribe to very different views of the role of the state in managing the economy and to the place of individual rights and privileges and political rights and freedoms. The paradox, then, will be if these countries can continue to modernize so successfully without adopting many Western values. If they can, what does this do to one of the main themes of globalization—namely, the argument that globalization represents the spreading across the globe of a set of values? If these countries do continue to follow their own roads toward economic and social modernization, then we must anticipate future disputes between Western and non-Western values over issues like human rights, gender, and religion.

global governance
Governance that involves the regulation and coordination of transnational issue areas by nation-states, international and regional organizations, and private agencies through the establishment of international regimes. These regimes may focus on problem solving or the simple enforcement of rules and regulations.

cosmopolitan democracy
A condition in which international organizations, transnational corporations, and global markets are accountable to the peoples of the world.

paradox A seemingly absurd or self-contradictory statement that, when investigated or explained, may prove to be well founded or true.

We hope these arguments for and against the dominant way of representing globalization will cause you to think deeply about the utility of the concept in explaining contemporary world politics. The chapters that follow do not take a common stance *for* or *against* globalization. We will end by posing some questions that we would like you to keep in mind as you read the remaining chapters:

- Is globalization a *new* phenomenon in world politics?
- Which theory discussed earlier—and more in Part Two of this textbook—best explains the effects of globalization?
- Is globalization a positive or a negative development?
- Does globalization make the state obsolete?
- Does globalization make the world more or less democratic?

CASE STUDY 1.2 — Cell Phones, Poverty, Civil War, Okapi, and Prostitution

Mama Doudou is an entrepreneur. She sells bread and arranges prostitutes for 300 miners working in an illegal camp in the Okapi Faunal Reserve in eastern Congo, home to several endangered species including the okapi, a relative of the giraffe. The mining camp, called Kuwait, is one of some twenty illegal operations tucked away in the protected area. Mama Doudou gets paid in coltan, which is not a local currency but a commodity—a valuable mineral that helps sustain the high-tech world we depend on.

Coltan, short for columbite-tantalite, is rich in the element tantalum, an excellent conductor of electricity because it is highly resistant to heat. Abundant in eastern Congo, coltan is dug from streambeds by local residents and economic refugees from surrounding countries. Tons of this ore are flown in chartered flights to US and European refineries where the metal tantalum is extracted for use in the manufacture of capacitors. These are electronic components that control the flow of electric current inside circuit boards and help maintain the charge in a computer chip. Capacitors are found in many consumer products (e.g., laptop computers, pagers, cell phones, and computer game boxes) and in defense and security products (e.g., jet engines, night-vision goggles, and fiber optics).

So it is that consumer demand in wealthy societies for electronic toys, cell phones, and computers has fueled a mad scramble for coltan and other minerals across the globe, bringing the high-tech world face to face with thugs, rebels, pimps, prostitutes, poachers, corrupt political leaders, and people on the fringes of society just trying to survive. As major global corporations seek to fill a seemingly insatiable appetite for essential minerals, guerrillas and armed thugs are getting rich, protected and endangered species are being slaughtered, and innocent civilians are being exploited in the mines and killed in the civil war. Having found a way to survive this mess, Mama Doudou is taking advantage of the forces of globalization that bring the high-tech world to her illegal mining camp.

The Congo is a *failed state*. The government is totally ineffective, capable of providing only minimal services for its citizens. With no healthcare, no educational system, and no social services, many people die of infectious disease and malnutrition. A miner works about seven days a week, digging a kilo of coltan each day and earning as much as $2,000 a month, or about $70 a day. This is an incredible amount of money where people usually live on 20 cents a day. Mama Doudou charges high prices for her goods and services: a kilo of coltan for arranging a "temporary wife" for the duration of a miner's work in the camp, and roughly $27 for antibiotics that help control the accompanying gonorrhea.

Miners must now dig for a day to pay for food, and it takes several days to pay for the antibiotics. Mining activity has increased and the wars continue. And Mama Doudou and other entrepreneurs thrive.

For Discussion
1. How is this story a case of uneven globalization—where some countries or regions of the world benefit more than others by the global economy?
2. Is this a typical situation in a failed state? How would things change if the Congo had a stable government?
3. Are you part of the problem, and should you be part of the solution? Do consumers in the wealthy countries of the world have any responsibility here? Explain.

Sources: Karl Vick, "Vital Ore Plays Crucial Role in the Congo's War," Guardian Weekly *(April 5–11, 2001) p. 37;* Blaine Harden, "The Dirt in the New Machine," New York Times Magazine *(August 12, 2001) pp. 35–39.*

- Is globalization merely Western imperialism in a new guise?
- Does globalization make armed conflicts more or less likely?
- Last but not least, what will *your* role be in world politics? How will you choose to identify yourself and participate locally, nationally, and globally? Has globalization increased your opportunities to engage with the world?

Conclusion

We hope this introduction and the chapters that follow help you answer these questions. We also hope this book as a whole provides you with a good overview of the politics of the contemporary world. We leave you to decide whether or not globalization is a new phase in world politics and whether it is a positive or a negative development.

For many people, globalization means travel for business and the movement of goods and services. The departure board at a new terminal at Charles de Gaulle Airport in Paris will serve 8.5 million passengers a year. Global travel can lead to more awareness but not always understanding of foreign lands and cultures.

Returning to 9/11 and its aftermath, we think it important to conclude this chapter by stressing that globalization clearly is a very complex phenomenon that is contradictory and difficult to comprehend. Just as the Internet is for most of us a liberating force, so was it the way that those who planned all the various terrorist attacks communicated. Similarly, television can bring live stories right into our living rooms so that we understand more about the world. But on 9/11, television was also a means of communicating a very specific message about the vulnerability of the United States and ultimately a way of constructing the categories within which we reacted. Finally, maybe the most fundamental lesson of 9/11 is that not all people in the world share a view of globalization as a progressive force in world politics. Those who undertook the attacks were rejecting, in part, the globalization-as-Westernization project. *Globalization is therefore not one thing.*

How we think about it will reflect not merely the theories we accept but also our own positions in this globalized world. In this sense, the ultimate paradox of 9/11 is that the answers to questions such as what it was, what it meant, and how to respond to it may themselves ultimately depend on the social, cultural, economic, and political spaces we occupy in a globalized world. That is, world politics suddenly becomes very personal: How does your economic position, your ethnicity, your gender, your culture, or your religion determine what globalization means to you?

CONTRIBUTORS TO CHAPTER 1: John Baylis, Anthony McGrew, Steve Smith, and Steven L. Lamy.

REVIEW QUESTIONS

1. Is globalization a new phenomenon in world politics?
2. In what ways are you linked to globalization?
3. How do ideas about globalization shape our understanding of the trend?
4. How can different levels of analysis lead to different explanations of the impact of globalization on global politics?
5. Why do theories matter?
6. International relations began as a problem-solving discipline in response to World War I. What are the global problems that now define our field of study?

FURTHER READING

There are several good introductory guides to globalization. The following provide a comprehensive discussion:

Enloe, C. (2007), *Globalization and Militarism: Feminists Make the Link* (Lanham, Md.: Rowman & Littlefield). A good analysis from a leading feminist of the connections between globalization and various forms of violence.

Hebron, L., and Stack, J. (2011), *Globalization* (Upper Saddle River, N.J.: Pearson).

Held, D., et al. (1999), *Global Transformations* (Cambridge: Polity Press). See also Held, D., and McGrew, A. (eds.) (2003), *The Global Transformations Reader*, 2nd ed. (Cambridge: Polity Press). Excellent essays that explore the impact of globalization in many issue areas.

McGrew, A., and Lewis, P. (1992), *Global Politics* (Cambridge: Polity Press). A good collection of essays about global politics and contains some very relevant chapters on the relationship among the three theories discussed in this chapter and globalization.

Ojeili, C. el-, and Hayden, P. (2006), *Critical Theories of Globalization* (London: Palgrave Macmillan). Not all believe that globalization is a positive process. These essays look at the negative aspects of globalization.

Rosenau, J. N., and Czempiel, E.-O. (1992), *Governance Without Government* (Cambridge: Cambridge University Press). A good collection of essays dealing with the political aspects of globalization.

Scholte, J. A. (2000), *Globalization: A Critical Introduction* (London: Macmillan). Offers an excellent overview.

Excellent critiques of the globalization thesis:

Held, D., and McGrew, A. (2002), *Globalization/Anti-globalization* (Cambridge: Polity Press). Covers most of the debates related to globalization and its critics.

Kaldor, M. (2003), *Global Civil Society: An Answer to War* (Cambridge: Polity Press). A powerful account of the relationship between globalization and international civil society.

Stiglitz, J. (2003), *Globalization and Its Discontents* (London: Penguin) and (2006) *Making Globalization Work* (New York: W. W. Norton). An excellent study by a Nobel prize–winning economist with specialization in development and the global economy.

INTERNET RESOURCES

Asian Development Bank
http://www.adb.org/
The website of the leading multilateral lending agency aimed at improving economic conditions in that continent.

Canadian International Council
http://www.canadianinternationalcouncil.org/
A foreign policy analysis website offering research articles on a range of topics.

G-8 Information Centre
http://www.g7.utoronto.ca/
The information clearing house of the organization of the eight largest capitalist economies.

International Atomic Energy Agency
http://www.iaea.org/
A United Nations-linked organization whose mission is to encourage the peaceful dissemination of nuclear technology. Since 1991, it has increasingly played a role in inspecting nuclear weapons programs.

International Monetary Fund
www.imf.org
Part of the Bretton Woods system, this multilateral organization helps manage the global economy.

Multinational Monitor
http://multinationalmonitor.org/monitor.html
A nongovernmental organization that provides news and information about MNCs and TNCs.

One World Online
http://us.oneworld.net/
A social networking site that links not-for-profit organizations with news and information.

UN Research Institute for Social Development
http://www.unrisd.org/
A UN clearinghouse for information about social economic matters.

Women in International Security
http://wiis.georgetown.edu/
A site that seeks to build links among women who do research in international security matters.

World Trade Organization
http://www.wto.org
The prime multilateral organization that sets the "rules of the game" in international trade.

TED Talks and Other Internet Videos
Sugata Mitra, "How Kids Teach Themselves" (www.ted.com)

National Geographic: Remembering 9/11

http://channel.nationalgeographic.com/series/
    remembering-9-11

Ten years after the events on September 11, *National Geographic*
    has compiled and made available primary source documents,
    stories, and interviews dealing with the events on that day and
    the changing international landscape since 2001.

Hole-in-the-Wall

http://www.hole-in-the-wall.com/

Despite its growing role as a major global player, India remains
    plagued by great poverty and high illiteracy rates. Hole-in-the-
    Wall, or "HiWEL" for short, actively works to install computers
    in impoverished areas for general use.

Carnegie Council: "The Next Convergence: The Future of Economic Growth in a Multispeed World"—Michael Spence

http://www.carnegiecouncil.org/resources/video/data/000397

In a rapidly globalizing world where the standard of living will see
    a massive surge forward within the next twenty years, Michael
    Spence draws on historical trends and future projections to
    map out global economic growth.

For more information, quizzes, case studies, and
other study tools, please visit us at **www.oup.com/
us/lamy**

THINKING ABOUT GLOBAL POLITICS

Why Should I Care?

In this chapter, we have discussed how forces of globalization
shape all of our lives. We know that these forces of globalization influence nation-states, but how do they shape your life and
the activities of your family and friends? How is your quality of
life shaped by global factors that have created a global economy
and a global consumer culture? How are your personal choices
influenced by the actions of distant actors and economic, political, and cultural conditions pushed by globalization?

PART ONE: YOU AS A GLOBAL CONSUMER

Consider the following questions in small groups with a focus on
how you are linked in a web of interdependence that may shape
the choices you make. Also understand that you are making
choices in different sectors of global society. It is like playing chess
on three or four different chessboards. You are making choices in
the economic sector, political sector, and cultural sector. In turn,
these choices affect social relations and have profound implications for the natural world, or the environmental sector.

1. With the iPod case in mind, consider how many items
   in your daily commodity basket (the sum total of goods
   and services purchased in a given time frame) are not
   local and are imported from a foreign country.
2. Do you think dependency on foreign goods and services matters? How might your choices influence people in your community and people in distant lands?
3. Individuals, like countries, need to avoid situations where
   their choices create an unhealthy dependency on foreign goods and services. For example, a country's dependency on oil makes it vulnerable to corporations and
   countries that supply it. It is okay to depend on products,
   but you hope this dependency has low political and
   economic costs. For example, our dependency on oil
   makes us vulnerable because it is too hard to find a substitute. This is called *vulnerability interdependency*. But

our dependency on good French wine can be replaced by
a dependency on good Chilean or Australian wine. The
cost of finding an alternative is low; thus, this is called
sensitivity interdependency. These sensitivity situations
are unavoidable in a global economy. Again, considering
your lifestyle, are you in the vulnerability or sensitivity category? Is it easy to stay in the sensitivity category?

PART TWO: ASSESSING YOUR POLITICAL CONNECTIONS

1. The entire world changed with the terrorist attacks
   against the United States, Spain, and the United
   Kingdom. How have global politics changed and how
   have these changes affected you and your family?
2. Identify four international events that have occurred in
   the last six months that have had a direct impact on
   political life in your country. Be specific about how these
   events have changed the game of domestic politics.
3. What about leadership in this world of global politics?
   When you consider the impact of globalization and the
   complex issues we all face as citizens in rich and poor
   states, what skills and competencies do you think leaders need to be successful in securing the interests of
   their citizens and providing for world order?

WRITING ASSIGNMENT: MORAL INTERDEPENDENCY

We have become so interdependent economically and politically, but do we recognize our moral responsibility to people
who are not our citizens? Do we have any responsibility for the
impact of our foreign policy decisions on other countries? For
example, in the pursuit of wealth and prosperity, we may trade
for oil with authoritarian regimes that oppress their citizens.
Are we also culpable? By providing that regime with financial
resources, are we contributing to its reign of terror?

2 | The Evolution of Global Politics

Those who cannot learn from history are doomed to repeat it.

—*George Santayana*

We learn from history that we learn nothing from history.

—*G. B. Shaw*

I f we were to write a brief list of world events in 2013, it might include the following:

• The global economic crisis has eased for the advanced economies, but the recovery may not be sustainable because real risks remain. The eurozone is vulnerable because of its banking system, and the polarized domestic political system creates economic risks and uncertainty in the United States. The effects include slowing economic growth in China and India.

• The depth of extreme poverty has fallen by 25 percent in the past thirty years for the developing world as a whole, but most of the drop has happened in China and India. According to the World Bank, those living in extreme poverty in the rest of the developing world are as poor as those in extreme poverty thirty years ago.

• The emergence of a new divide between rich and poor states related to climate change and *weather weirding*. The typhoon Haiyan ravaged the Philippines, and extreme weather events have devastated regions across the world. Yet, in the 2013 Warsaw Climate Change Conference, the world learned that Australia, Japan, and Canada downgraded their efforts at reducing carbon emissions. China and 132 states that belong to the G-77 bloc of developing states criticized the foot dragging by the global rich states and the primary source of carbon emissions.

• The aftermath of the Arab Spring has not resulted in stable democracies in the Middle East. In Egypt, the military overthrew the elected president, violence and instability continue to thwart efforts at building a stable government in Libya, and a civil war has ravaged Syria. The Assad government has used chemical weapons on Syrian citizens and now the world community is involved in a process of containing and destroying those outlawed weapons.

• The United States is coming out of the longest war in its history in Afghanistan, yet instability and violence continue to plague the region and our attempt at state building in Iraq seems to have failed. The United States has increased its use of unmanned drones in Pakistan, Yemen, and many African states.

Supporters of Egypt's ousted President Morsi held a demonstration in a suburb of Cairo, Egypt, in September 2013. The Egyptian military government has increased its crackdown on Islamists that support the ousted president.

- Religious extremist movements continue to use violence across the world. Al Shabaab attacked the Westgate shopping center in Nairobi, Kenya, killing seventy. France intervened in Mali to stop jihadi forces. Many of these new extremist groups are financed and trained by Al Qaeda.
- Representatives of the United States, Great Britain, China, France, Germany, Russia, and the European Union negotiated with Iran to limit its nuclear program and to contain the proliferation of nuclear weapons. Meanwhile, no one seems to be watching what North Korea may be doing with its nuclear program.

Add to our list the cycle of violence in Israel and Palestine, which is showing no sign of abating, and the problem of fragile states defined by political crises and economic underdevelopment, which contributes to the poverty and misery of hundreds of millions of people who have no food, shelter, or healthcare. Sometimes, it's difficult to imagine how things might ever improve; other times, it's easy to get caught up in the moment, when something significant or strange occurs on the world stage. Yet each of the events and enduring conditions listed here stems from a deeper world history, and knowing about these histories takes us a step closer to understanding global politics—past, present, and future.

Perhaps, despite our pessimistic list, the international system has actually moved in a positive direction. After all, countries that were enemies in 1944—including France, Germany, and Great Britain—are today working together to bring economic prosperity to the world as members of the European Union. The accumulation of human history—political change, economic progress, medical breakthroughs, the lives of ordinary people—are part of the fabric of struggle and cooperation, strife and comity.

Our goal in this chapter is to demonstrate, briefly, how the international system, and in some ways the global society, has evolved during the last 400 years. It is, of course, not possible to cover all of international political history in one chapter. Therefore, our attention here will be primarily on significant political events; in other chapters, we will discuss social and economic trends.

Introduction

The history of international relations did not begin in 1648, but as we'll explain, it's a good place to begin our story. Kingdoms, empires, city-states, and nation-states have for centuries interacted in the same kinds of patterns that emerged after the end of the Thirty Years' War (1618–1648).

In China, Africa, India, and ancient Greece, political units of various sizes had engaged in economic relations, exchanged ambassadors, and fought wars for centuries prior. And globalization is not a new phenomenon; it dates back to the premodern era, when the Silk Road constituted one of the first overland and transcontinental trade routes, connecting eastern, southern, and western Asia with the Mediterranean and European world. Similarly, early maritime trade routes, particularly the Indian Ocean trade route, played an important part in east-to-west exchanges of culture, language, and goods, all the way from the Roman period to the seventeenth century.

But we choose to begin with 1648 because an event during that year represents a major dividing line in history: the Peace of Westphalia, which ended the Thirty Years' War, established the principle of sovereignty. Crucial in delimiting the political rights and authority of monarchs, it added significantly to the developing template for the international system, now referred to as the "globalized system," that is a theme of this book: arrangements for governance, human rights, and economics that form the basis of the contemporary world.

In this chapter, we will discuss wars and political upheavals. It is a sweeping tale, covering the American and French Revolutions, two world wars, the end of European colonization of Africa and Asia, the Cold War and the changes in the international political system that followed its end, and the terrorist attacks of the early and mid-2000s. Our goal is to provide some background, or context, for you to understand the topics that we will examine in depth in Chapters 8 through 14.

After reading and discussing this chapter, you should have a better understanding of the origins of the modern international system. This is primarily a Western, Eurocentric system—one that spread even as former empires tried to contain European expansion. You will also have a better understanding of the Cold War and its effects on the world. Some have called the Cold War "World War III," as it was a global ideological battle for the hearts and minds of all peoples. If it was a war about two contending rule books—one being the US or Western view of capitalism and democratic governance and the other being the Soviet brand of socialism and authoritarian government—is the post–Cold War crisis about how to apply the Western rules? Some authorities have suggested that the current global war on terrorism is actually World War IV. This chapter encourages you to explore various dimensions of the US-led war on terrorism that is now centered in Afghanistan, Pakistan, and Somalia.

Most important, you'll gain a sense that history matters because it shapes political institutions and influences how leaders make decisions. Leaders in situations of uncertainty often refer to lessons from historical events. Analogical reasoning, or learning from history, is an important element of decision making in our complex international environment.

The Significance of the Peace of Westphalia

When Martin Luther nailed his Ninety-Five Theses to the door of the cathedral in Wittenberg, Germany, in 1517, he launched more than the **Protestant Reformation**. For the next century, monarchs across Europe found in religion a justification to begin wars that were actually about politics and economics. The **Thirty Years' War** (1618–1648) was the last of these religious conflicts in Europe and ostensibly began over a disagreement about the right of political leaders to choose a state religion. The opponents—including at various times Denmark, France, Austria, Sweden, Spain, and the principalities of the Holy Roman Empire—conducted most of their operations in Germany, killing tens of thousands of soldiers and civilians and devastating cities and farmland.

The **Peace of Westphalia** in 1648 not only ended this catastrophic conflict but also ushered in the contemporary international system by establishing the principle of sovereignty (a state's control and authority over its own territory). Political leaders, aware that the fighting had solved nothing and brought only widespread destruction, codified in the accord the right of the more than 300 German states that constituted the Holy Roman Empire to conduct their own diplomatic relations—a very clear acknowledgment of their sovereignty. They were also to enjoy "an exact and reciprocal Equality": the first formal acceptance of **sovereign equality** (the idea that countries have the same right to sovereignty) for a significant number of states.

Protestant Reformation A social and political movement begun in 1517 in reaction to the widespread perception that the Catholic Church had become corrupt and had lost its moral compass.

Thirty Years' War (1618–1648) The last of the great wars in Europe fought nominally for religion.

Peace of Westphalia (1648) Ended the Thirty Years' War and was crucial in delimiting the political rights and authority of European monarchs.

sovereign equality The idea that all countries have the same rights, including the right of noninterference in their internal affairs.

society of states An association of sovereign states based on their common interests, values, and norms.

balance of power In the international system, a state of affairs in which there is parity and stability among competing forces, and no one state is sufficiently strong to dominate all the others.

Peace of Utrecht (1713) The agreement that ended the War of the Spanish Succession and helped to consolidate the link between sovereign authority and territorial boundaries in Europe. This treaty refined the territorial scope of sovereign rights of states.

national self-determination The right or desire of distinct national groups to become states and to rule themselves.

Concert of Europe An informal institution created in 1815 by the five great powers of Europe (Austria, Britain, France, Prussia, and Russia), whereby they agreed on controlling revolutionary forces, managing the balance of power, and accepting interventions to keep current leaders in power. This system kept the peace in Europe from 1815 until World War I.

More generally, the peace may be seen as encapsulating the very idea of a **society of states**, an association of sovereign states based on their common interests, values, and norms. The participants of the conference, including ambassadors from the Netherlands, Spain, Sweden, France, Austria, and several of the larger German principalities, very clearly and explicitly took over from the papacy the right to confer international legitimacy on individual rulers and states and to insist that states observe religious toleration in their internal policies (Armstrong 1993, 30–38). The **balance of power**—parity and stability among competing powers—was formally incorporated in the **Peace of Utrecht**, which ended the War of the Spanish Succession (1701–1714), when a "just equilibrium of power" was formally declared to be the "best and most solid basis of mutual friendship and durable harmony."

The period from 1648 to 1776 saw the international system that had been taking shape over the previous 200 years come to fruition. Wars were frequent, if lacking the ideological intensity that religion brought to the Thirty Years' War. Some states, notably the Ottoman Empire, slowly declined; others, such as Britain and Russia, rose. Hundreds of ministates still existed, but it was the interaction among no more than ten key players that determined the course of events.

Yet despite constant change and many wars, Europe in its entirety constituted a kind of republic, as eighteenth- and nineteenth-century European writers argued. Some pointed to religious and cultural similarities in seeking to explain this phenomenon, but the central elements that all agreed on were a determination by all states to preserve their freedom, a mutual recognition of one another's right to an independent existence, and, above all, a reliance on the balance of power. Diplomacy and international law were seen as the other two key institutions of international society, as long as the latter was based clearly on state consent. As Torbjorn Knutsen (1997) points out, the Treaty of Westphalia supported a new view of international law among states: they moved from seeing it as divinely inspired to seeing it as a set of customs, conventions, and rules of conduct created and enforced by states and their leaders.

Revolutionary Wars

Against this background of a polite, nominally rule-based European international society, the American, French, and Haitian Revolutions (1776, 1789, and 1791, respectively) had profound consequences. In the case of the United States, one consequence was its eventual emergence as a global superpower in the twentieth century; the consequences of the French Revolution were more immediate. First, the revolutionary insistence that sovereignty was vested in the nation rather than in the rulers—especially dynastic imperial rulers like the Habsburgs—gave a crucial impetus to the idea of **national self-determination**. This principle would increasingly dominate international politics in the nineteenth and twentieth centuries and endanger imperial systems that were seen as denying the rights of nations (people connected by linguistic, ethnic, and cultural bonds) to become sovereign states themselves.

The second consequence of the French Revolution stemmed from the response of the main European powers. After the defeat of Napoleon in 1815, the leading states increasingly set themselves apart from the smaller ones as a kind of great powers' club. This system, known as the **Concert of Europe**, lasted until World War I. It was characterized by regular meetings of the club that had the aims of maintaining the European balance of power drawn up at the end of the Napoleonic Wars and reaching decisions on potentially divisive issues. The leading dynastic powers, Austria and Russia, wanted the concert to give itself the formal right to intervene against any revolution. Britain, which was the least threatened by revolution, strongly resisted this proposition on the grounds that such a move would violate the key principle of nonintervention. However, the concert

British troops charge unmounted Indian civilians during the Sepoy Rebellion in 1857.

unquestionably marked a shift away from the free-for-all and highly decentralized system of eighteenth-century international society toward a more managed, hierarchical system. This shift affected all three of the key institutional underpinnings of the Westphalian international society: the balance of power, diplomacy, and international law.

In 1814, the powers had already formally declared their intention to create a "system of real and permanent balance of power in Europe," and in 1815, during the **Congress of Vienna**, they carefully redrew the map of Europe to implement this system. The main diplomatic development was the greatly increased use of conferences to consider and sometimes settle matters of general interest. In a few technical areas, such as international postal services, telegraphy, and sanitation, permanent international organizations were set up. In international law, the powers sought to draft "a procedure of international legitimation of change" (Clark 1980, 91), especially in the area of territorial change. The great powers collectively made attempts to guarantee various treaties, such as those defining the status of Switzerland, Belgium, and Luxembourg. A great many treaties laid down rules governing various technical and economic issues as well as a few humanitarian issues, notably slavery and the treatment of those wounded in war.

However, while the concert did help bring some measure of peace and order to Europe, it was also one of the mechanisms whereby the European powers legitimized their increasing domination of Asia and Africa. For example, the **Congress of Berlin** of 1885 helped prevent a major war over rival European claims in Africa, but it also set out the rules governing "new acts of occupation." Pious sentiments about bringing the "benefits of civilization" to Africa meant little.

Developments external and internal to the European concert system brought about its demise. Externally, after the American Civil War, the United States began to become a world power. Two events indicate this changing status. First, President Teddy Roosevelt brokered the Treaty of Portsmouth, New Hampshire, that ended the Russo-Japanese War in 1905. Second, Roosevelt sent the new American battle fleet, called the Great White Fleet for its paint scheme, around the world in a cruise that lasted from December 1907 to

Congress of Vienna A meeting of major European leaders (1814–1815) that redrew the political map of Europe after the Napoleonic Wars. The congress was an attempt to restore a conservative political order in the continent.

Congress of Berlin A meeting of the European states that had an interest in colonizing Africa. The Berlin conference redrew the existing political map of Africa with a goal to avoid conflict between the European governments in Africa.

February 1909. The United States also intervened in Morocco and China, seeking equal access to regions where the Europeans already had influence.

Meanwhile, a critical internal change to the European concert system was the hardening of the Great Powers, as they were called, into two rival blocs after the Franco-Prussian War of 1870–1871. Previously, the balance-of-power mentality had meant that the major countries would realign themselves as necessary to keep any one power from becoming dominant. Bismarck's creation of the German Empire in 1871 caused a major imbalance in the concert system. His alliance system was flexible and complex, and it maintained order among European states, but with Bismarck out of power, less skilled leaders let the alliance rules and protocols lapse. France focused more on Europe and less on Africa, and the German kaiser let the Russians ally with Great Britain. One result of these developments was the carnage of World War I.

World Wars: Modern and Total

Wars on a global scale shocked international society. Although separated by twenty years, World Wars I and II have some similarities beyond mere geography (see Map 2.1). Changes in military technology shaped the ways combatants fought: machine guns, airplanes, and submarines all influenced operations. Both wars also featured controversies over the treatment of civilians. Indiscriminate bombing of cities occurred during both wars and reached its nadir with the British and American firebomb air raids on Germany and Japan. Yet one major distinction between the two world wars is this: the Nazi death camps were at the time without parallel in human history. Unfortunately, genocide and ethnic cleansing have since continued to plague the world.

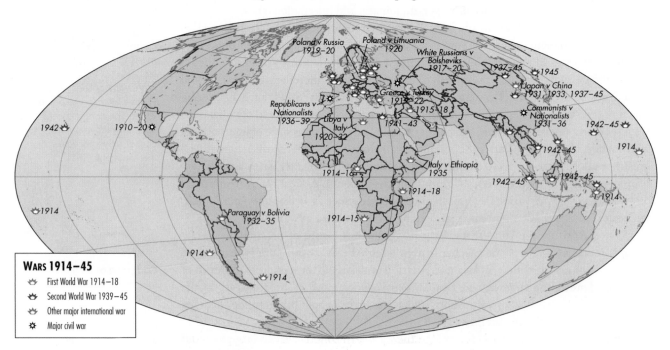

Map 2.1 Wars 1914–1945.

The two world wars were responsible for perhaps more than 80 million deaths. World War I was essentially a European territorial dispute, which, because of extensive European empires, spread as far afield as Africa and Southeast Asia. World War II also started as a European conflict but spread to the Pacific when Japan seized territory. In the interwar period, disputes broke out over territory in South America and East Asia, but elsewhere, the reluctance of the colonial powers to become embroiled in territorial disputes maintained an uneasy peace.

For the victorious Allies, the question of how World War I began became a question of how far the Germans and their allies should be held responsible. In 1919, at the Versailles Palace outside Paris, the victors imposed a statement of German war guilt in Article 231 of the final settlement, primarily to justify the reparations they demanded. Debates among historians about the war's origins have focused on political, military, and systemic factors. Some have suggested that responsibility for the war was diffuse, as its origins lay in complex dynamics of the respective alliances and their military imperatives. One of the more influential postwar interpretations, however, came from West German historian Fritz Fischer, who, in his 1967 book *Germany's Aims in the First World War*, argued that German aggression, motivated by the internal political needs of an autocratic elite, was responsible for the war.

However complex or contested the origins of the war are in retrospect, the motivations of those who fought are more explicable. The masses of the belligerent states shared nationalist beliefs and patriotic values. As they marched off to fight, most thought the war would be short, victorious, and, in many cases, glorious. The reality of the European battlefield and the advent of **trench warfare** determined otherwise. Defensive military technologies, symbolized by the machine gun, triumphed over the tactics and strategy of attrition, though by November 1918 the Allied offensive finally achieved the rapid advances that helped bring an end to the fighting. It was total war in the sense that whole societies and economies were mobilized: men were conscripted into armies, and women went to work in factories. The western and eastern fronts remained the crucibles of the fighting, although conflict spread to various parts of the globe. Japan, for example, went to war in 1914 as an ally of Britain.

In response to German aggression on the high seas and domestic public opinion that supported the Allies, the United States entered the war in 1917 under President Woodrow Wilson. His vision of international society and world order, articulated in his **Fourteen Points**, would drive the agenda of the Paris Peace Conference in 1919. The overthrow of the Russian tsar in February 1917 by what became known as the Provisional Government,

trench warfare Warfare in which armies dug elaborate defensive fortifications in the ground, as both sides did in World War I. Because of the power of weapons like machine guns and rapid-fire cannons, trenches often gave the advantage in battle to the defenders.

Fourteen Points President Woodrow Wilson's vision of international society, first articulated in January 1918, included the principle of self-determination, the conduct of diplomacy on an open (not secret) basis, and the establishment of an association of nation-states to provide guarantees of independence and territorial integrity (League of Nations).

After a rapid German advance into France in August 1914, troops on both sides created extensive networks of defensive trenches. Millions of combatants died.

armistice A cease-fire agreement between enemies in wartime. In the case of World War I, the armistice began at 11 a.m. on November 11, 1918.

Treaty of Versailles, 1919 Formally ended World War I (1914–1918).

League of Nations The first permanent collective international security organization aimed at preventing wars and resolving global problems. The League failed due to the unwillingness of the United States to join and the inability of its members to commit to a real international community.

liberal democracy A government that champions freedom of the individual, constitutional civil and political rights, and laissez-faire economic arrangements.

and the seizure of power by the Bolsheviks in November 1917, soon led Russia's new leaders to negotiate withdrawal from the war. Germany no longer fought on two fronts but faced a new threat as the United States mobilized resources. With the failure of Germany's last great military offensive in the west in 1918 and with an increasingly effective British naval blockade, Germany agreed to an **armistice** (cease-fire).

The **Treaty of Versailles**, which formally ended the war, established the **League of Nations**, specified the rights and obligations of the victorious and defeated powers (including the notorious regime of reparations on Germany), and created the "Mandate" system under which "advanced nation-states" were given legal authority over colonial peoples. It failed, however, to tackle what was for some the central problem of European security after 1870: a united and frustrated Germany. The treaty precipitated German revenge by creating new states out of former German and Austrian territories and devising contested borders. The League of Nations failed because the major powers—namely, France, Great Britain, and the United States—were not able to set aside their national interests for the good of a collective global interest. France sought to punish Germany, Great Britain was focused on its empire, and the United States did not want anything to do with settling European conflicts.

For some scholars, 1914–1945 represents two acts in a single play, or a thirty-year war. Marxist theorist E. H. Carr, for example, saw the period from 1919 to 1939 as a twenty-year crisis, which he believed resulted from an unrealistic and utopian peace treaty that did not address the real causes of the war. Economic factors were also crucial contributors to the outbreak of World War II. World War I boosted production levels for Japan and the United States, but it destroyed production facilities in Europe. Britain and France demanded reparations from Germany to pay for their reconstruction.

The Great Depression of the 1930s, though not caused by World War I, also contributed to the outbreak of World War II. It destroyed not only the US economy but the global economy. The damage it caused lowered the prestige of **liberal democracy** (a representative form of democracy), thereby strengthening extremist forces. Long-term consequences of the Depression included widespread unemployment and economic stagnation. Global trade and financial transactions increased, but this growing interdependence of national economies did not result in free trade; instead, protectionist policies (e.g., tariffs to protect domestic interests) increased. The resulting change in the international political system helped bring about the collapse of the trade, finance, and economic management systems.

The effect on German society was particularly significant. All modernized states suffered mass unemployment, but in Germany, inflation was acute. Economic and political instability provided the ground in which support for the Nazis took root. By 1933, Adolf Hitler had achieved power, and the transformation of the German state began. There remain debates about how far Hitler's ambitions were carefully thought through and how much he seized opportunities. A. J. P. Taylor provided a controversial analysis in his 1961 book *Origins of the Second World War*, in which he argued that Hitler was no different from other German political leaders. What was different about Germany this time

In 1923, the German Weimar Republic created after World War I suffered from hyperinflation. The currency was so worthless that children used it as building blocks. This economic collapse led to political unrest and helped the Nazis come to power.

was the particular philosophy of Nazism and ideas of racial supremacy and imperial expansion.

British and French attempts to negotiate with Hitler culminated in the **Munich Agreement of 1938**. In an effort to appease Germany, Britain and France acquiesced to Hitler's territorial claims over the Sudetenland in Czechoslovakia, but within months, Germany had seized the rest of Czechoslovakia and was preparing for war on Poland. Since then, **appeasement** has generally been seen as synonymous with a craven collapse before the demands of dictators—encouraging, not disarming, their aggressive designs. Recent debates about appeasement have focused on whether there were realistic alternatives to negotiation, given the lack of military preparedness to confront Hitler.

By 1939, the defensive military technologies of World War I gave way to armored warfare and air power, as the German **blitzkrieg** brought speedy victories over Poland and in the west. Hitler was also drawn into the Balkans and North Africa in support of his Italian ally, Mussolini. The invasion of the Soviet Union in June 1941 plainly demonstrated the scale of fighting and scope of Hitler's aims. Although Germany had massive early victories on the eastern front, winter saw a stalemate and the mobilization of Soviet peoples and armies. German treatment of civilian populations and Soviet prisoners of war reflected Nazi ideas of racial supremacy and resulted in the deaths of millions. German anti-Semitism and the development of concentration camps gained new momentum after a decision on the "Final Solution of the Jewish Question" in 1942. The term **Holocaust** entered the political lexicon of the twentieth century, as the Nazis attempted the **genocide** of the Jewish people and other minorities, such as the Roma, in Europe.

By 1941, German submarines and American warships were in an undeclared war. The imposition of American economic sanctions on Japan precipitated Japanese military preparations for a surprise attack on the US fleet at Pearl Harbor on December 7, 1941. When Germany and Italy declared war on America in support of their Japanese ally, President Franklin Roosevelt decided to assign priority to the European over the Pacific theater of war. After a combined strategic bombing offensive with the British against German cities, the Allies launched a second front in France, which the Soviets had pressed for.

Defeat of Germany in May 1945 came before the atomic bomb was ready. In an effort to shorten the war, avoid an invasion of Japan, and push the Japanese government to surrender, the United States dropped the first atomic bomb on Hiroshima on August 6, 1945, and the second on Nagasaki on August 9, 1945. The United States was the first and is still the only state to use these weapons of mass destruction in war. The destruction of the two Japanese cities remains enormously controversial. Aside from voicing moral objections to bombing civilian populations, historians have engaged in fierce debate about why the bombs were dropped.

When World War II ended, the United States and the Soviet Union remained as the two dominant countries in world politics. For some people in the United States, their homeland largely

Munich Agreement of 1938 An agreement negotiated after a conference held in Munich between Germany and the United Kingdom and other major powers of Europe along with Czechoslovakia. It permitted the Nazi German annexation of Czechoslovakia's Sudetenland, an area along the Czech border that was inhabited primarily by ethnic Germans.

appeasement A policy of making concessions to a territorially acquisitive state in the hope that settlement of more modest claims will assuage that state's expansionist appetites.

blitzkrieg The German term for "lightning war." This was an offensive strategy that used the combination of mechanized forces—especially tanks—and aircraft as mobile artillery to exploit breaches in an enemy's front line.

On August 6, 1945, the United States dropped an atom bomb on Hiroshima, killing 140,000 and unleashing a weapon system that the world is still trying to control. Now, with the number of nuclear weapons in the world, we can destroy the world as we know it. How can we control these weapons?

Holocaust The attempts by the Nazis to murder the Jewish population of Europe. Some 6 million Jewish people were killed in concentration camps, along with a further million that included Soviet prisoners, Roma, Poles, communists, homosexuals, and the physically or mentally disabled.

genocide The deliberate and systematic extermination of an ethnic, national, tribal, or religious group.

superpower A state with a dominant position in the international system. It has the will and the means to influence the actions of other states in favor of its own interests, and it projects its power on a global scale to secure its national interests.

untouched by the destruction of the war, the country seemed poised to take its proper position as world leader. For the leaders of the Soviet Union, the world looked ready for the expansion of the Soviet style of rule. In the next section, we examine the process of decolonization of Western European holdings. This process provided both countries, soon to be called **superpowers**, with many opportunities to expand their influence. American hegemony in the world economy ran from 1938 to 1973 (see also Chapter 12). The United States was willing to commit resources to stabilize the world economy and build global political structures to manage trade, development, and financial affairs.

Legacies and Consequences of European Colonialism

The effects of World War II helped cause the demise of European imperialism in the twentieth century (see Map 2.2, Table 2.1, and Map 2.3). More than marking an end of Western European dominance in world politics, the end of imperialism seemed to be the death knell for the European style of managing international relations. This change took place against the background of the Cold War, which we will discuss in the next section. But it's important first to appreciate the context of decolonization because it reflected and contributed to the decreasing importance of Europe as the arbiter of world affairs.

The belief that national self-determination should be a guiding principle in international politics had early marked a transformation of attitudes and values; during the age of imperialism, political status accrued to imperial powers. However, after 1945, imperialism became a term of disgrace. Colonialism of the past and the new UN Charter (which established the United Nations) were increasingly recognized as incompatible,

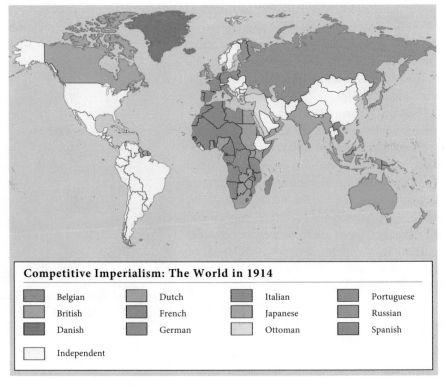

Competitive Imperialism: The World in 1914

■ Belgian		■ Dutch		■ Italian		■ Portuguese	
■ British		■ French		■ Japanese		■ Russian	
■ Danish		■ German		■ Ottoman		■ Spanish	
■ Independent							

Map 2.2 Former Colonial Territories.

Table 2.1
Principal Acts of European Decolonization, 1945–1980

Country	Colonial State	Year of Independence
India	Britain	1947
Pakistan	Britain	1947
Burma (Myanmar)	Britain	1948
Sri Lanka	Britain	1948
Indonesia	Netherlands	1949
Cambodia	France	1953
Indochina (Vietnam and Laos)	France	1954
Ghana	Britain	1957
Malaya (Malaysia)	Britain	1957
French African colonies*	France	1960
Congo (Zaire)	Belgium	1960
Nigeria	Britain	1960
Sierra Leone	Britain	1961
Tanganyika (Tanzania)	Britain	1961
Uganda	Britain	1962
Algeria	France	1962
Rwanda	Belgium	1962
Kenya	Britain	1963
Guinea-Bissau	Portugal	1974
Mozambique	Portugal	1975
Cape Verde	Portugal	1975
São Tomé	Portugal	1975
Angola	Portugal	1975
Zimbabwe	Britain	1980

*Including Cameroon, Central African Republic, Chad, Gabon, Ivory Coast, Madagascar, Mali, Mauritania, Niger, Senegal, and Upper Volta.

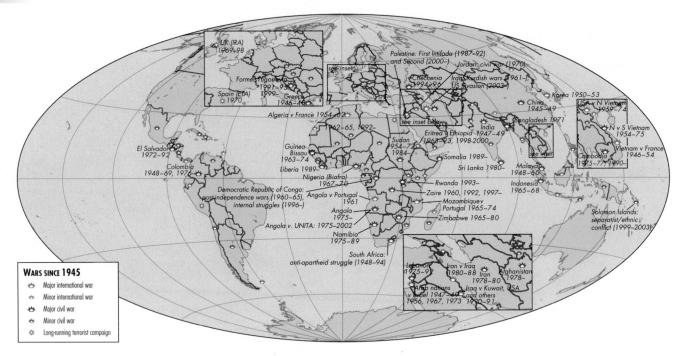

Map 2.3 Wars Since 1945.

As European colonial control was largely destroyed between 1945 and 1970, new nation-states were created. One result was an increase in localized wars, mainly arising from boundary disputes, and in civil wars caused by conflicts between different ethnic groups or between those with conflicting religious or political beliefs. Note that many of these wars directly or indirectly involved the United States and Soviet Union. An estimated 25–30 million people died in these wars, two-thirds of whom were civilians.

though independence was often slow and sometimes marked by prolonged and armed struggle, especially in many African states. The Cold War also complicated and hindered the transition to independence. Various factors influenced the process of decolonization: the attitude of the colonial power, the ideology and strategy of the anti-imperialist forces, and the role of external powers. Political, economic, and military factors played various roles in shaping the transfer of power. Different imperial powers and newly emerging independent states had different experiences of withdrawal from empire.

There was no one pattern of decolonization in Africa and Asia, and the paths to independence reflected attitudes of colonial powers, the nature of local nationalist or revolutionary movements, ethnic and racial factors, and, in some cases, the involvement of external states, including the Cold War protagonists. How far these divisions were created or exacerbated by the imperial powers is an important question in examining the political stability of the newly independent states. Equally important is how capable the new political leaderships in these societies were in tackling their political and economic problems.

Unlike decolonization in South Asia, the decolonization process in Africa was complicated by the number of European states involved in formal empire and the different national interests of these colonizing states. After World War II, only two countries in the continent were not under European rule: Liberia, which was colonized by former American slaves, and South Africa, a dominion of the British Empire since 1910. The economic crises created by the war forced the British, French, and Belgians to exploit the riches of their colonies. Portugal, led by the dictator Antonio Salazar, saw its colonies Angola, Mozambique, and Guinea as essential elements in Portugal's economic and political survival. Belgium held on to its colonies in Central Africa until 1960, and France worked to assimilate its colonies into a French imperial order. The British strategy was to devolve more authority to local elites and create a more informal empire. The first independent colony was the Gold Coast, now known as Ghana, in 1957, and other British colonies followed: Nigeria and Sierra Leone and later Gambia.

The 1960s was a period of accelerated decolonization and the beginning of many internal conflicts in Africa. Many of these new states were created to fail. They did not have adequate political or economic structures, and they were culturally diverse, with little or no loyalty toward any newly created nation-state. Furthermore, these new states had small populations, few experienced and educated leaders, and no political and economic independence. Each was still dependent on its former colonial masters. This dependency still shapes the domestic and foreign policies of these states today.

With the end of the Belgian Congo, the new Democratic Republic of the Congo was embroiled in a civil war, with the Russians and Americans supporting opposing forces. Here the leader of the pro-Western province of Katanga, Moise Tshombe, greets mercenaries fighting to support his secession from the Congo.

In Asia, the relationship between nationalism and revolutionary Marxism was a potent force. In Malaya (now part of Malaysia), the British defeated a communist insurgent movement (1948–1960). In Indochina, a peninsula in Southeast Asia consisting of Burma (Myanmar), Thailand, Malaya, Laos, Cambodia, and Vietnam, the French failed to do likewise (1946–1954). For the Vietnamese, resentment toward centuries of foreign oppression—Chinese, Japanese, and French—soon focused on a new imperialist adversary, the United States. Early American reluctance to support European imperialism gave way to incremental and covert commitments, and then, from 1965, to open military and political support of the newly created state of South Vietnam.

American leaders and a very influential anticommunist interest community spoke of a domino theory, in which if one state fell to communism, the next would be at risk. Chinese and Soviet support provided additional Cold War contexts. Washington failed, however, to coordinate limited war objectives with an effective political strategy and, once victory was no longer possible, sought to disengage from Vietnam through "peace with honor." The Tet (Vietnamese New Year) offensive of the Vietcong guerrillas in 1968 marked a decisive moment, convincing many Americans that the war would not be won, though it was not until 1973 that American forces finally withdrew, two years before South Vietnam was defeated. Many wars in Asia and Africa started as colonial wars and quickly became proxy wars in the Cold War struggle between the superpowers.

The global trend toward decolonization was a key development in the twentieth century, though one frequently offset by local circumstances. Yet while imperialism withered, other forms of domination, or **hegemony**, took shape. Simply stated, hegemony means a state has the capacity and the will to shape and govern the international system. Both the United States and the Soviet Union were vying for global hegemony during the Cold War. The notion of hegemony has been used to criticize the behavior of the superpowers, most notably with Soviet hegemony in Eastern Europe and American hegemony in Central America. For both countries, this struggle for dominance, regardless of the term used, was the central element of the period we discuss in the next section, the Cold War.

hegemony A system regulated by a dominant leader, or political (and/or economic) domination of a region. It also means power and control exercised by a leading state over other states.

Cold War

The rise of the United States as a global power after 1945 was of paramount importance in international politics. Its conflict with the Soviet Union provided one of the crucial dynamics in world affairs—one that affected, directly or indirectly, every part of the world. In the West, historians have debated with vigor and acrimony which country was responsible for the collapse of the wartime alliance between Moscow and Washington. The rise of the USSR as a global power after 1945 is equally crucial in this period. Relations between Moscow and its Eastern European "allies," with the People's Republic of China (PRC), and with revolutionary forces in the third world have been vital issues in world politics as well as key factors in Soviet-American affairs. If one feature of the **Cold War** was its **bipolar** structure, another was its highly divided character, born out of profoundly opposing views about the best way of organizing society: the Western system of market capitalism or the Eastern bloc's centrally planned economies.

Yet for all its intensity, the Cold War was very much a managed conflict in which both sides recognized the limits of what they could do. Certainly, policy makers in the East and the West appeared to accept in private—if not in public—that their rival had legitimate security concerns. The Cold War was thus fought within a framework of informal rules. This framework helps explain why the conflict remained "cold"—at least in terms of general war between the United States and the Soviet Union, since millions of people died during the period of 1945 to 1990 in what have been called "brushfire" or "proxy" wars in Africa and Asia.

Indeed, how and why the Cold War remained cold have been subjects of much academic debate. Few, however, would dispute the fact that whatever else may have divided the two superpowers—ideology, economics, and the struggle for global influence—they were in full agreement about one thing: the overriding need to prevent a nuclear war that neither could win without destroying the world and themselves. In the end, this is why the superpowers acted with such caution for the greater part of the Cold War era. In fact, given the very real fear of outright nuclear war, the shared aim of the two superpowers was not to destroy the other—though a few on both sides occasionally talked in such terms—but rather to contain the other's ambitions while avoiding anything that might lead to dangerous escalation (only once, in 1962, with the Cuban Missile Crisis, did the two superpowers come close to a nuclear exchange). This situation in turn helps explain another important feature of the Cold War: its stalemated and hence seemingly permanent character.

Some historians date the origins of the Cold War to the Russian Revolution of 1917, but most focus on events between 1945 and 1950. Whether the Cold War was inevitable, whether it was the consequence of mistakes and misperceptions, and whether it reflected the response of Western leaders to aggressive Soviet intent are central questions in debates about the origins and dynamics of the Cold War. Until 1989, these debates drew from Western archives and sources and reflected Western assumptions and perceptions. With the end of the Cold War, greater evidence has emerged of Soviet and US motivations and understanding.

Onset of the Cold War

The start of the Cold War in Europe reflected failure to implement the principles agreed on at the 1945 wartime conferences of Yalta and Potsdam. The futures of Germany and various Central and Eastern European countries, notably Poland, were issues of growing tension between the

Cold War The period from 1946 to 1991 defined by ideological conflict and rivalry between the United States and the Soviet Union. This was a global struggle for the hearts and minds of citizens around the world that was characterized by political conflict, military competition, proxy wars, and economic competition.

bipolar An international political order in which two states dominate all others. It is often used to describe the nature of the international system when the two superpowers, the Soviet Union and the United States, were dominant powers during the Cold War.

WHAT'S YOUR WORLDVIEW

The United States and the USSR fought many proxy wars across the globe. One writer lists some fifty-eight wars from 1945 to 1989 (Holsti 1991). Roughly 52 percent of the current armed conflicts began during the Cold War. Given these statistics, is it correct to call the period 1945 to 1989 a "Cold War"?

former wartime allies. Reconciling principles of national self-determination with national security was a formidable task. In the West, there was growing feeling that Soviet policy toward Eastern Europe was guided not by historic concern with security but by ideological expansion. In March 1947, the Truman administration sought to justify limited aid to Turkey and Greece with rhetoric designed to arouse awareness of Soviet ambitions and a declaration that America would support those threatened by Soviet subversion or expansion. The **Truman Doctrine** and the associated policy of **containment** expressed the self-image of the United States as inherently defensive. These were underpinned by the **Marshall Plan** for European economic recovery, proclaimed in June 1947, which was essential to the economic rebuilding of Western Europe. In Eastern Europe, democratic socialist and other anticommunist forces were undermined and eliminated as Marxist-Leninist regimes, loyal to Moscow, were installed. The only exception was in Yugoslavia, where the Marxist leader, Marshal Tito, consolidated his position while maintaining independence from Moscow. Subsequently, Tito's Yugoslavia was to play an important role in the third world Nonaligned Movement (a group of states pursuing a policy of neutrality toward the superpowers).

The first major confrontation of the Cold War took place over Berlin in 1948 (see Table 2.2 for a list of Cold War crises). During the Yalta and Potsdam Conferences, Germany and Berlin were divided among the four victorious powers: the United States, the Soviet Union, Great Britain, and France. The former German capital was left deep in the heart of the Soviet zone of occupation (East Berlin), and in June 1948, Stalin sought to resolve its status by severing road and rail communications. West Berlin's population and political autonomy were kept alive by a massive airlift. Stalin ended the blockade in May 1949. The crisis saw the deployment of American long-range bombers in Britain, officially described as "atomic capable," though none were armed with nuclear weapons. United States military deployment was followed by political commitment enshrined in the **North Atlantic Treaty Organization (NATO)** treaty signed in April 1949. The key article of the treaty—that an attack on one member would be treated as an attack on all—accorded with the principle of collective self-defense enshrined in Article 51 of the UN Charter. In practice, the cornerstone of the alliance was the commitment of the United States to defend Western Europe. In reality, this soon meant the willingness of the United States to use nuclear weapons to deter Soviet aggression. For the Soviet Union, political encirclement soon entailed a growing military, and specifically nuclear, threat.

Although the origins of the Cold War were in Europe, events and conflicts in Asia and elsewhere were also crucial. In 1949, the thirty-year Chinese civil war ended in victory for the communists under Mao Zedong. This had a major impact on Asian affairs and on perceptions in both Moscow and Washington. In June 1950, the North Korean attack on South Korea was interpreted as part of a general communist strategy and as a test case for American resolve and the will of the United Nations to withstand aggression. The resulting American and UN commitment, followed in October 1950 by Chinese involvement, led to a war lasting three years in which more than 3 million people died before prewar borders were restored. North and South Korea themselves remained locked in seemingly perpetual hostility, even after the Cold War.

The US Air Force brings milk to citizens of Berlin during the Soviet road blockade of the city in 1948. This may have been the first time the world saw the true intentions of the Soviet Union and its totalitarian regime.

Truman Doctrine A statement made by US President Harry Truman in March 1947 that it "must be the policy of the United States to support free people who are resisting attempted subjugation by armed minorities or by outside pressures."

containment An American political strategy for resisting perceived Soviet expansion.

Marshall Plan Officially known as the European Recovery Program, it was a program of financial and other economic aid for Europe after World War II. Proposed by Secretary of State George Marshall in 1948, it was offered to all European states, including the Soviet Union.

North Atlantic Treaty Organization (NATO) The organization established by treaty in April 1949 comprising twelve (later sixteen) countries from Western Europe and North America. The most important aspect of the NATO alliance was the American commitment to the defense of Western Europe. Today, NATO has twenty-eight member states.

Table 2.2
Cold War Crises

Years	Crisis	Key Actors
1948–1949	Berlin	USSR/US/UK
1950–1953	Korean Conflict	North Korea/South Korea/US/People's Republic of China
1954–1955	Taiwan Strait	US/People's Republic of China
1961	Berlin	USSR/US/NATO
1962	Cuba	USSR/US/Cuba
1973	Arab-Israeli War	Egypt/Israel/Syria/Jordan/US/USSR
1975	Angola	US/ USSR/Cuba/China/South Africa
1979–1992	Afghanistan	USSR/US/Saudi Arabia/Pakistan
1979–1990	Nicaragua-El Salvador	US/USSR/Cuba

Conflict, Confrontation, and Compromise

One consequence of the Korean War was the buildup of American forces in Western Europe, lest communist aggression in Asia distract from the American-perceived real intent in Europe. The idea that communism was a monolithic political entity controlled from Moscow became an enduring American fixation not shared in London and elsewhere. Western Europeans nevertheless depended on the United States for military security, and this dependency deepened as the Cold War confrontation in Europe was consolidated. The rearmament of the Federal Republic of Germany in 1954 precipitated the creation of the **Warsaw Pact** in 1955, an agreement of mutual defense and military aid signed by communist European states of Eastern Europe under Soviet influence. The military buildup continued apace, with unprecedented concentrations of conventional and, moreover, nuclear forces. By the 1960s, there were some 7,000 nuclear weapons in Western Europe alone. NATO deployed nuclear weapons to offset Soviet conventional superiority, and Soviet short-range, or "theater nuclear," forces in Europe compensated for overall American nuclear superiority.

Warsaw Pact An agreement of mutual defense and military aid signed in May 1955 in response to West Germany's rearmament and entry into NATO. It comprised the USSR and seven communist states (though Albania withdrew support in 1961). The pact was officially dissolved in July 1991.

The death of Stalin in March 1953 portended significant consequences for the USSR at home and abroad. Stalin's eventual successor, Nikita Khrushchev, strove to modernize Soviet society, and in the process, he helped unleash reformist forces in Eastern Europe. While Poland was controlled, the situation in Hungary threatened Soviet hegemony, and in 1956, the intervention of the Red Army brought bloodshed to the streets of Budapest and international condemnation on Moscow. Soviet intervention coincided with an attack on Egypt by Britain, France, and Israel, precipitated by Colonel Nasser's nationalization of the Suez Canal in a manner that displeased Britain, the former colonial occupier. The French took part in the attack because Nasser's government was providing support to anti-French rebels in Algeria. The British government's actions provoked fierce domestic and international criticism and the most serious rift in the "special relationship" between Britain and the United States. President Eisenhower was strongly opposed to the actions of the US allies, and in the face of what were effectively US economic sanctions (a threat to cut off American oil exports to Britain), the British abandoned the operation as well as their support for the French and Israelis.

Khrushchev's policy toward the West mixed a search for political coexistence with the pursuit of ideological confrontation. Soviet support for movements of national liberation aroused fears in the West of a global communist challenge. American commitment to **liberal democracy** and national self-determination was often subordinated to Cold War perspectives as well as to US economic and political interests. The Cold War saw the growth of large permanent intelligence organizations, whose roles ranged from estimating intentions and capabilities of adversaries to covert intervention in the affairs of other states. Crises over Berlin in 1961 and Cuba in 1962 marked the most dangerous moments of the Cold War. In both, there was a risk of direct military confrontation and, certainly in October 1962, the possibility of nuclear war. How close the world came to Armageddon during the Cuban Missile Crisis and exactly why peace was preserved remain matters of debate among historians and surviving officials.

The events of 1962 were followed by a stabler period of coexistence and competition. Nuclear arsenals, nevertheless, continued to grow. Whether this is best characterized as an **arms race** or whether internal political and bureaucratic pressures drove the growth of nuclear arsenals is open to interpretation. For Washington, commitments to NATO allies also provided pressures and opportunities to develop and deploy their own shorter-range (tactical and theater) nuclear weapons. The global nuclear dimension increased with the emergence of other nuclear-weapon states: Britain in 1952, France in 1960, and China in 1964. Growing concern at the spread, or proliferation, of nuclear weapons led to the negotiation of the Nuclear Nonproliferation Treaty (NPT) in 1968, wherein states that had nuclear weapons committed themselves to halt the arms race, and those that did not possess them promised not to develop them. Despite successes of the NPT, by 1990, several states had developed or were developing nuclear weapons, notably Israel, India, Pakistan, and apartheid South Africa. (South Africa later gave up its nuclear weapons program and remains the only state to have done so.)

The Rise and Fall of Détente

At the same time that America's commitment in Vietnam was deepening, Soviet-Chinese relations were deteriorating. Indeed, by 1969, the People's Republic of China and the Soviet Union had fought a minor border war over a territorial dispute. Despite (or because of) these tensions, the foundations for what became known as **détente** were laid between the Soviet Union and the United States and for what became known as **rapprochement** between China and the United States. Both terms, long a part of the language of diplomacy, refer to the processes by which countries seek to improve their relations. Détente in Europe had its origins in the **Ostpolitik** of German chancellor Willy Brandt and resulted in agreements that recognized the peculiar status of Berlin and the sovereignty of East Germany. For his efforts, which finally bore fruit with the end of the Cold War in 1989, Brandt won the Nobel Peace Prize. Soviet-American détente had its roots in mutual recognition of the need to avoid nuclear crises and in the economic and military incentives in avoiding an unconstrained arms race. Both Washington and Moscow also looked toward Beijing when making their bilateral calculations.

In the West, détente was associated with the political leadership of President Richard Nixon and his adviser Henry Kissinger, who were also instrumental in Sino-American rapprochement. This new phase in Soviet-American relations did not mark an end to political conflict, as each side pursued political goals, some of which were increasingly

liberal democracy States with democratic or representative governments and capitalist economies that are promoters of multilateralism and free trade. Domestic interests, values, and institutions shape foreign policy.

arms race A central concept in realist thought. As states build up their military to address real or perceived threats to their national security, they may create insecurity in other states. These states in turn develop their military capacities and thus begin an arms race. This never-ending pursuit of security creates the condition we know as a security dilemma.

détente The relaxation of tension between East and West; Soviet-American détente lasted from the late 1960s to the late 1970s and was characterized by negotiations and nuclear arms control agreements.

rapprochement The reestablishment of more friendly relations between the People's Republic of China and the United States in the early 1970s.

Ostpolitik The West German government's "Eastern Policy" of the mid- to late 1960s, designed to develop relations between West Germany and members of the Warsaw Pact.

Did Mao Zedong and Richard Nixon change the balance of Cold War politics when they shook hands in Beijing in 1972?

intercontinental ballistic missiles (ICBMs) Weapons system the United States and Soviet Union developed to threaten each other with destruction. The thirty- to forty-minute flight times of the missiles created a situation that is sometimes called "mutually assured destruction" (MAD) or "the balance of terror."

incompatible with the aspirations of the other super-power. Both sides supported friendly regimes and movements and subverted adversaries. All this came as various political upheavals were taking place in the third world (see Table 2.1). The question of how far the superpowers could control their friends, and how far they were entangled by their commitments, was underlined in 1973 when the Arab-Israeli War embroiled both the United States and the Soviet Union in what became a potentially dangerous confrontation. Getting the superpowers involved in the war—whether by design or serendipity—helped create the political conditions for Egyptian-Israeli rapprochement. Diplomatic and strategic relations were transformed as Egypt switched its allegiance from Moscow to Washington. In the short term, Egypt was isolated in the Arab world. For Israel, fear of a war of annihilation fought on two fronts was lifted. Yet continuing political violence and terrorism, and the enduring enmity between Israel and other Arab states, proved insurmountable obstacles to a more permanent regional settlement.

In Washington, Soviet support for revolutionary movements in the third world was seen as evidence of duplicity. Some American politicians and academics claim that Moscow's support for revolutionary forces in Ethiopia in 1975 killed détente. Others cite the Soviet role in Angola in 1978. Furthermore, the perception that the USSR was using arms control agreements to gain military advantage was linked to Soviet behavior in the third world. Growing Soviet military superiority was reflected in growing Soviet influence, it was argued. Critics claimed the Strategic Arms Limitation Talks (SALT) process enabled the Soviets to deploy multiple independently targetable warheads on their large **intercontinental ballistic missiles (ICBMs)**, threatening key American forces. America faced a "window of vulnerability," critics of détente claimed. The view from Moscow was different, reflecting different assumptions about the scope and purpose of détente and the nature of nuclear deterrence. Other events were also seen to weaken American influence. The overthrow of the shah of Iran in 1979 resulted in the loss of an important Western ally in the region, though the ensuing militant Islamic government was hostile to both superpowers.

December 1979 marked a point of transition in East-West affairs. NATO agreed to deploy land-based Cruise and Pershing II missiles in Europe if negotiations with the Soviets did not reduce what NATO saw as a serious imbalance. Later in the month, Soviet armed forces intervened in Afghanistan to support their revolutionary allies. The USSR was bitterly condemned in the West and in the third world for its actions and soon became committed to a protracted and bloody struggle that many compared to the American war in Vietnam. In Washington, President Carter, who had sought to control arms and reduce tensions with the USSR, hardened his view of the Soviet Union. The first reaction was the Carter Doctrine, which clearly stated that any Soviet attack on countries in the Persian Gulf would be seen as a direct attack on US vital interests. Another result was the Carter administration's decision to boycott the 1980 Summer Olympics in Moscow. Nevertheless, Republicans increasingly used foreign and defense policy to attack the Carter presidency. Perceptions of American weakness abroad permeated domestic politics, and in 1980, Ronald Reagan was elected president. He was committed to a more confrontational approach with the Soviets on arms control, third world conflicts, and East-West relations in general.

From Détente to a Second Cold War

In the West, critics of détente and arms control, some of whom would later advise the George W. Bush presidential administration, argued in the 1970s and 1980s that the Soviets were acquiring nuclear superiority. Some suggested that the United States should pursue policies and strategies based on the idea that victory in nuclear war was possible. The election of Ronald Reagan in 1980 was a watershed in Soviet-American relations. Ronald Reagan had made it clear during the election campaign that the United States would take a tough stance in its relations with the Soviet Union. In two monumental speeches delivered in March 1983, Reagan stated that the Soviet Union was the "focus of evil in the modern world," and he coined the phrase "evil empire" to describe the USSR. In the second speech, he outlined his idea for a strategic defense against Soviet missiles. One issue that Reagan inherited, and which loomed large in the breakdown of relations between East and West, was nuclear missiles in Europe. NATO's decision to deploy land-based missiles capable of striking Soviet territory precipitated a period of great tension in relations between NATO and the USSR and political friction within NATO.

Reagan's own incautious public remarks reinforced perceptions that he was as ill informed as he was dangerous in matters nuclear, though key arms policies were consistent with those of his predecessor, Jimmy Carter. On arms control, Reagan was disinterested in agreements that would freeze the status quo for the sake of getting agreement, and Soviet and American negotiators proved unable to make progress in talks on long-range and intermediate-range weapons. One particular idea had significant consequences for arms control and for Washington's relations with its allies and its adversaries. The **Strategic Defense Initiative (SDI)**, quickly dubbed "Star Wars" after a new movie, was a research program designed to explore the feasibility of space-based defenses against ballistic missiles. The Soviets appeared to take SDI very seriously and claimed that Reagan's real purpose was to regain the nuclear monopoly of the 1950s. The technological advances claimed by SDI proponents did not materialize, however, and the program was eventually reduced and marginalized, although never fully eliminated from the US defense budget.

The resulting period of tension and confrontation between the superpowers has been described as the second cold war or the end of détente and compared to the early period of confrontation and tension from 1946 to 1953. In Western Europe and the Soviet Union, there was real fear of nuclear war. Much of this fear was a reaction to the rhetoric and policies of the Reagan administration. The world viewed American statements on nuclear weapons, military intervention in Grenada in 1983, and an air raid against Libya in 1986 as evidence of a new belligerence. Reagan's policy toward Central America and his support for the rebel Contras in Nicaragua were sources of controversy within the United States and internationally. The International Court of Justice (ICJ), a judicial court of the United Nations (which we'll discuss in Chapter 6), found the United States guilty of violating international law in 1986 for sowing sea mines in Nicaraguan harbors. The Reagan administration ignored this ruling, claiming the ICJ lacked jurisdiction in this situation.

Strategic Defense Initiative (SDI) A controversial strategic policy advocated by the Reagan administration and nuclear physicists such as Edward Teller, who helped create the hydrogen bomb. The plan, which is often derisively nicknamed "Star Wars," called for a defensive missile shield that would make Soviet offensive missiles ineffective by destroying them in flight.

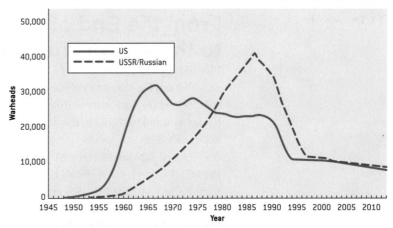

US-USSR/RUSSIAN NUCLEAR STOCKPILE, 1945–2013.

The Reagan administration's use of military power was nonetheless limited: rhetoric and perception were at variance with reality. Some operations ended in humiliating failure, notably in Lebanon in 1983 after a truck bomb attack on the US Marine barracks in Beirut. Nevertheless, there is evidence that the Soviet leadership took very seriously the words (and deeds) of the Reagan administration and believed that Washington was planning a nuclear first strike. In 1983, Soviet air defenses shot down a South Korean civilian airliner in Soviet airspace. The American reaction and the imminent deployment of US nuclear missiles in Europe created a climate of great tension in East-West relations.

Throughout the early 1980s, the ill health of a series of Soviet leaders (Brezhnev, Andropov, and Chernenko) inhibited Soviet responses to the American challenge and the American threat. In 1985, however, Mikhail Gorbachev became general secretary of the Soviet Communist Party, a position that gave him control over the state. Gorbachev's "new thinking" in foreign policy and his domestic reforms created a revolution both in the USSR's foreign relations and within Soviet society. At home, **glasnost** (or openness) and **perestroika** (or restructuring) unleashed nationalist and other forces that, to Gorbachev's dismay, were to destroy the Union of Soviet Socialist Republics.

Gorbachev paved the way for agreements on nuclear and conventional forces that helped ease the tensions of the early 1980s. In 1987, he traveled to Washington to sign the Intermediate Nuclear Forces (INF) Treaty, banning intermediate-range nuclear missiles, including Cruise and Pershing II. This agreement was heralded as a triumph for the Soviet leader, but NATO leaders, including Margaret Thatcher and Ronald Reagan, argued that it was vindication of the policies pursued by NATO since 1979. The INF Treaty was concluded more quickly than a new agreement on cutting strategic nuclear weapons, in part because of continuing Soviet opposition to SDI. And it was Reagan's successor, George H. W. Bush, who concluded a **Strategic Arms Reductions Treaty (START)** agreement that reduced long-range nuclear weapons (though only back to the level they had been in the early 1980s). Gorbachev used agreements on nuclear weapons as a means of building trust and demonstrated the serious and radical nature of his purpose. However, despite similar radical agreements on conventional forces in Europe (culminating in the Paris agreement of 1990), the end of the Cold War marked success in nuclear arms control rather than nuclear disarmament. The histories of the Cold War and of the atomic bomb are very closely connected, but although the Cold War is now over, nuclear weapons are still very much in existence. We will discuss the issues surrounding nuclear weapons in Chapter 8.

From the End of the Cold War to the War on Terrorism

The first major global conflict after the Cold War ended was the 1990 Iraqi invasion of neighboring Kuwait. After some attempts to find an Arab solution, the United States led a comprehensive multilateral diplomatic and military effort to punish Saddam Hussein for his actions and to signal to the world that this kind of violation of international law would not stand. The war to liberate Kuwait lasted only forty-two days, and an international coalition of diplomats and military forces helped define the "New World Order" that President George H. W. Bush had talked about since taking office in 1989. The United States wisely included the Soviet Union in its plans and effectively used the UN Security Council to pass more than twelve resolutions condemning the actions of Iraq. What the first President Bush created was a US-led global coalition that was supported by all five permanent members of the Security Council (China, France, the Russian Federation,

glasnost A policy of greater openness pursued by Soviet leader Mikhail Gorbachev from 1985, involving more toleration of internal dissent and criticism.

perestroika Gorbachev's policy of restructuring, pursued in tandem with glasnost and intended to modernize the Soviet political and economic system.

Strategic Arms Reductions Treaty (START) Negotiations between the United States and Soviet Union over limiting nuclear arsenals began in 1982 and progressed at a very slow pace over eight years. The eventual treaty in 1991 broke new ground because it called for a reduction of nuclear arms rather than just a limit on the growth of these weapons.

the United Kingdom, and the United States)—a first since the establishment of the United Nations. The majority of the world was behind this action. The invasion of Kuwait was illegal under international law, and the major powers were willing to work together to protect and promote a "rule-based system."

So it was that the world in 1990 was full of promise (especially for the victors of the Cold War) but full of potential risk as well. It was also replete with the sources of further conflict. This New World Order, as US President George H. W. Bush called it, existed briefly between two eras: one defined by an ongoing struggle between two competing secular ideologies and another shaped by an emerging clash between two conceptions of civilization itself.

The Cold War divided the world for more than forty years, threatened humanity with near destruction, and led to the death of at least 25 million people, mostly in the highly contested zone that came to be referred to as the "third world" during the Cold War. Yet in spite of these dangers and costs, the Cold War in its core areas still managed to create a degree of stability that the world had not experienced since the early part of the twentieth century. For this reason, many came to view the bipolar order after 1947 as something that was not merely the expression of a given international reality but also desirable and defensible. Indeed, as we will see in Chapter 3, some realists seemed to celebrate the superpower relationship on the grounds that a world with two balancing powers, each limiting the actions of the other, was likely to be a far stabler world than one with several competing states.

What happened in Eastern Europe in 1989, of course, produced enormous shock waves. The world at the time was already undergoing dramatic changes, mainly the result of radical new policies introduced by Soviet leader Mikhail Gorbachev. Many people hoped that Gorbachev's several reforms would make the world a safer and more humane place. Hardly anybody, though, seriously anticipated the collapse of communism and the destruction of the Berlin Wall. Moreover, few believed that this revolutionary process could be achieved peacefully. Policy makers had not planned for it, and the intelligence agencies in the West had completely missed the signs of change in the Soviet bloc. It was all rather surprising, if not disturbing, for those who had thought this superpower rivalry would never end without some nuclear confrontation. Now world leaders had to remake the world and find ways to integrate former enemies back into the West.

The tasks they confronted certainly seemed very great, ranging from the institutional one of devising new tasks for bodies such as NATO, the United Nations, and the European Union (created in 1992) to the more economic challenge of facilitating the transition in countries that had little experience running **market democracies**. Some wondered whether a US-led Atlantic Alliance could survive in an environment where there was no longer a well-defined threat. Certainly, many questioned the need for high military spending, arguing that if the world was now becoming a safer and more integrated place, what then was the purpose of spending billions on weapons?

When the Soviet Union dissolved, many of its allies across the world lost their power as well. The pro-Soviet military junta in Ethiopia fell from power in 1991, and statues of Lenin were torn down.

market democracies
See *liberal democracies.*

WHAT'S YOUR WORLDVIEW

With the end of the Cold War, many analysts talked optimistically about a "peace dividend"—that is, a chance to shift spending from military to social programs like education, health, and job training. Many European states and NATO partners cut their spending, but the United States did not cut military spending and shift funding to domestic priorities. Why do you think this happened? Do you think US leaders feared a new rival like China, or did they anticipate the need for a strong military to support their hegemonic position?

Globalization: Challenging the International Order?

If the Cold War period was marked by a clear and sharp divide between opposing socio-economic systems operating by radically different standards, then the post–Cold War order could readily be characterized as one in which many states were compelled to play by a single set of rules within an increasingly competitive world economy. The term most frequently used to describe this new order was *globalization*, a notion that had barely been used before 1989 but now came to be employed ever more regularly to define an apparently new system of international relations.

Globalization, however, seemed to mean different things to different theorists. Thus, for one school, the hyperglobalists, it was assumed to be undermining borders and states—quite literally abolishing the Westphalian system, which had begun to crystallize over 330 years ago, as we read at the beginning of this chapter. Thomas Friedman (2000) argued that globalization has changed world politics forever, giving individuals more tools to influence markets and governments and create networks that challenge the power of states. Others—the skeptics—took a less cataclysmic view. Globalization, they agreed, was providing a different context within which international relations was now being played out. But it would be absurd to conclude that it was doing away with the state or destroying the underlying logic of **anarchy**. Anthony Giddens (2000) reminded us that globalization might pull power away from the state, but it might also empower local groups who want to defend their position in this global society. Some writers were even skeptical of whether there was anything especially novel about globalization. **Capitalism**, after all, had always been a global system. Since the sixteenth century, interdependence had been one of capitalism's more obvious features. So why assume that there was much new about the phenomenon simply because academics and publicists talked about it with greater frequency?

Such skepticism, however, did not prevent its many critics and equally influential defenders from engaging in an extended and at times heated debate about the impact of globalization on global inequality, climate change, and the more general distribution of power in the international system. It also made very little difference as to what governments tended to say and do. Globalization, they insisted with growing regularity, was a fact of economic life. There was no escaping its logic. The only thing one could do (using the oft-repeated words of President Clinton) was to "compete not retreat." Moreover, if one did not do so, the future for one's own people, and by implication one's state, was bleak. United Kingdom prime minister Tony Blair agreed and even appeared to use the menace of globalization as a means of attacking those in Europe who would defend old economic ways. In a world of global competition, Blair observed, there was really very little choice. Europe either had to reform or decline. There was no other way.

But if there was little meeting of minds among politicians and academics, there was little doubt of the impact globalization was having on the world economy, in particular on its three central-core locations in North America, Europe, and East Asia. Here, at least, the theoretical debate about the novelty, existence, and meaning of the phenomenon was being resolved, as this very special triad of economic power (over 80 percent of the world's total) experienced reasonable growth, increased economic interdependence, and massive wealth creation. No doubt the process caused great national uncertainty as firms became ever more internationalized. For example, with the creation of high-speed information technologies, a firm, whether large or small, could have its management

anarchy A system operating in the absence of any central government. It does not imply chaos but, in realist theory, the absence of political authority.

capitalism A system of production in which human labor and its products are commodities that are bought and sold in the marketplace.

offices in one country, its design staff in another, and its production facilities in a third. Many US corporations, encouraged by federal tax code, led the way in this process.

There was also something distinctly unethical about an apparently unregulated economic process that literally made billions for the few (especially those in the financial sector) while generating insecurity for the many. However, this was a price well worth paying—or so its defenders inferred—if there was to be any semblance of economic progress. In a world where extreme competition ruled and money moved at the flick of a switch, there was only one thing worse than being part of this runaway system—and that was not being part of it.

From Superpower to Hyperpower: US Primacy

If a one-world economy operating under the same set of highly competitive rules was at least one consequence of the end of the Cold War, another was a major resurgence of American self-confidence in a new international system where it seemed to have no serious rival. This was not only a development that few had foretold (in the 1970s and 1980s, many analysts believed that the United States was in decline); it was one that many had thought impossible (most realists in fact believed that after the Cold War the world would become genuinely multipolar). It was also a situation many feared on the grounds that an America with no obvious peer competitor would act more assertively and with less restraint. That aside, all of the most obvious indicators by the late 1990s—military, economic, and cultural—seemed to point to only one conclusion: as a result of the Soviet collapse, followed in short order by the economic crisis in Japan and Europe's manifest failure to manage the conflict in the former Yugoslavia, the United States by the turn of the century had been transformed from a mere superpower (its designation hitherto) to what the French foreign minister Hubert Vedrine in 1998 termed a **hyperpower**. Former secretary of state Madeleine Albright may have also agreed, in her own way, with this assessment, although she used more diplomatic language; she called the United States "the indispensable power" in global politics.

This claim to unilateral privilege was linked to a particularly bleak view of the world shared by many, though not all, US policy makers. The Cold War may have been over, they agreed: America may have emerged triumphant. But this was no reason to be complacent. To repeat a phrase often used at the time, although the "dragon" in the form of the USSR had been slain, there were still many "vipers and snakes" lurking in the tall grass. Among the five most dangerous and pernicious of these were various rogue states (Iran, Iraq, North Korea, Libya, and Cuba), the constant threat of nuclear proliferation (made all the more likely by the disintegration of the USSR and the unfolding nuclear arms race between Pakistan and India), and the threat of religious fundamentalists and ideological extremists (all the more virulent now because of the fallout from the last great battlefield of the Cold War in Afghanistan). Indeed, long before 9/11, the dangers posed by radical Islamism were very well known to US intelligence, beginning with the bombing of the US Marine barracks in Beirut, Lebanon, in October 1983, that caused the deaths of almost 300 American personnel. The devastating bombing of the World Trade Center in 1993 and the US embassies in Tanzania and Kenya five years later, as well as the audacious attack on the USS *Cole* in 2000, all pointed to a new form of **terrorism** that could be neither deterred nor easily defeated by conventional means.

Yet in spite of these several threats, there was no clear indication that the United States was eager during the 1990s to project its power with any serious purpose. The United States may have possessed vast capabilities, but there appeared to be no real desire in a post–Cold War environment to expend American blood and treasure in foreign adventures.

hyperpower The situation of the United States after the Cold War ended. With the Soviet Union's military might greatly diminished and China having primarily only regional power-projecting capability, the United States was unchallenged in the world.

terrorism The use of violence by nonstate groups or, in some cases, states to inspire fear by attacking civilians and/or symbolic targets and eliminating opposition groups. This is done for purposes such as drawing widespread attention to a grievance, provoking a severe response, or wearing down an opponent's moral resolve to effect political change.

GLOBAL PERSPECTIVE

Perception, Continuity, and Change After January 20, 2009

The study of global politics depends to a great extent on perception. How we think about the world often determines what we think is important. This habit of mind helps explain how political leaders and opinion makers in the United States were unprepared for the two key events of the late twentieth century: the collapse of the Soviet Union and the rise of militant Islamic fundamentalism. The signs of the two events were in plain sight if you knew what to look for.

In the case of Islamic fundamentalism, certainly if you lived in a country with a large Muslim population, you would have been aware of the growing appeal of fundamentalist strains of Islam. The Wahabi sect in Saudi Arabia, for instance, forms the basis for society there. Egypt has had problems with violence linked to the Muslim Brotherhood since the time of British colonization. Indeed, the Brotherhood is often blamed for the assassination of President Anwar Sadat. In Afghanistan, the United States itself helped arm Islamic fundamentalists in their war against the Soviet invasion during the 1980s. The trend was visible every day in public as people rejected European styles of dress: more men grew beards, and more women adopted the clothing styles the fundamentalists preferred.

If North American and European leaders were not ready for the impact of Islamic fundamentalism, how unprepared are people in the rest of the world for trends that are resulting from the Arab Spring, the killing of Osama bin Laden, or the end of the war in Iraq? Will there be continuity or change in the Arab states, and will the current American administration abandon the unilateral strategies of the Bush years in favor of the multilateralism that framed the intervention in Libya and seems to be shaping the sanctions policies aimed at Iran? If we start with the global war on terrorism, we can see that some things now are the same, and some are not. For example, in the early months of 2009, the Obama administration continued to use Predator drone aircraft to attack suspected Islamic militants in tribal areas in Pakistan along the Afghanistan border. Operation Geronimo, which resulted in the death of Osama bin Laden, was launched without the permission of Pakistani leaders. Pakistani officials objected to drone attacks during the Bush years, but President Obama decided that the raids must continue, and it is likely these kinds of attacks will continue with or without the support of Pakistan. A major change in US policy could be seen, however, in the fundraising efforts to rebuild Palestinian

homes in Gaza. Moreover, as the United States increased the number of its troops in Afghanistan to fight the resurgent Taliban, officials in Washington also quietly expressed their dissatisfaction with the actions of the Karzai government there. Both were major changes from the policy of the Bush administration.

Change is not always in a direction that you can control. One result of the Arab Spring is the move away from autocratic regimes toward democratic systems. Elections in Tunisia and Egypt have put Islamic parties in power. A moderate Islamic party won more than 40 percent of the vote in the 2011 elections in Tunisia. The Muslim Brotherhood's Freedom and Justice Party

The Nobel Peace Prize committee members chose US president Barack Obama as their honoree in 2009. What must be done to fulfill the promise that the committee saw in the election of Obama?

Continued

GLOBAL PERSPECTIVE | Perception, Continuity, and Change After January 20, 2009 *continued*

and the ultraconservative Salafis together won more than 70 percent of the seats in the new Egyptian parliament in early 2012. However, in 2013, the Egyptian military overthrew the legally elected government led by President Morsi. The United States and its allies in the West and in the Middle East are in a political bind. Do they support religious parties that represent extremist religious views, or do they support nondemocratic forces like the Egyptian military that overthrow an elected government? Since the experience of September 11 it has been difficult for the United States and its allies to work with Islamist parties.

For people outside the United States, it is difficult to assess the meaning of apparent continuity or change in US foreign policy. One source of this difficulty is the perception popular in the developing world that the United States is the global hegemonic oppressor. People have been socialized by family members, schools, and political officials to blame the United States for all their sufferings.

This is a perception that may not be based on fact, and it could be as incorrect as the perception that all Muslims are terrorists or that Islamic fundamentalism did not pose a threat to Europe and the United States. Perceptions and images are often more powerful than reality.

For Discussion

1. Images die a slow death. Many people in the West still distrust the Russians because of the Cold War, which has been over since the late 1980s. How do we overcome the perceptions and misperceptions that shape our views of other cultures?

2. Do you think countries like the United States and other major powers need an enemy? Does it serve political interests and maybe economic interests to have such a foe? Explain.

3. Do you think the United States and the West will be able to work with the Islamist parties in Egypt, Tunisia, Iraq, and Afghanistan? Why or why not?

The desire sank even further following the debacle in Somalia in 1993: the death of eighteen US soldiers there created its own kind of syndrome that made any more US forays abroad extremely unlikely. The United States after the Cold War was thus a most curious hegemon. On the one hand, its power seemed to be unrivaled (and was); on the other, it seemed to have very little idea about how to use this power other than to bomb the occasional rogue state when deemed necessary (as in former Yugoslavia), while supporting diplomatic solutions to most problems when need be (as in the cases of the Middle East and North Korea). The end of the Cold War and the disappearance of the Soviet threat may have rendered the international system securer and the United States more powerful, but it also made the United States a very reluctant warrior. In a very important sense, the United States during the 1990s remained a superpower without a mission.

The attack on the USS *Cole* in 2000 by Al Qaeda members using a motorboat containing a large bomb is what international security specialists call an example of asymmetrical warfare. Why did the leaders of the United States and other Western democracies ignore the growing threat of Islamic militants prior to September 11, 2001?

Europe in the New World System

If the most pressing post–Cold War problem for the United States was how to develop a coherent global policy in a world where there was no single major threat to its interests, then for Europe, the main issue was how to manage the new enlarged space that had been created as a result of the events in 1989. Indeed, while more triumphant Americans would continue to proclaim that it was they who had won the Cold War in Europe, it was Europeans who were the real beneficiaries of what had taken place in the late 1980s.

Civilians escorted by Kenyan police and soldiers escape the Westgate Mall in Nairobi, Kenya, that was attacked by Al Shabaab, a radical Islamic group supported by Al Qaeda. Kenya had sent peacekeeping troops to Somalia.

There were sound reasons for thinking this way. A continent that had once been divided was now whole again. Germany had been peacefully united. The states of Eastern Europe had achieved one of the most important of international rights: the right of self-determination. The threat of war with potentially devastating consequences for Europe had been eliminated. Naturally, the transition from one order to another was not going to happen without certain costs, borne most notably by those who would now have to face up to life under competitive capitalism. And the collapse of communism in some countries was not an entirely bloodless affair, as events in former Yugoslavia (1990–1999) revealed only too tragically. With that said, a post–Cold War Europe still had much to look forward to.

Although many in Europe debated the region's future, policy makers themselves were confronted with the more concrete issue of how to bring the East back into the West, a process that went under the general heading of enlargement. In terms of policy outcome, the strategy scored some notable successes. Indeed, by 2007, the European Union had grown to twenty-seven members, and NATO was one less at twenty-six, with most of the new members coming from the former Soviet bloc. The two bodies also changed their clublike character in the process, much to the consternation of some people in the original member states, who found the entrants from the former Soviet bloc to be as much trouble as asset. In fact, according to critics—both politicians and academics—enlargement had proceeded so rapidly that the essential core meaning of both organizations had been lost. The European Union, it was now argued by some, had been so keen to enlarge that it had lost the will to integrate. NATO meanwhile could no longer be regarded as a serious military organization with an integrated command structure. One significant aspect of this was the "out of area" problem that limited NATO activities to Europe itself. This would change after September 11, 2001. Still, it was difficult not to be impressed by the capacity of NATO and the European Union in their new roles. These institutions had helped shape part of Europe during the Cold War and were now being employed to help manage the relatively successful (though never easy) transition from one kind of European order to another. For those who had earlier disparaged the part institutions might play in preventing anarchy in Europe, the important roles played by the European Union and NATO seemed to prove that institutions were essential.

Europe, it was generally recognized, remained what it had effectively been since the end of World War II: a work in progress. The problem was that nobody could quite agree when, if ever, this work would be completed and where, if anywhere, the European Union would end. Some analysts remained remarkably upbeat. The European Union's capacity for dealing with the consequences of the end of the Cold War, its successful introduction of a single currency (the euro, in January 2002), and its ability to bring in new members all pointed to one obvious conclusion: the European Union's future was assured. A few even speculated that the new twenty-first century would itself be European rather than American. Many, however, were more skeptical. After a decade-long period of expansion and experimentation, Europe, they believed, had reached a dead end. It was more divided than united over basic constitutional ends, and it faced several challenges—economic, cultural, and political—to which there seemed to be no easy answers. Indeed, according to some commentators, European leaders not only confronted older issues that remained unsolved, but they also faced a host of new ones (e.g., Turkish membership in the European Union, how to integrate its 13 million Muslim citizens, and rising economic competition from China) to which they had no ready-made solutions. Europe, by the beginning of the twenty-first century, may have been well aware of where it was coming from, but it had no blueprint for where it wanted to go. In some ways, Europe had "lost the plot."

Russia: From Yeltsin to Putin

One of the many problems facing the new Europe after the Cold War was how to define its relationship with postcommunist Russia, a country confronting several degrees of stress after 1991 as it began to transform itself from a Marxist superpower with a planned economy to a democratic country that was liberal and market oriented. As even the most confident of Europeans accepted, none of this was going to be easy for a state that had experienced the same system for nearly three-quarters of a century. And so it proved during the 1990s, an especially painful decade during which Russia lost its ability to effectively challenge the United States and was instead a declining power with diminishing economic and ideological assets. Furthermore, there was not much in the way of economic compensation. On the contrary, as a result of its speedy adoption of Western-style privatization, Russia underwent something close to a 1930s-style economic depression, with industrial production plummeting, living standards sinking, and whole regions once devoted to Cold War military production experiencing free fall.

President Boris Yeltsin's foreign policy, meanwhile, did little to reassure many Russians. Indeed, his decision to get close to Russia's old capitalist enemies gave the distinct impression that he was selling out to the West. This made him a hero to many outside Russia. However, to many ordinary Russians, it seemed as if he (like his predecessor Gorbachev) was conceding everything and getting very little in return. Nationalists and old communists, still present in significant numbers, were especially scathing. Yeltsin and his team, they argued, had not only given away Russia's assets at "discount prices" to a new class of **oligarchs**, but he was also trying to turn Russia into a Western dependency. In short, he was not standing up for Russia's national interest.

oligarchs A term from ancient Greece to describe members of a small group that controls a state.

Whether his successor Vladimir Putin, a former official in the KGB, had a clear vision for Russia when he took over the presidency matters less than the fact that, having assumed office, he began to stake out very different positions. These included greater authoritarianism and nationalism at home, a much clearer recognition that the interests of Russia and those of the West would not always be one and the same, and what turned into a persistent drive to bring the Russian economy—and Russia's huge natural resources—back under state control. This did not lead to turning back the clock to Soviet times. What it did mean, though, was that the West's leaders could no longer regard the country as a potential strategic partner. Certainly, Western governments could not assume that Russia would forever be in a state of decline. The West must instead confront a state with almost unlimited supplies of oil and gas and with a leadership determined to defend Russia's interests and to restore Russia to a position of global leadership.

Still, the West had less to fear now than during the Cold War proper. Economic reform had made Russia dependent on the West (though some Western countries, like Germany, depended on Russia for their energy requirements). Furthermore, the official political ideology did not in any

WHAT'S YOUR WORLDVIEW

One of Russia's concerns today is the expansion of NATO with the addition of many of the former Soviet-bloc countries, like Poland, Hungary, and the Czech Republic. Even Estonia, Latvia, Lithuania—all former republics in the USSR—have joined NATO. Many Russians feel surrounded by the potential adversaries and are concerned with the growing influence of the United States on their borders. Given this sentiment, why did the Bush administration insist on this expansion? With the end of the Cold War, is there even a need for NATO?

The "stare-down" at the G-8 summit in Northern Ireland between the leaders of two powerful states may reveal the deep divisions between President Obama and President Putin over the conflict in Syria and the negotiations over Iran's nuclear weapons. Now one might add the serious disagreement over Russian policy toward Ukraine.

way challenge Western institutions or values. The world had changed forever since 1991. Nor was Russia the power it had once been during Soviet times. Indeed, not only was it unable to prevent some of its former republics from either signing up to former enemy institutions like NATO or moving more openly into the Western camp, but by 2007, it was effectively encircled by the three Baltic republics to the northwest, an increasingly pro-Western Ukraine to the south, and Georgia in the Caucasus. Adding to its potential woes was the fact that many of its more loyal, regional allies ran highly repressive and potentially unstable governments: Belarus, Turkmenistan, and Azerbaijan, for example.

Meanwhile, in Chechnya, Russia faced an insurgency beginning in 1994 that not only revealed deep weaknesses in the Russian military but also brought down Western outrage on its head—perhaps not to the point of causing a rupture but certainly enough to sour relations. Many in the United States and a few in Europe were compelled to conclude that while Russia may have changed in several positive ways since the collapse of the USSR in 1991, at the end of the day, it still remained historic Russia with an authoritarian outlook, a disregard for human rights, and an inclination toward empire. A new future may have beckoned, but the heavy hand of the past continued to influence relations between Russia and the West.

East Asia: Primed for Rivalry?

If perceived lessons from history continue to play a crucial role in shaping modern Western images of post-Soviet Russia, then the past also plays a part in defining the international relations of East Asia—and a most bloody past it has been. The time following World War II was punctuated by several devastating wars (in China, Korea, and Vietnam), revolutionary insurgencies (in the Philippines, Malaya, and Indonesia), authoritarian rule (nearly everywhere), and revolutionary extremism (most tragically in Cambodia). The contrast with the postwar European experience could not have been more pronounced. In fact, scholars of international relations have been much taken with the comparison, pointing out that whereas Europe managed to form a new liberal security community during the Cold War, East Asia did not. In part, this was the result of the formation of the European Union and the creation of NATO (organizations that had no equivalents in Asia). But it was also because Germany managed to effect a serious reconciliation with its immediate neighbors while Japan (for largely internal reasons) did not. The end of the Cold War in Europe transformed the continent dramatically, but this was much less true in East Asia, where powerful communist parties continued to rule—in China, North Korea, and Vietnam—and at least two outstanding territorial disputes (a less important one between Japan and Russia and a potentially far more dangerous one between China and Taiwan) continued to threaten the security of the region.

For all these reasons, East Asia, far from being primed for peace, was still ripe for new rivalries. Europe's very bloody past between 1914 and 1945, went the argument, could easily turn into Asia's future. This was not a view shared by every commentator, however. In fact, as events unfolded, this uncompromisingly tough-minded realist perspective came under sustained criticism. Critics did not deny the possibility of future disturbances: How could they, given Korean division, North Korea's nuclear weapons program, and China's claim to

Taiwan? But several factors did suggest that the region was not quite the powder keg some thought it to be.

The first and most important factor was the great economic success experienced by the region itself. The sources of this have been much debated, with some people suggesting that the underlying reasons were cultural and others that they were directly economic (cheap labor plus plentiful capital); a few believed they were the byproduct of the application of a nonliberal model of development employing the strong state to drive through rapid economic development from above. Some have also argued that the United States played a crucial role by opening its market to East Asian goods while providing the region with critical security on the cheap. Whatever the cause or combination of causes, the fact remains that East Asia by the end of the twentieth century had become the third-largest powerhouse in the global economy, accounting for nearly 25 percent of world **gross domestic product (GDP)**.

Second, although many states in East Asia may have had powerful memories of past conflicts, these were beginning to be overridden in the 1990s by a growth in regional trade and investment. Indeed, even though East Asia carried much historical baggage (some of this deliberately exploited by political elites in search of legitimacy), economic pressures and material self-interest appeared to be driving countries in the region together rather than apart. The process of East Asian economic integration was not quick—the **Association of Southeast Asian Nations (ASEAN)** was only formed in 1967. Nor was integration accompanied by the formation of anything like the European Union. However, once regionalism began to take off during the 1990s, it showed no signs of slowing down.

A third reason for optimism lay with Japan. Here, in spite of an apparent inability to unambiguously apologize for past misdeeds and atrocities—a failure that cost it dearly in terms of **soft power** (see Chapter 5) influence in the region—its policies could hardly be characterized as disturbing. On the contrary, having adopted its famous peace constitution in the 1950s and renounced the possibility of ever acquiring nuclear weapons (Japan was one the strongest upholders of the original 1968 Nonproliferation Treaty), Japan demonstrated no interest in upsetting its neighbors by acting in anything other than a benign manner. Furthermore, by spreading its considerable largesse in the form of aid and large-scale investment, it went some of the way in fostering better international relations in the region. Even its old rival China was a significant beneficiary, and by 2003, more than 5,000 Japanese companies were operating on the Chinese mainland.

This leads us, then, to China itself. Much has been written about "rising China," especially by analysts who argue—in classical realist fashion—that when new powerful states emerge onto the international stage, they are bound to disturb the existing balance of power. China looks benign now, they agree. It will look different in a few years' time—once it has risen. Again, though, there may be more cause for guarded optimism than pessimism, largely because China itself has adopted policies (both economic and military) whose purpose clearly is to reassure its neighbors that it can rise peacefully and thus effectively prove the realists wrong. It has also translated policy into action by supporting regional integration, exporting its considerable capital to other countries in East Asia, and working as a responsible party rather than a spoiler inside regional multilateral institutions. Such policies are beginning to bear fruit, with greater numbers of once-skeptical neighbors—even possibly Japan—viewing China as a benevolent instrument of development rather than a threat.

gross domestic product (GDP) The sum of all economic activity that takes place within a country.

Association of Southeast Asian Nations (ASEAN) A geopolitical and economic organization of several countries located in Southeast Asia. Initially formed as a display of solidarity against communism, it has since redefined its aims and broadened to include the acceleration of economic growth and the promotion of regional peace.

soft power The influence and authority deriving from the attraction that a country's political, social, and economic ideas, beliefs, and practices have for people living in other countries.

WHAT'S YOUR WORLDVIEW

Both China and India are gaining power and influence in global affairs. Both countries are members of the G-20, and both have strong economies that were not devastated by the recent economic crisis. These two states are also increasing their military spending, including the expansion of their naval power. Some experts argue that this is only the beginning of a shift of global power toward Asia. What do you think? Is this a real challenge to other major powers or just a rebalancing of the world?

Sailors from China's North Sea Fleet soldiers stand on a guided missile destroyer and a missile frigate at a military port in Qingdao in East China's Shandong province. Japan, Korea, the United States, and India are aware of China's naval buildup and are responding in kind. Will this arms race and resulting *security dilemma* increase the chances for conflict in the region?

In the end, however, all strategic roads in China (and in East Asia as a whole) lead to the one state whose presence in the region remains critical: the United States of America. Though theoretically opposed to a unipolar world in which there is only one significant global player, the new Chinese leadership has pursued a most cautious policy toward the United States. No doubt some Americans will continue to be wary of a state run by the Communist Party, whose human rights record can hardly be described as exemplary. However, as long as China continues to act in a cooperative fashion, there is a good chance that relations will continue to prosper. There is no guaranteeing the long-term outcome. With growth rates around 10 percent per year, with its apparently insatiable demand for overseas raw materials, and with enormous dollar reserves at its disposal, China has already changed the terms of the debate about the future of international politics. Of course, it remains to be seen what effects the global economic collapse that began in 2008 will have on China; and for some time to come, China may remain what one observer has called a "colossus with feet of clay," overly dependent on foreign investment and still militarily light years behind the United States. But even such a colossus presents a set of challenges that did not exist in the much simpler days of the Cold War. Indeed, one of the great ironies of international history may be that China as a rising capitalist power playing by the rules of the market may turn out to be more of a problem for the West than China the communist power in those far-off days when it denounced the imperialists across the ocean and called on Asians to drive Americans out of the region.

Latin America: Becoming Global Players

In the great ideological struggle between the United States and the Soviet Union, Latin American countries were expected to be client states of the United States and to take pro-US positions in disputes with the Soviet Union. Cuba was the pariah state because of its alliance with the USSR and its communist government. Any government that strayed from the US orbit was usually replaced in a covert coup or overthrown by local forces loyal to the United States. Often, these US loyalists were wealthy families connected to a multinational corporation or military leaders trained in the United States and dependent on the United States for weapons and other material support. The United States tried to overthrow the regimes in Cuba and Nicaragua, and it was successful in removing pro-communist leaders in Guatemala, Chile, and Grenada. Unfortunately for the US image in Latin America today, many of the authoritarian military leaders in Latin America were supported by the United States. The economic and strategic interests of the United States were more important than human interests within Latin American states.

A patron-client relationship between the United States and Latin America developed early in the nineteenth century. The Monroe Doctrine (1823) stated that any European country attempting to intervene in the Americas would be seen as an aggressor, and the United States would respond in kind. President Theodore Roosevelt added his corollary in 1904 that proclaimed the US right to intervene in cases of "flagrant wrongdoing" by a Latin American government. This usually meant a country was acting against US interests. The United

NUMBER OF WARS IN PROGRESS SINCE 1950.

Based on what you have read in this chapter, what accounts for these trends—for the increases, spikes, and decreases?

States clearly treated the countries in this region as client states serving US political and economic interests.

Since 9/11, the United States seems to have forgotten most of Latin America, and other countries have become more influential than the United States in the region. Meanwhile, Brazil, Venezuela, and Chile have become important global and regional players. Brazil, owing in part to its energy and manufacturing industries, has become an important member of the newly emerging Brazil, Russia, India, and China (BRIC) powers, and its soft power diplomacy campaigns have landed it the 2014 World Cup and the 2016 Summer Olympics. Chile has become a major player in global trade and in regional and global institutions such as the Organization of American States and the United Nations. As a very stable social democratic state, Chile is emerging as an active middle power in global politics.

Venezuela under the late president Hugo Chavez presented a challenge to US leadership if not hegemonic practices in Latin America. He has increased trade and investment with China, conducted military exercises with Russia, and created an alternative economic development program that is allocating five times more aid than the United States in Latin America.

Because of the war on terrorism and the Bush Doctrine's emphasis on unilateralism and preemptive war, the popularity of the United States was hurt badly during the George W. Bush administration. The European Union is now the largest investor in the region, and trade with China increased tenfold from 2000 to 2007. The United States continues to be identified with both obsolete and failed policies in the region. The US policy of not recognizing and actually boycotting Cuba is considered obsolete, and the US war on drugs and its immigration policies have been expensive and alienating failures.

The War on Terrorism: From 9/11 to Iraq and Afghanistan

The end of the Cold War marked one of the great turning points of the late twentieth century, but 9/11 was a reminder that the international order that had come into being as a result was not one that found ready acceptance everywhere. Bin Laden was no doubt motivated by far more than a dislike of globalization and American primacy. As many analysts have pointed out, bin Laden's vision was one that pointed back to a golden age of Islam rather than forward to something modern. That said, his chosen method of attacking the United States using four planes, his use of video to communicate with followers, his employment of the global financial system to fund operations, and his primary goal of driving the United States out of the Middle East could hardly be described as medieval. United States policy makers certainly did not regard him as some odd throwback to earlier times. Indeed, the fact that he threatened to use the most modern and dangerous weapons—namely, weapons of mass destruction—to achieve his objectives made him a very modern threat, one that could not be dealt with by the kind of traditional means developed during the Cold War. As the administration of George W. Bush constantly reiterated, this new danger meant that old strategies, such as containment and deterrence, were no longer relevant. If this was the beginning of a "new global war on terrorism," as some seemed to argue at the time, then it was unlikely to be fought using policies and methods learned between 1947 and 1989.

The very peculiar character of this new nonstate network threat, led by a man whose various pronouncements owed more to holy texts than to anything else, made it difficult for some in the West to understand the true character of radical Islamic movements and their use of terrorist tactics. A few, in fact, believed that the threat was more speculative than serious, more functionally useful for the United States in its quest for global preeminence than actually genuine. Furthermore, as the controversial war on terrorism unfolded—first in Afghanistan and then in other parts of the world—a few critics of a more radical persuasion began to wonder where the real danger lay. Indeed, as the United States began to flex its military muscle and widened the war on terrorism to include Iraq, Iran, and Pakistan, some began to turn their critical attention away from the original threat posed by radical Islamic terrorism and toward the United States itself. In this way, the original target of 9/11—the United States—was transformed from the early status of victim into the imperial source of most of the world's growing problems.

The various controversies surrounding the Bush administration's responses to international terrorism should not, however, obscure one simple fact: the impact that 9/11 had on both the United States and US foreign policy more generally. Most obviously, the new threat environment provided the United States with a fixed point of reference around which to organize its international affairs; and organize it did, in the shape of building close relations with those many states—Russia, India, Pakistan, and China perhaps being the more important— that were now prepared to join it in waging a global war against terror. After the 9/11 attacks, the Bush administration officials felt compelled to act in a far more assertive fashion abroad. Indeed, some of Bush's more conservative supporters believed that one of the reasons for the attack on the United States in the first place was that it had not been assertive enough in the 1990s. Finally, in what some saw as a near revolution in US foreign policy, policy makers in the Bush administration seemed to abandon the defense of the status quo in the Middle East. The events of 9/11, they argued, had changed the original formula whereby the United States turned a blind eye to autocratic regimes that existed in the region in exchange for cheap oil and stability. United States dependency on these two commodities was no longer enough, said the neoconservatives in government, in the news media, and in academia, to justify the United States making deals with states like Saudi Arabia that produced the dangerous ideologies that had inspired those who had flown the planes on 9/11 or who directly or indirectly had given (and were still giving) aid and comfort to terrorists around the world.

In this way, the intellectual ground was prepared for the war against Iraq in 2003. The war, though, remains something of a conundrum. After all, Iraq had not been involved in 9/11; the regime itself was secular; and it shared the same goal as the United States in at least one respect—that of seeking to contain the geopolitical ambitions of Islamic Iran. For all these reasons, different analysts have identified rather different factors to explain the war, including the ideological influence exercised by the neoconservatives on President Bush, America's close relationship with Israel, and America's desire to control Iraq's oil. No doubt all these things fed into the final decision (see the Case Study in this chapter). However, one is still left with more questions than easy answers, with possibly the most credible answer being the less conspiratorial one: the United States went to war partly because it thought it would win fairly easily, partly because it got its intelligence wrong, and partly because some political leaders thought—rather unwisely— that building a new regime in Iraq would be just as easy as getting rid of the old one.

Whatever the original calculations made by those who planned this war, it was clear by 2009 that this "war of choice" was a strategic blunder that neither delivered stable democracy to Iraq nor inspired others in the region to undertake serious political reform. It also had the doubly dangerous consequence of disturbing the whole of the Middle East, while making it possible for Iran to gain even greater influence in the region than it had before. In fact, by undermining the old regime in Iraq, the United States effectively created a vacuum into which an increasingly self-confident Iranian regime has marched.

CASE STUDY : The Iraq War and Its Origins

International relations, as a field, has always been concerned with the origins of wars. Long-term changes in the balance of power, fear of encirclement, imperial ambition—not to mention misperception and ideology—have all been employed at one time or another to explain why states engage in military action. The Iraq War presents a useful, and possibly difficult, test case for various theories of war origins. Several competing explanations have been advanced so far to explain the US decision to go to war against Iraq in 2003. These include, among others, the official argument that Iraq represented a serious and potentially rising threat to a critically important region; the more materialist thesis that the United States was determined to secure direct control of Iraq's massive reserves of oil; and the popular claim that the war was the product of pressures arising from within the United States itself—here identified as the Israel lobby, the ideologically inclined neoconservatives, and their various supporters on the Christian Right. This coalition was joined by a few liberals who wanted a regime change and Saddam Hussein punished as a brutal dictator.

2013 was the tenth anniversary of British participation in the invasion of Iraq. Here George Bush and Tony Blair meet to finalize the British role in this war of choice. How did British citizens react to this decision to support the United States?

The student of world politics, however, is still left with a number of unanswered questions. First, would the war have happened without the quite unexpected election of George W. Bush in late 2000? That is, did the president make a huge difference to the decision taken? Second, could Bush have then led the United States into war without the profound shock created by the equally unexpected attack of 9/11? Considered this way, wasn't the war largely the byproduct of fear and insecurity? Third, what role did British prime minister Tony Blair play? Indeed, was this a war made possible by an alliance with a middle power? Fourth, would it have been feasible at all if various American writers and policy makers had not thought the United States so powerful that it could more or less do anything in the world? That is, to what extent did the notion of the "unipolar moment" contribute to the final decision to go to war? Furthermore, were the intellectual grounds for the war not also laid by those during the post–Cold War period who thought it wise to promote democracy and encouraged others to intervene in the internal affairs of sovereign states for humanitarian purposes? Finally, to what extent could one argue that the Iraq War was in the US national interest; and if it was, then why did so many realists oppose the war?

For Discussion

1. The debates about the role of think tanks like the Project for a New American Century and individuals like William Kristol, Richard Perle, and Paul Wolfowitz in shaping the Bush Doctrine will continue for years. How important are policy advisers like these, and when do they have the most influence?

2. Did the ideas of George W. Bush, Dick Cheney, and Colin Powell matter in shaping US policy? Were their advisers just as important? Explain.

3. Some experts have suggested that the Bush Doctrine was very Wilsonian in that it was aimed at rebuilding the Middle East based on American values of liberal democracy. Is there anything new about a country wanting to project its values? Could this have been done without the preemptive use of force? Explain.

4. Although thousands of troops remain in Iraq, the Iraq War is now officially over. Was it worth the human and financial costs? Why or why not?

Finally, as a result of their action in Iraq, the United States and its allies provided radical Islamists around the world with a rallying point that they appear to have exploited with some skill. The bombings of transit systems in London (2005) and Madrid (2004) were no doubt the result of many factors; however, few now believe they were entirely unconnected to what had been happening in the Middle East since 2003.

After the 9/11 attacks, Al Qaeda was given sanctuary by the Taliban government in Afghanistan. The United States immediately demanded that the leaders of this terrorist network be turned over to the United States for trial. The Taliban refused, and on October 7, 2001, the US military invaded Afghanistan, destroyed Al Qaeda's terrorist training camps, and overthrew the Taliban-controlled government. NATO members invoked Article 5 and came to the aid of the United States.

> The Parties agree that an armed attack against one or more of them in Europe or North America shall be considered an attack against them all and consequently they agree that, if such an armed attack occurs, each of them, in exercise of the right of individual or collective self-defence recognised by Article 51 of the Charter of the United Nations, will assist the Party or Parties so attacked by taking forthwith, individually and in concert with the other Parties, such action as it deems necessary, including the use of armed force, to restore and maintain the security of the North Atlantic area.

Currently, NATO maintains the International Security Assistance Force (ISAF), which consists of 130,000 troops at a cost of about $100 billion a year. Since 2009, the United States has moved away from a counterinsurgency policy that put an emphasis on protecting civilians, providing services, and nation building toward more direct military action: increasing airstrikes in both Afghanistan and Pakistan, the use of drones for surveillance and attacks on suspected terrorist leaders, a dramatic increase in covert operations, and the use of special forces surprise attacks on terrorist camps in the tribal regions that extend

When the US invaded Afghanistan in October 2001, they hired fighters from the Northern Alliance to defeat the Taliban. Here soldiers celebrate near Tora Bora, Afghanistan.

into Pakistan. Clearly, the United States and its allies have decided that the stick is more effective than the carrot, and the decision has been made to use lethal force to drive the Taliban to the negotiating table.

With the successful covert operation that resulted in the killing of Osama bin Laden in 2011, many citizens in NATO countries were wondering why their men and women continued to fight and die for a corrupt and ineffective government in Afghanistan. Suicide bombers continued to kill civilians who cooperated with the United States and the Afghan government, and the Taliban increased their attacks and found refuge in mountain tribal regions that extend into Pakistan. One of the most dangerous terrorist groups, the Haqqani network, is based in Pakistan and funded by the Pakistani intelligence agency, the Inter-Services Intelligence directorate (ISI). The Afghanistan government claims that the ISI has supported a fivefold increase in insurgent attacks since 2006.

The United States and Pakistan are allies, but they have different interests in Afghanistan. The United States hopes that when it withdraws, Afghanistan will be a relatively stable, prosperous, and democratic state that is no longer an incubator for terrorists. Pakistan does not want a strong Afghanistan that might be governed by ethnic Tajiks, who are traditionally allies of India. We must remember that India and Pakistan are rivals in this region and both have nuclear weapons. When the United States and NATO withdraw, peace and stability in this region may not yet be achieved.

With or without the war in Afghanistan, however, the West would still be confronted by a challenge in the form of violent radical Islam. This is a movement that not only feeds off Western blunders and policies (especially American ones in the Middle East and South Asia) but is also based on a set of cultural values, state practices, and historical grievances that make it almost impossible to deal with effectively—without compromising what it means to be part of the West. Herein, though, lay another problem: how precisely to define this conflict.

It was certainly fashionable to characterize it as one between two different "civilizations" (a term originally made popular by American writer Samuel Huntington in 1993). Nevertheless, there was something distinctly uncompromising about a conflict between those on the one side who supported democracy, **pluralism**, individualism, and a separation between state and church and those on the other who preached intolerance and supported **theocracy** while calling for armed struggle and **jihad** against the unbeliever. Not that these views were shared by all Muslims. Indeed, these radical views were roundly condemned by the overwhelming majority of Muslim clerics and followers of Islam. Still, as the antagonism unfolded, there seemed to be enough disaffected people in enough societies—including Western ones—to make this aggressive ideology an occasional but potent threat. The way the world in general, and the West in particular, chose to deal with it was likely to determine the shape of international relations for many years to come.

Conclusion

In this chapter, we have seen some of the trends and events that created the contemporary globalized system. War (both "hot" and "cold"), revolutions, and colonization and its collapse each had a role in the evolution of international society. The irony might be found in this fact: religion played a role in both 1648 and 2001. The signatories of the Peace of Westphalia wanted to remove religion from European international politics. Members of Al Qaeda want to bring religion back into global politics.

The Peace of Westphalia in the seventeenth century created an international system in Europe that many people at the time believed would make for more orderly politics on the

pluralism A political theory holding that political power and influence in society do not belong just to the citizens nor only to elite groups in various sectors of society but are distributed among a wide number of groups in the society. It can also mean a recognition of ethnic, racial, and cultural diversity.

theocracy A state based on religion.

jihad In Arabic, *jihad* means "struggle." Jihad can refer to a purely internal struggle to be a better Muslim or a struggle to make society more closely align with the teachings of the Koran.

continent. In the same way, the end of the Cold War in the twentieth century seemed to prom-ise a more peaceful world. But as we have seen in this chapter, these hopes went unfulfilled. The effects of revolutions, wars, and European imperialism have revealed the hollow nature of the European international system. Moreover, during the Cold War—while much of the attention of politicians and academics in the developed world was focused on the US-USSR confrontation—other wars, economic trends, and social movements around the world were too often ignored. As a result, the euphoria in Western Europe and the United States that fol-lowed the end of the Soviet Union soon gave way to a new set of challenges and threats. And many of the new challenges were quite old, such as the persistence of poverty in underdevel-oped nations.

We'll explore these issues in depth later in Parts Three (Global Actors) and Four (Global Issues). But first, in Part Two, we will examine theories that we can use to approach these issues more thoughtfully, helping us better understand and explain our ever-changing po-litical world.

CONTRIBUTORS TO CHAPTER 2: David Armstrong, Michael Cox, Len Scott, and Steven L. Lamy.

REVIEW QUESTIONS

1. Was the international system of nineteenth-century Europe merely a means of legitimizing imperialism? Explain.

2. How did the method by which European colonies in Africa and Asia gained their independence determine their postindependence internal politics?

3. Why did the United States become involved in wars in Asia after 1950? Illustrate your answer by reference to either the Korean War or the Vietnam War.

4. How have scholars of international relations attempted to explain the end of the Cold War?

5. Why did liberal theorists predict that the world would become a stabler place after the end of the Cold War, and why did realists disagree with them?

6. If the United States won the Cold War, why did it have such problems defining a grand strategy for itself after 1989 and before 9/11?

7. How has globalization since the Cold War changed the basic character of world politics?

8. How successfully has Europe adapted to the challenges facing it since the end of the Cold War?

9. How has the war on terrorism changed global politics?

FURTHER READING

Bisley, N. (2006), *Rethinking Globalization* (Basingstoke: Palgrave). The single best volume on the subject.

Booth, K., and Dunne, T. (eds.) (2002), *Worlds in Collision* (Basingstoke: Palgrave). This is a collection of short, well-written essays on the world after 9/11.

Burstein, D., and de Keijzer, A. (1998), *Big Dragon: The Future of China* (New York: Simon & Schuster). In spite of the title, this is a relatively balanced account of China.

Cox, M., Ikenberry, G. J., and Inoguchi, T. (eds.) (2000), *American Democracy Promotion: Impulses, Strategies, and Impacts* (Oxford: Oxford University Press). This book looks at a critically important and neglected facet of US foreign policy.

Held, D., et al. (2005), *Debating Globalization* (Cambridge: Polity Press). A useful collection of opposing views.

Kaldor, M. (1999), *New and Old Wars: Organized Violence in a Global Era* (Cambridge: Polity Press). This book explains why millions have died in "small" wars since the end of the Cold War.

Knutsen, T. L. (1997), *A History of International Relations Theory* (Manchester: Manchester University Press). A comprehensive history of the development of international relations theory and its analytic tradition.

Leonard, M. (2005), *Why Europe Will Run the Twenty-First Century* (London: Fourth Estate). A now unfashionably opti-mistic perspective on the future of Europe.

Mann, J. (2004), *Rise of the Vulcans: The History of Bush's War Cabinet* (New York: Viking Press). An indispensable background on how the Bush administration viewed the world at large after 2001.

O'Meara, P., Mehlinger, H. D., and Krain, M. (eds.) (2000), *Globalization and the Challenges of a New Century* (Bloomington: Indiana University Press). This is a very useful collection of many well-known essays about global order and disorder.

Reynolds, D. (2000), *One World Divisible: A Global History Since 1945* (New York: W. W. Norton). If you don't know your history, this is the book you need to read to help you understand the last sixty years.

Ruthven, M. (2002), *A Fury for God: The Islamist Attack on America* (London: Granta Books). This is a fine analysis of the ideology of radical Islamism.

Sifry, M. L., and Cerf, C. (eds.) (2003), *The Iraq Reader* (New York: Touchstone Books). The best collection on the debate to go to war.

Video Suggestions

Black and White in Color (Home Vision, 1976). The 1976 Academy Award–winning film satire on racism, colonialism, and war. The French and Germans living in the Ivory Coast decide to fight the European war in their colonies.

Crucial Turning Points of World War II (Reader's Digest, 1997). A historical documentary detailing the fifteen crucial battles that changed the course of war and altered America's destiny forever.

Empires: Napoleon (PBS, 2000). A film that documents Napoleon's rise from obscurity to victories that made him a hero in France.

The French Revolution (History Channel, 2005). A historical documentary that explores the history, causes, and timeline of the French Revolution.

Goodbye Lenin! (Sony Pictures Classics, 2003). A fictional account of the fall of the Berlin Wall from the East German perspective.

Paths of Glory (United Artists, 1957). Directed by Stanley Kubrick, this fictional account of World War I follows Colonel Dax and his French soldiers, who refuse to continue an impossible attack.

Race for the Superbomb (PBS, 1999). A detailed account of the nuclear arms race during the Cold War.

The Target for Tonight (Classic Pictures Entertainment, 2004). A documentary series that provides personal accounts from both sides during World War II, with an emphasis on civilians and cities targeted during the war.

War and Peace in the Nuclear Age (Boston: WGBH-TV, 1988). A thirteen-part series on the origins and evolution of the nuclear competition during the Cold War.

White Light/Black Rain: The Destruction of Hiroshima and Nagasaki (HBO, 2007). Details the horrific human costs of atomic warfare.

Why We Fight (Sony, 2005). Explores the anatomy of US war fighting and the factors that push US militarism.

Witness: Voices from the Holocaust (Stories to Remember, 1999). Urges us to listen to and never forget these voices.

Woodrow Wilson: American Idealist (History Channel, 2007). The life of Woodrow Wilson and his experience as a leader during World War I.

INTERNET RESOURCES

Cold War International History Project: The Woodrow Wilson International Center for Scholars
http://wwics.si.edu/index.cfm?topic_id=1409&fuseaction=topics.home
The online resource center for Cold War research from a leading US institute.

Intelligence Resource Program
http://www.fas.org/irp/
The federation of American scientists site contains fascinating material on most aspects of collection, analysis, and uses of information that states collect on each other.

Resources Page for Website of Professor Vincent Ferraro, Mount Holyoke College
http://www.mtholyoke.edu/acad/intrel/feros-pg.htm#documents
A definitive collection of material on all aspects of US foreign policy, plus links to information about foreign governments, research institutes, TNCs, and NGOs of all kinds.

United States Holocaust Memorial Museum
http://www.ushmm.org/
The museum's online collections offer a chance for people to remember the horrors of the Holocaust.

Carnegie Council: "The Origins of Political Order: From Prehuman Times to the French Revolution"—Francis Fukuyama

http://www.carnegiecouncil.org/resources/video/
 data/000391

Francis Fukuyama looks at the link between natural political
 evolution during these periods and any connections to state
 strength today.

Carnegie Council: "The World Ahead: Conflict or Cooperation?"—Richard K. Betts

http://www.carnegiecouncil.org/resources/video/data/000383

Drawing on Fukuyama's, Mearsheimer's, and Huntington's theories of world order and civilization interaction, Betts looks at
 these "academic forecasters" and their successes and failures

in predicting political climates. His thesis: although grand theories have limitations, good guesses and correct answers are
 possible.

Carnegie Council: "Putin, Power, and the New Russia"—Marshall I. Goldman

http://www.carnegiecouncil.org/resources/video/data/000065

Gazprom, Russia's primary oil and gas company, is helping propel
 Russia into a new era of economic growth.

For more information, quizzes, case studies and other study tools, please visit us at **www.oup.com/us/lamy**

THINKING ABOUT GLOBAL POLITICS

Understanding and Resolving International Conflicts

INTRODUCTION

In this exercise, you will be asked to analyze several conflict situations from the perspective of different state and
nonstate actors or players directly or indirectly involved in a
given conflict. First, we ask you to explore the causes of this
conflict, and second, we ask you to consider possible ways
of managing or resolving the conflict. You might have to do
some research to find answers to our questions. This is a
great opportunity to explore the wide variety of sources on
the web and in your university or college library.

PROCEDURE

This is a cooperative learning exercise. In groups of three or
four, begin by reviewing the list of Cold War conflicts in this
chapter and the list of conflicts in Chapter 8, Figure 8.1.

1. Review the list of Cold War conflicts and identify those
   that might still be going on. For those that have ended,
   how did they end? What were the reasons these conflicts were resolved?
2. Now look at the list of conflicts from 1946 to 2009. Pay
   particular attention to conflicts that began after the Cold
   War and respond to the following questions:
   a. Who is involved in this conflict? Primary actors?
      Secondary actors?

   b. What do these actors claim are the causes of the
      conflict?
   c. What other factors serve to accentuate the conflict
      and increase its lethality?
3. In Chapters 1 and 4, we introduce you to levels of analysis: tools for explaining decision making and the behavior of states in the international system. Since war
   and conflict are a constant in the international system,
   we can use levels to explain why wars begin and how
   they might end. With your cooperative learning team,
   come up with plausible explanations for the start of
   each conflict. Was it caused by the leader's desire for
   power (level 1) or the state's need for oil (level 2) or
   the fear of a neighbor's military buildup or the security dilemma (level 3)? Now share your list of plausible
   explanations with the rest of the class. See if you can
   reach agreement on the most frequent reasons that
   countries go to war. Are there any patterns that develop? You might also check your ideas with the work
   of historians or official records on the war. If we know
   why countries go to war, can we anticipate and even
   prevent future wars?

Continued

THINKING ABOUT GLOBAL POLITICS *continued*

4. Now, with some understanding of why wars begin, let's review several examples of peacemaking efforts. There are many examples of conflicts that have ended peacefully. Select at least two of these conflicts and identify the factors that helped all the parties reach an acceptable peace. For example, was one party defeated and forced to accept a peace agreement, like Japan and Germany in World War II, or was peace achieved because a third party offered mediation and assistance, like Norway did to help reach a peace agreement in Sri Lanka?

WRITING ASSIGNMENT

What has this exercise taught you about the difficulties of preventing future wars and the problems associated with peacemaking? Do you think peace, defined as an absence of war, is a utopian dream? Must we live in a world where all we can hope to do is manage conflict and prevent systemic war?

Theories of Global Politics

In this part, we discuss the main theories that try to explain global politics. We have two main aims: first, we want you to grasp the primary themes of the theories that have been most influential. To this end, we have included chapters on the leading theoretical perspectives in global politics: *realism* and *liberalism* in Chapter 3 and *Marxism*, *feminism*, and *constructivism* in Chapter 4. Of these, realism has been by far the most influential theory, but it has also attracted fierce criticism. Most of the history of international relations theory has seen a dispute between realism and its liberal and Marxist rivals, with the debate between realism and liberalism being the most longstanding and well developed. The primary critical approaches of international relations—Marxism, feminism, and constructivism—are so called because they are critical of the core assumptions that define the dominant theoretical traditions: realism and liberalism. By the end of this part, you should be able to assess the comparative strengths and weaknesses of the various theories and approaches discussed here. Our second aim is to provide the overview of theory that you need to assess the significance of globalization for world politics.

After reading these chapters, you will be in a better position to see how theories of global politics might interpret globalization and other global conditions and issues in different ways. You should be able to decide for yourself which interpretation you find most convincing. You will then be better able to sort through evidence in the remaining parts of the book to determine whether globalization marks a new, distinct stage in global politics requiring new theories.

The neoconservatives who dominated the George W. Bush administration sought to rebuild Afghanistan and spread democracy. Here a young woman displays her dyed finger after voting in 2009. Unfortunately, elections have not created a stable government.

3 | Realism and Liberalism

A nation's survival is its first and ultimate responsibility; it cannot be compromised or put to risk.

—*Henry Kissinger*

Though it be true that democratic government will make wars less likely, it will not eliminate all causes of conflict between nations, and if the enormous sacrifices of this war are not to be made in vain, not merely must democracy triumph in individual states, but in the society of states as well.

—*Woodrow Wilson*

There are several "states of concern" for the leading world powers, and North Korea may present one of the most difficult problems for those concerned with national security and the control of nuclear weapons. A quick review of recent North Korean actions suggests that no state is able to control this intransigent state and its leaders. In early May 2009, North Korea test-fired six missiles after detonating a nuclear device several days earlier. South Korean spy satellites captured images that showed the North Koreans moving missiles to launch pads close to the demilitarized zone. One of the suspected missiles is the type that is capable of reaching US territory.

The then secretary of defense Robert Gates, attending a regional security conference in Singapore, stated that these nuclear tests and missile launches were a direct threat to US national security. He was adamant in stating that the United States would not accept North Korea as a nuclear state. Meanwhile, the armed attacks on South Korea by the North have continued. In March 2010, a North Korean torpedo sank the *Cheonan*, a South Korean warship, killing forty-six people. In November 2010, a North Korean artillery barrage hit the island of Yeonpyeong in South Korean territory. These attacks heightened immediate concerns in South Korea, Japan, and other East Asian states. In November of 2013—the three-year anniversary of the North Korean shelling of the South Korean border island of Yeonpyeong—the North Korean regime threatened to turn South Korea's presidential office into a "sea of fire." In the same month, the North Korean government restarted

A South Korean military officer displays fragments of shells that North Korea fired at a South Korean island in November 2010. The South reacted with calls for more troops on potential targets, and North Korea stridently warned South Korea about any military provocations. The new leadership in North Korea has maintained a hostile position toward the West. Are we headed for a nuclear showdown in this region?

a nuclear reactor that is capable of producing plutonium for bombs. The United States does not fear a North Korean nuclear attack but worries that North Korea will sell its technology to terrorist networks or other states. The North Korean government is in direct violation of international rules and has rejected attempts by the International Atomic Energy Agency (IAEA)—the international agency in charge of controlling the proliferation of nuclear arms—to inspect its nuclear sites and prevent the production of weapons-grade nuclear material.

From the realist perspective, negotiations and diplomacy have costs as well as benefits. Realists believe one must always negotiate from strength and be prepared to act with force or the threat of force when dealing with rogue states that have no intention of following international rules. Realists claim that the basic flaw of liberal thinking is that North Korea can be talked out of these weapons. The power, prestige, and influence of the United States and liberal institutions like the IAEA are being undermined by North Korea. Realists argue that the major powers must put pressure on North Korea by choking off its ability to export and import weapons and military equipment, cut off all access to financial resources, and pressure China to rein in its North Korean ally. Liberal thinkers still hold out hope for arms control talks and the promise that North Korean leaders will want to end their intransigence and join the international community of nation-states.

As we will discuss in this chapter, both realism and liberalism are effective theories by which we can more closely examine interactions among states. Both have become important in the study of international relations at universities around the world. Yet both have their limitations as well. You will see that the basis for both theories is a very different understanding about human nature, the goal of a state's policy, and the nature of the international system.

Introduction

In Chapter 1, we asked you to consider your personal worldview, or perspective on global events and conditions, which can result from your experiences, education, personal identity, citizenship, and other factors. In this chapter, we begin to present the concept of **theory**. By theory, we mean a set of propositions that help us understand events or behaviors. You are subconsciously using theories all the time. Like pairs of sunglasses that can block different amounts of sunlight, a theory can limit what we see yet also help us see certain characteristics better. Another good analogy is the various methods a doctor might use to look at the body—x-ray, inspection with the naked eye, MRI, thermal imaging, and so on. Each method highlights or reveals certain features but cannot show other things.

Theories of international relations can help us understand international relations in many ways (see Table 3.1). As we will see in this chapter, the theories called realism and liberalism have an impact on the ways political leaders view and understand the world. We do not mean that a leader one day announces, "I am a realist" or "I am a liberal" and then follows a recipe for foreign policy. Instead, we believe that theories can help us look at actions and be able to describe and explain events. Theories can also help us predict future actions on the basis of what has occurred in the past. But we must keep in mind that the theories we use—like sunglasses—might also restrict what we think.

theory A proposed explanation of an event or behavior of an actor in the real world. Definitions range from "an unproven assumption" to "a working hypothesis that proposes an explanation for an action or behavior." In international relations, we have intuitive theories, empirical theories, and normative theories.

Table 3.1

Riding the Waves of IR Theory

How has the field of international relations developed? Why have we accepted some worldviews and theories at one time and rejected them a few years later? What is the relationship between real-world events and theory? How do these theories shape our view of the world?

Wave I: The Beginnings—The Roots of International Relations Theory (Early BCE to Fifteenth Century)

Issues: governance, empires, fideism, the nature of man, military strategy, and war

Voices: Kautilya, Kung-san Yang, Homer, Herodotus, Thucydides, Sun Tzu, Plato, Aristotle, and Cicero

Later voices: St. Augustine, St. Thomas Aquinas

Debate: realism vs. idealism

Wave II: The Secular State and the Westphalian International System (1500 to 1700)

Issues: feudalism to nation-state, nationalism, colonialism/empires, trading states, international law, and international society

Voices: Machiavelli, Hobbes, and Grotius

Debate: realism vs. rule of law (international society)

Wave III: European Hegemony—Ideas and Power (1800–1914)

Issues: the age of reason and enlightenment problem solving

The state as the rational instrument for human progress

Empire and Balance of Power—the struggle for power and markets, war and peace, human rights, arms races, and the security dilemma

Voices: Rousseau, Smith, Bentham, Locke, Kant, Marx, Lenin, and Luxemburg

Debate: realism, idealism, and international society (Grotians or those who seek reform or the creation of a "rule-based" system)

Wave IV: Responding to War—Visions of Community (1919–1939)

Issues: causes of war, rebuilding the system, disarmament, and world peace

Beginning of foreign policy analysis—sources of foreign policy behavior

Voices: Carr, Toynbee, Wilson, Weber, and Angell

Debate: realism, liberal internationalism, and idealism

The birth of modern international relations—problem-solving discipline

Wave V: Resurgence of Realism—US Hegemony in Policy and Academic World (1945–1970)

Issues: security studies, integration, international organizations, development studies, and conflict studies

Voices: Morgenthau, Herz, Niebuhr, Kennan, Kissinger, Mitrany, Bull, Wight, and Deutsch

Emergence of the English School of IR Debate: realism vs. liberalism

Wave VI: A Methods Debate—Transnationalism and Liberal Institutionalism (1970–1980s)

Issues: poets vs. counters—quantitative/qualitative debate, global society, the global market and global institutions, and third world dependency

Liberalism: importance of trade and cooperation, interdependence, democracy and peace, and the possibilities of change and progress.

Debate: realism vs. liberalism . . . some neo-Marxism

Continued

Table 3.1 (*continued*)

Riding the Waves of IR Theory

Wave VII: Methods Debates Continue, Globalization and Governance, and Human Security (1990s–present)

Issues: rationalism vs. reflectivism, the neoliberal and neorealism debates, the emergence of global civil society, and questions of world order

Problem-solving theory: as described by Robert Cox, those who seek to maintain the system (SM) and those who seek to reform the system (SR). Both accept the international relations system as it exists today.

Critical theory: emancipatory project

Normative issues and ethics and foreign policy

Constructivism—out of the liberal tradition

Debate: realism vs. neorealism, neoliberalism, English School, and WOMP and other utopians

Key Questions

- Is the field of international relations truly international? Are we listening to all voices?
- Has globalization changed the agenda of international relations?
- Why do global problems like poverty and war persist?
- What factors push the field from one wave to another?
- Why is realism so persistent?

Theories are essential in your development as an informed critical thinker and an effective decision maker. One of the basic skills of citizenship in this era of globalization is to be able to *describe, explain, predict, and prescribe* (DEPP) from these different theoretical positions. The DEPP skills are essential for you as a scholar in this field. They also will help determine your level and form of *participation* in the global system. Thus, after you finish reading and discussing this chapter, you should know how realists and liberals *describe, explain, predict, prescribe, and participate* in (DEPPP) global politics.

With the military establishment a powerful political actor in both India and Pakistan, will nationalism and military leaders who embrace realist views of global politics lead both countries into a major regional conflict?

What Is Realism?

Over the centuries, various world leaders have sought to create international rules to make life more stable and predictable by decreasing outbreaks of violent aggression. As you will recall from Chapter 2, the Peace of Westphalia (1648) established a principle that still governs international relations: sovereignty. The key European nations who signed the peace treaties agreed that only a legitimate government could exercise control over its citizens and territory, could act independently and flexibly in its relations with other states, and could craft its own strategies and policies aimed at securing perceived national interests. By inference, no state could interfere in the domestic affairs of any other state. Of course, the principle of sovereignty applied more to the continent of Europe and less to societies anywhere else on Earth; nevertheless, sovereignty was—and still is today—a critically important concept.

By declaring some regions of the world sovereign and agreeing that sovereign states could not legally interfere with the internal business of other sovereign states, political leaders *thought* they had solved the problem of foreign wars. However, this attempt to eliminate war failed early and often: within a year of the Peace of Westphalia, England invaded Ireland; within four years, the English and the Dutch were at war; within six years, Russia and Poland were at war; and so it went.

With this reality in mind, it is relatively easy to understand why the earliest perspective on international relations, referred to as **realism**, is based on the following three assumptions:

1. States are the only actors in international relations that matter.
2. A policy maker's primary responsibility is to create, maintain, and increase national **power**—the means available to a state to secure its national interests—at all costs.
3. No central authority stands above the state. The anarchic nature of the international system is an essential assumption for realist thinkers and, in fact, for most liberal thinkers and even some critical-approach thinkers.

The world perceived by realists is lawless, competitive, and uncertain. In fact, one influential philosopher who helped define realism, Thomas Hobbes, published this pessimistic observation about life in his political treatise *Leviathan*: "The life of man is solitary, poor, nasty, brutish and short." The only way to avoid misery and anarchy, according to Hobbes (1651), was to have a strong ruler of a strong state impose order and provide protection from external attack.

The Essential Realism

In later sections, we will see how realism can be regarded as a broad theoretical umbrella covering a variety of perspectives, each with its own leading authors and texts. Despite the numerous denominations, keep in mind that, essentially, all realists subscribe to the following three S's: *statism*, *survival*, and *self-help*. Let's discuss these three essential elements in more detail and also examine some of realism's shortcomings.

Statism

For realists, the state is the main actor, and sovereignty is its distinguishing trait. The meaning of the sovereign state is inextricably bound up with the use of force. In terms of its internal dimension, to illustrate this relationship between violence and the state, we need to look no further than Max Weber's famous definition of the state as "the monopoly of the legitimate use of physical force within a given territory" (M. J. Smith 1986, 23). Within this territorial space, **sovereignty** means that the state has supreme authority to make and enforce laws. This is the basis of the unwritten contract between individuals and the state. According to Hobbes, for example, we trade our liberty in return for a guarantee of security (safety and protection of a way of life). Once security has been established, **civil society** can begin—a society of individuals and groups not acting as participants in any government institutions or in the interests of commercial companies. But in the absence of security, people are in the state of nature where there can be no business, no art, no culture, no society. The first move for the realist, then, is to organize power domestically. Only after power has been organized can community begin.

Realist international theory assumes that, domestically, the problem of order and security is solved. However, in the real world—in the relations among independent sovereign

---

realism The theoretical approach that analyzes all international relations as the relation of states engaged in the pursuit of power. Realists see the international system as anarchic, or without a common power, and they believe conflict is endemic in the international system.

power This is a contested concept. Joseph Nye (2011) states that power is the capacity to do things and, in social and political situations, to affect others to get the outcome one wants. Sources of power include material or tangible resources and control over meaning or ideas.

WHAT'S YOUR WORLDVIEW

Do you think Hobbes's pessimism about life applies to our society in the twenty-first century? Have we advanced at all since the seventeenth century?

sovereignty The condition of a state having control and authority over its own territory and being free from any higher legal authority. It is related to, but distinct from, the condition of a government being free from any external political constraints.

civil society The totality of all individuals and groups in a society who are not acting as participants in any government institutions or acting in the interests of commercial companies.

states—insecurities, dangers, and threats to the very existence of the state loom large. Realists primarily explain this on the basis that the very condition for order and security—namely, the existence of a sovereign world government—is missing from the international realm.

Realists claim that in this condition of anarchy, states compete with other states for power and security. The nature of the competition is viewed in zero-sum terms; more for one state means less for another. This competitive logic of power politics makes agreement on universal principles difficult, apart from the principle of nonintervention in the internal affairs of other sovereign states. But realists suspend even this principle—as we saw in the previous chapter, designed in seventeenth-century Europe to facilitate coexistence— and argue that in practice, nonintervention does not apply in relations between great powers and their regional neighbors. As evidenced by the most recent behavior of the United States in Afghanistan and Iraq, modern hegemonic (dominant) states are able to influence events far beyond their borders, overturning the nonintervention principle on the grounds of national security and international order.

Given that the first move of the state is to organize power domestically and maintain law and order and the second is to accumulate power internationally, it is self-evidently important to consider in more depth what realists mean by their ubiquitous fusion of politics with power. It is one thing to say that international politics is a struggle for power, but this merely begs the question of what realists mean by power. The famous classical realist Hans Morgenthau offers the following definition of power: "Man's control over the minds and actions of other men" (1948/1955, 26). There are two important points that realists make about the elusive concept of power. First, power is a relational concept; one does not exercise power in a vacuum but in relation to another entity. Second, power is a relative concept; calculations need to be made not only about one's own power capabilities but also about the power that other states possess. Yet the task of accurately assessing the power of states is infinitely complex. Too often, power calculations are reduced to counting the number of troops, tanks, aircraft, and naval ships a country possesses in the mistaken belief that this translates into the ability to get other actors to do something they would not otherwise do.

Survival

The second principle that unites realists is the assertion that in international politics the preeminent goal is survival. Although realists disagree as to whether the accumulation of power is an end in itself, one would think there is no dissenting from the argument that security is states' ultimate concern. Survival is held to be a precondition for attaining all other goals, whether these involve conquest or merely independence. According to Kenneth Waltz, "beyond the survival motive, the aims of states may be endlessly varied" (1979, 91). Yet, as we will see in a later section of this chapter, a recent controversy among structural realists has arisen over the question of whether states are in fact principally *security* or *power* maximizers.

Niccolò Machiavelli tried to make a science out of his reflections on state survival. He wrote the short and engaging book *The Prince* to codify a set of maxims that would enable leaders to maintain their hold on power. In important respects, we find two related Machiavellian themes recurring in the writings of modern realists; both derive from the idea that international politics requires different moral and political rules from those of domestic politics. The first is the task of understanding what realists believe to be the true nature of international politics; the second is the need to protect the state at all costs (even if this may mean the sacrifice of one's own citizens). These concerns place a heavy burden on the shoulders of state leaders. In the words of Henry Kissinger, the academic realist who became secretary of state during the Nixon presidency, "a nation's survival is its first and ultimate responsibility; it cannot be compromised or put to risk" (1977, 204). Their guide must be an **ethic of responsibility**: the careful weighing of consequences and the realization that individual immoral acts might need to be carried out for the greater good.

Think, for instance, of the ways governments frequently suspend the legal and political rights of suspected terrorists in view of the threat they pose to national security. For example, the United States altered its longstanding treaty obligations against torture and imprisoned what Bush administration officials called "enemy combatants" in the US Navy base at Guantánamo Bay. An ethic of responsibility is frequently used as a justification for breaking the laws of war, as in the case of the British nighttime firebombing raids on Nazi Germany or the US decision to drop nuclear bombs on Hiroshima and Nagasaki in 1945. The principal difficulty with the realist formulation of an *ethics* (as opposed to ethic) of responsibility is that, while instructing leaders to consider the consequences of their actions, it does not provide a guide for how state leaders should weigh the consequences (M. J. Smith 1986, 51).

Not only does realism provide an alternative moral code for state leaders, proponents claim, it also suggests a wider objection to the whole enterprise of bringing **ethics** into international politics. (Morality is what is good, right, and proper, and ethics is the examination, justification, and analysis of morality as custom or practice.) Starting from the assumption that each state has its own particular values and beliefs, realists argue that the state is the supreme good and there can be no community beyond borders. This moral relativism has generated a substantial body of criticism, particularly from some liberal theorists who endorse the notion of universal human rights.

ethic of responsibility For realists, it represents the limits of ethics in international politics; it involves the weighing up of consequences and the realization that positive outcomes may result from amoral actions.

ethics Ethical studies in international relations and foreign policy include the identification, illumination, and application of relevant moral norms to the conduct of foreign policy and assessing the moral architecture of the international system.

Self-Help

Kenneth Waltz's *Theory of International Politics* (1979) brought to the realist tradition a deeper understanding of the international system itself. Unlike many other realists, Waltz argued

Why is the US military prison at Guantánamo Bay, Cuba, still holding prisoners? These protesters were taking part in a demonstration in front of the White House and reminding President Obama of his campaign promise to close the prison and stop torture.

that international politics is not unique due to the regularity of war and conflict because this is also familiar in domestic politics. The key difference between domestic and international orders lies in their structure. In the domestic polity, citizens usually do not need to defend themselves. In the international system, there is no higher authority, no global police officer, to prevent and counter the use of force. Security can therefore be realized only through **self-help**. In an anarchic structure, "self-help is necessarily the principle of action" (Waltz 1979, 111). But in the course of providing for one's own security, the state in question will automatically be fueling the insecurity of other states.

The term given to this spiral of insecurity is the **security dilemma**. According to Nick Wheeler and Ken Booth, security dilemmas exist "when the military preparations of one state create an irresolvable uncertainty in the mind of another as to whether those preparations are for 'defensive' purposes only (to enhance its security in an uncertain world) or whether they are for offensive purposes (to change the status quo to its advantage)" (1992, 30). This scenario suggests that one state's quest for security is often another state's source of insecurity. States find it very difficult to trust one another and often view the intentions of others in a negative light. Thus, the military preparations of one state are likely to be matched by neighboring states. The irony is that at the end of the day, states often feel no securer than before they undertook measures to enhance their own security. Hence, insecurity becomes a self-fulfilling prophecy.

In a self-help system, structural realists argue that the balance of power, or parity and stability among competing powers, will emerge even in the absence of a conscious policy to maintain it (i.e., prudent statecraft). Waltz argues that balances of power result irrespective of the intentions of any particular state. In an **anarchic system** populated by states with leaders who seek to perpetuate themselves, alliances will be formed that seek to check and balance the power against threatening states. Classical realists, however, are likelier to emphasize the crucial role state leaders and diplomats play in maintaining the balance of power. That is, the balance of power is not natural or inevitable; the leaders of states construct it.

There is a lively debate among the various kinds of realists concerning the stability of a balance-of-power system. This is especially the case today, as many argue that the balance of power has been replaced by an unbalanced unipolar order. It is questionable whether other countries will actively attempt to balance against the United States as structural realism might predict. Certainly, the Obama administration has pledged to return to the United States' past policy of seeking multilateral cooperation and to end the unilateralism of its predecessor. But whether it is the contrived balance of the Concert of Europe in the early nineteenth century or the more fortuitous balance of the Cold War, balances of power are broken—either through war or peaceful change—and new balances emerge. What the perennial collapsing of the balance of power demonstrates is that states are at best able to mitigate the worst consequences of the security dilemma but are not able to escape it. The reason for this terminal condition, say realists, is the absence of trust in international relations.

Historically, realists have illustrated the lack of trust among states by reference to Enlightenment thinker Jean-Jacques Rousseau's parable of the stag hunt. In *Man, the State and War*, Kenneth Waltz revisits the parable:

> Assume that five men who have acquired a rudimentary ability to speak and to understand each other happen to come together at a time when all of them suffer from hunger. The hunger of each will be satisfied by the fifth part of a stag, so they

self-help In realist theory, in an anarchical environment, states cannot assume other states will come to their defense even if they are allies. Each state must take care of itself.

security dilemma In an anarchic international system, one with no common central power, when one state seeks to improve its security it creates insecurity in other states.

anarchic system A realist description of the international system that suggests there is no common power or central governing structure.

WHAT'S YOUR WORLDVIEW

Realists would say that leaders of states will cooperate if they see the possibility of mutual gains. Reciprocity—the idea that if you follow the rules, then others will—also encourages cooperation. Do you think there are limits to cooperation? What factors work against cooperation in addressing global problems like climate change and poverty?

GLOBAL PERSPECTIVE

Russia and Realism

The year 2009 began quite cold for millions of people in Europe. Western Europeans shivered while the governments of Russia and Ukraine squabbled over the price of natural gas that Gazprom, the Russian state monopoly, charged Ukraine for its supply of this prime heating fuel. Because Ukrainian prime minister Yulia Timoshenko's government refused to meet Russia's price, Gazprom closed the valves on all the pipelines routed through that country and, by extension, on all of its Western European customers.

On the face of it, this crisis was a business dispute about supply and demand. Russian-owned Gazprom offered its product to Ukraine for less than it charged its other European customers; under the late-2008 proposal from Gazprom, Ukraine would pay $250 for each 1,000 cubic meters of gas, but other Europeans had to pay more than $500 for the same amount. Timoshenko's government complained that this was an unjustified increase. Gazprom's reaction to this rejection was a counteroffer of $418 per unit.

Realist theory provides a clear explanation for this dispute: both countries are former Soviet republics, and this dispute is part of the end of that empire. Nationalists in both Moscow and Kyiv, goes this argument, were using the price of natural gas in an attempt to satisfy domestic political pressures in a game of international power politics. For many Russians, the implosion of the USSR was a humiliation. Instead of being the leaders of the country, Russians were forced to negotiate with other nationalities such as the Chechens, with whom Russia fought two wars in the 1990s, and the Ukrainians. By shutting off the heat for millions in Europe, Russia could show that it still mattered in international politics. For Ukrainians, supplies of natural gas were yet another unwanted example of how Russians were trying to continue their hated hegemony over the former Soviet republics. By standing up to the Russian giant, Ukraine's leaders were asserting the Ukrainian nationalist agenda.

In the end, Russia won. The terms of the new ten-year contract promised to supply Ukraine gas at a starting price of $360 per 1,000 cubic meters for the first quarter of 2009. For many Russians, this is a satisfying result. Fifteen years ago, as the program of economic shock therapy faltered, Russians leaders had to ask the IMF and World Bank for

A critical element of power is the possession of natural resources like oil and natural gas. Russia's gas monopoly, Gazprom, provides vital energy supplies to all of Europe as this control room map suggests. Does this powerful monopoly give Russian political leaders some influence in European politics?

loans in exchange for radical restructuring of the economy. One ultranationalist politician called it a humiliation and "paying for the sausages." With its vital natural gas, Russia now held the cards, and it was the European leaders who had to ask for help. Experts predict that the next crisis may also involve Ukraine. In 2014, Ukraine had a choice to make. Sign a free trade agreement with the European Union or join the Russian commonwealth. The turmoil over this decision resulted in the annexation of Crimea by Russia and a potential civil war over the future of Ukraine as an independent state or a part of Russia.

For Discussion

1. Many experts describe Russia as a state capitalist system in which the purpose of the economy is to enrich the state. Given its rich supply of energy resources, is Russia likely to become more influential in global politics? Explain.

2. If you were a leader of the European Union, how might you prevent Russia from using its control of natural gas as a political tool to get what it wants in the system?

3. Given the Russian strategy suggested in this story, can we speculate on what might happen as the world decides how the Arctic and all of its resources might be exploited?

"agree" to cooperate in a project to trap one. But also the hunger of any one of them will be satisfied by a hare, so, as a hare comes within reach, one of them grabs it. The defector obtains the means of satisfying his hunger but in doing so permits the stag to escape. His immediate interest prevails over consideration for his fellows. (1959, 167–168)

Waltz argues that the metaphor of the stag hunt provides a basis for understanding the problem of coordinating the interests of the individual versus the interests of the common good and the payoff between short-term interests and long-term interests. In the self-help system of international politics, the logic of self-interest mitigates against the provision of collective goods, such as "security" or "free trade." In the case of the latter, according to the theory of **comparative advantage**, all states would be wealthier in a world that allowed freedom of goods and services across borders. But individual states, or groups of states like the European Union, can increase their wealth by pursuing **protectionist** policies, such as tariffs on foreign goods, as long as other states do not respond in kind. Of course, the logical outcome is for the remaining states to become protectionist, international trade to collapse, and a subsequent world recession to reduce the wealth of each state. Thus, the question is not whether all will be better off through cooperation but rather who will likely gain more than another. It is because of this concern with relative-gains issues that realists argue that cooperation is difficult to achieve in a self-help system.

One Realism or Many?

So far in this chapter, we have treated the realist lens as if it were a unified set of beliefs and propositions; it is, however, not at all that way, as both the model's supporters and critics have pointed out. The belief that there is not one realism but many leads logically to a delineation of different types of realism. The simplest distinction we can make is to differentiate realism into three historical periods. While these different periods suggest a neat historical sequence, they are problematic insofar as they close down the important question of divergence within each historical phase. Rather than opt for the neat but intellectually unsatisfactory system of historical periodization, we outline here our own representation of realisms that makes important connections with existing categories deployed by other thinkers in the field. A summary of the varieties of realism outlined appears in Table 3.2.

Classical Realism

The **classical-realist** lineage begins with Thucydides' representation of power politics as a law of human behavior. The classical realists argued that the drive for power and the will to dominate are the fundamental aspects of human nature. The behavior of the state as a self-seeking egoist is understood to be merely a reflection of the characteristics of the people that comprise the state. Therefore, it is human nature that explains why international politics is necessarily power politics. This reduction of realism to a condition of human nature is one that frequently reappears in the leading works of the doctrine, most famously in the work of Hans Morgenthau. Classical realists argue that human nature explains the essential features of international politics, such as competition, fear, and war. The important point for Morgenthau is, first, to recognize that these laws exist and, second, to devise the most appropriate policies that are consistent with the basic fact that human beings are flawed creatures. For both Thucydides and Morgenthau, the essential continuity of the power-seeking behavior of states is rooted in the biological drives of human beings.

Another distinguishing characteristic of classical realism is its adherents' belief in the primordial character of power and ethics. Classical realism is fundamentally about the

comparative advantage A theory developed by David Ricardo stating that two countries will both gain from trade if, in the absence of trade, they have different relative costs for producing the same goods. Even if one country is more efficient in the production of all goods than the other (absolute advantage), both countries will still gain by trading with each other as long as they have different relative efficiencies.

protectionist An economic policy of restraining trade between states through methods such as tariffs on imported goods, restrictive quotas, and a variety of other government regulations designed to allow "fair competition" among imports and goods and services produced domestically.

classical realism The belief that it is fundamentally the nature of people and the state to act in a way that places interests over ideologies. The drive for power and the will to dominate are held to be fundamental aspects of human nature.

Table 3.2
A Taxonomy of Realisms

Type of Realism	Key Thinkers	Key Texts	Big Idea
Classical Realism (Human Nature)	Thucydides (ca. 430–406 BCE)	*The Peloponnesian War*	International politics is driven by an endless struggle for power that has its roots in human nature. Justice, law, and society either have no place or are circumscribed.
	Machiavelli (1532)	*The Prince*	Political realism recognizes that principles are subordinated to policies; the ultimate skill of the state leader is to accept, and adapt to, the changing power-political configurations in global politics.
	Morgenthau (1948)	*Politics Among Nations*	Politics is governed by laws that are created by human nature. The mechanism we use to understand international politics is the concept of interests defined in terms of power.
Structural Realism (International System)	Rousseau (ca. 1750)	*The State of War*	It is not human nature but the anarchical system that fosters fear, jealousy, suspicion, and insecurity.
	Waltz (1979)	*Theory of International Politics*	Anarchy causes logic of self-help, in which states seek to maximize their security. The stablest distribution of power in the system is bipolarity.
	Mearsheimer (2001)	*Tragedy of Great Power Politics*	The anarchical, self-help system compels states to maximize their relative power position.
Neoclassical Realism	Zakaria (1998)	*From Wealth to Power*	The systemic account of world politics provided by structural realism is incomplete. It needs to be supplemented with better accounts of unit-level variables such as how power is perceived and how leadership is exercised.

struggle for belonging, a struggle that is often violent. Patriotic virtue is required for communities to survive in this historic battle between good and evil, a virtue that long predates the emergence of sovereignty-based notions of community in the mid-seventeenth century. Classical realists therefore differ from contemporary realists in the sense that they engaged with moral philosophy and sought to reconstruct an understanding of virtue in light of practice and historical circumstance.

Thucydides was the historian of the Peloponnesian War, a conflict between two great powers in the ancient Greek world, Athens and Sparta. Though he was a disgraced general on the losing side, Thucydides' work has been admired by subsequent generations of realists for its insights into many of the perennial issues of international politics. One of the

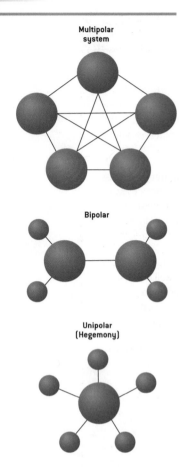

Multipolar system

Bipolar

Unipolar (Hegemony)

POWER, POLITICS, AND POLARITY.

Which of these power arrangements best represents the world today? What about the world of the early twentieth century? Nineteenth century? How does theory help us understand these global power dynamics?

structural realism (neorealism) A theory of realism that maintains the international system and the condition of anarchy or no common power push states and individuals to act in a way that places interests over ideologies. This condition creates a self-help system. The international system is seen as a structure acting on the state with individuals below the level of the state acting as agency on the state as a whole.

significant episodes of the war between Athens and Sparta is known as the "Melian dialogue" and provides a fascinating illustration of a number of key realist principles. Case Study 3.1 reconstructs Thucydides' version of the dialogue between the Melians and the Athenian leaders who arrived on the island of Melos to assert their right of conquest over the islanders. In short, what the Athenians are asserting over the Melians is the logic of power politics and the duty of a hegemon to maintain order. Because of their vastly superior military force, they are able to present a fait accompli to the Melians: either submit peacefully or be exterminated. Citing their neutrality in the war, the Melians for their part try to buck the logic of power politics, appealing in turn with arguments grounded in justice, God, and their lack of support for the Spartans. As the dialogue makes clear, although at a military disadvantage and bound to lose, the Melians chose to fight. Their defeat became the basis for a maxim of realism: "The strong do what they have the power to do and the weak accept what they have to accept."

How is a leader supposed to act in a world animated by such malevolent forces? The answer given by Machiavelli is that all obligations and treaties with other states must be disregarded if the security of the community is under threat. Moreover, imperial expansion is legitimate, as it is a means of gaining greater security. Other classical realists, however, advocate a more temperate understanding of moral conduct. Mid-twentieth-century realists such as Butterfield, Carr, Morgenthau, and Wolfers believed that wise leadership and the pursuit of the national interest in ways that are compatible with international order could mitigate anarchy. Taking their lead from Thucydides, they recognized that acting purely on the basis of power and self-interest without any consideration of moral and ethical principles frequently results in self-defeating policies. After all, as Thucydides showed, Athens suffered an epic defeat while following the realist tenet of self-interest.

Structural Realism, or Neorealism

Structural realists, sometimes called **neorealists**, concur that international politics is essentially a struggle for power, but they do not endorse the classical-realist assumption that this is a result of human nature. Instead, structural realists attribute security competition and interstate conflict to the lack of an overarching authority above states and the relative distribution of power in the international system. Kenneth Waltz, the best-known structural realist, defines the structure of the international system in terms of three elements—organizing principle, differentiation of units, and distribution of capabilities. He identifies two different organizing principles: anarchy, which corresponds to the decentralized realm of international politics, and hierarchy, which is the basis of domestic order. He argues that the units of the international system are functionally similar sovereign states; hence, unit-level variation is irrelevant in explaining international outcomes. It is the third tier, the distribution of capabilities across units, that is, according to Waltz, of fundamental importance to understanding crucial international outcomes. According to structural realists, the relative distribution of power in the international system is the key independent variable to understanding important international outcomes such as war and peace, alliance politics, and the balance of power. Many structural realists are interested in providing a rank ordering of states so as to differentiate and count the number of great powers that exist at any particular point in time. The number of great powers in turn determines the structure of the international system. For example, during the Cold War from 1945 to 1989, there were two great powers—the United States and the Soviet Union—that constituted the bipolar international system.

How does the international distribution of power impact the behavior of states, particularly their power-seeking behavior? In the most general sense, Waltz argues that states, especially the great powers, must be sensitive to the capabilities of other states. The possibility

| CASE STUDY | The Melian Dialogue: Realism and the Preparation for War | **3.1** |

BACKGROUND

Thucydides, the former Athenian general and historian, wrote that the history of the Peloponnesian War was "not an essay which is to win applause of the moment, but a possession of all time." Most realists find references to all of their core beliefs in this important document. The Melians were citizens of the Isle of Melos, which was a colony of Sparta. The Melians would not submit to the Athenians as many of the other islands had. Athens was a dominant sea power, and Sparta was more of a land power. At first, Melos tried neutrality, but Athens attacked and plundered the territory and then sent envoys to negotiate. A short excerpt from the dialogue appears below (Thucydides 1954/1972, 401–407). Note that the symbol [. . .] indicates one or more line breaks from the original text.

THE CASE

ATHENIANS: Then we on our side will use no fine phrases saying, for example, that we have a right to our empire because we defeated the Persians. [. . .] You know as well as we do that, when these matters are discussed by practical people, the standard of justice depends on the equality of power to compel and that in fact the strong do what they have the power to do and the weak accept what they have to accept.

MELIANS: . . . You should not destroy a principle that is to the general good of all men—namely, that in the case of all who fall into danger there should be such a thing as fair play and just dealing . . .

ATHENIANS: This is no fair fight, with honor on one side and shame on the other. It is rather a question of saving your lives and not resisting those who are far too strong for you.

MELIANS: It is difficult . . . for us to oppose your power and fortune . . . Nevertheless we trust that the gods will give us fortune as good as yours . . .

ATHENIANS: Our opinion of the gods and our knowledge of men lead us to conclude that it is a general and necessary law of nature to rule whatever one can. This is not a law that we made ourselves, nor were we the first to act upon it when it was made. We found it already in existence, and we shall leave it to exist forever among those who come after us. We are merely acting in accordance with it, and we know that you or anybody else with the same power as ours would be acting in precisely the same way. [. . .] You seem to forget that if one follows one's self-interest one wants to be safe, whereas the path of justice and honor involves one in danger. [. . .] This is the safe rule—to stand up to one's equals, to behave with deference to one's superiors, and to treat one's inferiors with moderation.

MELIANS: Our decision, Athenians, is just the same as it was at first. We are not prepared to give up in a short moment the liberty which our city has enjoyed from its foundation for 700 years.

ATHENIANS: . . . You seem to us . . . to see uncertainties as realities, simply because you would like them to be so.

For Discussion

1. As you think of all the assumptions of realism discussed in this chapter, how many of these do you see articulated in this brief dialogue?
2. Later in this dialogue, the Athenians tell the Melians that "the strong do what they will and the weak do what they must." Do you think this phrase is still relevant today?
3. Melos was an ally of the great military power, Sparta. What should Sparta do once it finds out what Athens has done? What theory informed your strategy?

that any state may use force to advance its interests results in all states being worried about their survival. According to Waltz, power is a means to the end of security. In a significant passage, Waltz writes, "Because power is a possibly useful means, sensible statesmen try to have an appropriate amount of it." He adds, "In crucial situations, however, the ultimate concern of states is not for power but for security" (1989, 40). In other words, rather than being power maximizers, states, according to Waltz, are *security* maximizers. He argues that power maximization often proves to be dysfunctional because it triggers a counterbalancing coalition of states.

offensive realism A structural theory of realism that views states as power maximizers.

defensive realism A structural theory of realism that views states as security maximizers—more concerned with absolute power as opposed to relative power. According to this view, it is unwise for states to try to maximize their share of power and seek hegemony.

A different account of the power dynamics that operate in the anarchic system is provided by John Mearsheimer's theory of **offensive realism**, which is another variant of structural realism. While sharing many of the basic assumptions of Waltz's structural-realist theory, frequently termed **defensive realism**, Mearsheimer differs from Waltz when it comes to describing the behavior of states. Most fundamentally, "offensive realism parts company with defensive realism over the question of how much power states want" (Mearsheimer 2001, 21). According to Mearsheimer, the structure of the international system compels states to maximize their relative power position. Thus, offensive realists are power maximizers. Under anarchy, he agrees that self-help is the basic principle of action. Yet he also argues that not only do all states possess some offensive military capability, but there is a great deal of uncertainty about the intentions of other states. Consequently, Mearsheimer concludes that there are no satisfied or status quo states; rather, all states are continuously searching for opportunities to gain power at the expense of other states. Contrary to Waltz, Mearsheimer argues that states recognize that the best path to peace is to accumulate more power than anyone else. Indeed, the ideal position, although one that Mearsheimer argues is impossible to achieve, is to be the global hegemon of the international system. Yet because Mearsheimer believes that global hegemony (domination) is impossible, he concludes that the world is condemned to perpetual great-power competition.

Contemporary Realist Challenges to Structural Realism

Although offensive realism makes an important contribution to realism, some contemporary realists are skeptical of the notion that the international distribution of power alone can explain the behavior of states. Since the end of the Cold War, a group of scholars have attempted to move beyond the parsimonious—economical or frugal—assumptions of structural realism. They have incorporated a number of additional factors at the individual and national levels into their explanation of international politics. While systemic factors are recognized to be an important influence on the behavior of states, so are factors such as the perceptions of state leaders, state-society relationships, and the motivations of states (we will learn more about the various levels of analysis—*individual, national, systemic,* and *global*—in Chapter 5). This group of **neoclassical-realist** scholars are attempting to build a bridge between international structural factors and unit-level factors, which many classical realists of the 1930s and 1940s emphasized (Rose 1998). According to Stephen Walt, the causal logic of neoclassical realism "places domestic politics as an intervening variable between the distribution of power and foreign policy behavior" (2002, 211).

neoclassical realism A version of realism that combines both structural factors such as the distribution of power and unit-level factors such as the interests of states.

One important intervening variable is leaders themselves—namely, how they perceive the international distribution of power. There is no objective, independent reading of the distribution of power: rather, what matters is how state leaders derive an understanding of the distribution of power. Structural realists assume that all states have a similar set of interests, but neoclassical realists such as Randall Schweller (1996) argue that historically this is not the case. He argues, with respect to Waltz, that the assumption that all states have an interest in security results in neorealism exhibiting a profoundly status quo bias. Schweller returns to the writings of realists such as Morgenthau and Kissinger to remind us of the key distinction that they made between status quo and states seeking system change. Neoclassical realists would argue that the fact

WHAT'S YOUR WORLDVIEW

In our global system with new technologies, opportunities for travel, and transnational networks willing to use weapons of mass destruction to challenge nation-states, can any state guarantee security for its citizens?

that Germany was a revisionist state in the 1930s and a status quo state since the end of World War II is of fundamental importance to understanding its role in the international system. Not only do states differ in terms of their interests, but they also differ in terms of their ability to extract and direct resources from the societies they rule. Fareed Zakaria (1998) introduces the intervening variable of state strength into his theory of state-centered realism. State strength is defined as the ability of a state to mobilize and direct the resources at its disposal in the pursuit of particular interests. Neoclassical realists argue that different types of states possess different capacities to translate the various elements of national power into state power. Thus, contrary to Waltz, all states cannot be treated as "like units" with similar goals, interests, and values.

As Brazil grows as an economic leader in global politics, it has increased its military strength and its involvement in many UN peacekeeping efforts around the world, including in Haiti, Timor-Leste, and the Ivory Coast.

Given the varieties of realism that exist, it is hardly surprising that the overall coherence of the realist tradition of inquiry has been questioned. The answer to the question of "coherence" is, of course, contingent on how strict the criteria are for judging the continuities that underpin a particular theory. It is perhaps a mistake to understand traditions as a single stream of thought, handed down in a neatly wrapped package from one generation of realists to another. Instead, it is preferable to think of living traditions like realism as the embodiment of both continuities and conflicts. Despite the different strands running through the tradition, there is a sense in which all realists share a common set of propositions.

In the next section, we will examine liberalism, another tradition within the field of international relations theory. We will see that realism and liberalism share certain assumptions about the international systems but disagree strongly about others.

What Is Liberalism?

The leaders of the victorious states in World War I—the United States, the United Kingdom, and France—realized that national interactions needed to change substantially to avoid a second devastating war. They decided to adapt the underlying principles of the political and economic **liberalism** they had been practicing domestically since the seventeenth and eighteenth centuries to international relations. Liberal thought is grounded in the political and economic philosophies articulated by several scholars—Immanuel Kant, John Locke, Jean-Jacques Rousseau, whose ideas also inform realist thinking, and Adam Smith, among others—who viewed the world from a very different perspective from Thucydides and Hobbes. These liberal thinkers argued that human nature is good, not evil; that states can thrive best in a world governed by morality and law; and that reason and rationality will compel states to cooperate to achieve mutually held goals in peace. Envisioning a world where compliance with the principles of liberalism would facilitate more harmonious relationships among global actors, the United States, the United Kingdom, and France sought to recast the rules of international relations as they drafted the 1919 Treaty of Versailles at the end of World War I and then the charter for the League of Nations.

liberalism A theoretical approach that argues for human rights, parliamentary democracy, and free trade—while also maintaining that all such goals must begin *within a state*.

THEORY IN PRACTICE

The Prisoner's Dilemma

Game theorists are mathematicians interested in non-zero-sum games that focus on the strategic interaction between rational actors who can pursue either competitive or collaborative strategies. Their interaction produces a much more complex situation than is found in the purely competitive market setting; yet, by distilling the detail and working with a theoretical model, we can better understand the underlying dynamics of a complex situation, such as market failures, arms races, or any agreement that requires some form of collective agreement.

The Prisoner's Dilemma is a popular interpretation of this non-zero-sum game. It's a game in which two people each have two options whose outcome depends on the simultaneous choice made by the other—for example, whether to confess to a crime. A typical scenario would unfold something like this: A prison warden once had two prisoners. The warden required a voluntary confession of at least one of the prisoners before he could hang either one. So he summoned the first prisoner (A) and offered him his freedom *and* a big cash reward if he would confess at least one day before the second prisoner (B). Then an indictment could be prepared, and the second prisoner could be hanged. If prisoner B should confess at least a day before him, however, the first prisoner was told, then prisoner B would be freed and given the cash reward—and that he (prisoner A) would be hanged instead.

"And what if we both should confess on the same day?" asked prisoner A. "Then you each will keep your life but will get ten years in prison," the warden responded.

"And if neither of us should confess?" "Then both of you will be set free—without any reward, of course."

But, are you willing to bet your life that your fellow prisoner—that crook—will not confess and pocket the reward? Now go back to your solitary cell and think about your answer until tomorrow." The second prisoner in his interview was told the same, and each man spent the night alone considering his dilemma (Deutsch 1968, 120).

Here the two actors are confronted with two possible strategies, generating a situation with four possible outcomes. Being rational, the prisoners can place these outcomes on a preference ranking. The matrix here reveals the preference rankings for the two prisoners. Both prisoners will pursue the strategy which will optimize their position in light of the strategies available to the other prisoner. To avoid being hanged, both prisoners

will confess and end up in prison for ten years, thereby demonstrating how individual rationality leads to collective irrationality. The suboptimal outcome could only be avoided if the two prisoners possessed a mechanism which allowed them to collaborate.

We know that in the United States, the study of international political economy is dominated by rational choice approaches. Rational means that, for a group or individual, this was the optimal choice. The prisoner's dilemma payoff structure may apply to any agreement or global issue that requires a global or collective response, such as new regulations governing banking practices. To some actors in the banking industry, the optimal choice may be to defect rather than cooperate

		A	
		Silent	**Confess***
B	**Silent**	3, 3‡	4, 1
	Confess*	1, 4	2, 2†

Key

* Dominant strategy: both players have dominant rather than contingent strategies. A strategy becomes dominant if it is preferable to the alternative strategy no matter which strategy the other player adopts.

† Denotes an equilibrium outcome.

‡ A Pareto optimal outcome: Vilfredo Pareto (1848–1923) was an Italian sociologist and economist who developed a criterion for identifying when an exchange between two parties has reached its most efficient or optimum point. He argued, in essence, that the point is reached when one party is better off and the other party is no worse off than before the exchange took place.

In this figure, cell numerals refer to ranked preferences: 4 = best, 1 = worst. The first number in each cell refers to A's preference, and the second number refers to B's preference.

Continued

THEORY IN PRACTICE   *continued*

because of the short-term advantages of unilateral action over cooperation. This raises another problem addressed by the prisoner's dilemma: Without a collective will to enforce rules and the means to punish those who defect, states will not see cooperation as the optimal choice. Of course, what may seem irrational to the outside observer may seem perfectly rational to the people in power who are making the decision.

For Discussion

1. Critics of game theory suggest that human nature does not work this way. Beliefs, values, and previous experiences play a major role in shaping how we act, and it is hard to be rational all of the time. What do you think about this criticism?
2. What do we gain from this sort of rigorous and rational analysis? What is lost?
3. Can you think of decision-making situations where game-theoretic models work really well in explaining behavior?
4. Does this form of analysis travel well? That is, does it apply to decision making in all cultural situations?

Just as realism derives from the observations and interpretations of political situations, so does liberalism. The seeds of a liberal perspective had been sown in the wake of the fifteenth century's so-called Age of Discovery, which fostered the rampant expansion of global commerce as states, explorer entrepreneurs, and trading companies became involved in the business of exchanging goods and services. Commerce across political and cultural boundaries was never just a simple matter of private individuals swapping one commodity for another (otherwise known as *barter*) or for money. To engage in commerce, these pioneer global traders had to negotiate the terms of trade—that is, how much of one commodity was worth how much of another, or how much money; they had to abide by new and different cultural norms and legal systems; and they had to bargain with political leaders to gain and maintain market access. In other words, trade formed linkages that transcended political, social, cultural, and economic boundaries.

As trade expanded to include the exchange of a wider variety of commodities from all over the world, so did the linkages. Over time, a complex web of connections evolved along with the multitude of formal and informal agreements needed to facilitate commerce. As economic and social interactions crossed political boundaries with increasing frequency, trade and immigration patterns rendered realist guidelines decreasingly useful to policy makers. It was no longer so easy to engage in unilateral actions without experiencing economic repercussions, as World War I had emphatically demonstrated.

In the end, however, realism prevailed. Its logic, combined with the realities of the world, led to its continued domination of global and foreign policy making. The major world powers of the twentieth century were not willing to abandon unilateralism. The United States never ratified the treaty creating the League of Nations (due to concerns about future entanglements in European wars), France sought revenge over Germany, and the United Kingdom sought to limit the power of the League. Then, one by one, Germany, Japan, and Italy violated Versailles Treaty covenants with impunity. No country was able *and* willing to provide the leadership that might have prevented renewed belligerence; Japan, Germany, and Italy sought to regain lost power by acquiring resources and invading other states, in a style reminiscent of Athens and Sparta, through aggression. President Woodrow Wilson, the leader of liberal thinking at the end of the war, naively believed that France and the United Kingdom would give up their territorial ambitions because they depended on US economic support.

The world was soon consumed by war again. World War II, like its predecessor, committed combatant and noncombatant alike to the national cause of winning. When it finally ended in 1945, Europe and Japan lay in smoldering ruins, and the nuclear age had dawned. In a desperate effort to end the war and to signal to others evidence of its military might, the United States dropped atomic bombs on Hiroshima and Nagasaki, Japan, triggering a profound and fundamental change in international and human relations. Now no country was safe from war. Leaders and citizens alike feared the possible consequences of combat, whether over resources such as territory or economic markets or over political ideas and values. The introduction of **weapons of mass destruction**—biological, chemical, or nuclear weapons capable of nearly unfathomable lethality and incapable of discriminating between combatants and civilians—meant that future conflicts might lead to the extinction of the human race.

As World War II came to an end, key decision makers in the United States experienced their own transformation. They now recognized that the United States needed to be an active player on the world scene; they also saw that the United States had the financial and military power to enforce a new world order based on its political and economic visions. Moreover, they realized that, in a world where sovereignty remained the reigning principle, decisions affecting two or more states required the participation of all affected stakeholders and the backing of the rule of law. Embedded in this **multilateralist** approach to global governance is a principle of political liberalism—namely, that the "governed" (in this case, states) should have a say in the development of those rules, norms, and principles by which they will be governed. And so, as they endeavored to avoid an even more calamitous World War III, the political leaders of the United States and its allies created a whole host of international governmental organizations (IGOs) to manage global relations in key political and economic arenas and, in the long run, to govern an anarchic system. The mandates of these IGOs were informed by **liberal internationalism**, a combination of

- democratic values (political liberalism),
- free trade markets (economic liberalism),
- multilateral cooperation (multilateralism), and
- a rule-based international society that respects sovereignty and human rights.

We will discuss these principles further as we define the boundaries of liberal thinking and begin to understand how neoliberalism—and radical liberalism—have since evolved their own set of arguments from the liberal tradition.

Defining Liberalism

In essence, liberalism argues for human rights, parliamentary democracy, and free trade—while also maintaining that all such goals must begin *within a state*. The early European liberals thought that reforms within one's own country would be the first step in a long process that could eventually extend to world affairs. Although the belief in the possibility of progress is one identifier of a liberal approach to politics (Clark 1989, 49–66), there are other general propositions that define the broad tradition of liberalism.

Perhaps the appropriate way to begin this discussion is with a four-dimensional definition (Doyle 1997, 207). First, all citizens are equal before the law and possess certain basic rights to education, access to a free press, and religious toleration. Second, the legislative assembly of the state possesses only the authority invested in it by the people, whose basic rights it may not abuse. Third, a key dimension of the liberty of the individual is the right to own property, including productive forces. Fourth, liberalism contends that the most effective system of economic exchange is one that is largely market driven and not one that

---

weapons of mass destruction A category defined by the United Nations in 1948 to include "atomic explosive weapons, radioactive material weapons, lethal chemical and biological weapons, and any weapons developed in the future which have characteristics comparable in destructive effects to those of the atomic bomb or other weapons mentioned above."

multilateralism The process by which states work together to solve a common problem.

liberal internationalism A perspective that seeks to transform international relations to emphasize peace, individual freedom, and prosperity and to replicate domestic models of liberal democracy at the international level.

Engaging with the

WORLD

Global Zero: A World Without Nuclear Weapons

This global citizens' movement is committed to the total elimination of nuclear weapons. As its website suggests, governments spend over $1 trillion on nuclear weapons, which in the wrong hands could lead to the end of life as we know it. This organization has opportunities for interns and volunteers. Many college and university campuses have Global Zero organizations. Check out http://www.globalzero.org.

is subordinate to bureaucratic regulation and control, either domestically or internationally. When these propositions are taken together, we see a stark contrast between liberal values of individualism, tolerance, freedom, and constitutionalism and realism's conservatism, which places a higher value on order and authority and is willing to sacrifice the liberty of the individual for the stability of the community.

Although in the past many writers have tended to view liberalism as a theory of domestic government, what is becoming more apparent is the explicit connection between liberalism as a *domestic* political and economic theory and liberalism as an *international* theory. Properly conceived, liberal thought on a global scale embodies a domestic political and economic system *operating at the international level.* Like individuals, states have different characteristics; some are bellicose and war prone, whereas others are tolerant and peaceful. In short, the identity of the state determines its outward orientation. Liberals see a further parallel between individuals and sovereign states. Although the character of states may differ, all states in a global society are accorded certain "natural" rights, such as the generalized right to nonintervention in their domestic affairs. We see this in the "one state, one vote" principle in the UN General Assembly (see Chapter 6 for more on the United Nations).

On another level, the domestic analogy refers to the extension of ideas that originated inside liberal states to the international realm, such as the coordinating role played by institutions and the centrality of the rule of law to the idea of a just order. In a sense, liberal thinkers seek to create an international system that embodies the values and structures of liberal democratic governments. Liberals concede that we have far to go before this goal can be reached. Historically, liberals have agreed with realists that war is a recurring feature of the anarchic states system. But unlike realists, they do not identify **anarchy** as the cause of war. How, then, do liberals explain war? As Table 3.3 demonstrates, certain strands of liberalism see the causes of war located in **imperialism**, others in the failure of the balance of power, and still others in the problem of undemocratic regimes. And can we prevent war through collective security, commerce, or world government? While it can be productive to think about the various strands of liberal thought and their differing prescriptions (Doyle 1997, 205–300), given the limited space permitted to deal with a broad and complex tradition, the emphasis here is on the core concepts of international liberalism and the way these relate to the goals of order and justice on a global scale.

Unlike what we learned about realism, liberalism is at its heart a doctrine of change and belief in progress. As can be seen from a critical appraisal of the fourfold definition presented earlier, liberalism pulls in two directions: its commitment to freedom in the economic and social spheres leans in the direction of a minimalist role for governing institutions, while the democratic political culture required for basic freedoms to be safeguarded requires robust and interventionist institutions. This has variously been interpreted as a tension between different liberal goals and more broadly as a sign of rival and incompatible conceptions of liberalism. Should a liberal polity—no matter what the size or scale—preserve the right of individuals to retain property and privilege, or should liberalism elevate equality over liberty so that resources are redistributed from the strong to the weak? These are the very issues being raised by those in the global Occupy movement on one side and the US Tea Party on the other. When we are looking at politics on a global scale, it is clear that inequalities are far greater while at the same time our institutional capacity to do something about them is that much less. As writers on globalization remind us, the intensification of global flows in trade, resources, and people has weakened the state's capacity to govern. Closing this gap requires nothing short of a radical reconfiguration of the relationship between territoriality and governance.

anarchy A system operating in the absence of any central government. It does not imply chaos but, in realist theory, the absence of political authority.

imperialism The practice of foreign conquest and rule in the context of global relations of hierarchy and subordination. It can lead to the establishment of an empire.

Table 3.3
A Taxonomy of Liberalism: Levels of Analysis

Images of Liberalism	Public Figure/ Period	Causes of Conflict	Determinants of Peace
First image (human nature)	Richard Cobden (mid-19th century)	Interventions by governments domestically and internationally disturbing the natural order.	Individual liberty, free trade, prosperity, interdependency.
Second image (the state)	Woodrow Wilson (early 20th century)	Undemocratic nature of international politics, especially foreign policy and the balance of power.	National self-determination, open governments responsive to public opinion, collective security.
Third image (the structure of the system)	I. Kant (18th century)	The balance-of-power system.	A world government with powers to mediate and enforce decisions.

The Essential Liberalism

Enlightenment A movement associated with rationalist thinkers of the eighteenth century. Key ideas (which some would argue remain mottoes for our age) include secularism, progress, reason, science, knowledge, and freedom. The motto of the Enlightenment is "*Sapere aude!*" (Have courage to know!) (Kant 1991, 54).

Immanuel Kant and Jeremy Bentham were two of the leading liberals of the **Enlightenment**. Both were reacting to the barbarity of international relations, or what Kant graphically described as "the lawless state of savagery," at a time when domestic politics was at the cusp of a new age of rights, citizenship, and constitutionalism. Their abhorrence of the lawless savagery led them individually to elaborate plans for "perpetual peace." Although written more than two centuries ago, these manifestos contain the seeds of core liberal ideas, in particular the belief that reason could deliver freedom and justice in international relations. For Kant, the imperative to achieve perpetual peace required the transformation of individual consciousness, republican constitutionalism, and a federal contract between states to abolish war (rather than to regulate it, as earlier international lawyers had argued). This federation can be likened to a permanent peace treaty rather than a "superstate" actor or world government. Kant's conditions for world peace, and Woodrow Wilson's for peace after World War I that were clearly influenced by Kant's ideas, are presented in Table 3.3.

Kant's claim that liberal states are peaceful in their international relations with other liberal states was revived in the 1980s. In a much-cited article, Michael Doyle argued that liberal states have created a "separate peace" (1986, 1151). According to Doyle, there are two elements to the Kantian legacy: restraint among liberal states and "international imprudence" in relations with nonliberal states.

democratic peace thesis A central plank of liberal-internationalist thought, the democratic peace thesis makes two claims: first, liberal polities exhibit restraint in their relations with other liberal polities (the so-called separate peace), but second, they are imprudent in relations with authoritarian states. The validity of the democratic peace thesis has been fiercely debated in the international relations literature.

Although the empirical evidence seems to support the **democratic peace thesis**, it is important to bear in mind the limitations of the argument. In the first instance, for the theory to be compelling, believers in the thesis need to provide an explanation of why war has become unthinkable between liberal states. Kant had argued that if the decision to use force was taken by the people rather than by the prince, then the frequency of conflicts would be drastically reduced. Democratic or liberal states tend not to go to war with other liberal or democratic states, but they *will* go to war with nonliberal or undemocratic states. Historical evidence supports this point. Thus, Kant's idea that democratic states will not go to war cannot be supported.

An alternative explanation for the democratic peace thesis might be that liberal states tend to be wealthy and therefore have less to gain—and more to lose—by engaging in conflicts than poorer, authoritarian states. Perhaps the most convincing explanation of all is the simple fact that liberal states tend to be in relations of amity with other liberal states. War between Canada and the United States is unthinkable, perhaps not because of their liberal democratic constitutions but because they are friends with a high degree of convergence in economic and political matters (Wendt 1999, 298–299). Indeed, war between states with contrasting political and economic systems may also be unthinkable because they have a history of friendly relations. An example here is Mexico and Cuba, which maintain close bilateral relations despite their history of divergent economic ideologies.

WHAT'S YOUR WORLDVIEW

Liberal internationalism emerged as a dominant perspective after the two world wars. After these conflicts, most states wanted to return to a rule-based system that promotes democracy and free trade. Yet, historically, this view does not last. What are some possible reasons that liberal-internationalist thinking does not prevail?

Irrespective of the scholarly search for the reasons that liberal democratic states are more peaceful, it is important to note the political consequences of this hypothesis. Francis Fukuyama wrote an article entitled "The End of History" that celebrated the triumph of liberalism over all other ideologies, contending that liberal states were stabler internally and more peaceful in their international relations (1989, 3–18). Other defenders of the democratic peace thesis were more circumspect. As Doyle recognized, liberal democracies are as aggressive as any other type of state in their relations with authoritarian regimes and stateless peoples (1995a). The behavior of the United States after September 11, 2001, illustrates this possibility. How, then, should states inside the liberal zone of peace conduct their relations with nonliberal regimes? How can the Kantian legacy of restraint triumph over the historical record of international imprudence on the part of liberal states? These are fascinating and timely questions that will be taken up in the final section of the chapter.

Two centuries after Kant first called for a "pacific federation," the validity of the idea that democracies are more pacific continues to attract a great deal of scholarly interest. The claim has also found its way into the public discourse of Western states' foreign policy, appearing in speeches made by US presidents as diverse as Ronald Reagan, Bill Clinton, George W. Bush, and Barack Obama. Less crusading voices within the liberal tradition believe that a legal and institutional framework must be established that includes states with different cultures and traditions. At the end of the eighteenth century, Jeremy Bentham advocated such a belief in the power of law to solve the problem of war. "Establish a common tribunal" and "the neces-

free trade An essential element of capitalism that argues for no barriers or minimal barriers to the exchange of goods, services, and investments among states.

sity for war no longer follows from a difference of opinion" (Luard 1992, 416). Like many liberal thinkers after him, Bentham showed that federal states such as the German Diet, the American Confederation, and the Swiss League were able to transform their identity from one based on conflicting interests to a more peaceful federation. As Bentham famously argued, "between the interests of nations there is nowhere any real conflict."

Because liberal politics and capitalism are intimately linked, many writers believe, with Adam Smith, that the elimination of tariffs, duties, and other restrictions on imports would be a vital step in dissemination of liberalism's program. For example, Cobden's belief that **free trade** would create a more peaceful world order is a core idea of nineteenth-century liberalism. Trade brings mutual gains to all the players irrespective of their size or the nature of their economies. It is perhaps

With the United States focused on state building in Iraq and Afghanistan and the global war on terrorism, its Central American neighbors are moving on to discuss ways to work together to achieve security in stability in the region. This type of regional cooperation fits well with the tenets of liberal internationalism, that capitalism and democracy will create zones of peace and cooperation.

not surprising that this argument found its most vocal supporters in Britain. The supposed universal value of free trade brought disproportionate gains to the hegemonic power. There was never an admission that free trade among countries at different stages of development would lead to relations of dominance and subservience. Indeed, since World War II, this is one of the problems that both the General Agreement on Tariffs and Trade (GATT) and its successor, the World Trade Organization (WTO), have faced. (See Chapters 11 and 12 for more information on these international organizations.)

Like free trade, the idea of a "natural harmony of interests" in international political and economic relations came under challenge in the early part of the twentieth century. The fact that Britain and Germany had highly interdependent economies before World War I (1914–1918) seemed to confirm the fatal flaw in the association of economic interdependence with peace. From the turn of the century, the contradictions within European civilization, of progress and exemplarism on the one hand and the harnessing of industrial power for military purposes on the other, could no longer be contained. Europe stumbled into a horrific war killing 15 million people. The war not only brought an end to three **empires** but also was a contributing factor to the Russian Revolution of 1917.

World War I shifted liberal thinking toward a recognition that peace is not a natural condition but one that must be constructed. In a powerful critique of the idea that peace and prosperity were part of a latent natural order, the publicist and author Leonard Woolf argued that peace and prosperity required "consciously devised machinery" (Luard 1992, 465). But perhaps the most famous advocate of an international authority for the management of international relations was Woodrow Wilson. According to this US president, peace could only be secured with the creation of an international organization to regulate the international anarchy. Security could not be left to secret bilateral diplomatic deals and a blind faith in the balance of power. Just as peace had to be enforced in domestic society, the international domain needed a system of regulation for coping with disputes and an international force that could be mobilized if nonviolent conflict resolution failed. In this sense, more than any other strand of liberalism, idealism rests on the idea that we can replicate the liberalism we know domestically at the international level (Suganami 1989, 94–113).

Along with calls for free trade and self-determination, in his famous "Fourteen Points" speech addressed to Congress in January 1918, Wilson argued that "a general association of nations must be formed" to preserve the coming peace; the League of Nations was to be that general association. For the League to be effective, it needed to have the military power to deter aggression and, when necessary, to use a preponderance of power to enforce its will. This was the idea behind the **collective security** system that was central to the League of Nations. Collective security refers to an arrangement where "each state in the system accepts that the security of one is the concern of all, and agrees to join in a collective response to aggression" (Roberts and Kingsbury 1993, 30). It can be contrasted with an alliance system of security, where a number of states join together, usually as a response to a specific external threat (sometimes known as "collective defense"). In the case of the League of Nations, Article 16 of the League's charter noted the obligation that, in the event of war, all member states must cease normal relations with the offending state, impose sanctions, and, if necessary, commit their armed forces to the disposal of the League Council should the use of force be required to restore the status quo.

The League's constitution also called for the self-determination of all nation-states, another founding characteristic of liberal-idealist thinking on international relations. Going back to the mid-nineteenth century, self-determination movements in

empire A distinct type of political entity, which may or may not be a state, possessing both a home territory and foreign territories. This may include conquered nations and colonies.

collective security An arrangement where "each state in the system accepts that the security of one is the concern of all, and agrees to join in a collective response to aggression" (Roberts and Kingsbury 1993, 30).

Greece, Hungary, and Italy received support among liberal powers and public opinion. Yet the default support for self-determination masked a host of practical and moral problems that were laid bare after Woodrow Wilson issued his proclamation. What would happen to newly created minorities within a territory who felt no allegiance to the new state created by this emphasis on self-determination? How would minorities be protected if the majority population denied them rights? Could a democratic process adequately deal with questions of identity—who was to decide what constituency was to participate in a ballot? And what if a newly self-determined state rejected liberal-democratic norms?

US president Woodrow Wilson, a liberal internationalist, thought the key to international security was an international organization, the League of Nations. Why did the League fail?

Although the organization was able to mediate relatively minor disputes—over the Åland Islands, for example—the overall experience of the League of Nations as a peacekeeper was a failure. While the moral rhetoric at the creation of the League was decidedly liberal and idealist, in practice states remained imprisoned by self-interest in the style of realism. There is no better example of this than the US decision not to join the institution it had created. With the Soviet Union initially outside the system for ideological reasons, the League of Nations quickly became a debating society for the member states. Hitler's decision in March 1936 to reoccupy the Rhineland, a designated demilitarized zone according to the terms of the Treaty of Versailles, effectively pulled the plug on the League's life-support system (it had been put on the critical list following the Manchurian crisis in 1931 and the Ethiopian crisis in 1935).

According to the realist's version of the history of the discipline of international relations, the collapse of the League of Nations dealt a near-fatal blow to liberal idealism. There is no doubt that the language of liberalism after 1945 was more pragmatic; how could anyone living in the shadow of the Holocaust be optimistic? Yet familiar core ideas of liberalism—belief in the benefits of progress, free trade, and respect for human rights—remained. Even as World War II raged, key political leaders in Europe and North America recognized the need to replace the League with another international institution with responsibility for international peace and security. Only this time, in the case of the United Nations, there was an awareness of the need for a consensus between the great powers for enforcement action to be taken. The framers of the UN Charter therefore included a provision (Article 27) allowing any of the five permanent members of the Security Council the power of veto. This revision constituted an important modification to the classical model of collective security (A. Roberts 1996, 315). The framers of the UN Charter also acknowledged that security was more than guns and thus created the Economic and Social Council (see Chapter 6) to build what became known as *human security*, which we will examine in Chapter 10. With the ideological polarity of the Cold War, the UN procedures for collective security were stillborn (as either of the superpowers and their allies would veto any action proposed by the other). It was not until the end of the Cold War that a collective security system was put into operation, following the invasion of Kuwait by Iraq on August 2, 1990.

An important argument advanced by liberals in the early postwar period concerned the state's inability to cope with modernization. David Mitrany (1943), a pioneer **integration** theorist, argued that transnational cooperation was required to resolve common problems. His

integration A process of ever-closer union between states in a regional or international context. The process often begins with cooperation to solve technical problems.

functionalism An idea formulated by early proponents of European integration that suggests cooperation should begin with efforts aimed at resolving specific regional or transnational problems. It is assumed that resolution of these problems will lead to cooperation, or spillover, in other policy areas.

transnational nonstate actor Any nonstate or nongovernmental actor from one country that has relations with any actor from another country or with an international organization.

pluralism The political theory that holds political power and influence in society do not belong only to the citizens or to elite groups in various sectors of society but are distributed among a wide number of groups in the society. It can also mean a recognition of ethnic, racial, and cultural diversity.

interdependence A condition where states (or peoples) are affected by decisions taken by others. Interdependence can be symmetric (i.e., both sets of actors are affected equally), or it can be asymmetric (i.e., the impact varies between actors). If political or economic costs of interdependence are high, a state is in a vulnerable position. If costs are low, it is a situation of sensitivity interdependence.

relative gains One of the factors that realists argue constrain the willingness of states to cooperate. States are less concerned about whether everyone benefits (absolute gains) and more concerned about whether someone may benefit more than someone else.

core concept was **functionalism**, meaning the likelihood that cooperation in one sector would lead governments to extend the range of collaboration across other sectors. This process is known as *spillover*. As states become more embedded in an integration process, the benefits of cooperation and the costs of withdrawing from cooperative ventures increase. The history of the European Union supports Mitrany's assertion.

Academic interest in the positive benefits from transnational cooperation informed a new generation of scholars (particularly in the United States) in the 1960s and 1970s. Their argument was not simply about the mutual gains from trade but that other **transnational nonstate actors** were beginning to challenge the dominance of sovereign states. Global politics, according to pluralists (as they are often called, using a term from the study of domestic politics), was no longer an exclusive arena for states, as it had been for the first 300 years of the Westphalian states system. The inability of the United States to win the Vietnam War—not simply an academic pursuit—provided the impetus to this research because that conflict seemed to challenge realism's central claims about power determining outcomes in international politics. In one of the central texts of this genre, Robert Keohane and Joseph Nye (1972) argued that the centrality of other actors, such as interest groups, transnational corporations (e.g., Shell Oil or AIG), and nongovernmental organizations (NGOs), like Oxfam or Human Rights Watch, had to be taken into consideration. They also asserted that military power had a declining utility in international politics. The overriding image of international relations is one of a cobweb of diverse actors linked through multiple channels of interaction.

Although the phenomenon of transnationalism was an important addition to the international relations theorists' vocabulary, it remained underdeveloped as a theoretical concept. Perhaps the most important contribution of **pluralism** was its elaboration of **interdependence**. Due to the expansion of capitalism and the emergence of a global culture, pluralists recognized a growing interconnectedness in which "changes in one part of the system have direct and indirect consequences for the rest of the system" (Little 1996, 77). Absolute state autonomy, so keenly entrenched in the minds of state leaders, was being circumscribed by interdependence. Such a development brought with it enhanced potential for cooperation as well as increased levels of vulnerability.

In his 1979 work *Theory of International Politics*, neorealist Kenneth Waltz attacked the pluralist argument about the decline of the state. He argued that the degree of interdependence internationally was far lower than the constituent parts in a national political system. Moreover, the level of economic interdependence—especially between great powers—was less than what existed in the early part of the twentieth century. Waltz concludes that "if one is thinking of the international-political world, it is odd in the extreme that 'interdependence' has become the word commonly used to describe it" (1979, 144).

In the course of their engagement with Waltz and other neorealists, early pluralists modified their position. Neoliberals, as they came to be known, conceded that the core assumptions of neorealism were indeed correct: the anarchic international structure, the centrality of states, and a rationalist approach to social scientific inquiry. Where they differed was apparent primarily in the argument that anarchy does not mean durable patterns of cooperation are impossible; the creation of international regimes matters here, as they facilitate cooperation by sharing information, reinforcing reciprocity, and making defection from norms easier to punish. Moreover, in what became the most important difference between neorealists and neoliberals, the latter argued that actors would enter into cooperative agreements if the gains were evenly shared. Neorealists disputed this hypothesis, saying that what matters is a question not so much of mutual gains as of **relative gains**: a neorealist (or structural-realist) state needs to be sure that it has more to gain than its rivals from a particular bargain or regime.

Neoliberalism

There are two important arguments that set **neoliberalism** apart from democratic peace liberalism and the liberal idealism of the interwar period. First, academic inquiry should be guided by a commitment to a scientific approach to theory building. Whatever deeply held personal values scholars maintain, their task must be to observe regularities, formulate hypotheses as to why that relationship holds, and subject these to critical scrutiny. This separation of fact and value puts neoliberals on the positivist or social scientific research side of the methodological divide. Second, writers such as Keohane are critical of the naive assumption of nineteenth-century liberals that commerce breeds peace. A free trade system, according to Keohane, provides incentives for cooperation but does not guarantee it. Here he is making an important distinction between cooperation and harmony. "Co-operation is not automatic," Keohane argues, "but requires planning and negotiation" (1989b, 11).

Neoliberal institutionalism (or institutional theory) shares many of the assumptions of neorealism; however, its adherents claim that neorealists focus excessively on conflict and competition and minimize the chances for cooperation even in an anarchic international system. Neoliberal-institutional organizations such as the Bank for International Settlements, the International Monetary Fund (IMF), and the World Bank are both the mediators and the means to achieve cooperation among actors in the system. Currently, neoliberal institutionalists are focusing their research on issues of global governance and the creation and maintenance of institutions associated with managing the processes of globalization.

For neoliberal institutionalists, the focus on mutual interests extends beyond trade and development issues. With the end of the Cold War, states were forced to address new security concerns like the threat of terrorism, the proliferation of weapons of mass destruction, and an increasing number of internal conflicts that threatened regional and global security. Graham Allison (2000) states that one of the consequences of the globalization of security concerns like terrorism, drug trafficking, and pandemics like HIV/AIDS is the realization that threats to any country's security cannot be addressed unilaterally. Successful responses to security threats require the creation of regional and global regimes that promote cooperation among states and the coordination of policy responses to these new security threats.

Robert Keohane (2002a) suggests that one result of the 9/11 terrorist attacks on the United States was the creation of a very broad coalition against terrorism involving a large number of states and key global and regional institutions. Neoliberals support cooperative multilateralism and are generally critical of the preemptive and unilateral use of force as is condoned in the 2002 Bush Doctrine. Most neoliberals would believe that the US-led war with Iraq undermined the legitimacy and influence of global and regional security institutions that operated so successfully in the first Gulf War (1990–1991) and continue to work effectively in Afghanistan.

The neoliberal-institutional perspective is more relevant in issue areas where states have mutual interests. For example, most world leaders believe that we will all benefit from an open trade system, and many support trade rules that protect the environment. Institutions have been created to manage international behavior in both areas. The neoliberal view may have less relevance

> **neoliberalism** Theory shaped by the ideas of commercial, republican, sociological, and institutional liberalism. Neoliberals see the international system as anarchic but believe relations can be managed by the establishment of international regimes and institutions. Neoliberals think actors with common interests will try to maximize absolute gains.

Liberal theory holds that networks of cooperation involving citizens in a variety of occupations exist to help strengthen state-to-state ties. Here Bill Gates speaks during a session at the World Economic Forum in Davos, Switzerland. As government funds dry up in the global economic crisis, wealthy individuals and their foundations may play a greater role in global politics.

CASE STUDY 3.2 — The Power of Ideas: Politics and Neoliberalism

BACKGROUND

A very good example of the hegemonic power of the United States, many Marxists would argue, is the success that it has had in getting neoliberal policies accepted as the norm throughout the world.

THE CASE

The set of policies most closely associated with the neoliberal project (in particular, reduction of state spending, currency devaluation, privatization, and the promotion of free markets) are, revealingly, known as the Washington Consensus. Many would argue that these are commonsense policies and that third world countries that have adopted them have merely realized that such economic policies best reflect their interests. However, Marxists would argue that an analysis of the self-interest of the hegemon and the use of coercive power provide a more convincing explanation of why such policies have been adopted.

The adoption of neoliberal policies by third world countries has had a number of implications. Spending on health and education has been reduced, they have been forced to rely more on the export of raw materials, and their markets have been saturated with manufactured goods from the industrialized world. It does not take a conspiracy theorist to suggest that these neoliberal policies are in the interests of capitalists in the developed world. There are three main areas where the adoption of neoliberal policies in the third world is in the direct interest of the developed world. First, there is the area of free trade. We need not enter into arguments about the benefits of free trade, but it is clear that it will always be in the interest of the hegemon to promote free trade; this is because, assuming it is the most efficient producer, its goods will be the cheapest anywhere in the world. It is only if countries put up barriers to trade to protect their own production that the hegemon's products will be more expensive than theirs. Second, there is the area of raw materials. If third world countries are going to compete in a free trade situation, the usual result is that they become more reliant on the export of raw materials (because their industrial products cannot compete in a free trade situation with those of the developed world). Again, this is in the interest of the hegemon, as increases in the supply of raw material exports mean that the price falls. Additionally, where third world countries have devalued their currency as part of a neoliberal package, the price of their exported raw materials goes down. Finally, when third world governments have privatized industries, investors from North America and Europe have frequently been able to snap up airlines, telecommunications companies, and oil industries at bargain prices. Duncan Green (1995) gives an eloquent description of the impacts of neoliberalism on Latin American countries.

If neoliberal policies appear to have such negative results for third world countries, why have they been so widely adopted? This is where the coercive element comes in. Through the 1970s and 1980s and continuing to today, there has been a major debt crisis between the third world and the West. This debt crisis came about primarily as a result of excessive and unwise lending by Western banks. Third world countries were unable to pay off the interest on these debts, let alone the debt itself. They turned to the major global financial institutions, such as the IMF, for assistance. Although the IMF is a part of the UN system, it is heavily controlled by Western countries, in particular the United States. For example, the United States has 18 percent of the votes, while Mozambique has only 0.07 percent. In total, the ten most industrialized countries have more than 50 percent of the votes.

OUTCOME

For third world countries, the price of getting assistance was that they would implement neoliberal policies. Only once these were implemented, and only on the condition that the policies were maintained, would the IMF agree to provide aid to continue with debt repayment.

Hence, Marxists would argue that a deeper analysis of the adoption of neoliberal policies is required. Such an analysis would suggest that the global acceptance of neoliberalism is very much in the interests of the developed world and has involved a large degree of coercion. That such policies seem "natural" and "commonsense" is an indication of the hegemonic power of the United States.

For Discussion

China's economic policies are based on state control of the economy. All capitalist activities serve the interests of the nation-state. This system, called the Beijing Consensus, is seen as a challenge to the dominance of the neoliberal Washington Consensus. Will China's economic success encourage other nation-states to take more control over their economies?

in areas in which states have no mutual interests. Thus, cooperation in military or national security areas, where someone's gain is perceived as someone else's loss (a zero-sum perspective), may be more difficult to achieve.

Liberalism in Practice: Globalization

When applying liberal ideas to international relations today, we find two clusters of responses to the problems and possibilities posed by globalization. Before outlining these responses, let's quickly recall the definition of liberalism set out at greater length earlier, the four components being *juridical equality*, *democracy*, *liberty*, and the *free market*. As we will see, these same values can be pursued by very different political strategies.

The first response we'll address is that of the **liberalism of privilege** (Richardson 1997, 18). According to this perspective, the problems of globalization need to be addressed by a combination of strong democratic states in the core of the international system, robust regimes, and open markets and institutions. For an example of the working out of such a strategy in practice, we need look no further than the success of the liberal hegemony of the post-1945 era. The US writer G. John Ikenberry is an articulate defender of this liberal order. In the aftermath of World War II, the United States took the opportunity to embed certain fundamental liberal principles into the rules and institutions of international society. Most important, and contrary to realist thinking, US leaders chose to forfeit short-run gains in return for a durable settlement that benefited all the world's states.

According to Ikenberry, the United States signaled the cooperative basis of its power in a number of ways. First, in common with liberal-democratic principles, the United States was an example to other members of international society insofar as its political system is open and allows different voices to be heard. Moreover, foreign policy, like domestic policy, is closely scrutinized by the media, public opinion, and political committees and opposition parties. Second, the United States advocated a global free trade regime in accordance with the idea that free trade brings benefits to all participants (it also has the advantage, from the hegemon's point of view, of being cheap to manage). Third, the United States appeared, to its allies at least, as a reluctant hegemon that would not seek to exploit its significant power-political advantage. Fourth and most important, the United States created and participated in a range of important international institutions that constrained the country's actions. The Bretton Woods system of economic and financial accords (which, following World War II, created the IMF, World Bank, and GATT/WTO) and the NATO security alliance are the best examples of the highly institutionalized character of American power in the post-1945 period. Advocates of this liberal hegemonic order note that it was so successful that allies were more worried about abandonment than domination.

The post-1945 system of regulatory regimes and institutions has been successful in part simply because it exists. Once a set of institutional arrangements becomes embedded, it is very difficult for alternatives to make inroads. There are two implications that need to be teased out here. One is the narrow historical "window" that exists for new institutional design; the other is the durability of

liberalism of privilege The perspective that developed democratic states have a responsibility to spread liberal values for the benefit of all peoples of the earth.

NATO leaders attending the 2012 summit in Chicago discussed a wide range of topics, including an exit strategy for Afghanistan and the establishment of a new "Smart Defense" initiative that includes pooling resources for the production of weapons and the joint management of weapons, ammunitions, and other security resources.

existing institutions. "In terms of American hegemony, this means that, short of a major war or a global economic collapse, it is very difficult to envisage the type of historical breakpoint needed to replace the existing order" (Ikenberry 1999, 137).

Let us accept for a moment that the neoliberal argument is basically correct: the post-1945 international order has been successful and durable because US hegemony has been liberal. The logic of this position is one of institutional conservatism, meaning that to respond effectively to global economic and security problems, there is no alternative to working within the existing institutional structure. This is a manifesto for managing an international order in which the Western states that paid the start-up costs of the institutions are now experiencing significant returns on their institutional investment.

At the other end of the spectrum, many critics of the liberal international order see the current order as highly unresponsive to the needs of weaker states and peoples. The 2011 UN Development Program report, *Sustainability and Equity: A Better Future for All*, states that income distribution has worsened in most of the world, with Latin America the most unequal region in income terms. However, according to the Multidimensional Poverty Index (MPI), a more sophisticated measure of poverty (which factors in access to clean water, cooking fuel, and health services), the ten poorest countries are in sub-Saharan Africa. Niger, with 92 percent of its population considered poor, leads in this category, followed by Ethiopia and Mali. The South Asian states of India, Pakistan, and Bangladesh have the largest number of MPI poor.

Given that liberalism has produced such unequal gains for the West and the rest, it is not surprising that the hegemonic power has become obsessed with the question of preserving and extending its control of institutions, markets, and resources, just as realists predicted it would. When this hegemonic liberal order comes under challenge, as it did on 9/11, the response is uncompromising. It is notable in this respect that President George W. Bush mobilized the language of liberalism against Al Qaeda, the Taliban, and also Iraq. He referred to the 2003 war against Iraq as "freedom's war," and the term "liberation" is frequently used by defenders of Operation Iraqi Freedom.

Despite the neoconservative ideology underpinning the most recent Bush presidency, the official discourse of US foreign policy overlaps in interesting ways with a number of liberal values and ideas (Rhodes 2003). For example, a key opening theme in Bush's speech at the West Point graduation ceremony in June 2002 was how force can be used for freedom: "We fight, as we always fight, for a just peace." Bush then went on to locate this argument in historical context. Prior to the twenty-first century, great-power competition manifested itself in war. Today, "the Great Powers share common values" such as "a deep commitment to human freedom." In his State of the Union address of 2004, he even declared that "our aim is a democratic peace."

The tendency for liberalism to embrace imperialism has a long history (Doyle 1986, 1151–1169). We find in Machiavelli a number of arguments for the necessity for republics to expand. Liberty increases wealth and the concomitant drive for new markets; soldiers who are at the same time citizens are better fighters than slaves or mercenaries; and expansion is often the best means to promote a state's security. In this sense, contemporary US foreign policy is no different from the great expansionist republican states of the premodern period such as Athens and Rome. Few liberals today would openly advocate imperialism, although the line between interventionist strategies to defend liberal values and privileges and imperialism is very finely drawn. Michael Doyle advocates a policy mix of forcible and nonforcible instruments that ought to be deployed in seeking regime change in illiberal parts of the world.

WHAT'S YOUR WORLDVIEW?

The new liberal economic order has left many countries and their people in poverty. Are there ways to create programs that give capitalism a more human face? What do you think could be done to address global poverty?

This strategy of preserving and extending liberal institutions is open to a number of criticisms. For the sake of simplicity, we will gather these under the umbrella of **radical liberalism**, which sees liberalism as benefiting only a few states and individuals. Table 3.4 summarizes the core assumptions of realism, liberalism, and radical liberalism/utopianism. Proponents of radical liberalism object to the understanding of liberalism embodied in the neoliberal defense of contemporary international institutions. The liberal character of those institutions is assumed rather than subjected to critical scrutiny. As a result, the incoherence of the purposes underpinning these institutions is often overlooked. The kind of economic liberalization advocated by Western financial institutions, particularly in economically impoverished countries, frequently comes into conflict with the norms of democracy and human rights. Three examples illustrate this dilemma.

New security challenges involve protecting vulnerable populations and providing basic human needs. These Kenyan children lost their parents to HIV, and 69 percent of global HIV victims are in sub-Saharan Africa. Radical liberals would support more funding for these types of programs and less funding for neoliberal infrastructure projects—people, not buildings, should be the priority.

First, the more the West becomes involved in the organization of developing states' political and economic infrastructure, the less those states can be accountable to their domestic constituencies. The critical democratic link between the government and the people is therefore broken (Hurrell and Woods 1995, 463). Second, to qualify for Western aid and loans, states are often required to meet harsh economic criteria requiring cuts in many welfare programs. The example of the poorest children in parts of Africa having to pay for primary school education (Booth and Dunne 1999, 310)—which is their right according to the Universal Declaration of Human Rights—is a stark reminder that economic liberty and political equality are frequently opposed. Third, the inflexible response of the IMF, World Bank, and other international financial institutions to various crises in the world economy has contributed to a backlash against liberalism. Richard Falk puts this dilemma starkly: there is, he argues, a tension between "the ethical imperatives of the global neighborhood and the dynamics of economic globalization" (1995a, 573). Radical liberals argue that the hegemonic institutional order has fallen prey to the neoliberal consensus, which minimizes the role of the public sector in providing for welfare and elevates the market as the appropriate mechanism for allocating resources, investment, and employment opportunities.

A second line of critique that radical liberals pursue focuses not so much on the contradictory outcomes but on the illiberal nature of the regimes and institutions. To put the point bluntly, there is a massive **democratic deficit** at the global level; policy decisions are not subject to review by citizens. Only fifteen members of international society can determine issues of international peace and security, and five of the fifteen can exercise a power of veto. Thus, it is hypothetically possible for up to two hundred states in the world to believe that military action ought to be taken, but such an action would contravene the UN Charter if one of the permanent members cast a veto. If we take the area of political economy, the power exerted by the West and its international financial institutions perpetuates structural inequality. A good example here is the issue of free trade, which the West has pushed in areas where it gains from an open policy (e.g., in manufactured goods and financial services) but resisted in areas where it stands to lose (e.g., agriculture and textiles). At a deeper level, radical liberals worry that *all* statist models of governance are undemocratic, as elites are notoriously self-serving.

radical liberalism The utopian side of liberalism best exemplified by the academic community called the World Order Models Project (WOMP). These scholars advocate a world in which states promote values like social justice, economic well-being, peace, and ecological balance. The scholars see the liberal order as predatory and clearly in need of transformation.

democratic deficit Leaders have created many policy-making institutions at the global, regional, and national levels with policy-making power led by individuals who are appointed and not elected. Thus, policy decisions are not subject to review by citizens.

Table 3.4

Realism, Liberalism, and Radical Liberalism/Utopianism: A Review of Core Assumptions

	Realism	Liberalism	Radical Liberalism/ Utopianism
Main Actors	States	States	States
		Nonstates	Nonstates
		Groups	Groups and Individuals
Central Concern	Relative Power	Welfare, Security	Peace, Social Justice, and Human Security
Typical Behavior	Self-Help	Cooperation	Promotion of Ideas
Basis for Power	Tangible Resources (Military/Economic)	Issue Specific Both Hard and Soft Power	Political Legitimacy and Value of Ideas
Nature of Interstate Relations	Unregulated Competition Limited Alliances	Interest-Based Regimes Coordination and Collaboration among States	Norm-Based Regimes
Ideal State of the World	Stability Through Balance of Power	Equitable System Managed by RO/IO	World Community

These sentiments underpin the approach to globalization taken by writers such as Daniele Archibugi, David Held, and Mary Kaldor, who believe that global politics must be democratized (Held and McGrew 2002). Held's argument is illustrative of the analytic and prescriptive character of radical liberalism in an era of globalization. His diagnosis begins by revealing the inadequacies of the "Westphalian order" (or the modern states system that is conventionally dated from the middle of the seventeenth century). During the latter stages of this period, we have witnessed rapid democratization in a number of states, but this has not been accompanied by democratization of the contemporary states system (Held 1993). This task is increasingly urgent given the current levels of interconnectedness because "national" governments are no longer in control of the forces that shape their citizens' lives (e.g., the decision by one state to permit deforestation has environmental consequences for all states). After 1945, the UN Charter set limits to the sovereignty of states by recognizing the rights of individuals in a whole series of human rights conventions. But even if the United Nations had lived up to its charter in the post-1945 period, it would still have left the building blocks of the Westphalian order largely intact—namely, the hierarchy between great powers and the rest (symbolized by the permanent membership of the Security Council), massive inequalities of wealth among states, and a minimal role for nonstate actors to influence decision making in international relations.

In place of the Westphalian and UN models, Held outlines a **cosmopolitan model of democracy.** This requires, in the first instance, the creation of regional parliaments and the extension of the authority of such regional bodies (e.g., the European Union) that already exist. Second, human rights conventions must be entrenched in national parliaments and

cosmopolitan democracy
A condition in which international organizations, transnational corporations, and global markets are accountable to the peoples of the world.

monitored by a new International Court of Human Rights. Third, reform of the United Nations, or its replacement, with a genuinely democratic and accountable global parliament "is necessary." Without appearing too sanguine about the prospects for the realization of the cosmopolitan model of democracy, Held is nevertheless adamant that if democracy is to thrive, it must penetrate the institutions and regimes that manage global politics.

Radical liberals place great importance on the civilizing capacity of global society. While the rule of law and the democratization of international institutions are core components of the liberal project, it is also vital that citizens' networks are broadened and deepened to monitor and cajole these institutions. These groups form a linkage among individuals, states, and global institutions. It is easy to portray radical-liberal thinking as utopian, but we should not forget the many achievements of global civil society so far. The evolution of international humanitarian law and the extent to which these laws find compliance are largely due to the millions of individuals who are active supporters of human rights groups like Amnesty International and Human Rights Watch (Falk 1995b, 164). Similarly, global protest movements have been responsible for the heightened sensitivity to environmental degradation everywhere.

Conclusion

In this chapter, we learned that realism provides what its advocates call a "parsimonious" model of global politics. It tells us that if we look for a few simple factors in any event, crisis, or pattern of interactions, we can understand why leaders picked a certain path of action. For realists, global politics is an endless struggle for dominance and power. Power can be control over something tangible, like resources and territory or power, or it can be a struggle for an intangible, like prestige. Realism is valuable because it helps us understand some kinds of interactions. However, because of its pessimistic opinion about human nature, realist theory tends to see enemies or competitors everywhere. The doctrine assumes that all leaders of all countries are constantly on the verge of war. Although it shares some of realism's ideas about international systemic anarchy, liberalism offers a less violent explanation for global politics. Many proponents of the liberal perspective believe that long-term international cooperation is possible and will lead to human material and spiritual progress.

We turn in the next chapter to several approaches that are more recent intellectual inventions. These theories that we call "critical" suggest other ways of interpreting global events.

CONTRIBUTORS TO CHAPTER 3: Tim Dunne, Brian C. Schmidt, and Steven L. Lamy.

REVIEW QUESTIONS

1. How does the Melian dialogue (see first Case Study in this chapter) represent key concepts such as self-interest, balance of power, alliances, capabilities, empires, and justice?

2. Is realism anything more than the ideology of powerful, satisfied states?

3. How would a realist explain the origins of the war on terrorism?

4. What is the debate between defensive and offensive realism?

5. How might realists explain the impact globalization has on world politics?

6. Should liberal states promote their values abroad? Is force a legitimate instrument in securing this goal?

7. Are democratic peace theorists right but for the wrong reasons?

8. Whose strategy of dealing with globalization do you find more convincing: those who believe that states and institutions should maintain the current order or those who believe in reform driven by international or regional organizations or global civil society?

9. Are liberal values and institutions in the contemporary international system as deeply embedded as neoliberals claim?

FURTHER READING

For a general survey of the realist tradition:

Smith, M. J. (1986), *Realist Thought from Weber to Kissinger* (Baton Rouge: Louisiana State University Press). An excellent discussion of many of the leading realist thinkers.

Twentieth-century classical realism:

Carr, E. H. (2001), *The Twenty Years' Crisis 1919–1939: An Introduction to the Study of International Relations* (London: Palgrave). An important critique of liberal idealism.

Morgenthau, H. J. (1948), *Politics Among Nations: The Struggle for Power and Peace* (New York: Alfred A. Knopf). A foundational text for the discipline of international relations.

Structural realism:

Mearsheimer, J. (2001), *The Tragedy of Great Power Politics* (New York: W. W. Norton). This is the definitive account of offensive realism.

Waltz, K. (1979), *Theory of International Politics* (Reading, Mass.: Addison-Wesley). This is the exemplar for structural realism.

Neoclassical realism:

Rose, G. (1998), "Neoclassical Realism and Theories of Foreign Policy," *World Politics* 51: 144–172. An important review article that is credited with coining the term *neoclassical realism*.

Liberalism in international relations:

Doyle, M. (1997), *Ways of War and Peace* (New York: W. W. Norton). One of the best textbooks on the principal theories of international relations. There are more than 100 pages of analysis on liberalism in the book. See also, in a shorter and modified form, his article: Doyle, M. (1986), "Liberalism and World Politics," *American Political Science Review* 80(4): 1151–1169.

Held, D., and McGrew, A. (eds.) (2002), *The Global Transformation Reader*, 2nd ed. (Cambridge: Polity Press). A useful collection of essays with many contributors who represent radical liberalism.

Nye, J. (2011), *The Future of Power* (New York: Public Affairs). A comprehensive review of hard and soft power and the various ways it is used in international relations.

Video Suggestion

Film: *The Fog of War*: Robert McNamara, former secretary of defense under President Kennedy, discusses America's use of military force (Cuban Missile Crisis, Vietnam War).

INTERNET RESOURCES

Internet Classics Archive
http://classics.mit.edu/index.html

Online Library of Liberty
http://oll.libertyfund.org/

Perseus Digital Library
http://www.perseus.tufts.edu/hopper/

Oxford Bibliographies Online
http://oxfordbibliographiesonline.com/
An expert guide to the best available scholarship.

Academic Earth
http://www.academicearth.org/lectures/search/international%20affairs/

TED Talks and Other Online Videos

Harvard Professor Joseph Nye on power and foreign policy: http://www.ted.com/speakers/joseph_nye.html

Former UN Diplomat and Indian Diplomat Sahshi Tharoor on the rise of India and soft power: http://www.ted.com/talks/shashi_tharoor.html

Economist Martin Jacques talks about the economic and political rise of China: http://www.ted.com/talks/martin_jacques_understanding_the_rise_of_china.html

Carnegie Council: "How Wars End: Why We Always Fight the Last Battle"—Gideon Rose
http://www.carnegiecouncil.org/resources/video/data/000369
Rose points out that the United States' impressive military track record is rivaled by an equally unimpressive track record of dealings with other states outside war.

Carnegie Council: "The Crisis of American Foreign Policy: Wilsonianism in the Twenty-First Century"—Anne-Marie Slaughter
http://www.carnegiecouncil.org/resources/video/data/000115
Ann-Marie Slaughter attacks the idea that George W. Bush was largely influenced by the Wilsonian goal of exporting/promoting democracy overseas.

Woodrow Wilson Center: The National Conversation
http://www.wilsoncenter.org/event/search-national-security-narrative-for-the-21st-century
Anne-Marie Slaughter, Steve Clemons, and Brent Scowcroft are only several of the contributors to this new initiative at the Woodrow Wilson Center discussing defense and diplomacy tactics.

For more information, quizzes, case studies and other study tools, please visit us at **www.oup.com/us/lamy**

A Summit on Global Problems

GOAL
This analytic exercise provides an opportunity for you to explore alternative views of global problems. By conducting careful research, you will gain an understanding of how theories shape policy priorities. What might realists, liberals, or Marxists think about what issues are most important?

EXPECTATIONS
In this exercise, you will work with your team members to research, synthesize, and apply basic data as well as compare values and assumptions about how the world works. Based on your research and analysis, you and your team will also be expected to write concise policy recommendations. Your professor may decide how best to divide the classroom into eight (or however many) teams to represent a number of diverse countries.

SCENARIO
You have been asked to participate in a significant international event: a summit conference aimed at identifying and then proposing solutions to global problems. These problems threaten our international stability and influence or affect most citizens in the world.

The agenda for this conference will be decided by eight nation-states, and the agenda will determine what issues are discussed and in what order. The nation-states are the United States, India, France, Brazil, Russia, Norway, Saudi Arabia, and China. Your task is to find out how leaders in each country see the world and how they rank global issues or problems.

PROCEDURE
This is a cooperative learning project. With your team, choose which one of these countries you will represent. Then, as a team, you should complete the following tasks:

1. Using academic journals and the official websites of countries, NGOs, and foreign policy think tanks, find answers to the following questions: What are your nation-state's policy priorities and what worldview prevails? What position has your country supported in economic, political, military, and sociocultural policy issue areas?
2. Once you know something about your country, consider which theories of international relations are consistent with your country's past and present policy priorities. Are the leaders of your country realists, liberals, Marxists, feminists, or something else?

3. As a group representing your country and its worldview,* develop an agenda of policy issues that you would like the summit to address. For example, you might include human rights issues, war and violence, and global poverty. Consider the order in which you would want these issues to be addressed and why.
4. Be prepared to explain the causes of these problems and suggest effective policy responses that are consistent with your country's interests and priorities.

DISCUSSION
After preliminary work with your country team, you will come together with the entire group of eight nation-states with the purpose of developing a specific list of policy priorities that a global summit must address. Only six items may appear on the final agenda for the global conference. In this eight-nation-state preliminary summit, you are to do the following:

1. Present your country's suggestions to the groups of eight nation-states.
2. Evaluate and critically review the agenda items presented by the other seven countries.
3. After your discussion of each state's list, the entire class should try to reach consensus on only six policy problems for the upcoming summit. The method of selecting these issues is left to the class and your professor. The goal is to reach agreement on six issues; however, this may not be possible.

FOLLOW-UP
1. Were you able to reach consensus on six items? Why or why not?
2. Were some issues more acceptable than others?
3. Did your national interest prevent acceptance of some issues?
4. Are there some global problems that are better left to a few powerful and influential states? Why? Which states?

---

*A worldview represents basic values and assumptions people use to describe the world around them. An individual uses his or her worldview to identify problems and evaluate and analyze policies aimed at responding to these problems. Also, from worldviews emerge theories that we use to explain issues and events. For example, a Marxist would most likely explain persistent inequality by focusing on the failures of capitalism.

4 | Critical Approaches

Philosophers have only interpreted the world in various ways; the point, however, is to change it.

—*Karl Marx*

Theory is always *for* some one, and *for* some purpose.

—*Robert W. Cox*

Take a moment to consider this photograph of the Moroccan delegates taking part in a demonstration at the World Social Forum, a meeting that brings together global activists who are critical of the present global political and economic system. Use your computers to find out more about this forum, and answer the following questions:

- Who belongs to the organizations attending this forum, and what factors are they struggling against?
- Who at this forum is protesting the current system and why?
- Why would political leaders like the president of Brazil support protests against the system that put them in power?
- What alternatives to the status quo are the forum's attendees promoting, and how can theory help us understand these alternative visions of the future?

In this chapter, we will show you how to ask other kinds of questions: about the connections between social relations and political structures, about money—who controls it, for example—and about the critical concept that has guided our study so far, which is to say the state. The perspectives on international relations that we call "critical" ask us to reconsider our assumptions about politics. You will learn that many people in this world do not accept the dominant theories that define the international system; they therefore seek change or transformation. We hope you will also learn that it is important to understand all theoretical views. If we decided to discard or marginalize these critical approaches, we would abandon the intellectual goal of being careful and comprehensive critical thinkers. We would also abandon the people behind these ideas, theories, and ways of knowing. The narratives of those on the margins are as important as

The World Social Forum was held in Tunisia in 2013. While Davos, Switzerland, brings together the rich and famous in an economic summit, the World Social Forum brings together representatives from the poor, the marginalized, and those who seek peace and global equality by ending war and closing the gap that separates rich and poor. These two goals help to define the field of international relations.

those in the center of power. In addition, these critical theories offer alternatives to state-centric and power-politics theories.

In Chapter 3, we saw how realism and liberalism gained dominance in the study of international relations during the twentieth century. Both theories offer valuable insights into the interplay of states; however, as we saw, both realism and liberalism have certain shortcomings. With the exception of Marxism, the perspectives we examine in this chapter have recently become part of the international relations discourse, in part as a response to these shortcomings but also in reaction to a different set of stimuli. Indeed, Marxism, feminist theory, and constructivism can each provide important tools to understand trends and events in global politics and globalization in ways that realism and liberalism cannot. Many might ask, why spend time on Marxism since the Soviet Union collapsed? Most socialists or Marxists have two very convincing answers. First, the Soviet Union never provided a model of the ideal socialist or Marxist society. Michael Harrington (1989, 79), an American socialist, describes Soviet socialism as follows:

> [Soviet] Socialism was a bureaucratically controlled and planned economy that carried out the function of primitive accumulation and thus achieved rapid modernization. The state owned the means of production, which made some people think it must be socialist; but the party and the bureaucracy owned the state by virtue of a dictatorial monopoly of political power.

Harrington called the Soviet system a moral disaster for socialism. It was a totalitarian state and not an ideal expression of Marxism.

A second reason is globalization. Marx and Engels (1848) described how increasing interdependence will inevitably create a single global market and a global consumer culture.

> The need for a constantly expanding market for its products chases the bourgeoisie over the surface of the globe. In place of wants, satisfied by the production of country, we find new wants, requiring for their satisfaction the products of distant lands and climes.

A global economy shifts the key elements of Marxist thought from the domestic level to the global level.

We have emphasized the point that theory matters because we all embrace theories that help us understand the world and explain how and why things happen. Critical views might help you understand the meaning of the difference between momentary and structural violence, as Mark Twain eloquently presents in *A Connecticut Yankee in King Arthur's Court*. Twain distinguishes between physical violence and structural violence as he tells the story of two "Reigns of Terror":

> . . . If we could but remember and consider it; the one wrought murder in hot passions, the other in heartless cold blood; the one lasted mere months, the other had lasted a thousand years; the one inflicted death upon a thousand persons, the other upon a hundred millions; but our shudders are all for the "horrors" of the . . . momentary Terror, so to speak; whereas, what is the horror of swift death by the axe compared with lifelong death from hunger, cold, insult, cruelty and heartbreak? A city cemetery could contain the coffins filled by that brief Terror

which we have all been so diligently taught to shiver at and mourn over, but all France could hardly contain the coffins filled by that older and real Terror—that unspeakable bitter and awful Terror which none of us has been taught to see in its vastness or pity as it deserves. (1917, chap. 13)

Critical perspectives ask us to focus on the reign of terror that lasts a thousand years.

Introduction

Chapter 3 introduced the interparadigm debate between realism and liberalism. This debate, though mainstream, by no means covers the complete range of issues linked to globalization that any contemporary approach to global politics needs to address. Instead, the debate tends to be a rather conservative and scholarly exercise, a study of the status quo. It gives the impression of open-mindedness and intellectual pluralism, when in fact realism in its various forms often dominates university departments and academic journals. One factor that proponents of realism stress is its ability to describe everyday life as most people understand it. Thus, they can dismiss other views as value laden, or normative (promoting certain norms and values), to be negatively compared with the allegedly scientific objectivity of realism. The approaches discussed in this chapter convincingly challenge that assertion of objectivity.

In the past fifteen to twenty years, the dominance of the mainstream theories has changed dramatically in two ways. First, there has been a lively academic debate between advocates of structural realism, or neorealism, and advocates of neoliberalism. This debate within the mainstream of scholarly thinking has exposed the shortcomings of both approaches. The second change has been the steadily growing intellectual appeal of a range of new approaches, which complemented the longstanding Marxist criticism of a capitalist-dominated international system. In part, these changes reflect a transformed world. The end of the Cold War system in the early 1990s significantly reduced the credibility of realism, especially in its structural-realist guise, where the stability of the bipolar system was seen as an enduring feature of global politics. The most obvious failure was the inability of either of the mainstream theories—realism or liberalism—to predict the end of the Cold War. To be fair to the scholars, however, we must remember that leaders of states around the world—and their intelligence agencies and military planners—did not expect the collapse of the Soviet Union that brought an end to the Cold War. As the bipolarity of the international system dramatically disappeared, so too did the explanatory power of the theory that most relied on it.

But this was not by any means the only reason for the rise of new approaches. There are three other obvious reasons. First, realism's dominance was called into question by a resurgence of its historical main competitor, liberalism, in the form of neoliberal institutionalism, as we discussed in Chapter 3. The debate between the two now comprised the mainstream of the discipline. Second, there were other changes under way in world politics that made the development of new approaches important, as discussed in Chapter 2 under the heading

WHAT'S YOUR WORLDVIEW

In Chapter 2, we discussed how the Cold War ended—specifically, what transpired and how the events unfolded. But how did ideas, as distinct from actions, also help end the Cold War? More recently, how have ideas shaped global politics during the global economic crisis?

Emanuele Kant

One of the founders of the English School, Martin Wight, introduced scholars to three theoretical traditions: Machiavellians (realists), Grotians (liberal reformers), and Kantians (radical liberals or idealists). Many of the critical theorists embrace Kantian ideas such as the possibility of peace and the universal values of human rights, justice, and the categorical imperative. In foreign policy, the categorical imperative means that states act according to the principle that a state's actions should be the maxim but which all states base their actions.

"Globalization: Challenging the International Order?" Whatever the explanatory power of realism, it did not seem very good at dealing with economic, sociological, and cultural issues, such as the rise of nonstate actors, race and gender politics, transnational social movements, and information technology. In short, new approaches were needed to explain these features of global politics, even if proponents of realism still claimed that their theory was good at analyzing power politics among states. Third, there were major developments under way in other academic disciplines in the social sciences and philosophy that attacked the underlying methodological (i.e., how to undertake study) assumption of realism, a position known as **positivism**. This is the idea that political scientists can conduct research following the scientific method that guides the physical sciences like physics, chemistry, and biology. In its place, a host of alternative ways of thinking about the social sciences were being proposed, and the academic field of international relations simply caught up. Since then, scholars have proposed many alternative approaches as more relevant to global politics in the twenty-first century. In this chapter, we will examine the three most influential alternatives to realism and liberalism (see Table 4.1).

After reading and discussing this chapter, you will have a better understanding of critical voices—those that question the assumptions of the dominant theories and paradigms. Marxists ask us to look at the world from the perspective of workers and not the owners; feminists ask us to look at the lives of women; and constructivists ask us to consider how ideas, images, and values shape our worldview and our construction of reality.

The Essential Marxism

We turn our attention first to **Marxism**, the oldest of the challengers. Marxist ideas inspired many political movements in the developing world in the period of decolonization through the 1970s and 1980s. Although the Communist Party state of the Soviet Union is gone and never reached the goal of a pure expression of Marxism, and the authoritarian Chinese Communist Party permits a form of capitalism in China, the central ideas of Marxism can still help us understand the inequality that characterizes the globalized economy.

A Marxist interpretation of world politics has been influential since the mid-1800s. In his inaugural address to the Working Men's International Association in London in 1864, Karl Marx told his audience that history had "taught the working classes the duty to master [for] themselves the mysteries of international politics." However, despite the fact that Marx himself wrote copiously about international affairs, most of this writing was journalistic in character. He did not incorporate the international dimension into his theoretical description of capitalism. This omission should perhaps not surprise us. The sheer scale of the theoretical enterprise in which he was engaged, as well as the nature of his own methodology, inevitably meant that Marx's work would remain contingent and unfinished.

Marx was an enormously prolific writer whose ideas developed and changed over time. The *Collected Works* produced by Progress Publishers in Moscow, for instance, contains fifty volumes of very thick books. Hence, it is not surprising that his legacy has been open to numerous interpretations. In addition, real-world developments have led to the revision of his ideas in light of experience. A variety of schools of thought have emerged that claim Marx as a direct inspiration or whose work can be linked to Marx's legacy.

Four strands of contemporary Marxist thought have made major contributions to thinking about global politics. Before we discuss what is distinctive about these approaches, it is important that we examine their essential commonalities.

positivism The position arguing that we can explain the social world as effectively as natural and physical scientists explain phenomena.

Marxism A theory critical of the status quo, or dominant capitalist paradigm. It is a critique of the capitalist political economy from the view of the revolutionary proletariat, or workers. Marxists' ideal is a stateless and classless society.

Table 4.1

Alternative International Relations Theories at the Beginning of the Twenty-First Century

	Central Idea	View of International System	Key Authors
Marxism: Dependency School	Global capitalist system eliminates harmony of interests of workers.	Core-periphery relationship. Unfair terms of international trade. Underdevelopment in periphery.	Prebisch, Frank, Cardoso, O'Donnell
Marxism: World-System	Expansion of European capitalist system. Systems have life cycle, new ones develop.	Hegemonic powers. Core-periphery-semiperiphery relationship. Exploitation on a global scale, semiperiphery elites benefit.	Wallerstein, Chase-Dunn
Constructivism	Seeks to understand change. Ideas are social creations. Relationships result from historical processes. Ideas can evolve, replace older ways of thinking.	A process. Result of hegemonic ideas. Can change as a result of evolving ideas.	Onuf, Walker, Wendt
Liberal Feminism	Change women's subordinate position in existing political systems.	Improve women's representation in INGOs. End gender bias in INGOs and NGOs.	Caprioli, Enloe, Elshtain, Tickner, Tobias
Socialist and Marxist Feminism	Ideas about gender relations impact economic relations.	States encourage gendered division of labor.	Chin, Hennessy, Ingraham, Whitworth
Standpoint Feminism	Ideas about gender are social constructs.	Ideas about gender shape international system.	Hartsock, Prügl, Zalewski
Postmodern Feminism	Perceptions of gender determine positions on gender. Dichotomized language.	Distinctions like order/anarchy, public/private, developed/underdeveloped linked to gender.	Fausto-Sterling, Hooper, Kinsella, Longino
Postcolonial Feminism	Effects of colonial experience on gender identity.	Challenges Western portrayals of third world women. Globalization perpetuates colonial-era gender-based exploitation.	Mohanty, Spivak

First, all the theorists discussed in this section share with Marx the view that the social, political, and economic world should be analyzed as a totality. The academic division of the social world into different areas of inquiry—history, philosophy, economics, political science, sociology, international relations, and so on—is both arbitrary and unhelpful. None can be understood without knowledge of the others: the social world has to be studied as a whole. Given the scale and complexity of the social world, this requirement clearly makes great demands of the analyst. Nonetheless, for Marxist theorists, the disciplinary boundaries that characterize the contemporary social sciences need to be transcended if we are to generate a proper understanding of the dynamics of global politics.

Another key element of Marxist thought, which underlines this concern with interconnection and context, is the materialist conception of history. The central contention here is that economic development is effectively the motor of history. The central dynamic that Marx identifies is tension between the means of production (e.g., labor, tools, technology) and relations of production (technical and institutional relationships) that together form the **economic base** of a given society. As the means of production develop—for example, through technological advancement—previous relations of production become outmoded, limiting effective utilization of the new productive capacity. This limitation in turn leads to a process of social change that transforms relations of production to better accommodate the new configuration of means. For example, computer-driven machines for manufacturing might replace auto-factory workers, or the workers' jobs might be moved to a country where labor and production costs are lower. Workers are still needed, but fewer, and most of those must be retrained to repair computers or develop software and no longer make car doors. The recent crisis in the US auto industry are still having profound negative effects in industrial cities like Detroit and Cleveland, forever changing the political, economic, and social landscape. In other words, developments in the economic base act as a catalyst for the broader transformation of society as a whole. This is because, as Marx argues in the preface to his *Contribution to the Critique of Political Economy*, "the mode of production of material life conditions the social, political and intellectual life process in general." Thus, the legal, political, and cultural institutions and practices of a given society reflect and reinforce—in a more or less mediated form—the pattern of power and control in the economy. It follows logically, therefore, that change in the economic base ultimately leads to change in the "legal and political **superstructure**."

And so, as you might have guessed by now, **class** plays a key role in Marxist analysis. Marx defines class as "social relations between the producers, and the conditions under which they exchange their activities and share in the total act of production" (Marx 1867). For most Americans, class is simply a way of designating an individual's position within the income distribution of a society. We talk about upper, middle, and lower income classes, and these represent income groups in our society. For Marxists, your income does not determine your class. Instead, your class is defined by your position within the hierarchy of production. In contrast to liberals, who believe that there is an essential harmony of interest between various social groups, Marxists hold that society is systemically prone to class conflict. Indeed, *The Communist Manifesto*, which Marx coauthored with Friedrich Engels, argues that "the history of all hitherto existing societies is the history of class struggle" (Marx and Engels 1848). In capitalist society, says Marx, the main axis of conflict is between the bourgeoisie (the capitalists) and the proletariat (the workers).

The Marxist perspective on globalization seeks to describe the ways inequality affects the lives of millions of

economic base For Marxists, the substructure of the society is the relationship between owners and workers. Capitalists own the means of production and control technology and resources. The workers are employed by the capitalists, and they are alienated, exploited, and estranged from their work and their society.

superstructure The government or political structure that is controlled by those who own the means of production.

class A social group that in Marxism is identified by its relationship with the means of production and the distribution of societal resources. Thus, we have the bourgeoisie, or the owners or upper classes, and the proletariat, or the workers.

The founders of "scientific socialism," Karl Marx and Friedrich Engels, together in a park that was once in communist-controlled East Berlin. Can you think of ways in which socialist ideas still influence politics in your country?

people. Marx and his coauthor Engels predicted that capitalism would spread around the world and then, and only then, would the proletariat become aware of their exploitation as workers, alienation from their government, and estrangement from society ruled by the bourgeoisie. In this situation, globalization might be the catalyst for awareness and eventual transformation. As we see in the data presented in Table 4.2, for example, despite the wealth generated in the global economy in the ten years prior to the economic depression of 2008–2009, that prosperity did not improve the living conditions of most of the world's population.

Despite his commitment to rigorous scholarship, Marx did not think it either possible or desirable for the analyst to remain a detached or neutral observer of this great clash between capital and labor. As he argued in a famous phrase that encouraged student radicals around the world in the 1960s, "philosophers have only interpreted the world in various ways; the point, however, is to change it" (Marx 1888). Marx was committed to the cause of emancipation. He was not interested in developing an understanding of the dynamics of capitalist society simply for the sake of it. Rather, he expected such an understanding to make it easier to overthrow the prevailing order and replace it with a communist society—a society in which wage labor and private property are abolished and social relations transformed.

> **WHAT'S YOUR WORLDVIEW**
>
> *Has globalization increased worker exploitation and therefore the likelihood of revolution according to Marxist political thought? How would liberals respond to Marxist accusations?*

It is important to emphasize that the essential elements of Marxist thought are also contested. That is, they are subject to much discussion and disagreement even among contemporary writers who have been influenced by Marxist writings. There is disagreement as to how these ideas and concepts should be interpreted and how they should be put into operation. Analysts also differ over which elements of Marxist thought are most relevant, which have been proven to be mistaken, and which should now be considered as outmoded or in need of radical overhaul. Moreover, there are substantial differences between them in terms of their

Table 4.2

Indicators of World Inequality

- Worldwide, more than 1.2 billion people live on less than $1 per day. ✗
- In 1990, the average American was thirty-eight times richer than the average Tanzanian. By 2005, this had risen to sixty-one times richer.
- More than 1.1 billion people lack access to clean water.
- Average incomes in more than fifty developing countries are now at a lower level than they were in 1990. In twenty-one countries, a larger proportion of the people are hungry. In fourteen countries, a higher proportion of children are dying before reaching the age of five, and in thirty-four countries, life expectancy has decreased.
- Tariffs on manufactured goods from the developing world are four times higher than those on manufactured goods from other OECD countries.
- One-sixth of the world's adults are illiterate (two-thirds of the world's illiterates are women).
- In the developed world, subsidies to agricultural producers are six times higher than overseas development aid.
- More than 10 million children die every year from easily preventable diseases.
- A child born in Zambia today is less likely to live past the age of thirty than a child born in 1840 in England.
- In Africa, only one child in three completes primary education.
- In sub-Saharan Africa, a woman is 100 times more likely to die in childbirth than women in high-income OECD countries.
- African countries pay out $40 million every day on debt repayment.

Sources: World Bank, United Nations Development Program, Jubilee Research.

GLOBAL PERSPECTIVE   What Makes a Theory "Alternative" or Critical?

If you grew up in the United States, you have probably internalized a combination of the liberal and realist perspectives. To keep with our simile that theories are like eyeglasses, you are in essence wearing bifocals, combining both liberal and realist visions of different worlds. You probably think that you live in a basically peaceful and law-abiding society with a free market economic system in which anyone can become rich. This is the rough outline of the liberal model. And while you have this view of the domestic situation, you most likely look at international events quite differently. Here the realist model describes what you see: if countries are not at war, then they are constantly seeking some kind of an advantage—in trade negotiations, for example. Individuals and states are self-interest oriented, and international politics is a constant struggle for power and material resources; even in trade negotiations, self-help and self-interest rule.

But for someone who grew up in the former Eastern bloc of communist countries, the view of your society could be quite different, especially if that person were a child of a member of the ruling Communist Party. For that person, Marxism, not capitalism, is the dominant political-economic model. In fact, in some ways, the theory of Marxism in the USSR was like a religion: it had an explanation for history, it described how to live properly, and it offered a utopian workers' paradise as a reward for living correctly.

A Marxist could look at life in the United States and see exploitation everywhere. Workers in factories are alienated from the products they make. Without an employee discount, for instance, an assembly line worker at a General Motors factory could never even think about owning the car that went by on the conveyor belt. Schools are designed to create good future workers by teaching the benefits of arriving on time, being polite to the teacher, and submitting perfect homework. The income gap between rich and poor is wide and getting wider.

For this imagined child of the Communist Party in the USSR, life is very good and not based on exploitation. There are special shops for party members, where shortages of meat are rare and you can purchase white bread, not the rough rye loaves found in other stores. You would probably also attend school with other children like yourself and have science labs with the latest equipment, while being taught by instructors who do not seem bored with their work. When you catch the flu in the winter, you do not have to wait in long lines for your turn to see the doctor in a clinic.

The Marxist perspective on international affairs would sound a bit like realism but with a socialist spin. For where realism sees constant struggles for power, the Marxist doctrine of the USSR saw capitalist encirclement of the Soviet Union and the exploitation of the developing world. The doctrine preached class warfare on a global scale, and the USSR extended foreign aid in "fraternal cooperation" with its socialist friends.

Imagining still that you were a student born into the USSR: in your classes on foreign relations, you would learn that the "correlation of forces" was beginning to turn in the direction of the socialist world. You would also learn that your country was peace loving and had pledged that it would never use nuclear weapons first in a war with the capitalist NATO countries.

Of course, this is a stylized reality we've asked you to imagine, but it was done to prove a point: what is "alternative" depends on your perspective. An alternative perspective can also be critical of the status quo. In all likelihood, you, this hypothetical student in the USSR, would know that you had a privileged status in society. You might be uncomfortable with it because you could see the exploitation of people in the "workers' paradise": tiny apartments with a shared bathroom down the hall; food shortages; drab clothing selections; a yearlong wait to purchase a car, and then no choice of color. In the workplace, people seem like the assembly line workers in the capitalist West: bored and underpaid. A popular joke in the 1970s Soviet Union was "we pretend to work, and the state pretends to pay us."

However, for all its shortcomings, it would be *your* Marxist perspective, and you might feel very good about it; meanwhile, it would be the liberal capitalist model that you considered perilous until perhaps 1989, when you would learn what it meant to see things from the other perspective.

For Discussion

1. We suggest in the text that the Soviet Union was an authoritarian/totalitarian state capitalist system and not truly a communist or Marxist society. Its authoritarianism made it an alternative to democracy. What examples are there, if any, of Marxist societies? Is Marxism at all relevant today?

2. Does realism help us understand Russian society better than Marxism? Why or why not? What about utopian societies?

3. What examples do we have, if any, of experiments in utopian societies? Would you say a real Marxist society was utopian?

attitudes toward the legacy of Marx's ideas. The work of the more contemporary Marxists, for example, draws far more directly on Marx's original ideas than does the work of the critical theorists. Indeed, the critical theorists would probably be more comfortable being viewed as post-Marxists than as straightforward Marxists. But even for them, as the very term post-Marxism suggests, the ideas of Marx remain a basic point of departure.

The Origins of World-System Theory

As we noted earlier, Marx did not devote much attention in his writing to the international aspects of capitalism, in particular leaving out the European colonial occupations of Asia and Africa. In fact, Marx seemed to think that colonization might help move the people of the non-European world out of their premodern modes of production and into the capitalist mode. This in turn would create conditions of exploitation that would spark a proletarian revolution of the kind Marx and Engels predicted in *The Communist Manifesto*.

World-system theory identifies the world system as the basic unit of analysis in international relations (see Table 4.3). The idea of a world system refers to the international division of labor; this approach divides the world into core states, semiperiphery states, and periphery states. The origins of this theory can be traced back to the first systematic attempt to apply the ideas of Marx to the international sphere—that is, to the critique of **imperialism** advanced by a number of thinkers at the start of the twentieth century (see Brewer 1990). The best-known and most influential work to emerge from this debate is the pamphlet written by Lenin, published in 1917, called *Imperialism: The Highest Stage of Capitalism*. Lenin accepted much of Marx's basic thesis but argued that the character of capitalism had changed since Marx published the first volume of *Capital* in 1867 (Marx 1992). Capitalism had entered a new stage—its highest and final stage—with the development of **monopoly capitalism**. Under monopoly capitalism, a two-tier structure had developed within the world economy: a dominant core exploiting a less-developed periphery. With the development of a core and periphery, there was no longer an automatic harmony of interests among all workers. The bourgeoisie in the core states could use profits derived from exploiting the periphery to improve the lot of their own proletariat. That is, the capitalists of the core could pacify their own working class through the further exploitation of the periphery.

The idea of **dependency**, or the fact that the social and economic development of underdeveloped countries is conditioned by external forces, is an important assumption of world-system theory. Writers from the Latin American dependency school explored Lenin's views, especially the notion of core and periphery, in greater depth. In particular, Raul Prebisch, though not a Marxist scholar, argued that states in the periphery were suffering as a result of what he called "the declining terms of trade." He suggested that the price of manufactured goods increased more rapidly than that of raw materials. So, for example, year by year, more tons of coffee are required to pay for a refrigerator. As a result of their reliance on primary goods, states of the periphery become poorer relative to those of the core. Writers such as Guillermo O'Donnell, Andre Gunder Frank, and Fernando Henrique Cardoso extended these arguments further. It is from the framework built by such writers that contemporary world-system theory emerged.

The Key Features of Wallerstein's World-System Theory

To outline the key features of world-system theory, we begin with the work of perhaps its most prominent protagonist, Immanuel Wallerstein. For Wallerstein, history has been marked

> **WHAT'S YOUR WORLDVIEW**
>
> *Marxists believe that globalization has created an uneven distribution of wealth, power, and influence. Do you think it is possible to manage and reform globalization to address the growing disparities? What examples are there of NGOs or governments attempting to address these concerns?*

world-system theory A theory emphasizing that world systems, and not individuals or states, should be the basic unit of analysis. Thus, the political and economic structure of the world shapes global politics. "World system" refers to the international division of labor, which divides the world into core countries, semiperiphery countries, and periphery countries.

imperialism The practice of foreign conquest and rule in the context of global relations of hierarchy and subordination. It can lead to the establishment of an empire.

monopoly capitalism A term introduced by Lenin suggesting that competitive capitalism had been replaced by large corporations that control the market in specific sectors.

dependency theory A school of thought that offers explanations for economic development and underdevelopment. Dependency theorists emphasize that social and economic development is conditioned by external forces—namely, the domination of underdeveloped states by more powerful countries.

Table 4.3

General Assumptions of Realism, Liberalism, Utopian/World-Order Models, and World-System Theory

	Realism	Liberalism	Utopian/World-Order Models	World-System Theory
Principal actors in world affairs	Nation-states (the more powerful, the more important)	Nation-states, international and regional organizations, and nongovernmental organizations	Nation-states, international and regional organizations, and nongovernmental organizations	Nation-states, regional and international organizations based on the principle of one state, one vote
Primary concern of leaders	Maintaining power relative to other states	International security broadly defined to include economic, political, and sociocultural concerns	The implementation of policies generally reflective of the specific human-centric ideals such as social justice, economic well-being, and ecological balances	Addressing the problem of inequality and human misery by changing the world's economic system and finding a way out of the power struggle between the US and the USSR
Policy behavior used to secure policy goals	Self-help	Cooperative (multilateral) behavior through international or regional institutions	Locally decentralized power structures with an emphasis on individual participation and the promotion of human-centric goals and ideals; internationally, multilateral institutions where participation is not limited to states	Multilateral efforts aimed at presenting the rich states with an impression that the poor states are united and cooperate to create a more equitable system
Source of power and influence	Military, economic, and political resources and capabilities	Expertise and capabilities within regional and international institutions (e.g., agenda setting); specific strength in a particular interest area (e.g., trade)	Ability to gain confidence of citizens by providing for their basic needs and ensuring order and stability	Ability to use international to influence the policy actions of rich states; control of commodities (e.g., oil)

Continued

by the rise and demise of a series of world systems. The modern world system emerged in Europe at around the turn of the sixteenth century. It subsequently expanded to encompass the entire globe. The driving force behind this seemingly relentless process of expansion and incorporation has been capitalism, defined by Wallerstein as "a system of production for sale in a market for profit and appropriation of this profit on the basis of individual or collective ownership" (1979, 66). Within the context of this system, all the institutions of the social world are continually being created and re-created. Furthermore, and crucially, it is not only the elements within the system that change. The system itself is historically bounded. It had a beginning, has a middle, and will have an end.

In terms of the geography of the modern world system, in addition to a core-periphery distinction, Wallerstein identified an intermediate "semiperiphery." According to

Table 4.3 (*continued*)
General Assumptions of Realism, Liberalism, Utopian/World-Order Models, and World-System Theory

	Realism	Liberalism	Utopian/World-Order Models	World-System Theory
View of relations with other states	Zero-sum competition is the norm; cooperative behavior possible, but national interest still rules	Nation-states coordinate their activities and cooperate in specific policy areas; the challenge of common crisis situations requires multilateral efforts	Nation-states act according to specific international norms guaranteed by multilateral enforcement institutions	Poor states are exploited by rich states. The core states control the international policy agenda and use the poor states to enhance their position in the international hierarchy. The poor states must work together to change the international system. This cooperation is hindered by the tendency for the global powers to create spheres of influence and encourage regional differences
Preferred world future	The best the world can hope for is a balance of power where stability is guaranteed by deterrence and numerous alliances	A community of nation-states, not unlike the European Community, where state members encourage the integration of policy-making authority in specific issue areas; these institutions would encourage cooperative behavior and multilateral efforts aimed at protecting the welfare of citizens throughout the world	A global federation based on human-centric interests, not national interests	A more equitable international system and a global political system in which all countries, regardless of size, cultural composition, or ideological orientation, enjoy equal access to decision-making institutions

Source: Steven L. Lamy, International Relations: Contending Perspectives *(Boulder, Col.: Lynne Rienner, 1988) USC School of International Relations.*

Wallerstein, the semiperipheral zone displays certain features characteristic of the core and others characteristic of the periphery. Although dominated by core economic interests, the semiperiphery has its own relatively vibrant indigenously owned industrial base. Because of this hybrid nature, the semiperiphery plays important economic and political roles within the modern world system. In particular, it provides a source of labor that counteracts any upward pressure on wages in the core and also provides a new home for industries that can no longer function profitably in the core (e.g., car assembly and textiles). The semiperiphery also plays a vital role in stabilizing the world political structure.

Another theorist, Robert W. Cox, provides a transition from contemporary Marxism to more recent theoretical developments. In his 1981 article "Social Forces, States, and World Orders: Beyond International Relations Theory," Cox analyzes the state of international

World-system theorists proposed that goods, such as boots made in Vietnam, are made in the periphery for sale in the core. Is there evidence to suggest that globalization will increase the division between rich and poor or reduce the gap between core and periphery?

problem-solving theory
Realism and liberalism are problem-solving theories that address issues and questions within the dominant paradigm or the present system. How can we fix capitalism? How can we make a society more democratic? These are problem-solving questions that assume nothing is wrong with the core elements of the system.

critical theory Theories that are critical of the status quo and reject the idea that things can be fixed under the present system. These theories challenge core assumptions of the dominant paradigm and argue for transformation and not just reform.

WHAT'S YOUR WORLDVIEW

Do you think critical theories like Marxism and feminism are no longer important for you, as a student of global politics, to explore? Why or why not?

relations theory as a whole and one of its major subfields, international political economy. This article became an important wedge in the process of toppling realism's dominance in international relations. The sentence that has become one of the most often-quoted lines in all of contemporary international relations theory reads as follows: "Theory is always *for* some one, and *for* some purpose" (1981, 128). This echoes Marx's statement we cited earlier that philosophy must change the world. It expresses a worldview that follows logically from a broad Marxist position that has been explored in this section. If ideas and values are (ultimately) a reflection of a particular set of social relations and are transformed as those relations are themselves transformed, then this suggests that all knowledge of political relations must reflect a certain context, a certain time, a certain space. Thus, politics cannot be objective and timeless in the way some traditional realists and contemporary structural realists, for example, would like to claim.

One key implication is that there can be no simple separation between facts and values. Whether consciously or not, all theorists inevitably bring their values to bear on their analysis. This leads Cox to suggest that we need to look closely at each theory, each idea, and each analysis that claims to be objective or value-free. We need to ask who or what it is for and what purpose it serves. He subjects realism, and in particular its contemporary variant structural realism, to an extended criticism on these grounds.

According to Cox, these theories are for, or serve the interests of, those who prosper under the prevailing order—that is, the inhabitants of the developed states and, in particular, the ruling elites. Their purpose, whether consciously or not, is to reinforce and legitimate the status quo. They do this by making the current configuration of international relations appear natural and immutable. When realists (falsely, according to Cox and many other analysts) claim to be describing the world as it is, as it has been, and as it always will be, what they are in fact doing is reinforcing the ruling hegemony in the current world order. In the same way, according to a contemporary neoliberal argument, blindly accepting globalization as a beneficial process reinforces the hegemony of the countries, corporations, and their stockholders.

Cox extends his argument by contrasting **problem-solving theory** with **critical theory**. Problem-solving theory accepts the parameters of the present order while attempting to fix its problems and thus helps legitimate an unjust and deeply iniquitous system. Critical theory attempts to challenge the prevailing order by seeking out, analyzing, and, where possible, assisting social processes that can potentially lead to transformation of the existing system.

Third World Socialists

Following World War II, many former European colonies declared independence, with leaders like Kwame Nkrumah (1909–1972), the first prime minister and president of Ghana, and Julius Nyerere (1921–1999), the first president of Tanzania. To build sovereign states, they rejected prevailing economic theories of the day—especially Soviet-style socialism and Western capitalism—in favor of political-economic development strategies based on autarchy (economic self-sufficiency), which were sensitive to the history, values, experience, resources, and specific attributes of each region. They recognized that, for most developing states, the major resources are people and land, so states must intervene to replace exploitation with citizen access to economic resources and opportunities. Finally, they stressed the importance of producing for local consumption, presciently fearing that development strategies requiring rapid industrialization or reliance on export-driven industries would increase dependency levels.

Although defined by different experiences and context, Nyerere, Nkrumah, Gandhi, and Mao Zedong (Mao Tse-Tung) led socialist and populist revolutions against former colonial powers. Subsequently, they battled new "colonizing" economic forces that increased their countries' dependency on the North, thereby reducing their power and independence in the international system. Each of these third world socialist movements shared five critical elements:

1. Intensely nationalistic, they targeted all forms of colonialism and foreign economic domination.
2. As radical movements, they rejected exploitation and injustice and were willing to use force to initiate change.
3. Capitalism was identified with imperialism, an immoral system, wherein wealth accumulation came at the expense of others.
4. Their inspiration was the masses—city workers and rural peasants—whose needs should have been served by the political and economic systems that govern them.
5. They were socialist, meaning the state owned much of the core industries, but not orthodox Marxist-Leninist.

Feminist Theory

Often misunderstood as an attack on men, **feminist theory** provides useful tools with which to analyze a range of political events and policy decisions. In this section, we offer an overview of five main types of feminist theory, which have become common since the mid-1980s: liberal, socialist/Marxist, standpoint, postmodern, and postcolonial. The title of this section, "Feminist Theory," is both deliberate and misleading. It is deliberate in that it focuses on the socially constructed roles that women occupy in world politics. It is misleading because this question must be understood—as we noted in the previous section—in the context of the construction of differences between women and men and contingent understandings of masculinity and femininity. In other words, the focus could more accurately be on gender than on women because the very categories of women and men, and the concepts of masculinity and femininity, are highly contested in much feminist research. Similarly, distinctions such as liberal and socialist are slightly misleading because, as we will discuss in more detail later, these categories do not exactly correspond to the diverse thinking of feminist scholars, especially in contemporary work, in which elements from each type are often integrated.

The term *gender* usually refers to the social construction of the difference between men and women. Although it is a complex concept, here is one way to think of it: biology determines your sex; a mix of social and cultural norms, as well as your own sense of identity, determines your gender. Some of the theories covered in this section assume natural and biological (e.g., sex) differences between men and women. Some of the approaches do not. What all of the most interesting work in this field does, however, is analyze how gender both *affects* global politics and *is an effect of* global politics. That is, feminist theorists examine how different concepts (e.g., the state or sovereignty) are "gendered" and in turn how this gendering of concepts can have differential consequences for men and women (Steans 1998). It is important to note that feminists have always been interested in how understandings of gender affect the lives of men and women (Brittan 1989; Seidler 1989; Connell 1995; Carver 1996; Zalewski and Parpart 1998). As with all

feminism A political project to understand so as to end women's inequality and oppression. Feminist theories tend to be critical of the biases of the discipline. Many feminists focus their research on the areas where women are excluded from the analysis of major international issues and concerns.

Engaging with the
W⬤RLD
Global Fund for Women

The Global Fund for Women is a publicly supported, non-profit grant-making foundation that advances women's human rights by funding women-led organizations worldwide. They provide general operating support grants to organizations working at the local, regional, and national levels to enable women and girls to reach their potential and live free of discrimination and violence. Internship opportunities are designed for undergraduate and graduate students to provide firsthand experience with an international grant-making foundation committed to global women's rights.

Summer Internship Duration: They host student interns generally from June to August for unpaid assignments of up to 40 hours/week. The number of internship positions available will be determined every spring according to team needs. Any opportunities will be posted on their website.

Special Internship Programs: The organization also serves as a hosting agency for other formal internship programs from educational institutions that provide funding to student programs related to philanthropy.

theoretical traditions, there are different shades of feminism that combine with some of the more traditional theoretical ideas in global politics. We will discuss five forms, or varieties, of feminist thinking.

Feminist theory in international relations originally grew from work on the politics of development and peace research. But by the late 1980s, a first wave of feminism, **liberal feminism**, was more forcefully posing the question of "where are the women in global politics?" The meaning of liberal in this context is decidedly *not* the same as the meaning we discussed in Chapter 3. This definition is more in line with traditional views of liberalism that put equal and nondiscriminatory liberty at the center of the international debate.

In the context of feminism, the term *liberal* starts from the notion that the key units of society are individuals, that these individuals are biologically determined as either men or women, and that these individuals possess specific rights and are equal. Thus, one strong argument of liberal feminism is that all rights should be granted to women equally with men. Here we can see how the state is gendered insofar as rights, such as voting rights and the right to possess property, have been predicated solely on the experiences and expectations of men—and typically, a certain ethnic/racial class of men. Thus, taking women seriously made a difference to the standard view of global politics. Liberal feminists look at the ways women are excluded from power and prevented from playing a full part in political activity. They examine how women have been restricted to roles critically important for the functioning of things but not usually deemed important for theories of global politics. To give you an example of political discrepancies by gender, Table 4.4 shows the percentage of women in national parliaments by region in 2013.

To ask "where are the women?" was at the time quite a radical political act, precisely because women were absent from the standard texts of international relations, and thus they appeared invisible. Writers such as Cynthia Enloe (1989, 1993, 2000) began from the premise that if we simply started to ask "where are the women?" we would be able to see their presence in and importance to global politics, as well as the ways their exclusion from global politics was presumed a "natural" consequence of their biological or natural roles. After all, it was not that women were actually absent from global politics. Indeed, they played absolutely central roles either as cheap factory labor, as prostitutes around military bases, or as tourist hotel maids.

The point is that traditional international theory either ignored these contributions or, if it recognized them at all, designated them as less important than the actions of states*men*. Enloe demonstrated just how critically important were the activities of women—for example, as wives of diplomats and soldiers or as models of correct European behavior—to the functioning of the international economic and political systems both during the era of European colonialism and afterward. She illustrated exactly how crucial women and the conventional arrangements of "women's and men's work" were to the continued functioning of international politics.

Most specifically, Enloe documented how the concept and practice of militarization influenced the lives and choices of men and women around the world. "Militarization," she writes, "is a step-by-step process by

liberal feminism A position that advocates equal rights for women but also supports a more progressive policy agenda, including social justice, peace, economic well-being, and ecological balance.

Feminist thinkers ask "where are the women?" as a means to understand power relationships. In places like Saudi Arabia, women are not even allowed to drive cars. Here a woman uses a loophole in the law to drive a dune buggy. What factors might cause a state to limit the rights and privileges available to women?

Table 4.4
Percentage of Women in National Parliaments by Region in 2013 (as of October 2013)

	Regional Averages		
	Single House or Lower House	**Upper House or Senate**	**Both Houses Combined**
Nordic countries	42.0%	—	—
Americas	24.8%	25.0%	24.9%
Europe—OSCE member countries (including Nordic countries)	24.5%	22.6%	24.1%
Europe—OSCE member countries (excluding Nordic countries)	22.8%	22.6%	22.8%
Sub-Saharan Africa	21.1%	18.8%	21.7%
Asia	19.1%	13.8%	18.5%
Arab States	17.8%	7.6%	15.9%
Pacific	13.1%	39.8%	15.9%

*Regions are classified by descending order of the percentage of women in the lower or single house.
Source: http://www.ipu.org/wmn-e/arc/world011013.htm

which a person or a thing gradually comes to be controlled by the military or comes to depend for its well-being on militaristic ideas" (2000, 3; also see Elshtain 1987; Elshtain and Tobias 1990). Enloe is an example of a scholar who begins from a liberal premise—that women and men should have equal rights and responsibilities in global politics—but draws on socialist feminism to analyze the role of economic structures and on standpoint feminism to highlight the unique and particular contributions of women.

A second strand of feminist theory is **socialist/Marxist feminism**, which insists on the role of material and primarily economic forces in determining the lives of women. This approach is also sometimes known as *materialist feminism* (Hennessy and Ingraham 1997). For Marxist feminism, the cause of women's inequality is found in the capitalist system; overthrowing capitalism is the necessary route for the achievement of the equal treatment of women (Sargent 1981). Socialist feminism, noting that the oppression of women occurred in precapitalist societies and continues in capitalist societies, differs from Marxist feminism in that it introduces a second central material cause in determining women's unequal treatment—namely, the patriarchal system of male dominance (Braun 1987; Gottlieb 1989). According to Marxist feminists, then, capitalism is the primary oppressor; for socialist feminists, it is capitalism plus patriarchy. For socialist/Marxist feminists, the focus of a theory of global politics would be on the patterns by which the world capitalist system and the patriarchal system of power lead to women being systematically disadvantaged compared to men. The approach, therefore, has much in common with postcolonial

socialist/Marxist feminism Because of its insistence on the role of material and primarily economic forces in determining the lives of women, this approach is also sometimes known as *materialist feminism* (Hennessy and Ingraham 1997). For Marxist feminism, the cause of women's inequality is found in the capitalist system; overthrowing capitalism is the necessary route for the achievement of the equal treatment of women (Sargent 1981).

THEORY IN PRACTICE 4.1

Gendered Perspective on Human Rights: The Worst Places in the World to Be Born a Woman

In an age when women's rights and suffrage movements have been largely successful in the developed world, the lack of basic human rights for women in developing countries is often overshadowed. The classical political and civil rights (e.g., freedom of speech, freedom of association, freedom from arbitrary arrest) assume that the rights bearer will be living or would wish to live a life of active citizenship, but until very recently, such a life was denied to nearly all women in nearly all cultures. These rights are nonexistent for billions of women in the developing world today. Even in developed countries, women still face the fact that human rights treaties are cast in a language that assumes the rights bearer is a man and the head of a household. But a 2011 survey compiled by the Thomson Reuters Foundation has shown the range of dangers for women worldwide to be much worse.

Women in India strike against what they call a rape culture. In early 2013, a woman was gang raped on a bus and later died. The government was reluctant to punish the men guilty of this crime, and a global campaign to protect women and end rape began. These women are protesting the more recent rape of a photojournalist.

This survey, based on responses from more than 200 aid professionals, academics, health workers, policy makers, journalists, and development specialists chosen for their expertise in gender issues, ranks the top five most dangerous places in the world for women. The survey is conducted on the basis of six risk factors, including health, discrimination and lack of access to resources, cultural and religious practices, sexual violence, human trafficking, and conflict-related violence.

In light of these risk factors, Afghanistan has been ranked the world's most dangerous place to be born a woman. In Afghanistan, women must face a daily reality in which female public officials are the target of violence and killings, healthcare is inadequate, and poverty is extreme.

Following Afghanistan, the Democratic Republic of the Congo (DRC), Pakistan, India, and Somalia stand in descending order as the five worst places for women in the world. The DRC has been called the "rape capital of the world" by the United Nations, and the violence perpetrated by militia groups and soldiers on all sides of the war there continues today. This violence is largely due to a fragile state and the ongoing struggle for Congo's rich mineral resources, in which militias aim to destabilize and dismantle communities by destroying the women at the heart of them.

Third on this list is Pakistan, and that ranking is based on cultural, tribal, and religious practices harmful to women. These practices include acid attacks, forced underage marriage, and honor killings against women and men who violate strict societal codes and bring

dishonor to their families. Honor killings alone number 1,000 a year.

The survey ranks India as the fourth most dangerous country for women due to high levels of human trafficking for sex or labor and a significant number of forced marriages. Because parents prefer to have boys rather than girls, infanticide is a growing problem.

Somalia, the fifth worst place for women, is a country that is politically and economically unstable. It is a failed state that suffers from drought, famine, and civil unrest. In human terms, it suffers from high levels of maternal mortality, rape, and female genital mutilation (FGM), and all citizens—men and women—have limited access to education and healthcare. In Somalia today, 95 percent of women face FGM, mostly

Continued

between the ages of four and eleven. Due to a lack of healthcare and hospitals, only 9 percent of women give birth in a health facility, and the odds of dying from childbirth are fifty-fifty.

This survey points to the great deal of progress that still must be made toward gender equality worldwide as well as the dire need to protect basic human rights that are violated daily. The chief executive of the Thomson Reuters Foundation claims that more hidden dangers, such as lack of education and poor access to healthcare, "are just as deadly, if not more so, that physical dangers like rape and murder."

Emerging initiatives such as TrustLaw Woman, an organization launched by the Thomson Reuters Foundation, seek to protect human rights for women worldwide. With the aim of creating accountability

for crimes against women, Trust-Law links up local NGOs and social entrepreneurs with established law firms that are prepared to offer legal advice pro bono.

But the protection of women's rights is a continuing problem for the international human rights regime, in part because many atrocities go undocumented and unaddressed in the developing world. For this reason, global civil society must take a central role in determining accountability for these crimes and pressuring governments to take active measures against the abuse of women's rights.

For Discussion

1. Why do you think it is so difficult to protect the rights of all human beings regardless of gender, race, religion, or sexual identity?

2. Some might suggest that governments are not doing their job if they fail to protect all citizens, not just their own. Many NGOs are attempting to fill this gap. Is this attempt by NGOs good or bad for the future of the international system? Why?

3. In a time of economic crisis, are states likely to cut back on measures that protect human rights? Why or why not? Is this something that realists or liberals might object to or support?

4. We expect states to provide security, and yet failed or fragile states cannot protect their citizens. Who should provide protection for women and children and why? What would radical liberals say about the need to protect citizens?

Source: http://www.trust.org/trustlaw/womens-rights/dangerpoll/

feminism, which is discussed later in this section. Both are especially insightful when it comes to looking at the nature of the world economy and its differential advantages and disadvantages that apply to women. But postcolonial feminism, as we will see, criticizes socialist/Marxist feminism for presuming the "sameness" of patriarchy throughout the world and across time.

The third version of feminist theory we'll discuss is **standpoint feminism** (Zalewski 1993; Hartsock 1998). This variant emerged out of socialist feminism and the idea of a particular class system. The goal was to think about how women as a class might be able to envision politics from a perspective denied to those who benefited from the subordination of women. Drawing on socialist-feminist interpretations of structure, standpoint feminism began to identify how the subordination of women, as a particular class, by virtue of their sex rather than economic standing (although the two are seen as related), possessed a unique perspective—or standpoint—on global politics as a result of their subordination. This first insight was later developed to consider how the knowledge, concepts, and categories of global politics were predicated on a norm of masculine behavior and masculine experiences and therefore represented not a universal standard but a highly specific, particular standard.

Standpoint feminists argue that seeing the world from the standpoint of women radically alters our understanding of that world. We can appreciate this when we think about the gendered effects of free trade on the global economy: women work as underpaid employees in factories around the world; harried single-parent-family women shop for those products as bargains at the local Wal-Mart; and female register workers scan those low-priced items

standpoint feminism
Drawing on socialist-feminist interpretations of structure, standpoint feminism began to identify how the subordination of women led to a unique perspective—or standpoint—on global politics.

WHAT'S YOUR WORLDVIEW ?

How would your view of the wars in Iraq and Afghanistan change if you analyzed the wars based on the role of women and the impact of women in all the societies involved?

but are blocked from promotion because of gender bias in the workplace. Standpoint feminism has undergone dramatic changes since its first articulation to incorporate the critiques of women of color, who argued that, as socialism had presumed class identity as a primary affiliation, standpoint feminism presumed sex identity as the primary affiliation of all women and, accordingly, the single source of their oppression. The standpoint position also runs the risk of "essentializing," or fixing the views and nature of women, by saying that *this one perspective* is how *all* women see the world (Gioseffi 2003). For example, it is unlikely that Hillary Rodham Clinton, Condoleezza Rice, Sarah Palin, and Queen Latifah all share the same beliefs about politics. Nonetheless, despite these dangers, standpoint feminism has been very influential in showing just how male dominated the main theories of global politics are.

In an important book, J. Ann Tickner (1992) examines the ways gendered identities have shaped international politics in security, economics, and environmental policy areas. Looking at war and peace, for example, Tickner demonstrates how the seemingly objective rules of Morgenthau's realism in fact reflect conventional ideas of masculine values and definitions of reality rather than feminine ones. Tickner reformulates these same rules, taking women's (as opposed to men's) experiences as the starting point. Her point is to show that traditional Western European and North American notions of "proper" gender roles have underpinned decisions about security.

PERCENTAGE OF WOMEN LEGISLATORS AROUND THE WORLD.
What does this graph suggest about the feminist movement worldwide? Do you find these percentages as expected or surprising?

postmodern feminism A position that criticizes the basic distinction between sex and gender that earlier feminist theories found useful.

sex and gender Sex is biological difference, born male or female; the sex act; sexual difference. Gender is what it means to be male or female in a particular place or time; the social construction of sexual difference.

postcolonial feminism A position that works at the intersection of class, race, and gender on a global scale. It especially analyzes the gendered effects of transnational culture and the unequal division of labor in the global political economy.

The fourth version is **postmodern feminism**, which develops the work of poststructuralism (especially that of Michel Foucault and Jacques Derrida) to analyze specifically the concept of gender. Essentially, postmodern feminism criticizes the basic distinction between **sex and gender** that earlier feminist theories found so useful in thinking about the roles of men and women in global politics and in analyzing the gendered concepts of global politics itself. This distinction between sex and gender was useful because it allowed feminists to argue that the position of women and men in the world was not natural but highly contingent and dependent on the meaning given to biological differences. Yet, while extremely useful, the acceptance of the sex-gender distinction retained the binary opposition of male-female and presumed that, while gender was constructed, sex was wholly natural. However, as a number of scholars demonstrated, what we understood sex to be, what biological differences were, was heavily influenced by our understanding of gender—that is, that sex was as constructed as gender (Fox-Keller 1985; Haraway 1989, 1991; Longino 1990; Fausto-Sterling 1992, 2000). This does not mean that our biological bodies or "the determination of sex" is not important. Rather, it suggests that "understanding this process leads to questions concerning how sex and gender operate to create the reality through which bodies materialize as sexed, as sexualized . . . as objects of knowledge and subjects of power" (Kinsella 2003, 296; also see Kinsella 2005a, 2005b, 2006).

The final form of feminism to mention is **postcolonial feminism**. Postcolonial feminists work at the intersection of class, race, and gender on a global scale. They especially analyze the gendered effects of transnational culture and the unequal division of labor in the global political economy. From this perspective, it is not good enough to simply demand (as liberal feminists do) that men and women should have equal rights in a Western-style democracy. Such a move

CASE STUDY : Sexual Violence

For more than a decade, the women and children in the Kivu region in eastern Congo have fallen victim to the highest rates of sexual violence in the entire world, perpetrated from all sides of armed conflict. Rape is used as a weapon of war and is considered more effective than guns or bombs because it "destroys the fabric of society from within," according to Melanne Verveer, the US State Department's ambassador-at-large for global women's issues.[a] But these heinous crimes often go unnoticed and undocumented because of the fear that plagues victims of sexual violence.

Chouchou Namegabe, a Congolese journalist, seeks to stop the silence and inspire action against Congo's rape epidemic by creating a safe space for survivors of sexual violence to tell their story anonymously on the radio talk show she started in 2001. When asked to share what her listeners in Congo have heard, Chouchou gave the horrific testimony of one woman who was "kidnapped with her five children. She was brought in the forest, and every day, she was raped in front of her children. And when she was hungry, they killed her child, and they forced her to eat the flesh of her child. Every day, they killed one of her children. And she was forced to eat the flesh of her children. She was asking to be killed, but they refused. They say we can't give you such a good death."[b]

Although stories like this are incomprehensible to most people in the developed world, it is incredibly important for them to be disseminated so that action can be taken against such violence. There is no reason that inhabitants in developed nation-states should be sheltered from the stories of the realities faced by Congolese citizens and the citizens of many other developing countries on a daily basis. Women in war-torn regions are also in dire need of adequate protection and a means of sharing their testimonies with the world so that something can be done to put an end to the violence.

Leading feminist theorist Cynthia Enloe argues that women are often victims of "militarization," or a "step-by-step process by which a person or thing gradually comes to be controlled by the military" or dependent on "militaristic ideas."[c] Militarization is obvious in the lives of women serving in the military or married to men who serve, but it often spreads to affect civilian female populations as well. The use of rape as a tool of warfare is one of the most shocking forms of female militarization, yet its victims often remain nameless and voiceless, allowing the mass injustice to go unnoticed. Military rape is not only a women's issue but also a *political* issue, shaping the security infrastructure and propagating militaristic values. It is clear these female civilians bear the brunt of wartime brutality; it is less clear what role the international community can play in generating reform.

Cases of sexual violence are often random acts committed by individual soldiers who rape out of a sense of entitlement; it is seen merely as one of the spoils of war. But in armed conflict, rape is also often a military tactic, a combat tool used to humiliate individuals and specific ethnic communities, devastate families, and destroy social structures. Perpetrators thrive in lawless societies that provide little recourse for the survivors of these attacks. Whether explicitly ordered by military commanders or implicitly overlooked and thus permitted, rape is an inexcusable violation of international human rights.

Military-sanctioned rape has been reported in Bosnia, Japan, Chile, Argentina, the Philippines, Guatemala, Iraq, Israel, India, Rwanda, Haiti, Bhutan, China, Turkey, and Indonesia; however, the country most associated currently with military rape remains the Democratic Republic of the Congo (DRC). Due to a long war involving extreme levels of sexual violence, the DRC has been named "The Worst Place on Earth to Be a Woman."[d] Sexual violence in the Congo has garnered a robust international response from both individuals and international organizations. In 2007, the United Nations established the UN Action Against Sexual Violence in Conflict to guide advocacy, resource mobilization, and joint programming around the issue. In addition, the International Criminal Court, established in 2002, included rape and sexual violence among its list of war crimes and crimes against humanity; however, rape was not used as a grounds for prosecution until 2009. Jean-Pierre Bemba Gombo, a politician, businessman, and militia leader in the DRC, is the first to be on trial in The Hague for committing systematic and widespread crimes of sexual violence. While the road to ending this injustice is long and arduous, Bemba's prosecution may represent progress in exposing the severity of sexual violence in conflict and strengthening regimes that protect human security and represent the voice of women in world politics.

Yet the primary questions remain: How can the international community change the ethical norms and practices associated with warfare? Will international organizations and judicial bodies be effective? Can any imposed action from the international community make a difference, or does the answer lie in a long process of internal change, educational advancement, and social revolution regarding gender roles?

Continued

CASE STUDY | Sexual Violence *continued*

For Discussion

1. We have rules of war and treaties that are aimed at preventing the use of rape and torture during conflicts. Why do these practices persist? How can we do a better job enforcing these rules?
2. If you were to begin a campaign aimed at educating people about this complex issue and trying to persuade governments to act, who would you have in your coalition and why?
3. Any form of humanitarian intervention remains very controversial, but with the Responsibility to Protect (R2P) agreement, we now have a responsibility to act. Do you think this will help at all? Why or why not?

WORKS CITED

"Bemba Trial Test Rape as a War Crime." 2009. Amnesty International. http://www.amnesty.org.au/svaw/comments/20168/

Enloe, Cynthia H. 2000. *Maneuvers: The International Politics of Militarizing Women's Lives*. Berkeley: University of California Press.

Kristoff, Nicholas D. "From Oprah to Building a Sisterhood in Congo," *New York Times*, February 3, 2010. http://www.nytimes.com/2010/02/04/opinion/04kristof.html?WT.mc_id=yt_nyt628&WT.mc_ev=click

"Stop Rape Now Brochure," UN Action Against Sexual Violence in Conflict. http://www.stoprapenow.org/uploads/aboutdownloads/1282162584.pdf

"The Trial of Jean-Pierre Bemba Gombo," The Open Society Justice Initiative, 2011. www.bembatrial.org

[a] http://peacemagazine.org/archive/v25n4p06.htm
[b] http://www.theworld.org/2011/09/namegabe-rape-sexual-violence-congo/
[c] Enloe, *Maneuvers*, 3.
[d] http://www.nytimes.com/2010/10/04/world/africa/04congo.html?ref=congothedemocraticrepublicof

---

patriarchy A persistent societywide structure within which gender relations are defined by male dominance and female subordination.

constructivism An approach to international politics that concerns itself with the centrality of ideas and human consciousness. As constructivists have examined global politics, they have been broadly interested in how the structure constructs the actors' identities and interests, how their interactions are organized and constrained by that structure, and how their very interaction serves to either reproduce or transform that structure.

ignores the way poor women of color in the global South or developing world remain subordinated by the global economic system—a system that liberal feminists were slow to challenge. The concerns and interests of feminists in the West and those in the rest of the world may not, therefore, so easily fit together. Postcolonial feminists are also critical of Western, privileged academic intellectuals (men and women) who claim to speak for the oppressed, a form of cultural imperialism with important material effects. Perhaps the most influential postcolonial feminist scholar in this vein is Gayatri Spivak, who combines Marxism and feminism to interpret imperialism, past and present, and ongoing struggles for decolonization. In an influential essay "Can the Subaltern Speak?" Spivak (1988) acknowledged the ambiguity of her own position in a privileged Western university and argued that elite scholars should be wary of homogenizing the "subaltern" and trying to speak *for* them in their "true" voice (what she calls a form of "epistemic violence"). The term *subaltern* refers to subordinated groups and, in this instance, to underprivileged women in the global South. In not recognizing the heterogeneity of experience and opinion of these diverse women, goes the argument, seemingly benevolent and well-meaning academics are at once patronizing in their desire to redeem them and unwittingly complicit in new forms of colonialism. Some postmodernists have also been criticized along similar lines for being too Western-centric and gender blind. Thus, the combination of colonialism and **patriarchy** has made it doubly difficult for the resistance and agency of the subordinated groups to be heard and recognized.

Constructivism

Constructivist scholars emphasize the importance and power of ideas. Most writers who call themselves **constructivists** argue that our actions and words make society, and society in turn

Jane Addams and the Women's International League for Peace and Freedom

The Women's Peace Party (WPP), led by activist Jane Addams (1860–1935), was one of the first groups to protest against World War I. On January 10, 1915, more than 3,000 people met in Washington, D.C., and endorsed a platform that inspired President Wilson's Fourteen Points for peace; their planks included the following (Addams and Joslin 1922/2002, 6–7):

1. Convene a meeting of neutral nations to promote peace.
2. Limit arms production and nationalize the arms industries.
3. Oppose militarism in the US.
4. Promote peace through education.
5. Insist on democratic control over foreign policy.
6. Extend suffrage to women, thereby humanizing governments.
7. Replace the "balance of power system" with a "concert of nations" system.
8. Develop a global governance system based on the rule of law, not coercion.
9. Deploy non-force options to control rivals.
10. Work to eliminate the causes of war, like poverty.
11. Appoint a commission of experts to promote international peace.

Addams and her colleagues strongly believed that, if an international organization had been in place when dialogue among European powers failed, it could have mediated the dispute before it exploded into a major war.

The WPP became the American section of the pacifist Women's International League for Peace and Freedom (WILPF), which was established in the Netherlands in spring 1915 as a federation of women organized in twenty-one countries. Participants argued that the choice "between violence and passive acceptance of unjust conditions" was a false one. As true Kantians, they believed that "courage, determination, moral power, generous indignation, active good-will, and education can be used to secure goals rather than violence" (Addams and Joslin 1917/2002, 145–146). Delegates of WILPF visited fourteen countries—both belligerent and neutral—to urge leaders to end the war and to address the causes of violence in the international system. Repeatedly, they confronted the dominance of realist thinking:

> We heard the same opinion expressed by these men of the governments responsible for the promotion of the war; each one said that his country would be ready to stop the war immediately if some honorable method of securing peace were provided; each one disclaimed responsibility for the continuance of war; each one predicted European bankruptcy if the war were prolonged, and each one grew pale and distressed as he spoke of the loss of his gallant young countrymen . . . (Addams and Joslin 1917/2002, 11).

Considered by many to be the "most dangerous woman in America" for her opposition to the US entry into World War I and her challenges of the world's leaders and their vested interests, Addams was awarded the Nobel Peace Prize in 1935 for her efforts aimed at ending the war and providing relief for the victims of war.

For Discussion

1. What organizations are promoting both a pacifist and feminist agenda in today's global politics debates?
2. How important were pacifist groups in the period between World War I and World War II?
3. Women like Jane Addams played an important role in both American and international politics. Why do students of international relations never hear about her?
4. Why does the study of global politics often neglect the contributions of individual people? How do their contributions matter?

shapes our actions and words. Ideas, beliefs, and values influence the identities and interests of states and the eventual selection of policies and strategies that transform our world. As part of this process, we construct rules that first identify for us the key players (i.e., who has agency) in a given situation, recognizing that no one actor in the international system is an agent in all policy situations; then those rules instruct, direct, and commit actors to take certain actions. For example, realist rules during the Cold War dictated that all states were subservient to and would follow the lead of the United States or Soviet Union. However, actual practice does not always comply with the rules: frequently, states found areas where these superpowers had little interest—such as development or peacekeeping—and established a niche to serve their interests. The George W. Bush administration tried to assert a similar pattern of hegemonic rules after the attacks of September 11, 2001, with phrases like "coalition of the willing" and "you are either with us or you are with the terrorists."

Over time, rules and practices can form a stable pattern that serves the interests of key agents. These patterns become "institutions." The Cold War was a twentieth-century institution, and the global economy is a good example of a twenty-first-century institution. Its rules and practices are based on neoliberal free market capitalism that best serves the interests of corporations, global economic institutions, and the wealthy states. The wealthy states' power in the system is based on both material factors (e.g., control of resources) and discursive power (based on knowledge and the control of language and ideas within a society).

A leading constructivist, Alexander Wendt, seeks to understand "how global politics is socially constructed" (1995, 71). Famous for his claim that "anarchy is what states make of it" (1992, 391), Wendt argues that anarchy in the international system does not have to result in competition, security dilemmas, arms races, or conflict. States have plenty of options; they are only limited by rules, practices, and institutions that they themselves have created. How a country reacts to anarchy reflects its particular understanding of that condition.

Constructivists argue that the international system is defined by socially constructed realities, and therefore, to understand the system, one must focus on shared rules, practices, meanings, identities, and norms. These help define the system for each actor. These factors define the interests, identities, preferences, and actions of each state in the system. By emphasizing the social construction of reality, we also are questioning what is frequently taken for granted. This raises several issues. One is a concern with the origins of social constructs that now appear to us as natural and are now part of our social vocabulary. After all, the notion of sovereignty did not always exist, as we learned in Chapter 2; it was a product of historical forces and human interactions that generated new distinctions regarding where political authority resided. In addition, the category of weapons of mass destruction (WMD) is a modern invention. Although individuals have been forced to flee their homes throughout the course of human history, the political and legal category of "refugees" is only a century old. To understand the origins of these concepts requires attention to the interplay between existing ideas and institutions, the political calculations by leaders who had ulterior motives, and morally minded actors who were attempting to improve humanity.

Also of concern to constructivist thinkers are alternative pathways. Although history appears path dependent, which is to say that world history can be seen as patterned and somewhat predictable, there are contingencies—historical accidents and human intervention that can force history to change course. The events of 9/11 and the response by the Bush administration arguably transformed the direction of global politics. But how would the world be different today if Al Gore had taken the presidential oath of office in January 2001 before those attacks?

This interest in possible and counterfactual worlds works against historical determinism. Wendt's (1992) claim that "anarchy is what states make of it" calls attention to how different beliefs and practices will generate divergent patterns and organization of global politics. A world of nonviolent activists like Mahatma Gandhi would be very different from a world of violent extremists like Osama bin Laden.

Constructivists also examine how actors make their activities meaningful. Following Max Weber's insight that "we are cultural beings with the capacity and the will to take a deliberate attitude toward the world and to lend it *significance*" (1949, 81), constructivists attempt to recover the meanings that actors give to their practices and to the objects they create. Constructivists argue that culture, rather than private belief, informs the meanings people give to their action. Sometimes, constructivists have presumed that such meanings derive from a hardened culture. But because culture is fractured and society comprises different interpretations of what is meaningful activity, scholars need to consider these cultural fault lines. To pinpoint or fix any precise meaning is largely a political and temporary accomplishment; it is not to discover some transcendent truth.

Some of the most important debates in global politics are about how to define particular activities. Development, human rights, security, humanitarian intervention, sovereignty—topics that we discuss in later chapters—are important orienting concepts that can have any number of meanings. States and nonstate actors have rival interpretations of the meanings of these concepts and will fight to try to have their preferred meaning collectively accepted.

Global social movements based on *normative ideas* such as peace, justice, and ecological balance drive groups like Greenpeace to protest against drilling in the fragile Arctic region. Thirty activists protesting the drilling by the Russian energy company were arrested and held by the Russian government. The Arctic 30—including Swedish activist Dima Litvinov—were released in November after a global campaign by other governments and global social movements representing human rights groups, advocates of international law, and environmentalists.

Indeed, the fact that these meanings are fixed through politics, and that once these meanings are fixed they have consequences for the ability of people to determine their fates, suggests an alternative way of thinking about power. Most international relations theorists treat power as the ability of one state to compel another state to do what it otherwise would not and tend to focus on the material technologies, such as military firepower and economic statecraft, that have this persuasive effect. Constructivists have offered two important additions to this view of power. The forces of power go beyond **material**: they also can be **ideational** or discursive. Ideational power is more than control over meaning; it is also the acceptance of ideas or a way of life. The notion that *your* way of thinking is the norm is but one example of ideational power.

Consider the issue of **legitimacy**. States, including great powers, crave legitimacy—the belief that they are acting according to and pursuing the values of the broader international community. There is a direct relationship between state legitimacy and the costs associated with a course of action: the greater the legitimacy, the easier time state leaders will have convincing others to cooperate with their policies. The smaller the legitimacy, the more costly the action. This means, then, that even great powers will frequently feel the need to alter their policies to be viewed as legitimate—or bear the consequences. Further evidence of the constraining power of legitimacy is offered by the tactic of "naming and shaming" by human rights activists. For example, Iran's release of a US reporter in 2009, who was charged with spying, shows how the international media and NGOs dedicated to promoting and protecting press freedoms can be influential in changing government policy. Similarly, human rights advocates led by Mia Farrow used the threat of a boycott of the 2008 Olympics to persuade China to stop jailing dissidents and persecuting religious and ethnic minorities. China did allow for some changes, but because of its economic and political power, it was able to ignore calls for major reforms. If states did not care about their legitimacy—about their reputation

material Things we can see, measure, consume, and use, such as military forces, oil, and currency.

ideational Refers to ideas like democracy, capitalism, peace, and social justice.

legitimacy An authority that is respected and recognized by those it rules and by other rulers or leaders of other states. The source of legitimacy can be laws or a constitution and the support of the society.

Constructivists assert that ideas shape how we view the world. Tony Benn, was a longtime member of Parliament and political leader of the most socialist wing of the Labour Party. He spent his life promoting progressive causes. He served as the president of Stop the War Coalition. What would constructivists say about his worldview given his practices?

and the perception that they were acting in a manner consistent with prevailing international standards—then such a tactic would have little visible impact. It is only because law-breaking governments want to be perceived as acting in a manner consistent with international norms that they can be taunted into changing their conduct.

Other scholars look for points of connection and evaluate the relative strengths of each approach to see when they might be combined to enrich our understanding of the world. One possibility is strategic social construction (Finnemore and Sikkink 1998). Actors attempt to change the norms that subsequently guide and constitute state identities and interests. Human rights activists, for instance, try to encourage compliance with human rights norms not only by naming and shaming those who violate these norms but also by encouraging states to identify with these norms because it is the right thing to do. Another possibility is to consider the relationship between the normative structure and strategic behavior. Some use constructivism to elucidate how identity shapes the state's interests and then turn to rational choice for understanding strategic behavior. In this view, the American identity shapes national interests, and then the structure of the international system informs America's strategies for pursuing those interests. Yet some scholars go further and argue that the cultural context shapes not only identities and interests of actors but also the very strategies they can use as they pursue their interests. That is, although "game" metaphors are most closely associated with **game theory** and rational choice, some constructivists also argue that the normative structure shapes important features of the game, including the identity of the players and the strategies that are appropriate.

game theory A branch of mathematics that explores strategic interaction.

And as it turns out, not all is fair in love and war—or any other social endeavor, for that matter. For decades, Arab nationalism shaped the identities and interests of Arab states, contained norms that guided how Arab leaders could play the game of Arab politics, and encouraged Arab leaders to draw from the symbols of Arab politics to try to maneuver around their Arab rivals and further their own interests. They had very intense rivalries, and as they vied for prestige and status, they frequently accused each other of being a traitor to the Arab nation or harming the cause of Arabism. But rarely did they use military force. Until the late 1970s, the idea of relations with Israel was a taboo violated by Egyptian Anwar Sadat's trip to Jerusalem in 1977 and separate peace treaty in 1979. Arab states did not respond through military action but rather by evicting Egypt from the Arab League, and then Sadat paid the ultimate price for his heresy when he was assassinated in 1981 by supporters of the Muslim Brotherhood, who were reacting to Sadat's actions but also their own suppression within Egypt. But how does constructivism

WHAT'S YOUR WORLDVIEW **?**

What is your image of the world? How do you construct the world in which we live? Is it a peaceful and hopeful place with a chance for reform, or is it a place of violence, despair, and misery? Whose ideas do you embrace in your construction of the world?

help us understand how and why things change? Proponents of constructivism scolded structural-realist and neoliberal-institutionalist scholars for their failure to explain contemporary global transformations. The Peace of Westphalia, for instance, helped establish sovereignty and the norm of noninterference, but in recent decades, various processes have worked against the principle of noninterference and suggested how state sovereignty is conditional on how states treat their populations. **World orders** are created and sustained not only by great-power preferences but also by changing understandings of what constitutes a legitimate **international order**. Until World War II, the idea of a world organized around **empires** was not illegitimate—but now it is.

Conclusion

Although the proponents of the critical theories presented in this chapter seek to challenge the conventionally dominant theories of international relations, their work does more than that. In addition to offering new critical ways to view the field, these critical theories, if combined with aspects of realism and liberalism, give us a richer understanding of international processes (as summarized in Table 4.5). We can see, for example, that war might not result only from countries' struggle for material power but also from the power of ideas or constructed notions of a proper masculine role in society. A student of international relations who aims to become a critical thinker must consider all theoretical perspectives in attempting to understand our world.

In the final part of this book, we will explore contemporary issues of globalization. As you read, think of the various theories as glasses to help you see the central problem of each issue. You should be open to multiple interpretations of events and remember that no one theory can explain everything because, by accepting a single theory as your basis for understanding and explaining global politics, you are excluding other perspectives that might also be valid.

Table 4.5
Some Models of the International System

	Realist	Liberal, Institutionalist	Marxist	Constructivist, Feminist
Primary unit	State	States, NGOs, MNCs, TNCs	State	Various
International system is . . .	Anarchic	Self-interestedly cooperative	Based on capitalist exploitation	Various: sum of ideas, a fiction, gendered
Leaders are . . .	Rational	Rational	Capitalists	Biased

CONTRIBUTORS TO CHAPTER 4: Stephen Hobden, Richard Wyn Jones, Steve Smith, and Steven L. Lamy.

world order A wider category of order than the international. It takes as its units of order, not states, but individual human beings, and assesses the degree of order on the basis of the delivery of certain kinds of goods (be they security, human rights, basic needs, or justice) for humanity as a whole.

international order The normative and the institutional pattern in the relationship between states. The elements of this may be thought to include such things as sovereignty, the forms of diplomacy, international law, the role of the great powers, and the codes circumscribing the use of force. It is a shared value and condition of stability and predictability in the relations of states.

empire A distinct type of political entity, which may or may not be a state, possessing both a home territory and foreign territories. This may include conquered nations and colonies.

REVIEW QUESTIONS

1. Why have critical theoretical approaches become more popular in recent years?
2. How would you explain the continuing vitality of Marxist thought in a post–Cold War world?
3. How did Lenin's approach to international relations differ from that of Marx?
4. What is Wallerstein's notion of a semiperiphery? Why might it be useful?
5. Feminists define gender as a social construction. What does this mean? What kinds of questions does international relations feminism try to answer using gender as a category of analysis?
6. Women's participation at the highest levels of international and national policy making has been extremely limited. Do you think this is important for understanding global politics?
7. Do you think women's roles—as diplomats' and soldiers' wives, domestic servants, sex workers, homemakers, and home-based workers—are relevant to the business of international politics? If so, how?
8. What is the core concept of constructivism?
9. What do you think are the core issues for the study of global change, and how does constructivism help you address those issues? Alternatively, how does a constructivist framework help you identify new issues that you had not previously considered?
10. Why has international relations ignored issues concerning race for so long? What does postcolonialism suggest on the subject?
11. What is it about Marxism, constructivism, and feminism that makes them a threat to realism and liberalism?
12. Which of the three critical approaches discussed in this chapter do you think offers the best account of global politics? Why?

FURTHER READING

Campbell, D. (1998), *Writing Security: United States Foreign Policy and the Politics of Identity*, rev. ed. (Manchester: Manchester University Press). This important book shows how the identity of the United States is constructed through perceptions of danger in foreign policy discourse.

Chowdhry, G., and Nair, S. (eds.) (2002), *Power, Postcolonialism, and International Relations: Reading Race, Gender, and Class* (London: Routledge). An edited volume looking at how the intersection of race, class, and gender structures much of world politics.

Enloe, C. (1989), *Bananas, Beaches and Bases: Making Feminist Sense of International Politics* (London: Pandora). This was the classic text charting the way forward for feminist international relations.

Gilroy, P. (1993), *The Black Atlantic: Modernity and Double Consciousness* (Cambridge, Mass.: Harvard University Press). A look at the unique racial and cultural identity of black people forced to move from their native countries to the West and how Europeans were also affected by this cultural exchange.

Said, E. (1979), *Orientalism* (New York: Vintage). A decisive postcolonial text showing how colonial literary and artistic texts create the "other" with devastating material consequences.

Walker, R. J. B. (1993), *Inside/Outside: International Relations as Political Theory* (Cambridge: Cambridge University Press). An important early contribution to postmodern international relations theory, which challenged some of the central categories of the discipline.

INTERNET RESOURCES

Following are four sources of primary texts of philosophy that can be useful to students for outside reading assignments:

Internet Classics Archive
http://classics.mit.edu/index.html

Online Library of Liberty
http://oll.libertyfund.org/

Perseus Digital Library
http://www.perseus.tufts.edu/hopper/

Project Gutenberg
http://promo.net/pg/

Marxists Internet Encyclopedia
www.marxists.org

The source for anything to do with the past, present, and future of Marx and his followers. Includes biographical sketches, texts, and letters. The latter includes letters from Jenny Marx to Engels and others.

UN WomenWatch: Women and Peace and Security

http://www.un.org/womenwatch/feature/wps/

The UN site for information on all aspects of women in international politics.

TED Talk: Paul Collier on Postconflict Recovery

http://www.ted.com/talks/lang/eng/paul_collier_s_new_rules_for_rebuilding_a_broken_nation.html

Oxford professor of economics and an expert on African economies discusses strategies for postconflict recovery. How do you rebuild broken nation-states?

TED Talk: Paul Collier on the "Bottom Billion"

http://www.ted.com/talks/paul_collier_shares_4_ways_to_help_the_bottom_billion.html

The gap between the world's poor and rich is only growing, and Collier asks a good question: If you're poor, is it better to be a cow in Europe? This video is best applied in conjunction with Table 4.2.

TED Talk: Madeleine Albright: "On Being a Woman and a Diplomat"

http://www.ted.com/talks/madeleine_albright_on_being_a_woman_and_a_diplomat.html

Madeleine Albright, former secretary of state under Bill Clinton, discusses the hurdles and privileges of being a female politician.

Carnegie Council: "Superfusion: How China and America Became One Economy and Why the World's Prosperity Depends on It"—Zachary Karabell

http://www.carnegiecouncil.org/resources/video/data/000295

Zachary Karabell's talk on China's rise through the help of US corporate investment helps illustrate what many economists and scholars consider to be the decay of Wallerstein's core–periphery distinction with respect to China.

For more information, quizzes, case studies and other study tools, please visit us at **www.oup.com/us/lamy**

THINKING ABOUT GLOBAL POLITICS

Meeting of the Minds

INTRODUCTION

You have now read and discussed the contributions of a number of both mainstream and critical theorists in the field of international relations. These theorists all see the world differently, and all of them would have different views on what is going on in the world if they were alive today. So why not invite several of these theorists to your class for a discussion about contemporary issues?

This is not a new idea. Polymath Steve Allen, the originator of the *Tonight Show*, created a talk show that featured guests from across time and cultures. He brought back Socrates, Plato, Marie Antoinette, Voltaire, Marie Curie, and others to talk about their contributions to their disciplines or their worldviews as great leaders. Can you imagine Machiavelli and Kant talking about what they would do to stop extremists in the so-called *global war on terrorism*? Mr. Allen used direct quotations to construct conversations when possible and used factual information to provide accurate pictures of each of the famous visitors. He stated, "*Meeting of the Minds* encourages the viewer and reader, who may be historically illiterate, to become more familiar with the great thinkers and doers of the past and to whet their appetites for more research and study."

Now it is your turn. Use this exercise to review the core assumptions of the key theoretical voices that you have discussed in class and are important to our field of study.

PROCEDURE

1. Divide into small groups of three to five students. Each group will either select or be assigned a theorist for the discussion. Select from foundational and contemporary theorists discussed in the text or others you have read about. For example:

Foundational Voices

Realists	Liberals	Radical Liberals/ Utopians	Marxists
Thucydides	Grotius	Abbe St. Pierre	Marx
Machiavelli	Bentham	William Penn	Lenin
Hobbes	deVattel	Kant	Luxembourg

Develop a similar list for modern voices.

Continued

2. Develop a full profile by doing research on the writings and positions taken by your chosen or assigned theorist. Try to use his or her words and not someone's interpretations. Primary documents and original works would be best. Please do not use *Wikipedia*. The creative part of this exercise is the creation of a script that speculates on what these theorists will say about current events.

DISCUSSION

The instructor or a student will play the role of Steve Allen or, to update things, Jay Leno or Ellen DeGeneres. A team of students who work together to develop questions for the guests can play this role of talk show hosts. Yes, there should be three or four guests on this program.

What should the talk show host ask? Use the issue chapters in the book to develop questions about current global challenges like poverty, trade wars, financial meltdowns, human rights, and ongoing conflicts around the world. You can also use the headlines for the week.

Once everyone is ready, take one or two classes and have that discussion.

After the discussion is complete, review it and critique the quality of the contributions for each theorist. Were the answers useful, and did they represent the real views of the theorists?

Ask each group to turn in their notes to see how well they did their research.

If thoughtfully and thoroughly prepared, these notes will make great study sheets for an exam that might include questions about these theorists.

FOLLOW-UP

This kind of theory review works really well as part of review sessions for a final. If you have teaching assistants and a large lecture course, you can stage the talk shows during discussion sessions.

PART THREE

Global Actors

In this part of the book, we present an overview of the primary actors in the global system and the ways they interact. Our first goal is to give you information about the numerous kinds of actors. We begin with Chapter 5 on making *foreign policy*. We show the ways factors such as nationalism, resources, and type of state influence the actors who make foreign policy. Building on this foundation, Chapter 6 looks at *international law and international organizations*. In this chapter, you will see the limits and possibilities for collective action in global politics. Our second goal is to show you that global politics is more than simply the interactions of states in various policy areas. Therefore, the last chapter of this part, Chapter 7, looks at the important role that *nongovernmental organizations and transnational social movements* play in global politics.

Protesters at the UN Framework Convention on Climate Change in Warsaw, Poland, wear masks of the German chancellor Angela Merkel and US president Barack Obama. They were critical of the only modest progress toward an agreement that would effectively deal with climate change. The divide between rich and poor states was apparent in the positions taken by the delegates.

Statecraft is the strategy of power. Power is the capacity to direct the decisions and actions of others. Power derives from strength and will.

—*Charles Freeman*

It is possible to achieve goals only by persuasion, eloquence, threats and—if need be—intimidation.

—*Abba Eban*

Small states are not usually seen as leaders in global politics. At times, they might play a major role in a regional organization or as part of a coalition in an international organization, but they rarely lead major global policy debates. Global factors affect both small and large states, however, and therefore play a role in shaping the foreign policy of all states. Here, Philippines climate commissioner Naderev Sano, a delegate to the 2013 UN Framework Convention on Climate Change, is asking the world to create and implement policies that will address the dangers presented by global climate change. The Philippines was recently devastated by Typhoon Haiyan. Climate change cannot be blamed for a specific weather event, but the melting of Arctic ice, increases in CO_2 levels, and warming of the oceans have contributed to unusual and severe weather events. Sea level is projected to rise three feet by the end of the century—and that would be the end of this sovereign state with its own culture, language, and history. Other states in the Pacific face similar challenges. Citizens in Papua New Guinea and the Solomon Islands have been forced to flee their homes due to rising tides, and Tuvalu, Kiribati, and the Marshall Islands may vanish entirely within the next fifty years.

Climate change, a global phenomenon, is shaping the foreign policy priorities of many small developing states like the Philippines and Vietnam as well as Asian middle powers like Japan and South Korea, and even European middle powers like Sweden, Norway, and Denmark. The Pacific Small Island Developing States was established in 2007 as an informal group of eleven island countries. They list their first challenge as climate change and they use the

Philippine climate commissioner Naderev Sano at the UN Framework Convention on Climate Change in Warsaw asks the world to consider the destruction from Typhoon Haiyan on the Philippines and the possible impact of climate change. Like many vulnerable developing states, countries like the Philippines are trying to shape the final agreement so it includes funds for emissions control and for dealing with the damage from climate change. The developing and developed states remain divided on the policy solutions.

forums of the United Nations to promote their national and regional interests. Ambassador Marlene Moses of Nauru suggested that these eleven states share vulnerabilities such as their size and remoteness, and that their "low-lying nature exposes them to adverse effects of climate change," which has a major impact on national security. Since 2009, the UN Assembly has recognized the link between climate change and global security. Most states put military and economic security over environmental policies that might address the causes of climate change. The small states of the Pacific, the European members of the Arctic Council, and the participants in the 2013 African Climate Conference hope to convince the rest of the world that global consumerism is altering Earth's climate and threatening human survival, especially in vulnerable states.

As we will see in this chapter, there may be both concrete and abstract limits to what one person can accomplish in foreign policy. We will discuss the methods that political leaders around the world use in pursuit of their foreign policy goals, including promoting and securing what they see as the national interests of their countries. All countries in the post–Cold War world—rich and poor, large and small, democratic and authoritarian—operate within the same set of limits and possibilities in the domestic and international arenas.

Introduction

Each of the theories we examined in Chapters 3 and 4 describes the behavior of an actor called the state. As you will recall from Chapter 1, there is a lot of disagreement in international relations theory about what we mean by "the state." But for this chapter, we need to begin by accepting that the state *exists* and that it is the most important actor in the contemporary globalized international system so that we can better understand the relationship among nations and states, nationalism and national interests, and globalization and global politics. (As a review, we define *state* as a legal territorial entity, *nation* as a community of people who share a common sense of identity, and *nation-state* as a political community in which the state claims legitimacy on the grounds that it represents the nation.) Only by accepting that the state exists will we be able to discuss the process by which the system of states interacts. We call this process **foreign policy**.

We begin this chapter with a definition of foreign policy and explore the questions of who makes foreign policy and what we expect from it. We then present a brief overview of levels of analysis and the study of foreign policy behavior. Here we show you how to explain *why* states make certain choices over others. In the next section of the chapter, we offer an analytic framework of the foreign policy process, providing an overview of how most states make foreign policy. We go on to explore **statecraft**, the methods and tools that governmental leaders use to secure and promote their national interests. We also consider the growing importance of soft power in the post–Cold War era, which is defined more by globalization and global challenges. We will see how, in global politics, foreign policy actors often pursue different goals simultaneously because foreign policy connects domestic politics and international relations. For example, a leader might advocate human rights policy to satisfy domestic interest groups but maintain trade relations with an authoritarian state because of its need for natural resources. In the final section of the chapter, we look at foreign policy styles and traditions across great, middle, and small states around the world.

foreign policy The articulation of national interests and the means chosen to secure those interests, both material and ideational, in the international arena.

statecraft The methods and tools that national leaders use to achieve the national interests of a state.

After reading and discussing this chapter, you will have a sense of how most states make foreign policy and the factors that shape it—how citizens and their leaders articulate, promote, and eventually secure their national interests. You will have a deeper understanding of levels of analysis, categories of analytic tools that students and scholars in our field use to explain the foreign policy of all states. You will also be introduced to some of the strategies, tools, and approaches that states use to secure their interests and promote their ideas and values in our global system.

What Is Foreign Policy?

States pursue many goals, including more power, prestige, and resources. Foreign policy is the articulation of **national interests** (the goals of a nation-state) and the means chosen to secure those interests, both material and ideational, in the international arena. **Material interests** may be trade agreements, energy resources, and even control over strategic territory. **Ideational interests** include the promotion of values, norms, and policy ideas that enhance the security and prosperity of a nation-state. The national interests of any state are shaped by individuals (especially political leaders or elites), interest groups, geographic position, traditions, norms, and values. International events, global factors such as the Internet and climate change, and the actions of both friends and enemies can also influence a country's national interests.

States, Nationalism, and National Interests

Since foreign policy aims to secure a country's national interests and promote its values, it is critically important to understand the relationship among states, nationalism, and national interests. To do so, we must keep in mind the following points:

1. From about the mid-seventeenth century, an order of sovereign, territorial states known as the Westphalian system (discussed in Chapter 2) developed in Europe.
2. The rise of nationalism from the late eighteenth century rationalized this state order, later extending beyond Europe until the whole world was organized as a series of nation-states. International relations were, and to many still are, primarily relations among nation-states.
3. Globalization may undermine this political order by eroding sovereign territorial power and by creating competing identities and multiple loyalties.

With these points in mind, we will first outline key concepts and debates concerning nationalism and nation-states, which will inform our discussion of foreign policy.

Nationalism is the idea that the world is divided into nations, and these nations provide the overriding focus of political identity and loyalty that in turn demands **national self-determination**. Nationalism can be considered as ideology, as politics, and as sentiments. Definitions of nationalism usually frame it as ideology, a political worldview. **Civic nationalism** is defined by a common citizenship regardless of ethnicity, race, religion, gender, or language. All citizens are united in their loyalty toward and identity with a nation-state. They also embrace a set of political practices, traditions, and values that we call a political culture. Civic nationalism and **ethnonationalism** differ in the fact that civic nationalism maintains loyalty to the state and lacks a racial or ethnic element, whereas ethnonationalism is defined by loyalty toward a specific ethnic community such as a language or religious community. Ethnic nationalists generally seek to create their own sovereign nation-state separate from the state in which they reside. There are French-speaking Canadians and Dutch-speaking Belgians who argue for their own country. We are reminded by the civil

national interest The material and ideational goals of a nation-state.

material interest The physical goals of state officials as they set foreign and domestic policy.

ideational/ideal interest The psychological, moral, and ethical goals of a state as it sets foreign and domestic policy.

nationalism The idea that the world is divided into nations that provide the overriding focus of political identity and loyalty, which in turn should be the basis for defining the population of states. Nationalism also can refer to this idea in the form of a strong sense of identity (*sentiment*) or organizations and movements seeking to realize this idea (*politics*).

national self-determination The right or desire of distinct national groups to become states and rule themselves.

civic nationalism The idea that an association of people can identify themselves as belonging to the nation and have equal and shared political rights and allegiance to similar political procedures.

enthnonationalism A strain of nationalism marked by the desire of an ethnic community to have absolute authority over its own political, economic, and social affairs. Loyalty and identity shift from the state to an ethnic community that seeks to create its own state.

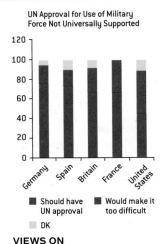

UN Approval for Use of Military
Force Not Universally Supported

■ Should have   ■ Would make it
   UN approval   too difficult
■ DK

**VIEWS ON
MULTILATERALISM
AND INTERVENTION.**

Is the era of unilateralism over?

wars in Sri Lanka, Bosnia, and Rwanda that ethnic conflicts can be very difficult to resolve because of the power of ethnic identity and the dangers of chauvinism and ethnocentrism.

However, we might ignore nationalist ideology unless it becomes significant. This can happen if nationalism shapes people's sense of identity: nationalism as sentiments. It can also happen if nationalism is taken up by movements able to form nation-states: nationalism as politics empowered via self-determination. Nationalism is an important element of any country's foreign policy and the formation of national interests.

Ideas, defined by Goldstein and Keohane (1993) as beliefs held by individuals, matter (1) when they provide road maps for decision makers who are formulating and implementing policy and (2) when they become embedded in institutions that are part of the foreign policy process. Consider how all states interpret the concept of sovereignty or define human rights. Ideas and interests help us explain the actions of all states. In the case of the United States, many Americans believe that it is a nation unlike all others, with values and traditions that other states should emulate; this is often called "American exceptionalism." Many of the original settlers to the United States, especially in the New England colonies, brought with them an idea that they had a covenant with God to create a new nation that would lead humanity to greatness. In his introduction to Reinhold Niebuhr's critically important book *The Irony of American History*, international relations scholar Andrew Bacevich (2008, x–xi) describes the American view of exceptionalism:

> As a Chosen People with what Niebuhr refers to as a "Messianic consciousness," Americans came to see themselves as set apart, their motives irreproachable, their actions not to be judged by standards applied to others.

This notion of exceptionalism has often translated into a foreign policy that promotes US values and traditions across the world and frames all US actions as blessed by a higher

Do governments matter? Belgium, a state made up of three nations—Flemish, French, and German regions—was without a national government from June 2010 until December 2011. Here citizens march in Brussels in January 2011 in support of national unity, drawing attention to Belgium's record-breaking length of time without a government.

power. Presidents from Washington to Obama have sought to promote US democracy and free market values around the world. At the end of the two world wars, both Woodrow Wilson and Franklin Roosevelt sought to build an American-led, rule-based international system that reflected US interests and ideals. More recently, the Clinton administration embraced the idea of American exceptionalism as reflected in its foreign policy. Clinton, inspired by Wilsonian ideals, believed that the United States should use its power and resources to enlarge the number of capitalist and democratic states. Similarly, the aggressive promotion of US values and traditions around the world was part of the foreign policy of G. W. Bush, who described his administration's goals in his second inaugural address: "It is the policy of the United States to seek and support the growth of democratic movements and institutions in every nation and culture, with the ultimate goal of ending tyranny in our world."

Of course, this idea of exceptionalism and national purpose is not unique to the United States. In Russia, after the fall of the Soviet Union, some argued for Russian exceptionalism based on a more humanitarian, postcapitalist, Russian spiritualism. Raymond Aron (1966) suggested that security, power, glory, and ideals are "heterogeneous objectives" that shape a country's national interests. Every state has a vision about how the world should be ordered, but only a few have the means to follow through with their beliefs about order, security, and justice. In short, this is how nationalism can shape foreign policy as a sentiment and political ideology.

Nationalist sentiments can be held by elites within a society or by the masses. Some nationalist ideas appeal only to a small portion of the population, whereas others have popular resonance. In terms of politics, nationalism can be state strengthening or state subverting. **State-strengthening nationalism** accepts an existing state as broadly legitimate but seeks to strengthen it, internally by "purifying" the nation and reforming government and externally by reclaiming "national" territory and extending power. **Secessionist nationalism** aims to create a new state, usually by separation from a larger state and sometimes by unifying smaller states. This type often includes ethnonationalism, in which loyalty and identity shift to an ethnic community (e.g., a religious group) that seeks to create its own state. The relationship of nationalism to global politics varies with these types. **Mass nationalism**, using ethnic ideas to subvert an existing state, is very different from **elite nationalism**, using civic ideas to strengthen an existing state.

Robert Cooper (2000) provides an interesting view of the evolution of the nation-state and the role of nationalism in a global age. Cooper suggests that the world can be divided into three types of states: premodern, modern, and postmodern states. In **premodern states**, individuals are more loyal to subnational, religious, and ethnic communities. People do not always identify as citizens of these very weak states, which are essentially what we call **failed (collapsed)** or **fragile states**. Afghanistan, Zimbabwe, Somalia, North Korea, and Iraq are examples (see Table 5.1). These states do not have a monopoly of force at home and lack complete control over their own territory. They are also incapable of executing meaningful agreements with other countries. Similarly, premodern states do not have the capacity to provide even the basic services for their citizens. Their key governing institutions are unstable and ineffective. These are states that have minimal or nonexistent foreign policies except for the relationships they have with states that provide them with aid and essential services. Often, these relationships are dependent ones, and they are with a former colonial power.

Modern states are traditional nation-states with control over their territory and the ability to protect their citizens and provide services that allow for the accumulation of wealth. China, India, and Brazil are examples of modern states. Their foreign policies tend to be dominated

state-strengthening nationalism The use of nationalist ideology to bolster or reform a government or seek to regain territory at the expense of other states.

secessionist nationalism The use of nationalist ideology to create a new state, often by seceding from an existing multiethnic state.

mass nationalism The use of nationalist ideology to encourage separation from an existing state. This is a tactic often employed with secessionist nationalism.

elite nationalism The use of nationalist ideology to encourage unity within an existing state. This is often a tactic that state-strengthening nationalists use.

premodern state A state within which the primary identity of citizens or subjects is to national, religious, or ethnic communities.

failed or collapsed state A state that does not command the primary loyalty of its citizens or subjects because it does not meet its basic responsibilities. Such a state has no monopoly of force at home and lacks complete control over its own territory.

fragile state A state that has not yet failed but whose leaders lack the will or capacity to perform core state functions.

modern state A political unit within which citizens identify with the state and see the state as legitimate. This state has a monopoly over the use of force and is able to provide citizens with key services.

Table 5.1
The Failed State Index 2013

Rank	State	Symptoms
1.	Somalia	jihadist terrorism, piracy, poverty, food insecurity
2.	Congo, D.R	civil war, massive human rights abuses, disease, mass rape and torture
3.	Sudan	civil war, authoritarian government, terrorism, poverty, overdependence on oil
4.	South Sudan	poverty, corruption, food shortages, armed conflict, human rights abuses
5.	Chad	poverty, influx of refugees, radicalized youth population, tribal/religious conflicts
6.	Yemen	jihadist terrorism, human rights abuses, external interference, poverty, disease, lack of food and clean water
7.	Afghanistan	violent protests, assassinations by Taliban, external interference, drug trade
8.	Haiti	corruption, forced evictions, poverty, crime, continued inability to cope with effects of natural disasters
9.	Central African Republic	natural disasters, inadequate infrastructure, terrorism, violent protests, governmental coups
10.	Zimbabwe	economic collapse, humans rights abuses, political instability and corruption
11.	Iraq	destroyed infrastructure, terrorism, ethnic conflict, external interference

Source: Fund for Peace, Failed State Index (http://ffp.statesindex.org/rankings-2013-sortable).

by economic interests and a desire to become a major power in their region so that they gain a seat at the table with other global leaders or major powers. In these states, citizens identify with the state, and nationalism tends to be very high. For example, the 2008 Olympics in China gave world viewers an indication of the strength of Chinese nationalism. India's acquisition of nuclear weapons, its rise as a leader of the G-20 economic group, and the favorable nationalist reaction within India serve as another example of the relationship between nationalism and foreign policy in a modern state.

postmodern state
A political unit within which citizens are less nationalistic and more cosmopolitan in their outlook on both domestic and foreign policy.

Postmodern states include the states that make up the liberal Western world. The United States and the European states provide the best examples. Postmodern states are linked with other states in both formal and informal arrangements at the regional and global levels. Citizens are less nationalistic and more cosmopolitan in their outlook on both domestic and foreign policy. Indeed, in most postmodern states, the distinction between domestic and foreign policies is virtually nonexistent. Policy-making authority is shared among a variety of actors at the local, national, regional, and international levels. For example, the European Union now develops common foreign policy positions, and most postmodern states depend on NATO for their external security. Postmodern states share, trade, and borrow sovereignty with other public and private actors. Not surprisingly, these states tend to support calls for global governance and efforts aimed at resolving global problems, like the **Kyoto Protocol** (an international agreement linked to the UN Framework Convention on Climate Change) and the **International Criminal Court (ICC**; the first permanent, treaty-based, international criminal court).

These same states took the lead to promote the 2005 UN resolution that established the new "responsibility to protect" initiative, which fundamentally challenges the traditional Westphalian view of national sovereignty. The Responsibility to Protect Doctrine (R2P) was first adopted as a norm by a UN high-level panel in 2004. Next the 2005 Report of the UN Secretary-General was submitted and approved by all of the heads of states and government representatives attending the sixtieth session of the UN General Assembly, agreeing to the R2P principle. Further, the UN Security Council Resolution 1674, affirmed in April 2006, provided for protection of civilians in armed conflict but again supported the R2P principle. The R2P Doctrine clearly prescribes that states have the responsibility to protect civilians from violence and deprivation and to prevent further violations of human security. When a state fails to protect its citizens, the responsibility shifts to the international community.

While modern states are all consumed with economic growth and building up their power and authority at home and abroad, postmodern states are multilateralists, busy building regional and global regimes to deal with the security challenges presented by modern and premodern states. Premodern (failed or fragile) states—which former US secretary of defense Robert Gates called "the main security challenge of our time" in 2010—can become incubators for terrorism, and they provide profitable homes for drug sales, human trafficking, arms trading, and even piracy. Many are also kleptocracies, or states ruled by corrupt leaders who are stealing the state's resources and using its police and security forces to repress any dissidents. In a kleptocracy, corrupt leaders benefit if the state is failed or fragile, as there are no institutions of government to punish them for their crimes. A revolution is often the only way to get rid of these corrupt leaders. The Arab Spring led to the end of three kleptocracies: Egypt, Tunisia, and Libya.

Foreign policy decisions result from premodern, modern, and postmodern political circumstances. It should be noted that even in undemocratic or authoritarian states, domestic interests such as those favored by military leaders, government bureaucrats, and business leaders shape both domestic and foreign policy. Citizens might not have as much to say about what their leaders decide to do in the international system, but bureaucratic agencies and elites do have a voice. Consider how the Chinese business community has worked to open up the communist regime in that country. The leaders of a state may often seem like Janus, the Roman god of doors and beginnings, who had two aspects—one facing inward and the other outward. As we will see later in this chapter, the foreign policy process is essentially that: the act of balancing domestic and international factors.

Kyoto Protocol An international agreement, linked to the UN Framework Convention on Climate Change, which sets binding targets for thirty-seven industrialized countries and the European community for reducing greenhouse gas emissions. The protocol commits these countries to stabilize GHG emissions, while the convention only encourages them to do so.

International Criminal Court (ICC) The first permanent, treaty-based, international criminal court, established to help end impunity for the perpetrators of the most serious crimes of concern to the international community. The ICC is governed by the Rome Statute and an independent international organization.

To enhance their prestige and global image, leaders of nation-states try to secure the sponsorship of major global conferences and cultural and sporting events. Brazil will sponsor the 2014 World Cup and the 2016 Olympics. Unfortunately, security is a critical element for these events, and no host country can afford to allow a major terrorist attack. Brazilian federal police like those outside Maracana Stadium will provide law and order, safety, and security for people coming to these events.

CASE STUDY : Refugees

BACKGROUND

Who is a refugee? As refugees, can they be called citizens of any country? Why does this category matter and how has it changed? How do refugee issues challenge those making foreign policy? Do we have a responsibility to protect and provide food and shelter to refugees who are not our citizens? There are many ways to categorize people who leave their homes, including migrants, temporary workers, displaced peoples, and refugees.

THE CASE

Prior to the twentieth century, "refugee" as a legal category did not exist, and it was not until World War I that states recognized people as refugees and gave them rights. Who was a refugee? Although many were displaced by World War I, Western states limited their compassion to Russians who were fleeing the Bolsheviks (it was easier to accuse a rival state of persecuting its people); only they were entitled to assistance from states and the new refugee agency, the High Commissioner for Refugees. However, the high commissioner took his mandate and the category and began to apply it to others in Europe who also had fled their country and needed assistance. Although states frequently permitted him to expand into other regions and provide more assistance, states also pushed back and refused

A girl from southern Somalia in a refugee camp in Mogadishu, Somalia. United Nations experts predict that as many as 750,000 people will starve in this current drought-induced crisis. Refugees present a moral and practical dilemma for the international community. Do states have a responsibility to feed and protect refugees?

to give international recognition or assistance to many in need—most notably, when Jews were fleeing Nazi Germany. After World War II and as a consequence of mass displacement, states reexamined who could be called a refugee and what assistance they could receive. Because Western states were worried about having obligations to millions of people around the world, they defined a refugee as an individual "outside the country of his origin owing to a well-founded fear of persecution" as a consequence of events that occurred in Europe before 1951. This definition excluded those outside Europe who were displaced because of war or natural disasters due to events after 1951. Objecting to this arbitrary definition that excluded so many, the new refugee agency, the UN High Commissioner for Refugees, working with aid agencies and permissive states, seized on events outside Europe and argued that there was no principled reason to deny to others what was given to Europeans. Over time, the political meaning of refugee came to include anyone who was forced to flee his or her home and crossed an international border. Eventually, states changed the international legal meaning to reflect the new political realities.

In the contemporary era of Rwanda, Darfur, and Bosnia after the Cold War, we are likely to call someone a refugee if he or she is forced to flee home because of circumstances caused by others, without having to cross an international border. To capture the idea of those who flee but are still in their homeland, we use the term "internally displaced peoples." Indeed, the concept of refugees has expanded impressively over the last 100 years, and the result is that there are millions of people who are now entitled to forms of assistance that are a matter of life and death. Watching this world tragedy unfold has led many states to support the human security movement and the October 2005 UN resolution on the responsibility to protect (see Chapter 10).

OUTCOME

One reason states wanted to differentiate "statutory" refugees from internally displaced peoples is because they have little interest in extending their international legal obligations to millions of people and do not want to become too involved in the domestic affairs of states. For example, in the

Continued

CASE STUDY : Refugees *continued*

early 1990s, refugees fleeing the civil war in Yugoslavia flooded into Germany. However, the German government was already paying for the reunification with East Germany and could not afford to support more refugees at the time. Therefore, because of domestic political reasons, the German government had to look to other states for a solution to a foreign policy problem. The German government chose to lobby for intervention by the European Union, NATO, and the United Nations.

For Discussion

1. Do states have a responsibility to accept political refugees?
2. Should states intervene in other states to alleviate refugee crises?
3. Should domestic political considerations—such as electoral politics—shape the foreign refugee policy of a state?

Foreign Policy from Different Perspectives

So which interests are *national*? Why these interests over others? Who determines these interests? In broad terms, a state's national interests fall into the following categories:

1. Security: the survival of the society, maintaining independence, and protecting territory
2. Economic welfare: economic well-being and market stability
3. Prestige: status, image, and level of respect and trust
4. Promoting values and political ideology: making the world like you
5. Expanding territory or control over vital resources: increasing power or resources
6. Seeking peace and stability: playing a role in maintaining world order and being a rule maker

As we have seen so far in this book, however, different theoretical views provide different perspectives on both issues and policies, even within the same broader theory. Neoclassical realists, for example, believe that domestic political interests play a role in shaping foreign policy, and thus, a state's priorities may change. For classical realists, however, national interests are relatively unchangeable over time. Hans Morgenthau argued that a state's national interest is the pursuit of power and that power, once acquired, is used to secure material aims, protect social and physical quality of life, and promote specific ideological or normative goals. As we saw in Chapter 3, classical realists like Morgenthau believe in a state-centric international system in which states act as a single coherent actor that pursues national interests in a rational manner. Here, "rational" means selecting a policy path that maximizes benefits for the state and minimizes risks. Morgenthau and his disciples considered "national interest as the pursuit of power" the essence of politics.

For all realists, the principal national interest is national security, or maintaining the integrity of a country's territory and its economic, political, and cultural institutions. Power is essential for national security, and most realists define power in military terms. Morgenthau argued that to understand foreign policy one needs to understand the "political and cultural context within which foreign policy is formulated" and that interests and ideas shape foreign policy actions and priorities. He quotes the noted scholar Max Weber to make his point: "Interests (material and ideal), not ideas, dominate directly the actions of men. Yet the

WHAT'S YOUR WORLDVIEW

Is nationalism essential for a state to be strong and to take on global leadership? Does excessive nationalism diminish efforts toward multilateralism and cooperative problem solving?

'images of the world' created by these ideas have very often served as switches determining the tracks on which the dynamism of interests kept actions moving" (1960, 9).

Robert Pastor (1999) argues that a state's leaders rank their foreign policy goals from *vital* or *essential* to *desirable*. From his realist view, Pastor ranks national interests as follows:

1. National security that includes the defense of borders and the prevention of external influence over domestic affairs.
2. The pursuit of economic interests and securing vital resources.
3. The defense of a country's traditions and values, and the promotion of its ideals in the international system.
4. The implicit and explicit effort to make the world more like itself.

The objectives of foreign policy, according to many realists, must be defined in terms of material national interests and must be supported by adequate power. Military power is the dominant coin of the realm from a realist view; however, in this era of globalization, the tools of statecraft have changed in both their utility and efficacy. All major states today, for instance, have substantial armed forces, yet all states face the potential of attacks by terrorist groups, and a strong military is not always an effective deterrent.

As we discussed in Chapter 3, proponents of the liberal perspective on international relations also believe that a state's power is not measured by force alone. Liberals seek power not only in terms of military power; power and influence in the international system may also depend on diplomacy and skills of persuasion. For liberals, a state may be able to secure its national interests by (1) maintaining rule of law in the international system and (2) empowering international institutions and regimes that promote global governance in policy areas such as economic development and global finance. Liberal internationalists like former Canadian foreign minister Lloyd Axworthy (2003, 5) have taken bold steps to reform the international system and shift foreign policy priorities from narrow national interests to a much more universal focus on human security and human interests. Axworthy described a goal that many liberal middle powers have embraced:

> We propose a way of seeing the world and tackling global issues that derives from serving individual human needs, not just those of the nation-state or powerful economic interests.

Liberal internationalism in this case has evolved to embrace a more Kantian or normative view of national priorities and interests.

Constructivists, meanwhile, believe that state interests and foreign policy goals are "defined in the context of internationally held norms and understandings about what is good and appropriate" (Finnemore 1996b, 2). Awareness that this normative context changes over time helps us understand shifts in foreign policy behavior. For example, the more internationalist context that came with the end of the Cold War supported a shift from ideological conflict to engagement and cooperation, and as a result, many states returned to their own traditions and values as guideposts for foreign policy.

Marxists and many utopians, on the other hand, believe that foreign policy is generally controlled by economic and political elites who also control power at home. National interests are determined by the wealthy and powerful, not the average citizen. This belief leads to the conclusions that (1) wars are fought primarily for economic reasons and (2) the goal of a country's development-assistance programs is to make poor countries dependent on the donor state, keeping them in the position of providing cheap labor, cheap resources, and a welcome place for foreign investors. Utopians such as the academics who comprised the World Order Models Project (WOMP) advocate a foreign policy that shifts national interests to more global interests such as peace, social justice, economic well-being, and ecological balance.

Who Makes Foreign Policy?

We need to always remind ourselves that human beings have agency in foreign policy. It is not the state that decides; it is individuals representing the state. Leaders, bureaucrats, members of parliament, and ministers make decisions, and these decisions are shaped by a variety of factors. Think about the last time you went to a diner. Did you order just anything that came to your mind? No, you probably ordered from a menu, and the menu was written by someone who was influenced by a number of factors such as market prices for food, the cooking skills required, his or her own tastes, and the tastes of the diner's clientele. Foreign policy decision makers are also given a menu—one that is shaped by past events, national attributes, policy decisions made by both internal and external actors, and the nature of global politics. The values and beliefs of the individual clearly shape the final decisions. We discuss the various factors that shape foreign policy decision making later in this chapter when we discuss levels of analysis.

When exploring the question of who makes foreign policy, we are interested in those who make decisions on behalf of states or organizations within a state. Both public and private actors may shape foreign policy. At each phase of the foreign policy process, which we'll discuss shortly—initiation, formulation, implementation, and evaluation—different actors will become involved and attempt to shape policy. Each policy issue area may attract different constellations of actors.

It is important to start with individuals in formal government positions: foreign ministers, a secretary of state in the United States, or a key minister of trade or defense. Generally, members of the executive branch or the prime minister's cabinet are the ones who *initiate* foreign policy, and they work through the legislature and parliament to *formulate* the policy. Government agencies generally work with the private sector or other governments to *implement* policy decisions. Private actors such as banks, transnational enterprises, nongovernmental organizations (NGOs), universities, and think tanks may play a role in any part of the foreign policy process. Other governments and regional and international organizations may also be involved in helping formulate and implement foreign policy. Nongovernmental organizations and corporations do not directly make policy, but they can have a profound influence on public officials who do make the final policy decisions.

> **WHAT'S YOUR WORLDVIEW**
>
> *Who do you think determines a country's foreign policy priorities? What are your country's top foreign policy interests, and are they what you would expect them to be?*

What Do We Expect from Foreign Policy?

National interests are usually related to what we, as citizens, expect from our governments. At the basic level, we want the state to protect our borders, provide internal security and a system of law and order, and support and maintain a means of exchange or a marketplace. This is the point at which domestic and international policy distinctions begin to blur. Foreign policy and domestic policies are clearly interdependent in this global age. Most foreign policy experts believe that citizens expect their state's foreign policy to deliver in seven areas (Hill 2003, 44–45):

1. Protecting citizens living or traveling in a foreign country.
2. Projecting an image or identity in the international system that enhances a state's prestige and makes that state's values, beliefs, and traditions attractive to other states in the international system.

3. Maintaining the "status quo" in terms of providing stability and protecting citizens against external threats.
4. Advancing prosperity and providing the ways and means for accumulating wealth.
5. Assisting leaders in making decisions about whether to intervene in a global crisis or get involved in an alliance or international institution.
6. Providing support for international negotiations aimed at creating and maintaining a stable world order.
7. Working toward protecting the global commons (e.g., oceans) and for providing global public goods (e.g., clean air).

A variety of internal and external actors and structures influence and shape these foreign policy goals. Globalization has pushed domestic and foreign policy processes into a complex and interconnected relationship. Domestic societies are more exposed to external or international developments, and foreign policies both shape and are shaped by domestic developments. In capitals across the world, foreign policy leaders talk about policy issues that are transnational in nature, like migration, poverty, environmental challenges, and trade. In crafting government policies to slow global warming, for example, political leaders must contend with the demands of business and industry groups and those of concerned citizens at home—not to mention demands that leaders, corporations, and citizens of other states bring to negotiations. These leaders also understand how domestic interests often prevent the realization of foreign policy goals. One of the most difficult issues for foreign policy leaders is how to make bold foreign policy decisions without alienating a powerful domestic group that might influence the next election. For example, the leaders of the world knew that genocide was taking place in Darfur, and yet few states were willing to intervene in the area to stop the killing. Humanitarian intervention presents a difficult policy choice for most leaders. It is hard to convince domestic groups to sacrifice blood and treasure for people from distant lands.

Now that we've covered some foundational aspects of what foreign policy is, who makes it, and what we expect from it, we revisit levels of analysis (introduced in Chapter 1) to look at *why* states make the foreign policy decisions they do.

Levels of Analysis in Foreign Policy

As a student of foreign policy, you might be interested in finding answers to puzzles or unexpected actions by a state. Why did North Korea's leaders decide to develop nuclear weapons? Why do Nordic governments give so much development assistance? Why did China's government seek influence with the regime in Sudan that supported—or did little to stop—the killing in Darfur? These are complex issues, but some explanations are better than others. Foreign policy analysis is the search for factors or variables that explain the most about a state's behavior. Scholars doing research in this area are interested in questions like the following: Why do states behave in a certain way? What factors explain a state's behavior? Why do leaders pick one option over another? If a state spends a significant amount of money on its military, what factors explain that choice? Although there are always questions about "agency," or which actors actually make foreign policy, foreign policy analysis offers plausible explanations for foreign policy behavior. We say plausible explanations because this is not an exact science: the social scientist trying to explain foreign policy puzzles can never replicate the certainty of the natural scientist working in the lab and controlling all the variables. Yet if the social scientist can identify factors that shape foreign policy, it might help us better

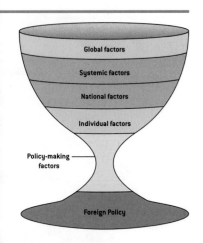

LEVELS OF ANALYSIS IN FOREIGN POLICY.

Many factors influence foreign policy. As a scholar, one must consider each level when trying to explain the behavior of nation-states.

understand the foreign policy process and even predict how states might behave in similar situations. In this section, we will discuss one such approach to the agency question: levels of analysis.

In Chapter 1, we discussed how some research in international relations attempts to replicate the research methods and assumptions of the natural sciences. The idea here is that one can develop theories, test them by gathering evidence, and find useful explanations for the decisions made by leaders. Foreign policy analysis, a subfield of international relations, puts the individual at the center of decision making. Most studies of decision making begin with the assumption that all decision makers act rationally or always act to maximize benefits and minimize costs. In his classic study of decision making in a crisis situation, *Essence of Decision*, Graham Allison (1971) introduces three models, or analytic tools, for explaining decision making. The first, the rational-actor model, or RAM, provides a useful example of using rationality. The other two models, organizational behavior and bureaucratic politics, are second-level or domestic-level tools. Unfortunately, some foreign policy decision makers cannot meet the requirements of rationality. For example, it may not be possible for policy makers to know all of their options and assign values to those options. They may lack access to information essential to selecting policies that result in value maximization. Thus, other factors, like a decision maker's belief system, the political structure of a state, or the distribution of power in the international system, may influence the range of choices and the eventual policy choice.

Most texts suggest that there are three levels of analysis: *individual*, or the human dimension; *national* attributes, or the domestic factors; and *systemic* conditions, or the nature of the international system. A number of scholars have added a fourth level that focuses on *global* conditions or factors (see Table 5.2). Discussions about the importance of globalization and technological innovations like the Internet suggest that these are potentially factors that influence decisions made by national leaders.

Individual, or the Human Dimension

We assume that all leaders are rational actors (i.e., always selecting a policy path that maximizes benefits and minimizes costs), but other factors like beliefs, personality images, and perceptions also shape decision making. Foreign policy research suggests that these other factors or filters are most important in a crisis situation, a decision requiring secrecy and thus involving few actors, or a decision demanding a quick response. This level is also important when a leader is given a great deal of latitude to make a decision and when the decision maker has an interest or expertise in foreign policy. To act rationally, leaders must be able to know all of their options, be capable of assigning values to these options, and have enough information to select the higher valued options. Those who use these other idiosyncratic factors like *belief systems* or *personality types* to explain behavior do not believe any decision maker can be rational all of the time. Most decision makers operate in an environment of uncertainty with imperfect information. Many leaders talk about "going with their gut" when they are making decisions in crises, but they are usually relying on previous experience (e.g., analogical reasoning) or their worldview (e.g., realism, liberalism, Marxism, feminism, constructivism). Leaders filter information through their worldviews, which include both principled and causal beliefs, and generally seek programs that fit with these beliefs. For example, former British prime minister Margaret Thatcher, with a strong realist belief system, convinced George H. W. Bush to take the 1990 Iraqi invasion of Kuwait seriously and respond militarily. She also decided to use force rather than diplomacy to take back the Falkland Islands after the Argentine invasion in 1982.

Table 5.2
Levels of Analysis: Explaining the Behavior of Global Actors

Level One: Individual, or the Human Dimension

- Bounded rationality/cybernetics
- Biological explanations
- Motivation/personality
- Perception/images
- Belief systems/information processing

Level Two: National Attributes, or the Domestic Factors

Changing elements:
- Power capabilities
- Domestic politics: finding coalitions for policy and support for retaining power
- Decision-making styles and structures: bureaucratic politics and organizational behavior

More permanent elements:
- Size and resource base
- Geographic factors
- Political structure
- Economic system
- Political culture

Level Three: Systematic Conditions, or the Nature of the International System

- Level of anarchy or order
- Distribution of power
- Obligations, treaties, alliances
- Regimes or governing arrangements

Level Four: Global Factors

- Global social movements
- Environmental conditions and challenges
- Media and popular cultural forces
- Decisions by transnational nonstate actors such as transnational enterprises and international NGOs
- Ideas, values, and norms that transcend culture and time

National Attributes, or the Domestic Factors

At the domestic or national level, researchers look at a country's history and traditions and at its political, economic, cultural, and social structures. Regime type—such as whether a state is a parliamentary democracy or authoritarian with unelected leaders and a strong single-party bureaucracy—shapes the choice of foreign policy strategies. The role of political parties and interest groups or NGOs within a society is also an important variable at the domestic level. An area of study that crosses over to some of the constructivist research in foreign policy is the focus on cultural values. Valerie Hudson (2007) suggests that national identity and cultural variables may be more important today than systemic factors like balance of power in shaping foreign policy. Citizens in social democratic states with political cultures that promote social justice and economic well-being expect their foreign policy programs to advance these same values.

Changing elements that shape policy include military power, economic wealth, and demographic factors. More permanent elements like geographic location and resource base also matter. A powerful variable in many democratic societies is domestic politics, or electoral calculations. Politicians often find that they are unable to achieve their desired goals because of demands of the election cycle. A further complication is the role of bureaucracies in the policy process. Unelected civil servants can influence outcomes the politicians want. Academic work includes many such examples, beginning with Graham Allison's study of the Cuban missile crisis, *Essence of Decision*. In his exploration of crisis decision making within the Kennedy administration, Allison found that **standard operating procedures (SOPs)**, or the way things are usually done in an organization, are major determinants of foreign policy behavior. Large organizations employ SOPs to respond to a range of events. For instance, when a natural disaster like a hurricane or earthquake happens, agencies have plans ready to provide the correct kind of assistance. Normally, a state's agencies of all kinds—military, intelligence, foreign affairs— have SOPs ready for every foreseeable eventuality. Bureaucratic politics, Allison's third model, suggests that within every government, bureaucratic agencies compete with one another for control over resources and policy. The eventual result of this competition is the policy.

standard operating procedures (SOPs) The prepared-response patterns that organizations create to react to general categories of events, crises, and actions.

Systemic Conditions, or the Nature of the International System

The anarchic nature of the international system—its lack of a central authority—may be the most important factor at this level. However, as we have seen in this book, countries take individual and collective actions to cope with this lack of a global central authority. Thus, treaties, alliances, and trade conventions, which states agree to abide by, are seen as systemic constraints. These are formal contracts created by states in an attempt to provide order in the system.

A country's behavior is also shaped by more informal systemic constraints based on traditions, common goals, and shared norms. For example, most states respect the sovereignty of all states, and most follow the rule of international law. These laws cannot be enforced, but states abide by them because they expect others to do the same. This notion of **reciprocity** is the primary incentive for states to support a rule-based international system. The distribution of power in the system (e.g., unipolar, bipolar, multipolar, nonpolar) and the nature of order (e.g., balance of power, collective security) are also important system-level factors. Neorealists believe that the lack of a common power or a central government at the global level is the defining element of international relations, and a state's foreign policy is aimed primarily at survival in this anarchic system. Kenneth Waltz describes this anarchic condition of the system (1959, 238):

reciprocity A form of statecraft that employs a retaliatory strategy, cooperating only if others do likewise.

> Each state pursues its own interests, however defined, in ways it judges best. Force is a means of achieving the external ends of states because there exists no consistent, reliable process of reconciling the conflicts of interest that inevitably arise among similar units in a condition of anarchy.

Liberals, on the other hand, believe that anarchy forces states to create rules and develop regimes or governing arrangements aimed at encouraging cooperation and multilateralism. Today, many liberals focus on more effective global governance across policy areas. As the world has learned with the very recent global economic crisis, rules and regulations that govern all markets are indeed essential.

Global Factors

These variables are often confused with system-level factors. Simply stated, the difference is that global factors are not necessarily created by states, whereas systemic factors are.

Global-level variables can be the outcome of decisions or technology made by individuals, interest groups, states, or nonstate actors. For example, social media, created and used by private actors, played a major role in organizing opposition forces in Egypt, Tunisia, Libya, and Syria. Global factors may also be the results of natural conditions. These factors cannot be traced to the actions of any one state or even group of states. In fact, they usually challenge the ideas of boundaries and sovereignty. The Internet and resulting information revolution, the movement of capital by multinational banks, CNN broadcasts, and the revolutionary ideas of religious fundamentalists all represent global factors that might shape policy behavior. These factors are pushed and promoted by the process of globalization. Environmental conditions such as pollution, pandemics, global warming, and drought can also have a global impact on foreign policy; for example, they may lead to new alliances or to conflicts over the control of critical resources. As writers such as Peter Gleik and Michael Klare have shown, there is a very real possibility of "water wars" in the Middle East and Africa. These conditions may be the result of actions taken by specific national or transnational actors, but the effects are felt globally.

For our last example of global factors, consider how the Internet and other forms of telecommunication technology have been used by both radical groups and humanitarian groups to rally support for their causes and to challenge the power of key states. No one state owns the Internet or the various messaging services, and yet these can be valuable tools aimed at shaping foreign policy.

Social scientists may combine variables to reach an explanation of a particular foreign policy decision. But social science researchers want to isolate key variables or factors that explain the decision made. They are guided by the goals of precision and parsimony (thrift). Advocates of the scientific approach, or **positivists**, want to be able to say that US policy toward Iraq, for example, can best be explained by looking at the personality of George W. Bush or the power of the Defense Department and the office of the vice president in shaping policy. Each of these bureaucratic organizations made the case for war. What is exciting about research in our field is that there is always disagreement about which variables explain the most. Thus, someone could say with equal certainty that US economic interests—namely, our dependency on oil—offer a better explanation for the decisions to launch a "war of choice," something we will discuss more in Chapter 8. The strength of anyone's argument is based on the quality of the empirical evidence that one collects to support the hypothesis being tested. We use the work of historians, public policy records, government documents, interviews, budgets, and journalists' accounts to gather evidence to confirm or reject our hypotheses.

We should remember that by explaining foreign policy, we might be able to predict what states would do in a given situation. Likewise, we can use previous decisions as analogs and make suggestions or prescriptions for future foreign policy. Next we turn to a discussion of how foreign policy is accomplished. We will examine the strategies and tools that states might use to secure their goals and meet their priorities in the international system.

positivists Analysts who use the scientific method to structure their research.

The Foreign Policy Process

So far, we have examined the explanations and influences of foreign policy, answering questions of why and what for; in this section, we'll get down to the nuts and bolts and look at the process of how foreign policy comes about. You may be surprised to learn that the foreign policy–making apparatus of most democratic countries is basically the same. Political systems tend to divide the responsibility for decision making between members of the executive branch, which carries out the policies, and the deliberative or legislative branch, which sets spending priorities and guidelines for the executive to follow. Deliberative bodies often have a responsibility to oversee the actions of the executive branch. Both branches of government might subdivide responsibility further into geographic regions, economic sectors, or military affairs. In addition to the governmental actors with legal authority, there are also any number of individuals and groups outside the government structure that might seek to influence the policy process. The actors that comprise this informal sector vary by issue area, but they can include business groups, religious groups, news media, and private citizens.

As we suggested earlier in the chapter, even authoritarian or totalitarian states have decision-making processes in which government ministries debate issues and work with private interests to promote specific policy positions. Leaders rarely act alone and create a foreign policy that adheres specifically to their own interests. For example, the intransigence of North Korea and Iran in their defiance of the United States and the international community is supported by military leaders and various bureaucrats within each state. However, in both states, there are also oppositional groups.

Four Phases of Foreign Policy Making

The study of foreign policy making assumes that governmental officials with the legal authority to act do so in a logical manner. Political scientists call this the "rational-actor model" of foreign policy making. Proponents of this model assert that a government's foreign policy officials are able to (1) define a problem, (2) develop responses to the problem, (3) act upon one or more of the responses, and then (4) evaluate the effectiveness of the policy. In the following sections, we'll discuss these four phases in more depth.

Phase One: Initiation or Articulation Phase

Issues are often first articulated or otherwise promoted by media and interest groups attempting to influence the policy-making process. Information about a foreign policy issue is disseminated, and as public awareness of an issue increases, this informed public may pressure elected officials to either act on the issue or, in some cases, stay clear of the problem.

Both internal (or formal) and external (or informal) actors may push a certain position and pressure leaders to take action. For example, in the case of the conflict and genocide in Darfur, NGOs using the Internet provided the public with information about the atrocities. These same NGOs initiated further global-awareness campaigns with celebrities and notable public leaders that attracted the attention of major media outlets and many elected officials who recognized the importance of the issue for either moral reasons or more pragmatic electoral calculations.

Individuals and research institutes (often called "think tanks"; see Table 5.3) can initiate a debate about a foreign policy issue. Once public awareness increases, attentive members of the public might pressure a government to act. A natural disaster or an unexpected tragedy or crisis might also inspire some official reaction from governments. For example, in general, the US public is not very supportive of increasing foreign aid, but if a flood or earthquake devastates an area, US citizens generally want the government to supply emergency aid. New technologies like the Internet and cell phones may contribute to the democratization of foreign policy. Today, citizens in industrialized states have an opportunity to be better informed than ever before, and they are presented with a variety of options to become actively involved in a particular issue area. Citizen involvement also now transcends borders: global or transnational social movements have mobilized citizens to work to end hunger, forgive debt, and end the use of certain weapons. These campaigns have

Table 5.3
Some US Foreign Policy Think Tanks

> **Brookings Institution** is a highly authoritative nonprofit public-policy organization whose mission is to conduct high-quality independent research and provide innovative, practical recommendations that strengthen American democracy; foster the economic and social welfare, security, and opportunity of all Americans; and secure a more open, safe, prosperous, and cooperative international system.
>
> **Council on Foreign Relations** is an independent, nonpartisan membership organization, think tank, and publisher dedicated to being a resource for its members, government officials, business executives, journalists, educators and students, civic and religious leaders, and other interested citizens to help them better understand the world and the foreign policy choices facing the United States and other countries. The council publishes *Foreign Policy*, a leading journal of international affairs and US foreign policy.
>
> **Heritage Foundation** is a conservative-leaning think tank committed to building an America where freedom, opportunity, prosperity, and civil society flourish.
>
> **Carnegie Endowment for International Peace (CEIP)** is one of America's leading institutions for researching and analyzing international affairs and making recommendations for US foreign policy. The CEIP, with over 100 employees, is headquartered in Washington, D.C., with offices in four other countries.
>
> **RAND Corporation** is a nonprofit think tank formed to offer research and analysis to the United States armed forces. The organization has since expanded to work with other governments, private foundations, international organizations, and commercial organizations on a host of nondefense issues.
>
> **American Enterprise Institute (AEI)** is a conservative think tank, founded in 1943. Its mission is "to defend the principles and improve the institutions of American freedom and democratic capitalism—limited government, private enterprise, individual liberty and responsibility, vigilant and effective defense and foreign policies, political accountability, and open debate."
>
> **Center for American Progress** is a liberal political-policy research and advocacy organization. Its website describes it as "a nonpartisan research and educational institute dedicated to promoting a strong, just and free America that ensures opportunity for all."

been successful in their efforts to persuade governments to use official foreign policy tools to address their concerns. For example, Bono, the lead singer from the musical group U2, spent time with the late Senator Jesse Helms and other members of Congress as a representative of the Jubilee Movement that urged wealthy states to forgive the debts of poor states. Other celebrities have joined members of the domestic Christian Coalition to increase awareness of the issues surrounding poverty and third world debt and to lobby both the executive branch of government and members of Congress.

Global and domestic actors also have an impact on policy makers in authoritarian or nondemocratic states. China continues to be a favorite target for human rights groups, and they have had some impact on Chinese domestic policies. Tragically, many of these NGOs have had no impact on policy makers in failed states like Zimbabwe or extremist states like Sudan and Somalia.

Phase Two: The Formulation of Foreign Policy

The formulation phase involves the creation of an official government policy. Internal and external actors—individuals, interest groups, corporations, and foreign governments—initiate policy debates and put pressure on policy makers to act. The formulation phase is when parliaments, executive offices, ministries, and bureaucratic agencies work to develop an effective foreign policy. The idea to forgive the debt of third world countries is now discussed by relevant agencies within a government. Now the legislative branches debate the cost and benefits of forgiving debt, and specialists in various financial departments provide the essential information for the final policy position.

Specialists inside and outside government provide the essential information for policy makers. Often, in the policy-making process, the original intention of the policy is loaded with other priorities that might help the politician get reelected or might help a bureaucracy gain more power and more resources. In noncrisis situations, foreign policy is formulated much like domestic policy. It is a complex process involving legislatures, executive agencies, ministries and departments, and a wide variety of interest communities.

In crisis situations, foreign policy is made by a smaller group of individuals and agencies. Since the end of World War I, in the United States and many other Western democracies, the executive branch or cabinet has taken over the foreign policy process. Foreign ministries, defense departments, and special advisers to the prime minister or president are usually charged with responding to a crisis. In the administration of George W. Bush, decisions about the war in Iraq were made by a group of advisers scattered in the National Security Council, the vice president's office, and the Defense Department—while the State Department was often left out or its ideas dismissed by the president's inner circle.

Although in most democracies elected members of legislatures serve on committees with foreign policy oversight, most of these committees react to policy plans formulated by the head of government and that person's advisers. Most legislative bodies do have budget responsibilities and can use this power to support or change foreign policy priorities. However, shrewd leaders who appeal to the public for support of their foreign policy actions can neutralize the legislature's power of the purse. For example, few members of the US Congress challenged funding for military actions or aid programs for an important ally, for fear of being called antimilitary or unpatriotic. Generally, when dealing in areas of foreign policy, the old adage applies: "Partisanship ends at the water's edge." After 9/11, it was very easy for the Bush administration to get congressional support for any program that could be framed as part of the global war on terror. Prime Minister Blair had the same advantages after the July attacks in Britain. United States presidents since the end of World War II used the Cold War and the containment of communism around the world as justifications for financing an expansionary foreign policy. Hundreds of anticommunist organizations, the defense industries, and many ethnic communities, such as Polish and Hungarian Americans, kept pressure on US leaders to never ease up on the Soviet Union.

Phase Three: Foreign Policy Implementation

Once a policy is decided in a legislature or in a department or ministry, it is usually assigned to policy actors in a ministry or department and other affiliated actors in the field. These actors are expected to implement the policy. For example, if Congress passes a bill allocating funds for development assistance or foreign aid, the money is sent to the most appropriate agency: in this case, the US Agency for International Development (USAID), which receives the funds and distributes them to its various field offices. The money is then given to development projects that may have been organized by local governments, NGOs, and development agencies from other countries. It is not unusual for countries to form coalitions with local communities, NGOs, and other aid agencies. Funds are not always spent on intended projects, and they are often not spent at all. Corruption, project delays, new priorities, and leadership changes often get in the way of intended consequences. United States agencies intending to reduce poverty in developing countries must deal with a variety of factors that might delay a program or prevent it from reaching its goals.

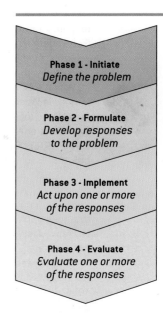

Phase 1 - Initiate
Define the problem

Phase 2 - Formulate
Develop responses to the problem

Phase 3 - Implement
Act upon one or more of the responses

Phase 4 - Evaluate
Evaluate one or more of the responses

A TYPICAL DECISION-MAKING PROCESS.
What do we mean by rational actor? What about this model suggests rationality? Of course, this graphic is a simplification. Can you draw a more complex process model, or flowchart, based on what you have read so far? What other steps or loops would your model depict?

GLOBAL PERSPECTIVE | Central America: A Perpetual Pursuit of Union?

THE ISSUE

The foreign policies of Central American states can seem to present a paradox. The outside observer sees a number of small countries with a common history, a relatively high degree of common identity, and apparently everything to gain from integration. So why haven't they integrated? This is a case of particularistic domestic goals undermining what seems to some outside observers a logical regional option.

BACKGROUND

Following independence, the Captaincy-General of Guatemala became the Federal Republic of Central America (1823–1839) before splitting into Guatemala, El Salvador, Honduras, Nicaragua, and Costa Rica. Restoration of this union has been a constant theme in integrationist discourse. Yet Central America was more a collection of communities than a clearly defined overarching entity. Non-Guatemalan elites resisted leadership by Guatemala, and Costa Rica early on showed a tendency toward isolationism. Nationalism grew, conflict undermined unionism, and outside involvement was often unhelpful. Various sources of division thus coexisted with a powerful mythology of union.

A first Central American Peace Conference in Washington, convened in 1907 to help end local conflicts, led to a short-lived Central American Court of Justice (1908–1918). The Organization of Central American States (ODECA) was created in 1951 with the goal of re-creating regional unity. The first organizations of functional cooperation emerged around this time. Some twenty-five such bodies now exist, covering everything from water to electrical energy and creating a complex web of regional interactions. Formal economic integration began in 1960 with the Central American Common Market (CACM). Intraregional trade grew, but the system entered crisis at the end of the 1960s. Efforts at reform in the 1970s were overtaken by political crises and conflicts. In the 1980s, integration became associated with the Central American peace process. In this context of confidence building, a Central American Parliament was created as a forum for regional dialogue. In 1991, with conflicts in El Salvador and Nicaragua ended, the

Cold War over, and a new wave of regional integration across the world, a new period began with the Central American Integration System (SICA). This aimed to provide a global approach to integration, with four subsystems—political, economic, social, and cultural.

RECENT HISTORY

The institutional system is concentrated around the presidential summits. The Central American Parliament is directly elected but has no powers. It does not include Costa Rica. As of 2006, only El Salvador, Honduras, and Nicaragua participated in the Central American Court of Justice. There have been repeated discussions of institutional reform. By 2005, intraregional trade represented around 27 percent of exports and 12 percent of imports. Most goods originating in Central American countries enjoy free circulation. The same levels of external tariff were being applied for 95 percent of goods. General negotiations for a Central American customs union began in 2004. The future is also being shaped by international agreements. The Central American countries signed a free trade agreement with the United States in 2004 modeled on the North American Free Trade Agreement (NAFTA). In 2006, they also began to

Effective regional cooperation has eluded the countries of Central America. With a growing divide between rich and poor and a very competitive global economy, the leaders of this region must address quality-of-life issues such as education, health, housing, and employment.

Continued

negotiate an association agreement with the European Union, including a free trade agreement. The pursuit of union continues at the international level, but it is hindered by goals and motivations found at the individual and domestic levels of analysis.

For Discussion

1. Does it make sense for Central America to have its own political and economic union, or should it be part of a larger Latin American union? Consider

how BENELUX (or Belgium, Luxembourg, and the Netherlands) merged into the original European Community.

2. Globalization may force countries into creating larger common markets. In what other policy areas would a union make sense?

3. What would the United States and Mexico think about such a union?

4. What are the internal and external factors working either for a union or against more cooperation?

Phase Four: Foreign Policy Evaluation

Policy evaluation is the final step in the process, and it is rare that this step occurs. Although the review provision might be built into the program, the administrators of the policy might have a personal interest in keeping the program active. The media may focus their attention on the policy outcomes if the policy program was a success or a failure. All interested parties will have a position and will try to influence future decisions in this policy area. Often, the very public and private actors involved in the previous phases of the policy process will be involved in the evaluation of policy outcomes.

Most legislatures conduct public hearings related to major foreign policy expenditures. These hearings can become particularly important if a policy program has failed or had a major impact on a society. Consider, for instance, the Iraq Study Group's hearings on the Iraq War or congressional committee hearings on the future of NATO or US trade policy toward China. Congress tends to use every opportunity to evaluate the foreign policy activities of a particular administration. In some political systems, like the United Kingdom and Canada, the prime minister must face the parliamentary opposition during a legislative session called "question time." This is a form of evaluation that generally attracts a great deal of public attention and comments from opposition politicians.

Another form of evaluation that usually triggers policy actions is comprehensive studies done by universities, think tanks, research institutions, and NGOs. Human Rights Watch, Greenpeace, the International Crisis Group, the International Committee of the Red Cross, and hundreds of other interest groups provide policy makers with comprehensive studies on just about every foreign policy issue area (see Chapter 7 for more on NGOs). To illustrate, in 2007 the Red Cross (ICRC) released a report on the "treatment of high value detainees" being held by the CIA. This report may have a major impact on future decisions about how to treat individuals taken prisoner in the war on terrorism.

Foreign Policy Strategies and Tools

The organized statements of goals and beliefs that political leaders formulate and the methods they intend to employ to achieve those goals are called foreign policy strategies or **doctrine**. For the political leaders of a state, a foreign policy doctrine acts as a kind of GPS for charting policy strategies and determining national priorities. The doctrine guides decisions such as where to invest critical resources to secure long- and short-term goals.

doctrine A stated principle of government policy, mainly in foreign or military affairs, or the set of beliefs held and taught by an individual or political group.

Bilateral and multilateral diplomacy is a critical aspect of foreign policy in this complex world. EU high representative Catherine Ashton played a key role in negotiations with Iran's foreign minister Mohammad Javad Zarif. The negotiations also involved the United States, China, France, Britain, Russia, and Germany. The final agreement reached in November 2013 was a foreign policy achievement for the European Union.

Most states have coherent foreign policy strategies to attain both material and ideational goals. For example, after emerging from apartheid and exclusive white rule in the late 1980s, the new South African state has developed a foreign policy that promotes human rights across the world and supports an African Renaissance. Similarly, after years of rule by military dictators, Chile has decided on an activist foreign policy based on the theme of "diplomacy for development." The hope is that this policy will help Chile overcome its structural constraints of size and geographic location and allow it to develop a niche as a regional leader and an honest broker in international affairs.

All countries have three kinds of foreign policy tools to choose from: sticks, carrots, and sermons. "Sticks" refer to threats, "carrots" to inducements, and "sermons" to what diplomats might call "moral suasion." We could also add the power that comes with having a positive image or reputation in the international system. Being an honest broker, or a moral leader seeking to help resolve regional conflicts, can also become a source of power in the international world. Norway, for example, took the lead to resolve the Middle East conflict and the conflict in Sri Lanka. Norwegian leaders are supported in these endeavors because Norwegian citizens see it as their responsibility to the global community. Norwegian nationalism includes a strong sense of internationalism. It is important to remember that, because of differences in resources, population, and level of economic development, some countries might not be able to use some or any of the options we discuss in the following sections.

Sticks: Military and Economic Tools

In the international system of the realist perspective that influences many political leaders, states must secure their interests by military power. Since there is no common power or central government and no agreement on rules governing the system, some countries use force or the threat of force to secure their interest and gain more power and influence in the international system. Other military tools include military aid or assistance, sharing intelligence, alliances, military research, and technological innovations (see Table 5.4). Sometimes, the decision to deploy a weapon system can be a stick for diplomats to use. The G. W. Bush administration supported the development and deployment of a ballistic missile defense system in Eastern Europe to defend Europe against missiles from Iran or terrorist groups in the Middle East. Perhaps fearing growing US power and influence in the region, the Russian government saw the installation of such a defense system as a menace to Russia's security needs. In response, the Obama administration offered the Russians a carrot by declining to build the missile defense system.

Countries will adopt some weapons system to deter their enemies, but many countries seek military power to protect their interests in what international relations specialists call a "self-help world." Unfortunately, spending scarce national resources on military equipment does not guarantee safety. For instance, the United States enjoys military hegemony in the world today and spends more on its military than any other nation-state. Yet the sale of

Table 5.4
Five Largest Suppliers and Recipients of Major Conventional Weapons, 2008–2012

Supplier	Share of Global Arms Exports (%)	Main Recipients (Share of Supplier's Transfers)	Recipient	Share of Global Arms Imports (%)	Main Suppliers (Share of Recipient's Transfers)
USA	30	South Korea (12%)	**India**	12	Russia (79%)
		Australia (10%)			UK (6%)
		UAE (7%)			Uzbekistan (4%)
Russia	26	India (35%)	**China**	6	Russia (69%)
		China (15%)			France (13%)
		Algeria (14%)			Ukraine (10%)
Germany	7	Greece (10%)	**Pakistan**	5	China (50%)
		South Korea (10%)			US (27%)
		Spain (8%)			Sweden (5%)
France	6	Singapore (21%)	**South Korea**	5	USA (77%)
		China (12%)			German (15%)
		Morocco (10%)			France (5%)
China	5	Pakistan (55%)	**Singapore**	4	US (44%)
		Myanmar (8%)			France (30%)
		Bangladesh (7%)			German (11%)

Source: SIPRI fact sheet http://books.sipri.org/product_info?c_product_id=455.

weapons by private actors and even many states has created real security challenges for the entire world. New security challenges presented by global terrorism networks have resulted in a number of new security arrangements and the sharing of both technical resources and military personnel. NATO, for example, has expanded its mandate to address the wars in both Iraq and Afghanistan. The United States is funding some of these efforts and providing new technology, equipment, and training for its partners in the current war in Afghanistan.

The use of foreign policy sticks is not limited to leaders who have adopted the realist perspective on global politics. Liberals also recognize the importance of military tools of statecraft. Woodrow Wilson did not shy away from using America's military resources to help end World War I. However, he called for a collective security arrangement with the League of Nations. Wilson also supported arms control treaties and pushed for more rules of war. Even today, progressive-liberal states like Canada, the Netherlands, and Denmark are active members of NATO and have willingly deployed their armed forces in Iraq and Afghanistan. Many middle and small powers are active participants in peacekeeping forces in conflict regions around the world. Collective humanitarian interventions and peacekeeping are military tools that are becoming more important in areas where states have failed to provide basic security or are disintegrating. The United Nations has some seventeen current peacekeeping operations, eight in Africa alone.

A new form of warfare may present major challenges for both liberals and realists. Cyberwarfare, or an attack on a country's computer and information systems, could be aimed at causing an economic collapse. Russia used cyberattacks in Estonia and Georgia to weaken confidence in these governments and make their citizens and leaders feel vulnerable to outside forces. This form of warfare is likely to increase. China has used this form of warfare to attack computer systems in the United States, and Israel used a computer worm to disrupt Iran's nuclear program. Military resources are not much help here. How do you prevent this kind of attack and protect vital information networks? Most states are not well prepared for such an attack, and the perpetrators could be states, terrorist networks, or a single computer expert.

In addition to military inducements, states can employ economic sticks. This type of influence can include **economic sanctions**, boycotts, **arms embargoes**, and punitive tariffs. Sanctions are used to both alter domestic politics and influence the foreign policy behavior of a target state. In the war on terrorism, the United States froze bank and investment assets from Afghanistan and Iraq as well as several Islamic charity organizations. Blocking access to multilateral lending institutions such as the World Bank and investment restrictions have become major tools in attempts to influence state behavior at home and abroad. Economic sanctions can involve the buying and selling of large quantities of a target state's currency to manipulate its exchange rate and create an economic crisis. Additionally, restrictions on travel and business are often used to force change in a society.

The best example of an effective sanction effort was the global cultural, political, and economic boycott of South Africa during its apartheid regime. Currently, members of the UN Security Council are using sanctions to punish North Korea for its production and testing of nuclear weapons. Sanctions imposed on Iran for pursuing nuclear weapons seemed to have worked. The major powers are meeting with the leaders of Iran and there is a slight chance that Iran might abandon its potential nuclear weapons program. The US and the European Union have imposed sanctions on the Syrian government for its use of chemical weapons and its behavior in the civil war. They have also imposed sanctions on the Russian Government for its annexation of Crimea and its aggressive behavior toward Ukraine. Similarly, the United Nations has initiated sanctions against Iran for its refusal to submit to inspections by the International Atomic Energy Agency. Part of NATO's war against Libya involved the freezing of all the Libyan funds in foreign banks. Economic tools need not be all negative, however. States often use the promise of material assistance to reach a desired goal.

Carrots: Foreign Assistance

Most of the wealthy states in the international system are donor states, or states that give a significant amount of development assistance or aid to less wealthy or poor states. For donor states, development assistance is a means of pursuing foreign policy objectives. There are at least five forms of foreign assistance:

1. *Project aid* provides a grant or loan to a country or an NGO for a specific project.
2. *Program aid* is given to a government to create certain policy conditions in the recipient country, such as opening a market or supporting balance of payments.
3. *Technical assistance* provides a country with equipment or technicians in a given policy area.

4. *Humanitarian* or *disaster assistance* provides states funds for food, materials, medicine, and other basic supplies.
5. *Military* or *security aid* is often given to allies or partners in programs like the war on terrorism or to those participating in UN peacekeeping activities.

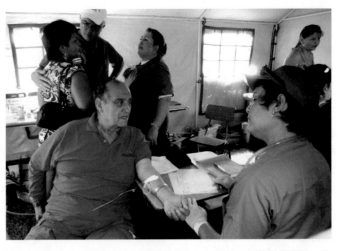

Twenty-six Cuban doctors set up a field hospital in central Chile to treat earthquake survivors. Cuban medical teams offer high-quality care to those in need all around the world. Why do you think the United States continues to restrict travel to and trade with Cuba? Could it be all about votes in Florida?

As we will discuss more fully in Chapter 13, states give aid for a variety of purposes, but most states tie their aid to national interests such as security, economic growth, or prestige. Food aid helps the hungry, but it also helps farmers in the donor state who sell their crops and cattle to the government. Even the most generous states use this economic tool to serve some of their own domestic interests. Assistance programs include the sharing of expertise and technology. Giving humanitarian assistance may also enhance a state's prestige and its image in the international system. Christine Ingebritsen (2006, 283) argues that the small countries of Scandinavia, consistently major donors, have played a pivotal role in promoting global social justice and strengthening norms of ethical behavior (see Chapter 10). These small and middle powers have used carrots such as development assistance, trade agreements, and other nonforce resources to encourage peaceful resolution of conflict, promote multilateralism, and work toward a more equitable distribution of global wealth. A typical Nordic aid program might include funding for public health and education, environmental protection, promotion of human rights and democracy, and family planning. The Nordic countries also give a high percentage of their aid to multilateral organizations and NGOs working in developing regions of the world (see Figure 5.1). About 40 percent of UNICEF's budget comes from Nordic countries, and organizations like Oxfam and Save the Children receive funds from Nordic governments.

Development assistance or aid programs in the United States are administered by the US Agency for International Development (USAID). Under the Clinton administration, the

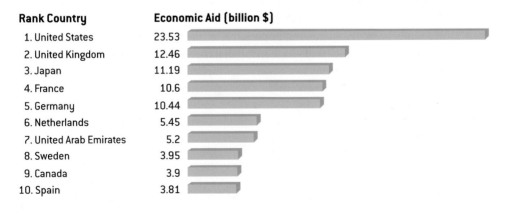

Rank Country	Economic Aid (billion $)
1. United States	23.53
2. United Kingdom	12.46
3. Japan	11.19
4. France	10.6
5. Germany	10.44
6. Netherlands	5.45
7. United Arab Emirates	5.2
8. Sweden	3.95
9. Canada	3.9
10. Spain	3.81

Figure 5.1 Top Ten Foreign Aid Donors.
Do you see a pattern among the countries on this list? What motivates these states to give such large amounts of aid?

number of USAID goals were trimmed from thirty to five. These reflected the neoliberal goals of the administration for the enlargement of democratic and capitalist states:

1. Provision of human relief
2. Stabilization of population growth
3. Promotion of democracy
4. Environmental protection
5. Economic growth

These goals changed slightly with the G. W. Bush administration. Namely, a focus was placed on preventing HIV/AIDS, and family planning programs were no longer supported.

Other economic tools include trade agreements, the provision of loans, and the sharing of development or trade experts. Countries give economic resources in two main methods: directly to another country, in what are called "bilateral agreements," or indirectly through global institutions like the World Bank, the International Monetary Fund (IMF), and a variety of regional development banks like the Asian Development Bank. World Bank aid in the developing world can finance a range of projects, such as rural electrification or creating an export-driven agricultural market.

Sermons: Diplomatic Messaging and the Use of the Media

Military and economic sticks address material interests. "Sermons" address ideal interests. These might include *demarches*, or simple warnings, directives, or position statements sent to governments as a form of moral suasion. A charismatic leader giving a speech to the world can be a powerful diplomatic tool. President Obama's speech on June 4, 2009, given in Cairo, Egypt, addressed a global audience and was a clear attempt to convince the Muslim world that the US policy toward Islam was going to change. Minutes after its completion, the US government had it on the Internet in several languages. We have yet to see the full impact of this particular speech will succeed; as a kind of public diplomacy, it is an effective use of modern media and global communications to serve political purposes.

Raymond Aron, a renowned international relations scholar, called diplomacy the art of convincing without the use of force. Will Rogers, a famous American author and public intellectual, offered a more colorful yet truthful definition: diplomacy is the art of saying "nice doggie" until you can find a stick. **Diplomacy** plays a critical role in the preservation of peace and world order. Many experts consider it a lost art undermined by advanced communications, summit meetings, the increasing importance of international and regional organizations, and the demands of a global media industry that is persistently looking for information and often exposing secret agreements. Traditional diplomatic historians assert that diplomacy performs four important functions:

1. Communication among actors
2. Negotiation
3. Participation in regional and international organizations
4. Promotion of trade and other economic interests

Diplomats today must deal with a host of new global challenges that require cooperation among state and nonstate actors. Diplomatic meetings aimed at addressing global challenges like climate change, terrorism, organized crime, human rights, and international investments are becoming major sources of power for countries with basic knowledge, scientific expertise, and the means to implement the policies. The role states play in

diplomacy The process by which international actors communicate as they seek to resolve conflicts without going to war and find solutions to complex global problems.

the development of global regimes (see Chapter 8) is an important source of power in this era of globalization. Small and middle powers tend to value the role of diplomacy and use some of their most qualified foreign policy experts in diplomatic roles.

Public diplomacy is fast becoming an important foreign policy tool. In the past, this form of diplomacy might have been called propaganda, but today, it involves telling the world about the positive characteristics of your society. These educational, cultural, and informational programs are also an important source of power. Countries can provide funds for educational exchanges of students, faculty, and diplomats. The US Fulbright Program, for example, sends students and scholars from the United States around the world and brings foreign scholars to the United States. International foundations can also provide this type of funding. One example is the Aga Khan International Scholarship Foundation, which provides scholarships each year for postgraduate studies to outstanding students from developing countries.

US vice president Joe Biden spoke in South Korea about the US rejection of China's self-declared "air defense identification zone" in the East China Sea. Biden reaffirmed the US commitment to allies like South Korea, Japan, and Taiwan. These countries and others in the region will likely come into conflict with China over this expanded air defense identification zone. China reserves the right to deny access to any aircraft.

Concerts, book tours, movies, and art exhibits are all part of a country's efforts to promote its values and cultural attributes. During the Cold War, the US Information Agency sponsored tours of jazz bands to the Soviet Union and other communist countries. Media sources are also ways to promote a state's interests and make a state attractive to others. For example, the BBC and the Voice of America provide global radio programs that attract listeners and learners across the world, and during the Cold War, Radio Moscow provided a Soviet perspective on news events.

Finally, in a world of nuclear weapons and internal wars that kill both civilians and soldiers, **coercive diplomacy** has become a valuable foreign policy tool because "it seeks to persuade an opponent to cease his aggression" rather than go to war (George 1991, 5). In 1990, the first Bush administration used a strategy of coercive diplomacy in an attempt to get Saddam Hussein to leave Kuwait. The Bush administration made a clear demand, or *ultimatum*, that the Iraqi government ignored. The administration then took a variety of steps that involved the buildup of forces, economic sanctions, and diplomatic maneuvers in the United Nations. This strategy of gradually turning the screw was aimed at getting Iraq to see how costly a war with the United States and a coalition of forces representing some thirty-six countries would be. In this case, coercive diplomacy failed because Iraq did not back down, and the US-led coalition destroyed the Iraqi military with the blessings of the United Nations and most of the world community.

Soft and Hard Power in Foreign Policy

One way to understand the methods of foreign policy making is to think of both carrots and sticks as **hard power** tools. However, these inducements and threats are only part of the diplomatic process in the international system. Harvard professor and former Clinton administration official Joseph Nye introduced the concept of **soft power**, or the ability to "shape the preferences of others" (2004, 5–15). Soft power, as Nye presented the concept, tries to co-opt people and countries rather than threaten or coerce them. Political leaders can use soft power to encourage cooperation and to shape what other states want in the international system. A country's culture and ideology are important sources of soft power.

public diplomacy The use of media, the Internet, and other cultural outlets to communicate the message of a state.

coercive diplomacy The use of diplomatic and military methods that force a state to concede to another state. These methods may include the threat of force and the mobilization of the military to gradually "turn the screw" but exclude the actual use of force. The implication is that war is the next step if diplomacy fails.

hard power The material threats and inducements leaders employ to achieve the goals of their state.

soft power The influence and authority deriving from the attraction that a country's political, social, and economic ideas, beliefs, and practices have for people living in other countries.

"Never forget Srebrenica" is the message on this poster as a Dutch activist participates in a 2007 memorial in The Hague to the victims of Europe's worst massacre since World War II. The failure of Dutch troops to protect Bosnian Muslims in the designated safe area of Srebrenica still haunts the people of the Netherlands, and this event shapes the foreign policy of the country today.

Nye asserts that the soft power of any country is based on three sources: (1) its culture, (2) its political values, and (3) its foreign policy. If a country's culture is attractive to others, it can be a source of power. Similarly, if a country's political values—like democracy and respect for human rights—are attractive to other citizens and other states, then that country can gain power and influence in the international system. Finally, a country with a moral foreign policy can also have power and influence in the international system. From this view, we see that the United States may have lost its international standing because of its use of torture and prisoner abuse in Iraq and secret prisons around the world; when the United States lost moral credibility, its foreign policy activities were more likely to be seen as unethical by most of the global community. Nye suggests that if a country promotes values that other states want, leadership will cost less.

Soft power is not merely the same as influence. After all, influence can also rest on the hard power of threats or payments. Soft power is more than just persuasion, or the ability to move people by arguments, though that is an important part of it. It is also the ability to attract, and attraction often leads to acquiescence. Simply put, in behavioral terms, soft power is *attractive power*.

Both hard- and soft-power tools will be an important part of any future leader's foreign policy doctrine and policy agenda. In this **nonpolar** world (Haas 2008), where no one state or group of states controls all power and authority, and where power and influence are distributed among a variety of state and nonstate actors, it will be harder to control these actors and even harder to build multilateral alliances to respond to global challenges. With no clear concentration of power in many policy areas, the number of threats and vulnerabilities is likely to increase, and states will need to work harder to maintain order and stability. Most experts predict that all states and transnational actors will need to combine resources to address the

nonpolar An international system in which power is not concentrated in a few states but is diffused among a variety of state and nonstate actors.

most significant global problems the world faces. The entire global effort aimed at addressing climate change, for example, will require major collective action. Globalization may not have changed enduring national interests such as security and prosperity, but it has certainly changed how states pursue these interests.

Foreign Policy Styles and Traditions

No examination of how foreign policy works would be complete without a discussion of various styles and traditions, as well as the various ways great powers, middle powers, and weak states may differ in their approaches. Analysts of foreign policy behavior often assert that factors such as the geographic size of a country, its resource base, and its population can determine the kind of foreign policy—or style—a country will undertake. A **foreign policy style** is often the result of how a country deals with other members of the international community. When this style continues over a long period of time, we call it a **foreign policy tradition**. The foreign policy style and tradition include a common set of public assumptions about the role of the state in the international system. A tradition includes national beliefs about how the world works and what leaders must do to secure their national interests. Styles and traditions promote different foreign policy strategies, and each suggests different sets of policy priorities. In this section, we discuss some aspects of foreign policy style and foreign policy tradition.

Great Powers, Middle Powers, and Small States

The foreign policy of all states is aimed at securing national interests and responding to the needs, values, and interests of their citizens. All states seek a role, or *niche*, in the international system. James Rosenau (1981) suggested that all states develop a strategy for adapting to the conditions created by the international system. Smaller states with limited resources and little capacity to influence other powers by unilateral actions are likely to select an acquiescent strategy. This strategy suggests they will adapt their interests to fit with the interests of larger and more powerful regional or global leaders. Consider, for example, the role of "client states" and alliances during the Cold War. These states followed the lead of the United States or Soviet Union and were rewarded with the promise of security and prosperity in the form of aid, military assistance, and trade agreements.

States that were once global leaders and even hegemonic powers at times seek policies aimed at preserving their power and status in the international system. This preservative strategy is employed by countries like the United Kingdom and France. Preservative policies include taking a leadership role in international and regional organizations, identifying issues that need attention, and taking the lead in responding to these challenges. The United Kingdom's efforts to lead the debt-relief campaign and France's role in the Middle East peace talks are examples of this behavior.

The most powerful states seek to retain and possibly increase their power and authority by adapting a **promotive foreign policy**. The United States and the Soviet Union promoted their views, values, and interests after World War II as they competed for the hearts and minds of all citizens around the globe. Each superpower created an alliance structure that divided the world into two armed camps with the capacity to destroy the world as we know it. After the Cold War, the US leaders talked about establishing a new world order that served the interests of the United States and its allies. Some experts talked about the unipolar moment, a time when the United States could promote its values, traditions, and interests to create a peaceful and prosperous world.

foreign policy style Often shaped by a state's political culture, history, and traditions, this describes how a country deals with other states and how it approaches any decision-making situation. For example, does it act unilaterally or multilaterally? Does it seek consensus on an agreement or does it go with majority rule?

foreign policy tradition A tradition that includes national beliefs about how the world works and a list of national interests and priorities based on these beliefs. It also refers to past actions or significant historical events that act as analogs and give guidance to leaders about what strategy would best secure their national interests.

WHAT'S YOUR WORLDVIEW

Do you think power gives rise to responsibility? Should powerful states be expected to right the world's wrongs and solve the world's problems?

promotive foreign policy A foreign policy that promotes the values and interests of a state and seeks to create an international system based on these values.

THEORY IN PRACTICE

The Impact of Globalization on Different Kinds of States

The Asian economic crisis of 1997 highlights states' different capacities for responding to globalization. Even though all states in the region were affected by the crisis, their responses suggested that some enjoyed more choice or sovereignty than others. Indonesia, Thailand, and Korea turned to the International Monetary Fund for assistance, which was conditional on several policies mostly defined by the IMF, itself in Washington, D.C. Malaysia, meanwhile, formulated its own strategy for adjustment and imposed policies such as capital controls, which Washington greatly disapproved of. Although globalists and skeptics alike treat all states as equal in their arguments about globalization, we should question whether this equality is true. (Globalists think that globalization is changing the world and undermining the authority of states, whereas skeptics still see the state as the primary actor in global politics and believe the state can and will manage the processes of globalization.)

One way to think about the impact of globalization is to distinguish between strong states and weak states. At the extreme end, strong states shape the rules and institutions that have made a global economy possible. We have already seen the way US policies shaped the creation, implementation, and breakdown of the Bretton Woods system. A more general description of strong states is that they can control—to some degree—the nature and speed of their integration into the world economy. Into this category we might place not only relatively strong industrialized countries but also developing countries such as Brazil, Malaysia, China, Iraq, and Iran. In all of these cases, globalization is having a powerful effect, as evidenced by the restructuring of national and private industries in industrialized countries, the past decade of economic liberalization in Brazil, and, in a radically different way, through international coercive interventions in Iraq. Yet, at the same time, in each of these countries, there are high protective barriers in important sectors of the economy and serious debates about capital controls and the regulation of international capital. The capacity of these countries to control their integration into the world economy is doubtless related to their size, resources, geostrategic advantages, and economic strength. However, interestingly, it also seems related to their national ideology and the domestic power of the state. One characteristic that all strong states have in common is that they guard with equal ferocity their independence in economic policy, foreign policy, human rights, and security issues.

Weak states, by contrast, suffer from a lack of choice in their international economic relations. They have little or no influence in the creation and enforcement of rules in the system, and they have exercised little control over their own integration into the world economy. For example, in the aftermath of the debt crisis of the 1980s, many weak states opened up their economies, liberalized, and deregulated, more as a result of coercive liberalization than of a democratic policy choice. In the 1990s, this continued with what an international economist called "forced harmonization," whereby, for instance, in the case of trade negotiations on intellectual property, developing countries were coerced into an agreement that transferred "billions of dollars' worth of monopoly profits from poor countries to rich countries under

India has become a major economic power, taking advantage of the widening and deepening of globalization. The increase in global trade and the growth of technological industries and services have not touched all citizens. In Mumbai, a plane flies over the filthy Mithi River, which is flanked by slums.

Continued

the guise of protecting the property rights of inventors" (Rodrik 1999).

Distinguishing among states according to their capacity to shape and respond to globalization is vital in analyzing the impact on the global economy. The example of the collapse of the international financial system in late 2008 demonstrates that some states, in particular the United States, are rule makers in the world economy, whereas less powerful states are rule *takers*.

For Discussion

1. Based on this situation, do you think globalization is uneven or predatory, or are the benefits shared equally? Why?
2. In the very recent economic crisis, have regional organizations like the European Union or global organizations like the International Monetary Fund been able to respond effectively? Explain.
3. Our international system is based on nation-states, but to our global economy, borders and sovereignty are almost meaningless. Do we need more effective global regimes? Why or why not?

There are always states that believe the existing international system is unfair, oppressive, violent, and alienating. These states seek to transform the international system by promoting an **intransigent foreign policy**. They do not accept the rules of the game and mobilize their resources to challenge the great powers in the international system. During the 1960s and 1970s, leaders of the Nonaligned Movement (NAM)—namely, Cuba, Pakistan, India, and Indonesia—pushed intransigent policy programs challenging the dominant rules of the game. Today, North Korea and Iran are challenging great-power rules—namely, the rules that restrict the number of states with nuclear weapons.

To a certain extent, these four **adaptation strategies** describe the foreign policies of states today. States adapt to circumstances and events and the structure of the system. Some international relations theorists propose that the choice from among these strategies is linked to a given country's size or influence in the international system. This assertion has been, at times, the center of a significant debate among academics. Although it is clear that countries choose a foreign policy strategy because of their resources and needs, it is not always the case that size determines a particular policy option. A brief overview of what we might expect from great, middle, and small powers follows. States are constantly adapting to changes in the international system and to the domestic factors that might limit a state's ability to act in the system or, conversely, provide opportunities for more active participation.

intransigent foreign policy A foreign policy that challenges the rules established by the great powers or rule-making states.

adaptation strategies Changes in foreign policy behavior in reaction to changes in the international system or international events and adjusting national goals to conform to the effects of events external to that state.

Great-Power Foreign Policy

Most of the research about **great-power** politics and foreign policy is shaped by traditional realist assumptions about world politics and as a result tends to ignore cases that contradict the academic goal of a parsimonious theory. It is also, as we learned in Chapter 3, an arguably bleak perspective because it sees enemies everywhere. For example, John Mearsheimer (2001, 29–32), an influential realist scholar, contends that great powers always seek to maximize their share of world power, and all great powers seek hegemony in the international system.

For all great powers, survival is the primary goal. These states all think strategically about how to survive in a system where all states are potential threats. More specifically, the goals of great powers include advancing the economic and political interests of their people and maintaining the rules and institutions in the international system that serve their interests. The United States and its allies created the primary institutions of global governance after World War II. The only significant challenge to that system was advanced by the Soviet Union. Some have called the Cold War a war about whose rule book

great power A state that has the political, economic, and military resources to shape the world beyond its borders. In most cases, such a state has the will and capacity to define the rules of the international system.

would be followed. With the end of the Cold War, there is now only one rule book, and the battle is over which rules to apply and how to apply them. Countries invited to the G-8 and G-20 meetings are all great global powers and great regional powers. They meet once a year to debate best ways to respond to economic crises, humanitarian challenges and security issues, and what they decide in these areas will affect the entire world.

Mistrust and uncertainty force states to act always in accordance with their own self-interest. Mearsheimer (2001, 33) suggests that great powers act "selfishly in a self-help world." This means the foreign policies of great powers are focused on gaining power and authority in the military world and beyond. Great powers seek to lead in all policy sectors. The dominant currency is military power, and all great powers must respond to the **security dilemma**. Without any form of central authority in the international system, states must seek security through military power and security alliances. Since all states are potential threats, foreign policy for great powers might be described as a "ceaseless competition" for security, power, and authority in all policy sectors.

Middle-Power Foreign Policy

Relying again on realist assumptions and definitions, a scholar might focus on national attributes such as land area, resource base, population, and military capabilities to distinguish **middle powers** from small or weak states and great powers. However, in a world where power and influence are no longer solely defined in terms of physical attributes and military strength, a state's behavior or experience in various policy situations may provide better insights into how that state sees itself and how others see its role in the international system. Most middle powers are liberal states with social democratic political systems and economies based on trade. This means their survival and prosperity depend on global stability and order. These states seek incremental reform by extending a liberal world order, which they see as the most effective way to achieve both human and national security. Canada, Australia, and the Nordic countries are great examples of active middle powers.

In describing the importance of a "behavioral" measure of middle powers, Cooper, Higgott, and Nossal (1993) describe their attributes as follows:

A. *Catalysts*: States that provide resources and expertise to take leadership roles in global initiatives.
B. *Facilitators*: States that play active roles in setting agendas in global policy discussions and building coalitions for collaborative responses.
C. *Managers*: Middle powers that support institution building at the international level and encourage support for existing international organizations and multinational activities.

The same authors quote Gareth Evans, a former Australian minister for foreign affairs and trade, in describing a concept called **niche diplomacy**. This form of middle-power activism "involves concentrating resources in specific areas best able to generate returns worth having, rather than trying to cover the field" (Cooper et al. 1993, 25–26).

The middle powers, because of their position and past roles in international affairs, have very distinctive interests in the future order. Middle powers are activists in

security dilemma In an anarchic international system, one with no common central power, when one state seeks to improve its security, it creates insecurity in other states.

middle powers These states, because of their position and past roles in international affairs, have very distinctive interests in world order. Middle powers are activists in international and regional forums, and they are confirmed multilateralists in most issue areas.

niche diplomacy Every state has its national interests and its areas of comparative advantage over other international actors. This is its area of expertise and where it has the greatest interest. Hence, this is where the state concentrates its foreign policy resources.

No good deed goes unpunished! It is common for middle powers to see themselves as problem solvers. Norway has taken the lead in trying to end conflicts in the Middle East with the Oslo Accords and in the Sri Lankan civil war. In Sri Lanka in 2009, pro-government forces demonstrate against the Norwegians for not punishing pro-Tamil demonstrators.

international and regional forums, and they are confirmed multilateralists in most issue areas. They actively support an equitable and pluralistic rule-based system. They are, for the most part, trading states and thus favor a relatively open and stable world market. Since stability is so important to them, most middle powers see themselves as global problem solvers, mediators, and moderators in international disputes (Holbraad 1984; Wood 1998). Middle powers usually play a leadership role in regional organizations (e.g., the European Union) and in functionally specific institutions such as the World Health Organization (WHO) and the Development Assistance Committee (DAC) of the Organisation of Economic Co-operation and Development (OECD).

Middle powers like Canada play an important role in humanitarian activities across the world. As a leader of the human security movement, Canada works frequently with NGOs to respond to natural disasters and long-term human crises. Here, Canadian Armed Forces help an NGO, *Action Against Hunger,* deliver food aid in the Philippines after the November 2013 typhoon.

A third view of middle powers places an emphasis on the **normative orientation** of this group of states. Although subject to much criticism, the image of middle powers as potentially wiser and more virtuous than other states is usually promoted by national leaders and progressive interest groups to gain domestic support for international activism and to enhance the reputation of their states in the international community. This image of global moral leaders, bridging the gap between rich and poor communities, fits well with the egalitarian social democratic values of most Western middle powers. Robert Cox (1989, 834–835) argues that the traditional normative aims of middle powers—namely, greater social equity and a call for more diffusion of power in the system—might give them more leverage as principled problem solvers in continuing economic and political challenges faced by all states in the system today.

normative orientation In foreign policy, promoting certain norms and values and being prescriptive in one's foreign policy goals.

The middle powers may play a critical role as the catalysts of problem-solving initiatives or the managers of regimes initiated by greater powers with less interest for internationalism and little domestic support for egalitarian goals and values.

Small-State Foreign Policy

Researchers agree that small states are defined by a small land mass, GNP, and population. In addition, they usually do not have large military forces or the resources to have a significant impact on global politics. However, if they act in concert with other states, it is possible for small states to have an impact on the system. For example, the like-minded states that played a pivotal role in the formation of the International Criminal Court (ICC) included a coalition of small and middle powers.

Small states can also identify a niche and develop expertise in a given policy area. Most wealthy small states, like Belgium or New Zealand, often focus their foreign policy on trade and economic issues. They will also participate in regional organizations and at times take leadership roles in crisis situations. New Zealand, along with Australia and the island state of Vanuatu, took the lead to create a nuclear-free zone in the Pacific in 1985. The Reagan administration's response to this action demonstrates the limits to small-state actions: when the New Zealand Labour government banned nuclear-capable US Navy ships from its harbors, the United States terminated security cooperation with the country. Belgium is one of the most active members of the European Union, NATO, and every other regional and international organization. Because of its colonial past, it has worked with many African states in development and peacekeeping activities.

It should be stated that with the end of the Cold War and the intensity of forces of globalization, there has been a change in the valuation of states' capacities and their potential influence in the international system. After all, military power may not be as important as policy expertise or technology in this new world where new security challenges include climate change, pandemics, poverty, and cyberwarfare. Foreign policy in a **nonpolar world** (i.e., power is diffused and held by a variety of state and nonstate actors) is less constrained by the structure of the system and allows for more flexibility and independence. Globalization has also increased the number of opportunities for citizen participation, and technology like the Internet makes it much easier to organize for a specific cause or policy position and to promote a small state's national interest in the global community.

nonpolar world A world in which there are many power centers, and many of them are not nation-states. Power is diffused and in many hands in many policy areas.

Some small states have taken on the role of norm entrepreneurs in the international system. Christine Ingebritsen et al. (2006, 275) describes this role:

> Thus, Scandinavia, a group of militarily weak, economically dependent small states, pursues "social power" by acting as a norm entrepreneur in the international community. In three policy areas (the environment, international security, and global welfare), Scandinavia has acted to promote a particular view of the good society.

Other attributes of small-state foreign policy include the following (Henderson et al. 1980, 3–5):

- Most small states have limited financial and human resources and thus have to decide carefully when and where to participate. Generally, this means a limited global role and a focus on their geographic region and the interests of their own citizens.
- With limited resources (their citizens), most small states focus on economic and trade issues.
- Small states generally take an active role in regional and international organizations. Multilateralism is a preferred strategy, and small states consider it the best way to secure their interests.
- Small states can play critical roles in alliances and in global policy regimes. Many of these states have resources and expertise, and they seek roles as global problem solvers in policy areas of importance to their domestic population.

A UN resolution sponsored by the French government authorized an increase in French and African Union troops attempting to prevent further violence between Christian and Muslim groups in the Central African Republic. The entire population is suffering from the violence. Fragile or failed states may present the biggest foreign policy challenges for global institutions like the UN and for the major powers.

As the space between domestic and foreign policy sectors blurs or even disappears, domestic politics and the interests of citizens play a greater role in shaping foreign policy. In both small and middle powers, what citizens expect from states at home has a significant influence on how these states behave internationally.

Conclusion

In this chapter, we provided an overview of the primary issues and actors in the foreign policy process. We saw that many variables shape the world of diplomacy in the contemporary international system: material needs, ideas, and people themselves. The rational-actor model offers one way to understand the policy-making process. We also considered different styles and traditions in foreign policy. In the following chapters, we will turn to specific topics that comprise the critical challenges in the international system; for example, we will see how globalization is undermining the autonomy of the nation-state. International and regional organizations like the United Nations and the European Union, nongovernmental organizations (NGOs), and multinational corporations are each eroding the nation-state's power; they influence some of the core policy areas that were once the sole responsibility of nation-states. This trend is an important factor shaping relations in the contemporary world, as we will examine in depth in the next chapters.

CONTRIBUTOR TO CHAPTER 5: Steven L. Lamy.

REVIEW QUESTIONS

1. Why has nationalism spread across the world in the last two centuries?
2. How has the rise of the modern state shaped the development of nationalism?
3. In what ways do personal characteristics affect outcomes in the rational-actor model?
4. What are the four levels of analysis? How are they used to explain the behavior of states?
5. How do bureaucracies influence the foreign policy process?
6. Do small states have any power and influence in the international system?
7. "Contemporary globalization erodes nation-state sovereignty but does *not* undermine nationalism." Discuss.
8. Who are the actors in creating foreign policy? What are the phases?
9. What is a foreign policy doctrine?
10. Do you think the foreign policy process is shifting away from the state?

FURTHER READING

Goldstein, J., and Keohane, R. (1993), *Ideas and Foreign Policy. Beliefs, Institutions and Political Change* (Ithaca, N.Y.: Cornell University Press). A collection of essays that help us understand the importance of worldviews, causal beliefs, and principled beliefs in shaping foreign policy.

Henderson, J., Jackson, K., and Kennaway, R. (1980), *Beyond New Zealand: The Foreign Policy of a Small State* (Auckland, NZ: Methuen). A case study of the foreign policy of a small state that provides useful ideas that apply to other small states.

Hill, C. (2003), *The Changing Politics of Foreign Policy* (Houndmills, Basingstoke: Palgrave Macmillan). Excellent review of the analytic and theoretical issues in the field of foreign policy analysis.

Hudson, V. (2007), *Foreign Policy Analysis: Classic and Contemporary Theory* (Lanham, Md.: Rowman & Littlefield). One of the few texts that reviews the history of foreign policy analysis and also reviews key research that is framed by levels of analysis.

Ingebritsen, C., Neumann, I., Gstöhl, S., and Beyer, J. (2006), *Small States in International Relations* (Seattle: University of Washington Press). A recent study of small states, primarily the Nordic states, that focuses on their role as norm entrepreneurs in the post–Cold War world.

Johansen, R. C. (1980), *The National Interest and the Human Interest* (Princeton, N.J.: Princeton University Press). An analysis of US foreign policy decision making in four cases

from the mainstream realist view that are compared with a more utopian World Order Models Project view of the same issues. It is Machiavelli versus Kant.

Mead, W. R. (2001), *Special Providence: American Foreign Policy and How It Changed the World* (New York: Alfred A. Knopf). Excellent study of the history of US foreign policy traditions and the four traditions that shape debates and policies.

Mearsheimer, J. J. (2001), *The Tragedy of Great Power Politics* (New York: W. W. Norton). A study of great powers in the post–Cold War world written by one of the leading realist thinkers.

Morgenthau, H. J. (1962), *Politics Among Nations* (New York: Alfred A, Knopf). The most important modern realist text that shaped US foreign policy after World War II and maybe the most influential text in shaping world politics.

Rosenau, J. N. (1980), *The Scientific Study of Foreign Policy* (London: Nichols). An early study that helped shape the study of foreign policy analysis.

Slaughter, A.-M., Jentleson, B., Daalder, I., et al. (July 2008), *Strategic Leadership: Framework for a Twenty-First-Century National Security Strategy* (Washington, D.C.: Center for a New American Security). The game plan for the Obama administration's foreign policy that was written by some of the most prominent liberal internationalist thinkers in the United States.

INTERNET RESOURCES

Most state members of the international community have official websites. Here is a sample:

Australian Ministry of Foreign Affairs
http://www.dfat.gov.au/

Chinese Ministry of Foreign Affairs
http://www.fmprc.gov.cn/eng/default.htm

French Ministry of Foreign Affairs
http://www.diplomatie.gouv.fr/en/

Indian Ministry of External Affairs
http://meaindia.nic.in/

Japanese Ministry of Foreign Affairs
http://www.mofa.go.jp/

New Zealand Ministry of Foreign Affairs and Trade
http://www.mfat.govt.nz/

Nigerian Ministry of Foreign Affairs
www.mfa.gov.ng

Norwegian Ministry of Foreign Affairs
http://www.regjeringen.no/en/dep/

Saudi Arabian Ministry of Foreign Affairs
http://www.mofa.gov.sa/

(Please note that most countries have official websites with English language pages.)

Brookings Institution
http://www.brookings.edu

The Brookings Institution is a nonprofit public policy organization based in Washington, D.C. Their mission is to conduct high-quality, independent research and, based on that research, to provide innovative, practical recommendations that strengthen American democracy, foster the economic and social welfare, security and opportunity of all Americans, and secure a more open, safe, prosperous, and cooperative international system.

Council on Foreign Relations (CFR)
www.cfr.org

The website of the Council on Foreign Relations (CFR) is designed to be an online resource for everyone in these turbulent times who wants to learn more about the complex international issues challenging policy makers and citizens alike.

The Fund for Peace
http://www.fundforpeace.org

This independent, nonpartisan research and educational organization works to prevent war and alleviate the conditions that cause conflict. The organization promotes sustainable security through research, training and education, engagement of civil society, bridging bridges across diverse sectors, and developing innovative technologies and tools for policy makers. This site has a failed-state index and other pertinent info.

International Coalition for the Responsibility to Protect
www.responsibilitytoprotect.org/

The Responsibility to Protect (RtoP or R2P) is a new international security and human rights norm to address the international community's failure to prevent and stop genocides, war crimes, ethnic cleansing, and crimes against humanity.

Carnegie Council: "The Fear: Robert Mugabe and the Martyrdom of Zimbabwe"—Peter Godwin
http://www.carnegiecouncil.org/resources/audio/data/000630

Peter Godwin, a native of Zimbabwe (Rhodesia), discusses his states evolution and present life under Robert Mugabe.

Carnegie Council: "The End of Arrogance: America in the Global Competition of Ideas"—Bruce W. Jentleson
http://www.carnegiecouncil.org/resources/video/data/000373

In the midst of global power shifts, Jentleson explores how the United States should shift its foreign policy to cope with the changing global landscape.

TED Talk: David Brooks: "The Social Animal"
http://www.ted.com/talks/david_brooks_the_social_animal.html

David Brooks explores how we act and why; his discussion can be extended to levels of analysis and decision making.

TED Talk: Joseph Nye: "Global Power Shifts"
http://www.ted.com/talks/joseph_nye_on_global_power_shifts.html

Nye explores his proposed alternative to traditional hard power (military)—soft power. With global power shifts occurring, Nye suggests that maybe the perfect balance between hard and soft power is "smart power."

TED Talk: Shashi Tharoor: "Why Nation's Should Pursue 'Soft' Power"
http://www.ted.com/talks/shashi_tharoor.html

Tharoor sees India's greatest possible contribution through "the power of example" or "soft" power; increasingly, the world will see the soft-power battle between Bollywood and Hollywood. "It's not the side with the bigger army, it's the one with the better story."

For more information, quizzes, case studies and other study tools, please visit us at **www.oup.com/us/lamy**

THINKING ABOUT GLOBAL POLITICS

Designing a New World Order

BACKGROUND

The significant changes in the political and economic landscape in Europe and the former Soviet Union, the unprecedented collective response to Iraqi aggression in Kuwait, and the puzzling failure of the major powers to respond effectively to aggression in Somalia, Rwanda, and the former Yugoslavia suggest that it may be time for the rule-making actors in the international system to establish a new set of standards and rules of behavior in a new world order. This new system of explicit and implicit rules and structures will replace the East-West Cold War "bipolarity," or the "balance of nuclear terror." Many leaders, including former presidents the first Bush and Clinton, have frequently invoked the concept of "new world order" as a justification for foreign policy decisions. However, there does not seem to be any consensus in the United States or in other nation-states about the structure of this new world order. Some world leaders have called for a series of discussions about the future of world politics in an effort to prevent US hegemony and avoid drifting toward a new era of competition and anarchy. They want to know their role in this new system. Who will be the new rule makers? How will order be maintained? What are the rules? What are the new security challenges? These are some of the questions leaders are asking.

EXPECTATIONS

In this small-group discussion exercise, you will explore various world-order models, review how changes in the structure of the system might influence or shape foreign policies of states, and then make a case for a new US global strategy and a new world order.

PROCEDURE

1. Review the options presented in the "World-Order Models" section below. You may want to review historical periods when these systems were in operation (not all systems of order presented on this sheet have been implemented).
2. With reference to a traditional realist's three system-level challenges and constraints—order, anarchy, and the security dilemma—which world-order system would you find most effective for US interests? What about the interests of other major powers (e.g., Japan, Germany, Russia, and Great Britain)? What about the concerns of developing states or the South?
3. Discuss the nature of foreign policy under each system structure. For example, how would the foreign policy of major, middle, and small powers be influenced if the system moved from bipolarity to hegemony? Review each possible system structure and its influence on foreign policy.

WORLD-ORDER MODELS

One-Country Rule: One country governs the rest of the world, controlling all resources, industry, and trade. The superpower determines the national interest of all other nations and the interest of the world; all are defined in terms of the superpower's interests.

Bipolar: Two superpowers have divided the world. Each controls a large group of countries and controls the resources, industry, and trade within its bloc. Relations between the two blocs are determined by the superpowers to serve their own interests.

Polycentrism: Each country has its own government and controls its own resources, industry, and trade. There are no international organizations or alliances; every country operates in its own interest.

Regionalism: Countries located in the same part of the world have formed regional governments that control resources, industry, and trade within each region. Relations between regions are governed by regional interests.

World Law: All nations of the world have established a world authority that makes laws against international violence and has agencies to enforce these laws, keep the peace, and resolve conflicts. Individual nations control their own resources, industry, internal security, and trade. The world authority acts only to prevent the use of violence in relations between nations.

Some Other Order: Draw your own model of an international system. Specify how international relations, trade, and security are handled in your model. Why is your model better than any of the other models?

DISCUSSION AND FOLLOW-UP

If time permits, in small groups, discuss what you think will be the major issues facing the world's leaders in the next ten years. Then try to reach consensus on a system structure (i.e., world-order model) that you feel will create an international environment that will enable states to constructively and effectively respond to these issues.

6 | Global and Regional Governance

Den Norske Nobelkomite
har overensstemmende med
reglene i det av
ALFRED NOBEL
den 27 november 1895
opprettede testamente tildelt
Barack H. Obama
Nobels Fredspris
for 2009

Oslo 10 desember 2009

Only in a universal union of states can the property and rights of states become settled and a true state of peace come into being.

—*Immanuel Kant*

This is an ungoverned world. The UN has no autonomous power; it is what its members want it to be, and usually its members don't want it to be anything much . . . When it is said that it is better if things are done multilaterally, too often this means accepting the lowest common denominator.

—*Stanley Hoffmann*

In his first address to the leaders of all the member states of the United Nations, President Barack Obama called for a real change in global politics and a renewal of commitment to multilateralism, international organizations, and the rule of law. President Obama also promised that the United States would lead a new era of global engagement and collective action. He referred to the founders of the United Nations, who in 1945 believed that the world could solve the most pressing problems only by working together. Dedicated to preventing another world war, the United Nations was built on the principle that peace could be achieved only with the cooperative efforts of the entire world. It is the only international organization with a global mandate.

President Obama outlined a policy agenda for global action that would be led by the United Nations and all of its members. This four-pillar agenda focused on the most critical issues that threaten peace and stability in the world today.

- His first pillar called for the end of nuclear proliferation and the prevention of a nuclear arms race. He mentioned the importance of the Nuclear Nonproliferation Treaty and of the United Nations and the International Atomic Energy Agency (IAEA).
- The second pillar focused on the pursuit of peace and the end of violence and terrorism in the world. Here the president talked about the importance of UN peacekeeping and peace enforcement.
- The third pillar emphasized the importance of global cooperation to clean up the environment and preserve the planet. International and regional organizations will play a critical role in formulating treaties and rules that protect the environment.

In December 2009, President Barack Obama received the Nobel Peace Prize not for his past actions but for his promises to change the tone and direction of US foreign policy. Has he fulfilled the promises made in his Nobel acceptance speech?

- Finally, President Obama's fourth pillar addressed the economic crisis that has hurt people in both rich and poor states. The World Health Organization and the UN Development Programme, as well as the World Trade Organization, the International Monetary Fund, and the World Bank, will need to work with regional organizations like the European Union, the Asian Development Bank, and the African Union to increase economic growth and find ways to address global poverty.

President Obama, like other world leaders, is calling for global engagement and acknowledging the necessity of working together through international organizations in this age of globalized challenges. Most world leaders embrace the idea that by following the concept of rule of law and by working through international organizations, it is possible to create a safer world order.

Introduction

Leaders in all countries face the challenge of managing the processes of globalization. States seek to create international institutions and laws that enable them to secure their national interests in a more globalized society. **Global governance** describes the formal and informal processes and institutions that guide and control the activities of both state and nonstate actors in the international system; global governance does not mean the creation of a world government. After all, this governance is not always led by states, nor is it always led by international organizations that are created by states. Indeed, multinational corporations and even nongovernmental organizations (NGOs) create rules and regulations to govern behavior in some policy areas. For example, banks will set up informal rules for exchanging currencies, and NGOs have set up ethical rules for fundraising and intervention in crisis regions. As demonstrated by the work of Elinor Ostrom, 2009 Nobel Prize winner in economics, sometimes private, nongovernmental groups can do a better job of creating rules for governing a shared resource. In this case, the state is the primary actor but not the only one in global governance. (In Chapter 7, we will discuss transnational and nongovernmental actors further.)

In this complex and increasingly global system, states are working with international and regional organizations like the United Nations and the European Union and with nonstate actors like Shell, Nike, Oxfam, Save the Children, and Amnesty International through diplomacy, international law, and regimes or international governing arrangements to solve common regional and global problems. Scholar Cary Coglianese suggests that international organizations and international law are critical in responding to three types of problems (2000, 299–301):

1. Coordinating global linkages: In this area, rules and laws are critical for managing the exchanges of information, products, services, money, and finance, and even for managing collective responses to criminal activity.
2. Responding to common problems: The global community faces common problems like global warming, poverty, human rights abuses, refugees, and pandemics, all of which require some form of coordination and collective policy response.
3. Protecting core values: Institutions and laws are essential for protecting and promoting core values like equality, liberty, democracy, and justice across the world.

The problems just listed and others increase with globalization. States will undoubtedly become more dependent on international and regional institutions like the United Nations or the African Union to promote international and regional cooperation in these

global governance The regulation and coordination of transnational issue areas by nation-states, international and regional organizations, and private agencies through the establishment of international regimes. These regimes may focus on problem solving or the simple enforcement of rules and regulations.

critical areas. The global system is a legal order with strong enforcement mechanisms and institutions capable of coordinating responses to global crises. The legal effectiveness and problem-solving success depend on voluntary compliance by both state and nonstate actors. If the laws, regimes, and institutions are considered fair and legitimate by global actors, compliance will be high and the processes of globalization will be more effectively managed. In addition, states adhere to laws because of the principle of reciprocity, or the notion that if a state agrees to abide by the rulings of regional or international organizations or of other states, then others will do the same. Here we mean **international laws**, or the body of legal standards, procedures, and institutions that govern the interactions of sovereign states. **Regimes** are governing arrangements that guide states as well as transnational actors and institutions (described in detail in the next section); they are sets of rules, norms, and practices that shape the behavior of all actors in a given issue area.

With the world trapped in a seemingly endless economic crisis, French lawyer and financial expert Christine Lagarde took over as managing director of the International Monetary Fund in 2011. How important are global institutions as we search for solutions to this crisis?

international law The formal rules of conduct that states acknowledge or contract between themselves.

regime A set of implicit or explicit principles, norms, rules, and decision-making procedures around which actors' expectations converge in a given area of international relations. Often simply defined as a governing arrangement in a regional or global policy area.

Regionalism has become a pervasive feature of international affairs. According to the World Trade Organization (WTO), by July 2005, only one WTO member—Mongolia—was not party to any regional trade agreement, and a total of 489 such agreements had been ratified. Regional peacekeeping forces have become active in some parts of the world. Since the 1970s, regionalism has become one of the forces challenging the traditional centrality of states in international relations.

That challenge comes from two directions. The word *region* and its derivatives denote one distinguishable part of some larger geographic area. Yet the term is used in different ways. On the one hand, regions are territories within a state, occasionally crossing state borders. On the other, regions are particular areas of the world, covering a number of different sovereign states. We will focus on this latter description of regionalism in our discussion.

In this chapter, we discuss three linked topics. First, we introduce the basics of international law that provide a framework for the interactions of states in global politics. Next we turn to the United Nations, the largest international organization with a mandate to prevent world wars and protect human rights. In the final section, we discuss the concept of regional integration with a focus on the European Union, the most successful and comprehensive regional organization. We will also briefly discuss the African Union and the Organization of American States.

After reading and discussing this chapter, you will have an understanding of how international law has developed as an important institution in global politics and how it shapes the behavior of all actors in the system. You will explore the UN system in detail and have a better idea of how the various branches of the United Nations contribute to global governance. Finally, you will be introduced to several regional organizations, and you will review the development of the European Union and its integration process.

International Law

In this section, we consider the practice of modern international law and the debates surrounding its nature and efficacy. For our purposes, there is one central question: What is the relationship between international law and international politics? If the power and interests of states are what matters, as we discussed in Chapter 5, then international law is either a servant of the powerful or an irrelevant curiosity. And yet, if international law does *not* matter, then why do states and other actors devote so much effort to negotiating new legal regimes and augmenting existing ones? Why does so much international debate revolve around the legality of state behavior, around the applicability of legal rules, and around the legal obligations incumbent on states? And why is compliance with international law so high, even by domestic standards? There seems to be a paradox at work.

Our starting point, therefore, should be made clear: international law is best understood as a core international institution—a set of norms, rules, and practices created by states and other actors to facilitate diverse social goals from order and coexistence to justice and human development. It is, however, an institution with distinctive historical roots, and understanding these roots is essential to grasping its unique institutional features.

International Order and Institutions

Realists portray international relations as a struggle for power, a realm in which states are "continuously preparing for, actively involved in, or recovering from organized violence in the form of war" (Morgenthau 1985, 52). Although war has certainly been a recurrent feature of international life, it is a crude and deeply dysfunctional way for states to ensure their security or realize their interests. Because of this, states have devoted as much, if not more, effort to liberating themselves from the condition of war than to embroiling themselves in violent conflict. Creating some modicum of international order has been an abiding common interest of most states most of the time (Bull 1977, 8).

To achieve international order, states have created international institutions. People often confuse institutions and organizations, incorrectly using the two terms interchangeably. **International institutions** are commonly defined as complexes of norms, rules, and practices that "prescribe behavioral roles, constrain activity, and shape expectations" (Keohane 1989a, 3; see Table 6.1). International law is an international institution. **International organizations**, like the United Nations, are physical entities that have staffs, head offices, and letterheads. International institutions can exist without any organizational structure; the 1997 Ottawa Convention banning landmines is an institution, but there is no landmines head office. Many institutions have organizational dimensions, though. The World Trade Organization (formerly the General Agreement on Tariffs and Trade) is an institution with a very strong organizational structure. While institutions can exist without an organizational dimension, international organizations cannot exist without an institutional framework, as their very existence presupposes a prior set of norms, rules, and principles that empower them to act and which they are charged to uphold. If states had never negotiated the Charter of the United Nations, the organization could not exist, let alone function.

In modern international society, states have created three levels of institutions. There are deep constitutional institutions, such as the principle of sovereignty, which define the terms of legitimate statehood. Without the institution of sovereignty, the world of independent states and the international politics it engenders would not exist. States have also created fundamental institutions, like international law and **multilateralism** (three or more states working together), which provide the basic rules and practices that shape how states solve cooperation and coordination problems. These are the institutional norms, techniques, and structures that states and other actors invoke and employ when they have common ends they want to achieve or clashing interests they want to contain. Lastly, states have developed issue-specific institutions or regimes, such as the Nuclear

international institutions Complexes of norms, rules, and practices that prescribe behavioral roles, constrain activity, and shape expectations.

international organization Any institution with formal procedures and formal membership from three or more countries. The minimum number of countries is set at three, rather than two, because multilateral relationships have significantly greater complexity than bilateral relationships.

multilateralism The process by which states work together to solve a common problem.

Table 6.1
Levels of International Institutions

Constitutional institutions

Constitutional institutions comprise the primary rules and norms of international society without which society among sovereign states could not exist. The most commonly recognized of these is the norm of sovereignty, which holds that within the state, power and authority are centralized and hierarchical, and outside the state no higher authority exists. The norm of sovereignty is supported by a range of auxiliary norms, such as the right to self-determination and the norm of nonintervention.

Fundamental institutions

Fundamental institutions rest on the foundation provided by constitutional institutions. They represent the basic norms and practices that sovereign states employ to facilitate coexistence and cooperation under conditions of international anarchy. They are the rudimentary practices states reach for when seeking to collaborate or coordinate their behavior. Fundamental institutions have varied from one historical system of states to another, but in the modern international system, contractual international law and multilateralism have been the most important.

Issue-specific institutions, or *regimes*

Issue-specific institutions, or *regimes*, are the most visible or palpable of all international institutions. They are the sets of rules, norms, and decision-making procedures that states formulate to define legitimate actors and legitimate action in a given domain of international life. Examples of regimes are the Nuclear Nonproliferation Treaty, the Framework Convention on Climate Change, the Ottawa Convention on antipersonnel landmines, and the International Covenant on Civil and Political Rights. Importantly, issue-specific institutions or regimes are concrete enactments of fundamental institutional practices such as international law and multilateralism.

Nonproliferation Treaty (NPT), which enact fundamental institutional practices in particular realms of interstate relations. The NPT is a concrete expression of the practices of international law and multilateralism in the field of arms control.

We are concerned here with the middle strata of fundamental institutions. "Fundamental institutions are the elementary rules of practice that states formulate to solve the coordination and collaboration problems associated with coexistence under anarchy" (Reus-Smit 1999, 14). In modern international society, a range of such institutions exists, including international law, multilateralism, bilateralism, diplomacy, and management by the great powers. Since the middle of the nineteenth century, however, the first two institutions (international law and multilateralism) have provided the basic framework for international cooperation and the pursuit of order.

How do states develop international law? Why do states follow international law if there is no international government to enforce these laws? Why is international law not given a higher priority in the study of

Winston Churchill, Harry Truman, and Josef Stalin met in 1945 in Potsdam, Germany, to map out the strategy for ending World War II, rebuilding Europe, and creating the institutions that might govern the international system. How did the ideological conflict between the USSR and the West undermine these efforts?

international relations? These are important questions that might help us understand the development of international law as an international institution.

The principal mechanism modern states employ to legislate international law is multilateral diplomacy, which is commonly defined as cooperation among three or more states based on, or with a view to formulating, reciprocally binding rules of conduct. It is a norm of the modern international legal system that states are obliged to observe legal rules because they have consented to those rules. A state that has not consented to the rules of a particular legal treaty is not bound by those rules. The only exception concerns rules of customary international law, and even then, implied or tacit consent plays an important role in the determination of which rules have customary status.

In many historical periods and in many social and cultural settings, the political and legal realms have been entwined. For instance, the absolutist conception of sovereignty bound the two realms together in the figure of the sovereign. In the modern era, by contrast, the political and legal realms are thought to be radically different, with their own logics and institutional settings. Domestically, this conception informs ideas about the constitutional separation of powers; internationally, it has encouraged the view that international politics and law are separate spheres of social action. This has not only affected how the academic disciplines of international relations and law have evolved but also how state practice has evolved.

Realists generally believe that international law should serve the interests of the powerful states. This belief has led to criticisms of international law and of international organizations like the United Nations, which protects the interests of major powers by focusing decision-making power in the Security Council. As we will discuss, some non-Western states claim that many of these international laws do not account for their interests, traditions, and values.

Criticisms of International Law

From one perspective, international law is easily cast as a Western, even imperial, institution. As we have seen, its roots lie in the European intellectual movements of the sixteenth and seventeenth centuries. Ideas propagated at that time drew on ideas that could be traced back to ancient Greek and Roman thought. They also made a clear distinction between international laws that were appropriate among Christian peoples and those that should govern how Christians related to others—peoples in the Muslim world, the Americas, and, later, Asia. The former were based on assumptions of the inherent equality of Christian peoples, and the latter on the inherent superiority of Christians over non-Christians.

Further evidence of this Western bias can be found in the "standard of civilization" that European powers codified in international law during the nineteenth century (Gong 1984). According to this standard, non-Western polities were granted sovereign recognition only if they exhibited certain domestic political characteristics and only if they were willing and able to participate in the prevailing diplomatic practices. The standard was heavily biased toward Western political and legal institutions as the accepted model. On the basis of the standard, European power divided the world's peoples into "civilized," "barbarian," and "savage" societies, a division they used to justify various degrees of Western authority.

Many claim that Western bias still characterizes the international legal order. Critics point to the Anglo-European dominance of major legal institutions, most notably the UN Security Council, and international human rights law, which they argue imposes a set of Western values about the rights of the individual on non-Western societies. According to this argument, Western powers use their privileged position on the Security Council to intervene in the domestic politics of weak, developing countries.

There is truth in these criticisms. However, the nature and role of international law in contemporary world politics are more complex than they first appear. To begin with, at the heart of the modern international legal system lies a set of customary norms that uphold the legal equality of all sovereign states as well as their rights to self-determination and nonintervention. Non-Western states have been the most vigorous proponents and defenders of these cardinal legal norms, and their survival as independent political entities depends on the continued salience of such principles. Second, non-Western peoples were more centrally involved in the development of the international human rights regime than is commonly acknowledged. The **Universal Declaration of Human Rights** (1948) was the product of a deliberate and systematic process of intercultural dialogue involving representatives of all of the world's major cultures (Glendon 2002). The **International Covenant on Civil and Political Rights** (1966), which is often portrayed as a reflection of Western values, was shaped in critical ways by newly independent postcolonial states (Reus-Smit 2001a). What's more, international human rights law has been an important resource in the struggles of many peoples against repressive governments and against institutions such as colonialism.

From International to Supranational Law?

As long as international law was designed primarily to facilitate international order—to protect sovereign states from outside interference—it remained a relatively circumscribed, if essential, institution in four ways.

1. States were the primary *subjects* of international law, the principal bearers of rights and obligations: "The classic view has been that international law applies only to states" (Higgins 1994, 40). The 1933 Montevideo Convention on the Rights and Duties of States establishes the "state as a person of international law," defines what constitutes a state, and lays down the principal rights and obligations enjoyed by states (Weston et al. 1990, 12).

2. Related to the preceding, states were the primary *agents* of international law, the only actors empowered to formulate, enact, and enforce international law. International law was thus viewed as an artifact of state practice, not the legislation of a community of humankind.

3. International law was concerned with the regulation of interstate relations. How states interacted with one another fell within the purview of international law; how they operated within their territorial boundaries did not. This distinction was enshrined in the twin international norms of self-determination and nonintervention.

4. The scope of international law was confined—or attempted to be confined—to questions of order, not justice. The principal objective of international law was the maintenance of peace and stability based on mutual respect for each state's territorial integrity and domestic jurisdiction; issues of distributive justice and the protection of basic human rights lay outside its brief.

Since the end of the Cold War, states have sought to move beyond the simple pursuit of international order toward the ambitious yet amorphous objective of global governance, and international law has begun to change in fascinating ways. First, although states are "still at the heart of the international legal system" (Higgins 1994, 39), individuals, groups, and organizations are increasingly recognized as subjects of international law. The development of an expansive body of international human rights law, supported by evolving mechanisms of enforcement, has given individuals as well as some collectivities (e.g., minority groups or

Universal Declaration of Human Rights (1948) A declaration set forth by the UN General Assembly after World War II as the first global regime that states all humans beings are inherently entitled to a certain set of universal rights.

International Covenant on Civil and Political Rights (1966) A covenant set forth by the UN General Assembly that proclaims the "recognition of the inherent dignity and of the inalienable rights of all members of the human family as the foundation of freedom, justice and peace in the world" (ICCPR Preamble).

The genocide of World War II brought about a global understanding that states should respect human rights and that the repression of ethnic minorities within a state is not to be tolerated. Here a soldier from the Karen National Union, an ethnic rebel group in Myanmar, prepares for a battle with government forces. Does the international community have a responsibility to prevent the repression of such groups?

indigenous peoples) clear rights under international law. And recent moves to hold individuals criminally responsible for violations of those rights indicate the clear obligations individuals bear to observe basic human rights. Examples include the war crimes tribunals that we discuss later in this chapter for Rwanda and the former Yugoslavia, the creation of a new International Criminal Court (ICC), and the fourteen cases the ICC is pursuing against war criminals like the leaders of the Lord's Resistance Army and the sons of General Qaddafi for crimes against humanity.

Second, nonstate actors are becoming important *agents* in the international legal process. Although such actors cannot formally enact international law and their practices do not contribute to the development of customary international law, they often play a crucial role in

- shaping the normative environment in which states are moved to codify specific legal rules,
- providing information to national governments that encourages the redefinition of state interests and the convergence of policies across different states, and
- actually drafting international treaties and conventions.

This last role was first seen when the International Committee of the Red Cross drafted the 1864 Geneva Convention (Finnemore 1996b, 69–88). More recently, nonstate actors aided in the development of the Ottawa Convention on antipersonnel landmines in 1997 (Price 1998) and in the creation of the International Criminal Court (ICC), which began its operations in 2003.

Third, international law is more concerned with global, not merely international, regulation. Where the principles of self-determination and nonintervention once erected a fundamental boundary between the international and domestic legal realms, this boundary is now being breached by the development of international rules that regulate how states should behave within their territories. International law is a crucial element of global governance. Notable here are international trade law, the growing corpus of international environmental law, and the previously mentioned body of international human rights law. The penetration of these laws through the boundaries of the sovereign state is facilitated by the growing tendency of national courts to draw on precepts of international law in their rulings.

Finally, the rules, norms, and principles of international law are no longer confined to maintaining international order, narrowly defined. Not only does the development of international humanitarian law indicate a broadening of international law to address questions of global justice, but recent decisions by the UN Security Council have treated gross violations of human rights by sovereign states as threats to international peace and security, thus legitimating action under Chapter 7 of the UN Charter. (An example is the 2006 international intervention in East Timor, where a conflict over discrimination in the military expanded to violence throughout the country.) In doing so, the Security Council implies that international order depends on the maintenance of at least minimum standards of global justice.

Because of these changes, it has been suggested that international law may be gradually transforming into a system of supranational law—that is, one that transcends national boundaries or governments. Once states are no longer the only subjects and agents of international law, once international law is involved in global regulation, and once its scope has been extended to encompass issues of justice as well as order, it has broken the bounds of both its initial intent and original practice. These changes have not yet prompted the rewriting of international legal texts, and both international lawyers and international relations scholars are responding cautiously, but current developments have injected new excitement and energy into the field of international law, which many previously regarded as moribund. International relations scholars are taking a fresh look at the role of legal norms in shaping world politics, something often dismissed as idealism.

This desire to promote a rule-based global society that would protect the rights of humankind and prevent the scourge of war led world leaders to create the United Nations in 1945. We now turn to a discussion of this important international institution.

The United Nations

The **United Nations (UN)** has the unique status of being the largest international organization, or what some call a **supranational global organization**, and the only one that has a universal focus. Other international organizations with more specific responsibilities include the World Bank, the International Monetary Fund, and the World Trade Organization. The states that comprise the United Nations created a group of international institutions, which include the central system located in New York; the Specialized Agencies, such as the World Health Organization (WHO) and the International Labor Organization (ILO); and the Programmes and Funds, such as the United Nations Children's Fund (UNICEF) and the United Nations Development Programme (UNDP). When created more than half a century ago in the aftermath of World War II, the United Nations reflected the hope for a just and peaceful global community.

Unlike the other international organizations that we will discuss in the next chapter, the United Nations is the only global institution with legitimacy that derives from universal

United Nations Founded in 1945 following World War II, it is an international organization composed of 193 member states dedicated to addressing issues related to peace and security, development, human rights, humanitarian affairs, and international law.

supranational global organization An authoritative international organization that operates above the nation-state.

state sovereignty The concept that all countries are equal under international law and that they are protected from outside interference; this is the basis on which the United Nations and other international and regional organizations operate.

Responsibility to Protect Resolution supported by the United Nations in 2005 to determine the international community's responsibility in preventing mass atrocities, reacting to crises, protecting citizens, rebuilding, and preventing future problems.

nonstate actor Any participant in global politics that is neither acting in the name of government nor created and served by government. Terrorist networks, NGOs, global crime syndicates, and multinational corporations are examples.

membership and a mandate that encompasses security, economic and social development, and, more specifically, the protection of human rights and the environment. Yet the United Nations was created by states for states, and the relationship between **state sovereignty** and the protection of the needs and interests of people has not been fully resolved. This debate was complicated by the 2005 UN decision to support the **Responsibility to Protect** resolution (R2P). This resolution was meant to resolve the impasse between people who believe the outside world has the power to intervene in countries where human security is threatened and those who believe sovereignty precludes any outside intervention. The meaning of sovereignty and the limits of UN action have remained key issues. Since the founding of the United Nations, there has been an expansion of UN activities to address conditions within states, an improvement in UN capacity in its economic and social work, and an increased tendency to accord the United Nations a moral status. Threats to global security addressed by the United Nations now include interstate conflict and threats by **nonstate actors** as well as political, economic, and social conditions within states.

Despite the growth in UN activities, however, there are some questions about the relevance and effectiveness of the United Nations. The failure by the United States and the United Kingdom to get clear UN Security Council authorization for the war in Iraq in 2003 led to well-publicized criticism of the United Nations and a crisis in international relations. Yet the troubled aftermath of the invasion and persistent questions about the legitimacy of a war that was not sanctioned by the United Nations show that the United Nations has acquired important moral status in international society.

San Francisco was the scene of the signing of the UN Charter in 1945. Has the time come to revise the document and reform the United Nations?

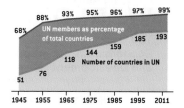

After describing the history and main organs of the United Nations, this section will look at the changing role of the United Nations in addressing matters of peace and security and then matters of economic and social development. We will also focus on how the United Nations' role has evolved in response to changes in the global political context and on some of the problems that it still faces.

A Brief History of the United Nations and Its Principal Organs

The United Nations was established on October 24, 1945, by fifty-one countries as a result of initiatives taken by the governments of the states that had led the war against Italy, Germany, and Japan. As early as 1939, American and British diplomats were discussing the need for a more effective international organization like the United Nations. It was intended to be a **collective security** organization. Often illustrated with the example of the stag hunt found in an essay by Jean-Jacques Rousseau (described in Chapter 3), this concept of collective security is simple: members of an organization agree that if one of them commits an offense to peace, all members of the organization will fight the aggressor. Unfortunately, as we will see later in this chapter, the Cold War bipolar international system undermined the effectiveness of the United Nations in security affairs.

By 2011, 193 states were members of the United Nations—nearly every state in the world. Notable exceptions include Western Sahara and Kosovo (neither of which is recognized as a self-governing territory), Taiwan (which is not recognized as a separate territory from China), and Palestine and Vatican City (both of which have nonmember observer status). When joining, member states agreed to accept the obligations of the **United Nations Charter**, an international treaty that set out basic principles of international relations. According to the charter, the United Nations had four purposes: to maintain international peace and security; to develop friendly relations among nations; to cooperate in solving international problems and in promoting respect for human rights; and to be a center for harmonizing the actions of nations. At the United Nations, all the member states—large and small, rich and poor, with differing political views and social systems—had a voice and a vote in this process. Interestingly, while the United Nations was clearly created as a grouping of states, the charter referred to the needs and interests of peoples as well as those of states (see Table 6.2).

In many ways, the United Nations was set up to correct the problems of its predecessor, the **League of Nations**. The League of Nations had been established after World War I and was intended to make future wars impossible, but it lacked effective power. There was no clear division of responsibility between the main executive committee (the League Council) and the League Assembly, which included all member states. Both the League Assembly and the League Council could only make recommendations, not binding resolutions, and these recommendations had to be unanimous. Any government was free to reject any recommendation. Furthermore, there was no mechanism for coordinating military or economic actions against miscreant states. Key states, such as the United States, were not members of the League. By World War II, the League had already failed to address a number of acts of aggression.

The structure of the United Nations was intended to avoid some of the problems faced by the League of Nations. The United Nations has six main organs: the Security Council, the General Assembly, the Secretariat, the Economic and Social Council, the Trusteeship Council, and the International Court of Justice (see Figure 6.1).

INTERGOVERNMENTAL ORGANIZATIONS.
There are 196 countries in the world and 193 are members of the United Nations. If the UN Security Council continues to block effective action like preventing mass atrocities in Darfur and punishing the Syrian government for using chemical weapons, do you think countries will quit the UN?

collective security An arrangement where "each state in the system accepts that the security of one is the concern of all, and agrees to join in a collective response to aggression" (Roberts and Kingsbury 1993, 30).

United Nations Charter (1945) The legal regime that created the United Nations. The charter defines the structure of the United Nations, the powers of its constitutive agencies, and the rights and obligations of sovereign states party to the charter.

League of Nations The first permanent collective international security organization aimed at preventing future wars and resolving global problems. The League failed due to the absence of US membership and the inability of members to commit to a real international community.

The Organisation of Economic Co-operation and Development

The OECD, which was founded in 1961 and currently has thirty-four member countries, promotes policies to improve the economic and social well-being of people around the world. Through the OECD's Student Ambassador Program, an on-campus, yearlong ambassadorship, you can engage with the OECD and plan activities to raise awareness. The OECD works with governments to understand what drives economic, social, and environmental change; measures productivity and global flows of trade and investment; and analyzes and compares data to predict future trends. To learn more about getting involved, check out www.oecd.org.

Table 6.2

The UN Charter Contains References to Both the Rights of States and the Rights of People

The Preamble of the UN Charter asserts that "We the peoples of the United Nations [are] determined [. . .] to reaffirm faith in fundamental human rights, in the dignity and worth of the human person, in the equal rights of men and women and of nations large and small."

Article 1(2) states that the purpose of the United Nations is to develop "friendly relations among nations based on respect for the principle of equal rights and self-determination of peoples and to take other appropriate measures to strengthen universal peace."

Article 2(7) states that "Nothing contained in the present Charter shall authorize the United Nations to intervene in matters which are essentially within the domestic jurisdiction of any state."

Chapter VI deals with the "Pacific Settlement of Disputes."

Article 33 states that "The parties to any dispute, the continuance of which is likely to endanger the maintenance of international peace and security, shall, first of all, seek a solution by negotiation, enquiry, mediation, conciliation, arbitration, judicial settlement, resort to regional agencies or arrangements, or other peaceful means of their own choice."

Chapter VII deals with "Action with Respect to Threats to the Peace, Breaches of the Peace, and Acts of Aggression."

Article 42 states that the Security Council "may take such action by air, sea, or land forces as may be necessary to maintain or restore international peace and security." The Security Council has sometimes authorized member states to use "all necessary means," and this has been accepted as a legitimate application of Chapter VII powers.

Article 99 authorizes the secretary-general to "bring to the attention of the Security Council any matter which in his opinion may threaten the maintenance of international peace and security."

United Nations Security Council The council made up of five permanent member states (sometimes called the P-5)—namely, Great Britain, China, France, Russia, and the United States—and ten nonpermanent members. The P-5 all have a veto power over all Security Council decisions.

veto power The right of the five permanent members of the Security Council (United States, Russia, China, France, and Great Britain) to forbid any action by the United Nations.

The Security Council

The **UN Security Council** was given the main responsibility for maintaining international peace and security. It was made up initially of eleven states and then, after 1965, of fifteen states. It includes five permanent members (sometimes called "the P-5"), namely, France, the Russian Federation (previously the Soviet Union), the United Kingdom, the United States—the victors in World War II—and China, as well as ten nonpermanent members. (China was first represented by Nationalist China and not the People's Republic of China.) In contrast to the League of Nations, the United Nations recognized great power prerogatives in the Security Council, offering each of the P-5 a **veto power** over all Security Council decisions. The convention emerged that abstention by a permanent member is not regarded as a veto. Unlike with the League, the decisions of the Security Council are binding and must only be passed by a majority of nine of the fifteen members. However, if one permanent member dissents, the resolution does not pass.

The five permanent members of the Security Council were seen as the major powers when the United Nations was founded, and they were granted a veto on the view that if the great powers were not given a privileged position, the United Nations would not work. This recognition of a state's influence being proportional to its size and political and military power

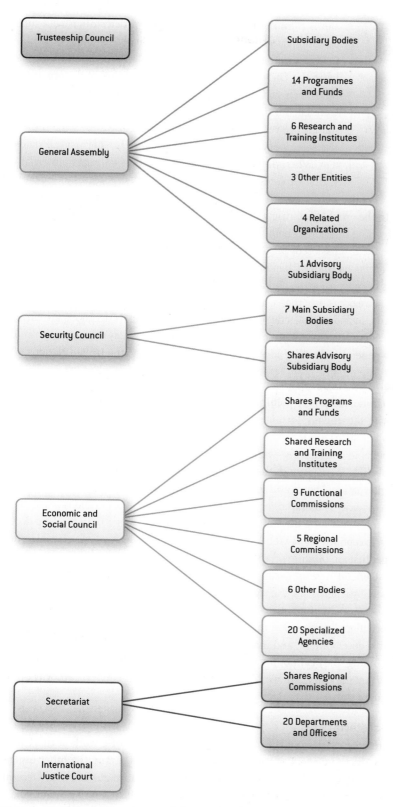

Figure 6.1 The Structure of the United Nations

stems from the realist notion that power determines who rules in the international system. Indeed, this tension between the recognition of power politics through the Security Council veto and the universal ideals underlying the United Nations is a defining feature of the organization. There have been widespread and frequent calls for the reform of the Security Council, but this is very difficult. In both theoretical and policy terms, the inability to reform the Security Council also shows the limits of a collective security system and liberal thinking that suggests all states are equal.

When the Security Council considers a threat to international peace, it first explores ways to settle the dispute peacefully under the terms of Chapter VI of the UN Charter. It may suggest principles for a settlement or may suggest mediation. In the event of fighting, the Security Council tries to secure a cease-fire. It may send a peacekeeping mission to help the parties maintain the truce and to keep opposing forces apart (see the discussion of peacekeeping below). The council can also take measures to enforce its decisions under Chapter VII of the charter. It can, for instance, impose economic sanctions or order an arms embargo. (See Chapter 5 for a discussion of these foreign policy tools.) On rare occasions, the Security Council has authorized member states to use all necessary means, including collective military action, to see that its decisions are carried out. The council also makes recommendations to the General Assembly on the appointment of a new secretary-general and on the admission of new members to the United Nations.

The General Assembly

United Nations General Assembly Often referred to as a "parliament of nations," it is composed of all member states, which meet to consider the world's most pressing problems. Each state has one vote, and a two-thirds majority in the General Assembly is required for decisions on key issues. Decisions reached by the General Assembly only have the status of recommendations and are not binding.

The recognition of power politics through veto power in the Security Council can be contrasted with the universal principles underlying the other organs of the United Nations. All UN member states are represented in the **General Assembly**—a "parliament of nations"—which meets to consider the world's most pressing problems. Each member state has one vote. A two-thirds majority in the General Assembly is required for decisions on key issues such as international peace and security, the admission of new members, and the UN budget. A simple majority is required for other matters. However, the decisions reached by the General Assembly only have the status of recommendations rather than binding decisions. One of the few exceptions is the General Assembly's Fifth Committee, which makes decisions on the budget that are binding on members.

The General Assembly can consider any matter within the scope of the UN Charter. There were 156 items on the agenda of the sixty-first session of the General Assembly (2006–2007), including topics such as globalization, the role of diamonds in fueling conflict, international cooperation in the peaceful uses of outer space, peacekeeping operations, sustainable development, and international migration. Since General Assembly resolutions are nonbinding, they cannot force action by any state, but the assembly's recommendations are important indications of world opinion and represent the moral authority of the community of nation-states.

The Secretariat

United Nations Secretariat The Secretariat carries out the administrative work of the United Nations as directed by the General Assembly, Security Council, and other organs. The Secretariat is led by the secretary-general, who provides overall administrative guidance.

The **Secretariat** carries out the substantive and administrative work of the United Nations as directed by the General Assembly, the Security Council, and the other organs. It is led by the secretary-general, who provides overall administrative guidance. In December 2006, Ban Ki-moon from South Korea was sworn in as the eighth secretary-general. The Secretariat consists of departments and offices with a total staff of 8,900 under the regular budget and a nearly equal number under special funding.

On the recommendation of the other bodies, the Secretariat also carries out a number of research functions and some quasi-management functions. Yet the role of the Secretariat remains primarily bureaucratic, and it lacks the political power and the right of initiative of, for instance, the Commission of the European Union. The one exception is the power of the secretary-general, under Article 99 of the Charter, to bring to the Security Council's attention situations that are likely to lead to a breakdown of international peace and security. This article, which at first may not appear to invest much power, was the legal basis for the remarkable expansion of the diplomatic role of the secretary-general compared with its League predecessor. The secretary-general is empowered to become involved in a large range of areas that can be loosely interpreted as threats to peace, including economic and social problems and humanitarian crises.

The Economic and Social Council

The **Economic and Social Council (ECOSOC)**, under the overall authority of the General Assembly, is intended to coordinate the economic and social work of the United Nations and the UN family of organizations. It also consults with **nongovernmental organizations (NGOs)**, thereby maintaining a vital link between the United Nations and **civil society**. Subsidiary bodies of ECOSOC include functional commissions, such as the Commission on the Status of Women; regional commissions, such as the Economic Commission for Africa; and other bodies (see Figure 6.1).

Along with the Secretariat and the General Assembly, ECOSOC is responsible for overseeing the activities of a large number of other institutions known as the United Nations system, including the Specialized Agencies and the Programmes and Funds. The Specialized Agencies, such as the World Health Organization (WHO) and the International Labor Organization (ILO), have their own constitutions, regularly assessed budgets, executive heads, and assemblies of state representatives. They are self-contained constitutionally, financially, and politically and are not subject to the management of the central system.

The Programmes and Funds are much closer to the central system in the sense that their management arrangements are subject to direct General Assembly supervision, can be modified by assembly resolution, and are largely funded on a voluntary basis. Since the establishment of the United Nations in 1945, a number of new issues have come onto the international agenda, such as the rights and interests of women, climate change, resource depletion, population growth, terrorism, and the spread of HIV/AIDS. Frequently, those issues led to a new organization in the Programmes and Funds. Examples of Programmes and Funds include the United Nations Development Programme (UNDP) and the United Nations Children's Fund (UNICEF).

Whereas the League of Nations attributed responsibility for economic and social questions to the League Assembly, the Charter of the United Nations established ECOSOC to oversee economic and social institutions. This change was a consequence of thinking in more functionalist terms. Functionalism is a liberal idea that suggests states will cooperate in functionally specific areas like a health pandemic and, if successful, cooperative activity will "spill over" into other policy areas (see Chapter 4). Organizations were set up to deal with specific economic and social problems. However, ECOSOC was not given necessary management powers. It can only issue recommendations and receive reports from the Specialized Agencies. In consequence, the United

United Nations Economic and Social Council (ECOSOC) This council is intended to coordinate the economic and social work of the United Nations and the UN family organizations. The ECOSOC has a direct link to civil society through communications with nongovernmental organizations (NGOs).

nongovernmental organization (NGO) An organization, usually a grassroots one, with policy goals but not governmental in makeup. An NGO is any group of people relating to each other regularly in some formal manner and engaging in collective action, provided the activities are noncommercial and nonviolent and are not on behalf of a government.

civil society (1) The totality of all individuals and groups in a society who are not acting as participants in any government institutions, or (2) all individuals and groups who are neither participants in government nor acting in the interests of commercial companies.

WHAT'S YOUR WORLDVIEW

With nation-states reluctant to send their own forces into harm's way and no real international force, how will the UN and other global institutions respond to humanitarian challenges and weak and vulnerable states?

Nations' economic and social organizations have continually searched for better ways of achieving effective management.

The Trusteeship Council

Trusteeship Council Upon creation of the United Nations, this council was established to provide international supervision for eleven trust territories administered by seven member states in an effort to prepare them for self-government or independence. By 1994, all trust territories had attained self-government or independence, and the council now meets on an ad hoc basis.

When the United Nations was created, the **Trusteeship Council** was established to provide international supervision for eleven trust territories administered by seven member states and to ensure that adequate steps were taken to prepare the territories for self-government or independence. By 1994, all trust territories had attained self-government or independence either as separate states or by joining neighboring independent countries. The last to do so was the trust territory of the Pacific Islands, Palau, which had been previously administered by the United States under special rules with the United Nations called a Strategic Trust. Its work completed, the Trusteeship Council now consists of the five permanent members of the Security Council. It has amended its rules of procedure to allow it to meet when necessary.

The International Court of Justice

International Court of Justice (ICJ) The main judicial organ of the United Nations consisting of fifteen judges elected jointly by the General Assembly and Security Council. The ICJ handles disputes between states, not individuals and states, and although a state does not have to participate in a case, if it elects to do so it must obey the decision.

The **International Court of Justice (ICJ)** is the main judicial organ of the United Nations. Consisting of fifteen judges elected jointly by the General Assembly and the Security Council, the court decides disputes between countries. Participation by states in a proceeding is voluntary, but if a state agrees to participate, it is obligated to comply with the court's decision. The court also provides advisory opinions to other UN organs and Specialized Agencies on request. Only states may bring cases before the ICJ. If people who live in one state want to bring a suit against another state, they must get their home state to file the suit.

Three factors reduce the effectiveness of the ICJ. First, the competence, or jurisdiction, of the court is limited, as noted, to cases that states bring against states. The court's statutory jurisdiction extends to anything related to a state's undertakings by signing the UN Charter and any matter related to a ratified treaty. If a state is not a signatory, there can be no recourse to the good offices of the ICJ. In addition, if the United Nations itself is a party to the case, at least one state party of the ICJ must be an applicant as well. This happened with the South West Africa cases of the 1970s. A second factor that reduces the ICJ's effectiveness is the question of compulsory jurisdiction. States that are party to the ICJ statute are bound by compulsory jurisdiction if they agree to it; this is the "option-clause" problem. For example, in the *Aerial Incident of July 27, 1955 (Israel v. Bulgaria)*, the court found that Bulgaria was not liable for damages because its compulsory jurisdiction option had expired. A third factor—the state reservations—limits the effectiveness of the ICJ and follows from the option-clause problems. For not only may a state let its compulsory jurisdiction lapse, but it can also refuse to accept the ICJ jurisdiction if the state claims that its own existing national law covers the issue before the courts. This occurred, for example, in a 1957 case in which Norway sued France over a debt owed to Norwegian investors. France claimed that its domestic legal system had jurisdiction in the matter, and Norway lost.

The International Criminal Court is an independent international organization that is not part of the United Nations. We will discuss it in Chapter 10.

WHAT'S YOUR WORLDVIEW

Given the global economic troubles the world now faces, should the United Nations create an Economic Security Council? What could it do, and could it be effective?

Maintenance of International Peace and Security

The performance of the United Nations in questions of peace and security has been shaped by the global political context. Clearly, there have been changes in international society since the United Nations was founded in 1945 that have had an impact on the UN system. The Cold War between the United States and the Soviet Union hampered the functioning of the UN Security Council because the veto could be used whenever the major interests of the United States or Soviet Union were threatened. From 1945 to 1990, 193 substantive vetoes were invoked in the Security Council, compared with only 19 substantive vetoes from 1990 to 2007. Furthermore, while the UN Charter provided for a standing army to be set up by agreement between the Security Council and consenting states, the East-West Cold War rivalry made this impossible to implement. The end result was that the UN Security Council could not function in the way the UN founders had expected.

Since member states could not agree on the arrangements laid out in Chapter VII of the charter, especially with regard to setting up a UN army, a series of improvisations followed to address matters of peace and security. First, a procedure was established under which the Security Council agreed to a mandate for an agent to act on its behalf. This occurred in the Korean conflict in 1950 and the Gulf War in 1990, when action was undertaken principally by the United States and its allies.

Second, there have been many instances of what analysts call "classical peacekeeping," which involves the establishment of a UN force under UN command to be placed between

The UN Foundation was established with a gift of $1 billion from the founder of CNN, Ted Turner. He is a champion of public and private partnerships. Here he is giving Indian Congress Party president Sonjay Gandhi an award. The UN Foundation links the UN's work with others around the world. What does this mean in practice?

disputing parties after a cease-fire. Such a force uses its weapons only in self-defense, is established with the consent of the host state, and does not include forces from the major powers. No reference to peacekeeping exists in the UN Charter, but classical peacekeeping mandates and mechanisms are based on Chapter VI of the charter. This mechanism was first used in 1956, when a UN force was sent to Egypt to facilitate the exodus of the British and French forces from the Suez Canal area and then to stand between Egyptian and Israeli forces. Since the Suez crisis, there have been a number of classical peacekeeping missions—for instance, monitoring the Green Line in Cyprus, in the Golan Heights (on the border between Syria and Israel), and after the decade-long Iraq-Iran War. The primary drawback to this kind of peacekeeping operation is that it is not effective if the war parties do not want peace. Further, once these peacekeeping missions are initiated, they are very difficult to conclude.

peace enforcement
Designed to bring hostile parties to agreement and may occur without the consent of the parties.

Third, a new kind of peacekeeping, sometimes called multidimensional peacekeeping or **peace enforcement**, emerged after the end of the Cold War. These missions are more likely to use force to achieve humanitarian ends, and their mandates are sometimes based on Chapter VII of the UN Charter. This type of peacekeeping has been used when order has collapsed within states; it therefore addresses civil wars as well as international conflict. A key problem has been that the peacekeepers have found it increasingly difficult to maintain a neutral position and have been targeted by belligerents. Examples include the intervention in Somalia in the early 1990s and intervention in the former Yugoslavia in the mid-1990s. In both cases, until the European Union, NATO, or the United States was directly involved in the operations, peace was not achieved. Even after the US intervention in 1993 in Somalia, sadly best known for the Black Hawk Down incident, the country remains a failed state characterized by clan-based violence.

In the early 1990s, after the end of the Cold War, the UN agenda for peace and security expanded quickly. The secretary-general at the time, Boutros Boutros-Ghali, outlined a more ambitious role for the United Nations in his seminal report *An Agenda for Peace* (1992). The report described interconnected roles for the United Nations to maintain peace and security in the post–Cold War context. These included four main kinds of activities: (1) **preventive diplomacy**, which involves confidence-building measures, fact finding, and preventive deployment of UN authorized forces; (2) **peacemaking**, designed to bring hostile parties to agreement, essentially through peaceful means; (3) **peacekeeping**, which is the deployment of a UN presence in the field with the consent of all parties (this refers to classical peacekeeping); and (4) **postconflict peace building**, which ideally will develop the social, political, and economic infrastructure to prevent further violence and to consolidate peace. However, when all peaceful means have failed, peace enforcement authorized under Chapter VII of the charter may be necessary, and it may occur without the consent of the parties in conflict.

preventive diplomacy
Measures that states take to keep a disagreement from escalating.

peacemaking Active diplomatic efforts to seek a resolution to an international dispute that has already escalated.

peacekeeping The interposition of third-party military personnel to keep warring parties apart.

postconflict peace building
Activities launched after a conflict has ended that seek to end the condition that caused the conflict.

United Nations peacekeeping went through a rapid expansion in the early 1990s. In 1994, UN peacekeeping operations involved nearly 80,000 military personnel around the world, seven times the figure for 1990 (Pugh 2001, 115). In 2011, the total number of peacekeeping personnel (military and police) in the UN's fifteen ongoing peacekeeping operations was just over 98,022, representing contributions from 114 different countries (see Table 6.3).

Increased Attention to Conditions Within States

The new peacekeeping was the product of a greater preparedness to intervene within states. This shift challenged the traditional belief that diplomats should ignore the internal affairs of states to preserve international stability. An increasing number of people believed that the international community, working through the United Nations, should address individual

Table 6.3
UN Peacekeeping Operations in 2013

Location	Origin of Operation	Location	Origin of Operation
Western Sahara	1991	South Sudan	2011
Haiti	2004	Ivory Coast	2004
Congo (DR)	2010	Kosovo	1999
Darfur	2007	Liberia	2003
Syria	1974	Mali	2013
Cyprus	1964	Middle East (UNTSO)	1948
Lebanon	1974	India & Pakistan	1949
Sudan	2011		

Sources: http://www.un.org/en/peacekeeping/resources/statistics/factsheet.shtml.

political and civil rights as well as the right to basic provisions like food, water, healthcare, and housing. Under this view, violations of individuals' rights were a major cause of disturbances in relations among states: a lack of internal justice risked international disorder. The United Nations reinforced this new perception that pursuing justice for individuals, or ensuring **human security**, was an aspect of national interest. (See Chapter 10 for more information on the topic of human security.)

In some states, contributions to activities such as peacekeeping were defended in terms of national interest. Indeed, states like Canada and Norway could justify their contributions to peacekeeping as a "moral" course of action, but these contributions also served their national interests by enhancing their status in the international community. The Japanese also responded to moral pressure founded in national interest when they contributed substantially to defraying the cost of British involvement in the 1990–1991 Gulf War. This act can be explained in terms of the synthesis of morality and interest. For some states, reputation in the United Nations had become an important national good.

These actions reflected an increasing concern with questions of justice for individuals and conditions within states. Yet in the past, the United Nations had helped promote the traditional view of the primacy of international order between states over justice for individuals, so the new focus on individual rights was a significant change. What accounts for this change?

First, the international environment had changed. The Cold War standoff between the East and the West had meant that member states did not want to question the conditions of the sovereignty of states. Jeanne Kirkpatrick's (1979) influential essay, which recommended tolerating abhorrent dictatorships in Latin America in order to

human security The security of people, including their physical safety, their economic and social well-being, respect for their dignity, and the protection of their human rights. Simply put, it is freedom from fear and freedom from want.

United Nations peacekeeping forces—called the Blue Helmets—are supposed to protect refugees. Here General Romero Dallaire talks to UN Chief of Staff Iqbal Riza in Kigali, Rwanda, just before the killing of 1 million Tutsis and moderate Hutus in 1994. The United Nations failed to prevent and stop this genocide. Why did this happen?

THEORY IN PRACTICE

Neoconservatives and the United Nations

THE CHALLENGE

For analysts from the realist school of thought, states exist in an anarchic, self-help world, looking to their own power resources for national security. This was the perspective of the neoconservatives who dominated the George W. Bush administration. They subscribed to a strain of realist thinking that is best called hegemonist; that is, they believed the United States should use its power solely to secure its interests in the world. They were realists with idealistic tendencies, seeking to remake the world through promoting—by force, if necessary—freedom, democracy, and free enterprise.

Paul Wolfowitz, an important voice in the neoconservative camp, wrote that global leadership was all about "demonstrating that your friends will be protected and taken care of, that your enemies will be punished, and those who refuse to support you will live to regret having done so."[a] Although it would be wrong to assume that all realist thinkers and policy makers are opposed to international organizations such as the United Nations, most are wary of any organizations that prevent them from securing their national interests. The belief is that alliances should be only short-term events because allies might desert you in a crisis. For some realists, such as the Bush neoconservatives, committing security to a collective security organization is even worse than an alliance because, in a worst-case situation, the alliance might gang up on your country. Even in the best-case situation, it would be a bad idea to submit your military forces to foreign leadership.

OPTIONS

In its early years, prior to the wave of decolonization in Africa and Asia, the United Nations' US-based realist critics did not have the ear of the country's political leadership. Presidents Truman and Eisenhower both found a way around the USSR's Security Council veto by working

The UN headquarters in Manhattan. Does the United States have any advantages as the host of the UN headquarters? Disadvantages?

through the General Assembly, a body that at the time was very friendly to the United States and its goals. However, with the end of European control of Africa and Asia, the General Assembly changed. The body frequently passed resolutions condemning the United States and its allies. One result was a growing movement to end US involvement in the United Nations, especially among the key foreign policy advisers to President Reagan.

APPLICATION

United States president George W. Bush, himself a critic of multilateralism, chose, in a controversial recess appointment, John Bolton to be the US ambassador to the United Nations. Bolton had worked in the

administrations of Presidents Reagan and the elder Bush, but his appointment as a UN envoy was a surprise to many in the international diplomatic community, primarily because he was such a staunch opponent of multilateral organizations in general, with the United Nations drawing his most specific vituperation.

In the 1980s, the intellectual explanation for this antipathy toward the United Nations had a logic based on problems that the organization itself would later recognize to a certain extent. Reagan administration critics did not like what they said was the socialist ideological bias found in programs of the UN Educational, Scientific, and Cultural Organization (UNESCO) and the fact that the head of UNESCO was a critic of US foreign policy in Central America. United States critics also did not like the pro-abortion policy of some UN-sponsored development programs. In 1985, the US delegate to the UN's Nairobi Conference on the status of women was President Reagan's daughter Maureen, who often cast the sole dissenting vote on measures designed to improve women's lives. Political realists saw no tangible benefit for the United States to remain active in the United Nations once the leaders in Washington could no longer count on a UN rubber stamp for US policies. For a number of years, the United States did not pay its dues to the United Nations. Only after Richard Holbrooke, the US ambassador to the United Nations in the Clinton administration, negotiated a reduction in the American contribution to

Continued

THEORY IN PRACTICE *continued*

the United Nations in 2000 did the United States repay its arrears with the help of prominent media businessman Ted Turner.

The rejection of UN-style multilateralism revived with the Bush presidency in 2001. The Bush foreign policy advisers did not like the peacekeeping operation in the former Yugoslavia. In her criticism of Clinton foreign policy, National Security Adviser Rice said the United States would not send its troops to countries for nation building. More important, the Bush administration did not want to have its hands tied when dealing with Iraq and its

alleged store of nuclear, chemical, and biological weapons. President Bush and his top advisers believed that sanctions—an important weapon in the UN's moral-suasion arsenal—would never force Iraq to disarm and that only force could do so. The irony is that, after the 2003 invasion, the US's own weapons inspectors could find no evidence that Iraq had any of the banned weapons.

For Discussion

1. What might be a Marxist criticism of the United Nations and its operations?

2. Is there any way to overcome realists' belief of international anarchy and the impossibility of global governance?

3. Some utopians believe that a world government would end war and provide answers to other global challenges. Do you agree or disagree? Why or why not?

4. Do the five permanent members of the Security Council have too much power over the operations of the organization?

[a]Paul Wolfowitz, "Remembering the Future," *National Interest*, no. 59 (Spring 2000), p. 41.

---

fight communism, was a reasonable report of the situation at that time. Unsavory right-wing regimes in Latin America were tolerated because they were anti-Soviet, and interfering in the other's sphere risked escalation of conflict (Forsythe 1988, 259–260).

Second, the process of decolonization had privileged statehood over justice. The United Nations respected the claims of colonies to become states and had elevated the right to statehood above any tests of viability, such as the existence of a nation, adequate economic performance, defensibility, or a prospect for achieving justice for citizens. This unconditional right to independence was enunciated in the General Assembly Declaration on the Granting of Independence to Colonial Countries and Peoples in 1960. A convention emerged that the claims of elites in the putative states could be a sufficient indication of popular enthusiasm, even when the elites were crooks and the claims misleading.

Charles Beitz was one of the first to question this convention when he concluded that statehood should not be unconditional and that attention had to be given to the situation of individuals after independence (Beitz 1979). Michael Walzer and Terry Nardin produced arguments leading to similar conclusions: states were conditional entities in that their right to exist should depend on a criterion of performance with regard to the interests of their citizens (Walzer 1977; Nardin 1983). Such writings helped alter the moral content of diplomacy.

The new relationship between order and justice was, therefore, a product of particular circumstances. After the Cold War, the international community began to sense that threats to international peace and security did not emanate only from aggression between or among states. Rather, global peace was also threatened by civil conflict (including refugee flows and regional instability), humanitarian emergencies, violations of global standards of human rights, and other conditions such as poverty and inequality.

More recently, other types of non-state-based threats, such as terrorism and the proliferation of small arms and weapons of mass destruction,

WHAT'S YOUR WORLDVIEW

Why would a country decide to participate in a UN peacekeeping operation? What factors would motivate participation in such a collective action?

have an increasingly prominent place on the UN security agenda. Partly due to the terrorist attacks in the United States in 2001 as well as the impasse reached in the UN Security Council over Iraq in 2003, then secretary-general Kofi Annan named a high-level panel to examine the major threats and challenges to global peace. The 2004 final report, *A More Secure World: Our Shared Responsibility*, emphasized the interconnected nature of security threats and presented development, security, and human rights as mutually reinforcing. Many of the report's recommendations were not implemented, but some were, notably the establishment of a new UN Peacebuilding Commission.

The UN Peacebuilding Commission was established in December 2005 as an advisory subsidiary body of the General Assembly and the Security Council. It was proposed first by the secretary-general's High-Level Panel on Threats, Challenges, and Change in December 2004 and again in the secretary-general's report *In Larger Freedom* in March 2005 (United Nations 2005). This panel and report argued that existing mechanisms at the United Nations were insufficient in responding to the particular needs of states emerging from conflict. Many countries, such as Liberia, Haiti, and Somalia in the 1990s, had signed peace agreements and hosted UN peacekeeping missions but reverted to violent conflict. The Peacebuilding Commission aims to provide targeted support to countries in the volatile postconflict phase to prevent the recurrence of conflict. It proposes integrated strategies and priorities for postconflict recovery toward the goal of improving coordination among the myriad of actors involved in postconflict activities. The establishment of the Peacebuilding Commission is indicative of a growing trend at the United Nations to coordinate security and development programming.

The organizational committee of the Peacebuilding Commission is made up of thirty-one member states, and the first session was held in June 2006. The Peacebuilding Support Fund, with a target of $250 million, is designed to support the activities of the commission. Country-specific meetings look at postconflict strategies, priorities, and programming. The first two states that the Peacebuilding Commission considered were Sierra Leone and Burundi.

Intervention Within States

As the international community more clearly understood issues of peace and security to include human security and justice, it expected the United Nations to take on a stronger role in maintaining standards for individuals within states. One difficulty in carrying out the new tasks was that it seemed to run against the doctrine of nonintervention. **Intervention** was traditionally defined as a deliberate incursion into a state, without its consent, by some outside agency to change the functioning, policies, and goals of its government and achieve effects that favor the intervening agency (Vincent 1974).

intervention The direct involvement within a state by an outside actor to achieve an outcome preferred by the intervening agency without the consent of the host state.

At the founding of the United Nations, sovereignty was regarded as central to the system of states. States were equal members of international society and were equal with regard to international law. Sovereignty also implied that states recognized no higher authority than themselves and that there was no superior jurisdiction. The governments of states had exclusive jurisdiction within their own frontiers, a principle that was enshrined in Article 2(7) of the UN Charter. Intervention in the traditional sense was in opposition to the principles of international society, and it could only be tolerated as an exception to the rule.

In earlier periods, however, states had intervened in one another's business and claimed they had a right to do so. The United States refused to accept any curtailment of its right to intervene in the internal affairs of other states in its hemisphere until 1933, when it conceded the point at the Seventh International Conference of American States. The US position was very similar to the Brezhnev Doctrine of the 1970s, which held that the Soviet Union had the

CASE STUDY : The 2003 Intervention in Iraq

In March 2003, a US-led coalition launched a highly controversial war in Iraq, which removed Saddam Hussein from power. The justification for war stressed Iraq's possession of weapons of mass destruction in defiance of earlier UN resolutions. Unlike in Kosovo, gross violations of human rights were not given as a main justification for the invasion until later. Yet the failure to find weapons of mass destruction in Iraq as well as the ongoing civil war have fueled the claims of critics that the war was unjustified.

There was no agreement over whether the UN Security Council authorized military action in Iraq. American and British diplomats pointed to UN Security Council Resolution 687 of 1991, which required the destruction of Iraqi weapons of mass destruction under UN supervision, and UN Security Council Resolution 1441 of 2002, which threatened "serious consequences"

Prior to the invasion of Iraq in 2003, the International Atomic Energy Agency (IAEA) took a lead role in the nuclear weapons inspections regime. What might the IAEA report have said that would have convinced German foreign minister Joschka Fischer (shown here outside a Security Council meeting) to keep his country out of the war?

if this were not done. Yet efforts to reach a Security Council resolution in the winter of 2003 that would clearly authorize the use of force against Iraq were unsuccessful. France and Russia threatened to veto a second Security Council resolution authorizing force.

The decision of the US and British administrations, along with a small number of allies, to use force against Iraq without clear UN authorization undermined the credibility of the United Nations. This action renewed the fears that great powers like the United States and the United Kingdom would be willing at any time to act without UN authorization. The Bush administration's National Security Strategy of September 2002 states that "[W]e will be prepared to act apart when our interests and unique responsibilities require" (NSS 2002, 31).

Nonetheless, the aftermath of the invasion and the continued difficulties in establishing security in Iraq highlight the need for international cooperation. The

United Nations enhances the legitimacy of military action and can also help share in global risks, burdens, and strategies for rebuilding.

For Discussion

1. Why do you think the second Bush administration did not follow the path of the first Bush administration by using the United Nations and encouraging multilateralism?

2. After this Iraq War, do you think the United States or other major powers will likely intervene in other states unilaterally? Why or why not? Is unilateralism a thing of the past?

3. How effective can the United Nations be as a provider of security and a protector of human rights and international law?

4. Do you think powerful states like the United States should be able to remove leaders they think are unacceptable? Why or why not?

right to intervene in the member states of the socialist commonwealth to protect the principles of socialism.

Much earlier, the British had insisted on the abolition of slavery in their relations with other states. They stopped ships on the high seas and imposed the abolition of slavery as a condition in treaties (Bethell 1970). There were also occasions when states tried to bind other states to respect certain principles in their internal affairs. A number of states in eastern Europe, such as Hungary and Bulgaria, were bound to respect the rights of minorities within their frontiers based on agreements made at the 1878 Congress of Berlin by the great powers. In practice, then, intervention was a common feature of international politics.

By the 1990s, some believed that there should be a return to this earlier period when intervention was justified, but it was felt that a wider range of instruments should be used to protect generally accepted standards. Supporters of this idea insisted on a key role for the United Nations in granting a license to intervene. It was pointed out that the UN Charter did not assert merely the rights of states but also the rights of peoples: statehood could be interpreted as being conditional on respect for such rights. There was ample evidence in the UN Charter to justify the view that extreme transgressions of human rights could be a justification for intervention by the international community.

The major pronouncements of the UN General Assembly on humanitarian assistance referred to the primary responsibility of states for dealing with complex crises within their frontiers. A 1991 General Assembly resolution implied some relaxation of this principle when it held that "the sovereignty, territorial integrity, and national unity of States must be fully respected in accordance with the Charter of the United Nations. In this context, humanitarian assistance should be provided with the consent of the affected country and in principle on the basis of an appeal by the affected country" (A/RES/46/182). The use of the phrase "in principle" and the term "should" imply that there could be occasions where intervention was necessary even when consent in the target state was not possible. In the Outcome Document of the 2005 World Summit, the General Assembly said that if national authorities are "manifestly failing to protect their populations from genocide, war crimes, ethnic cleansing and crimes against humanity" and if peaceful means are inadequate, the international community could take collective action through the UN Security Council according to Chapter VII of the charter (A/RES/60/1, para. 138 and 139). This document echoes recommendations from the Responsibility to Protect, the 2001 final report of the International Commission on Intervention and State Sovereignty.

Yet the number of occasions when a UN resolution justified intervention due to gross infringements of the rights of individuals has remained limited. The justification of intervention in Kosovo represented a break from the past because it included a clear humanitarian element. Kosovo was arguably the first occasion international forces were used in defiance of a sovereign state to protect humanitarian standards. NATO launched the air campaign in March 1999 in Kosovo against the Republic of Yugoslavia without a mandate from the Security Council since Russia had declared it would veto such action. Nonetheless, NATO states noted that by intervening to stop ethnic cleansing and crimes against humanity in Kosovo, they were acting in accordance with the principles of the UN Charter.

WHAT'S YOUR WORLDVIEW

Much was written about the need to invoke the Responsibility to Protect (R2P) doctrine to help the citizens of Libya. NATO members cited R2P to justify intervention. Meanwhile, in early 2014, some 150,000 have died in the conflict in Syria. Why has the world done very little about this civil war and the death of innocents?

The Iraq War in 2003 was another case, although the legality of intervention under existing Security Council resolutions is contested, especially in view of the failure to obtain a second UN Security Council resolution to give an explicit mandate for the action (see the Case Study in this chapter). The US action against Afghanistan in 2001 is an exceptional case in which the UN Security Council acknowledged the right of a state that had been attacked—referring to the events of 9/11 in the United States—to respond in its own defense.

Arguably, earlier instances of intervention did not explicitly breach sovereignty. The 1991 Security Council resolution sanctioning intervention in Iraq (S/Res/688) at the end of the Gulf War did not breach Iraqi sovereignty insofar as its implementation depended on Saddam

Hussein's consent. The 1992 Security Council resolution (S/Res/733) that first sanctioned UN involvement in Somalia was based on a request by Somalia. A later resolution (S/Res/794) authorizing the United States to intervene in Somalia did not mention the consent of Somali authorities, but by that time, a central Somali government did not exist.

The difficulty in relaxing the principle of nonintervention should not be underestimated. For instance, the United Nations was reluctant to send peacekeepers to Darfur without the consent of the Sudanese government and continues to avoid intervention in South Sudan. Some fear a slippery slope whereby a relaxation of the nonintervention principle by the United Nations will lead to military action by individual states without UN approval. It could be argued that the action against Iraq in 2003 illustrates this danger (see the Case Study in this chapter). There are significant numbers of non-UN actors, including regional organizations, involved in peace operations, and several states are suspicious of what appears to be the granting of a license to intervene in their affairs.

A growing readiness by the United Nations to intervene within states to promote internal justice for individuals would indicate a movement toward global governance and away from unconditional sovereignty. There have been some signs of movement in this direction, but principles of state sovereignty and nonintervention remain important. There is no clear consensus on these points. There is still some support for the view that Article 2(7) of the UN Charter should be interpreted strictly: there can be no intervention within a state without the express consent of the government of that state. Others believe that intervention within a country to promote human rights is only justifiable on the basis of a threat to international peace and security. Evidence of a threat to international peace and security could be the appearance of significant numbers of refugees or the judgment that other states might intervene militarily. Some liberal internationalists argue that this condition is flexible enough to justify intervention to defend human rights whenever possible. Many states and nonstate actors argued for NATO intervention in Libya in 2011 by invoking the new norm of responsibility to protect that was articulated in the 2005 UN resolution.

Overall, then, the UN's record on the maintenance of international peace and security has been mixed. On the one hand, there has been a stronger assertion of the responsibility of international society, represented by the United Nations, for gross offenses against populations. Nonetheless, the practice has been patchy. Intimations of a **new world order** in the aftermath of the Gulf War in 1991 quickly gave way to despondency with what were seen as failures in Somalia, Rwanda, other parts of Africa, and the former Yugoslavia and increasing disagreement about the proper role of the United Nations in Kosovo, Iraq, Libya, and Syria. Compared with the enthusiasm about the potential for the United Nations in the early 1990s, the debates and disagreements at the time of the war in Iraq in 2003 were striking.

new world order The post–Cold War rhetoric of President George Herbert Walker Bush, who called for a new world order based on neoliberal values of democracy, capitalism, and the rule of law. After periods of turmoil or war, the victors often call for a new world order based on their values, beliefs, and interests.

Economic and Social Questions

As described, there has been an increased tendency to view threats to peace and security not only in terms of aggression between or among states but also in terms of civil conflict within states, threats emanating from nonstate actors, and threats relating to economic and social conditions within states. This view incorporates the belief that conditions within states, including human rights, justice, development, and equality, have a bearing on global peace. The more integrated global context has meant that economic and social problems in one part of the world may affect other areas. Furthermore, promoting social and economic development is an important UN goal in itself. The preamble of the UN Charter talks of promoting "social progress and better standards of life in larger freedom" and the need to "employ international

GLOBAL PERSPECTIVE — The United Nations and Environmental Protection

THE ISSUE

The United Nations is an organization of states that claim the right of sovereign equality. In practical terms, this means that if the leaders of a country do not want to act on a UN resolution, declaration, or action plan, the leaders can assert the right to make a national-level decision. On matters of peace and war, this can, perhaps, be excused as protecting the national interest in an uncertain self-help world.

However, should national interest *not* apply to the topic of environmental protection? Many problems of pollution are becoming globalized as industrial production moves around the world. What has the United Nations done to stop pollution?

BACKGROUND

The UN Conference on Environment and Development (Earth Summit) held in 1992 in Rio de Janeiro was unprecedented for a UN conference in both its size and its scope of concerns. Representatives from 172 countries and more than 2,400 NGOs discussed ways to help reach the goal of sustainable development in the global community. The Rio Earth Summit was held twenty years after the first UN Conference on the Human Environment in Stockholm. That 1972 conference had stimulated the creation of national environmental ministries around the world and established the UN Environment Programme (UNEP).

The central concern of the Rio Earth Summit was the need for broad-based, environmentally sustainable development. As a result of the summit, 108 governments adopted three major agreements concerned with changing the traditional approach to development. These agreements included the Rio Declaration on Environment and Development (a series of principles defining the rights and responsibilities of states), the Statement of Forest Principles, and Agenda 21 (a comprehensive program of action to attain sustainable development on a global scale). In addition, the UN Framework Convention on Climate Change and the Convention on Biological Diversity were signed by many governments.

RECENT HISTORY

The UN Commission on Sustainable Development was formed after the 1992 Earth Summit to ensure follow-up and to report on the implementation of Earth Summit agreements at the local, national, regional, and international levels. A five-year review of Earth Summit progress took place in New York in 1997, and a ten-year review took place at the World Summit on Sustainable Development held in Johannesburg in 2002. There were significant divisions at the Johannesburg Summit. The conference was thought to be too large, and the outcome was generally seen as disappointing. Nonetheless, by 2002, it was clear that environmental questions were prominent on the UN agenda.

In June 2012 the world gathered again in Rio for the Rio+20 Summit on Environmental Sustainability. The conference did not produce any major agreements or commitments, but it did provide a global platform for environmentalists to push a green agenda. The governments, corporations, and not-for-profit organizations participating in the conference reached some hopeful results. First, participants established Sustainable Development Goals (SDGs) in areas of economic, social, and environmental policy to follow on the Millennium Development Goals, which lapse in 2015. The summit also resulted in 713 voluntary pledges of $513 billion from public, private, and NGO actors. These pledges are to fund sustainable public transportation systems, energy projects, and creating national and local green economy jobs. Those concerned about the environment will wait to see if these pledges are met.

Were these UN-level actions successful in fighting environmental problems? If you believe that the UN's greatest tool is moral suasion, then yes, the United Nations has taken a leading role in seeking to apply pressure to national governments to get them to regulate polluters in their countries. However, as you will see in Chapter 14, actions, not only moral suasion, are needed to solve the menace of the world's environmental problems.

For Discussion

1. The 1992 Earth Summit introduced us to the strategy of sustainable development and the concept of foresight capacity. Simply put, foresight capacity asks you to consider how your choices today will affect future generations. Do you ever consider how your future grandchildren will be affected by your choices as a consumer today? If so, how? If not, why not?

2. National interests, especially economic interests, seem to crowd out any attempt to protect the environment. What could you do to convince national leaders that environmental issues should take priority? For example, would you frame them as a security issue?

3. Given the global track record on creating rules to protect the environment and given very weak enforcement efforts in many areas, what are the chances of future action on climate change?

machinery for the promotion of the economic and social advancement of all peoples."

The number of institutions within the UN system that address economic and social issues has risen significantly since the founding of the United Nations. Nonetheless, the main contributor states have been giving less and less to economic and social institutions. By the mid-1990s, the regular assessed budget for the United Nations and the budget for peacekeeping operations were in crisis. This situation was mitigated only when the United States agreed, under certain conditions, to repay what it owed the United Nations and returned to full funding in December 2002.

In 2000, the United Nations convened a Millennium Summit, where heads of state committed themselves to a series of measurable goals and targets, known as the Millennium Development Goals (MDGs). These goals, to be achieved by 2015, include reducing by half the number of people living on less than $1 a day, achieving universal primary education, and reversing the spread of HIV/AIDS and malaria (A/55/L.2). Since 2000, the United Nations has been integrating the MDGs into all aspects of its work at the country level, but progress on reaching the MDGs has been very uneven.

The governments of Norway and Denmark agreed to transport chemical weapons out of Syria. The plan for destroying these weapons was a joint project of the Organization for the Prohibition of Chemical Weapons (OPCW) and the UN. This is a great example of multilateral cooperation at the national and international levels.

The Reform Process of the United Nations

In his important book *The Parliament of Man* (2006), Paul Kennedy suggests that any reform of the United Nations will need to be partial, gradual, and carefully executed. He argues that the need to make the United Nations more effective, representative, and accountable to its members is greater today than it was in the past because of a number of global developments, including the following:

1. The emergence of new great powers like India and Brazil and older powers like Japan and Germany which have been left out of the Security Council. Are the current members of the Security Council willing to add new members or even change the decision-making structure?

2. The presence of truly global issues that threaten the world as we know it. These include environmental degradation, terrorism, the proliferation of weapons of all kinds, and the persistence of global poverty. Is the United Nations interested in or capable of responding to these issues?

In the mid- to late 1990s, alongside growing UN involvement in development issues, the UN economic and social arrangements underwent reform at two levels: (1) the country (field) level and (2) the general or headquarters level.

Country Level

The continuing complaints of NGOs about poor UN performance in the field served as a powerful stimulus for reform. A key feature of the reforms at the country (field) level was the adoption of Country Strategy Notes. These were statements about the overall development process tailored to the specific needs of individual countries. They were written on the basis of discussions among the Specialized Agencies, Programmes and Funds, donors, and the host country and described the plans of the various institutions and donors in a particular country. The merit of the Country Strategy Notes is that they clearly set out targets, roles, and priorities.

Another reform at the country level was the strengthening of the resident coordinator, usually an employee of the UN Development Programme (UNDP). He or she became the responsible officer at the country level and was provided with more training to fulfill this role. Field-level officers were also given enhanced authority so that they could make decisions about the redeployment of funds within a program without referring to headquarters. There was also an effort to introduce improved communication facilities and information sharing. The activities of the various UN organizations were brought together in single locations, or "UN houses," which facilitated interagency communication and collegiality. The new country-level approach was called an "integrated programs" approach. The adoption of the Millennium Development Goals framework has also helped country field staff achieve a more coherent approach to development. This can be contrasted to earlier arrangements whereby the various agencies would work separately on distinct projects, often in ignorance of each other's presence in the same country.

Headquarters Level

Since the Security Council is the main executive body within the United Nations, with primary responsibility for maintaining international peace and security, it is not surprising that many discussions of UN reform have focused on the Security Council.

The founders of the United Nations deliberately established a universal General Assembly and a restricted Security Council that required unanimity among the great powers. Granting permanent seats and the right to a veto to the great powers of the time—the United States, the Soviet Union (now Russia), France, the United Kingdom, and China—was an essential feature of the deal.

The composition and decision-making procedures of the Security Council were increasingly challenged as membership of the United Nations grew, particularly after decolonization. Yet the only significant reform of the Security Council occurred in 1965, when the council was enlarged from eleven to fifteen members and the required majority from seven to nine votes. Nonetheless, the veto power of the permanent five (P-5) members was left intact.

The Security Council does not reflect today's distribution of military or economic power, and it does not reflect a geographic balance. Germany and Japan have made strong cases for permanent membership. Developing countries have demanded more representation on the Security Council, particularly South Africa, India, Egypt, Brazil, and Nigeria. However, it has proved impossible to reach agreement on new permanent members. Should the European Union be represented instead of Great Britain, France, and Germany individually? How would Pakistan feel about India's candidacy? How would South Africa feel about a Nigerian seat? What about representation by an Islamic country? These issues are not easy to resolve. Likewise, it is very unlikely that the P-5 states will relinquish their veto. Nonetheless, although large-scale reform has proved impossible, there have been changes in Security Council working procedures that have made it more transparent and accountable to the member states.

Did you see the movie *Contagion*? Margaret Chan, director-general of the World Health Organization, has stated that WHO can do more to eradicate infectious diseases. Should the organization be more than an information clearinghouse if this means states must share their sovereignty over the health of citizens?

If the UN role in economic and social affairs at the country level was to be effective, reform was also required at the headquarters level. The UN family of economic and social organizations has always been a polycentric system. Historically, there was no organization or agent within the system that was capable of managing the wide range of economic and social activities under the UN umbrella. Reform efforts in the 1990s focused on the reorganization and rationalization of the Economic and Social Council (ECOSOC).

In the UN Charter, the powers given to the General Assembly and ECOSOC were modest. The ECOSOC could only issue recommendations and receive reports. By contrast, UN reform in the mid- to late 1990s allowed the ECOSOC to become more assertive and to take a leading role in the coordination of the UN system. The ECOSOC was to ensure that General Assembly policies were appropriately implemented on a systemwide basis. The ECOSOC was given the power to make final decisions on the activities of its subsidiary bodies and on other matters of systemwide coordination in economic, social, and related fields (A/50/227, para. 37).

One of the ECOSOC's responsibilities was to review common themes in the work of the nine functional commissions, such as the Commission on Narcotic Drugs, the Commission on Sustainable Development, and the Commission on the Status of Women. The reform effort aimed to eliminate duplication and overlap in the work of the functional commissions. The ECOSOC would integrate their work and provide input to the General Assembly, which was responsible for establishing the broader economic and social policy framework. The boards of the Programmes and Funds were also reformed to enhance their day-to-day management.

Overall, economic and social reorganization meant that the two poles of the system were better coordinated: the pole where intentions are defined through global conferences and agendas and the pole where programs are implemented. Programs at the field level were better integrated, and field officers were given enhanced discretion. The reform of the ECOSOC sharpened its capacity to shape broad agreements into cross-sectoral programs with well-defined objectives. At the same time, the ECOSOC acquired greater capacity to act as a conduit through which the results of field-level monitoring could be conveyed upward to the functional commissions. These new processes had the effect of strengthening the norms, values, and goals of a multilateral system.

The European Union and Other Regional Organizations

The "new regionalism" taking place since the late 1980s has been a response to new forms of globalization as well as to the new multipolar environment after the end of the Cold War. Various common features could be seen in the 1990s. Regional arrangements tended to be more open than before in terms of economic integration, as well as more comprehensive in scope. The new open regionalism indeed seemed to lose some of the very defining characteristics of regionalism, forming part of "a global structural transformation in which non-state actors are active and manifest themselves at several levels of the global system [and] can therefore not be understood only from the point of view of the single region" (Hettne 1999, 7–8).

Yet regionalism may also be seen as one of the few instruments available to states to try to manage the effects of globalization. If individual states no longer have the effective capacity to regulate in the face of uncontrolled movements of capital, then regionalism may be seen as a means to regain some control over global market forces—and to counter the more negative social consequences of globalization. The debate is far from over.

The Process of European Integration

European Union (EU) The union formally created in 1992 following the signing of the Maastricht Treaty. The origins of the European Union can be traced back to 1951 and the creation of the European Coal and Steel Community, followed in 1957 with a broader customs union (the Treaty of Rome, 1958). Originally a grouping of six countries in 1957, "Europe" grew by adding new members in 1973, 1981, and 1986. Since the fall of the planned economies in Eastern Europe in 1989, Europe has grown and now includes twenty-eight member states.

In Europe, regionalism after 1945 has taken the form of a gradual process of integration leading to the emergence of the **European Union**. It was initially a purely West European creation by the original six member states, born out of the desire for reconciliation between France and Germany in a context of ambitious federalist plans for a united Europe. Yet the process has taken the form of a progressive construction of an institutional architecture, a legal framework, and a wide range of policies, which in 2014 encompassed twenty-eight European states.

The European Coal and Steel Community was created in 1951 (in force in 1952), followed by the European Economic Community and the European Atomic Energy Community in 1957 (in force in 1958). These treaties involved a conferral of community competence, or standards, in various areas—the supranational management of coal and steel, the creation and regulation of an internal market, and common policies in trade, competition, agriculture, and transport. Since then, powers have been extended to include new legislative competencies in some fields such as the environment. Since the 1992 Treaty on European Union (the Maastricht Treaty, in force in 1993), the integration process has also involved the adoption of stronger forms of unification, notably monetary union, as well as cooperation in economic and employment policy and more intergovernmental cooperation in foreign and security policy.

From very limited beginnings, in terms of both membership and scope, the European Union has therefore gradually developed to become an important political and economic actor whose presence has a significant impact internationally and domestically (see Table 6.4). This gradual process of European integration has taken place at various levels, beginning with the signature and reform of the basic treaties. These are the result of intergovernmental conferences (IGCs), where representatives of national governments negotiate the legal framework for the EU institutions (see Table 6.5). Such treaty changes require ratification in each country and are the "grand bargains" in the evolution of the European Union.

Within this framework, the institutions have been given considerable powers to adopt decisions and manage policies, although the dynamics of decision making differ significantly across areas. There are important differences between the more integrated areas of economic regulation on the one hand and the more intergovernmental pillars of foreign policy and police or judicial cooperation in criminal matters on the other. In some areas, a country may have to accept decisions imposed on it by the (qualified) majority of member states. In other areas, it may be able to block decisions.

To understand the integration process, one needs to take account of the role played by both member states *and* supranational institutions. Moreover, member states are not just represented by national governments because a host of state, nonstate, and transnational actors participate in the processes of domestic preference formation and direct representation of interests in the key EU institutions. The relative openness of the European policy process means that political groups and economic interests will try to influence EU decision making if they feel that their position is not sufficiently represented by national governments. That is one reason the European Union is increasingly seen as a system of multilevel governance involving a plurality of actors on different territorial levels: supranational, national, and substate.

The complexity of the EU institutional machinery, together with continuous change over time, has spawned a lively debate among integration theorists (Rosamond 2000; Wiener and Diez 2004). Some approaches are applications of more general theories of international relations. For example, the literature on both realism and liberalism has contributed to theorizing integration. Other scholars have regarded the European Union as sui generis—in a category

Table 6.4
Important Agreements in the History of the European Union

Year	Treaty	Main Subjects
1951	Paris Treaty	Regulation of coal and steel production in the member states; creation of supranational institutions
1957	Rome Treaties	European Economic Community—creation of a customs union (removal of all intraunion duties and creation of a common customs tariff); plans for a common market and common policies; Euratom—cooperation in atomic energy
1986	Single European Act	Removal of all nontariff barriers to the movement of persons, goods, services, and capital (the 1992 program); foreign policy cooperation included in the treaty provisions
1992	Maastricht Treaty	Creation of the European Union, encompassing the European Community and two parallel pillars for Common Foreign and Security Policy (CFSP) and justice and home affairs; economic and monetary union (the euro)
1997	Amsterdam Treaty	Various institutional reforms; creation of the post of high representative for CFSP; provisions for enhanced cooperation
2001	Nice Treaty	Reform of commission and council (voting weights); expansion of majority voting
2009	Treaty of Lisbon	Initially known as Reform Treaty, replaced the abandoned Constitutional Treaty of 2005, it amends the Maastricht and Rome Treaties to comprise a constitutional basis for the EU, which aims to enhance the efficiency and democratic legitimacy of the Union and to improve the coherence of its action.

of its own—and therefore in need of the development of dedicated theories of integration. The most prominent among these has been neofunctionalism, which sought to explain the evolution of integration in terms of "spillover" from one policy sector to another as resources and loyalties of elites were transferred to the European level. As aspects of EU politics have come to resemble the domestic politics of states, scholars have turned to approaches drawn from comparative politics or the study of governance in different states.

However, the exchange between supranational and intergovernmental approaches has had the greatest impact on the study of European integration. Supranational approaches regard the emergence of supranational institutions in Europe as a distinct feature and turn these into the main object of analysis. Here the politics above the level of states is regarded as the most significant, and consequently, the political actors and institutions at the European level receive the most attention.

Intergovernmental approaches, on the other hand, continue to regard states as the most important aspect of the integration process, and consequently, they concentrate on the study of politics *between* and *within* states. But whatever one's theoretical preferences, most scholars would agree that no analysis of the European Union is complete without studying both the operation and evolution of the central institutions and the input from political actors in the member states. Academic debate in EU studies has also centered on a wider fault line in

Table 6.5
Institutions of the European Union

EU Institution	Responsibilities	Location
European Commission	Initiating, administering, and overseeing the implementation of EU policies and legislation	Brussels and Luxembourg
European Parliament (EP)	Acting as directly elected representatives of EU citizens, scrutinizing the operation of the other institutions, and, in certain areas, sharing with the council the power to determine EU legislation	Strasbourg (plenary sessions); Brussels (MEP offices, committee meetings, and some plenary sessions); Luxembourg (administration)
Council of Ministers	Representing the views of national governments and determining, in many areas jointly with the EP, the ultimate shape of EU legislation	Brussels (some meetings in Luxembourg)
European Council	Holding regular summits of the heads of state or government and the president of the commission, setting the EU's broad agenda, and acting as a forum of last resort to find agreement on divisive issues (note: different from the Council of Europe)	Brussels
European Court of Justice	Acting as the EU's highest court (supported by a Court of First Instance): annulment of Community acts, infringement procedures against member states for failing to comply with obligations, and preliminary rulings on the validity or interpretation of EC law on request from national courts	Luxembourg
European Central Bank	Setting the interest rates and controlling the money supply of the single European currency, the euro	Frankfurt am Main
Court of Auditors	Auditing the revenues and the expenditure under the EU budget	Luxembourg

President of European Central Bank Mario Draghi, right, and vice president Vitor Constancio chat during a European Finance ministers meeting at Zappeion Hall in Athens, on Wednesday, April 2, 2014. Draghi will need to deal with on-going Greek economic crisis.

the social sciences: the difference between rationalist and constructivist approaches. Constructivists have challenged the implicit rationalism of much integration research until the 1990s (see Chapter 3). Their critique focuses on the tendency of rationalist studies to privilege rational decision making over agenda setting and outcomes over process. The social-constructivist research agenda instead concentrates on the framing of issues *before* decisions about them are made and therefore emphasizes the role of ideas, discourses, and social interaction in shaping interests (Christiansen, Jørgensen, and Wiener 2001).

The prospect of an ever *wider* European Union has raised serious questions about the nature and direction of the integration process. The 2004 enlargement has generally been seen as a qualitative leap for the European Union. Concerns that the enlarged union, if not reformed substantially, would find it difficult to make decisions and maintain a reliable legal framework led to several attempts to reform the treaties. The most wide-ranging proposals and the most significant change in the language of integration came with the treaty establishing a constitution for Europe that EU governments signed in 2004. The very fact that the European Union should discuss something referred to in the media as a "European Constitution" is a sign of how far it has developed from its modest beginnings. However, the time may still not be right for such a project. The Constitutional Treaty was rejected in referendums in France and the Netherlands, raising serious doubts not only about this attempt at institutional reform but also about ambitions for a formal constitutional process more generally. In 2007, with intergovernmental negotiations about a revised "reform treaty," the European Union seemed likely to continue along the established path of a succession of gradual developments rather than big leaps.

After eight years of debate and several disappointing negative national votes, the European Union's reform treaty came into force on December 1, 2009. European Union leaders believe the now ratified Lisbon Treaty will rejuvenate the decision-making apparatus of all of the EU institutions, making the functioning of the twenty-eight-member union more efficient and democratic.

In the recent global economic crisis, Germany has emerged as the clear leader of the eurozone and the European Union. Some in Germany are talking about a remaking of the European Union that would include more financial union, including some control over the members' budgets and spending; creating a eurobonds program; renegotiating many of the treaties that bind the EU members together; and even going so far as to create a federal Europe. Once again, a major crisis may serve as a catalyst for greater European integration.

Other Regional Actors: The African Union and the Organization of American States

The **African Union (AU)** is the most important intergovernmental organization in Africa. It replaced the **Organization of African Unity (OAU)** in July 2002. At the time of this succession, fifty-three of the fifty-four African states were members (all but Morocco, which remains a nonmember at the time of this writing). The OAU was established in 1963 to provide a collective voice for Africa and to work to end all forms of colonization. It offered support to independence movements, worked to end apartheid in South Africa, and sought to reduce tensions among members and promote the peaceful resolution of disputes.

The OAU also sought to promote economic development and human rights and to improve the quality of life for all Africans. The record here is not good when you consider that eighteen of the twenty-one poorest countries in the world are in Africa, and some eight major conflicts are creating almost insurmountable human security problems across the continent. Many critics argue that the OAU was primarily a "talk shop" and was ineffective in many key areas. However, the OAU did succeed in encouraging its members to cooperate as a voting bloc in international organizations like the United Nations.

The African Union (AU) still must deal with many of the same challenges as it attempts to fulfill its vision of creating "an integrated, prosperous and peaceful Africa, driven by its own citizens and representing a dynamic force in the global arena." The African Union has carved out a bold set of objectives that clearly resemble the goals of other regional organizations. Again, it continues to fail to realize some of its key goals for the peoples of Africa. Peace security and stability, human rights and democratic governance, and sustainable development are AU priorities that are still not being met. The African Union has a long way

African Union (AU) Created in 2002 and consisting of fifty-four member states, this union was formed as a successor to the Organization of African Unity. It maintains fourteen goals primarily centered in African unity and security, human rights, peace security and stability, economy, sustainable development, and equality.

Organization of African Unity (OAU) A regional organization founded in 1963 as a way to foster solidarity among African countries, promote African independence, and throw off the vestiges of colonial rule. The Organization of African Unity had a policy of noninterference in member states, and it had no means for intervening in conflicts; as a result, this organization could be only a passive bystander in many violent conflicts.

to go to be considered a successful regional organization, and achieving this success may be even more difficult as major powers like China, India, the United States, and European states all compete for access to African resources and turn a blind eye to abuses of governance in many states.

Turning now to the Americas, the **Organization of American States (OAS)** is the world's oldest regional organization, founded in 1890. It was known at the time as the International Union of American Republics and changed its name to Organization of American States in 1948. Its charter states that the goals of the organization are to create "an order of peace and justice, to promote their solidarity, to strengthen their collaboration, and to defend their sovereignty, their territorial integrity, and their independence." The organization, which has thirty-five member states, may be more effective in the post-Cold War period. During the Cold War, the US obsession with communism drove the Organization of American States to intervene in the affairs of states and at times use extralegal activities to make certain that friendly governments stayed in power. Although the United States remains the dominant power, the Organization of American States could become a very effective regional organization and an influential part of global governance. The main pillars of the Organization of American States are democracy, human rights, regional security, and economic development. With rising powers like Brazil, Chile, and Argentina and the intransigent Venezuela, the Organization of American States could become a major player in global politics.

Organization of American States (OAS) A regional international organization composed of thirty-five member states. It is the world's oldest regional organization, founded in 1890 as the International Union of American Republics and changing its name to Organization of American States in 1948. The goals of this organization are to create "an order of peace and justice, to promote their solidarity, to strengthen their collaboration, and to defend their sovereignty, their territorial integrity, and their independence."

Conclusion

International and regional organizations and international law play an important role in the governance of our global society. These institutions provide the infrastructure of a truly global system in which it is possible to think about a global common good and a world where human interests trump national interests. There are three pillars of global governance (Muldoon 2004):

1. A political pillar that includes diplomacy, international law, and global and regional organizations like the United Nations, the World Trade Organization, and the European Union.
2. An economic pillar that includes multinational corporations, international banking and industry associations, global labor movements, and global economic movements.
3. A social pillar that includes actors within the global civil society, such as NGOs, and global social movements, like the Jubilee Movement led by U2 and Radiohead that sought to get states to forgive developing countries' debt.

Clearly, international and regional organizations play a critical role in governing the policy areas that transcend the nation-state. The effectiveness and perhaps the fairness of global policy will often depend on the efficacy of international law. Thus, all these institutions play a role in the governance of this global society.

As we have seen in this chapter, the capacity of the United Nations in its economic and social work, its development work, and its management of peacekeeping and postconflict reconstruction has expanded since the 1990s. Nonetheless, the predominance of US military power, the possibility that the United States will act again without clear UN authorization, the heightened concern over terrorism and weapons of mass destruction, the inability to respond effectively to the crisis in Darfur, and the pervasiveness of inequality and injustice across the world signal that further changes and adaptations within the UN system will be necessary.

With regard to regional organizations, the European Union is the best example of how far the integration process can go and how much sovereignty states are willing to share or surrender. The prospect of an ever-wider European Union has raised serious questions about the nature and direction of the integration process. The most wide-ranging proposals and the most significant change in the language of integration came with the treaty establishing a constitution for Europe that EU heads of state or government signed in 2004. The very fact that the European Union should discuss something referred to in the media as a European Constitution is a sign of how far it has developed from its modest beginnings. However, the time may still not be right for such a project.

For all of these reasons, international law and international organizations remain works in progress.

CONTRIBUTORS TO CHAPTER 6: Devon Curtis, Christian Reus-Smit, Paul Taylor, and Steven L. Lamy.

REVIEW QUESTIONS

1. Can you think of factors, in addition to the ones listed in the chapter, that may have contributed to the rise of modern international law in the last two centuries?
2. If states create institutions to sustain international order, why do wars and other conflicts persist?
3. What do you think are the strengths and weaknesses of the international legal system?
4. What have been the driving forces behind processes of regional integration and cooperation?
5. What impact have processes of regional integration had on the state?
6. Compare and contrast European integration with regional cooperation in other areas of the world.
7. How does the United Nations try to maintain world order?
8. How has UN peacekeeping evolved?
9. Has reform of the economic and social arrangements of the United Nations been effective?
10. Does increased UN activity undermine the sovereignty of states?

FURTHER READING

Archer, C. (2001), *International Organisations*, 3rd ed. (London: Routledge). A succinct survey of the range of international institutions and their main purposes.

Barker, J. C. (2000), *International Law and International Relations* (London: Continuum). A good survey on the relationship between international law and international relations.

Berdal, M., and Economides, S. (eds.) (2007), *United Nations Interventionism, 1991–2004* (Cambridge: Cambridge University Press). Includes case studies of eight UN operations and discusses the impact of the "new interventionism" on international order.

Byers, M. (2000), *The Role of Law in International Politics* (Oxford: Oxford University Press). An excellent collection of advanced essays on the politics of international law.

Cassese, A. (2001), *International Law* (Oxford: Oxford University Press). An excellent international legal text by a leading scholar and jurist.

Claude, I. L., Jr. (1984), *Swords into Plowshares: The Progress and Problems of International Organization*, 4th ed. (New York: Random House). A classic text on the history of international institutions, particularly concerned with their role in war and peace. Useful for the history of the United Nations.

Dodds, F. (ed.) (1997), *The Way Forward: Beyond Agenda 21* (London: Earthscan). An account of the involvement of the UN system in the issues raised in the functional commissions, such as social development, the status of women, and environmental protection.

Goldsmith, J. L., and Posner, E. A. (2006), *The Limits of International Law* (New York: Oxford University Press). A vigorous critique of the institution of international law and its capacity to produce substantial goods for international society.

Higgins, R. (1994), *Problems and Process: International Law and How We Use It* (Oxford: Oxford University Press). A very good introduction to international law by a justice of the International Court of Justice.

Karns, M., and Mingst, K. (2004), *International Organizations: The Politics and Processes of Global Governance* (Boulder, Colo.: Lynne Rienner). A comprehensive overview of the main actors and processes of global governance.

Kennedy, P. (2006), *The Parliament of Man: The Past, Present, and Future of the United Nations* (New York: Random House). A review of the origins and evolution of the United Nations and a discussion of its future challenges.

Kratochwil, F. (1989), *Rules, Norms, and Decisions* (Cambridge: Cambridge University Press). The most sustained and advanced constructivist work on international legal reasoning.

Lynch, C., and Loriaux, M. (eds.) (2000), *Law and Moral Action in World Politics* (Minneapolis: University of Minnesota Press). A good collection of essays on the relationship between international law and ethics.

Malone, D. (ed.) (2004), *The UN Security Council: From the Cold War to the Twenty-First Century* (Boulder, Colo.: Lynne Rienner). Discusses the history of the UN Security Council and major UN operations.

Muldoon, J. P., Jr., (2004), *The Architecture of Global Governance: An Introduction to the Study of International Organizations* (Boulder, Colo.: Westview Press). Excellent combination of theoretical views and historical applications of international order and international organization.

Reus-Smit, C. (ed.) (2004), *The Politics of International Law* (Cambridge: Cambridge University Press). An edited collection that presents a constructivist perspective on international law, illustrated by a range of contemporary case studies.

Roberts, A., and Kingsbury, B. (eds.) (1993), *United Nations, Divided World: The UN's Roles in International Relations*, 2nd ed. (Oxford: Clarendon Press). An important collection of readings by practitioners and academics.

Taylor, P., and Groom, A. J. R. (eds.) (2000), *The United Nations at the Millennium* (London: Continuum). A detailed account of the institutions of the central UN system.

Thakur, R. (2006), *The United Nations, Peace and Security* (Cambridge: Cambridge University Press). Discusses the changing role of UN peace operations.

Von Glahn, G. (1995), *Law Among Nations: An Introduction to Public International Law*, 7th ed. (New York: Addison-Wesley). A traditional yet comprehensive introduction to international law by a political scientist.

SELECTED DOCUMENTS RELATED TO THE CHANGING ROLE OF THE UNITED NATIONS SYSTEM

Development of the economic and social organizations:

A/32/197, December 1977. The first major General Assembly resolution on reform of the economic and social organizations.

A/48/162, December 1993. A major step toward reform of the economic and social organization of the United Nations, especially ECOSOC.

Development of the UN's role in maintaining international peace and security:

SC Res. 678, November 1990. Sanctioned the use of force against Saddam Hussein.

SC Res. 816, April 1993. Enforced the no-fly zone over Bosnia in that it permitted NATO warplanes to intercept Bosnian Serb planes in the zones.

SC Res. 1160, 1199, and 1203. Contained arguments relevant to the action on Kosovo.

SC Res. 1244 contained the agreement at the end of the bombing.

Development of humanitarian action through the United Nations:

SC Res. 688, April 1991. Sanctioned intervention at the end of the Gulf War to protect the Kurds in northern Iraq.

SC Res. 733, January 1992. Sanctioned UN involvement in Somalia. A/46/182, April 1992, is the major document on the development of the machinery for humanitarian assistance.

SC Res. 794, December 1992, sanctioned American intervention in Somalia under Chapter VII of the UN Charter. The government of Somalia had ceased to exist in the eyes of the member states of the Security Council.

SC Res. 1441, November 2002, resolution on Iraq that threatened serious consequences if Saddam Hussein failed to reveal his weapons of mass destruction to the team of UN inspectors.

INTERNET RESOURCES

The network of websites regarding international law and international organizations provides reliable information for students to use in their work. Here is a sample of these websites:

European Union
http://europa.eu/

International Court of Justice
http://www.icj-cij.org/

International Criminal Court
http://www.icc-cpi.int/

UN High Commissioner for Refugees
http://www.unhcr.org/cgi-bin/texis/vtx/home

UN High Commissioner of Human Rights
http://www.ohchr.org/EN/Pages/WelcomePage.aspx

UN Office of Peacekeeping Operations
http://www.un.org/Depts/dpko/dpko/dpko.shtml

UN Peacebuilding Commission
www.un.org/peace/peacebuilding/

United Nations Internet Portal
www.un.org

Organization of American States
www.oas.org

African Union
www.au.int

Carnegie Council: "The Unfinished Global Revolution: The Pursuit of a New International Politics"—Mark Malloch Brown
http://www.carnegiecouncil.org/resources/video/data/000375

Malloch is a firm believer in the idea that "countries can get second chances"; he explores how international institutions can be facilitators for human and state growth.

Carnegie Council: "Five to Rule Them All: The UN Security Council and the Making of the Modern World"—David L. Bosco
http://www.carnegiecouncil.org/resources/video/data/000269

David Bosco explores the power of the UN Security Council and how political divisions within the council are its only real check.

For more information, quizzes, case studies and other study tools, please visit us at **www.oup.com/us/lamy**

THINKING ABOUT GLOBAL POLITICS

Theory Pursuit: A Structured Review of Realism, Liberalism, and Critical Approaches

GOAL
In this competitive exercise you will be exploring the core assumptions of realism, liberalism, and the critical approaches discussed in this text. After completing it, you should have a useful study guide for the course.

PROCEDURE
Part A: The Preparation
Step One: Your instructor forms teams of three or four students.

Step Two: Each team discusses a strategy for developing questions and answers for the competition.

Step Three: Each team member develops nine questions, three questions for each of the theoretical traditions: realism, liberalism, and critical approaches. You must also provide complete answers to these questions, based on readings and lectures. Include full and proper citations so that your answers can be checked.

Part B: The Competition
Step Four: The competition takes place in class. Teams ask each other questions, and the team with the most correct answers will advance to the class championship. Just as in most professional and college sports competitions, the instructor might have preliminary rounds of competition and then a championship round. Attending these sessions is an excellent opportunity for you and your classmates to review materials. Just listening to this competition will be an excellent review for the final!

FOLLOW-UP
If the instructor decides to grade this exercise, the focus should be on the quality of your questions and, most importantly, the quality of the references that you used in your research. The purpose is to provide you an opportunity to carefully explore and review the text and other class readings, which will help you prepare for future examinations.

The steady concentration of power in the hands of states that began in 1648 with the Peace of Westphalia is over, at least for a while.

—*Jessica T. Mathews*

NGOs and other civil society actors are now perceived not only as disseminators of information or providers of services but also as shapers of policy, be it in peace and security matters, in development or in humanitarian affairs. The involvement of NGOs and other actors, such as parliamentarians, local authorities and business leaders, in the United Nations global conferences demonstrates this. It would now be difficult to imagine organizing a global event and formulating multilateral agreements and declarations without the active participation of NGOs.

—*Kofi Annan, Former UN Secretary-General*

In the previous chapter, we considered the role of international governmental organizations—institutions whose members are governments (e.g., the United Nations, World Trade Organization, International Monetary Fund, and World Bank)—in the quest for global governance and influence in global politics. We also examined several regional organizations with governments as their members (the European Union, African Union, and Organization of American States). In this chapter, we turn to major actors in the global system that are not nation-states or organizations with governments as their primary or only members.

Amnesty International, the International Campaign to Ban Landmines, and Doctors Without Borders all have been awarded the Nobel Peace Prize for their contributions to humanity. These nongovernmental organizations (NGOs) have stepped in to protect human rights where governments have failed, to limit the impact of war on civilians, or to respond to medical emergencies and address the causes of pandemics. Nongovernmental organizations and other nonstate actors provide information, expertise, and services that many governments cannot offer. The list of such actors is growing as governments fail to provide basics like education for all, clean water, or even minimal healthcare. Global networks of NGOs are playing a greater role in maintaining human security in many fragile or failed states. As a noted scholar has remarked, "National governments are not simply losing autonomy in a globalizing economy.

Myanmar democracy icon Aung San Suu Kyi (left) hands out donations to Buddhist nuns at the National League for Democracy (NLD) headquarters in Myanmar in 2010.

They are sharing powers with businesses, with international organizations, and with a multitude of citizens groups, known as NGOs" (Mathews 1997).

As the issues we face become more transnational and more complex, there is a need for building global networks that include both governments and non-state actors. For example, the Bill and Melinda Gates Foundation, the Howard G. Buffett Foundation, and the Belgian government are working with the World Food Program (WFP) to transform how the WFP buys food. The new program buys from small local farmers. This initiative, Purchase for Progress (P4P), is focusing on farmers in Central America and sub-Saharan Africa and is providing services that we expect governments to offer.

But not all nonstate actors are working to achieve positive change. Others include terrorist organizations and criminal networks, which challenge governments and, in some cases, control territory and act as if they have legitimate governmental authority (as the Taliban and Al Qaeda elements did in the 2009 occupation of the Swat Valley in Pakistan). With the globalized spread of technology and the greater interconnectedness of the world, terrorist networks and global crime syndicates are becoming increasingly powerful and more difficult than ever to fight.

Here we will take a close look at some of the most important transnational actors—their various approaches, activities, and structures—to see how they are transforming our world.

Introduction

In Chapter 1, we argued that globalization has profoundly changed the game of global politics and made it more complex. Every state is playing on four different game boards—economic, political, military, and cultural—and on each of these boards, there are different actors, interests, and sources of power and influence. We want you to understand that states, whose actions are shaped by national interests, share policy spaces with a variety of transnational **nonstate actors** (participants in global politics that are not states) that have interests of their own. These nonstate actors are doing what states cannot or will not do, and in many cases, they are the catalysts for positive change and the sources of innovation. Of course, some nonstate actors are criminal networks or terrorist groups that may seek to undermine the authority of states or overthrow the government. Realists, most liberal thinkers, and even some critical-approach thinkers argue that the global system is anarchic—meaning that there is no common power that governs the global system—but some actors manage the contemporary global system in their areas of policy interests and provide a form of governance in those areas. The main categories of political actors in the global system are these:

nonstate actor Any participant in global politics that is not a state. Examples include INGOs, IGOs, MNCs, global crime syndicates, and terrorist networks.

- 196 national governments, including 193 members of the United Nations
- Some 65,000 multinational corporations (MNCs), such as Toyota, Royal Dutch Shell, Microsoft, De Beers, and Nestlé, which have more than 821,000 subsidiaries all over the globe that employ over 90 million people and produce about 25 percent of the world's gross product
- More than 5,000 think tanks and research institutes that provide information and expertise to public and private actors that make critical policy decisions

- 246 intergovernmental organizations (IGOs), such as the United Nations, NATO, the European Union, and the Arctic Council
- Approximately 7,500 international nongovernmental organizations (INGOs), such as Amnesty International, World Vision, and the Global Policy Forum, plus a number of global social movements and transnational advocacy networks (TANs), such as the International Campaign to Ban Landmines and the Network of Young People Affected by War
- Thousands of philanthropic foundations that provide funding for global projects in areas such as human security, education, science and technology, and global security

Governing arrangements called regimes (which we discussed in Chapter 6) have not replaced states as the principal actors in global politics. But states often share or even transfer sovereignty to regimes and to the international or regional organizations that often manage these regimes. Intergovernmental organizations such as the International Monetary Fund and the European Union are playing a major role in the European economic crisis, working closely with the governments of France and Germany to create a stronger European regime by promoting strict adherence to fiscally conservative banking policies. Intergovernmental organizations are generally considered nonstate actors, but their members are all states. This means they are not part of civil society, which encompasses the space between the public (governmental or state) sector and the private (for-profit or corporate) sector.

Our discussion in this chapter will focus on the other nonstate actors—civil-society and for-profit actors—that are critical players in global politics. These include INGOs, TANs (coalitions of NGOs), social movements, MNCs, foundations, universities, think tanks, and individuals. An example is the Occupy Wall Street movement, which quickly became an international movement in 2011, with over 2,500 total communities in more than eighty-two countries. Its central aim is to address issues of social and economic inequality, including the concentration of power in the economic elite and the widening gap between rich and poor. Members of this social movement work to influence the policy of many governments and intergovernmental organizations, such as the United Nations and the World Bank. Another example of a nonstate actor is the coalition called the Red Campaign to find a cure for AIDS, which has partnered with another category of nonstate actors, MNCs. Nike, Google, the Gap, or Starbucks might provide funding and platforms to promote a coalition's ideas. All of these actors play a regular part in global politics. In addition, terrorists and other criminal groups are nonstate actors that have

Modern-day Robin Hoods? Rolling Jubilee, part of the Occupy movement that protested around the world in 2011 and 2012, spent $400,000 to buy $15 million of personal debts from banks and then set free those in debt. Most of the debt that was purchased was medical debt owed by 2,693 people across 45 states. The original Jubilee Movement aimed at forgiving third world debt.

an impact on quality of life and security across the globe, even though they are not considered legitimate participants in the system.

As we discussed in Chapter 3, realists suggest that states are the principal actors and that they define the agenda of global politics. Both liberals and critical theorists, however, suggest a more pluralistic approach that recognizes the importance of other actors in shaping national and international policies. This view draws on the study of domestic politics and is based on the assumption that all types of actors can affect political outcomes. Nobody can deny the large number of nonstate organizations that exist today and the range of their activities. The controversial question is whether to accept the pluralist assertions that the nonstate world has significance in its own right and that it affects the analysis of interstate relations. It is possible to adopt, as realists do, a state-centric approach and to *define* global politics as covering only the relations among states; a careful review of global politics, however, shows the limitations of such an approach.

For pluralist scholars, it is an unacceptable analytic bias to decide, before beginning research, that only states have any influence. In the early 1970s, international relations scholars Robert Keohane and Joseph Nye introduced the idea of **transnational relations**, defined as interactions across national boundaries when at least one actor is a nonstate actor. In the twenty-first century, even realists have accepted this view, and it has become harder to justify a state-centric approach that does not consider the role of transnational nonstate actors. Governments do interact, after all, with NGOs, MNCs, think tanks, and international organizations.

After reading and discussing this chapter, you will be able to identify the various categories of nonstate actors that are critical participants in global politics. You will be able to describe the specific resources and expertise these actors bring to policy debates and to policy formulation and implementation processes. You will also learn that, increasingly, these nonstate actors partner with states or even act alone to fill the void when governments fail to meet the basic human and security needs of their citizens. Finally, this chapter provides significant evidence that the era of international relations in which states acted with few constraints and limits on their power and authority—which has lasted for 360 years—may have come to an end. You will learn that states have become more dependent on partnerships with international and regional organizations and that their ability to address global challenges often requires working with NGOs and MNCs.

transnational relations
Interactions across national boundaries when at least one actor is a nonstate actor (as defined by Robert Keohane and Joseph Nye).

WHAT'S YOUR WORLDVIEW ?

In your view, which of the following two statements is valid? (1) When it comes to critical decisions about the well-being of states and citizens, only governments are at the table. (2) When governments face these critical decisions, it is nonstate actors like MNCs and transnational NGOs that have determined what is on the table.

The Growth of Global Civil Society

international nongovernmental organization (INGO) A formal nongovernmental organization with members from at least three countries.

civil society Citizens and groups that are neither in the public (governmental or state) sector nor the private (for-profit or corporate) sector and that engage in dialogue, debate, conflict, and negotiation.

The world of global activism is led by a number of nonstate actors, including a variety of **INGOs** (NGOs with members from at least three countries), philanthropic foundations that give money to global social movements, and powerful, wealthy, or famous individuals (e.g., Bill Gates, Bono, and the Dalai Lama) who use their expertise and resources to influence the formulation and implementation of public policy. All of these groups together make up what is known as a global or transnational civil society. Hurrell (2002, 146–147) describes transnational civil society as "Self-organized intermediary groups that are relatively independent of both public authorities and private economic actors." Anheier, Glasius, and Kaldor (2004) define global civil society as

a supranational sphere of social and political participation in which citizen groups, social movements and individuals engage in dialogue, debate, confrontation and negotiation with each other, with governments, international and regional governmental organizations and with multinational corporations.

Global civil society occupies the space between the state and the market, and it operates globally; it is not constrained by national boundaries. Religious organizations, schools and other educational institutions, trade unions, and service organizations like Rotary International make up a traditional list of civil-society actors. Scholars in this area (e.g., Keck and Sikkink 1998) have added to this list INGOs, research groups or epistemic communities, foundations, and media organizations. Global civil society also includes social movements and advocacy networks. A **social movement** is defined as a mode of collective action that challenges ways of life, thinking, dominant norms and moral codes; seeks answers to global problems; and promotes reform or transformation in political and economic institutions. Transnational social movements (TSMOs), often made up of NGOs and like-minded governments and international organizations, have led many successful global campaigns to address issues such as famine in Africa, landmines, and corporate social responsibility in developing countries.

social movement A mode of collective action that challenges ways of life, thinking, dominant norms, and moral codes; seeks answers to global problems; and promotes reform or transformation in political and economic institutions.

Transnational advocacy networks (TANs) are described as "networks of activists, distinguishable largely by the centrality of principled ideas or values in motivating their formation" (Keck and Sikkink 1998, 1). The advocates or activists in these networks "promote normative positions, lobby for policy reforms, and play an important role in policy debates over a wide variety of social issues" (Keck and Sikkink, 8–9). Both INGOs and governments can play a central role in these networks. The TANs and TSMOs have taken advantage of the forces of globalization to increase the political effectiveness of their various campaigns, and the ease of communicating online has contributed to their rise. These movements and networks, which target governments at all levels, in some cases provide critical resources for political change and innovation. Making connections with other actors across the world is much easier with social media, global media outlets, greater financial resources, and INGO links to governments, academic institutions, and even global corporations.

transnational advocacy network (TAN) A network of activists—often, a coalition of NGOs—distinguishable largely by the centrality of principled ideas or values in motivating its formation.

Although not, strictly speaking, part of the global civil society, MNCs have formed their own INGOs and probusiness networks to lobby for their own interests and to counter the increasingly effective efforts of more progressive INGOs and TANs. Most global corporations support trade-and-aid policies, which encourage open markets and provide stability and protection for their investments. These corporations and their INGOs are up against numerous public campaigns to make corporations more accountable to the public and to force them to address environmental concerns, human rights, and social justice issues.

Médecins Sans Frontières, or Doctors Without Borders, is a French secular humanitarian-aid nongovernmental organization. The organization won the Nobel Peace Prize, and it is best known for its projects in war-torn regions and developing countries facing endemic diseases. Here a nurse assists an Iraqi patient in Amman, Jordan. This is an NGO that respects no boundaries that prevent it from taking care of people in need. Kant would approve.

In the next sections of this chapter, we will introduce you to the major nonstate actors that are playing more important roles in the development of policy at the local, national, and global levels. In some cases, actors such as think tanks and research institutes provide expertise in the *formulation* of policy options. In other cases, actors such as NGOs may partner with states to *implement* policy decisions. We will explore who these actors are and what kind of power and influence they have.

Some scholars have suggested that power and authority have shifted from states and public authorities toward actors in the global civil society. Although it is true that INGOs do provide services and resources in areas where states have failed to provide for their citizens, filling those gaps is only part of what these actors do for the world. In many situations, INGOs, think tanks, foundations, and even MNCs act as innovators and catalysts for change. Understanding the complexities of the global economy requires understanding more than states and IGOs. This is the world of global politics, not simply international relations, and we need to understand the specific roles played by the many types of nonstate actors.

Multinational Corporations

multinational corporation (MNC) A firm with subsidiaries that extend the production and marketing of the firm beyond the boundaries of any one country.

Multinational corporations (MNCs) are firms with subsidiaries that extend the production and marketing of the firm beyond the boundaries of any one country. The foreign subsidiaries of an MNC are directly owned by the parent corporation. Multinational corporations are not included under the umbrella of civil society because they are for profit. Some experts use the terms *MNC* and *transnational corporation* interchangeably; however, Andrew Hines, an expert for BNET (now CBS Money Watch), makes a clear distinction between four types of international businesses:

1. *international companies* are simply importers and exporters with no investments or operations outside the home countries;
2. *multinational companies* have investments around the world, but they adjust their products and services to local markets;
3. *global companies* have investments and a presence in many countries, and they use the same brand and image in all markets;
4. *transnational companies* are complex organizations that invest in foreign operations, and although they have a central corporate office, they allow foreign markets to make decisions about marketing and research and development.

To simplify our analysis, we will focus on MNCs and assume that transnational corporations are similar in the role they play as global actors. Most MNCs have their origins in developed countries, and they invest throughout the world. The number of MNCs increased exponentially after World War II. Most MNCs at the time were from the United States, United Kingdom, Japan, Germany, and France. Recently, China, India, Russia, Brazil, and Korea have added MNCs to the market. Indeed, because of their interests in global markets and their interests in selling to the world, the nationality of MNCs may be irrelevant. As consumers, we look for the best products at the best price, and we usually make little noise about purchasing a product made by a foreign corporation. National leaders do not seem to be concerned when multinationals build factories in their country or when they purchase critically important industries. A simple but somewhat accurate description is that MNCs are global because they seek markets for investments, cheap but skilled labor, and access to resources essential for making their products. Multinational corporations have power because they control scarce and critically important economic resources, they have the ability to move resources around the world, and they have advantages in areas of marketing and consumer loyalty.

Generally, MNCs get a bad review as representatives of Western capitalist culture, guilty of exploiting labor and crowding out local businesses. Many MNCs are seen as enemies of the people, supporting oppressive governments and contributing to pollution, poverty, and corruption. This view may be both outdated in some cases and limited, however, and views of MNCs vary according to one's theoretical perspective. Liberals see MNCs as a positive force, spreading technology, efficiency, and wealth. Economic nationalists, or neomercantilists, argue that MNCs threaten national sovereignty and dilute national wealth. Finally, Marxists see MNCs as representatives of the core-capitalist states, creating dependencies in countries where they invest and helping create and maintain a core-periphery global economic structure. According to this view, MNCs participate in predatory globalization, or the search for investment opportunities in countries where labor is cheap and where laws aimed at protecting the welfare of workers and the environment are either not enforced or nonexistent. Essentially, Marxists argue that MNCs put profits above all else. But many NGOs work with MNCs to create opportunities for work in developing countries and to respond to human needs such as clean water, basic education, and healthcare. Multinational corporations also give many small local businesses access to markets, financial credits, and technological infrastructure.

The 1984 gas leak in Bhopal, India, was a terrible tragedy that continues to impact the quality of life for the people in the region. In 2012, these children live in a region with polluted water because of the former Union Carbide industrial complex. Transnational or global social movements often form around the injustices revealed by industrial disasters such as Bhopal.

The view of MNCs is changing because those who own and manage these corporations realize that they must provide a positive image if they are to attract customers. Their ability to attract customers and make profits depends in part on providing resources, expertise, and training to local populations. In many situations, MNCs have become partners in development by providing valuable resources for governments and their citizens. Many governments now compete for investments from MNCs. Not only do they provide jobs and help build infrastructure, MNCs are often engines of change and reform in corrupt and mismanaged governments.

One important question is why companies invest abroad. The decision to become a multinational firm is not only about access to markets; it is also about finding competitive advantages for the firm. These might be technological innovations and efficient production costs, for example, that make manufacturing more profitable at a foreign location. With information technology and inexpensive transportation costs, one might argue that there is no alternative to MNCs and corporate foreign direct investment (FDI). In fact, unless a country possesses large quantities of resources such as financial capital, raw materials, and access to technology, trying to cut off any sort of foreign investment can only lead to economic decline.

We have made the claim that MNCs are playing a more positive role in many developing countries. To continue this challenge to the more radical view that MNCs are only interested in profits, we will consider the case of India's economy, which is predicted to be as big as China's in ten to fifteen years. The 1.2 billion people living in India are becoming more affluent, more educated, and more politically active, and they are demanding more from both the public and private sectors. At the same time, MNCs are more concerned about attracting customers, and that means providing a good product and being good citizens in this market.

But India has had its share of problems with MNCs more interested in profit and less interested in the well-being of its workers and neighbors. One is reminded of the 1984 Bhopal gas tragedy at a Union Carbide factory that killed 3,800 people and left several thousand with permanent disabilities. Union Carbide, a US-based MNC, was one of the first US companies to invest in India, and it produced pesticides for India's agricultural sector. In the final settlement, Union Carbide paid out close to $500 million for victims and for building clinics and other facilities in the region.

Another MNC with a long history in India (more than 100 years) is Nestlé. This corporation has had to deal with charges of malpractice, corruption, and generally putting profits ahead of the needs and interests of its consumers. (See the Case Study in this chapter.) Nestlé India has seven factories that produce milk, which Indians drink in great quantities. One small factory in the Punjab region depends on about 180 farmers for its supply of milk, and those farmers were having problems with their animals. Nestlé brought in agronomists, veterinarians, and agricultural education experts to work with the local farmers to help maintain healthier herds that produced more milk. Nestlé clearly benefited, but so did the local farmers.

Hindustan Unilever, a subsidiary of the Anglo-Dutch MNC Unilever, also seems to have embraced the message of paying attention to the needs and interests of the consumer. Unilever created Project Shakti, which recruited 45,000 poor rural women as sales agents and trained them as "micro entrepreneurs." These women provide a valuable service by teaching their neighbors about nutrition and hygiene. Unilever wins, and so do these women who learn valuable skills and bring in an income to support their families.

Multinational corporations are also involved in a number of partnership projects with governments and INGOs. The US Agency for International Development (USAID) has been working since 2002 with Albanian farmers and Land O'Lakes, a food-producing MNC, to increase the quality of dairy products and to provide jobs for 12,000 farmers and dairy processors. In several Latin American countries, including Colombia and Ecuador, the Nature Conservancy, a US-based NGO, has been working with an MNC, FEMSA (along with the Inter-American Development Bank and the Global Environment Facility), to establish a social investment foundation that supports education, science, and technology. More than 50 million people will benefit from this partnership, which will work to restore forests and grasslands where clean water originates. FEMSA is the world's largest Coca-Cola bottling company and a major beer distributor in all of Latin America. The conservation trust fund established in Colombia is aimed at protecting rivers and watersheds that provide clean drinking water for people living in Bogotá.

Several factors are combining to make these public and private partnerships more likely in the future. Governments have fewer financial resources for global projects. Citizens are becoming more aware of vital global challenges and more critical of bad behavior by both public and private actors, and IGOS and INGOS are providing expertise and other resources to facilitate global responses to address these challenges.

INGOs as Global Political Actors

Nongovernmental organizations are autonomous organizations that are not instruments of any government, are not for profit, and are formal legal entities. These exist within societies as domestic NGOs, like the Sierra Club in the United States, or as international nongovernmental organizations (INGOs). They campaign for certain causes (e.g., Amnesty International for human rights), represent the interests of specific professionals (e.g., international trade unions), and include charitable organizations (e.g., CARE and Oxfam).

As long as nation-states have fought wars or famine has plagued societies, civil-society organizations have played a role in trying to find solutions to these problems.

CASE STUDY A Global Campaign:
The Baby Milk Advocacy Network

BACKGROUND

The prototype for global campaigning by NGOs has been the International Baby Food Action Network (IBFAN), which challenges the marketing of dried milk powder by the major food and pharmaceutical corporations. In the early 1970s, medical staff in developing countries gradually became aware that the death rate for babies was rising because of decreased breast feeding. If the family was poor and used insufficient milk powder, the baby was undernourished. If the water or the bottle was not sterile, the baby developed gastric diseases. Bottle feeding today causes around 1.5 million deaths a year.

In 2009, a mother in Cameroon holds a can of milk powder that she feeds her three-and-a-half-month-old daughter a few times a week. IBFAN challenges the marketing of milk powder by MNCs, citing research linking decreased breast feeding to an increased death rate for babies.

THE CASE

The question was first taken up by the *New Internationalist* magazine and War on Want (WoW) in Britain in 1973–1974. A Swiss NGO, the Third World Action Group (AgDW), then published a revised translation of WoW's report under the title "Nestlé Kills Babies." When Nestlé sued for libel, AgDW mobilized groups from around the world to supply evidence for their defense. The Swiss Court found AgDW guilty in December 1976 on one of Nestlé's four original counts on the technical basis that Nestlé was only indirectly responsible for the deaths.

The question moved to the United States when religious groups involved in Latin America fought another court case against Bristol-Myers. Increased awareness led to organization by a new group, the Infant Formula Action Coalition, of a boycott of Nestlé's products that spread to many countries. In the hope of diffusing the increasing pressure, the International Council of Infant Food Industries accepted a proposal by Senator Edward Kennedy for the WHO and UNICEF to hold a meeting on infant feeding in October 1979. Rather than seeing the issue depoliticized, the companies found they were facing demands to limit their marketing. The meeting also taught a group of NGOs how much they could benefit from working together with a common political strategy. They decided to continue to cooperate by forming IBFAN as a global advocacy network.

The new network was able to mobilize a diverse coalition of medical professionals, religious groups, development activists, women's groups, community organizations, consumer lobbies, and the boycott campaigners. Against intense opposition from the MNCs and the US administration, IBFAN succeeded in achieving the adoption of an International Code of Marketing of Breast-Milk Substitutes by WHO's assembly in May 1981. The key provisions of the code were that "there should be no advertising or other form of promotion to the general public" or any provision of free samples to mothers.

OUTCOME

According to UNICEF, since 1981, 84 countries have enacted legislation implementing all or many of the provisions of the Code and subsequent relevant World Health Assembly resolutions. In addition, 14 countries have draft laws awaiting adoption. The work of IBFAN continues along two tracks: it monitors and reports violations of the code by companies, including in countries where marketing is now illegal, and it also seeks to upgrade the law in countries that are only partially implementing the code.

This account is based on A. Chetley (1986), The Politics of Baby Foods (London: Pinter) and information at www .ibfan.org, the IBFAN website.

For Discussion

1. The global campaign against Nestlé led to this action network. Is this an effective way to shape national policy?
2. When and where do global campaigns work?
3. What is the "boomerang pattern," and what role did it play in the Nestlé campaign?

In 1874, there were thirty-two registered INGOs, and in 1914, there were more than a thousand. The International Red Cross was founded by Jean Henri Dunant in 1859 after the Battle of Solferino and was awarded the Nobel Peace Prize in 1917, 1944, and 1963. The Red Cross directed the implementation of the first Geneva Convention on the humane treatment of wounded soldiers and prisoners of war. Another INGO, Save the Children, formed after World War I, and Médecins Sans Frontières (Doctors Without Borders) started after the Biafran Civil War in Nigeria in the late 1960s. International nongovernmental organizations have been willing to work in crisis situations when governments are reluctant to become involved. The real growth in the number of INGOs took place in the 1990s. Simultaneously, INGOs began to work more closely with each other and with governments and IGOs like the World Bank and the United Nations.

National governmental organizations often act collectively in pursuit of their interests or values, and some scholars believe that they are shifting political power away from the state. National governmental organizations work with states and regional and international organizations, but most global politics scholars believe that the state no longer monopolizes the political world. Most of the NGOs working in what some have called the most idealist and "imagined" global communities are progressive organizations working to reform or transform the current global system. They aim to do so by making decision-making arenas more democratic, transparent, equitable, and environmentally friendly. As Rischard (2002) argues in his book on global problems, NGOs tend to work in three broad areas:

- *Sharing our planet*—issues such as global warming, ocean pollution, and biodiversity
- *Sharing our humanity*—issues that focus on global health, education, human rights, war, violence, and repression
- Governance, or *sharing our rule book*—issues that involve international laws and institutions

Thus, trade and investment rules promoted by neoliberal institutions like the WTO and the World Bank have become the target of concern for many global activists.

Not all INGOs support progressive changes, however. Some represent the status quo, and some support authoritarian or racist preferred futures. Transnational or multinational corporations sponsor NGOs and advocacy networks that are also a part of this global civil society. It might be useful now to review the key actors in this world and share some of the terminology used by scholars and practitioners in these contested areas of policy.

First, there are a variety of INGOs, differentiated by their purpose, organization, and sponsorship. These include:

- *BINGOs*: business and industry INGOs like the World Economic Forum, the World Business Council for Sustainable Development, and the Global Business Council on HIV and AIDS
- *GRINGOs*: government regulated and initiated INGOs; many authoritarian states sponsor these to keep watch on dissidents and the activities of foreign interests
- *QUANGOS*: sometimes called quasi INGOs because they receive most of their funds from public sources although they are still independent
- *RINGOS*: INGOs that are sponsored by religious groups and often promote religious norms and values; World Vision, CARITAS, and Norwegian Church Fund are examples

Next there are TANs, whose advocates or activists promote normative positions and campaigns, lobby for policy reforms, and often play an important role in "value-laden" debates over a wide variety of social issues (Keck and Sikkink 1998, 8–9). Both INGOs and governments can play a central role in these networks. For example, the International Campaign to Ban Landmines and the campaign in support of the International Criminal Court (ICC) were coalitions of INGOs and like-minded states. Transnational social movements, like the global antiapartheid movement and the ongoing antislavery movement, act the same as TANS in that both are global activist movements.

International nongovernmental organizations are generally seen as independent, altruistic, idealistic, and progressive. However, not all of them deal with issues such as war, floods, and refugees or promote democracy, human rights, and clean air. Not all INGOs are independent and progressive. There are many racist neo-Nazi INGOs, for example.

Transnational advocacy networks and transnational social movements have taken advantage of the forces of globalization to increase the political effectiveness of their various campaigns. Governments at all levels are the targets, and for many people across the globe, these movements and networks have become the focus of their political activism and political identity.

What kind of power do these INGOs have? How can they counter the economic and political power of global corporations? Do they have any influence over nation-states?

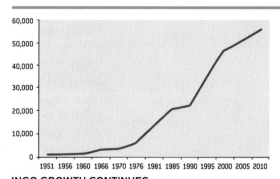

INGO GROWTH CONTINUES.
What impact does the growth of INGOs have on states?

Sources of INGO Power

A critical question is how much power INGOs and other transnational actors have to implement their own strategic plans and affect the policy of governments and intergovernmental organizations. We know that MNCs can use their money and the promise of jobs, investment, and access to new technologies to influence governments, but what about religious organizations like World Vision or think tanks like the Brookings Institute? Let's look at INGOs to assess their sources of influence.

In many societies, especially the pluralist social-democratic states (e.g., Sweden, Denmark, the Netherlands), domestic NGOs and INGOs play an important role as partners

in the policy process. Some NGOs are not as independent from public agencies as they claim to be. These so-called QUANGOs are often supported by governments to carry out policy programs that governments cannot or will not implement.

To illustrate, INGOs have played a critical role in implementing development-assistance programs throughout the world. The International Red Cross claims the INGOs working in the development and human security areas give out more money than the World Bank. Most of this money comes from governments and public agencies. From 1990 to 1994, the percentage of European Union aid that was distributed by NGOs rose from 47 percent to 67 percent. Organizations like Oxfam in the United Kingdom, World Vision (the largest privately funded Christian relief-and-development NGO), and Doctors Without Borders receive anywhere from 25 percent to 50 percent of their funding from various government

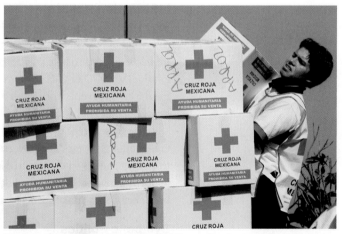

The International Committee of the Red Cross, often in association with its national counterparts, offers disaster-relief services in what is meant to be a nonpolitical manner. Here we see a member of the Red Cross stacking crates of food for victims of the devastating earthquake in Haiti in January 2010. How do states benefit by permitting NGOs to provide these essential services?

sources. International nongovernmental organizations are also supported by private sources like corporations and by philanthropic foundations. In December 2011, Google announced that it would provide $11.5 million in grants to ten organizations working to end the practice of slavery. This is about 25 percent of what Google was giving away to charitable organizations during the holiday season. The grant is to be used by a coalition on international antitrafficking organizations. The International Justice Mission (IJM) is the lead organization in this effort. More specifically, IJM in India, one of the fourteen field offices, will lead intervention and rescue missions. International Justice Mission is a human rights agency that rescues victims of slavery, sexual exploitation, and other forms of violent oppression. Prior to this gift, most of IJM funding came from private sources, and less than 1 percent of its funding had come from major corporations or corporate foundations. Another important member of this coalition is CNN and its CNN Freedom project that started in March 2011. CNN, a global media superpower, has broadcast more than 200 stories about human trafficking and modern-day slavery. This kind of exposure educates citizens and their leaders and pressures them to act.

Obviously, government funding increases the ability of INGOs to assist people in need and to help governments carry out some of their foreign policy goals. As governments are forced to cut back their workforce, many duties are being picked up by INGOs. Not only do INGO employees deliver services to the poor and protect citizens in conflict areas, but INGOs like Amnesty International and Human Rights Watch provide policy makers and interested citizens with valuable information and research reports that can be used to develop new laws and policy programs. Their research expertise gives them access to policy makers, and often, their ideas and interests become part of public policy. International nongovernmental organizations also provide an important source of ideas and innovation and may prompt governments to act in favor of their position or policy agenda.

Forms of INGO Power

Forms of INGO power discussed by Keck and Sikkink (1998) include information politics, symbolic politics, leverage politics, accountability politics, and global campaign politics. We will briefly discuss each of these.

Information Politics

International nongovernmental organizations and other civil-society actors use e-mail, fax machines, newsletters, and web pages to keep their followers informed, solicit donations, and mobilize citizens to take positions supporting their causes. During antiglobalization demonstrations at WTO or G-8 talks, many activists use digital cameras and audio streams to share the day-to-day events with other activists in distant lands. This builds support and a stronger sense of community among INGOs and other activist groups.

Another part of information politics is the research and studies that many INGOs provide media reporters and government officials. Because of their expertise and their access to critical players in crisis situations, NGOs can also provide important technical and strategic information. This information is often not available anywhere else and can be used to influence policy makers and to inform other activists.

Symbolic Politics

Activist leaders of INGOs identify a critical issue or event and provide explanations that frame the issue so it becomes a catalyst for growth of the movement. The shelling of a café in Sarajevo by Bosnian Serb forces during the civil war in Yugoslavia was used as a symbolic event by human rights INGOs who were demanding US intervention to stop the ethnic cleansing in Bosnia.

International nongovernmental organizations use their position in society and their role in crises that occur as a way of increasing awareness and expanding support for their cause. When the Red Cross, Doctors Without Borders, and the International Campaign to Ban Landmines were awarded the Nobel Peace Prize, it called attention to their cause and gave the groups more legitimacy throughout the world. International nongovernmental organizations and the transnational social movements they participate in often use big stories to gain public attention, more members, financial contributions, and the attention of those with political power. In the 1980s, Irish rock star Bob Geldof (who played Wall in the Pink Floyd–inspired movie) turned the world's attention to famine in western Africa. His activism led musicians in the United Kingdom, the United States, and Canada to each produce their own "We Are the World" records and sponsor a series of globally televised concerts to raise public awareness and collect funds for famine relief.

Some of these big stories that are picked up by the media are based on false or incomplete information. A good example is the 1995 Brent Spar incident. Greenpeace launched an attack on an obsolete oil rig, called the Brent Spar, in the North Sea to protest the decision by Shell to sink it. Greenpeace claimed that the environmental damage would be worse by sinking the rig than by towing it to shore and dismantling it there. Yet independent environmental studies did not support this position. These studies clearly showed that the environmental damage would be greater if the rig were towed to shore and dismantled. Still, Greenpeace continued with its campaign and forced the government of Germany and Shell Oil to dismantle the rig on land. Both traditional and social media sources can be used to turn the facts about natural disasters and the aftermath of war and violence into human stories.

Leverage Politics

International nongovernmental organizations often use material leverage (e.g., money or goods) or moral leverage to persuade governments to act in certain ways or to encourage other INGOs to support their position on an issue. They often shame governments into acting in a certain way. They are adept at using the media to expose hypocritical behaviors and to make certain the public is aware of unpopular practices by governments, transnational corporations, and other actors. With greater access to media and information technology, INGOs have greater access to larger audiences. These INGOs demand more accountability and have increasing power and influence. Simply stated, those INGOs with a significant number of members can influence votes and help to shape the domestic and foreign policy process.

Accountability Politics

International nongovernmental organizations are able to use a number of information and media sources to force governments and political leaders to follow up on their public promises. These groups act as watchdogs, making certain that political leaders follow through with commitments that they make when running for office or addressing a current public concern. Unfortunately, this pressure does not always work. Both George H. W. Bush and Bill Clinton promised to push China to improve its human rights record before they would support new trade relations. Once elected, both presidents caved in to trade interests and failed to address human rights concerns. Although INGOs are not always successful, they continue to use all of their resources to pressure governments to close the gap between promises and performances.

Global Campaign Politics

A relatively new tool for NGOs and other civil-society actors and like-minded governments is a global campaign that uses the media, local activist networks, and, if necessary, product boycotts like the one described in the Nestlé Case Study. The use of the social networking

Greenpeace activists boarded the Brent Spar oil platform in the North Sea in 1995. Recently, thirty Greenpeace activists were arrested for trespassing on a Russian Gazprom platform. Greenpeace uses these symbolic actions and its information resources to try to gain support for its positions on environmental issues.

sites on the Internet and the proliferation of NGOs across the world have made it easier to establish and maintain such campaigns. The One Campaign aimed at addressing global poverty and recent campaigns seeking to provide assistance to victims of natural disasters in New Orleans and Haiti have also benefited from what we know as celebrity diplomacy. We are all familiar with the role played by Bono, Radiohead, and Wyclef Jean in mobilizing public support for their humanitarian cause. Many of these global campaigns play on our love for music, film, and other forms of entertainment. With the Internet and social media, it is relatively easy to identify a global issue, build an organization, promote a particular set of values and actions, and raise both financial and volunteer support for your cause. It is even easier if you can link your cause to a major event or to the popularity of a certain artist or sports hero. Consider for a moment the actions of Norwegian speed skater Johann Olav Koss, who won three gold medals in the 1994 Winter Olympics in Lillehammer, Norway. Koss donated his bonus for his athletic accomplishments to Olympic Aid, an organization that was helping the victims of the war in Bosnia. He asked every Norwegian to give a donation for every gold medal won by Norway. Koss expanded his organization and called it Right to Play, a global organization that reaches 700,000 children in some twenty countries. Koss is not alone in his efforts to use sports to deal with societal problems like drug violence and global problems like poverty. An entire social movement called Sport for Development and Peace (SDP) has emerged and is supported by foundations, corporations, governments, and international organizations. To illustrate, Spirit of Soccer works to rid the world of "explosive remnants of war," Women Win advances women's rights in nineteen countries, and Football for Peace partners with Fédération Internationale de Football Association to promote peace and goodwill in fifty-five countries.

Celebrity Diplomacy

In 2005, *Time* magazine named Bono and Bill and Melinda Gates for their contributions to the global community. Bono, lead singer in the Irish rock group U2, has been described by James Traub of the *New York Times* as a "one-man state who fills his treasury with the global currency of fame." He has used this fame to lead major global campaigns to end global poverty. Andrew Cooper dedicates a great deal of space to these global activists in his book *Celebrity Diplomacy* (2008), in which he suggests that these well-known celebrities are part of a more open and robust process of diplomacy that is the opposite of the insulated and secretive world of traditional diplomacy. Cooper suggests this new form of diplomacy may be eroding the authority and legitimacy of more traditional forms of diplomatic activity. Cooper points out that the Latin root of the word *ambassador* is *ambactiare*, which means "to go on a mission," and many celebrities have embraced that theme and used their status and resources to achieve goals that reflect their own values. The International Campaign to Ban Landmines was headline news when Princess Diana became its international spokesperson. Angelina Jolie and Brad Pitt have become spokespersons for a variety of causes related to children and refugees; they have created a new charitable foundation to aid humanitarian causes around the world. The Jolie/Pitt Foundation gave away $2 million—$1 to Global Action for

Children (now defunct) and $1 million to Doctors Without Borders—to help families affected by HIV/AIDS and extreme poverty.

Not all celebrities are promoting progressive or cosmopolitan causes like global governance, social justice, human security, and protecting the environment. There are celebrities who represent more conservative political causes and movements, like the late Charlton Heston, president of the National Rifle Association. This is not a new phenomenon; countries have always used movie stars and entertainers to sell war bonds and promote public campaigns.

Celebrities, like any of us, use texts and blogs to communicate around the world, but they can also use their celebrity status to sell more than just movies and music. They sell ideas and normative values and positions to their adoring fans and use technology and global media to convince political leaders to embrace their positions. Traditional diplomats are very critical of these celebrity actions and suggest that they lack the expertise and dedication to the real goals of traditional diplomacy. Critics say it is okay for celebrities to raise funds for humanitarian issues, but they are not representatives of states and they need to be careful not to interfere with any official diplomatic agenda.

A new group of celebrities are the entrepreneurs who have made billions and have created foundations and philanthropic organizations to promote and fund their special causes. Two founders of eBay, Inc., Pierre Omidyar and Jeff Skoll, are at the top of the list of the new rich doing something for the world. The Omidyar Network operates more like a venture capital program investing some $1 billion in businesses and nonprofits that seek social change in developing countries. The Skoll Foundation has given three-year grants to some fifty-nine entrepreneurial groups who sponsor programs that promote peace and prosperity. *Barron's* magazine believes these two philanthropists may be having the biggest impact with their focus on supporting other philanthropists and social entrepreneurs, providing them with networking and leveraging opportunities. This is a very effective practice called **venture philanthropy**, and it is having an especially large impact in the developing world. British aviation magnate Richard Branson has focused his wealth on global social and environmental problems. He has established a green-energy carbon war room and a fund to reward scientists for finding new ways to control global warming and remove carbon from the environment.

As governments cut social programs at home and development assistance programs, and failed or fragile states are unable or unwilling to provide basic services for their citizens, foundations and individual philanthropists are willing to step up and fund water wells, schools, and hospitals. These incredibly wealthy individuals are also willing to support innovative programs that encourage local business development and local efforts to solve persistent societal challenges.

Global Foundations and Think Tanks

A **foundation** is a nonstate actor that is established as a charitable trust or a nonprofit INGO with the purpose of making grants to other institutions or to individuals for a variety of purposes (see Table 7.1). Many world leaders establish foundations when they leave office to continue to make a difference in global affairs. For example, the William J. Clinton Foundation has partnered with other INGOS, and through its Clinton Global Initiatives, it challenges governments to respond to major global challenges such as the

venture philanthropy
The practice of supporting philanthropists or social entrepreneurs by providing them with networking and leveraging opportunities.

foundation A type of nonstate actor that is established as a charitable trust or a nonprofit INGO with the purpose of making grants to other institutions or to individuals.

Pierre Omidyar, chairman and founder of eBay, Inc., at a panel session held during the 2010 Clinton Global Initiative in New York City. His Omidyar Network invests some $1 billion in businesses and nonprofits that seek social change in developing countries.

Table 7.1
Major Foundations with Significant Global Activities

Foundation	Region	Mission	Website
Kenya Community Development Foundation	Africa	To support sustainable community development.	www.kcdf.or.ke/
Trust Africa	Africa	To strengthen the global alliance for Africans by facilitating collaboration among African institutions, building long-term relationships with grantees, and maintaining close ties with the African diaspora.	www.trustafrica.org/
The Myer Foundation	Australia	To build a fair, just, creative, and caring society by supporting initiatives that promote positive change in Australia and in relation to its regional setting.	www.myerfoundation.org.au/
Aço Villares	Brazil	To provide arts, culture, and recreation education to Brazil.	www.villares.com.br/
Mohammed bin Rashid Al Maktoum Foundation	Dubai	To provide Arabs with opportunities to guide the region toward a knowledge economy.	www.mbrfoundation.ae/ENGLISH
Robert Bosch Foundation	Germany	To distribute grants to promote education, international understanding, science and research, and health and humanitarian aid.	www.bosch-stiftung.de/
The Infosys Foundation	India	To support the underprivileged sections of society in areas of healthcare, education, culture, destitute care, and rural development, and improve the welfare of people in rural areas of India.	www.infosys.com/infosys_foundation/
The Sasakawa Peace Foundation	Japan	To contribute to the welfare of humankind and the sound development of the international community.	www.spf.org/e/
Acción International	Latin America	To foster social and economic development in Latin American through business development.	www.accion.org/
Fondo Mexicano para la Conservation de la Naturaleza	Mexico	To conserve the environment and biodiversity as well as social and economic development.	www.fmcn.org.mx/ingles/home.htm
Stichting INGKA Foundation	Netherlands	To promote and support innovation in the field of architectural and interior design.	N/A

Continued

Table 7.1 (*continued*)
Major Foundations with Significant Global Activities

Foundation	Region	Mission	Website
Calouste Gulbenkian Foundation	Portugal	To support projects and programs in the fields of arts, charity, education, and science.	www.gulbenkian.org.uk/
Knut and Alice Wallenberg Foundation	Sweden	To promote research and education beneficial to Sweden.	www.wallenberg.com/kaw/in_english/
Adele Koller-Knüsli Foundation	Switzerland	To promote social and cultural projects and organizations.	N/A
Jacqueline Spengler Foundation	Switzerland	To support social and cultural projects in the region.	N/A
Himalaya Foundation	Taiwan	To bring financial management to philanthropic activities. Main areas of focus are academic exchange and healthcare.	www.himalaya.org.tw/EN/index.asp
Wellcome Trust	United Kingdom	To achieve extraordinary improvements in human and animal health by supporting the brightest minds in biomedical research and the medical humanities.	www.wellcome.ac.uk/
Bill and Melinda Gates Foundation	United States	To partner with and support people and organizations worldwide to tackle critical problems though its Global Development Program, Global Health Program, and United States Program.	www.gatesfoundation.org/
Ford Foundation	United States	To support visionary leaders and organizations on the front lines of social change worldwide.	www.fordfound.org/
William and Flora Hewlett Foundation	United States	To solve social and environmental problems at home and abroad by financing grants worldwide.	www.hewlett.org/
John D. and Catherine T. MacArthur Foundation	United States	To support creative people and effective institutions committed to building a more just, verdant, and peaceful world. Works to defend human rights, advance global conservation and security, make cities better places, and understand how technology is affecting children and society.	www.macfound.org/
The Annie E. Casey Foundation	United States	To foster public policies, human service reforms, and community supports that more effectively meet the needs of today's vulnerable children and families.	www.aecf.org/

Continued

Table 7.1 (*continued*)
Major Foundations with Significant Global Activities

Foundation	Region	Mission	Website
Pew Charitable Trusts	United States	To solve today's most challenging problems by applying a rigorous analytic approach to improving public policy, informing the public, and stimulating civic life.	www.pewtrusts.org/
The Rockefeller Foundation	United States	To support work that expands opportunity and strengthens resilience to social, economic, health, and environmental challenges.	www.rockefellerfoundation.org/
ExxonMobil Foundation	United States	To support initiatives in women's economic opportunity, math and science, and malaria prevention.	www.exxonmobil.com/Corporate/community_foundation.aspx
Open Society Foundations	United States	To build vibrant and tolerant democracies whose governments are accountable to their citizens by shaping public policies that assure greater fairness in political, legal, and economic systems and safeguard fundamental rights.	www.soros.org/
John Templeton Foundation	United States	To support research on subjects ranging from complexity, evolution, and infinity to creativity, forgiveness, love, and free will.	www.templeton.org/

need for education, safe drinking water, and clean air. Tony Blair, the former prime minister of the United Kingdom, has established the Tony Blair Faith Foundation to promote "respect and understanding about the world's major religions." The foundation works with students and universities to understand how globalization shapes religion and how religious norms and values may shape the forces of globalization. The Nelson Mandela Foundation was established in 1999 to continue the work of this great leader, especially in the areas of reconciliation in divided societies and social justice.

As they have in the past, foundations are likely to continue to have an important role in global politics. They do not simply step in and provide funding where the state has left a vacuum. Rather, foundations want to be change agents and encourage reform and innovation in societies across the globe. Some of the more successful and enduring foundations are in the United States, but many wealthy individuals in Europe and Asia have established foundations to help their countries and their neighbors. For example, the Bharti Foundation, founded by telecom billionaire Sunil Mittal, has opened over 200 schools to address the problem of illiteracy and has funded teacher training programs and libraries. Foundations play a major role in funding research institutes and communities of scholars and experts who are essential sources of information for those who formulate, implement, and eventually evaluate policy decisions and processes.

Most of what we know about complex global issues is presented to us by an **epistemic community**, or a network of professionals with expertise in an issue area that is recognized

epistemic community A network of professionals with expertise in an issue area that is recognized by policy makers as relevant to their work and critically important for formulating and implementing policy.

by policy makers as relevant to their work and critically important for formulating and implementing policy. For example, an epistemic community (also known as a knowledge society) might be looking at a major health issue like malaria. As described by Peter Haas (1992), members of this network of professionals share a set of normative and principled beliefs about what is important and what needs to be done. In this case, the experts want to find a way to eradicate malaria, and they share their research to find a solution. They also exchange causal beliefs and share notions of what is valid research and research methods. These experts review all of this research because they have a common purpose. Often, they work at universities, think tanks, and research institutes and are funded by foundations like the Bill and Melinda Gates Foundation. The Gates Foundation supports projects in more than 100 countries and gave $456 million to PATH Malaria Vaccine Initiative. Since 1994, the Gates Foundation has spent more than $15 billion on global health projects and close to $4 billion on global development projects.

Melinda Gates, co-chair of the Bill and Melinda Gates Foundation, talks to guests at the 2008 groundbreaking ceremony for the charity organization's headquarters in Seattle. The Gates Foundation, started by Microsoft Corp. founder Bill Gates and his wife Melinda Gates in 2000, is using its $37.3 billion endowment to fight diseases such as AIDS and malaria and to support numerous other causes throughout the world.

Other notable philanthropic foundations that have had a major impact on global politics include the Rockefeller Foundation, the Open Society Foundations, the MacArthur Foundation, the Ford Foundation, and the Aga Kahn Foundation. The Rockefeller Foundation has been involved in philanthropy to promote the "well-being of humanity" since 1913. Currently, it has embraced the theme of smart globalization, which is described as a "world in which globalization's benefits are more widely shared and social, economic, health, and environmental challenges are more easily weathered." The resources of the foundation focus on interrelated issue areas that include specific projects such as climate change, food security and a green revolution in Africa, prevention of disease, environmentally responsible transit, and investing to solve social and environmental problems.

Established in 1936 by Edsel Ford, son of Henry Ford, the founder of the Ford Motor Company, the Ford Foundation sponsors programs in over fifty countries. Since the foundation's beginning, it has sought to strengthen democratic values, reduce poverty and injustice, promote international cooperation, and advance human achievement. Some of the current initiatives include a program on protecting women's rights and, in the area of climate change and rural development, a project with the World Bank on reducing tropical deforestation. The MacArthur Foundation is best known for selecting outstanding individuals to receive their "genius grants" every fall, but the international programs of the foundation are given in more than sixty countries. Grants are given to programs in human rights, sustainable development, and peace and security. The current president of the foundation, Robert Gallucci, is a specialist on nuclear arms and served as the US ambassador in charge of nonproliferation talks with North Korea. Their Asia Security Initiative funds policy research involving academics and policy makers in Australia, Bangladesh, Switzerland, Japan, India, South Korea, China, and the United States.

Many of these foundations fund research institutes or think tanks and universities. **Think tanks** (also known as research institutes) vary in size, resource base, policy orientation, and political influence in either national or global politics. Some are scholarly and focus on nonpartisan research, and others represent a particular political position or ideology. Many focus on ideas like free market capitalism, socialism, or civic engagement (see Table 7.2).

think tank (or research institute) A body of experts providing advice and ideas on specific political or economic problems.

Table 7.2
Major Think Tanks with Significant Global Activities

Think Tank	Region	Mission	Website
Australian Institute of International Affairs (AIIA)	Australia	To promote interest in and understanding of international affairs in Australia.	http://www.aiia.asn.au/
Lowy Institute for International Policy	Australia	To generate new ideas and dialogue on international developments and Australia's role in the world.	http://www.lowyinstitute.org/
Bangladesh Institute of Development Studies (BIDS)	Bangladesh	To conduct policy-oriented research on development issues facing Bangladesh and other developing countries.	http://www.bids-bd.org/
Bruegel	Belgium	To contribute to European and global economic policy making through open, fact-based and policy-relevant research, analysis, and debate.	http://www.bruegel.org/
Egmont	Belgium	To provide analysis and suggest international policy options for both Belgian and foreign policy makers.	http://www.egmontinstitute.be/
Brazilian Center for International Relations (CEBRI)	Brazil	To study and debate crucial themes of Brazilian foreign policy and international relations.	http://www.cebri.com.br/
Centre for International Governance Innovation	Canada	To support research, form networks, advance policy debate, and generate ideas for multilateral governance improvements.	http://www.cigionline.org/
The North-South Institute	Canada	To eradicate global poverty and enhance social justice through research.	http://www.nsi-ins.ca/
Copenhagen Institute	Denmark	To support decision making through the analysis of trends that influence the future both in Denmark and internationally.	http://www.cifs.dk/en/
Åland Islands Peace Institute	Finland	To research peace and conflict issues.	http://www.peace.ax/en
European Union Institute for Security Studies	France	To research security issues of relevance to the European Union and provide a forum for debate.	http://www.iss.europa.eu/
German Institute of Global and Area Studies	Germany	To conduct research focused on political, economic, and social developments.	http://www.giga-hamburg.de/english/
Konrad Adenauer Foundation	Germany	To research scientific concepts, developing a basis for possible political action.	http://www.kas.de/wf/en/

Continued

Table 7.2 (*continued*)
Major Think Tanks with Significant Global Activities

Think Tank	Region	Mission	Website
Hellenic Foundation for European and Foreign Policy (ELIAMEP)	Greece	To provide a forum for public debate on issues of European integration and international relations.	http://www.eliamep.gr/en
Millennium Institute	Hungary	To promote systems literacy and dynamic modeling tools to attain sustainable development worldwide.	http://www.millennium-institute.org/
Institute for Defense Studies and Analyses (IDSA)	India	To promote national and international security through the generation and dissemination of objective research and knowledge on defense and security-related issues.	http://www.idsa.in/
Club of Rome	Italy	To identify and combat the most crucial problems facing humanity.	http://www.clubofrome.org/
The Asian Institute for Policy Studies	Korea Republic	To provide effective solutions to issues critical to Korea, East Asia, and the rest of the world.	http://www.asaninst.org/eng/index.php
African Progress Center	Kenya	To find practical and long-term solutions to strengthen freedom and democracy in Africa.	N/A
Netherlands Institute of International Relations Clingendael	The Netherlands	To identify and analyze emerging political and social developments for the benefit of government and the general public.	http://www.clingendael.nl/
Ecologic Foundation	New Zealand	To promote sustainable development.	http://www.ecologic.org.nz/
Sustainable Future Institute	New Zealand	To contribute strategic foresight through evidence-based research and policy analysis.	http://sustainablefuture.info/
Pakistan Institute of International Affairs (PIIA)	Pakistan	To encourage and facilitate the understanding of international affairs.	http://www.piia.org.pk/
Institute of Strategic Studies (ISSI)	Pakistan	To provide an in-depth understanding and objective analysis of regional and global strategic issues affecting international peace and security.	http://www.issi.org.pk/
Resources, Environment and Economics Center for Studies (REECS)	Philippines	To consult on environmental and resource economics.	http://www.reecs.org/
Centre for Eastern Studies (OSW)	Poland	To analyze the political, economic, and social situations in neighboring countries.	http://www.osw.waw.pl/en

Continued

Table 7.2 (*continued*)

Major Think Tanks with Significant Global Activities

Think Tank	Region	Mission	Website
Singapore Institute of International Affairs	Singapore	To research, analyze, and discuss regional and international issues.	http://www.siiaonline.org/
Stockholm International Peace Research Institute	Sweden	To research conflict, armaments, arms control, and disarmament.	http://www.sipri.org/
Taiwan Institute of Economic Research	Taiwan	To research domestic and foreign macro-economics and industrial economics.	http://english.tier.org.tw/
Gulf Research Center	United Arab Emirates (UAE)	To conducting scholarly, high-quality research focused on social sciences in the Gulf region.	http://www.grc.ae/
International Centre for Policy Studies (ICPS)	Ukraine	To contribute to the establishment of a robust framework for Ukraine's economic, social, and foreign policies.	http://www.icps.com.ua/eng
American Enterprise Institute for Public Policy Research	United States	To preserve and strengthen the foundations of a free society through rigorous inquiry, debate, and writing.	http://www.aei.org/
The Aspen Institute	United States	To enhance the quality of leadership through informed dialogue.	http://www.aspeninst.org/
Brookings Institution	United States	To improve the performance of American institutions, the effectiveness of government programs, and the quality of US public policies.	http://www.brook.edu/
Cato Institute	United States	To publish on the complete spectrum of policy issues.	http://www.cato.org/
Center for Defense Information (CDI)	United States	To find realistic and efficient military spending solutions.	http://www.cdi.org/
Center for International Private Enterprise	United States	To strengthen democracy around the globe through private enterprise and market-oriented reform.	http://www.cipe.org/
The Center for Strategic and International Studies (CSIS)	United States	To develop practical solutions to the world's greatest challenges and provide strategic insights and bipartisan policy solutions to policy makers.	http://csis.org/
Council on Foreign Relations	United States	To address significant foreign policy issues in major geographic areas.	http://www.cfr.org/

Continued

Table 7.2 (*continued*)
Major Think Tanks with Significant Global Activities

Think Tank	Region	Mission	Website
Economic Policy Institute	United States	To broaden discussions about economic policy to include the needs of low- and middle-income workers.	http://www.epi.org/
Economic Strategy Institute	United States	To ensure that globalization works with market forces to achieve maximum benefits rather than distorting markets or imposing costs.	http://www.econstrat.org/
Heritage Foundation	United States	To formulate and promote conservative public policies based on the principles of free enterprise, limited government, individual freedom, traditional American values, and a strong national defense.	http://www.heritage.org/
Institute for Global Communications	United States	To bring advanced communications technologies to grassroots organizations worldwide.	http://www.igc.org/
International Institute for Counter-Terrorism	United States	To facilitate international cooperation in the global struggle against terrorism.	http://www.ict.org.il/
Progressive Policy Institute	United States	To act as a forum for political commentary informed by rigorous analysis of evidence.	http://progressivepolicy.org/
Project on Defense Alternatives	United States	To adapt security policy to the challenges and opportunities of the post–Cold War era.	http://www.comw.org/pda/
RAND Corporation	United States	To improve policy and decision making through research and analysis of issue areas such as health, education, national security, international affairs, law and business, and the environment.	http://www.rand.org/
Third World Network	United States	To address issues relating to development, developing countries, and North-South affairs.	http://www.twnside.org.sg/
United States Institute of Peace	United States	To prevent and mitigate international conflict without resorting to violence.	http://www.usip.org/
World Resources Institutes	United States	To put ideas into action by working with governments, companies, and civil society to build solutions to urgent environmental challenges.	http://www.wri.org/

Although about 60 percent of think tanks are in the United States, Western Europe, and Canada, the Foreign Policy Research Institute (2007) sent surveys to over 5,000 think tanks in 169 countries and received 1,000 responses from 134 countries. This survey showed that think tanks are adapting to new global realities as they attempt to engage with and influence policy makers, the media, and the general public.

Think tanks have increased in number and influence as critical players in global politics, and their growing importance is due to a variety of factors. One obvious factor is the complexity of issues now facing policy makers. Most of the officials we elect or appoint to handle these issues are not experts. They depend on the epistemic communities that are often found within think tanks and research institutes. Another reason for the growth of these actors is that, although we are flooded with information, it is very hard to decide what information is reliable. Think tanks and research institutes with a long history of producing reliable information based on sound research offer public officials information they can use with confidence. These think tanks play a critical role by providing the following services:

- Disseminating research reports and other briefing documents
- Promoting specific policy strategies and ideas
- Providing essential information to political parties, public officials, policy bureaucracies, the media, and the general public
- Evaluating policy programs and decision-making processes

Many think tanks play the role of policy entrepreneurs where they advocate for a certain policy agenda and work with national and international partners to convince governments to adopt their ideas. Consider how influential the American Enterprise Institute and the British Adam Smith Institute might be in discussions about privatization, the importance of the free market, and limiting the size of government. In fact, many of the experts who work in these think tanks often become government officials when someone who shares their views is elected. In the Foreign Policy Research Institute's survey, think tanks around the world identified their key categories for research as domestic and international economics, national security, regional studies, and international cooperation and development.

Criminal and Terrorist Networks as Global Actors

Globalization has provided a number of opportunities for the spread of positive ideas as well as trade, travel, and communications. There is, of course, a dark side to globalization, and that is the opportunities it provides for criminal networks to expand their activities, increase their profits, and increase their number of victims. A variety of informal organizations and criminal gangs engage in violent or criminal behavior across the globe. A distinction can be made between activity that is considered criminal around the world—such as theft, fraud, personal violence, piracy, or drug trafficking—and activity that is claimed by those undertaking it to have legitimate political motives. In reality, the distinction becomes blurred when criminals claim political motives or political groups are responsible for acts such as terrorism, torture, or involving children in violence. For all governments, neither criminal activity nor political violence can be legitimate within their own jurisdiction and generally not in other countries.

Politically, the most important criminal industries are illicit trading in arms, drugs, and people. In a 2003 article in *Foreign Policy*, Moises Naim argues that the war on

- Africa (554, 8.4%)
- Asia (1194, 18%)
- Europe (1836, 27.8%)
- Latin America and the Caribbean (721, 11%)
- Middle East and North Africa (339, 5.1%)
- North America (1919, 29.1%)
- Oceania (40, 0.6%)

DISTRIBUTION OF THINK TANKS BY REGION, 2012.

Who shapes the policy agenda when European and North American research institutes dominate policy research?

Source: http://gotothinktank.com/dev1/wp-content/uploads/2013/07/2012_Global_Go_To_Think_Tank_Report_-_FINAL-1.28.13.pdf.

THEORY IN PRACTICE

A Transnational Challenge: The War on Drugs

For many people in the United States, the trade in illegal recreational drugs like marijuana is a joke, but in Mexico, it is not at all funny. Beginning in the 1960s, Mexico became a source of the weed in addition to being a transit country for other illegal drugs destined for US markets. The actions of the drug gangs were often simply another part of life along the border. However, something changed dramatically during 2008, and by early 2009, open warfare began between Mexican drug kingpins and the Mexican federal government. In a change from the past, the federal police often found themselves outgunned by the drug gangs, which were armed with machine guns and rocket-propelled grenades. In the terms you learned in this chapter, the transnational criminal gangs represent a direct challenge to the authority of the governments of Mexico and the United States. It has become a significant transnational problem.

The central propositions of the Westphalian system are that each country is sovereign and has a legitimate monopoly on the use of force within its own specific territory. The transnational character of the drug trade has undermined the ability of governments to control the use of force within their borders. In the case of Mexico and the United States, the televised images of shoot-outs provide vivid examples of this phenomenon. The interdependent nature of this relationship goes beyond the fact that the drugs are on their way to users in the United States. Mexican officials complain that lax gun-purchasing laws in the United States are part of the problem because so-called straw purchasers buy firearms in the United States and then ship them south of the border.

Modern globalized mass culture also has a role in this drug-war drama. Movies, music, and video games that seem to glorify the violent drug culture play an important, if unwitting, part in the erosion of governmental authority. It becomes "cool" to swagger like a gangster or to run up a high score on Grand Theft Auto. At parties

The war on drugs has been going on for a long time. This national police special forces team from Colombia was trained by US forces back in 1989.

on Thursday night at the dormitory or during a free period from high school, some think it is cool to have drugs.

In these overt and subtle ways, the norms on which the government's authority is based are diluted. In some regions of the world—the Golden Triangle of northern Myanmar and Thailand, Medellín in Colombia, and Afghanistan—the drug kingpins have their private armies and administer their own form of justice in the territories they control. The drug traffickers provide a stable, if illegal, income for many people. Ironically, the drug lords also provide an alternative form of government, with their own quasi legal code that features swift retribution for transgressions.

Paradoxically, the legitimacy of governments can be further undermined when their drug interdiction agencies cooperate to stem the international drug trade. We can see this at work in the relations of the United States with Mexico, Colombia, Bolivia, and Peru. For more than thirty

years, the US government has tried a number of means to control the supply of illegal drugs from these countries. These have included economic incentives to farmers to switch to legal crops, military assistance to the governments, and the application of herbicides to kill the illegal plants. All of these methods have failed to end the drug-based agribusiness and have aggravated the perception that the gringo from El Norte is continuing its meddling in the internal affairs of the Latin American countries.

Although some scholars who subscribe to the realist tradition might discount the significance of transnational actors as participants in international relations, it is clear that many of these actors do indeed have a substantial impact on a globalized society. They provide food aid, medical care, and development assistance. Unfortunately, some transnational agents also bring dangerous illegal drugs and narcoterrorism that present very real challenges to the legitimacy of the states.

For Discussion

1. How can states respond to the security challenges presented by criminal networks? Should this be a task for global institutions?

2. Mexico is an important state in North America. Could the activities of the drug lords undermine its stability and move it toward being a failed state?

3. This is a problem not only for Mexico but also for the United States. It is a classic transnational problem and is clearly a supply-and-demand issue: US citizens are consuming the drugs, and Mexican drug cartels are supplying them. What should both nation-states do to address this issue?

terrorism has obscured the importance of five other global wars that we are losing. The war on drugs may be the best known of these. In Mexico alone, the drug cartels control entire cities and regions, and more than 60,000 people have been killed from 2006 to 2012, according to Human Rights Watch. The United States spends some $40 billion a year on drug interdiction, intelligence gathering, and prevention programs, but global drug activities seem to grow exponentially, and now good portions of Latin America, Southeast Asia, South and Central Asia, and Africa are involved in the production and distribution of illegal drugs. The demand for drugs has not decreased, and drug users in Europe and North America have made this a major global industry, accounting for nearly 10 percent of world trade.

The second war we are losing involves the illegal arms trade. This includes the illegal trade in small arms, munitions, equipment like tanks and artillery, aircraft, and unmanned weapons such as drones. Illicit trade in small arms accounts for 20 percent of the global market.

The third war is the one that interests many in the business world, and that is the protection of intellectual property and the prevention of piracy and counterfeiting of products such as movies, music, computer or video games, and software. Inadequate laws and limited enforcement resources have allowed for the development of industries that produce near-perfect knockoffs that are less expensive and are readily purchased by consumers who want to be seen with global brands and do not seem to care much about the criminal nature of their consumer behavior.

The fourth and perhaps most unsettling war is the one involving human trafficking. This is more than just smuggling aliens into the European Union from Africa or Chinese into Canada. Many of these aliens actually pay to be smuggled into these areas for jobs and a better quality of life. However, the darker side is the trafficking in women and children for sex or for slavery. This is a very lucrative business, and the United Nations estimates that it is the fastest-growing business for global criminal networks.

Money laundering and smuggling money, gold coins, and other valuables are part of the fifth war we are losing. This involves helping individuals, criminal networks, and corporations hide funds from creditors, business partners, and government tax collectors. It also involves hiding funds collected from illegal activities.

Even when governments are strong and reasonably effective, their ability to respond to the threats presented by global criminal networks is hindered by inadequate laws, bureaucratic jurisdictional disputes, and enforcement strategies that work well at home but not in a more complex global environment.

Is it possible to win any of these wars against the powerful criminal networks? The answer is, of course, yes, but governments will not win without some serious thinking about how we organize states and how we think about the international system. World leaders must begin to share or even trade sovereignty and open their systems to global institutions sponsoring multilateral enforcement activities. This will not be easy, considering the woeful underfunding of Interpol, the primary multilateral agency with a mission to fight crime, and states are reluctant to give it more power. These criminal and terrorist networks are not limited by issues of sovereignty and notions of national interests; instead, they are governed by market forces, and they see any boundary or border as permeable. States must find ways to regulate these activities that are transboundary in nature and reach some agreement on a set of regulations that will be enforced in every market across the globe. Successful efforts to end these wars may also depend on a change in our attitudes about community and the individual. If we continue to promote

GLOBAL PERSPECTIVE | Nongovernmental Organizations and Protecting the Rights of Children

Do nongovernmental organizations matter? That is the central question of the academic disputes that you read about at the start of this chapter. As you saw, people on one side in this discourse believe that NGOs are important actors that influence a range of behaviors in international relations. On the other side are many realists who believe that governments are the most important—and some believe the only—actor that matters in the study of the discipline. Somewhere in the middle are analysts who think that, by combining the study of states and NGOs, we can begin to understand the complexities of international relations. This dispute is primarily a disagreement of the kind you learned about in Chapters 3 and 4: What is the proper unit of analysis in the study of globalization and international relations?

For children around the world, these academic exercises miss the point: NGOs matter. Without the work of NGOs to supply food, provide education, and promote awareness, the lives of children would be much worse. In countries around the world each day, children are forced to be soldiers in civil wars, children starve, children lack basic health services, children are forced to work in factories for less pay than adults, and children are physically abused and forced into sex slavery.

Each day, workers for local and transnational NGOs strive to improve living conditions for millions of people under the age of eighteen. Hundreds of organizations attempt to implement the UN Millennium Development Goals that you read about already in this book. Nongovernmental organizations also do the important task of holding each country accountable for its ratification of the 1989 Convention on the Rights of the Child. Because the United Nations is an organization of sovereign and nominally equal countries, as you saw in Chapter 6, it is sometimes unable to do as much as some governments would like. Nongovernmental organizations, because they are not responsible to national governments, can apply moral suasion through public-awareness campaigns to help people in need.

There are hundreds of NGOs working around the world to help children. Two of the more famous are Oxfam and Human Rights Watch, which focus on three main areas of children's rights: basic needs such as food, clothing, shelter, and healthcare; education; and security, including juvenile justice and ending war. Although these are also problems in industrialized countries, they represent greater challenges in the developing world where governments lack the resources to provide for these needs. For example, according to the website of Oxfam International (http://www.oxfam.org/), its thirteen member groups work in more than 100 countries helping people to help themselves by providing the tools and seeds for them to grow their own food. Oxfam also works in the area of arms control, seeking to encourage governments to stop expensive weapons sales and to redirect the money to basic human needs in developing countries.

Human Rights Watch has programs aimed at ending abuses of people regardless of age; however,

A young Sudan People's Liberation Army child soldier holds a gun during the demobilization of soldiers in southern Sudan, 2001.

Continued

the organization believes that children are at risk because of their vulnerable status in many societies. The group's website (http://www.hrw.org/en/category/topic/children's-rights) has grim stories about the horrible conditions that children face around the world: detention in "social protection centers" in Vietnam where they are forced to work long hours for much less than the prevailing local wage scale; being forced to fight in civil wars in Africa and Asia; or use as sex workers in some countries, where they are then denied access to medical care, including HIV/AIDS medicines. The Children's Rights Division of Human Rights Watch has worked with the International Criminal Court to try to end the use of child soldiers and sexual trafficking in children.

Academic analysts of international politics might disagree about the worth of NGOs in the study of international society, but NGOs clearly have a positive effect daily on the lives of millions of people who are most at risk. Nongovernmental organizations are able to assume tasks that governments are unable or unwilling to do themselves.

For Discussion

1. If states fail to protect children, is there not a place for NGO intervention?
2. Children and their rights are hardly the focus of most international relations discussions. How do NGOs bring these concerns to our attention?
3. As the agenda of international relations shifts to human security issues, or freedom from fear and freedom from want, how important will nonstate actors be in the future?

the goal of individual advancement over peace and stability in our communities, these wars may continue for a long time.

We will discuss terrorism and terrorist networks in depth in Chapter 9, so for now, we merely want to emphasize that terrorist organizations are nonstate actors that have an impact on all actors in the international system. Terrorism is very difficult to eliminate because groups using terrorism are usually parts of larger global networks that are decentralized and hydra headed. President George W. Bush described the battle against it as "fourth-generation warfare," which involves nation-states in wars with nonstate global networks. William S. Lind (2007, 3) elaborates:

> In broad terms, fourth-generation warfare seems likely to be widely dispersed and largely undefined; the distinction between war and peace will be blurred to the vanishing point. It will be nonlinear, possibly to the point of having no definable battlefields or fronts. The distinction between "civilian" and military may disappear.

Terrorist networks are global networks composed of many different groups who may or may not share a common ideological position. These groups are usually united only in their desire to overthrow a government or a regional or global system of governance or replace a way of life or a hegemonic ideology. The major groups fighting the United States and much of the Western world today are fighting the dominant political, economic, and cultural actors and their belief systems. This *new terrorism* is characterized by its global reach, decentralized structure, a seemingly wide-open targeting strategy with no regard for civilians, and more obscure and extreme goals and objectives. Radical groups who are likely to use terrorism to overthrow governments and kill innocent civilians in the process are often linked to NGOs and foundations that are supported by sympathetic states or by states seeking to keep extremists out of their lands.

WHAT'S YOUR WORLDVIEW

What policies would you recommend to the US government to limit the flow of drugs from other countries into the United States? Can this drug trade be controlled without the help of other state and transnational actors?

We should not forget that some states also support terrorist activities, and in some cases, their military or police forces are the terrorists. In the pursuit of national interests, states may not always follow the rules.

Terrorists, Guerrillas, and National Liberation

Political violence is most common when broadly based nationalist movements, ethnic minorities, or fundamentalist religious groups reject the legitimacy of a government. As we will see in Chapter 9, these groups are often called "terrorists" to express disapproval, "guerrillas" by those who are more neutral, or "national liberation movements" by their supporters. In the past, nationalists were usually able to obtain some external support. Now, because of widespread revulsion against political violence, national groups and ethnic minorities are subject to pressure to negotiate instead of fight. Political violence is more likely to be considered legitimate when a group has widespread support, when political channels have been closed to them, when the target government is exceptionally oppressive, and when the violence is limited to "military targets." Groups that fail to match these four characteristics only obtain very limited transnational support. When Palestinian groups first used terrorist methods, the Palestine Liberation Organization (PLO) gained attention but not support. When they limited these violent attacks in the mid-1970s, the PLO achieved membership in the Arab League along with observer status at the United Nations. However, suicide bombing targeted at civilians by some Palestinians during and since the second intifada of the late 1980s greatly reduced the PLO's international legitimacy.

Since September 11, 2001, the political balance has changed substantially. The scale of the destruction wrought by Al Qaeda that day did much to delegitimize *all* groups who use violence for political purposes. Historically, terrorism has mainly been an instrument of internal conflict within a single society, but Al Qaeda suddenly presented the world with a new threat of a transnational global network. Within a few years, they staged attacks in Kenya, Tanzania, Yemen, Saudi Arabia, the United States, Tunisia, Indonesia,

Long labeled a terrorist organization, the Palestinian Liberation Organization (PLO) gained observer status at the United Nations in 1974. The Palestinian Authority sits at the diplomatic table as an equal with states, including Israel and the United States.

Turkey, and Spain. And yet contemporary terrorism is not a single phenomenon. The Basque, Palestinian, Kashmiri, Tamil, and Chechnya disputes clearly have roots that are totally independent of one another and have little or no connection to Al Qaeda. There are different transnational processes for different conflicts generating terrorism. Even Al Qaeda itself is a disparate coalition of anti-American fundamentalist groups rather than a coherent disciplined organization.

Extensive political violence used by governments against their citizens was commonplace and immune from diplomatic criticism as recently as the 1970s. Because of a widespread desire to end impunity for individual government leaders, soldiers, and officials responsible for the horrors of large-scale political violence at the end of the twentieth century, a revolution has occurred in international law. Initially, temporary tribunals were established to cover atrocities in Yugoslavia and Rwanda. Then the ICC was created in July 2002 as a permanent institution to prosecute those who commit genocide, war crimes, or crimes against humanity. The ICC is a modification of the traditional interstate system because it was created by political campaigning of human rights NGOs, because bitter opposition from the sole "superpower" was defeated, and because the sovereign responsibility to prosecute criminals has been assumed by a global court. In September 2005, the United Nations went further, replacing state sovereignty with a collective global responsibility to protect (R2P) when national authorities are manifestly failing (General Assembly Resolution 60/1).

The Significance of Criminals, Terrorists, and Guerrillas

Before September 11, 2001, analysis of transnational criminals and guerrillas did not present a challenge to orthodox state-centric theory. Criminals seemed to be marginal because they were not legitimate and were excluded from normal international transactions. Pirates operating in the Strait of Malacca or off the coast of Somalia rarely became international news. The violent groups that gained military, political, and diplomatic status on a transnational basis could be presented as nationalist groups aspiring to gain their place in the interstate system.

Such arguments ignore the way globalization has changed the nature of sovereignty and the processes of government. The operations of criminals and other non-legitimate groups have become more complex, spread over a wider geographic area, and larger in scale because the improvements in communications have made it so much easier to transfer people, money, weapons, and ideas on a transnational basis.

WHAT'S YOUR WORLDVIEW

In its campaign against terrorism, the George W. Bush administration in the United States violated many critical tenets of international law and basic principles of human rights. Are these practices acceptable in the global war on terrorism, or do they serve the purposes of terrorist actors to undermine the moral authority of the US government?

Government attempts to control such activities have become correspondingly more difficult, as the case of the Somali pirates demonstrates. The legal concept of sovereignty may nominally still exist, but political practice has become significantly different. Now virtually every government feels it has to mobilize external support to exercise "domestic jurisdiction" over criminals. Defeat of Al Qaeda will not be achieved by military counterterrorism but by global political change that delegitimizes fundamentalism and violence. Oppressive action by governments is subject to extensive review under global human rights mechanisms and, in some situations, may be subject to prosecution at the ICC.

Conclusion

In this chapter, we looked at how the process of globalization is more than the interactions of governments and international and regional organizations comprising governments. Since the mid-nineteenth century, INGOs and other transnational actors like MNCs, foundations, think tanks, research institutes, and wealthy individuals and celebrity diplomats have played an increasingly important role in global affairs. Global corporations, banks, and investment firms make choices that challenge the sovereignty and power of states. The recent global economic meltdown gave the world clear insights into how difficult it is for governments to control investment flows, but INGOs, as members of global civil society, occupy the space between the governmental (public) world and the corporate (private) world. As many nation-states lack the resources or the political will to address significant global challenges, nonstate actors may either step up or push national leaders to act.

CONTRIBUTOR TO CHAPTER 7: Steven L. Lamy.

REVIEW QUESTIONS

1. With the increase in the number of INGOs and an increase in their activities, is power shifting away from the state?

2. In what policy areas are INGOs playing a major role? Are they filling in for nation-states, or are they providing additional services?

3. What are TANs? What kind of power do they have? How do they influence policy makers?

4. How do transnational companies affect the sovereignty of governments?

5. What measures could you use to compare the size of countries, TNCs, INGOs, and international organizations? Are countries always larger than transnational actors?

6. Explain the expansion in the number of INGOs engaging in transnational activities.

7. What role do think tanks play in global politics? What is an epistemic community?

8. What is celebrity diplomacy and why is it on the rise? Are celebrities effective diplomats?

9. What challenges do states face when trying to respond to the threats presented by criminal networks?

FURTHER READING

Case study materials:

Edwards, M., and Gaventa, J. (2001), *Global Citizen Action: Lessons and Challenges* (Boulder, Col.: Lynne Rienner). Focuses on broadly based campaigning networks, with six case studies on civil-society interaction with the international financial institutions and seven case studies on environment, human rights, and development campaigns.

Keck, M. E., and Sikkink, K. (1998), *Activists Beyond Borders: Advocacy Networks in International Politics* (Ithaca, N.Y.: Cornell University Press). A major contribution to the literature on the nature of modern transnational advocacy networks, with case studies on Latin America, the environment, and violence against women.

Risse-Kappen, T. (ed.) (1995), *Bringing Transnational Relations Back In* (Cambridge: Cambridge University Press). Provides a set of six case studies around the theme that transnational influence depends on the structures of governance for an issue area at both the domestic level and in international institutions.

Stone, D. (1996), *Capturing the Political Imagination: Think Tanks and the Policy Process* (London: Frank Cass). One of the only studies that looks at the importance of research institutes and their global influence.

Weiss, T. G., and Gordenker, L. (eds.) (1996), *NGOs, the UN and Global Governance* (Boulder, Col: Lynne Rienner). Six studies of NGO activity and three chapters addressing cross-cutting themes, set within a pluralist approach.

NOTES

1. Data on transnational corporations is given in annual reports from the United Nations. The figures quoted come from *World Investment Report 2006* (UNCTAD 2006b, 270–273 and 280–284). The numbers of different types of transnational and international organizations are from the *Yearbook of International Organizations 2005–2006*, vol. 5, p. 7 (Munich: Saur, 2006).

2. The *World Investment Report 2008* lists the 100 largest nonfinancial TNCs ranked by foreign assets: of these, 50 had global sales of $60 billion or more in 2007. Data for each country on GNP and population are given each year in the *World Development Indicators, 2006* (Washington, D.C.: World Bank).

3. *World Investment Report 2006*, Annex tables A.I.6 and A.I.11.

4. ECOSOC Resolution 288(X)B, Arrangements for Consultation with Nongovernmental Organizations, was passed in February 1950. It was amended and replaced by Resolution 1296(XLIV) in May 1968 and again by Resolution 1996/31 in July 1996.

INTERNET RESOURCES

Amnesty International
www.amnesty.org

Child Rights Information Network
www.crin.org

International Baby Food Action Network
www.ibfan.org

International Campaign to Ban Landmines
www.icbl.org

International Committee of the Red Cross
www.icrc.org

International Federation of Red Cross and Red Crescent Societies
www.ifrc.org

Multinational Monitor
http://multinationalmonitor.org/monitor.html

NGO Branch of the UN Secretariat
www.un.org/esa/coordination/ngo

NGOs with UN ECOSOC consultative status, as of September 1, 2009 (list)
http://esango.un.org/paperless/content/E2009INF4.pdf

One World Trust program on accountability in global governance
www.oneworldtrust.org

Oxfam International Trade Campaign
www.oxfam.org/en/campaigns/trade

Sustainable Development Issues Network
http://sdin-ngo.net/

World Federalist Movement
www.wfm-igp.org/site

Carnegie Council: "They Fight Like Soldiers, They Die Like Children: The Global Quest to Eradicate the Use of Child Soldiers"—Lt. Gen. Roméo A. Dallaire
http://www.carnegiecouncil.org/resources/audio/data/000648

Serving as UNAMIR commander during the Rwanda genocide, Dallaire saw the horrors of genocide and the use of child soldiers firsthand; he now offers insight on how the use of child soldiers in conflict can be stopped.

Carnegie Council: International Humanitarian Law and Non-State Actors
http://www.youtube.com/carnegiecouncil#p/u/168/
   BWgRaq_mhlo

This short video offers an overview of developments and loopholes in international law along with the rise of terrorist organizations.

For more information, quizzes, case studies and other study tools, please visit us at **www.oup.com/us/lamy**

Who Could Help Tomorrow? Twenty Global Problems and Global Issues Networks

This is a problem-based exercise that simply asks you to consider which public, private, and civil-society actors should pool their resources and effectively respond to global problems. The idea for this comes from a book by J. F. Rischard, *High Noon: 20 Global Problems, 20 Years to Solve Them* (New York: Basic Books, 2002). He is a vice president of the World Bank, and his book has been at the center of discussion at several major global conferences. Now it is your turn to think about these issues and possible solutions. Rischard believes that two major stresses present unprecedented problems and opportunities. These two are demographic changes, including population growth and income distribution, and the new global economy that includes a technological revolution and the globalization of production, trade, and investment. These stress factors contribute to a number of global challenges that require the attention of all citizens of the world. Here are the three issue areas and some specific challenges in each category.

Sharing our planet: Issues involving the global commons
Global warming; biodiversity and ecosystem losses; fisheries depletion; deforestation; water deficits; and maritime safety and pollution

Sharing our humanity: Issues requiring a global commitment
Poverty; peacekeeping; conflict prevention; counter-terrorism; education for all; global infectious diseases; the digital divide; and natural-disaster prevention and mitigation

Sharing our rule book: Issues needing a global regulatory approach
Reinventing taxation for the twenty-first century; biotechnology rules; global financial architecture; illegal drugs; trade, investment, and competition rules; intellectual property rights; e-commerce rules; and international labor laws and migration rules

Who can help solve or manage these problems? How about a coalition of public, private, and civil-society actors? According to Rischard, partnerships like these are the only way forward. Global coalitions or global information networks called GINs are similar in purpose to TANs and TSMOs. Each GIN enlists members from governments, international civil-society organizations, and businesses to address the issues that challenge global stability and often create real human-security problems.

In small groups of three or four, identify one of the problems or challenges in the three categories listed. In your group, discuss the nature of the problem and identify actors that you think could help respond to it. You need at least two actors in each of the three categories (six total actors): two governments, two NGOs, and two businesses. This is your problem-solving coalition, or GIN. Why did you select these actors? What resources or expertise do they bring to the problem-solving activities? How will each actor participate in the situation? How will each solve or manage the problem?

For example, if water pollution is the issue, maybe you should involve Canada and Saudi Arabia. Canada has large supplies of clean water, and Saudi Arabia has money to pay for the program and a need for water. Nongovernmental organizations might include the Global Water Campaign and Oxfam; businesses that sell water, like Nestlé and Coca-Cola, might also have skills, interests, and resources.

Your assignment is to put together the most effective coalition to respond to the potential crisis and tell us how it will work!

PART FOUR

Global Issues: Security

In the final two parts of the book, we present a wide-ranging overview of the main issues in contemporary global politics. These parts build on the previous three, which were designed to give you a comprehensive foundation for the study of contemporary global issues. As with the other parts, these last two parts have two aims: First, we want to give you an understanding of some of the more *important and pressing problems* that appear every day in the media headlines and that, directly and indirectly, affect our lives. These issues are the stuff of globalization, and they take a number of different forms. Our second aim is to raise further questions about the *nature of globalization*.

In Chapter 8, we consider *war and nuclear proliferation*, which pose dangers of global catastrophe. Next we consider how *terrorism* (Chapter 9), *human rights*, and *human security* (Chapter 10) are fundamentally linked to globalization. In Part Five, we will then turn to economic and environmental issues with global impacts, and you will see that all of these issues are intertwined and of crucial importance to global security and prosperity.

After reading and discussing Parts Four and Five, you should be able to answer critical questions about how globalization shapes global issues. Does it make it easier or harder to deal with the problems covered in these chapters? The picture that emerges shows globalization as a highly complex process, one that has sparked major disagreements about its significance and impact.

Have we seen the end of major land wars? Are people simply tired of the human and material losses? Consider the costs of moving personnel and equipment across Afghanistan, as shown in this photo from 2011.

8 | Security and Military Power

Only the dead have seen the end of war.

—*Plato*

I learned early on that war forms its own culture. The rush of battle is a potent and often lethal addiction, for war is a drug, one I ingested for many years. It is peddled by mythmakers—historians, war correspondents, filmmakers, novelists, and the state—all of whom endow it with qualities it often does possess: excitement, exoticism, power, chances to rise above our small stations in life, and a bizarre and fantastic universe that has a grotesque and dark beauty.

—*Chris Hedges*

Wars in the twenty-first century have been and continue to be conflicts within failed or fragile states. Insurgents seek to replace governments that are repressing their citizens, excluding them from political participation, and denying them access to any economic benefits. Not surprising, about 39 percent of these conflicts are in Africa, another 39 percent are in Asia, and most of the rest are in the Middle East. The world must deal with wars that seem to have no meaning.

Consider the war in the Democratic Republic of the Congo, which is the world's most lethal conflict since World War II. It has lasted more than fifteen years—although several rebel groups agreed to a cease-fire in late 2013—and taken the lives of more than 5.4 million people, including an estimated 2.7 million children. Some twenty rebel groups and armies from nine nation-states are fighting in a territory as large as all of Western Europe, often committing acts of sexual violence in their assaults. Ethnic or tribal disputes, poverty, and the lust for power and treasure all contribute to this war. Fundamentally, there is no government to respond, and even 20,000 UN peacekeepers have been unable to contain the conflict. In December 2013, the eighth UN peacekeeping mission in Africa began operations in the Central African Republic. The primary goal of the mission was to stop the sectarian violence, where Muslim and Christian groups preyed on each other, creating what UN officials called "pre-genocidal" conditions. Civil wars and sectarian conflicts like the conflicts in the DRC and the Central African Republic present the biggest security challenge to those who seek global order.

We have entered a period where the shape of war is changing. Nation-states are now unlikely to engage in wars of choice. The era

The ongoing conflict in the Democratic Republic of the Congo has killed millions and forced millions more to become refugees. How might this conflict influence your life?

of deploying large armies to fight large land wars may be over, replaced by precision strikes and drone raids. The new type of warfare lasts for years, is financially draining, costs thousands or even millions of lives, and poses extraordinary defensive challenges.

And although we seem to have become complacent over nuclear proliferation and the chances of a nuclear confrontation, the chances of a nuclear confrontation are still very real. Authoritarian states like North Korea and Iran are seeking to defend their interests in what they perceive as hostile environments, and nuclear powers like India and Pakistan are at each other's throat because of longstanding disputes over Kashmir. We must not forget that there are always radicals on the market for weapons of mass destruction.

Our material interests and lifestyle choices, if not our moral responsibilities, draw us all into these conflicts. In this chapter, we will examine national security, international or global security, and conflict from a number of academic perspectives. We will try to determine how the shape of war has changed in an age of globalization.

Introduction

Is international security possible to achieve given the kind of world this is? To consider this question, we need to first examine the causes of war, which is a raging debate in itself. For some writers, especially historians, the causes of war are unique to each case. Other writers believe it is possible to provide a wider, more generalized explanation: that the causes lie, for example, in human nature, in the internal organization of states, or in global anarchy. As we saw in Chapter 3, Kenneth Waltz and other structural realists put particular emphasis on the nature of global anarchy, but they also acknowledge individual and societal causes.

Here we return to our discussion of levels of analysis and contending explanations for why states go to war. War is rarely explained by a single variable; factors often combine and then lead to wars. In *Man, the State and War* (1959), Waltz suggests we look at the nature of men, the political and economic structure of states, and the nature of order in the international system. From his perspective, the international system is a permissive setting in which aggressive leaders of antagonistic countries see war as a proper solution to disputes.

The end of the Cold War reshaped the debate for some liberal and many critical theorists like constructivists and radical liberals (discussed in Chapter 4), who claimed to see the dawn of a new world order in the end of the ideological confrontation between East and West. For other analysts, however, realism or neorealism remained the best approach to thinking about international security. In their view, very little of substance had changed as a result of the events of 1989. The end of the Cold War initially brought an era of more cooperation among the superpowers. But this more harmonious phase in international relations was only temporary because countries still interacted in an anarchic system. For the thousands of people who have died in conflicts since the Cold War, events seemed to support the realist and neorealist worldviews. With the first Gulf War (1990–1991), the ongoing civil wars in Africa and Asia, and then the 9/11 attacks, it became increasingly clear that states and nonstate actors (including international terrorist groups) continued to view force as an effective way to achieve their objectives.

We begin with a look at the basic definitions and disagreements central to the field, including what is meant by *security,* and we probe the relationship between national security and international security. Then we examine the traditional ways of thinking about national security and the influence these ideas have had on contemporary thinking. We follow this examination with a survey of alternative ideas and approaches that have emerged in the literature in recent years. Next we turn to the pressing question of nuclear weapons proliferation, including a brief overview of these weapons and a discussion of attempts to prevent their spread in the years after the Cold War. Finally, we provide an assessment of these ideas about national security before returning to the central question of whether greater global security is more, or less, likely in the new century.

After reading and discussing this chapter, you should be able to define security and discuss different views of it, both mainstream and critical. You should also have a better understanding of new security challenges and the changing nature of war. While you read, remember that the world is filled with nuclear weapons that can destroy life as we know it. You will come away with a deeper understanding of the challenges that nuclear weapons and proliferation present to global peace and stability.

What Is Security?

Security is a contested concept. Analysts agree that it implies freedom from threats to core values (for both individuals and groups), but they disagree fundamentally about whether to focus primarily on *individual*, *national*, or *international* security. For much of the Cold War period, most writing on the subject centered on **national security**, which was defined largely in militarized terms. Both academics and political leaders tended to be most interested, as the realist model asserts, in the military capabilities of their states. More recently, however, this idea of security has been criticized for being ethnocentric (culturally biased), gendered, and too narrowly defined. Instead, a number of contemporary writers have argued for an expanded conception of security, one spreading outward from the limits of parochial national security to include a range of other considerations. It is known as the **widening school of international security** because it extends the definition of security to include economic, political, social, and even environmental issues.

Further, not all who study security issues focus on the tension between national and international security (see Table 8.1). Some argue that such an emphasis ignores the fundamental changes that have been taking place in world politics, especially in the aftermath of the Cold War. Others argue that much more attention should be given to "societal security." According to this view, growing regional integration is undermining the classical political order based on nation-states, leaving states exposed within larger political frameworks. We see this development in the European Union, and plans for an expanded North American Free Trade Agreement (NAFTA) might indicate a similar trend in the Western Hemisphere. At the same time, the fragmentation of various states, like the Soviet Union and Yugoslavia, has created new problems of boundaries,

security The measures taken by states to ensure the safety of their citizens, the protection of their way of life, and the survival of their nation-state. Security can also mean the ownership of property that gives an individual the ability to secure the enjoyment or enforcement of a right or a basic human need.

national security A fundamental value in the foreign policy of states secured by a variety of tools of statecraft including military actions, diplomacy, economic resources, and international agreements and alliances. It also depends on a stable and productive domestic society.

widening school of international security Sometimes called the Copenhagen school, these are authors who extend the definition of security to include economic, political, societal, and environmental policy areas.

Peacekeeping troops have multiple roles, including making certain that humanitarian relief supplies arrive safely. Can the world afford to help refugees and provide extensive humanitarian services?

Table 8.1

Comparing Worldviews

	Realist	Liberal	Global Humanist	Marxist
View of National Security as a Policy Issue	• Military power is essential in supporting the primary objective of a state's national interest: survival. • In an anarchic, state-centric system, war is inevitable. • Self-help: no other state or institution can be relied on to guarantee your survival.	• Nations should practice collective security as a means of cooperation and assured protection of national interest, sharing the use of resources. • Nations have shared responsibility for foreign policy successes as well as failures. • Wars undertaken for purposes of expediency are unjust. Defense of life and defense of property are just causes, but if the cause of war is unjust, all acts arising from it are immoral.* • Anticipatory self-defense is forbidden. • Complete security is impossible.	• Arms reduction is a desirable step toward disarmament. • The international norm against the use of nuclear weapons should be strengthened. • Security policy should be guided by a sense of human solidarity that transcends the nation rather than by a desire to maximize national military power. • Human interest should take priority over national interest.	• National security is the protection of those who own the means of production. • There is no need for a large, oppressive military force if people are not oppressed and exploited by a small and powerful group of capitalist elites. • Inequality is the main security threat in the global system.

Continued

minorities, and organizing ideologies that are causing increasing regional instability (Weaver et al. 1993, 196). These dual processes of integration and fragmentation have led to the argument that ethnonational groups, rather than states, should become the center of attention for security analysts.

Disagreements about definitions matter because these academic arguments often influence the policy decisions that political leaders make. If political leaders believe their primary responsibility is national security, then building a safe international system for all countries is of secondary importance. Consider the following definitions of security and their implications:

> In the case of security, the discussion is about the pursuit of freedom from threat. When this discussion is in the context of the international system, security is about the ability of states and societies to maintain their independent identity and their functional integrity. (Buzan 1991)

Table 8.1 (*continued*)
Comparing Worldviews

	Realist	Liberal	Global Humanist	Marxist
Economic Consequences	• Military funding should be a priority in a state's economy as a means of ensuring security.	• There should be a free trade economy among countries of all development levels.	• Military spending distracts from the effort to eliminate world poverty and the general achievement of economic and social well-being.	• Funding for social programs for those living on the margins favors institutions that maintain the status quo.
Human Rights Implications	• Military power is necessary to protect the rights of a nation's citizens. • National leaders are responsible for making decisions that will preserve a nation's security and thus the security of its citizens.	• The international system can seek to project values of order, liberty, justice, and tolerance as well as protect human rights.	• Maintaining present levels of military spending by superpowers perpetuates inequity of wealth. • Overemphasis on military power indirectly supports corrupt, elitist, and repressive foreign governments.	• The interest of the state is to marginalize those who seek change and to create laws that manage and control dissent in the name of national security.
Environment	• Production and operation of military equipment take priority over environmental hazards and concerns.		• Present arms buildups exacerbate the problems of wasteful resource depletion and unnecessary pollution.	• The natural world needs to be respected, not exploited and abused for the interests of a few.

*Murphy, Cornelius F., Jr. "The Grotian Vision of World Order." *American Journal of International Law* Jul. 76.3 (1982): 477–498. *JSTOR*. Web. Sept. 31, 2011. 481. http://www.jstor.org/stable/2200783.

Acceptance of **common security** as the organizing principle for efforts to reduce the risk of war, limit arms, and move towards disarmament, means, in principle, that co-operation will replace confrontation in resolving conflicts of interest. This is not to say that differences among nations should be expected to disappear . . . The task is only to ensure that these conflicts do not come to be expressed in acts of war, or in preparations for war. It means that nations must come to understand that the maintenance of world peace must be given a higher priority than the assertion of their own ideological or political positions. (Palme Commission 1982)

Other commentators argue that the emphasis on national and international security is less appropriate because a global society has begun to emerge in the post–Cold War era. Academics called "societal-security theorists" point to the fragmentation of some nation-states, and they argue that more attention should be given not to society at the ethnonational level but to global society or, as the Islamic movements after 2001 suggest, to religious affiliation. These writers argue that one of the most important contemporary trends is the

common security At times called cooperative security, it stresses noncompetitive approaches and cooperative approaches through which states—both friends and foes—can achieve security. Sometimes expresses the belief that until all people are secure from threats of war, no one is secure.

community A human
association in which members
share common symbols and
wish to cooperate to realize
common objectives.

broad process of globalization that is taking place. They accept that this process brings new
risks and dangers. These include international terrorism, a breakdown of the global monetary system, global climate change, and nuclear accidents. These threats to security, on a
planetary level, are viewed as largely outside the control of nation-states. Only the development of a global **community**, societal-security theorists believe, can deal with this adequately.

At the same time, other writers on globalization stress the transformation of the state
(rather than its demise) and the new security agenda in the early years of the new century.
In the aftermath of 9/11, and the new era of violence that followed it, Jonathan Friedman
argued that we are living in a world "where polarization, both vertical and horizontal, both
class and ethnic, has become rampant, and where violence has become more globalized
and fragmented at the same time, and is no longer a question of wars between states but
of sub-state conflicts, globally networked and financed, in which states have become one
actor, increasingly privatized, amongst others" (2003, ix). For many who feel like this, the
post–September 11 era is a new and extremely dangerous period in world history. Whether
the world is so different today from the past is a matter of much contemporary discussion. To consider this issue, we need to begin by looking at the way security has been
traditionally conceived.

Mainstream Approaches to Security

As we discussed in Chapter 2, from the Peace of Westphalia in 1648 onward, states have
been regarded as the only legitimate, and by far the most powerful, actors in the international
system. They have been the universal standard of political legitimacy, with no higher authority to regulate their interactions with one another. States have therefore taken the view that
there is no alternative but to seek their own protection in what has been described as a self-
help world. For most modern political leaders and academics, realism has been the analytic
lens best suited to understanding war and security. As a result, the assumptions of realism,
in all their permutations, have dominated discussions. The other lenses that we discuss in
the chapter must all respond to realism.

Realist Views on Security

In the historical debate about how best to achieve national security, writers like Thucydides,
Hobbes, Machiavelli, and Rousseau tended to paint a rather pessimistic picture of the implications of state sovereignty. They viewed the international system as a rather brutal arena
in which states would seek to achieve their own security at the expense of their neighbors.
According to this view, permanent peace was unlikely to be achieved. All that states could
do was try to balance the power of other states to prevent any one from achieving overall
hegemony. This was a view shared by writers like E. H. Carr and Hans Morgenthau, who
developed what became known as the realist (or "classical" realist) school of thought in the
aftermath of both world wars.

Other contemporary writers, like Kenneth Waltz and John Mearsheimer, share the realist's pessimistic view of international relations. The pessimism of these structural realists
rests on a number of key assumptions they make about the way the international system
works (see Chapter 3).

Key Structural-Realist Assumptions

The following assumptions, structural realists argue, produce a tendency for states to act aggressively toward one another:

- The international system is anarchic. This does not mean that it is necessarily chaotic. Rather, anarchy implies that there is no central authority capable of controlling state behavior.
- States claiming sovereignty will inevitably develop offensive military capabilities to defend themselves and extend their power. Hence, they are potentially dangerous to one another.
- Uncertainty, leading to a lack of trust, is inherent in the international system. States can never be sure of the intentions of their neighbors, and therefore, they must always be on their guard.
- States will want to maintain their independence and sovereignty, and as a result, survival will be the most basic driving force influencing their behavior.
- Although states are rational, they will often make miscalculations. In a world of imperfect information, potential antagonists will always have an incentive to misrepresent their own capabilities to keep their opponents guessing. This may lead to mistakes about real state interests.

> ### WHAT'S YOUR WORLDVIEW
>
> *Do regions of the world have their own unique set of security challenges, or are the structural realists correct when they argue that all states respond to anarchy and the security dilemma in the same fashion?*

According to this view, national security (or insecurity) is largely the result of the structure of the international system, and the condition of anarchy is highly durable. The implication is that international politics in the future is likely to be as violent as international politics in the past. In an important article entitled "Back to the Future," written in 1990, John Mearsheimer argued that the end of the Cold War was likely to usher in a return to the traditional multilateral, balance-of-power politics of the past. He predicted that if this happened, extreme nationalism and ethnic rivalries would lead to widespread instability and conflict. Mearsheimer viewed the Cold War as a period of peace and stability brought about by the bipolar structure of power that prevailed. With the collapse of this system, he argued that there would be a return to the kind of great-power rivalries that had blighted international relations since the seventeenth century.

Indeed, most contemporary structural-realist writers see little prospect of a significant improvement in security in the post–Cold War world. Pointing to the Gulf War in 1991, the violent disintegration of the former Yugoslavia and parts of the former Soviet Union, continuing violence in the Middle East, the Iraq War after the 2003 invasion, and the war in Afghanistan, they argue that we continue to live in a world of mistrust and constant security competition. They suggest there are two main factors that continue to make cooperation difficult, even after the changes of 1989. The first is the prospect of cheating; the second is the concern states have about what are called "relative gains."

The Problem of Cheating

Structural-realist writers do not deny that states often cooperate or that in the post–Cold War era there are even greater opportunities than in the past for states to work together. They argue, however, that there are distinct limits to this cooperation because the people who lead states have always been and remain fearful that others will attempt to gain advantages by cheating on any agreements reached. This risk is regarded as particularly important

Many small and middle powers recognize the importance of collective action and rely on regional and international organizations to provide security and stability. These Austrian troops are part of a NATO-led peacekeeping force in Kosovo. They are there to prevent ethnic violence before a 2012 election in Serbia.

given the nature of modern military technology, which can bring about very rapid shifts in the balance of power between states. "Such a development," Mearsheimer has argued, "could create a window of opportunity for the cheating side to inflict a decisive defeat on the victim state" (1994–1995, 20). States realize that this is the case, and although they join alliances and sign arms control agreements, they remain cautious and aware of the need to provide for their own national security in the last resort. For example, believing the country needed a missile-defense system, the Bush administration withdrew the United States in 2002 from the Anti-Ballistic Missile Treaty of 1972, which Russia and the United States had signed to limit the use of such defense systems.

The Problem of Relative Gains

Cooperation is also inhibited, according to many neorealist writers, because states tend to be concerned with **relative gains** rather than **absolute gains**. Instead of being interested in cooperation because it will benefit both partners, states always need to be aware of how much they are gaining compared with the cooperating state. Because all states will attempt to maximize their gains in a competitive, mistrustful, and uncertain international environment, the thinking goes, cooperation will always be very difficult to achieve and hard to maintain. We can see this thinking at work when we examine the acts that countries took in response to the global economic collapse that began in 2008. Although the situation needed coordinated actions, leaders seemed reluctant to take the first step for fear of harming their domestic economies, and they preferred to wait and see what other key players did first.

Liberal Institutionalists on Global Security

One of the main characteristics of the structural-realist approach to global security is the belief that international institutions do not have a very important part to play in the prevention of war. Institutions are seen as the product of state interests and the constraints imposed by the international system itself. According to this view, it is these interests and constraints that shape the decisions on whether to cooperate or compete rather than the institutions to which states belong.

Both political leaders and a number of international relations specialists have challenged such views, particularly following the end of the Cold War. British foreign secretary Douglas Hurd, for example, made the case in June 1992 that institutions themselves had played, and continued to play, a crucial role in enhancing security, particularly in Europe. He argued that the West had developed "a set of international institutions which have proved their worth for one set of problems" (Hurd, quoted in Mearsheimer 1994–1995). He went on to argue that the great challenge of the post–Cold War era was to adapt these institutions to deal with the new circumstances that prevailed.

Hurd's argument reflected a belief, widely shared among Western leaders, that a framework of complementary, mutually reinforcing institutions—the European Union, NATO, the Western European Union (WEU), and the Organization for Security and Co-operation in Europe (OSCE)—could be developed to promote a more durable and stabler European security system for the post–Cold War era. It is a view also shared by a distinctive group of academic writers active since the 1980s and early 1990s. These writers contend that a developing pattern of institutionalized cooperation among states opens up unprecedented opportunities to achieve greater international security in the years ahead. Although the past may have been characterized by frequent wars and conflict, they see important changes taking place in international relations that may relax the traditional security competition among states. Certainly, the fact that there has not been a war in Western Europe in more than sixty years supports this perspective.

relative gains One of the factors that realists argue constrain the willingness of states to cooperate. States are less concerned about whether everyone benefits (absolute gains) and more concerned about whether someone may benefit more than someone else.

absolute gains The notion that all states seek to have more power and influence in the system to secure their national interests. Offensive neorealists are also concerned with increasing power relative to other states. One must have enough power to secure interests and more power than any other state in the system—friend or foe.

Engaging with the
WORLD
Atlantic Council

Since the council's founding in 1961–1962, it has been a preeminent, nonpartisan institution devoted to promoting transatlantic cooperation and international security. It offers conferences and programs in the United States and Europe for faculty and students and has a very attractive internship program. Visit the council at http://www.acus.org/.

This approach, known as liberal institutionalism, argues that international institutions are much more important in helping achieve cooperation and stability than structural realists realize (see Chapter 3). Supporters of these ideas point to the importance of European economic and political institutions in overcoming the traditional hostility of European states. They also point to the developments within the European Union and NATO in the post–Cold War era and claim that, by investing major resources, states themselves clearly demonstrate their belief in the importance of institutions. The creation of the eurozone of shared currency and NATO's deployment of troops outside Europe provide evidence of this trend.

Since the end of the Cold War, NATO members have taken on new security tasks. Here, Turkish commandos have captured five pirates operating in the Gulf of Aden near Somalia.

As such, the liberal-institutionalist approach suggests that in a world constrained by state power and divergent interests, international institutions operating on the basis of reciprocity will be a component of any lasting peace. That is, international institutions themselves are unlikely to eradicate war from the international system, but they can play a part in helping achieve greater cooperation among states.

One question liberal institutionalists might examine is why war is absent in some parts of the contemporary world. The North Atlantic region, for example, has been described as a **security community**, a group of states for whom war has disappeared as a means of resolving disputes with one another, although they may continue to use war against opponents outside the security community. One common characteristic of these states is that they are all democracies. Philosophers like Kant and contemporary theorists like Michael Doyle and Bruce Russett have suggested that democracies will go to war, but they are not prepared to fight against another democracy. The assumption of this **democratic peace** argument is that where groups of democracies inhabit a region, war will become extinct in that region, and as democracy spreads throughout the world, war will decline. Further, democratic governments are likely to create regional or global organizations like NATO and the European Union, and liberal democratic states are more likely to promote and ratify arms control treaties that promote peace rather than war.

But how true is the assumption of the democratic peace argument? We must keep in mind the danger that wars will occur as democracies attempt to overthrow nondemocratic regimes in attempts to spread democracy. When neoconservative advisers in the Bush administration pushed the United States into the Iraq War in 2003, they argued that a democratic Iraq would become the seed from which democracy and therefore peace would grow in the Middle East. In cases like this, war ends up being fought in the name of peace.

security community A regional group of countries that have the same guiding philosophic ideals—usually liberal-democratic principles, norms, and ethics—and tend to have the same style of political systems.

democratic peace A central plank of liberal-internationalist thought, the democratic peace thesis makes two claims: (1) liberal polities exhibit restraint in their relations with other liberal polities (the so-called separate peace), but (2) they are imprudent in relations with authoritarian states. The validity of the democratic peace thesis has been fiercely debated in the international relations literature.

Critical Approaches to Security

We saw in Chapter 4 that many academics have developed theories attempting to explain international politics as something other than a struggle among power-seeking countries. These alternatives to both realism and some strains of liberalism became vibrant intellectual challenges to those mainstream ideas about the causes of war and peace.

The Constructivist Approach and War

Writers who describe themselves as "constructivists" often assert that international relations are affected not only by power politics but also by ideas. This assertion clearly places most

social structure An arrangement based on ideas, norms, values, and shared beliefs. According to constructivists, the social domain does not exist in nature but is constructed through processes of interaction and the sharing of meaning.

material structure An arrangement based on economic, political, and military resources.

constructivist thinkers in the liberal tradition. According to this view, the fundamental structures of international politics are **social** rather than strictly **material**. Constructivists therefore argue that changes in the nature of social interaction between states can bring a fundamental shift toward greater international security (see Chapter 4).

Constructivists think about international politics in a very different way from structural realists. The latter tend to view structure as made up only of a distribution of material capabilities. Constructivists, on the other hand, view structure as the product of social relationships. Social structures are made possible by shared knowledge, material resources, and practices. This means that social structures are defined in part by shared understandings, expectations, or knowledge. According to this perspective, the security dilemma is a social structure in which leaders of states are so distrustful that they make worst-case assumptions about one another's intentions. As a result, they define their interests in "self-help" terms. In contrast, a security community is a social structure composed of shared knowledge in which states trust one another to resolve disputes without war.

The emphasis on the structure of shared knowledge is important in constructivist thinking. Social structures include material things, like tanks and economic resources, but these acquire meaning only through the shared knowledge in which they are embedded. The idea of power politics, or **realpolitik**, has meaning to the extent that states accept the idea as a basic rule of international politics. According to social-constructivist writers, power politics is an idea that does affect the way states behave, but it does not describe all interstate behavior. States are also influenced by other ideas and **norms**, such as the rule of law and the importance of institutional cooperation and restraint. In his study "Anarchy Is What States Make of It" (1992), Wendt argues that security dilemmas and wars can be seen in part as the outcome of self-fulfilling prophecies. The "logic of reciprocity" means that states acquire a shared knowledge about the meaning of power and act accordingly. Equally, he argues, policies of reassurance can also help bring about a structure of shared knowledge that can help move states toward a more peaceful security community.

realpolitik First used to describe the foreign policy of Bismarck in Prussia, it describes the practice of diplomacy based on the assessment of power, territory, and material interests, with little concern for ethical realities.

norms These specify general standards of behavior and identify the rights and obligations of states. Together, norms and principles define the essential character of a regime, and these cannot be changed without transforming the nature of the regime.

Although constructivists argue that security dilemmas are not ruled by fate—or any higher autonomous power—they differ over whether they can be escaped. For some, the fact that structures are socially constructed does not necessarily mean that they can be changed. Many constructivist writers, however, are more optimistic. They point to the changes in ideas represented by perestroika and glasnost, concepts that Soviet Communist Party general secretary Mikhail Gorbachev introduced in the USSR during the second half of the 1980s, which led to a shared knowledge about the end of the Cold War. Once both sides accepted that the Cold War was over, it really was over. According to this view, understanding the crucial role of social structure is important in developing policies and processes of interaction that will lead toward cooperation rather than conflict. If there are opportunities for promoting social change, most constructivists believe it would be irresponsible not to pursue such policies.

Critical Security Studies: Feminism

Although constructivists and realists disagree about the relationship between ideas and material factors, they tend to agree on the central role of the state in debates about international security. Other theorists, however, believe that the state has been given too much prominence. Keith Krause and Michael C. Williams have defined critical security studies in the following terms: "Contemporary debates over the nature of security often float on a sea of unvoiced assumptions and deeper theoretical issues concerning to what and to whom the term *security* refers . . . What most contributions to the debate thus share are two inter-related concerns: what security is and how we study it" (1997, 34). What they also share is a wish to de-emphasize the role of the state and to reconceptualize security. For critical security theorists, states should not be the center of analysis because they are not only extremely diverse in character but also often part of the problem of insecurity in the international system. They can be providers of security, but they can also be a source of threat to their own people. According to this view, therefore, attention should be focused on the individual rather than the state. A number of different approaches make up critical security studies, however. These include feminist approaches, which we will discuss in the rest of this section.

Feminist writers challenge the traditional emphasis on the central role of the state in studies of international security. Although there are significant differences among feminist theorists, all share the view that books and articles on international politics in general, and international security in particular, have been written from a "masculine" point of view. In her work, Ann Tickner (1992, 191) argues that women have "seldom been recognized by the security literature" despite the fact that conflicts affect women as much as, if not more than, men. The vast majority of casualties and refugees in war are women and children, and as the recent war in Bosnia confirms, the rape of women is often used as a tool of war.

Feminist writers argue that if gender is brought more explicitly into the study of security, not only will new issues and critical perspectives be added to the security agenda, but the result will be a fundamentally different view of the nature of international security. According to Jill Steans, "Rethinking security involves thinking about militarism and patriarchy, maldevelopment and environmental degradation. It involves thinking about the relationship between poverty, debt and population growth. It involves thinking about resources and how they are distributed" (1998; see also S. Smith 1999, 72–101). If we look at the language used to describe war, we can see one way security is gendered. As Carol Cohn wrote in her important essay "Sex and Death in the Rational World of Defense Intellectuals" (1987), the defense-policy-making world tends to be dominated by men who employ sexual and other euphemisms to describe their work: "servicing the target" instead of "bombing it"; "collateral damage" instead of "dead civilians"; "patting the missile" instead of "getting a tour of a Trident missile–carrying submarine." Cohn and others write that this is the result of war being "man's work."

Conflicts like those in Bosnia and Sudan pose a critical problem for the international community of whether to intervene in the domestic affairs of sovereign states to safeguard minority rights and individual human rights (see Chapter 10). This dilemma reflects the historic transformation of human society that is taking place at the beginning of the twenty-first century. Although states continue to limp along, many global theorists argue that it is now increasingly necessary to think of the security of individuals and of groups within the emergent global society. Other writers on globalization, however, argue that states are not withering away but are being transformed as they struggle to deal with the range of new challenges—including those of security—that face them.

Marxist and Radical Liberal or Utopian Views on Security

We cannot make the mistake of dismissing Marxist ideas because the Soviet Union collapsed and China abandoned Mao's views of communism for Asian capitalism. Marxists believe that capitalism is the source of most of the world's security problems. Workers are exploited, and they are

"End the war in Afghanistan and stop the use of drones." Members of the Peace and Civil Rights Movement Berlin prepare for President Obama's visit in June 2013 and promote an alternative to current NATO and US security strategies and actions.

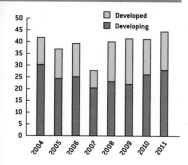

ARMS DELIVERY (IN BILLIONS OF DOLLARS). Which region accounts for the most arms delivery—the North or the South? Based on what you have studied so far in this course, how would you explain the trends you see in this graph?

Source: Conventional Arms Transfers to Developing Nations, 2004–2011 http://www.fas.org/sgp/crs/weapons/R42678.pdf (chart can be found on p. 36).

military-industrial complex The power and influence of the defense industries and their special relationship with the military. Both have tremendous influence over elected officials.

postmodernity An international system where domestic and international affairs are intertwined, national borders are permeable, and states have rejected the use of force for resolving conflict. The European Union is an example of the evolution of the state-centric system (Cooper 2003).

alienated and estranged from their societies. Thus, workers in poor states are prime targets for radical leaders planning to challenge the rich and the powerful by overthrowing governments that repress the voices of those on the margins. In a global economy, Marxists represent workers around the world and support a global revolution. Globalization has spread capitalist ideas as well as the ideas of those who see capitalism as the source of conflict and inequality. Many secular radicals are inspired by Marxist ideas and seek to create systems of governance that provide for basic human needs and address the inequalities within most societies. There are no states that are openly supporting Marxist revolutions across the world. However, there are anarchist and Marxist terrorist networks and cells that present a security challenge to all states. For these groups, the source of insecurity is poverty and the denial of access to societal resources.

For radical liberals or utopians, the major security concern may be the **military-industrial complex**, a term coined by US President Dwight D. Eisenhower as he warned the American public of the power and influence of the defense industries and their special relationship with the military. Part of this concern is over a strategic culture that emphasizes national security over human security. Current military budgets distract from efforts aimed at eliminating global poverty and providing for economic well-being and social justice. More than that, current military spending exacerbates the problems of environmental degradation and allows repressive elites to deny citizens basic human rights. The source of insecurity is found in realist thinking, in a worldview that puts national interests over human interests.

The Changing Character of War

In the contemporary world, powerful pressures are significantly changing national economies and societies. Some of these pressures reflect the impact of globalization, and others reflect the broader effects of **postmodernity** (in which domestic and international affairs are intertwined). The resulting changes have affected perceptions of external threats, and these changed perceptions have in turn influenced beliefs regarding (1) the utility of force as an instrument of policy and (2) the forms and functions of war. In the past two centuries, the modern era of history, some states have used war as a brutal form of politics (typified by the two world wars): a means to resolve certain issues in international relations. They have amassed military power for defense and deterrence and in support of their foreign and defense policies. In the post–Cold War period, however, the kinds of threats that have driven the accumulation of military power in the developed world have not taken the form of traditional state-to-state military rivalry; instead, they have been more amorphous and less predictable threats such as terrorism, insurgencies, and internal crises in other countries.

War has been a brutal experience for humanity. The cost in terms of lives lost defies understanding. About 14,400 wars have occurred throughout recorded history, claiming the lives of some 3.5 billion people. From 1815 to the present, there have been between 224 and 559 wars depending on the definition of war used (Mingst 2004, 198). (The Uppsala University Conflict Data Program and the International Peace Research Institute in Norway define wars as having at least 1,000 battle-related deaths per year, and they define conflicts as having at least 25 battle-related deaths per year.)

Since the end of the Cold War, however, the annual numbers of wars, battle deaths, and war-related massacres have all declined sharply compared with the Cold War period. Between 1989 and 1992, nearly 100 wars came to an end, and in terms of battle deaths, the 1990s were the least violent decade since the end of World War II. In 1992, more than fifty armed conflicts involving states were being waged globally, and by 2003, the number of conflicts had dropped to twenty-nine.

The Democratic Republic of the Congo

Events in the Democratic Republic of the Congo (DRC) since the end of the Cold War provide a good illustration of the complexities of contemporary conflict and the dangers of providing simple explanations of why wars occur. Between 1996 and 2006, in this "forgotten war" (sometimes called "Africa's World War"), nearly 4 million people lost their lives as a result of ethnic strife, civil war, and foreign intervention as well as starvation and disease. The key events are as follows.

In 1996, the conflict and genocide in neighboring Rwanda (in which 800,000 people died) spilled over into the Congo (named Zaire at the time). Rwandan Hutu forces, who fled after a Tutsi-led government came to power, set up bases in the eastern part of the country to launch attacks on Rwanda. This resulted in Rwandan forces invading the Congo with the aim of ousting the existing government of Mobutu Sese Seko and putting its own government under Laurent Désiré Kabila in power. This was achieved in May 1997. Kabila soon fell out with his backers in August 1998, however, and Rwanda and Uganda inspired a rebellion designed to overthrow him. This led to further intervention, this time by Zimbabwe, Angola, Namibia, Chad, and Sudan, in support of the Kabila government. Although a cease-fire was signed in 1999, fighting continued in the eastern part of the country. In January 2001, Kabila was assassinated and replaced by his son, Joseph Kabila. Fighting continued until 2003, partly due to ethnic divisions (the DRC is a country of 250 ethnic groups and 242 different languages) but also because of the continuing occupation of foreign troops (often engaged in the illegal mining of minerals and diamonds). These foreign troops frequently formed alliances with local militias to fight their enemies on DRC soil. Negotiations designed to broker a peace agreement eventually led to the Pretoria Accord in April 2003. As a result, some of the foreign troops left, but hostilities and massacres continued, especially in the east of the country, as rival militias backed by Rwanda and Uganda continued to fight and plunder the resources of the DRC.

On July 18, 2003, a transitional government was set up as a result of what was known as the Global and All-Inclusive Agreement. The agreement required parties to help reunify the country, disarm and integrate the warring factions, and hold elections. Continued instability, however, meant that the elections did not take place until July 2006, and even after these elections, the peace remained very fragile. New fighting between rebel groups and a corrupt and inefficient army began again in 2008. More than ten rebel groups were operating in the eastern region and were allegedly supported by Rwanda and Uganda. The most effective rebel group, the Congolese Revolutionary Army, or M23, advanced on the provincial capital city, Goma, and took control in late 2012. This prompted the UN to establish a peace-keeping mission of 3,000 African troops to support DRC forces. The M23 rebel forces held the capital city until December 2013, when the UN secured a regional peace agreement.

This conflict in the DRC highlights the utility of a broader definition of security and the importance of new ideas relating to human and societal security. It also illustrates the relative shift from interstate wars to intrastate conflicts, involving ethnic militias, in what are sometimes called failed states. Nevertheless, the war also highlights the continuing importance of conflict across state boundaries and traditional, regional balance-of-power rivalries.

For Discussion

1. With China increasing its presence in African countries, and the United States with bases and operations in some forty-nine African countries, could these civil wars escalate into conflicts involving the major powers?
2. Is the United Nations equipped to effectively respond to the human security challenges presented by failed states?
3. How are these civil wars the result of the failure of national governments to do what we expect them to do?

Conflicts within states, not between states, now make up 95 percent of all conflicts in the world. The Human Security Report of 2005 states that during the 1990s the number of wars declined, and these wars were less deadly. Today's wars are more low-intensity, asymmetric wars: major powers with the best equipment and technologically sophisticated weapons are fighting battles with poorly armed gangs and extremist networks in urban settings or in isolated rural regions.

For some observers, the current era has marked a major evolution in the structure of international relations, given the dramatic political changes after the Cold War and the dissolution of the Soviet Union. Changes in the international system on this scale are not common in history and, when they occur, can be expected to have a major impact on the mechanisms by which the international system is governed. At the same time, and partly as a result of the evolution of the international environment, changes are also occurring in the domestic attributes of many of the states that make up the international system. There has, for example, been a notable increase in the number of democratic political systems, but in the same period, many other states have disintegrated into civil wars and insurgency. The identity of the key players in international relations has also changed since the end of the Cold War. Some analysts

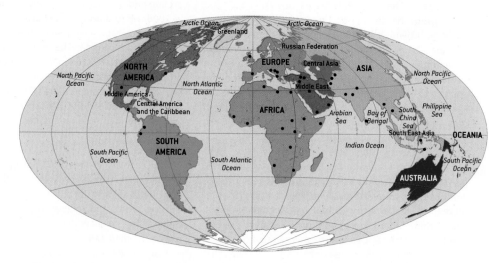

North America
Mexico War on Drugs (2006–present)
United States Cyber Warfare (2009–present)

South America
Guatemala War on Drugs (current)
Columbian insurgency (2002–2010)
El Salvador gang/drug conflicts (2010–present)

Europe
Basque country ERA (1959–2011)
Northern Ireland Real IRA (1997–present)
National Liberation Army–Macedonia (2001)
Russia v. Chechnya (1994–2009)
Kosovo (1998–1999)
Croatian conflict (1991–1995)

Middle East
Israel v. Palestinian conflict (1948–present)
Turkish–Kurdish conflict (1978–present)
Iraq Sunni–Shi'a conflict (ongoing)
Arab Spring (2010–present)
Yemen (2010–present)
Syrian conflict (2011–ongoing)

Oceania
East Timor (2006)
Indonesian conflicts (2002–present)

Africa
Lord's Resistance Army conflict (1989–present)
Sierra Leone (1991–2002)
Mozambique (1977–2002)
Angola (1975–2002)
Darfur and South Sudan (ongoing)
Somalia piracy (2005–present)
Democratic Rep. of Congo (1996–present)
Eritrea–Ethiopia (1998–2000)
Rwanda genocide (1994)
Ivory Coast (2002–present)

Asia
Cambodia Khmer Rouge (1975–1979)
India–Kashmir (1947–present)
US–Taliban (2001–present)
Afghanistan–Taliban (2001–present)
Tibet–China (1962–present)
Sri Lanka civil war (1983–2009)
Nepalese civil war (1996–2006)
Tajikistan civil war (1992–1997)
Myanmar (1948–present)

Figure 8.1 Selected States in Conflict with Nonstate Actors. *(Continued)*
60 countries are involved in wars with 512 nonstate insurgent groups.

Africa

Algeria: Three armed challenges, including the government versus Al Qaeda in the Islamic Maghreb and the Islamic Salvation Front

Angola: Conflict with the Front for the Liberation of the Enclave of Cabinda

Central African Republic: Seven armed challenges to the state, including Seleka, made up of five rebel groups, and recent conflicts between Christians and Muslims

Chad: A conflict between the government and Union of Resistance Forces

Democratic Republic of the Congo: Thirty-six different groups fighting against UN peacekeepers and the DRC government. The March 23 Movement reached a ceasefire agreement in November 2013.

Djibouti: A conflict with the Front for the Restoration of Unity and Democracy

Egypt: Six conflicts with groups such as the jihadist Salafists, Takfir wal-Hijra, and Al Qaeda in the Sinai Peninsula

Eritrea: Four armed conflicts

Ethiopia: Eight armed conflicts, including a challenge by the Ogaden National Liberation Front

Kenya: Two armed conflicts, including Al Qaeda–linked Somalia militia and the Mombasa Republican Council

Libya: Since the 2011 overthrow of Qaddafi, the new government is being challenged by four groups, including the Libyan Liberation Front and the Libyan Islamic Fighting Group

Mali: With assistance from France, fighting eleven conflicts against radical Islamists, including Al Qaeda in West Africa and the Islamic movement Ansar Dine

Mauritania: Two conflicts with Ansar Allah and Al Qaeda in the Islamic Maghreb

Nigeria: Five conflicts with groups including MEND (Movement for the Emancipation of the Niger Delta) and Boko Haram, an Islamic sect

Senegal: A conflict with the Movement of Democratic Forces of Casamance

Somalia: UN forces and the government fighting with at least ten groups, including Al Shabaab, Sufi militia Ahlu Sunna Waljamaca, and the Reewin Resistance Army

Sudan: involved in about twelve conflicts, including fights with the Sudan Liberation Army, Popular Defence Forces, and three groups in Darfur

South Sudan: The newest state in the international community is being challenged by sixteen different groups, including the National Transitional Council, formed by four rebel groups

Uganda: Conflicts with three groups, including the Lord's Resistance Army and Al Shabaab

Western Sahara: A longstanding conflict with the Polisario Front

Asia

Afghanistan: The government and the International Security Assistance Force (ISAF), which includes forty-nine countries, are in conflict with eight different groups, including the Haqqani network and Quetta Shura

Burma-Myanmar: The government is being challenged by twenty-eight different armed groups, including the Karen National Liberation Army and the Kachin Independence Army

China: One conflict with the East Turkestan Islamic Movement

India: The government is being challenged by thirty-three armed groups, including Islamic separatists of Jammu Kashmir Liberation Front and Maoists of Orissa

Indonesia: Four groups are challenging the government, including the Free Papua Movement and Jemaah Islamiah, linked to Al Qaeda

Kazakhstan: The government is fighting with the Kazakh Mujahideen

Kyrgyzstan: An Islamist group, Hizb ut-Tahrir, is in conflict with the government

Pakistan: The government is being challenged by twenty different armed groups, including Lashkar-e-Taiba, Punjab Taliban, and Balochistan Liberation Front

Philippines: The government is battling seven different groups, including Abu Sayyaf and the Moro Islamic Liberation Front

Sri Lanka: There are two internal conflicts with the Upsurging People's Force and the People's Liberation Front

Tajikistan: The government's armed forces are fighting with two groups, the Islamic Movement of Uzbekistan and Hizb ut-Tahrir

Thailand: The government is being challenged by three groups, including the Patani Liberation Army and the Runda Kumpulan Kecil (RKK)

Europe

France: The government is being challenged by the National Liberation Front of Corsica

Northern Ireland: The government must deal with the Ulster Defence Association, the Irish Republican Army, and seven other paramilitary groups

Russia: The government is being targeted by twelve insurgent groups, including Caucasus Mujahideen for Chechen independence and independence groups in Dagestan and Ingushetia

Middle East

Iran: There are five insurgent groups challenging the government, including two Sunni organizations and the Party of Free Life of Kurdistan

Iraq: The government is being challenged by over thirty insurgent groups, with support from the US and several militias

Israel: Stability in this country is challenged by forty-two insurgent organizations, including Hamas, the PLO, and the Palestinian Islamic Jihad

Lebanon: Hezbollah is one of ten groups that are challenging the government

Syria: Fifty-seven armed groups are involved in the civil war

Turkey: Mostly Kurdish rebels are working against the government

Yemen: Fourteen insurgent groups, including Al Qaeda in the Arabian Peninsula and Shia rebels, are attacking the government

North and South America

Columbia: Two insurgent groups, the National Liberation Army and Los Urabenos paramilitary group

Mexico: Most of the seventeen paramilitary groups represent various drug cartels

Figure 8.1 *(Continued)*

Americanization The spread of American values, practices, popular culture, and way of life.

contend the world has become temporarily subject to the hegemonic control of a single state, the United States, so that, for many, the processes of globalization and **Americanization** have become synonymous—and the response has been fierce cultural and political resistance.

Influential nineteenth-century strategist Carl von Clausewitz argued that the fundamental nature of war was immutable. The characteristics or form of war typical in any particular age might change, but the essential nature of war could not. For Clausewitz, the novel characteristics of war were not the result of new inventions but of new ideas and social conditions. In his view, wars were a socially constructed form of large-scale human group behavior and must be understood within the wider contexts of their political and cultural environments. If, indeed, wars are taking distinctive and perhaps novel forms in the post–Cold War world, this is a reflection of broader changes in the international system—including changing perceptions of threat—rather than war being the primary agent of those changes.

In an era of unprecedented communications technologies, new fields of warfare have emerged. Nonstate actors in the post–Cold War period have moved to transform both cyberspace and the global media into crucial battlegrounds, alongside terrestrial military and terrorist operations, so that war is now fought on a number of different planes of reality simultaneously, and reality itself is subverted in the cause of war through sophisticated strategies of informational and electronic deception. The battlefield of the past has now become the "battlespace": three-dimensional in the sense of including airpower and the use of space satellites, nondimensional in that it also embraces cyberspace and communications wavebands.

weapons of mass destruction A category defined by the United Nations in 1948 to include "atomic explosive weapons, radioactive material weapons, lethal chemical and biological weapons, and any weapons developed in the future which have characteristics comparable in destructive effects to those of the atomic bomb or other weapons mentioned above."

At the same time, the tangible capacity for making war has also been developing. Military technology with enormous destructive capacity is becoming available to more and more states. This is important not only because the technology to produce and deliver **weapons of mass destruction** is spreading but also because highly advanced conventional military technology is becoming more widely available. One of the effects of the end of the Cold War was that there was a massive process of disarmament by the former Cold War enemies. This surplus weaponry flooded the global arms market, much of it highly advanced equipment that sold off comparatively cheaply.

The Nature of War

Wars are fought for reasons. The Western understanding of war, following Clausewitz, is that it is instrumental, a means to an end. Wars in this perspective are not random violence; they reflect a conscious decision of engagement for a rational political purpose. Clausewitz defined war as an act of violence intended to compel one's opponent to fulfill one's will. Oftentimes, people who initiate wars rationalize them by appealing to common belief and value systems.

War is a form of social and political behavior. This was one of Clausewitz's central arguments. It remains true at the start of the twenty-first century, but only if we operate with a broad and flexible understanding of what constitutes politics. As our understanding of politics, and of the forms it can take, has evolved in the postmodern era, we should expect the same to be true of the character of war because that is itself a form of politics.

The US Air Force B-2 strategic bomber is designed to make it difficult for radar to see the aircraft.

The political nature of war has been evolving in recent decades under the impact of globalization, which has increasingly eroded the economic, political, and cultural autonomy of the state. Contemporary warfare takes place in a local context, but it is also played out in wider fields and influenced by nongovernmental organizations, intergovernmental organizations, regional and global media, and users of the Internet. In many ways, contemporary wars are fought partly on television, and the media therefore have a powerful role in providing a framework of understanding for the viewers of the conflict. Reaching beyond even the effect of twenty-four-hour-a-day television news channels desperate for items to broadcast, Al Qaeda, for instance, uses the Internet to disseminate its propaganda. The award-winning documentary *Control Room* showed how the 2003 invasion of Iraq became an exercise in the US government trying to restrict the images a globalized audience saw on its televisions. One effect of the constant coverage of international violence by the global media may be to gradually weaken the legal, moral, and political constraints against the use of force by making it appear routine, thereby reversing the moral questioning of war that was a feature of the second half of the twentieth century. The advent of such "war fatigue" might make recourse to war appear a normal feature of international relations.

Nevertheless, war, both in terms of preparation and its actual conduct, may be a powerful catalyst for change, but technological or even political modernization does not necessarily imply moral progress. Evolution in war, including its contemporary forms, may involve change that is morally problematic, as indeed is the case with the forces of globalization more generally. War is a profound agent of historical change, but it is not the fundamental driving force of history. A wide variety of factors can contribute to the outbreak of war, such as nationalism, class conflict, and human nature. These are the main drivers of change rather than war itself. War is not something imposed by an outside force; the willingness to go to war comes from within states and societies.

For many analysts, war's nature as the use of organized violence in pursuit of political goals always remains the same and is unaltered even by radical changes in political forms, in the motives leading to conflict, or by technological advances (Gray 1999b, 169). For Colin Gray, if war's nature were to change, it would become something else, so he, like Clausewitz, insists that all wars have the same political nature, one based fundamentally on the idea that war is a political act—the use of force for conscious political ends.

For Clausewitz and Gray, there is an important distinction between the *nature* and the *character* of war. The former refers to the constant, universal, and inherent qualities that ultimately define war throughout the ages, such as violence, chance, and uncertainty. The latter relates to the impermanent, circumstantial, and adaptive features that war develops and that account for the different periods of warfare throughout history, each displaying attributes determined by sociopolitical and historical preconditions while also influencing those conditions. Clausewitz also distinguished between the *objective* and *subjective* nature of war, the former comprising the elements common to all wars and the latter comprising features that make each war unique.

A number of questions follow from this survey of war in relation to its contemporary and future forms. Does the current era have a dominant form of war, and if so, what is it? In what ways are the processes associated with globalization changing contemporary warfare? In what ways are the characteristics of postmodernity reflected in contemporary modes of warfare?

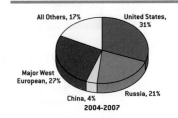

All Others, 17%   United States, 31%
Major West European, 27%
China, 4%   Russia, 21%
2004-2007

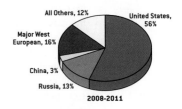

All Others, 12%   United States, 56%
Major West European, 16%
China, 3%
Russia, 13%
2008-2011

ARMS TRANSFER AGREEMENTS WORLDWIDE. The conventional arms suppliers here are shown as percentages. Do you notice a shift between the two date ranges compared here? Is it significant? How would you explain the relative stability of conventional arms suppliers worldwide?

Source: Conventional Arms Transfers to Developing Nations, 2004–2011 http:// www.fas.org/sgp/crs/weapons/ R42678.pdf (chart can be found on p. 29).

Reimaging War

Realism is often called the dominant, traditional, or mainstream theory of international relations. As we have seen in this book, this means the central assumptions of realism—anarchy, a self-help world, an enduring struggle for power—provide the framework for academic discussions of all aspects of the discipline. Foreign policy makers in all countries use the vocabulary of realism. However, unlike in the academic world, where an essay on political theory only receives a grade, in the world of political leaders, a political theory can have an impact on the lives of millions of people. What if politicians used

We now know the evidence to justify the invasion of Iraq in 2003 was false, and Secretary of State Colin Powell unknowingly presented false information to the UN. The French foreign minister Dominque Villepin, shown here with Powell in 2003, led the opposition in the United Nations. How do you think the invasion of Iraq affected the image of the United States?

one of the other theoretical perspectives, like constructivism or feminism?

Let's begin with what the former Bush administration in the United States called the "global war on terror." We see territory-based political units—countries in the customary Westphalian style of sovereign states—trying to defeat attacks from nonstate actors: terrorist organizations claiming their legitimacy from religious texts. This is not only an armed struggle; in terms of political theories, it is a confrontation between two kinds of theories, explanatory and constitutive. Leaders in Western Europe and the United States use the former when they look at the world; the followers of Islamic fundamentalist leaders employ the latter as they seek to create a new world with their ideas. This dichotomy in perspectives has practical policy implications. The United States leaders of the Bush administration, in line with the teaching of realism, believed that if they attacked terrorist strongholds and leaders around the world, they could defeat the terrorists. Islamists who employ terror as a means of conflict are equally convinced that the deaths of individual people will not kill the idea of re-creating the caliphate and, with it, the rule of Islamic law.

The alternative theories we have studied offer another take on events and ideas surrounding this global war on terror. They would begin by

pointing to the overall lack of success in the attempt to eliminate terrorists. Indiscriminate attacks by remotely piloted aircraft have killed people who were Muslims but not necessarily members of terrorist organizations. However, as news reports tell us, attacks on wedding ceremonies mistakenly believed by US mission planners to be Islamist cell meetings have created more anger directed against the United States and its interests around the world. A gendered perspective on the global war on terror would contend that the methods the Bush administration adopted are stereotypically masculinist: instead of seeking to open a dialogue with the Islamists, the United States followed a realist path, focusing on its own view of national security, and launched a military attack. The same set of alternative-theory lenses can help us understand events leading up to the 2003 US-led invasion of Iraq and the occupation of the country. Rejecting the consensus-building approach that his father (the former president) adopted prior to the 1991 Iraq War, George W. Bush made it clear early on that the invasion would happen whether or not UN arms control inspectors (permitted by Saddam Hussein's government) found the banned nuclear, biological, and chemical (NBC) weapons. Adopting the realist perspective, the Bush administration seemed convinced that Al Qaeda planned the September 2001 attacks with active material assistance from the Iraq government. The Americans were apparently convinced that such a coordinated event was beyond the capabilities of a nonstate actor operating out of Afghanistan. The Bush foreign

Continued

THEORY IN PRACTICE   *continued*

policy team labeled critics of their strategy as "not tough enough," "soft on terrorism," or "weak on security," all terms that attract the attention of advocates of the gendered perspective.

Perspective matters in the arena of public policy. Many pessimists tend to gravitate to the realist lens. They see a dangerous world in which war is always about to happen and their allies of today might desert them tomorrow. This is not to say that the alternative theories of

international relations are not pessimistic; for instance, some advocates of the gendered perspective see disheartening patterns of sexualized language to describe wars. And yet, if we do not try to use a range of theories to understand events, we might miss opportunities to learn or to make better policy choices. Certainly, both the global war on terror and the belief that Iraq had nuclear, biological, and chemical weapons demonstrate what can happen if leaders act on faulty assumptions.

For Discussion

1. Can you make a case for a non-force response to terrorists? Can we stop their activities without the use of force?

2. Was the Bush invasion justified? Answer from each theoretical perspective.

3. Since terrorism is a tactic used by many disgruntled individuals and groups, is it really possible for countries like the United States to win a war on terrorism? Why or why not?

The Revolution in Military Affairs

Although many observers have suggested that the character of war is changing significantly, their reasons for coming to this conclusion are often quite different. One school of thought focuses on the so-called **revolution in military affairs (RMA)**. The concept of the revolution in military affairs became popular after the dramatic American victory in the 1991 Gulf War. The manner in which superior technology and doctrine appeared to give the United States an almost effortless victory, if the Iraqi war deaths are ignored, suggested that future conflicts would be decided by the possession of technological advantages such as advanced guided weapons and space satellites. However, the subsequent popularity of the RMA concept has not produced a clear consensus on what exactly the RMA is or what its implications might be. Although analysts agree that RMAs involve a radical change or some form of discontinuity in the history of warfare, there is disagreement regarding how and when these changes or discontinuities take place or what causes them.

Proponents of RMA argue that recent breakthroughs and likely future advances in military technology mean that military operations will be conducted with such speed, precision, and selective destruction that the whole character of war will change, and this will profoundly affect the way military and political affairs are conducted in the next few decades. Most of the RMA literature focuses on the implications of developments in technology. In the conflicts in Kuwait (1991), Serbia (1999), and Iraq (2003), American technology proved vastly superior to that of the opponent. In particular, computing and space technology allowed the US forces to acquire information about the enemy to a degree never before seen in warfare and allowed precision targeting of weapon systems. Advanced communications allowed generals to exercise detailed and instant control over the developing battle and to respond quickly. The speed, power, and accuracy of the weapons made them carefully targeted so as to destroy vital objectives without inflicting unnecessary casualties on civilian populations, although absolute precision and reliability proved impossible to achieve. Opponents lacking counters to these technologies found themselves helpless in the face of overwhelming American superiority. However, the RMA emphasis on military technology and **tactics**, while understandable, risks producing an oversimplified picture of what is an extremely complex phenomenon in which nontechnological factors can play a crucial part in the outcome.

revolution in military affairs (RMA) The effect generated by the marriage of advanced communications and information processing with state-of-the-art weapons and delivery systems. It is a means of overcoming the uncertainty and confusion that are part of any battle in war.

tactics The conduct and management of military capabilities in or near the battle area.

In addition, most of the literature and debate on the RMA has been American and has tended to take for granted the dominance conferred by technological superiority. The current RMA is based on a particularly Western concept of fighting war and may be useful only in certain well-defined situations. For example, there is little discussion of what might happen if the United States were to fight a country that has a similar capability or is able to deploy countermeasures. There has been far less discussion of how a state might use unconventional or asymmetric responses to fight effectively against a more technologically sophisticated opponent. Asymmetry works both ways. **Asymmetric conflicts** since 1990 have been fought by US-led "coalitions of the willing" against Iraq (1991 and again in 2003), Yugoslavia, and Afghanistan. Because of the extreme superiority in combat power of the coalition, the battle phases of these asymmetric conflicts have been fairly brief and have produced relatively few combat deaths compared with the Cold War period. However, in the postconventional insurgency phases in Iraq and Afghanistan, the asymmetry has produced guerrilla-style conflict against the technological superiority of the coalition forces. Most battle deaths since 1945 have been caused by bullets and knives, not high-tech military equipment.

The conflicts in Iraq and Afghanistan (see the Case Study in this chapter) raised major questions about the pattern of warfare likely after the RMA. United States military supremacy across the combat spectrum does not translate well in wars against a network of radical terrorists. In Afghanistan, the United States has tried a counterinsurgency (COIN) strategy with mixed results. The current US leadership has turned now to a more direct counterterrorism (CT) strategy. The Obama administration's drawdown in troop strength and the reluctance of some NATO allies to continue sending troops to combat regions in Afghanistan have forced a shift from a more costly and time-consuming COIN policy to a more appropriate CT policy.

asymmetric conflicts In symmetrical warfare, armies with comparable weapons, tactics, and organizational structures do battle. Wars are fought on near-equal terms. When stakes are high and those actors in conflict are not equal in terms of weapons and technology, the weaker side adopts asymmetrical tactics. These include guerrilla warfare, roadside bombs, attacks on civilians, and other terrorist tactics.

The US uses drone warfare more extensively than any other country. It has drone bases in Afghanistan and in several African countries. This is a photo of the first drone landing on a nuclear aircraft carrier. This makes it possible for the US to use drones anywhere in the world.

A COIN policy involves fighting the enemy and stabilizing the country by helping develop an effective government. A COIN strategy might include

1. providing security for the local population and preventing attacks against civilians;
2. protecting infrastructure and providing safe regions for civilians;
3. helping local government provide basic services for citizens; and
4. helping shift loyalties from insurgents to local authorities.

Counterinsurgency is expensive, and it requires patience and a commitment on the part of occupation forces and the public who pay for this action to stay for a long time.

Counterterrorism, on the other hand, is more about direct military actions. It refers to the identification, tracking, and elimination of terrorist networks. This may be the future of warfare in asymmetrical situations. A CT strategy includes

1. using technology to hunt and track the enemy;
2. sharing intelligence with other states; and
3. targeting insurgent leadership with unmanned drones and covert operations.

Counterterrorism is an aggressive way to fight wars, but it requires fewer troops than COIN, and it does not require a long-term commitment to state building.

Postmodern War

Global society is moving from the modern to the postmodern age. This is a process that has been under way for several decades and is the result of a wide range of economic, cultural, social, and political changes that are altering the meaning of the "state" and the "nation." It has been marked by a shift from production to information as a core output of advanced economies. As this happens, it will affect the character of war. In some parts of the world, the state is deliberately transferring functions, including military functions, to private authorities and businesses, such as Blackwater (now known as Xe Services LLC) and other contractors in Afghanistan, for example. In other areas, these functions are being seized from the state by other political actors. Many of the world's armies are relying more on child soldiers, paramilitary forces, and private armies. At the same time, globalization has weakened the national forms of identity that have dominated international relations in the past two centuries, and it has reinvigorated earlier forms of political identity and organization, such as religious, ethnic, and clan loyalties.

The greatly increased role of the media is one feature of this evolution. Portable satellite dishes enabling live broadcasts make media far more important in terms of shaping or even constructing understandings of particular wars. Media warfare has made war more transparent. Each side now goes to great lengths to manipulate media images of the conflict, and journalists have effectively been transformed from observers into active participants, facing most of the same dangers as soldiers and helping shape the course of the war through their reporting. This reflects a broader change. Just as modernity and its wars were based on the mode of production, so postmodernity and its wars reflect the mode of information.

Another postmodern development has been the increased "outsourcing" of war to modern-day mercenaries and private contractors. Over the past decade, more and more states have contracted out key military services to private corporations. Privatized military

CASE STUDY : Asymmetric Conflict: The United States and Iraq, 2003–2011

BACKGROUND

On March 20, 2003, US-led coalition forces invaded Iraq with the stated objective of locating and disarming suspected Iraqi WMD. The coalition forces conducted a swift campaign, leading to the capture of Baghdad and the collapse and surrender of the Iraqi armed forces. President George W. Bush declared the official end of major combat operations on May 2, 2003. Although casualties during this conventional phase of fighting were historically low for a major modern war, the fighting quickly evolved into an insurgency in which guerrilla and terrorist attacks on the coalition forces and Iraqi civilian population were the norm. By the spring of 2007, the coalition had suffered around 3,500 deaths and 24,000 wounded. Estimates of total Iraqi war-related deaths ranged from 60,000 to a maximum figure of 650,000.

Having the ability to collect information about an enemy's capability does not mean that you have information about the enemy's intent. Was it moral for the United States to base its invasion of Iraq in 2003 on inaccurate or false intelligence reports?

THE CASE

The Iraq War illustrates a number of the themes that have been prominent in discussions of the possible future development of war. The rapid coalition victory saw the Iraqi armed forces shattered by the technological superiority of the advanced weapons and information systems of the US forces, suggesting that a revolution in military affairs was under way.

A central feature of the conflict was the American dominance of information warfare. This was both in the military sense, meaning the ability to use satellite systems for reconnaissance, communications, and weapons targeting, and in the postmodern sense, meaning the manipulation of the civilian communications and global media images of the war. The media manipulation helped produce an international understanding of the fighting that reflected what the US administration wished the world to perceive.

OUTCOME

The conflict did not end with the surrender of the regular Iraqi forces, however, confirming some of the arguments made by proponents of the "postmodern" and "new wars" (see the next section of this chapter). The ability to operate using complex informal military networks allowed the insurgency to conduct effective asymmetric warfare despite the overwhelming superiority of the US military technology. In addition, the insurgents were able to use the global media to manipulate perceptions of the strategy of terrorism and destabilization. The techniques used by the insurgents were brutal, ruthless, and targeted against the civilian population, in a campaign supported by outside forces and finance and sustained by an overtly identity-based campaign, again reflecting features of the postmodern and new-wars conceptions.

For Discussion

1. The United States has withdrawn most of its combat troops from Iraq, and yet sectarian violence continues and the government is very unstable. Was the war worth the loss of life?
2. The U. S. is now reducing its forces in Afghanistan. Does the U.S. experience in Iraq offer any lesson for the U.S. leaders?
3. Having the ability to collect information about an enemy's capability does not mean that you have information about the enemy's intent. Was it moral for the United States to base its invasion of Iraq in 2003 on intelligence reports?

firms (PMFs) like Xe Services LLC sell a wide range of war-related services to states, over-whelmingly in the logistical and security roles rather than direct combat. Hundreds of PMFs have operated in more than fifty countries since the end of the Cold War. The growth of PMFs reflects a broader global trend toward the privatization of public assets. Through the provision of training and equipment, PMFs have influenced the outcomes of several recent wars, including those in Angola, Croatia, Ethiopia, and Sierra Leone. Privatized military firms played a significant role in the 2003 US-led invasion of Iraq. They also have become the targets of criticism and lawsuits for wrongful death, as with the case of the Blackwater guards who in 2007 killed several unarmed Iraqi civilians.

Globalization and New Wars

Mary Kaldor has suggested that a category of **new wars** has emerged since the mid-1980s. Just as earlier wars were linked to the emergence and creation of states, the new wars are related to the disintegration and collapse of states, and much of the pressure on such states has come from the effects of globalization on the international system. As we noted earlier in the chapter, in the past decade, 95 percent of armed conflicts have taken place within states rather than between them. These new wars within rather than between states occur in situations where the economy of the state is performing very poorly or even collapsing. The tax revenues and power of the state decline dramatically and produce an increase in corruption and criminality. As the state loses control, access to weapons and the ability to resort to violence are increasingly privatized, paramilitary groups proliferate, organized crime grows, and political legitimacy collapses. One of the effects of these developments is that the traditional distinction between the soldier and the civilian becomes blurred or disappears altogether.

For Kaldor, a significant feature of these conflicts is the combatants' focus on questions of identity, which she sees as a result of the pressures produced by globalization. In the post-modern world, there has been a breakdown of traditional cleavages based on class and ideology and a greater emphasis on identity and culture. To the extent that war is a continuation of politics, therefore, war has become increasingly driven by questions of culture and identity. A major cause of the wars since 1990 has been the demands of various groups for national self-determination. Questions of identity in a broader sense have also underpinned recent wars. It can be argued that Islamic fundamentalists are fighting not for control of territory or political power in the traditional Westphalian sense but instead to defend or expand a particular cultural autonomy against the globalizing pressures of Westernization and secularism. They are, ironically perhaps, rejecting in a postmodernist way the seventeenth-century European concept of the state and replacing it with a tenth-century Middle Eastern concept of the state.

The relationship between identity and war is also shifting in terms of the gender and age of the combatants. The "feminization" of war has grown as women have come to play more visible and important roles, from auxiliaries in the late modern period to direct front-line roles in the postmodern period, from uniformed military personnel to female suicide bombers in Iraq and Israel. Children have also become more visible as participants rather than noncombatants in war. Helen Brocklehurst has drawn attention to the meaning and implications of the greater

new wars Wars of identity between different ethnic communities or nations, and wars that are caused by the collapse of states or the fragmentation of multiethnic states. Most of these new wars are internal or civil wars.

The civil war in Bosnia (1992–1995) drew the attention of the entire world. Ethnic cleansing, failed safe areas, and crimes against humanity horrified millions watching around the world. Serb snipers did not hesitate to shoot at civilians.

visibility of children as victims of war at many different levels. Child sol-diers can be found on every continent but have been particularly prevalent in recent African conflicts. In the civil war in Sierra Leone (1991–2002), nearly 70 percent of the combatants were younger than eighteen. Chil-dren fight in around three-quarters of today's armed conflicts through-out the world and may make up 10 percent of current armed combatants (Brocklehurst 2007, 373). Nearly one-third of the militaries that use child soldiers include girls in their ranks.

Many of the features of the new wars are not new; they have been common in earlier periods of history—ethnic and religious wars, for ex-ample, or conflicts conducted with great brutality. Looting and plunder have been a feature of most wars in history, and low-intensity conflicts have in fact been the most common form of armed conflict since the late 1950s. However, it can be argued that the initiators of the new wars have been empowered by the new conditions produced by globaliza-tion, which have weakened states and created parallel economies and privatized protection. These new wars are made possible by the inability of many governments to successfully ex-ercise many of the functions associated with the traditional Westphalian state. Such conflicts will typically occur in **failed states**—countries like Somalia, where the government has lost control of significant parts of the national territory and lacks the resources to reimpose con-trol. There are now some twenty clans that are fighting for control of Somalia and preventing people affected by the drought from getting help. Steven Metz (2004) has termed the coun-tries falling into this category the **third-tier states** of the global political system.

For some observers, the economic rationale, rather than politics, is what drives the new wars so that war has become a continuation of economics by other means. It is the pursuit of personal wealth, rather than political power, that is the motivation of the combatants. In some conflicts, therefore, war has become the end rather than the means.

failed states States that fail to provide basic services and provide for their citizens. These states cannot protect their boundaries, provide a system of law and order, and maintain a functioning marketplace and means of exchange.

third-tier states Sometimes called the "less-developed states" or the "premodern states." These countries fail to provide the basics, such as border protection, law and order, and maintenance of a functioning economy.

New Roles for NATO?

We may be on the verge of seeing a new role for NATO as an antiterrorist force and as a protector of civilians in failing or fragile states. Since 2001, NATO has taken two collective actions, one to respond to the terrorist attack on the United States and a second to protect Libyan civilians who were under attack by the Qaddafi regime. Cynics may argue that this is simply a way for the powerful states to maintain their control, but with the agreement on the Responsibility to Protect (R2P) at the 2005 World Summit (which we will discuss further in Chapter 10), it may mean that we will have more classic humanitarian interventions and more collective military actions.

On September 12, 2001, in an act of solidarity, the NATO allies invoked Article 5 of the Washington Treaty, which states that an attack on one constitutes an attack on all. Today, the NATO-led International Security Assistance Force is working to prevent Afghanistan from becoming a haven for terrorists. More than forty-eight countries have troops, police officers, and consultants of all types working to protect civilians and build the capacity of the Afghan government to take responsibility for security and for the other duties of government. Without this support, the Afghan government would not be able to counter the insurgency. Weary of a long war and a corrupt Afghan government, several NATO allies are pulling their troops out of Afghanistan, and even the United States is reducing its commitments after the assassination of bin Laden. NATO's experience here may lead it to intervene in other failed or fragile states.

Acting with the mandate provided by UN Security Council Resolutions 1970 and 1973, NATO began enforcing a no-fly zone over Libya in March 2011. Later in the month, NATO leaders announced that they would implement all aspects of the UN resolution and begin protecting civilians and civilian-populated areas under attack by the forces loyal to the Qaddafi regime. Operation Unified Protector was the first act of humanitarian intervention since the 1999 NATO action to protect Albanian Kosovars from ethnic cleansing. NATO fighter jets flew well over 20,000 sorties over Libya between April and October 2011, effectively supporting the rebels and the transitional government. The strikes ended when the dictator was captured and killed by members of the Libyan National Liberation Army. As of this writing, Libya is still under the transitional government. If the eventual replacement is a more representative government, the people of Libya may have control over their country's resources, and the West may have a new ally in North Africa.

Nuclear Proliferation and Nonproliferation

Although all wars since 1945 have been fought *without* the deployment of nuclear weapons, the issue of nuclear proliferation represents one of the more marked illustrations of the globalization of world politics. Only five states (China, France, Russia [Soviet Union], United Kingdom, and United States) are acknowledged by the Treaty on the Nonproliferation of Nuclear Weapons (NPT) as possessing nuclear weapons, but others have the capability to construct nuclear devices (see Table 8.2). This was emphasized in May 1998 when India and Pakistan, previously regarded as "threshold" or near-nuclear states, demonstrated their respective capabilities by conducting a series of nuclear tests followed by ballistic missile launches. These events highlighted another aspect of nuclear globalization: the potential emergence of a regionally differentiated world. While in some regions nuclear weapons have assumed a lower significance in strategic thinking than they once held, other regions may be moving in the opposite direction. In Latin America, the South Pacific, Southeast Asia, Africa, and Central Asia, the trend has been toward developing the region as a Nuclear Weapon Free Zone (NWFZ). In other regions, such as South Asia, the trend appears to be toward a higher profile for nuclear capabilities. What is unclear is the impact that nuclearization (i.e., nuclear weapons acquisition) in some regions will have on those moving toward denuclearization (i.e., a process of removing nuclear weapons).

Developments stemming from the dissolution of the Soviet Union have also raised novel problems. This is the only case where a previously acknowledged **nuclear weapon state (NWS)** has been subjected to political disintegration. At the time, there was little understanding of what the nuclear consequences would be from such a tumultuous state implosion, and only in hindsight can we judge its full significance. It was unquestionably a period of unprecedented nuclear transformation requiring long-term cooperation between previously hostile states. Less obvious is that this period of transition was facilitated by the foresight of policy makers from both sides of the former Cold War divide who had created a framework of arms control and disarmament agreements. Ensuring nuclear stability during this period might have been more difficult had it not been for policies such as the Cooperative Threat Reduction Program and agreements like the multilateral NPT and bilateral Strategic Arms Reduction Treaties (START) signed initially between the United States and the Soviet Union (and later between the United States and Russia).

nuclear weapon state (NWS) A state that is party to the nonproliferation treaty and has tested a nuclear weapon or other nuclear explosive device before January 1, 1967.

The Global Zero Movement

Not all efforts to reduce the number of nuclear weapons are sponsored by nation-states. The Global Zero Movement was founded in 2006 by Bruce Blair, a former Defense Department official and the founder of the World Security Institute. Blair's plan to eliminate

Leaders from two intransigent states meet. Iran's new president Hassan Rouhani meets with a top North Korean official, Kim Yong-nam, at the time of Rouhani's swearing-in ceremony in Teheran. Both states have defied the international nuclear nonproliferation regime. Talks in 2013 with Iran may contain its efforts to create nuclear weapons, but North Korea has them and a very unpredictable leader.

nuclear weapons was helped by a January 2007 opinion piece in the *Wall Street Journal*. That article, written by Henry Kissinger, Bill Perry, George Shultz, and Sam Nunn, all veterans of the US Cold War security establishment, asserted that nuclear weapons no longer made the world safer. In fact, the article stated that nuclear weapons now presented a source of intolerable risk, and only by a "concerted effort to free the world of nuclear weapons" would we reduce this risk of nuclear war.

This was at the same time that Obama and Medvedev began talks to reduce the number of nuclear warheads. In April 2009, Obama announced his position: "I state clearly and with conviction America's commitment to seek the peace and security of a world without nuclear weapons."

The Zero Movement continues to work to reduce the total number of nuclear warheads and reach agreement on a comprehensive verification and enforcement system. This NGO may not reach its goals, but it is making an effort to control the proliferation of nuclear weapons. Unfortunately, the rogue states that are seeking nuclear weapons, like Iran, and the terrorist networks that want weapons of mass destruction may not be listening.

Proliferation Optimism and Pessimism

One thesis that has sparked diverging responses asserts that the gradual spread of nuclear weapons to additional states should be welcomed rather than feared. The thesis is based on the proposition that, just as nuclear **deterrence** maintained stability during the Cold War, so can it induce stabilizing effects on other conflict situations. This argument is challenged by those who hold that more will be worse, not better, and that measures to stem nuclear proliferation represent the best way forward (Sagan and Waltz 1995, 2003). In a series of articles, two leading thinkers on nuclear matters, Kenneth Waltz and Scott Sagan, present the arguments. Waltz writes that a controlled spread of nuclear weapons in countries like Pakistan and India is better than a rapid arms race. He contends that leaders of the new nuclear weapons countries would show the same restraint that the United States and the Soviet Union demonstrated when they developed their nuclear arsenals.

deterrence The threat or use of force to prevent an actor from doing something the actor would otherwise do.

Sagan disagrees strongly with Waltz's argument. His argument is based on the internal political dynamics of the second generation of nuclear weapons states. According to Sagan, developing countries lack the stable political institutions that the United States and the Soviet Union had during the late 1940s and early 1950s. Instead, they have military-run or weak civilian governments, without the positive constraining mechanisms of civilian control, and military biases may serve to encourage nuclear weapons use—especially during a crisis.

The responses to nuclear proliferation encompass unilateral, bilateral, regional, and global measures that collectively have been termed the *nuclear nonproliferation regime*. Advocates of this regime argue that these measures (including treaties like the NPT, export controls, international safeguards, nuclear-supplier agreements, and other standard-setting arrangements) have constrained nuclear acquisition. Conversely, there have been several criticisms of this regime, and even some long-term supporters acknowledge it is in "need of intensive care" (Ogilvie-White and Simpson 2003). Among the criticisms are that it is a product of a bygone first nuclear age (1945–1990) and is not suited to the demands of the potentially more dangerous second nuclear age (1990–present); it is unable to alleviate the

Table 8.2
Chronology of Nuclear Development

1945	United States detonates the world's first nuclear weapon.	**1969**	Tlatelolco Treaty enters into force.
1946–1947	United States and Soviet Union submit plans for the international control of atomic energy to the newly formed United Nations Atomic Energy Commission (UNAEC).	**1970**	NPT enters into force.
1949	Soviet Union tests its first nuclear weapon.	**1971**	IAEA concludes the INFCIRC (Information Circular)/153 Safeguards Agreement; Zangger Committee also adopts a set of nuclear-export guidelines pursuant to the NPT.
1952	United Kingdom tests its first nuclear weapon.	**1972**	Anti-Ballistic Missile (ABM) Treaty is signed between United States and Soviet Union.
1953	President Eisenhower of the United States introduces his "Atoms for Peace" proposal to the UN General Assembly.	**1974**	India detonates a nuclear explosive device declared to be for peaceful purposes; Nuclear Suppliers Group (NSG) is formed.
1957	International Atomic Energy Agency (IAEA) inaugurated.	**1975**	First Review Conference of the NPT is held in Geneva; by the end of the year, 97 states are party to the treaty.
1958	European Atomic Energy Community (Euratom) begins its operation within the European Community.	**1978**	First UN Special Session on Disarmament (UNSSOD-1) provides the forum for the five nuclear weapon states to issue unilateral statements on negative security assurances.
1960	France becomes the fourth state to test a nuclear weapon.	**1980**	Second NPT Review Conference is held in Geneva.
1961	United Nations General Assembly adopts the "Irish Resolution" calling for measures to limit the spread of nuclear weapons to additional states.	**1983**	United States announces its Strategic Defense Initiative (SDI).
1963	Partial Test Ban Treaty (PTBT) enters into force.	**1985**	Third NPT Review Conference is held in Geneva; Treaty of Rarotonga creates South Pacific Nuclear-Free Zone.
1964	China becomes the fifth state to test a nuclear weapon.	**1987**	Missile Technology Control Regime (MTCR) is established.
1967	Treaty for the Prohibition of Nuclear Weapons in Latin America (the Tlatelolco Treaty) is opened for signature.	**1990**	Fourth NPT Review Conference is held in Geneva.
1968	Treaty on the Nonproliferation of Nuclear Weapons (the NPT) is opened for signature.	**1991**	A UN Special Committee (UNSCOM) is established to oversee the dismantling of Iraq's undeclared nuclear weapons program; United States announces its Safety, Security, Dismantlement (SSD) Program following the dissolution of the Soviet Union.

Continued

Table 8.2 (*continued*)
Chronology of Nuclear Development

1993	South Africa announces that it had produced six nuclear devices up until 1989 and then dismantled them prior to signing the NPT; Democratic People's Republic of Korea (DPRK) announces its intention to withdraw from the NPT following allegations concerning its nuclear program.	**2004**	A transnational nonstate nuclear supply network is discovered; Libya agrees unconditionally to dismantle its WMD infrastructure in compliance with international agreements; UN Security Council passes Resolution 1540.
1995	Review and Extension Conference of the NPT is held in New York; the 179 parties decide to extend the NPT indefinitely and also establish a new treaty review process and a set of principles and objectives for nonproliferation and disarmament.	**2005**	Seventh NPT Review Conference is held in New York.
1996	The Comprehensive Test Ban Treaty (CTBT) is opened for signature.	**2006**	DPRK announces that it has tested a nuclear weapon.
1997	First Preparatory Committee (PrepCom) for the new NPT treaty review process convenes in Geneva.	**2008**	Iran announces progress on its uranium-enrichment program; DPRK has successful test of Taep'o-dong-2C/3 ballistic missile.
1998	India and Pakistan conduct a series of nuclear and missile tests.	**2009**	Iran successfully launches a satellite into Earth orbit using booster based on DPRK Taep'o-dong-2C/3 ballistic missile. North Korea stalls six-party talks.
1999	United States announces its National Missile Defense (NMD) Act.	**2010**	North Korea constructs a light water reactor. Iran begins enriching up to 20% U-235 that can be used for nuclear weapons.
2000	Sixth NPT Review Conference is held in New York for the now 188 parties to the treaty; the five nuclear weapon states reiterate the undertaking "to accomplish the total elimination of their nuclear arsenals."	**2011**	Tohoku earthquake and tsunami causes extensive structural damage at the Fukushima nuclear power plant.
2002	Cuba becomes the 189 party to the NPT; The Hague Code of Conduct for missile-technology transfers is initiated.	**2013**	The International Atomic Energy Agency observes through satellite imagery that North Korea has restarted the Yongbyon reactor that is capable of producing weapons-grade plutonium.
			The five permanent members of the UN Security Council (US, UK, France, China, and Russia, plus Germany and the foreign policy representative from the European Union) meet with Iran to negotiate to halt the production of weapons-grade uranium. An agreement is reached and a plan to ease sanctions put into effect.
2003	The issue of noncompliance and responses to it become the focus of attention as the DPRK announces its "withdrawal" from the NPT and intervention occurs in Iraq.		

security dilemma that many states confront and, hence, does not address the security motivation driving nuclear weapons acquisition; and it is a discriminatory arrangement because the NPT only requires that the five NWSs pursue nuclear disarmament in good faith (under its Article VI), while all other parties—designated as **nonnuclear weapon states (NNWS)**—must forgo the acquisition of nuclear weapons.

Thus, there has always been a tension between two notions of the NPT: as primarily a nonproliferation measure (for preventing the emergence of additional nuclear-armed states) or as a means for achieving nuclear disarmament. This tension was in evidence during discussion at the NPT Conference in 1995, when the treaty was extended indefinitely after an initial twenty-five years in operation (under Article X). It was also featured at the NPT Review Conference in 2000, when the five NWSs reiterated their commitment to the goal of nuclear weapons elimination. India was a leading critic of this position, asserting that states have an inherent right to provide for their defense. During these dialogues, emphasis was placed on the need for all parties to improve transparency in their nuclear operations and for additional measures to enhance verification and compliance.

nonnuclear weapons state (NNWS) A state that is party to the Treaty on the Nonproliferation of Nuclear Weapons, meaning that it does not possess nuclear weapons.

Nuclear Weapons Effects

The effects of nuclear weapons are considerable. Because of this, the UN Commission for Conventional Armaments in 1948 introduced a new category, weapons of mass destruction (WMD), to distinguish nuclear weapons from conventional forms. More recently, another concept, known as CBRN (referring to chemical, biological, radiological, and nuclear capabilities), has appeared in academic and policy papers. Some analysts have also argued that the term *WMD* should be unraveled because each of the weapons types has different effects, with nuclear weapons being the true WMD (Panofsky 1998).

A nuclear weapon produces its energy in three distinct forms: blast, heat or thermal radiation, and nuclear radiation. Experience of nuclear testing has also indicated another feature of a nuclear weapon explosion, the phenomenon known as electromagnetic pulse (EMP). This can cause acute disruption to electronic equipment (Grace 1994, 1).

Extensive damage to human populations may result from a nuclear weapon detonation. Awareness of the effects stems from the two weapons dropped on Hiroshima and Nagasaki at the end of World War II, which remains the only time nuclear weapons have been used. What is also known is that the weapons that destroyed these Japanese cities were relatively small in comparison to the destructive forces generated by later testing of thermonuclear weapons. The largest weapon of this kind known to have been tested was estimated to be a fifty-megaton device (i.e., the equivalent of 50 million tons of TNT) produced by the Soviet Union in 1961. In recent years, there has been a trend away from nuclear weapons with large explosive potential toward designs with lower yields.

Nuclear Defense

The US Congress passed the National Missile Defense (NMD) Act in 1999. This act proposed that the United States develop the technical means to counter a possible small-scale ballistic missile attack on the US mainland. The announcement generated a range of reactions within the United States and elsewhere. The overall program cost and technical feasibility became central elements of the US domestic debate, for, unlike the 1983 Strategic Defense Initiative, which intended to use a range of technologies—including nuclear explosions—to intercept incoming missiles, the new Ballistic Missile Defense (BMD) system was developed primarily using kinetic energy. This means the intention is to hit an incoming missile with another defensive missile during its flight path. Such a system

Engaging with the

WORLD

Global Security Institute

The GSI offers a series of programs on disarmament as well as an internship program. It is dedicated to strengthening international cooperation and security based on the rule of law, with a particular focus on nuclear arms control, nonproliferation, and disarmament. Visit http://www.gsinstitute.org/gsi/you.html.

inevitably requires considerable early-warning and computational capabilities and a missile that is fast and maneuverable enough to hit a target potentially traveling at seven kilometers per second. International reaction to US missile-defense proposals met with concerns in Russia and China about the impact on stability if the Anti-Ballistic Missile (ABM) Treaty was eroded, and in Europe, similar reservations were expressed.

During the recent G. W. Bush administration, the United States eventually moved forward with a testing program for missile interceptors, withdrew from the ABM Treaty, negotiated a new agreement with Russia known as the Strategic Offensive Reductions Treaty (SORT), and began initial BMD deployments. Japan and Israel also decided to deploy missile defenses, while a debate emerged in Europe over the proposed stationing of US BMD in Poland, the Czech Republic, and possibly elsewhere. Russia responded negatively to the latter proposal because of concerns about the effects on stability in the region and its implications for arms control agreements. However, Vice President Biden signaled a change in US policy when he announced in Munich in February 2009 that the new Obama administration was reconsidering the BMD plans of the Bush administration. In an apparent effort to persuade Russia to play a more active role in halting the Iranian program to build nuclear weapons, the Obama administration announced in the late summer of 2009 that it would not build missile-defense installations in Poland and the Czech Republic. In March 2010, President Obama and Russian president Dmitry Medvedev reached agreement on a nuclear arms treaty that will cut nuclear weapons to the lowest levels since 1960s. This treaty replaces the Strategic Arms Reduction Treaty of 1991, and it is a positive step toward Obama's goal of reducing the global stockpile of nuclear weapons.

Theorizing Nuclear Proliferation

One question that has provoked interest is what constitutes nuclear proliferation: Is it a single decision to acquire a nuclear weapon, or is it a process that may stretch over several years, and, consequently, no one identifiable decision can be located? Research on what has been referred to as "the proliferation puzzle" has embraced several conceptual issues (Meyer 1984; Davis and Frankel 1993; Lavoy 1995; Ogilvie-White 1996; Hymans 2006). Much literature endorses the propositions derived from political realism, which asserts that in an anarchic international environment, states will seek nuclear weapons to enhance their security. However, insights from other theoretical positions have become more commonplace (see the chapters in Part Two). This has generated questions concerning what the level of analysis should be in studying nuclear proliferation. Should the focus be on the individual, the organization, the cultural group, the state, the international system, or some combination of these?

epistemic community
A knowledge-based transnational community of experts and policy activists.

The argument has also been advanced that norms, taboos, and **epistemic communities** have played an important role in the nuclear context (Adler 1992; Price and Tannenwald 1996). One viewpoint sees international norms as increasingly significant both as constraints on nuclear behavior and in setting appropriate standards among a range of actors. Similarly, some analysts stress the role played by culture and identity factors in fostering nonproliferation dialogues (Krause and Williams 1997). Scholars have also drawn attention to the important roles played by nongovernmental organizations (NGOs) and epistemic communities, referring to groups of individuals often from different disciplines and countries that operate as conduits for ideas on nonproliferation.

nuclear deterrence Explicit, credible threats to use nuclear weapons in retaliation to deter an adversary from attacking with nuclear weapons.

Another issue with enduring resonance concerns the question of what can explain nuclear "nonuse" since 1945. This debate started early in the nuclear calendar as authors like Bernard Brodie argued that nuclear weapons were useful only in their nonuse (Brodie 1946; C. S. Gray 1996). Over the years, the main explanation of nonuse has centered on the notion of **nuclear deterrence**: states have been deterred from using nuclear weapons because of concerns of retaliation in kind by adversaries. On the US side, this became known as *mutually assured destruction*, or MAD. Defense intellectuals in the United States believed that if both the United States and the Soviet Union were able to absorb a surprise nuclear attack and still retaliate with what the analysts called "unacceptable damage," then neither side would risk a preemptive strike.

WHAT'S YOUR WORLDVIEW

What, in your opinion, is the cause of nuclear proliferation? What theory best describes the causes of nuclear proliferation? What theory poses the best solution(s)?

Nuclear Motivations

Traditional analysis of the motivations for nuclear proliferation has focused at the state and interstate levels. For much of the post–World War II period, the pattern of nuclear weapon acquisition established by the five NWSs was considered the one most likely to be followed by any future proliferating state. Analysis of the motivational aspect consequently addressed the strategic, political, and prestige rationales that led these states to seek nuclear weapons. The strategic motivation focused on the role nuclear weapons played in World War II and its immediate aftermath, when initially they were seen as war-fighting or war-winning weapons. Later, attention shifted to the role nuclear weapons played in deterrence, leading to the assumption that one of the principal motivations for acquisition was the deterrence of other nuclear weapons–capable states. Similarly, the political and prestige benefits that nuclear weapons conferred on states with the wherewithal to manufacture them were also deemed significant. Nuclear weapons were seen as the most modern form of weaponry, and their custodians were automatically afforded a seat at the "best table of international affairs."

It is now more difficult to explain nuclear proliferation by focusing on a single variable. With reference to levels of analysis, specialists have argued that it is necessary to consider a range of factors that may influence nuclear weapons acquisition. These may include militarism and traditional technological factors, the availability of nuclear technology, and a cadre of trained nuclear scientists who encourage acquisition. Domestic politics, imperatives within a political party, or the domestic political situation may propel a state toward nuclear weapons. Diplomatic bargaining (i.e., that acquisition of a nuclear capability can be used to influence or bargain with both perceived allies and enemies) and nonintervention (i.e., that a nuclear capability can deter or prevent intervention by other states) are other factors.

Further complexity is added when attention is focused at the substate or **transnational actor** level because the motivations of nonstate actors may be different from those associated with states. In much traditional thinking, only states were considered to have the wherewithal to acquire nuclear capabilities. Nuclear commerce was conducted on a state-to-state basis, and it was states that entered into international arms control and disarmament treaties. Today, states are no longer the sole focus of attention as nonstate actors are also featured.

Studies conducted during the 1970s and 1980s on **nuclear terrorism** indicated that there were risks associated with particular groups acquiring a nuclear device or threatening to attack nuclear installations. One study by the International Task Force on Prevention of Nuclear Terrorism concluded that it was possible for a terrorist group to build a crude nuclear device provided it had sufficient quantities of chemical high explosives and weapons-usable fissile materials. More significantly, it was felt that such a group would be more interested in generating social disruption by making a credible nuclear threat than in actually detonating a nuclear device and causing mass killing and destruction (Leventhal and Alexander 1987). More recent occurrences have served to alter this latter judgment.

Events in the mid-1990s, such as the first bombing of the World Trade Center in New York in 1993 and the attack against the US government building in Oklahoma in April 1995, revealed the extent of damage and loss of life that could be caused. Although both instances involved traditional methods of inflicting damage, the use of nerve agents (chemical

transnational actor Any nongovernmental actor, such as a multinational corporation or one country's religious humanitarian organization, that has relations with any actor from another country or with an international organization.

nuclear terrorism The use of or threat to use nuclear weapons or nuclear materials to achieve the goals of rogue states or revolutionary or radical organizations.

The IAEA is intended to work with states to control the spread of nuclear technology and to assist states with nuclear emergencies. The nuclear power plants at Fukushima were inspected by the IAEA, but the Japanese are still concerned about safety following the 2011 nuclear accident. Are there safer energy options? Why do we not use them?

noncompliance The failure of states or other actors to abide by treaties or rules supported by international regimes.

weapons) in an underground train network in central Tokyo in March 1995 to cause both death and widespread panic has been viewed as representing a quantum change in methods. These concerns have intensified since the tragic events of September 11, 2001, when the World Trade Center was destroyed by a coordinated attack using civilian aircraft loaded with aviation fuel as the method of destruction. The attack not only produced mass casualties, but it also changed the assumption about terrorist use of CBRN capabilities (Wilkinson 2003).

Nuclear Capabilities and Intentions

The nuclear programs in Iraq, Iran, Pakistan, and North Korea have raised important issues concerning capabilities and intentions. These instances reveal the difficulties in obtaining consensus in international forums on how to respond to **noncompliance** and the problems associated with verifying treaty compliance in situations where special inspection or nuclear development arrangements are agreed. In the case of Iraq, a special inspection arrangement known as United Nations Special Committee (UNSCOM) was established following the 1991 Gulf War to oversee the dismantlement of the WMD program that had come to light as a result of the conflict. By the late 1990s, problems were encountered over access to particular sites, and UNSCOM inspectors were withdrawn. Disagreements also surfaced among the five permanent members of the UN Security Council concerning how to implement the UN resolutions that had been passed in connection with Iraq since 1991. These had not been resolved at the time of the 2003 intervention in Iraq, and subsequent inspections in that country were unable to find evidence of significant undeclared WMD.

The complexity associated with compliance is evident in the case of Iran. The country became the subject of attention from the International Atomic Energy Agency (IAEA) over delays in signing a protocol added to Iran's safeguards agreement requiring greater transparency by nonnuclear weapons states. Although Iran later did sign the protocol, the discovery by the IAEA of undeclared facilities capable of enriching uranium fueled speculation. In an effort to find a solution, a dialogue between Iran and the so-called EU-3 (France, Germany, and the United Kingdom) began in October 2003. While an agreement was reached in Paris in November 2004, the situation was not resolved, and by 2006, the UN Security Council passed resolutions, under Chapter VII of the UN Charter, requiring Iran to comply with its international obligations. The Iranian case is a destabilizing factor in regional—and international—politics. The Ahmadinejad government denounced Israel, with the former Iranian president himself calling for the destruction of the country. Thus, the difficulty of getting Iran to agree to verification mechanisms has complicated an already dangerous Middle East security picture. The current president of Iran, Hassan Rouhani, seems to be taking a more moderate stand on the nuclear weapons issue but as of early 2014, negotiations have not resulted in an end to Iran's nuclear program.

Post–Cold War Antiproliferation Efforts

In 1987, seven missile-technology exporters established identical export guidelines to cover the sale of nuclear-capable ballistic or cruise missiles. Known as the Missile

Technology Control Regime (MTCR), this supply arrangement seeks "to limit the risks of nuclear proliferation by controlling transfers of technology which could make a contribution to nuclear weapons delivery systems other than manned aircraft" (Karp 1995). Membership of the MTCR has expanded to include many of the major missile producers, and the guidelines now embrace missile systems capable of carrying chemical and biological payloads. Over time, concerns have been expressed about the long-term viability of the MTCR. Although observers acknowledge that the arrangement has fulfilled its initial purpose in slowing down missile proliferation, there are calls for new measures. Missile defenses are one means for dealing with the problem, but other suggestions include global or regional ballistic-test notification centers and multilateral arms-limitation measures for missiles with certain ranges. Also, in 2002, a new initiative, known as The Hague Code of Conduct, was launched (M. J. Smith 2002). The code seeks to develop standards of appropriate behavior in the transfer of missiles and missile parts.

At the time of the 1995 NPT Extension Conference, expectations were high that the documents adopted by consensus then would provide the foundation for strengthening the treaty. Events afterward indicated that this assessment was premature, as differences surfaced between the parties over how these documents should be interpreted. Similarly, in 1995, expectations were high that a CTBT would soon be agreed and implemented, but again, this proved premature. Although a CTBT was opened for signature in 1996, it has not entered into force. This will occur only when forty-four states (including the five NWSs and states such as India, Pakistan, and North Korea) have signed and ratified the treaty. This has meant that the success or failure of the CTBT depends on developments in several states. Further, not everyone agrees that this treaty is a worthwhile measure. Proponents claim that the restriction on nuclear testing will limit both **vertical** and **horizontal proliferation**. Critics of a CTBT argue that any such testing prohibition is unverifiable and will therefore be unable to constrain proliferation.

Problems have similarly been encountered over attempts to negotiate a Fissile Material Cutoff Treaty (FMCT). One issue has been whether the FMCT should only prevent future production of fissile materials or include an agreement to remove existing stockpiles. The verification provisions of any such treaty have also been the subject of differing proposals. One feature of this debate that inevitably will demand innovative thinking is how any excess fissile material can be disposed of, as safely and cost effectively as possible, given the large quantities involved.

vertical proliferation An increase in the number of nuclear weapons a state possesses and in other technologies used for delivery of weapons. Recently, concerns were raised about the production of tactical nuclear weapons like bunker busters that could be used to destroy caves and underground facilities in Afghanistan.

horizontal proliferation An increase in the number of actors who possess nuclear weapons.

The document tabled at the 1995 conference by the Arab states party to the NPT, known as the Resolution on the Middle East, calls on all states in the region to accede to the NPT. The debate over this resolution has highlighted how difficult it is to ensure universal adherence to the treaty. For although signatories to the NPT have increased to the point where 188 states are now party, Israel, India, and Pakistan have remained nonsignatories, and North Korea withdrew in 2003. Therefore, the question is how, if at all, the treaty can be made universal.

Thus, as the new millennium dawned, the context of nuclear proliferation was undergoing change. It became urgent to be more responsive to the complexities of globalized proliferation. This urgency generated measures like the Proliferation Security Initiative (PSI), established

We live in a world where controversy rules because we all see the world through different theoretical prisms or lenses. Here an activist for Greenpeace holds a banner outside a conference in Hong Kong in 2010. Nuclear weapons can destroy the world, and yet some leaders push nuclear power as safe. Who is right? Will this controversy ever end?

originally by eleven states in June 2003 and now involving fifteen, with sixty others participating on an ad hoc basis. The PSI is designed as a means to interdict trafficking in WMD, delivery systems, and related materials. There have also been calls to reappraise the prospects for creating new multilateral nuclear fuel centers (an idea that has been around for several decades). Regional safeguards organizations, such as the one established in the European Union (known as Euratom), provide possible models for facilitating greater regional oversight of nuclear energy developments.

Conclusion

Questions of war and peace are central to the existence of every country. In this chapter, we have examined the many ways academics analyze security affairs and how these ideas influence the decisions political leaders make on war and weapons procurement, especially nuclear weapons and nuclear proliferation. We have also explored several new war strategies the United States is using to shape its war-fighting policy, and we posed questions on whether the recent military intervention by NATO in Libya will set a precedent for future interventions. In the next chapter, we will turn to the globalizing of unconventional warfare through the use of terrorism.

CONTRIBUTORS TO CHAPTER 8: John Baylis, Darryl Howlett, and Steven L. Lamy.

REVIEW QUESTIONS

1. Why is security a contested concept?
2. What do neorealist writers mean by *structure*?
3. According to realists, why do states find it difficult to cooperate? How do constructivists explain cooperation?
4. What is distinctive about constructivist views of international security?
5. Is the tension between national and global security resolvable?
6. Has international security changed since 9/11? If so, how?
7. What are the main arguments for and against the proliferation of nuclear weapons?
8. What role do norms, taboos, and scientists play in the context of nuclear proliferation?
9. What nuclear-proliferation concerns have stemmed from the dissolution of the Soviet Union?
10. What chance do we have for controlling the proliferation of nuclear weapons?
11. What are COIN and CT? Where is war strategy going?
12. What is asymmetric warfare?
13. Do you think NATO and the United Nations will become more involved in fragile or failing states?

FURTHER READING

International and global security:

Waltz, K. N. (1954), *Man, the State and War* (New York: Columbia University Press). This is one of the best sources for the study of the causes of war; see also Garnett, J. C. (2006), "The Causes of War and the Conditions of Peace," in J. Baylis, J. Wirtz, E. Cohen, and C. S. Gray (eds.), *Strategy in the Contemporary World*, 2nd ed. (Oxford: Oxford University Press).

Buzan, B. (1983), *People, States and Fear* (London: Harvester). An excellent starting point for the study of national and international security. The book is written largely from a neorealist perspective.

Smith, M. J. (1986), *Realist Thought from Weber to Kissinger* (Baton Rouge: Louisiana State University Press). Covers the development of what has been described as classical realism and discusses some of the major thinkers in the field. For neoclassical approaches, Christensen, T. (1996), *Useful Adversaries: Grand Strategy, Domestic Mobilization and Sino-American Conflict, 1947–1958* (Princeton, N.J.: Princeton University Press); Schweller, R. (1998), *Deadly Imbalances: Tripolarity and Hitler's Strategy of World Conquest* (New York: Columbia University Press); Wohlforth, W. (1993), *The Elusive Balance: Power and Perceptions During the Cold War* (Ithaca, N.Y.: Cornell University Press); and Zakaria, F. (1998), *From Wealth to Power* (Princeton, N.J.: Princeton University Press). For an interesting account of "ethical realism," see Murray, A. J. H. (1997), *Reconstructing Realism: Between Power Politics and Cosmopolitan Ethics* (Edinburgh: Keele University Press), and

Lieven, A., and Hulsman, J. (2006), *Ethical Realism: A View of America's Role in the World* (New York: Pantheon Books).

Wendt, A. (1992), "Anarchy Is What States Make of It: The Social Construction of Power Politics," in *International Organization* 46(2). A very useful analysis of the constructivist perspective. See also Wendt, A. (1999), *Social Theory of International Politics* (Cambridge: Cambridge University Press).

Waever, O., Buzan, B., Kelstrup, M., and Lemaitre, P. (1993), *Identity, Migration and the New Security Agenda in Europe* (London: Pinter). Provides an original perspective for studying the kind of nonstate aspects of security that have affected Europe in the post–Cold War period.

Very useful discussions about the changing nature of security can be found in Bretherton, C., and Ponton, G. (eds.) (1996), *Global Politics: An Introduction* (Oxford, Blackwell); Terriff, T., Croft, S., James, L., and Morgan, P. (1999), *Security Studies Today* (Cambridge: Polity Press); Krause, K., and Williams, M. C. (eds.) (1997), *Critical Security Studies: Concepts and Cases* (London: UCL Press); Lawson, S. (ed.) (1995), *The New Agenda for Global Security: Cooperating for Peace and Beyond* (St. Leonards: Allen and Unwin); Kaplan, R. D. (2000), *The Coming Anarchy: Shattering the Dreams of the Post–Cold War* (New York: Random House); Booth, K., and Dunne, T. (2002), *Worlds in Collision: Terror and the Future of Global Order* (London: Palgrave); and Clark, I. (1999), *Globalization and International Relations Theory* (Oxford: Oxford University Press).

For a discussion of different theoretical approaches to security and some of the contemporary debates about security studies, see Collins, A. (ed.) (2006), *Contemporary Security Studies* (Oxford: Oxford University Press), and Smith, S. (December 1999), "The Increasing Insecurity of Security Studies: Conceptualizing Security in the Last Twenty Years," in *Contemporary Security Policy* 20(3). See also Stubbs, R. (April 2002), "The Many Faces of Asian Security," *Contemporary Southeast Asia* 24(1); and Tickner, J. A. (1992), *Gender in International Relations: Feminist Perspectives on Achieving Global Security* (New York: Columbia University Press).

The best guide to the use of the Internet on the subject of international security is Arkin, W. M. (1998), *The Internet and Strategic Studies* (Baltimore, Md.: Center for Strategic Education, the Paul Nitze School of Advanced International Studies, Johns Hopkins University).

Nuclear proliferation: theoretical aspects:

Buzan, B., and Herring, E. (1998), *The Arms Dynamic in World Politics* (London: Lynne Rienner). This text covers theoretical and empirical aspects associated with the arms dynamic in the context of nuclear weapons.

Campbell, K. M., Einhorn, R. J., and Reiss, M. B. (2004), *The Nuclear Tipping Point: Why States Reconsider Their Nuclear Choices* (Washington, D.C.: Brookings Institute Press). This volume explores the factors that lead states to reconsider their nuclear options.

Hymans, J. E. (2006), *The Psychology of Nuclear Proliferation* (Cambridge: Cambridge University Press). Using four case studies, the author draws on materials from the humanities, social sciences, and natural sciences to analyze nuclear decision making in the states chosen for study.

Sagan, S. D., and Waltz, K. N. (1995), *The Spread of Nuclear Weapons. A Debate* (New York and London: W. W. Norton, and 2nd ed. 2003). This book juxtaposes the contrasting arguments of the two authors concerning the spread of nuclear weapons.

Nuclear use and nonuse:

Herring, E. (ed.) (March 2000), *Preventing the Use of Weapons of Mass Destruction* (special issue), *Journal of Strategic Studies*, 23(1). The contributors to this volume concentrate on the issues associated with preventing the use of WMD.

Lavoy, P. R., Sagan, S., and Wirtz, J. J. (eds.) (2000), *Planning the Unthinkable: How New Powers Will Use Nuclear, Biological and Chemical Weapons* (Ithaca, N.Y.: Cornell University Press). The authors compare how military threats, strategic cultures, and organizations shape the way leaders intend to employ WMD.

Historical context and background:

Walker, W. (2004), *Weapons of Mass Destruction and International Order*, Adelphi Paper 370 (Oxford: Oxford University Press for the International Institute for Strategic Studies). This IISS paper addresses the "problem of order" associated with weapons of mass destruction by drawing on historical evidence and ideas.

Nonproliferation/antiproliferation measures:

Bosch, O., and Van Ham, P. (eds.) (2007), *Global Non-Proliferation and Counter-Terrorism* (Washington, D.C.: Brookings Institute Press). This volume assesses the impact of UN Security Resolution 1540.

Dhanapala, J., with Rydell, R. (2005), *Multilateral Diplomacy and the NPT: An Insider's Account* (Geneva: United Nations Institute for Disarmament Research). This book provides an analysis of the multilateral diplomacy surrounding the 1995 NPT Review and Extension Conference and is written by two authors who were closely involved in the negotiating process (one of whom was the president of that conference).

Simpson, J., and Howlett, D. (eds.) (1995), *The Future of the Non-Proliferation Treaty* (New York: St. Martin's Press). This explores the background issues associated with the NPT in the lead-up to the 1995 Review and Extension Conference.

Alternative nuclear futures:

Baylis, J., and O'Neill, R. (eds.) (2000), *Alternative Nuclear Futures* (Oxford: Oxford University Press). This edited volume provides an overview of the different positions related to the nuclear future.

The changing character of war:

Biddle, S. (2004), *Military Power: Explaining Victory and Defeat in Modern Battle* (Princeton, N.J.: Princeton University Press). An interesting and stimulating study of warfare since 1900, analyzing the techniques and technologies that have aided the offense and defense to achieve victory in modern wars.

Blank, S. J. (1996), "Preparing for the Next War: Reflections on the Revolution in Military Affairs," *Strategic Review* 24: 17–25. An analysis of the post–1990 revolution in military affairs, which argues cogently that to benefit from the technological advantages in the RMA, states must embrace necessary organizational and doctrinal changes.

Brocklehurst, H. (2006), *Who's Afraid of Children? Children, Conflict and International Relations* (Aldershot: Ashgate). A groundbreaking study of the place of children in modern warfare, exploring their roles as warriors, as victims, and as witnesses. The book raises searching questions about the meaning of childhood and child in the light of contemporary conflict.

Clausewitz, C. V. (1989), *On War*, M. Howard and P. Paret (ed. and trans.) (Princeton, N.J.: Princeton University Press). Clausewitz remains essential reading for the serious student of war.

Cohen, E. A. (2004), "Change and Transformation in Military Affairs," *Journal of Strategic Studies* 27(3): 395–407. An engaging article in which the author argues that the changes in the structures of military forces and the nature of battle mean there has been fundamental change in the character of war in the past two decades.

Coker, C. (2001), *Humane Warfare* (London: Routledge). A challenging book that argues the horrors of mid-twentieth-century warfare have led Western democracies to seek to fight "humane wars" characterized by minimal civilian and military casualties on both sides.

Duyvestyn, I., and Angstrom, J. (eds.) (2005), *Rethinking the Nature of War* (London: Frank Cass). A collection of excellent essays debating the changing nature of war in the post–Cold War era.

Gray, C. S. (2002), *Strategy for Chaos: Revolutions in Military Affairs and the Evidence of History* (London: Frank Cass). A very good introduction to the RMA debates with useful historical case studies of earlier RMAs.

Ignatieff, M. (1997), *The Warrior's Honor: Ethnic War and the Modern Conscience* (New York: Henry Holt). An examination of the motivations of "moral interventionists" such as aid workers, journalists, and peacekeepers, and those of the ethnic warriors with whom they engage in postmodern war zones.

Kaldor, M. (1999), *New and Old Wars: Organized Violence in a Global Era* (Cambridge: Polity Press). Kaldor argues that key features of the conflicts waged since 1990 allow them to be termed "new wars." Sadly, the long history of warfare demonstrates that there is little genuinely novel about such conflicts.

Record, J. (2004), *Dark Victory: America's Second War Against Iraq* (Washington, D.C.: US Naval Institute Press). This study presents the 2003 war against Iraq as a long-delayed completion of business begun in 1990–1991. Although he does not deal with the insurgency phase of the war, Record strongly advocates a comprehensive program for postwar reconstruction as a key to long-term success.

Van Creveld, M. (1991), *The Transformation of War* (New York: Free Press). An analysis that is particularly strong in bringing out the socioeconomic demands of modern warfare.

INTERNET RESOURCES

Battle of Salamis, Aeschylus
http://www.poetry-archive.com/a/the_battle_of_salamis.html
Poetry provides a most unacademic insight into war.

First World War.com—Vintage Photographs—Home Front
http://www.firstworldwar.com/photos/homefront.htm
Part of a larger private World War I hobbyist site, the photos are useful for student activities.

Global Security: Reliable Security Information
http://www.globalsecurity.org/
This website has an extensive selection of information about the armed forces of most countries. It also has current news from the world of international security.

Imperial War Museum
http://www.iwm.org.uk/
The definitive war museum has a large and growing online collection.

International Atomic Energy Agency
http://www.iaea.org
The international organization created to control the dissemination of nuclear technology. More recently at the center of debate regarding Iran's nuclear program.

International Institute for Strategic Studies
http://www.iiss.org/
An academic source for information about international policy.

International Physicians for the Prevention of Nuclear War

http://www.ippnw.org/

A leading NGO committed, as its name suggests, to ending the threat of nuclear war.

Carnegie Council: "Washington Rules: America's Path to Permanent War" —Andrew J. Bacevich

http://www.carnegiecouncil.org/resources/video/data/000347

Andrew Bacevich explores the costs of America's global power projection and interventionism and the resulting permanent war economy. He suggests that Washington look domestically for issues before acting globally.

Carnegie Council: "War"—Sebastian Junger

http://www.carnegiecouncil.org/resources/video/data/000402

After recording recent US military action in Afghanistan, Sebastian Junger shares his thoughts on the evolving dynamics and human relations of war.

Carnegie Council: "Terror and Consent: The Wars for the Twenty-First Century" —Philip Bobbitt

http://www.carnegiecouncil.org/resources/video/data/000073

Now, at the start of the twenty-first century, terrorism is inextricably linked with the popular conception of present-day wars. Philip Bobbitt suggests that it's time to rethink our conception of terrorism and instead focus on conflicts over global emerging markets.

Carnegie Council: "After START— What Next? David Speedie Interviews Jayantha Dhanapala"—David Speedie and Jayantha Dhanapala

http://www.carnegiecouncil.org/resources/video/data/000325

In this conversation, the post-START world since 1991 is discussed along with how the world can "get to zero."

TED Talk: Irwin Redlener on Surviving a Nuclear Attack

http://www.ted.com/talks/lang/eng/irwin_redlener_warns _of_nuclear_terrorism.html

Irwin Redlener traces the history of nuclear technology, what it was like living on the brink of nuclear war, and the persistence of nuclear threats today.

For more information, quizzes, case studies and other study tools, please visit us at **www.oup.com/us/lamy**

THINKING ABOUT GLOBAL POLITICS

Perspectives on the Arms Race

OBJECTIVE

The goal of this exercise is difficult to reach: consensus on a national security policy or national strategy for the United States with regard to nuclear weapons. After doing some research online and in your library, you will explore with your classmates the importance of worldviews in determining national interests. Your professor may put you into groups.

PROCEDURE

This is not a debate but a discussion. You should try to consider the assumptions of national security from all three significant groups participating in arms debates within the United States. These are the major groups:

> Arms advocates (realists)
>
> Arms control advocates (liberals)
>
> Disarmament advocates (select a critical perspective; see Chapter 4)

1. Review with your classmates the basic worldview positions and corresponding policy priorities of each group (reread Chapters 3 and 4).

2. Divide your class into three groups representing these views.
3. Explore these general questions in your discussion:
   a. What does the United States want its nuclear weapons to do?
   b. What should our nuclear strategy be?
   c. How can the United States use nuclear weapons to achieve its foreign policy and national security goals?

FOLLOW-UP

Take the evening to review your readings from the semester so far (both in this textbook and whatever supplemental readings your professor has assigned). Make a list of statements made in these materials that support your position, which you will use in your next class. During class, your professor may choose to have you (or a group leader) write these statements on the board and ask others in the class to respond to your selections.

9 | Terrorism

Asymmetry gives terrorists and cybercriminals their strength, since adversaries operate beyond accepted international norms and value systems on a plane where atrocity is a legitimate form of war.

—*Robert D. Kaplan*

With respect to terrorism, the locus of global concern is mainly restricted to Islamic countries with no willingness to address the terrorism of "covert operations" in the North, or to address the social causes of terrorism to the extent that recourse to such forms of political violence rests on injustices.

—*Richard Falk*

Since 2008, piracy and terrorism on the high seas has emerged as a major security issue, particularly in the Indian Ocean and the Gulf of Aden off the coast of Somalia. Between 2008 and 2012, some 799 ships were attacked and 168 hijacked. Although both academic and policy experts generally differentiate between terrorism and piracy because the former is political in nature and the latter is for personal gain, the case of Somalia may be different. Here the pirates are using terrorist tactics to provide for a region long forgotten by the failed state of Somalia, and there are some indications that they are collaborating with Islamic terrorists in the region. The pirates have held more than 3,000 people for ransom to date, and in 2009 alone pirates acquired some $70 million. In 2010 somewhere between $500,000 and $2 million was paid out in ransom. Not all the funds go to the pirates themselves. Part of the funding goes to those assisting on shore, some goes to bribes to prevent arrest, and a good portion goes to sponsors from other criminal networks.

In 2010, 90 percent of these hijackings took place off the coast of Somalia. Most of the pirates are from a semiautonomous region within Somalia called Puntland. Those who have become pirates claim they were forced into this life because of the civil war in Somalia and the persistence of poverty, compounded by the overfishing of Somali waters by countries taking advantage of the absence of law enforcement. These pirates do not see themselves as the bad guys. In their view, the real bandits are those who are exploiting the civil unrest in Somalia.

Global criminal networks—made up of individuals such as this pirate on the coast of Somalia in 2010—are forcing states to dedicate security forces to protect their trading routes. How might the activities of these networks influence what you pay for food and other essential commodities, such as gas?

Any solution to this form of terrorism must address the income that piracy brings. A coalition of regional and international organizations such as the United Nations, the European Union, and the African Union are working to address the problem of piracy. Their responses emphasize deterrence through the presence of patrol boats and the like, providing security on ships and enforcement of the rule of law. Because of these defensive actions, the pirate attacks have become more violent, and there is a legitimate concern that the pirates will begin to cooperate with Islamic terrorist groups in the region, such as Al Shabaab. For most countries this is both an economic and a political security issue. And those with ships in the region are willing to use force to eliminate those who use terrorist tactics to seize ships and hostages. This situation is not likely to end well for the pirates.

The Obama administration has stated that jihadists professing links to Al Qaeda in Mali, Nigeria, Somalia, Egypt, and Yemen will be pursued by the United States and its allies. In a letter to Congress in 2012, President Obama admitted military actions were taken against Al Shabaab in Somalia and Al Qaeda in Yemen. The pursuit of jihadists willing to use terrorist tactics now extends beyond Iraq, Afghanistan, and Pakistan.

Introduction

The relationship between terrorism and globalization is difficult to describe accurately, and the "global war on terrorism" is a misnomer. Terrorism is a tactic used by those who seek radical change through extralegal, violent means, such as rape, murder, and torture, to gain power, authority, and wealth or to impose their beliefs and values on others. Both terrorism and globalization are complicated in their own right and defy simple characterization. It is inaccurate to suggest that globalization is responsible for terrorism, but terrorists have exploited technologies associated with globalization. In particular, the Internet has improved the ability of terrorist groups to work together, share information, and reach out to previously unavailable audiences. Technology, however, cannot change the character of the terrorist message or the nature of the struggle. Terrorism, often called a weapon of the weak, is conducted by a minority of individuals who promote an extremist ideology and seek to destroy anyone who does not share their beliefs, values, or traditions. The global community is not powerless in the face of such violence. To succeed in preventing it, the global community must use the resources at its disposal collaboratively to diminish support for terrorism and demonstrate the illegitimacy of terrorist messages and aspirations. But it must do this while still respecting the values and institutions that terrorists seek to destroy.

After reading and discussing this chapter, you will be able to define terrorism, and you will understand that terrorism has been with us for a long time and is not practiced exclusively by any one ideological, religious, or ethnic community. You will also have a better understanding of how globalization can create conditions that might influence some individuals or groups to use terrorist tactics. You will learn that globalization may hinder or facilitate the use of terrorist tactics by those who seek change within states and in the international system. Finally, you will have a chance to review how states are now responding to terrorism.

Defining Terrorism

Terrorism and globalization share at least one quality—both are complex phenomena open to subjective interpretation. Definitions of terrorism vary widely, but all depart from a common point. **Terrorism** is characterized, first and foremost, by the use of violence.

terrorism The use of violence by nonstate groups or, in some cases, states, to inspire fear by attacking civilians and/or symbolic targets and eliminating opposition groups. This is done for purposes such as drawing widespread attention to a grievance, provoking a severe response, or wearing down an opponent's moral resolve to effect political change.

This tactic of violence takes many forms and often indiscriminately targets noncombatants. It has been around since ancient times, when the Sicarii of Judea carried out murders in resistance to Roman occupation. The purpose for which violence is used and its root causes are where most of the disagreements about terrorism begin. Historically, the term *terrorism* described state violence against citizens—for example, during the French Revolution or the Stalinist era of the Soviet Union. Over the past half-century, however, the definition of terrorism has evolved to mean the use of violence by small nonstate groups to achieve political change, although states do sometimes sponsor or engage in terrorist acts.

WHAT'S YOUR WORLDVIEW

Most people think that all groups that use terrorism are nonstate actors, but states can also use terrorist tactics. Do you think terrorism is a legitimate use of force if used by a state?

Terrorism differs from criminal violence in its degree of political legitimacy. Those sympathetic to terrorist causes suggest that violence, including the death of innocent people, is the only remaining option that can draw attention to the plight of the aggrieved. Such causes have included ideological, ethnic, and religious exclusion or persecution. Terrorists choose targets for the symbolic value of their destruction to motivate followers and to instill fear in the enemy's camp.

Defining terrorism can be difficult, as groups often advocate multiple grievances and compete with one another for resources and support. In addition, the relative importance of these grievances within groups can change over time. Those targeted by terrorists are less inclined to see any justification, much less legitimacy, behind attacks that are designed to spread fear by killing and maiming civilians. As a result, the term *terrorist* has a pejorative value that is useful in delegitimizing those who commit such acts.

Audrey Kurth Cronin, an academic authority on terrorism, has outlined different types of terrorist groups and their historical importance in the following way:

> There are *four types* of terrorist organizations currently operating around the world, categorized mainly by their source of motivation: left-wing terrorists, right-wing terrorists, ethnonationalist/separatist terrorists, and religious or "sacred" terrorists.

A Boston Marathon bombing survivor rolls her wheelchair near a memorial for the victims of the blast. No place in the world is immune from violence and terrorism, and no one seems to have an answer. What would you do to prevent the alienation and estrangement that motivates individuals and groups to use terrorist tactics?

All four types have enjoyed periods of relative prominence in the modern era, with left-wing terrorism intertwined with the Communist movement and currently practiced by Maoists in Peru and Nepal, right-wing terrorism employed by skinheads in several European countries drawing its inspiration from Fascism, and the bulk of ethnonationalist/separatist terrorism accompanying the wave of decolonization especially in the immediate post–World War II years and in places like Northern Ireland and Spain. Currently, "sacred" terrorism is becoming more significant . . . Of course, these categories are not perfect, as many groups have a mix of motivating ideologies—some ethnonationalist groups, for example, have religious characteristics or agendas—but usually one ideology or motivation dominates. (Cronin 2002–2003, 39)

Academics and political leaders have difficulty deciding what actions constitute terrorism, in part because the tactics of wars of **national liberation**, **guerrilla wars**, and asymmetric conflict can resemble those that terrorists use. The legitimacy of terrorist means and methods is the foremost reason for disagreement. Some people view terrorist acts as legitimate only if they meet the criteria associated with the just-war tradition that developed in Europe (see Chapter 8). These criteria, which relate to all applications of force, have been expanded to include a just cause, proportional use of violence, and the use of force as a last resort. For academics who study these issues, another problem is that the terrorists themselves, their justifications, and their methods do not fit conveniently into international relations theories. Realists, for example, suggest that the political violence used by terrorist groups is illegitimate because states alone have a monopoly on the legitimate use of physical force.

Terrorism expert Martha Crenshaw adopts an analytic, though subjective, approach to determining the legitimacy of terrorist acts of violence.

> The value of the normative approach [to terrorism] is that it confronts squarely a critical problem in the analysis of terrorism, and indeed any form of political violence: the issue of legitimacy. Terrorists of the left deny the legitimacy of the state and claim that the use of violence against it is morally justified. Terrorists of the right deny the legitimacy of the opposition and hold that the violence in the service of order is sanctioned by the values of the status quo . . . The need for scholarly objectivity and abstraction does not excuse us from the obligation to judge the morality of the use of force, whether by the state or against. (Crenshaw 1983, 2–4)

Yet even with the use of violence by states, there is disagreement on what constitutes the legitimate application of armed force. For example, during the 1980s, Libya sponsored terrorist acts as an indirect method of attacking the United States, France, and the United Kingdom. Those states in turn condemned Libyan sponsorship as contravening international norms and responded with the customary methods of international politics: sanctions, international court cases, and occasional uses of force. Disagreement associated with the invasion of Iraq in 2003, led by the United States, relates to interpretations of whether the conditions for just war were met before military operations began. Some suggest that the conditions were not met and that actions by the coalition should be considered an act of terrorism conducted by states, but leaders in the United States and the United Kingdom dismiss the charge on the basis of a greater evil that was removed. Violating international norms in the pursuit of terrorists runs the risk of playing into perceptions that the state itself is a terrorist threat. Critics suggest that US policy toward terrorist detainees and extraordinary renditions (sending suspected

national liberation A doctrine promoted by the Soviet Union and other nationalist groups that encouraged anticolonial or anti-Western insurgencies in the developing world.

guerrilla wars Conflicts or insurgencies that involve irregular forces. Fighters in these wars use unconventional methods of warfare, such as sabotage, ambushes, roadside bombs, and sniping.

WHAT'S YOUR WORLDVIEW

Why would an individual resort to terrorism? Why would people decide to join extremist groups and use terrorism to achieve their goals?

terrorists to foreign sites for detention) damage America's credibility as a global champion for individual rights and freedoms.

As with other forms of irregular, or asymmetric, warfare, terrorism is designed to achieve political change for the purpose of obtaining power to right a perceived wrong. However, according to some analysts, terrorism is the weakest form of irregular warfare with which to alter the political landscape. The reason for this weakness is that terrorist groups rarely possess the broader support of the population that characterizes insurgency and revolution, and the methods of terrorists often alienate potential supporters of the cause. Terrorist groups often lack support for their objectives because the changes they seek are based on radical ideas that do not have widespread appeal. To effect change, terrorists must provoke drastic responses that act as a catalyst for change or weaken their opponent's moral resolve.

In a few cases, terrorist acts have achieved (or appeared to achieve) relatively rapid change. The bombings in Madrid in 2004, for example, seemed to influence the outcome of elections in Spain in a dramatic fashion, and news-media editorials suggested that the attack was designed with just such a purpose in mind. An alternative explanation, however, is that many Spanish voters were already unhappy with their conservative government's support for the US invasion of Iraq; the train bombings, according to this interpretation, had no direct effect on voting behavior. Many terrorist leaders hope their actions will lead to disproportionate reactions by a state that in turn alienates public or international opinion and increases support for their cause.

Terrorist campaigns, however, often take years or decades to achieve meaningful results, and the amount and nature of force used can be problematic. Terrorist groups risk fading into obscurity if they do not alarm the public or conduct newsworthy attacks. However, attacks by terrorists that are too horrific, such as the publicized beheadings in Iraq after the US invasions, put support for terrorist causes at risk.

Although states can also engage in terrorist activities, we will focus our discussion of terrorism here on the use of violence by substate groups to inspire fear, by attacking civilians and/or symbolic targets, for purposes such as drawing widespread attention to a grievance, provoking a severe response, or wearing down their opponent's moral resolve to effect political change. Many of these substate groups have used various technologies to extend their reach to distant communities. These groups have become part of **transnational terrorist networks**.

As with definitions of terrorism, there is general agreement on at least one aspect of globalization. Technologies allow the transfer of goods, services, and information almost anywhere quickly and efficiently. In the case of information, the transfer can be secure and is nearly instantaneous. The extent of social, cultural, and political change brought on by globalization, including greater interconnectedness and homogeneity in the international system, remains the subject of much disagreement and debate, as other chapters in this book have outlined. These disagreements in turn influence discussion of the extent to which globalization has contributed to the rise of modern terrorism.

There is little doubt that the technologies associated with globalization have been used to improve the effectiveness and reach of terrorist groups. The relationship between globalization and terrorism is best understood as the next step in the evolution of political violence since terrorism became a transnational phenomenon in the 1960s. To understand the changes perceived in terrorism globally, it is useful to understand the evolution of terrorist events from primarily domestic to global phenomena.

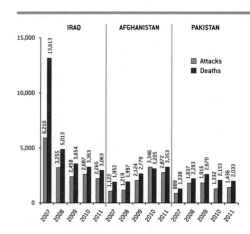

TERRORISTS INCIDENTS AND FATALITIES: IRAQ, AFGHANISTAN AND PAKISTAN.
What conclusions can you draw from studying these data? What does this graph say (if anything) about the "globalization of terrorism"?
Source: 2011 Report on Terrorism https://www.fas.org/irp/threat/nctc2011.pdf.

transnational terrorist networks Terrorists use existing global or transnational economic, transportation, and communication systems to manage and maintain terrorist organizations around the world. These networks facilitate the movement of followers and material to global locations.

Terrorism: From Domestic to Global Phenomena

Historically, nonstate terrorist groups have used readily available means to permit small numbers of individuals to spread fear as widely as possible. In the late nineteenth and early twentieth centuries, anarchists relied on railroads for travel and killed with revolvers and dynamite. Yet terrorists and acts of terrorism rarely had an impact beyond national borders, in part because the activists often sought political change within a specific country. Three factors led to the birth of transnational terrorism in 1968: (1) the expansion of commercial air travel, (2) the availability of televised news coverage, and (3) broad political and ideological interests among extremists that converged on a common cause. As a result, terrorism grew from a local to a transnational threat.

Air travel gave terrorists unprecedented mobility. For example, the Japanese Red Army trained in one country and attacked in another, as with the 1972 Lod Airport massacre in Israel. In the United States, some radicals forced airplanes to go to Cuba. Air travel appealed to terrorists for other reasons. Airport security measures, including passport control, were almost nonexistent when terrorists began hijacking airlines. These **skyjackings** suited terrorist purposes well. Hijacked airlines offered a degree of mobility, and therefore security, for the terrorists involved. States also acquiesced to terrorist demands, frequently for money, which encouraged further incidents. The success of this tactic spurred other terrorist groups, as well as criminals and political refugees, to follow suit. As a result, incidents of hijacking skyrocketed from five in 1966 to ninety-four in 1969.

Shared political ideologies stimulated cooperation and some exchanges between groups as diverse as the Irish Republican Army (IRA) and the Basque separatist organization Euzkadi Ta Askatasuna (ETA). Besides sharing techniques and technical experience, groups demanded the release of imprisoned "fellow revolutionaries" in different countries, giving the impression of a coordinated global terrorist network. The reality was that groups formed short-term relationships of convenience, based around weapons, capabilities, and money, to advance local political objectives. For example, members of the IRA did not launch attacks in Spain to help the ETA, but they did share resources.

Televised news coverage and the Internet also played a role in expanding the audience, who could witness the theater of terrorism in their own homes. People who had never heard of what was called "the plight of the Palestinians" became very aware of the issue after live coverage of incidents such as the hostage-taking conducted by Black September (a Palestinian paramilitary group) during the 1972 Munich Olympics. Although some considered media coverage to be "the oxygen that sustains terrorism," terrorists discovered that reporters and audiences lost interest in repeat performances over time. To sustain viewer interest and compete for coverage, terrorist groups undertook increasingly spectacular attacks, such as the seizure of Organization of Petroleum Exporting Countries (OPEC) delegates by Carlos the Jackal, whose real name was Ilich Ramírez Sánchez, in Austria in December 1975. Experts speculated that terrorist leaders understood the fine line they walked, however, as horrific, mass-casualty attacks might cross a threshold of violence. This possible concern may explain why few terrorist groups attempted to acquire or use weapons of mass destruction, including nuclear, chemical, and biological weapons.

The Iranian "Islamic Revolution" of 1979 was a watershed event in transnational terrorism. Although Israeli interests remained primary targets for attack due to continued sympathy for the Palestinian cause, a number of groups began to target citizens and symbols of the United States. Certainly, the kidnapping of fifty-three US workers in the

skyjacking The takeover of a commercial airplane for the purpose of taking hostages and using these hostages to bargain for a particular political or economic goal.

Terrorist attacks are nothing new in global politics. In 1972, Palestinian terrorist group Black September captured and killed eleven members of the Israeli Olympic team. Two West German policemen move into position to attempt to free the hostages.

Teheran embassy spurred this trend by demonstrating the inability of a global superpower to defend its embassy staff. The decade of terrorism from 1980 to 1990 included incidents such as suicide bombings (the US Marine barracks in Beirut, Lebanon, 1983—an attack that killed more than 200 service personnel) and skyjackings (TWA Flight 847, 1985, hijacked by Lebanese extremists). During this decade, three disturbing trends emerged: (1) fewer, but more deadly and indiscriminate, attacks; (2) increasing sophistication of attacks; and (3) a greater incidence of suicide attacks.

Marxist-Leninist groups discovered that their sources of support in Western Europe disappeared at the end of the Cold War, in part because the ideology had led to failure. In addition, national law enforcement and paramilitary forces were increasingly effective in combating terrorism. Other terrorist groups discovered that transnational attacks were counterproductive in achieving local aims. For example, ETA, the Basque ethnic separatist movement in Spain, and the IRA, the predominantly Catholic separatist group seeking independence from the United Kingdom, sought negotiations but still used terrorist attacks as a bargaining ploy and to remain visible domestically. Although Marxist-Leninist transnational terrorism has decreased in scale and intensity, militant Islamic terrorism, symbolized by the group Al Qaeda and enabled by globalization, has become a global phenomenon.

The Impact of Globalization on Terrorism

Al Qaeda, which translates from Arabic to "The Base" or "The Foundation," received global recognition as a result of its attacks conducted in New York and Washington on September 11, 2001. Over the past decade, experts have continuously debated what Al Qaeda is, what it represents, and the actual threat that it poses. For example, in early 2006, the Office of the Chairman of the Joint Chiefs of Staff in the Pentagon released the *National Military Strategic*

Al Qaeda Most commonly associated with Osama bin Laden, "The Base" (its meaning in Arabic) is a religious-based group whose fighters swear an oath of fealty to the leadership that succeeded bin Laden.

GLOBAL PERSPECTIVE

The Shanghai Cooperation Organization: Fighting Terrorism in the Former Communist Bloc

Although this is often missing from the headlines of North American press reports, terrorism is a threat to countries not directly involved in former president George Bush's global war on terror. Debates in the United States and Western Europe about the proper methods to stop attacks frequently center on matters of ethics and morality. To put it briefly, what *should* Western-style democracies do to confront terrorist groups, especially those with Islamist links that seek to destroy open societies based on tolerance? *Can* democracy and inclusive institutions survive if Western governments must occasionally bend their own laws to safeguard society?

Such questions of appropriate methods to combat terrorism tend not to restrain the governments of China and the former Soviet republics Russia, Kazakhstan, Kyrgyzstan, Tajikistan, and Uzbekistan, which together created the Shanghai Cooperation Organization (SCO) in June 2001. None of these countries are paragons of democratic virtue. Indeed, according to the annual survey of the human rights organization Freedom House, Kyrgyzstan ranks the highest of the six SCO countries, and it is only partly free (http://www.freedomhouse.org/template.cfm?page=363&year=2008).

Government officials in all of the countries regularly suppress and occasionally murder independent journalists who criticize those who hold political power.

Opposition political parties find their offices closed, their assets seized, their telephones tapped, and their members harassed and arrested. Religious minorities are often jailed if they practice their rituals in public. All of this sounds like the description of terror found at the beginning of this chapter: a state repressing its own subjects or citizens.

Yet from the time of its founding, the SCO called itself an antiterror institution, and its greatest threat is Islamist radical groups. Certainly, given the role that Taliban fighters played in defeating the Soviet invasion of Afghanistan in the 1980s and the Islamic aspect to the Russian war in Chechnya, it made sense that Russia would see an Islamic threat. However, media organizations in the United States miss the effect that separatist groups have in Chinese politics—for example, the Muslim Uighurs who live in the Sinkiang region in the west of the country. In Kyrgyzstan, Tajikistan, and Uzbekistan, Islam is the primary religious identification for more than 80 percent of people (https://www.cia.gov/library/publications/the-world-factbook/index.html). Each member state of the SCO must, therefore, take a different approach to its own Muslim problem. The leaders of the most Islamic states fear that a Taliban style of Sunni Islam might become popular and challenge the legitimacy of the secular governments. Both Russia and China fear that Islamic radicals might push for independence.

Thus, for SCO member states, the greatest threat is not external attack but internal collapse. As a result, terrorism and separatism are linked in the Shanghai Convention on Combating Terrorism, Separatism, and Extremism signed in June 2001. The SCO held its first joint antiterror war games in August 2003 in Kazakhstan. There was perhaps a message in the choice of host country for the exercise. Kazakhstan's population is about 30 percent Russian and has, after China and Russia, the fewest number of people who self-identify as Muslims: about 47 percent. Therefore, it is a country in which Russians have the most to fear from Islamic radicals, yet at the same time, the exercises might offend the fewest number of Muslims.

The Shanghai Cooperation Organization (SCO), which includes the leaders of Russia, China, and several Central Asian countries, frequently meets to discuss antiterrorist strategies and to explore regional issues with nearby countries. The former president of Iran, Mr. Ahmdinejad was accused by the US as a sponsor of terrorist networks in the Middle East. Why would the other SCO leaders support a country that promotes terrorist activities?

Continued

Despite the antiterrorist stand of the SCO, the Bush administration was wary of the motives of the group. Some US officials feared that China and Russia might apply pressure to the Central Asian states to have them force the United States to leave the bases it had in Kyrgyzstan in support of its war against the Taliban in Afghanistan. Neoconservatives in the United States who advocated the spread of democracy also expressed concerns that China and Russia might form an alliance similar to the Holy Alliance that Russia, Prussia, and Austria-Hungary created after the Napoleonic wars. That early-1800s alliance was strongly antidemocratic, repressing political and civil liberties. Some analysts believe that by seeking to slow an inevitable process of liberalism, the Holy Alliance brought about the destruction that it wanted to avoid.

For Discussion

1. Do you find it strange that authoritarian states want to fight terrorism? Might they respond to terrorism differently?
2. Could this coalition of authoritarian states actually work against the spread of democracy and the ending of global terrorism?
3. All the states in this coalition have significant Muslim populations. Are their concerns about internal order or global terrorism?

Plan for the War on Terrorism, which sought to characterize the fluid nature of the militant Islamic terrorism.

> There is no monolithic enemy network with a single set of goals and objectives. The nature of the threat is more complicated. In the GWOT [global war on terror], the primary enemy is a transnational movement of extremist organizations, networks, and individuals—and their state and non-state supporters—which have in common that they exploit Islam and use terrorism for ideological ends. The Al Qa'ida Associated Movement (AQAM), comprised of Al Qa'ida and affiliated extremists, is the most dangerous present manifestation of such extremism . . . The [Al Qaeda network's] adaptation or evolution resulted in the creation of an extremist "movement," referred to by intelligence analysts as AQAM, extending extremism and terrorist tactics well beyond the original organization. This adaptation has resulted in decentralizing control in the network and franchising its extremist efforts within the movement. (National Military Strategic Plan for the War on Terrorism [Unclassified], 13)

Part of the reason for the disagreement of terms stems from the fact that Al Qaeda, as the standard-bearer for militant Islam, has evolved considerably since the US invasion of Afghanistan. Immediately after 9/11, Al Qaeda was depicted as the center of a global nexus of terrorism connected to almost all terrorist groups. More recently, however, Al Qaeda has appeared less as a group and more as a global movement that markets and exploits its own form of militant Islam in a loose network of franchised cells and groups. Regardless of how one views Al Qaeda, one cannot dispute the influence of its message across national boundaries. Efforts to explain the vitality of global terrorism in general—and Al Qaeda in particular—focus on three areas linked to aspects of globalization:

- culture,
- economics, and
- religion.

Cultural Explanations

Culture helps explain many of the ethnic conflicts—violence between religious and language groups—across the world. The 1990s were a period of unprecedented ethnic violence and terrorism that included the genocide in Rwanda and the ethnic cleansing in the former Yugoslavia. Culture is also one way to examine why militant Islam's call for armed struggle has been successful in some countries.

Many fundamentalist groups believe that violence is the only method to preserve traditions and values against a cultural tsunami of Western products and **materialism**. Once sought after as an entry method to economic prosperity, Western secular, materialist values are increasingly rejected by those seeking to regain or preserve their own unique cultural identity. The phenomenon of rejecting the West is not new; one could argue that it began almost 200 years ago as the strength of the Ottoman Empire waned. Since then, the social changes associated with globalization and the spread of free market capitalism appear to be overwhelming the identity or values of groups who perceive themselves as the losers in the new international system. In an attempt to preserve their threatened identity and values, groups actively distinguish themselves from despised "others." At the local level, this cultural friction may translate into conflicts divided along religious or ethnic lines to safeguard **identity**.

According to one explanation, there is a set number of distinct civilizations globally. They include Confucian, Hindu, Islamic, Japanese, Latin American, Slavic-Orthodox, and Western (Huntington 1993, 25). Geography and cultural stability limit abrasion between some of the civilizations. Where individuals perceive their own civilization as weak, insecure, or stagnant and where interaction is high between weak and strong civilizations, conflict may be inevitable. Samuel Huntington suggests that a major fault line exists between the liberal Western civilization and an Islamic one "humiliated and resentful of the West's military presence in the Persian Gulf, the West's overwhelming military dominance, and . . . [unable] to shape their own destiny" (1993, 32).

Critics of Huntington suggest, among other things, that he ascribes a degree of homogeneity within the Islamic world (and among other areas and groups) that simply does not exist. Theologically and socially, the Islamic civilization contains a number of deep divisions that impede the cooperation required to challenge the West. The extremely bloody sectarian violence between Sunni and Shia in Iraq, which worsened significantly after the US invasion in 2003, is only one example of these very real fissures. Militant Islamic calls to kill noncombatants and fellow Muslims represent another internal fault line. Nonbelievers fall into the categories of infidels (those of different religion) and apostates (those Muslims who do not share their interpretation of the Koran). As a result, Osama bin Laden's unequivocal sanction to Abu Musab al-Zarqawi to kill Muslim Shia in Iraq in 2005 calls into question the morality of the means, and therefore the legitimacy, of bin Laden and militant Islam as the champions of Muslim values among the wider and moderate Islamic community.

Economic Explanations

Not everyone agrees that defense of cultural identity is the primary motivation for globalized terrorist violence. Some see economic aspects as the crucial motivating factor in the use of violence to effect political change. Although globalization provides access to a world market for goods and services, the net result has been perceived as a form of Western economic **imperialism**. The United States and the postindustrial states of Western Europe form the global North, or economic core that dominates international economic

---

materialism In this context, it is the spreading of a global consumer culture and popular-culture artifacts like music, books, and movies. Christopher Lasch called this the "ceaseless translation of luxuries into necessities." These elements are seen as undermining traditional cultural values and norms.

identity The understanding of the self in relationship to an "other." Identities are social and thus always formed in relationship to others. Constructivists generally hold that identities shape interests; we cannot know what we want unless we know who we are. But because identities are social and produced through interactions, identities can change.

imperialism The practice of foreign conquest and rule in the context of global relations of hierarchy and subordination. It can lead to the establishment of an empire.

institutions such as the World Bank, sets exchange rates, and determines fiscal policies. The actions and policies can be unfavorable to the underdeveloped countries, or global South, that comprise the periphery. Political decisions by the leaders of underdeveloped countries to deregulate or privatize industries to be competitive globally may lead to significant social and economic upheaval. The citizenry may shift loyalties to illegal activities such as terrorism if the state breaks its social contract (Junaid 2005, 143–144).

Wealth is also linked to personal security and violence. With little opportunity to obtain wealth locally, individuals will leave to pursue opportunities in other countries. The results are emigration and the rapid growth of burgeoning urban centers that act as regional hubs for the flow of global resources. Movement, however, is no guarantee that individual aspirations will be realized. In cases where they are not, individuals may turn to violence for criminal reasons (i.e., personal gain) or political reasons (i.e., to change the existing political system through insurgency or terrorism). Paradoxically, rising standards of living and greater access to educational opportunities associated with globalization may lead to increased expectations. If those expectations are unmet, individuals can turn to extreme political views and action against a system that denies them the opportunity to realize their ambitions. A prominent study suggests that a sense of alienation and lack of opportunity among some Muslim males is a contributing factor in their decision to turn to violence globally (Sageman 2004, 95–96).

Other views offer a broader explanation. In particular, the writings of revolutionary Frantz Fanon provide insights into the use of political violence to right economic wrongs (Onwudiwe 2001, 52–56). Shortly before his death in 1961, Fanon suggested in *The Wretched of the Earth* (1967/1990) that the end of colonialism would not end conflict between the West and the oppressed. This struggle would be replaced by another until the economic and power imbalances were removed (Fanon 1990, 74). According to the view that terrorist violence is motivated by inequalities of the global economy, the terrorist attacks against the World Trade Center in 1993 and 2001 were not reactions against the policies of the United States per se but rather were a blow against an icon of global capitalism. Statements by fringe groups, including neo-Nazis, anarchists, and the New, New Left, also suggest that globalization might be a stimulus for political violence (Rabasa, Chalk, et al. 2006, 86–93).

The explanation that recent terrorist violence is a reaction to economic globalization may be flawed, however, for a number of reasons. These reasons include the personal wealth and social upbringing of a number of members of global terrorist groups as well as trends in regional patterns of terrorist recruitment. Many former leaders and members of transnational terrorist groups, including the German Red Army Faction and the Italian Red Brigades, came from respectable middle- and upper-class families. The same holds true for a number of modern-day antiglobalization anarchists. Within militant Islamic groups, most of their leaders and senior operatives attended graduate schools around the globe in fields as diverse as engineering and theology and were neither

Former UN secretary general Kofi Annan speaks at an event at the UN European headquarters honoring the late South African president Nelson Mandela. Both men dealt with ethnic conflict and its aftermath. Annan was a UN official involved in the UN interventions in the former Yugoslavia and the failure to intervene in Rwanda. Mandela helped end the heinous system of apartheid that separated the races and brutalized the black population of South Africa.

WHAT'S YOUR WORLDVIEW

Poverty may not be a direct cause of terrorist activities, but do you think it contributes to attitudes that make people susceptible to recruitment by radical groups?

postmodern or new terrorists Groups and individuals subscribing to millennial and apocalyptic ideologies and system-level goals. Most value destruction for its own sake, unlike most terrorists in the past, who had specific goals, usually tied to a territory.

jihad In Arabic, *jihad* means "struggle." It can refer to a purely internal struggle to be a better Muslim or a struggle to make society more closely align with the teachings of the Koran.

poor nor downtrodden (Sageman 2004, 73–74). And like the Bolshevik leaders, bin Laden and others have been able to convince less fortunate people to die for the cause.

The links between terrorism and poverty also vary considerably by region. Many militant Islamic terrorists in Europe have employment rates and salaries that are close to EU averages for their age group (Bakker 2006, 41, 52). One might expect that the poorest region globally would account for a high percentage of terrorists, but this is not the case. Despite conditions that favor the outbreak of terrorist violence in sub-Saharan Africa against economic imperialism and global capitalism, the region has not proved a breeding ground for terrorism.

Religion and New Terrorism

In the decade prior to 9/11, a number of analysts perceived that fundamental changes were taking place in the character of terrorism. The use of violence to change state ideology or the representation of ethnic minority groups had failed in its purpose, and a new trend was emerging. **Postmodern** or **new terrorism** was conducted for different reasons altogether and seemed to be driven by the power of ideas like those that constructivist international relations theory describes (see Chapter 4). Motivated by promises of rewards in the afterlife, some terrorists are driven by religious reasons to kill as many of the nonbelievers and unfaithful as possible (Laqueur 1996, 32–33). Although suicide tactics had been observed in Lebanon as early as 1983, militant Islam had previously been viewed as a state-sponsored, regional phenomenon (Wright 1986, 19–21).

New terrorism, which some authors use to explain the global **jihad** (Arabic for "struggle"), is seen as a reaction to the perceived oppression of Muslims worldwide and the spiritual bankruptcy of the West. As globalization spreads and societies become more interconnected, Muslims have a choice: accept Western beliefs to better integrate or preserve their spiritual purity by rebelling. Believers in the global jihad view the rulers of countries such as Pakistan, Saudi Arabia, or Iraq as apostates who have compromised their values in the pursuit and maintenance of secular, state-based power. The only possible response is to fight against such influences through jihad. Jihad is understood by most Islamic scholars and imams to mean the internal struggle for purity spiritually, although it has also been interpreted historically as a method to establish the basis for just war. Extremists who espouse militant Islam, such as Osama bin Laden and his intellectual associate Ayman al-Zawahiri, did understand jihad in a different way. For the jihadi terrorist, there can be no compromise with either infidels or apostates.

The difference in value structures between secular and religious terrorists makes the responses to the latter difficult. Religious terrorists believe they have the mandate and sanction of the divine to commit otherwise illegal or immoral acts. They may kill themselves and others because they believe they will receive rewards in the afterlife. Differences in value structures make the deterrence of religious terrorism difficult, if not impossible, as secular states cannot credibly threaten materially the ideas that terrorists value spiritually. Secular terrorism has had as its goal the pursuit of power to correct flaws within society but retain the overarching system. Religious terrorism, by contrast, does not seek to modify but rather to replace the normative structure of society (Cronin 2002–2003, 41).

Religious explanations for the phenomenon of global terrorism have some of the same incongruities as cultural and economic explanations. Even if religion is a motivating factor, the ultimate purpose for which violence is used may be something else. A religious terrorist may have personal purposes, for example, such as promises of financial rewards for family members, gaining fame within a community, taking revenge for some grievance, or from a psychological standpoint, achieving a sense of fulfillment. Religiously inspired violence could also have political purposes, such as competing with other terrorist groups for popular support (Bloom 2005, 77–79) or convincing foreign occupiers to withdraw their forces (Pape 2006, 45–46). A common theme among jihadi statements is another political purpose: overthrowing apostate regimes and assuming political power. This is tied to the religious purpose, however, as political power is necessary to impose the militant Islamic form of **sharia law** within a state and restore the just and pure society of the caliphate (rule by those regarded as the successors of Muhammad).

The Intersection of Globalization, Technology, and Terrorism

Few challenge the point that terrorism has become much more pervasive worldwide due to the processes and technologies of globalization. The technological advances associated with globalization have improved the capabilities of terrorist groups to plan and conduct operations with far more devastation and coordination than their predecessors could have imagined. In particular, technologies have improved the capability of groups and cells in the following areas:

The American Imam Anwar al-Awlaki, the leader of Al Qaeda in the Arabian Peninsula and the mentor for many who led attacks against the West, was killed by a US airstrike in September 2011. In this photo from 2001, he is shown working with an interfaith community project at his mosque and school in Falls Church, Virginia. What might have motivated him to join Al Qaeda?

sharia law Traditional Islamic law of the Koran ("al Qur'an") and the "Sunna," which are the interpretations of the life of the Prophet Muhammad.

- proselytizing,
- coordination,
- security,
- mobility, and
- lethality.

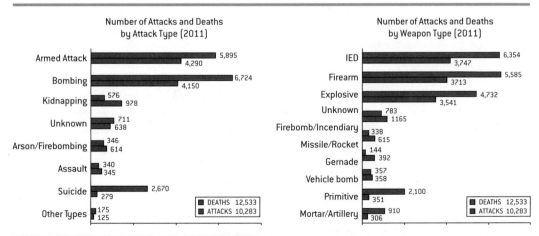

Number of Attacks and Deaths by Attack Type (2011)

- Armed Attack — 5,895 / 4,290
- Bombing — 6,724 / 4,150
- Kidnapping — 576 / 978
- Unknown — 711 / 638
- Arson/Firebombing — 346 / 614
- Assault — 340 / 345
- Suicide — 2,670 / 279
- Other Types — 175 / 125

DEATHS 12,533
ATTACKS 10,283

Number of Attacks and Deaths by Weapon Type (2011)

- IED — 6,354 / 3,747
- Firearm — 5,585 / 3713
- Explosive — 4,732 / 3,541
- Unknown — 783 / 1165
- Firebomb/Incendiary — 338 / 615
- Missile/Rocket — 144 / 392
- Gernade — 357 / 358
- Vehicle bomb — 2,100 / 351
- Primitive — 910 / 306
- Mortar/Artillery

DEATHS 12,533
ATTACKS 10,283

TERRORIST METHODS USED WORLDWIDE, 2011.
These data capture a snapshot of the major methods used by terrorists in fatal incidents. Based on what you have read in this chapter, is there anything in this graph that surprises you? Why or why not?
Source: pg. 13 of 2011 Report on Terrorism https://www.fas.org/irp/threat/nctc2011.pdf.

Proselytizing

Terrorist groups have traditionally sought sympathy and support within national boundaries or in neighboring countries as a means to sustain their efforts. Sustaining terrorist causes can be difficult, as terrorist messages, goals, and grievances tend to be extreme, and therefore less appealing than those of insurgents. For example, land reform, government corruption, or foreign occupation motivates more people to support or join insurgencies, whereas the radical political ideology espoused by groups such as the Japanese Red Army has less appeal in largely prosperous and stable democratic societies. In the past, states have had an advantage over terrorist groups in their ability to control information flows and therefore influence people's thoughts and beliefs. But terrorist leaders understand how the Internet has changed this dynamic: "We [know that we] are in a battle, and that more than half of this battle is taking place in the battlefield of the media. And that we are in a media battle in a race for the hearts and minds of our Umma [Muslim community]" (Office of the Director of National Intelligence 2005, 10).

The continued expansion of the number of Internet service providers, especially in states with relaxed or ambivalent content policies or laws, combined with capable and cheap computers, software, peripherals, and wireless technologies, has empowered individuals and groups to post tracts on or send messages throughout the Internet. One form of empowerment is the virtual presence that individuals have. Although prominent terrorists' physical presence can be removed through imprisonment or death, their virtual presence and influence are immortalized online.

Another form of terrorist empowerment brought on by globalization is the volume, range, and sophistication of propaganda materials. Terrorist groups were once limited to mimeographed manifestos and typed communiqués, but terrorist supporters and sympathizers now build their own websites. An early example was a website sympathetic to the Peruvian Tupac Amaru Revolutionary Movement. This website posted the group's communiqués and videos during the seizure of the Japanese embassy in Lima in 1996. Webmasters sympathetic to terrorist groups also control the content and connotation of the material posted on their websites. The website of the Sri Lankan group Liberation Tigers of Tamil Eelam, for example, posts items that cast the group as an internationally accepted organization committed to conflict resolution. Messages, files, and polemics can be dispatched to almost anywhere on the globe via the Internet or text messaging almost instantaneously.

For the purposes of spreading messages to the widest possible audience for those without Internet or text-messaging capabilities and when speed of communication is not a requirement or a possibility for security reasons, terrorists need not rely exclusively on virtual methods. Any computer of modest capabilities can be used by members of terrorist groups and their sympathizers to create propaganda leaflets and posters at very low cost in large quantities. Whereas offset-printing machines and photocopiers are difficult to move, a laptop computer and printer can be packed in a suitcase, increasing the mobility of the terrorist cell generating the material and making the cell more difficult to locate.

Terrorist groups in Chechnya and the Middle East have also made increasing use of video cameras to record the preparations for attacks and their results, including successful roadside bombings and the downing of helicopters. With the right software and a little knowledge, individuals or small groups can download or obtain digital footage and music and produce videos that appeal to specific groups. Video footage is useful in inspiring potential recruits and seeking donations by support elements within the organization. For example, terrorist recruiters distributed videos of sniper and other attacks against coalition forces in Iraq produced by the Al Qaeda media-production group As-Sahab. The competition among

THEORY IN PRACTICE

The Realist-Theory Perspective and the War on Terror

Debates about political theories have had an important role in government debates about how secular Western democracies can best fight terrorism. The realist tradition asserts that countries are the most important, sometimes the only, actors that matter in international politics. Many political scientists in the realist tradition also maintain that questions of morality should not restrain the actions of a country that is under threat of an attack. These components of realism can explain why the Bush administration was seemingly surprised by the September 11, 2001, attacks and why the government reacted the way it did to those events. For example, on August 6, 2001, National Security Adviser Rice gave President Bush a briefing that included a memo titled "Bin Laden Determined to Strike in US" that documented plans of the Al Qaeda organization.[*] This was the most recent of a series of warnings about possible terrorist attacks on the United States or on American interests around the world. Realist theory helps us understand why the Bush administration did not act aggressively on these reports: the theory asserts that *states* are the primary threat to other *states*. Despite the previous successful Al Qaeda attacks on the US embassies in Kenya and

Tanzania and the near sinking of the destroyer USS *Cole*, members of the Bush administration might have believed that a small nonstate group was not able to launch another attack. In addition, the Bush administration was preoccupied with North Korea's nuclear weapons program and an incident in which a Chinese fighter aircraft had damaged a US Navy maritime surveillance aircraft, forcing it to land in China. Logically for President Bush and his advisers, North Korea and China presented a more pressing threat to the United States.

Realist international relations theory also provides an explanation for the Bush administration's actions after September 11, 2001. If, as the memo said, bin Laden was determined to attack the United States, President Bush was equally determined that it would not happen again. Therefore, the United States soon attacked Afghanistan, seeking to depose the Taliban government that had offered sanctuary to bin Laden and other members of the Al Qaeda leadership. More telling, however, was the Bush administration's decision to label as "unlawful combatants" anyone that US military personnel captured and detain them at the US Navy base at Guantánamo, Cuba, or in secret

prisons around the world. The increasingly unpopular practice of *extraordinary rendition* was another component of the policy. Extraordinary rendition was the capture and transfer of suspected terrorists to unspecified foreign sites for purposes of detention and often torture. Although some nongovernmental human rights organizations called the actions violations of international law, the Bush administration, echoing a key aspect of the realist perspective, called the decisions morally necessary to protect the United States.

For Discussion

1. The terrorist challenge facing nation-states raises the enduring question of international relations: When is it appropriate for national leaders to violate international law and moral codes of conduct to protect their citizens? Is torture acceptable if it protects a nation-state?

2. Now we must deal with questions related to the morality of killing Osama bin Laden. Was it an illegal extrajudicial execution or a just kill?

[*]*The 9/11 Commission Report* (New York: W. W. Norton), p. 261.

global news outlets like CNN, MSNBC, and Al Jazeera ensures that the images of successful or dramatic attacks reach the widest audience possible.

Coordination

During the era of transnational terrorism, groups planned and conducted individual attacks or mounted multiple attacks from a single staging base. The technologies associated with globalization have enabled terrorist cells and groups to mount coordinated attacks in different countries. Indeed, a hallmark of militant Islamic groups is their ability to conduct multiple attacks in different locations. The simultaneous bombings of the US embassies in Kenya and Tanzania in 1998 are one example. Other examples include the synchronized detonation of ten of thirteen bombs on packed commuter trains in Madrid in March 2004 and three of the four underground bombings in July 2005 in London.

The technologies associated with globalization, including commercially available handheld radios and phones, have allowed terrorist cell members and groups to operate independently at substantial distances from one another and network together. The Global System for Mobile Communications (GSM) standard, for example, ensures that any compliant phone will work anywhere in the world where a GSM network has been established. E-mail and cell phone contact among geographically separated group members allows them to conduct their attacks in separate locations or converge on a specific target area. For example, the 9/11 hijackers used cheap and readily available prepaid phone cards to communicate between cell leaders and senior leadership and, according to at least one press account, to coordinate final attack authorization prior to the jets taking off from different locations.

Terrorist groups under pressure from aggressive countermeasures have used the latest technology to maintain their activities tactically and strategically. On a tactical level, bomb manufacturers for the IRA and Al Qaeda have demonstrated the ability to respond rapidly to electronic countermeasures. At the strategic level, Al Qaeda has continued to evolve despite losing its sanctuary and training camps in Afghanistan in December 2001. Instead of a hierarchical organization with fixed training bases, what has developed is a virtual global militant Islamic "community of practice" characterized by individuals exchanging information and discussing the best ways to coordinate and conduct attacks. Some Western analysts have labeled the current decentralized version of global terrorism "Al Qaeda 2.0." Cells form around individuals sympathetic to militant Islamic goals accessible via webcast or online jihadi discussion forums. At present, law enforcement officials believe that there are more than 5,000 active militant Islamic discussion sites along the lines of the now defunct Muntada al-Ansar al-Islami. Such diffuse violence can be thought of as a cruel variation on the environmentalist motto "Think globally, act locally," a motto that reinforces the perception of militant Islam's global depth, power, and reach.

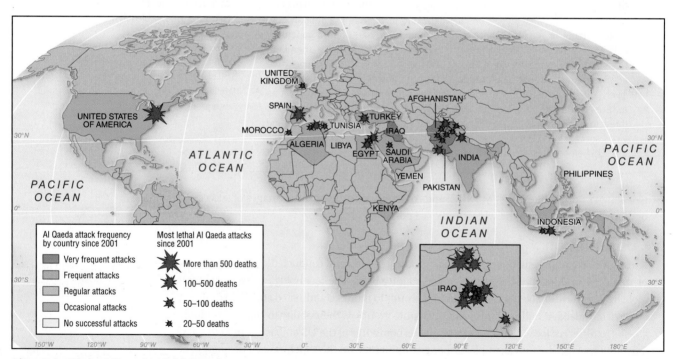

Map 9.1 Global Reach of Al Qaeda.

Can a nation-state respond to networks like this without global cooperation?

Security

Terrorist cells without adequate security precautions are vulnerable to discovery and detection. Translations of captured Al Qaeda manuals, for example, demonstrate the high value their writers place on security, including surveillance and countersurveillance techniques. The technological enablers of globalization assist terrorist cells and leaders in preserving security in a number of ways, including distributing elements in a coordinated network, remaining mobile, and utilizing clandestine or encrypted communications.

The security of terrorist organizations has historically been preserved by limiting communication and information exchanges between cells. This ensures that if one cell is compromised, its members only know each other's identities and not those of other cells. Thus, the damage done to the organization is minimized. Security is even more important to **clandestine** or **sleeper cells**, which remain dormant until activated by a message to carry out a mission. The use of specific codes and ciphers, known to only a few individuals, is one way of preserving the security of an organization. Although codes and ciphers inevitably have been broken and information obtained through interrogation, such activities take time. During that time, terrorist groups adjust their location and operating methods in an attempt to stay ahead of counterterrorist forces. Technological advancements, including faster processing speeds and software developments, now mean that those sympathetic to terrorist causes can contribute virtually through servers located hundreds or thousands of miles away.

Terrorist groups have been able to leverage technological developments designed to shield a user's identity from unauthorized commercial or private exploitation (Gunaratna 2002, 35). Concerns about infringements on civil liberties and privacy during the early years of the Internet led to the development of 64- and 128-bit encryption freeware that is extremely costly and time consuming to crack. In addition, access to hardware such as cell phones, personal data assistants, and computers can be restricted via the use of passwords. The use of Internet Protocol–address generators, anonymity-protection programs, and rerouted communications, as well as private chat rooms where password-protected or encrypted files can be shared, also provide a degree of security. In virtual jihadist discussion groups, youth sympathetic to the militant Islamic cause post information on circumventing electronic surveillance. They advise awareness of phishing and mobile-phone monitoring techniques and suggest using electronic "dead letters"—draft messages saved in shared third-party e-mail accounts, such as Hotmail—so that nothing is sent that could be intercepted.

clandestine or **sleeper cell**
Usually, a group of people sent by an intelligence organization or terrorist network that remains dormant in a target country until activated by a message to carry out a mission, which could include prearranged attacks.

Mobility

The reduced size and increased capabilities of personal electronics also give terrorists mobility advantages. Mobility has always been a crucial consideration for terrorists and insurgents alike, given the superior resources that states have been able to bring to bear against them. In open societies that have well-developed infrastructures, terrorists have been able to move rapidly within and between borders, and this complicates efforts to track them as they exploit the very societal values they seek to destroy.

The globalization of commerce has also improved terrorist mobility. The volume of air travel and goods that pass through ports has increased exponentially through globalization. Between states, measures have been taken to ease the flow of goods, services, and ideas to improve efficiency and reduce costs. One example is the European Schengen Agreement in which border security measures between EU member states have been relaxed to speed deliveries. Market demands for efficiencies of supply,

WHAT'S YOUR WORLDVIEW

Would you be willing to live with fewer personal freedoms if it meant better security? For example, would you accept rules that would allow governments to monitor your communications and your computer activity?

manufacture, delivery, and cost have complicated states' efforts to prevent members of terrorist groups from exploiting gaps in security measures. Additional mobility also allows terrorist groups to transfer expertise, as demonstrated by the arrest of three members of the IRA suspected of training counterparts in the Fuerzas Armadas Revolucionarias de Colombia (FARC) in Bogotá in August 2001.

The use of air travel by terrorists prior to 9/11 has been well documented. Mohamed Atta, for example, traveled extensively between Egypt, Germany, and the Middle East before the attacks. In this respect, the latest generation of terrorists resemble their transnational predecessors in exploiting travel methods for attacks. Terrorist use of transportation is not necessarily overt, as the volume of goods transported in support of a globalized economy is staggering and difficult to monitor effectively. For example, customs officials cannot inspect all of the vehicles or containers passing through border points or ports. To illustrate the scale of the problem, the United States receives 10 million containers per year, and one port, Los Angeles, processes the equivalent of 12,000 twenty-foot containers daily. Western government officials fear that terrorist groups will use containers as a convenient and cheap means to ship weapons of mass destruction. Incidents in Italy in 2001 and Israel in 2004 confirm that terrorist groups are aware of the convenience and cheapness of globalized shipping to improve their mobility.

improvised explosive device (IED) Usually, a homemade device or a crude booby trap, designed to cause death or injury, that can be made of a variety of explosive materials.

The terrorist group Aum Shinrikyo (currently known as Aleph), whose leader Shoko Asahara believed that the end of the world was near, released the nerve gas sarin on the Tokyo subway system in 1995, killing thirteen people and injuring thousands. How can any country anticipate and prevent these forms of terrorism?

Lethality

Globalization has undoubtedly had a troubling influence on terrorism, but the one element that concerns counterterrorism experts and practitioners the most is future catastrophic attacks using weapons of mass destruction. Since the end of the Cold War, some terrorist leaders have expressed both the desire and the will to use weapons of mass destruction. In 1995, Aum Shinrikyo, a Japanese group, released the nerve agent sarin in the Tokyo subway system, killing thirteen people and wounding more than 3,000. Evidence that US troops recovered in Afghanistan in 2001 outlined plans by Al Qaeda to produce and test biological and chemical weapons. In addition, a raid on a suspected Al Qaeda flat in London in 2004 revealed quantities of ricin, a toxin. Militant Islamic statements have mentioned, and one fatwa supports, the use of any means, including weapons of mass destruction, to kill as many infidels and apostates as possible. Globalized media, ironically, may have played a role in shaping terrorist plans. Al Qaeda leaders are alleged to have conjured up mass-casualty attacks as a result of spectacular special effects contained in Hollywood blockbuster movies.

In the absence of weapons of mass destruction, globalization has facilitated access to the weapons, resources, and proficiency required to conduct smaller but more lethal attacks. Terrorist groups from Chechnya to Sri Lanka have shared their expertise in manufacturing lethal bombs triggered by increasingly sophisticated and globally available remote control devices. Within Iraq, since 2003, terrorist groups have been able to obtain the knowledge and resources required to build sophisticated **improvised explosive devices (IEDs)**. Such IEDs range in scale and complexity. The United States, for example, claims that Iran supports terrorist violence in Iraq through the supply of specific IED technology. State sponsorship, however, may no longer be necessary in a globalized world. Digital videos

CASE STUDY : Cyberterrorism

BACKGROUND

In early January 2010, Google announced that a computer attack originating from China had penetrated its corporate infrastructure (in mid-December) and stolen information from its computers, most likely source code. The hackers had also accessed the Gmail accounts of some human rights activists and infiltrated the networks of thirty-three companies. Although it is difficult to pinpoint the origin of cyberattacks, the US National Security Agency traced the attacks first to servers in Taiwan and then to the Shanghai Jiaotong University and the Lanxiang Vocational School in China. The attacks on Google and other commercial and military targets indicate that China, like other countries including the United States, see the Internet and cyberespionage as a key part of the security arena. Rhetoric from Chinese military leaders also indicates that China is focusing its attention more and more on using cyberespionage to gather information to use against its economic, military, or social adversaries. In 2009, Senior Colonel Wang Wei, a professor at the Nanjing Military Academy, and Major Yang Zhen, a lecturer, noted that a sovereign state's political system, economic potential, and strategic objectives will be the primary targets attacked in any war against an information society. The Google hacking incident is only one of many similar cyberattacks originating from China.

THE CASE

Industries and other economic actors have become dependent on reliable, high-speed communications technology that allows for the instantaneous movement of capital, information, and ideas across the globe with the stroke of a key. The smooth functioning of all manner of government and critical infrastructure is now also contingent on the availability and dependability of communications technology. Unfortunately, in connecting people, the Internet also exposes them to vulnerabilities. As technology becomes more sophisticated and networks and information systems become more interdependent, there is increased risk of exploitation and disruption.

Most experts believe that terrorist groups and aggressive states do not currently have the capability to launch major cyberattacks, but they are close. Beyond cyberattacks, military planners are concerned about cyberwar, and one of the most notorious emerging powers in cyberspace is China. It is estimated that more than twenty other states have also developed a significant cyberwarfare capability, but China provides a useful case study because it has been more brazen in

its actions than Russia, France, or the United States, for example. According to the US Department of Defense, cyberwarfare is now an integrated part of China's military strategy, and People's Liberation Army officers are undergoing training in it at Chinese military academies.[*]

OUTCOME

The revolution in military affairs, which was so lauded in the 1990s and the early years of the twenty-first century, may prove to be the greatest vulnerability for the United States and other countries. Although the United States has focused on developing the world's greatest offensive capability in cyberspace, it has not developed an equally robust defensive capability. The development of and dependence on networked military systems—let alone critical national infrastructure—present significant weaknesses in modern military capability and strategic posture. Of particular concern is that potential adversaries' cyberwarriors may have already infiltrated these systems, leaving behind devices such as trapdoors (which allow hackers to return unnoticed and with greater ease at a later date) and logic bombs (which are programs hidden in software code and designed to eventually disrupt or destroy the software).

China is by no means alone in its motivation to build a cybercapability that can be used in conjunction with more conventional means of attack. Similarly, the United States is not the only country concerned about this new threat. All countries must guard against the need to engage in increased spending on the development of new and costly weapons systems.

[*]Tim Thomas, *Dragon Bytes: Chinese Information-War Theory and Practice* (Foreign Military Studies Office, Fort Leavenworth, Kan.: 2004), p. 140. Office of the Secretary of Defense, *Annual Report to Congress: Military Power of the People's Republic of China, 2008* (Washington, D.C.: 2008), p. 4.

For Discussion

1. Is it possible to defend against cyberattacks? Will this require a multinational response? Are states willing to share their defensive technologies with other states?

2. Do societies put themselves at a greater risk if they become more dependent on technology? Are we more vulnerable in a world that is so technologically connected?

3. Do cyber capabilities increase the power of smaller states and even groups within states and thus increase the vulnerabilities of even the great powers?

virtual jihad academy The use of the Internet to plan, promote, and propagate both physical attacks and cyberattacks as well as train and educate future followers or jihadists.

suggest that terrorists are already conducting distance learning through a **virtual jihad academy** in which prospective terrorists study everything from conducting ambush attacks to making and using IEDs to improve their effectiveness and lethality.

Combating Terrorism

States plagued by transnational terrorism responded individually and collectively to combat the phenomenon during the Cold War. These responses ranged in scope and effectiveness and included passing antiterrorism laws, taking preventive security measures at airports, and creating special-operations counterterrorism forces such as the West German Grenzschutzgruppe-9 (GSG-9). Successful rescues in Entebbe (1976), Mogadishu (1977), and Prince's Gate, London (1980), demonstrated that national counterterrorism forces could respond effectively both domestically and abroad. A normative approach to tackling the problem, founded on the principles of international law and collective action, was less successful. Attempts by the United Nations to define and proscribe transnational terrorism bogged down in the General Assembly over semantics (i.e., deciding on the definition of a terrorist), but other cooperative initiatives were successfully implemented. These included the conventions adopted through the International Civil Aviation Organization (ICAO) to improve information sharing and legal cooperation, such as The Hague Convention for the Suppression of Unlawful Seizure of Aircraft (1970). Another collective response to improve information sharing and collaborative action was the creation of the Public Safety and Terrorism Sub-Directorate within Interpol in 1985. However, most initiatives and responses throughout the 1980s were unilateral, regional, or ad hoc in nature.

Another TSA airport check and the most visible illustration of the impact of terrorism on the lives of all citizens who travel. Is it likely that these types of interventions will increase? Are citizens likely to face more oversight?

State leaders disagree on how best to deal with the current form of global terrorist violence. Much of the controversy relates to the nature of the threat and what approach should be taken to deal with it. Some national leaders view militant Islam as an intractable problem in which there can be no negotiation. After the 9/11 attacks, the leaders of the United States, Great Britain, and Australia suggested that all states should cooperate in a war on terror to deal with the threat. The stakes in what some have called "the Long War" consist of the preservation of basic freedoms and a way of life. To defeat terrorism, individual states have a responsibility to protect civilian populations while dealing with terrorist cells, supporters, and sympathizers within their own borders. Given the global, elusive, and adaptive character of the militant Islamic threat, the best approach for dealing with global terrorism is to pool resources in a coalition of the willing in which forces from the global North are seeking to improve the capabilities of specific partner states in the global South. The end result will be the development of a global counterterrorism network (GCTN) of states able to detect, track, and eliminate terrorist threats while nonmilitary efforts address the root causes of terrorism.

Other national leaders are less comfortable with the concept of "war" against the tactics of terrorism. In their view, actions by the military can only lead to terrorist reprisals, or worse—the return of terrorism to its original connotation, the sanctioned use of terror by the state to repress its own citizenry. In their eyes, terrorism is a crime that is best dealt with through law enforcement methods. By dealing with terrorism as a police problem, states uphold the rule of law, maintain the high moral ground, preserve democratic principles, and prevent the establishment of martial law. Military force should only be used in extreme circumstances, and even then, its use may have negative consequences. Terrorism is best dealt with inside state borders and through cooperative international law enforcement efforts to arrest suspects and provide them with due process. The law enforcement approach to terrorism must balance taking enough measures against terrorist groups without crossing over into the realm of "political justice, where the rules and rights enshrined in the principle of due process are either willfully misinterpreted or completely disregarded" (Chalk 1996, 98). To do little against domestic or global terrorism, in the name of upholding the rule of law, risks offering terrorist groups a sanctuary and the security of rights and laws.

The virtual opinion of a number of nongovernmental organizations (NGOs), members of blogs, and webmasters has also been critical of the war on terrorism. Those suspicious of the motives of the most recent Bush administration and the political elite of the United States range widely in their opinions. Conspiracy theorists online suggest that the war in Iraq, Afghanistan, and elsewhere is the first stage in the establishment of an Orwellian system that is constantly in conflict with the terrorist "other" to justify continued violation of personal privacy. More objective communities of practice and NGOs, such as Human Rights Watch, routinely provide monitoring and online reporting of suspected government human rights and civil liberties abuses. One example is the persistent attention paid to the status of terrorist detainees held in US custody at Guantánamo Bay.

Although disagreements still exist over how best to deal with terrorism philosophically, pragmatically the largest problems reside in locating terrorists and isolating them from their means of support. Locating and identifying terrorists are tedious and time-consuming processes that require collecting, assessing, and analyzing information from a range of sources. Information technologies associated with globalization have been useful in this process. Such technologies allow identification of terrorist patterns before and after attacks, with systems capable of performing calculations measured in the trillions per second (floating point operations, or flops). Terrorist finances and organizations are evaluated through link analysis to construct a more comprehensive picture of the way terrorist elements interact. In addition, huge volumes of information can be reduced and exchanged electronically among departments, agencies, and other governments or made available on secure servers whose capacities are measured in terabytes. For example, every day, the National Security Agency collects four times the amount of data in the Library of Congress. Discovering terrorist cells, however, has much to do with luck and pursuing nontechnical leads. State bureaucracies can impede or negate technical and resource advantages over terrorist groups.

Another outcome of the war on terrorism is the expanding role of the National Security Agency as it monitors phone traffic around the world. South Korean protesters denounce the US National Security Agency's alleged spying and demand that the South Korean government protest this activity by its ally. Do you think the US has gone too far? Does this hurt the image of the US among its friends?

To deal with global terrorism, the international community must address its most problematic modern aspects: the appeal of messages that inspire terrorists to commit horrific acts of violence. Killing or capturing individuals does little to halt the spread of extremist viewpoints that occurs under the guise of discussion and education. In the case of Islam, for example, radical mullahs and imams twist the tenets of the religion into a doctrine of action and hatred, where spiritual achievement occurs through destruction rather than personal enlightenment. For instance, suicide attacks offer the promise of private goods (spiritual reward) rather than public good (positive contributions to the community over a lifetime). Precisely how the processes and technologies of globalization can assist in delegitimizing the pedagogy that incites terrorists will remain one of the most vexing challenges for the international community for years to come.

The Death of Osama bin Laden and the End of the War on Terrorism?

The global effort to detect, deter, and protect against terrorist activity will continue. The May 2011 sanctioned killing of Osama bin Laden and more recent killing of two militant US citizens by US airstrikes (Anwar al-Awlaki and Samir Khan) have caused some to wonder if this war on terrorism is near an end. Al Qaeda is definitely weakened, if not disabled, as its leaders are being killed in Pakistan and Yemen.

May 3, 2011. Papers from around the world for sale in Islamabad, Pakistan, announce the killing of Osama bin Laden. How has his death affected the war on terrorism?

In addition, the Iraq War ended in December 2011, and President Obama announced the planned withdrawal of US troops from Afghanistan by 2014. The costs of the Iraq War were steep: an estimated 110,000 Iraqis killed, 4,400 US troops killed, more than 32,000 seriously wounded, and a financial cost in trillions of dollars. Unfortunately, the war in Afghanistan goes on, and this means terrorist activities in that region and around the world are likely to continue.

Robert Pape's (2006) work suggests that suicide terrorism is not a product of religious fundamentalism but a response to foreign occupation. Pape compiled data on seventy-one Al Qaeda suicide terrorists who carried out their attacks from 1995 through 2004. These data suggest that the terrorists felt harmed and humiliated by foreign military occupation or identified with the plight of those whose lands are being occupied by foreign forces. So, as long as the United States and its NATO allies are perceived to be occupying Afghanistan, terrorism within Afghanistan and around the world is likely to continue. Even if Al Qaeda is weak, other groups like the militant Haqqani network, which has been fighting foreign occupations of Afghanistan for more than thirty years, will continue to work with insurgents in Pakistan and Afghanistan to rid the region of Western military personnel.

International terrorism kills a few hundred people a year worldwide. As John Mueller notes in his provocative work *Overblown* (2006), this is about the same number of people who die in their bathtubs in the United States. Mueller suggests that the costs of terrorism arise chiefly from "fear and from overwrought responses" and that the economic costs of reaction are significantly higher than the costs inflicted by terrorists. Thus, terrorists have achieved their primary goal: creating fear in communities across the world and forcing many people to change their way of life. The war on terrorism will never be treated as a criminal problem unless we are resilient and address the conditions that cause people to seek violent solutions to their problems.

Conclusion

Terrorism remains a complex phenomenon in which violence is used to obtain political power to redress grievances that may have become more acute through the process of globalization. Globalization has improved the technical capabilities of terrorists and given them global reach, but it has not altered the fundamental fact that terrorism represents the extreme view of a minority of the global population. In other words, globalization has changed the scope of terrorism but not its nature. The benefits that globalization provides terrorists are neither one-sided nor absolute: the same technologies and processes also enable more effective means of states to combat terrorists. Global terrorists can succeed only through popular uprising or the psychological or physical collapse of their state-based adversary. Neither outcome is likely given the limitations of terrorist messages and capabilities. Terrorist and counterterrorist campaigns are characterized by prolonged struggle to maintain advantages in legitimacy domestically and internationally. The challenge for the global community will be in utilizing its advantages to win the war of ideas—to control what motivates and sustains those responsible for the current wave of terrorist violence.

CONTRIBUTORS TO CHAPTER 9: James D. Kiras and Steven L. Lamy.

REVIEW QUESTIONS

1. Why do various groups decide to use terrorist tactics? Critical theorists might say it is because they are denied access to public resources and opportunities or because government fails to represent their interests. Do you agree? Would realists and liberals agree?

2. When did terrorism become a truly global phenomenon, and what enabled it to do so?

3. In what ways are the technologies and processes associated with globalization more beneficial to states attempting to stop violence or groups attempting to engage in terrorist attacks?

4. Given that terrorism has been both a transnational and a global phenomenon, why has it not been more successful in effecting change within target states?

5. Of all the factors that motivate terrorists, is any one more important than others, and if so, why?

6. What has changed in terrorism over the past half-century, and have any factors remained the same? If so, what are they and why have they remained constant?

7. What role does technology play in terrorism, and will it change how terrorists operate in the future? If so, how?

8. Are we exaggerating the problems presented by terrorists? Is the issue overblown? Explain.

9. What is the primary challenge that individual states and the international community as a whole face in confronting terrorism?

10. How can globalization be useful in diminishing the underlying causes of terrorism?

FURTHER READING

Ganor, B. (2005), *The Counter-Terrorism Puzzle: A Guide for Decision Makers* (New Brunswick, N.J.: Transaction Books). Emphasizes the dilemmas and practical difficulties associated with various counterterrorism policy options.

Hoffman, B. (2006), *Inside Terrorism*, rev. and exp. ed. (New York: Columbia University Press). The best single-volume work on the development of terrorism, its evolution, and current and future prospects for defeating it.

Juergensmeyer, M. (2000), *Terror in the Mind of God: The Global Rise of Religious Violence* (Berkeley: University of California Press). Highlights similarities between religious leaders across faiths and sects in how they justify killing noncombatants.

Office of the Chairman of the Joint Chiefs of Staff (2006), *National Military Strategic Plan for the War on Terrorism* (Washington, D.C.: The Pentagon). The unclassified version of this document is available for downloading at www.strategicstudiesinstitute.army.mil/pdffiles/gwot.pdf.

Mueler, John, (2006), *Overblown: How Politicians and the Terrorism Industry Inflate National Security Threats, and Why We Believe Them* (New York: Free Press). This book presents an interesting argument about how the new version of the military-industrial complex, the "terrorism industry," and politicians have exaggerated the threat of terrorist attacks.

Rabasa, A., Chalk, P., et al. (2006), *Beyond al-Qaeda: Part 1, The Global Jihadist Movement*, and *Part 2, The Outer Rings of the Terrorist Universe* (Santa Monica, Cal.: RAND). This two-part report provides a comprehensive survey of current militant Islamic terrorist groups, the impact of Iraq on the global jihad, and the linkages between terrorism and organized crime. Available for downloading at www.rand.org/pubs/monographs/2006/RAND_MG429.pdf (Part 1) and www.rand.org/pubs/monographs/2006/RAND_MG430.pdf (Part 2).

Roy, O. (2004), *Globalized Islam: The Search for a New Ummah* (New York: Columbia University Press). A provocative work that challenges many of the assumptions about militant Islam as well as explanations for its rise.

Sageman, M. (2004), *Understanding Terror Networks* (Philadelphia: University of Pennsylvania Press). Analyzes Al Qaeda members based on information gathered from open sources and arrives at thought-provoking conclusions about the formation of the militant global jihad network.

Schmid, A. P., Jongman, A. J., et al. (1988), *Political Terrorism: A New Guide to Actors, Authors, Concepts, Data Bases, Theories, and Literature* (New Brunswick, N.J.: Transaction Books). A still useful, if at times overwhelming, reference work that highlights the problems associated with defining and studying terrorism.

INTERNET RESOURCES

Special Operations
www.specialoperations.com

Exhaustive collection devoted to all aspects of special operations, including national counterterrorism units and historical operations.

Terrorism Files
www.terrorismfiles.org

A useful collection of news items, terrorist group overviews, individuals, and incidents.

Terrorism Research Center
www.terrorism.com

This useful site has an excellent links section, including links to relevant reports and terrorism news.

This Is Baader-Meinhof
www.baader-meinhof.com

This site contains information related to transnational terrorism and, in particular, the German Baader-Meinhof group.

US State Department: Patterns of Global Terrorism Annual Report
http://www.state.gov/j/ct/rls/crt/2000/

Archived from 1995 onward, these reports contain valuable information and trends analysis on American perceptions of terrorism and the threat it poses.

Carnegie Council: "One Nation Under Surveillance: A New Social Contract to Defend Freedom Without Sacrificing Liberty" —Simon Chesterman
http://www.carnegiecouncil.org/resources/video/data/000380

Since the end of World War II, surveillance in the United States and the United Kingdom has seen a steady rise, tracking with technological advances. Simon Chesterman explores how surveillance can be balanced with national security objectives.

Carnegie Council: "Negotiating with Evil: When to Talk to Terrorists"—Mitchell B. Reiss
http://www.carnegiecouncil.org/resources/video/data/000361

Mitchell Reiss asks the question, "How far is the distance between the polished, well-tailored official that you're talking with and the underlying terrorist, the man who has done unspeakable harm to many innocent individuals? Is it ever possible to really bridge that divide?" He concludes that the distance is closer than one might expect.

Carnegie Council: "Captive: My Time as a Prisoner of the Taliban"—Jere van Dyk
http://www.carnegiecouncil.org/resources/video/data/000336

In 2008, Jere van Dyk, a CBS news reporter, was captured by the Taliban in Afghanistan. This is the story of how he survived.

TED Talk: Loretta Napoleoni: "The Intricate Economics of Terrorism"
http://www.ted.com/talks/lang/eng/loretta_napoleoni_the
_intricate_economics_of_terrorism.html

Using the Italian Red Brigades as a primary example, Loretta Napoleoni traces the funding of terrorist groups and the groups' links to money laundering.

For more information, quizzes, case studies and other study tools, please visit us at **www.oup.com/us/lamy**

THINKING ABOUT GLOBAL POLITICS

Why Terrorism? Developing Testable Hypotheses

OBJECTIVE
One of the tasks of a global politics analyst is to explain the behavior of nation-states and other actors in the international system. Our job is to solve puzzles and find answers to questions such as why the world failed to prevent the genocide in Rwanda and why the terrorist network led by Osama bin Laden decided to attack the United States. As social scientists, we look for patterns so we can develop testable hypotheses that explain behavior. To develop these, we might use levels of analysis, described in depth in Chapter 5, which we will do in this exercise to explore the question of why people become terrorists.

PROCEDURE
Step One
Review the four levels of analysis discussed in Chapters 1 and 5.
Step Two
Make a list of factors that might be reasons for individuals to use terrorist tactics. Factors at each level of analysis are potential *independent variables*, or factors that might explain the terrorist act. The terrorist act is the *dependent variable*, which is what we are trying to explain.
Step Three
Develop a plausible explanation for why people become terrorists. Use this typical hypothesis framework:

If *x* (independent variable) then *y* (dependent variable).

For example, at the individual level of analysis, you could hypothesize that an individual might join a terrorist group because of dogmatic beliefs (i.e., acceptance of beliefs as incontrovertibly true). This dogmatism might also explain why an individual would accept the use of force and violence as a means to an end. You now have a hypothesis that you can test.

FOLLOW-UP
What is exciting about research in our field is that there are always disagreements about which variables explain the behavior of an actor. The strength of a researcher's arguments is based on the quality of the evidence collected to support the hypotheses.

Consider the following foreign policy question:

Why did the United States sign a major trade agreement with China, rejecting arguments made by numerous NGOs and citizens for human rights?

Identify the dependent variable (what you are trying to explain), make a list of factors at each of the four levels of analysis, and select an independent variable (a factor that might explain the decision):

dependent variable: US signing of a trade agreement

example independent variable: interest group politics (Level II)

Look through the cases in this textbook, identify similar questions or unexpected behavior, and develop some plausible explanations.

10 Human Rights and Human Security

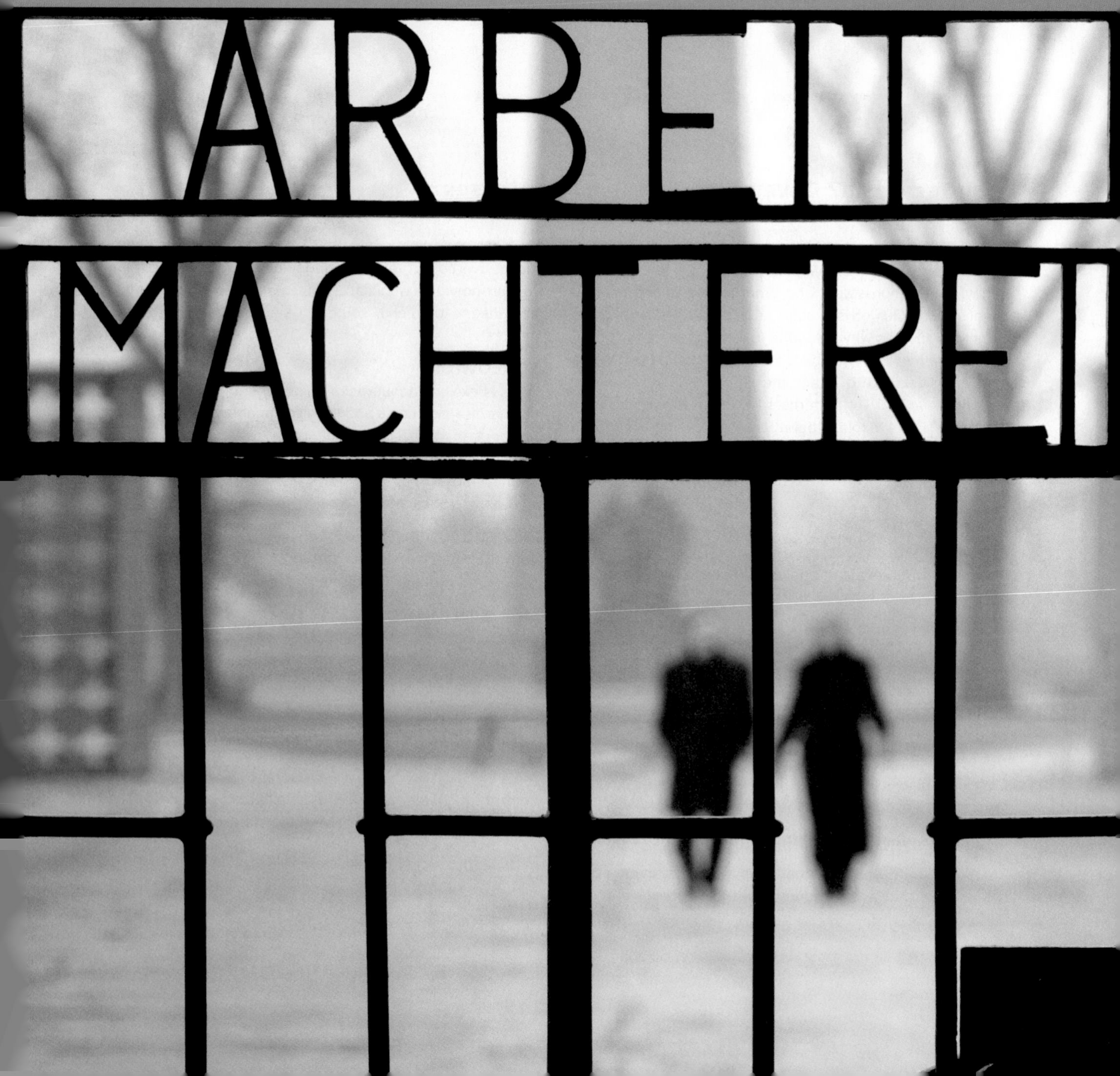

The crime of genocide should be recognized therein as a conspiracy to exterminate national, racial, or religious groups . . . The formulation of the crime may be as follows: Whoever, while participating in a conspiracy to destroy religious, national, or racial groups, undertakes an attack against life, liberty, or property of members of such groups is guilty of the crime of genocide.

—*Raphael Lemkin*

Human security naturally connects several kinds of freedom—such as freedom from want and freedom from fear, as well as freedom to take action on one's behalf.

—*Commission on Human Security*

The term *genocide* was created after World War II, as leaders of the antifascist coalition struggled to understand the magnitude of human tragedy before them. Immediately after the war, the victorious powers promised "never again" would countries stand by while tyrants massacred their own people or launched wars of aggression.

And yet sadly, since 1945, genocidal violence has occurred in the Congo, Cambodia, East Timor, Rwanda, Bosnia, Kosovo, Chechnya, Somalia, Darfur, and many other places. In this chapter, we will examine the linked concepts of human rights and human security, both of which emerged from the effects of World War II. We will see that there are many reasons for hope that the world community will be able one day to stop human rights abuses and provide security to all people. But because the successful promotion of both human rights and human security depends on the international community, there may be as many reasons to be pessimistic about the prospects for a better world. After all, protecting the rights of individuals can infringe on the prerogatives of governments and thus on the notion of sovereign equality of countries. As we have seen elsewhere in this book, however, globalization is changing many traditions in world affairs.

This tension between the rights of the *individual* and the rights of *society* is a significant barrier to the creation of human security. As we will see in the first section of this chapter, there were intellectual disagreements in the nineteenth and early twentieth

"Arbeit macht frei" literally means "work makes you free." This is a modern-day picture of the front gates leading into Auschwitz. In 1945, states pledged that genocide would never occur again. Have the states kept their promise?

centuries about answers to basic questions: What is a human right? What rights should be protected? And by whom? Must these rights be universal? We are still looking for answers to these questions. How can we discuss such a broad issue as global security on a smaller, human scale? What should it look like and why is it important? What opportunities still exist for political and military leaders to circumvent, undermine, and exploit international laws?

Introduction

As in other areas of the study of global politics, there are disagreements about human rights and human security. And like the debates in other areas, the splits tend to be down the same lines as the international relations theory we discussed in Chapters 3 and 4 (see Table 10.1). However, the fundamental question is a simple one. *Do countries have an obligation to improve the living conditions and protect the rights of people who live in other countries?*

Furthermore, if there is such an obligation, what are its legal foundations? And who would define the terms of human rights? Clearly, such rights would rest within a legal system. But whose? And what kind? Some of the contemporary disagreement about the obligation to promote human rights and human security stems from a history of colonialism. For example, the modern concept of individual human rights developed originally in Europe. Yet, as many European countries colonized other regions of the world (and even other parts of Europe), these rights were often not extended to other peoples who were seen as not human. Today, for many people who live in Africa and Asia, these human rights may appear to derive from their problematic colonial heritage. Why should it necessarily mean something different to be human in Africa than in Europe?

After reading and discussing this chapter, you will be able to define human rights, and you will understand their connection to the concepts of natural law and charter rights. You will have the tools to explore what responsibility states have to intervene in other states where rights are abused or suspended. You will also have an understanding of an important new concept in global politics—human security—and how it relates to human rights. You will know more about the history of humanitarian challenges and the variety of international responses to these challenges. Finally, you will understand the roles that various actors play in promoting and protecting human rights and human security.

What Are Human Rights?

The theory of **human rights** developed in Europe during the Middle Ages, and it rested on the idea of **natural law**—that humans have an essential nature. Natural law theorists differed on many issues, but they agreed on the following: (1) there are universal moral standards that support individual rights; (2) there is a general duty to adhere to these standards; and (3) the application of these standards is not limited to any particular legal system, community, state, race, religion, or civilization (Finnis 1980). These central propositions are the origin of modern rhetoric on *universal* human rights.

Natural law provided the theory, but in the rougher world of medieval political practice, rights had different connotations. There, rights were concessions extracted from a superior, probably by force. The Magna Carta (1215) is a case in point. In it, the barons of England obliged King John to grant to them and their heirs in perpetuity a series of liberties that are, for the most part, very specific and related to particular grievances. The Magna Carta is based

Engaging with the

WORLD

Reliefweb

This is a database of jobs, workshops, conferences, and courses in development, international policy, and assistance. It is a particularly useful resource for people who want to travel and to engage with the world. The majority of listings are conferences outside the United States, but there are over 400 listings most days. Check out reliefweb.int.

human rights The inalienable rights such as life, liberty, and the pursuit of happiness that one is entitled to because one is human.

natural law The idea that humans have an essential nature, which dictates that certain kinds of human goods are always and everywhere desired; because of this, there are common moral standards that govern all human relations, and these common standards can be discerned by the application of reason to human affairs.

Table 10.1
Comparing Worldviews

	Realist	Liberal	Utopian	Marxist
Impact on National Security	• Corporate and governmental leaders want international governments that support them, even if establishing these governments causes violence and repression.	• Citizens should have the right to self-determination and open governments that are responsive to public opinion. • Those holding sovereign power need to act responsibly. • An individual should submit to an established authority unless this authority violates an individual's conscience: disobedience is a lesser evil than the slaughter of the innocent.	• Self-determination increases the likelihood of long-term peace by facilitating the participation of all groups in the determination of their own affairs.	• The biggest security threat is global poverty and a capitalist system that rewards the rich and fails to provide employment and quality of life for those on the margins.
Economic Consequences	• Government activities should not advocate radical change, even if this change is designed to help abolish poverty for the lower classes.	• Through the reciprocity of mutual needs a great society of states develops, characterized by common norms and customs. These norms and customs are embodied in the law of nations and in natural law and are binding on all nations. States abide by these rules out of long-term, enlightened self-interest.	• Self-determination facilitates a more equitable sharing of the economic resources of the globe. • Collective responsibility and human equality apply both internally within a society and externally between societies.	

Continued

Table 10.1 (*continued*)
Comparing Worldviews

	Realist	Liberal	Utopian	Marxist
Human Rights Implications	• There should be no radical socioeconomic changes aimed at achieving human rights for the dispossessed.	• Humans are endowed equally with the right to do what is necessary for self-preservation, and to be the sole arbiters of what is necessary to expand their own liberty.	• Human rights are profoundly important guidelines for policy making. • Self-determination is a fundamental human right that contributes to spiritual and psychological well-being and should therefore be universally nurtured.	• A global capitalist class will allow for some human rights but none that would challenge its power and economic interests. The right to quality of life and access to societal resources or an equitable distribution of societal resources is not part of a capitalist system.
Environment	• Corporations focus resources and productive capacity on maximizing profit rather than fulfilling human needs.	• Rights involve protection of quality of life, and that includes clean air and water, and a healthy lifestyle. The rule of law can be used to protect the environment, and actions need to be taken collectively.	• If the rights of other societies are respected, productivity will eventually conform to meeting universal human needs. • Existing productive capacity for unessential goods should be converted into production of food and other essential items, leading to the better disposal of pollutants and conservation of resources.	• The environment is not a resource to be abused and exploited for the good of a few. It must serve the interests of all, and all should have access to environmental resources to create quality of life.

on the important principle that the subjects of the king owe him duty only if he meets their claims. This is clearly a political bargain or contract.

Although rights as part of natural law and those established by political contract are not inherently incompatible, these two kinds of rights are based on opposed principles. Whereas rights based on natural law are derived from the notion of human flourishing and are universal, **charter rights** are the result of a political contract and, by definition, are limited to the parties to the contract and thus restricted in time and space.

charter rights Civil liberties guaranteed in a written document such as a constitution.

The Liberal Account of Rights

The complex language of medieval thinking on rights carried over into the modern period. Political philosophers such as Hugo Grotius, Thomas Hobbes, and John Locke continued to use notions of natural law, albeit in radically different ways from their predecessors. Gradually, a synthesis of the concepts of natural rights and charter rights emerged. Known as the liberal account of rights, this position is made up of two basic components:

1. Human beings possess rights to life, liberty, the secure possession of property, the exercise of freedom of speech, and so on, which are inalienable—cannot be traded away—and unconditional. The only acceptable reason for constraining any one individual is to protect the rights of another.

2. The primary function of government is to protect these rights. Political institutions are to be judged on their performance of this function, and political obligation rests on their success in this. In short, political life is based on a kind of implicit or explicit contract between people and government.

liberal account of rights
The belief that humans have inherent rights that the state has a responsibility to protect.

From a philosophical and conceptual point of view, this position is easy to denigrate as a mishmash of half-digested medieval ideas. As G. W. F. Hegel and many subsequent communitarian thinkers have pointed out, it assumes that individuals and their rights predate society—and yet how could they exist without being part of a society? For philosopher Jeremy Bentham, the function of government was to promote the general good (which he called utility), and the idea that individuals might have the right to undermine this seemed to him madness, especially since no one could tell him where these rights came from; the whole idea was "nonsense upon stilts." Karl Marx, on the other hand, and many subsequent radicals pointed out that the liberal position stresses property rights to the advantage of the rich and powerful. All these points raise compelling questions, but they underestimate the powerful rhetorical appeal of the liberal position. Most people are less likely to be worried about the philosophical inadequacies associated with the liberal position on human rights than they are to be attracted by the obvious benefits of living in a political system based on or influenced by it.

One of the uncertain features of the liberal position is the extent to which the rights it describes are universal. For example, the French Revolutionary Declaration of the Rights of Man and of the Citizen clearly, by its very title, is intended to be of universal scope, but even here, the universalism of Article 1, "Men are born and remain free and equal in respect of rights," is soon followed by Article 3, "The nation is essentially the source of all sovereignty . . ." When revolutionary and Napoleonic France moved to bring the Rights of Man to the rest of Europe, the end result looked to most contemporaries remarkably like a French empire. The liberal position, while universal in principle, is particular in application, and it more or less takes state boundaries for granted.

The humanitarianism and international standard setting of the nineteenth and twentieth centuries brought these issues to the foreground. The Congress of Vienna of 1815 saw the great powers accept an obligation to end the slave trade, which was finally abolished by the

People around the world live with poverty and insecurity. The drug trade in developing countries provides jobs and income but also causes deadly violence. Drug gangs have taken control of vast regions of Mexico. Here more than 200 weapons were seized in a 2011 arrest in Mexico City.

Brussels Convention of 1890, while slavery itself was formally outlawed by the Slavery Convention of 1926. The Hague Conventions of 1907 and the Geneva Conventions of 1926 were designed to introduce humanitarian considerations into the conduct of war. The International Labor Office, formed in 1901, and its successor, the International Labor Organization, attempted to set standards in the workplace via measures such as the Convention Concerning Forced or Compulsory Labor of 1930.

In short, for Western European proponents of the liberal account of rights, human rights were intended to be protections for individuals against oppressive rulers, whether unelected monarchs or the choice of democratic majorities. The English and French colonizers of Asia and Africa took that notion of individual rights with them, and many believed it could take root in other cultures. As we will see, our modern notion of human rights is tied to the colonial experience, and over the centuries, this notion has evolved and been the subject of many disagreements.

Human Rights and State Sovereignty

Humanitarian measures taken together may provide a framework for some kind of global governance, but in many states, it is difficult to override a policy of **nonintervention**—not intervening in the affairs of other states—which is related to the notion of sovereignty. For example, abolishing the slave trade, which involved international transactions, was much easier than abolishing slavery, which concerns what states do to their own people; indeed, pockets of slavery survive to this day in parts of Africa, Asia, and the Middle East.

While sovereignty remains a norm of the system, humanitarian impulses have often been reduced to no more than laudable speech. One problem in realizing them is that a basic principle of international society is the sovereignty of states, which requires respect toward and noninterference with the institutions of member states. In nineteenth-century England, Manchester school radical liberals such as John Bright and Richard Cobden were bitterly critical of traditional diplomacy but supported the norm of nonintervention. They argued that their opponents, who claimed moral reasons in support of interventions, were in fact motivated by power politics. This is, of course, a familiar line of argument—one most likely, in the twenty-first century, to be directed at the American heirs of Britain's position in the world.

Cobden was a consistent anti-interventionist and anti-imperialist; other liberals were more selective. Gladstone's 1870s campaign to throw the Ottoman Empire out of Europe was based on the more common view that different standards applied between "civilized" and "uncivilized" peoples. In Gladstone's view, the Ottoman Empire—although since 1856 a full member of international society—could not claim the rights of a sovereign state because its institutions did not come up to the requisite standards. Indeed, this latter position was briefly established in international law in the notion of **standards of civilization**, a nineteenth-century, European discourse about what made a country civilized or uncivilized. Now, in the twenty-first century, this notion may disturb and unsettle us, yet current conventional thinking on human rights is based on very similar ideas.

The willingness of liberals to extend their thinking on human rights toward direct intervention characterized the second half of the twentieth century. The horrors of World War I stimulated attempts to create a peace system based on a form of international government, and although the League of Nations of 1919 had no explicit human rights provision, the underlying assumption was that its members would be states governed by the rule of law

nonintervention The principle that external powers should not intervene in the domestic affairs of sovereign states.

standards of civilization A nineteenth-century, European discourse about which values and norms made a country civilized or barbaric and uncivilized. The conclusion was that civilized countries should colonize barbaric regions for the latter's benefit.

and respecting individual rights. The UN Charter of 1945, in the wake of World War II, does have some explicit reference to human rights—a tribute to the impact, on the general thought climate, of the horrors of that war and, in particular, of the murder of millions of Jews, Roma people, and Slavs in the extermination camps of National Socialist Germany. In this context, the need to assert a universal position was deeply felt, and the scene was set for the burst of international human rights legislation during the postwar era.

International Human Rights Legislation

The post–World War II humanitarian impulse led to a flurry of lawmaking and standard setting, which gave rise to what are known as *generations* of rights. First-generation rights focus on individual rights such as free speech, freedom of religion, and voting rights—rights that protect the individual from the potential abuses of the state. Second-generation rights include social, economic, and cultural rights. This group of rights includes the right to employment, housing, healthcare, and education. First- and second-generation rights are covered by the Universal Declaration of Human Rights and the EU's Charter of Fundamental Rights. Third-generation rights are more focused on collective or group rights and have not been adopted by most states. These include the right to natural resources, the right to self-determination, the right to clean air, and the right to communicate. Many of these rights emerge from major global conferences that focus on transboundary issues such as the environment, racism, information and communications, and the rights of minorities and women.

Universal Declaration of Human Rights The principal normative document on human rights, adopted by the UN General Assembly in 1948 and accepted as authoritative by most states and other international actors.

The Universal Declaration of Human Rights

In 1948, the UN General Assembly established a baseline of human rights for its member states to follow. The **Universal Declaration of Human Rights** set out thirty basic political, civil, economic, and social rights that sought to define which specific rights all people share as humans. In the words of the Preamble to the declaration, "the peoples of the United Nations reaffirmed their faith in fundamental human rights, in the dignity and worth of the human person and of the equal rights of men and women . . ." The enumerated entitlements included freedom from torture, freedom of opinion, equal treatment before the law, freedom of movement within a country, the right to own property, the right to education, and the right to work.

There were two shortcomings in the Universal Declaration. First, it was nonbinding on the member states of the United Nations. Countries' leaders could pledge to support the goals of the document but then point to a range of political or economic problems that stopped them from full implementation. Article 29 bolstered their rationale for nonintervention: "Everyone has duties to the community in which alone the free and full development of his personality is possible." A second difficulty was the European origins of these rights. As the wave of decolonization swept Asia and Africa, newly independent countries eagerly embraced the tenets of human rights law. Unfortunately,

Under the 1993 Chemical Weapons Convention there is a worldwide ban on the production, stockpiling, and use of chemical weapons. A country using chemical weapons is breaking international law. Further, any country using chemical weapons is guilty of violating human rights. What if a leader uses these heinous weapons against its own citizens? Syria has allegedly killed hundreds using chemical weapons. Why has the world done nothing?

as civil strife threatened to split some of these countries, some leaders blamed it on the pattern of oppression that the colonizers had created, and they used the provisions of Article 29 as the political justification for postcolonial repression.

Despite its shortcomings, the Universal Declaration of Human Rights is, symbolically, a central piece of legislation. This was the first time in history that the international community had attempted to define a comprehensive code for the internal government of its members. During the late 1940s, the West dominated the United Nations, and the contents of the declaration represented this fact, with its emphasis on political freedom. The voting was forty-eight for and none against. Eight states abstained, for interestingly different reasons.

South Africa abstained. The white-dominated regime in South Africa denied political rights to the majority of its people and clearly could not accept that "all are born free and equal in dignity and rights" (Article 1), claiming it violated the protection of the domestic jurisdiction of states guaranteed by Article 2(7) of the UN Charter. This is a clear and uncomplicated case of a first-generation (political) rights issue.

The Soviet Union and five Soviet-bloc countries abstained. Although Stalin's USSR was clearly a tyranny, the Soviet government did not officially object to the political freedoms set forth in the declaration. Instead, the Soviet objection was to the absence of sufficient attention to social and economic rights by comparison to the detailed elaboration of "bourgeois" freedoms and property rights. The Soviets saw the declaration as a Cold War document designed to stigmatize socialist regimes—a not wholly inaccurate description of the motives of its promulgators.

Saudi Arabia abstained. It was one of the few non-Western members of the United Nations in 1948 and just about the only one whose system of government was not, in principle, based on some Western model. Saudi Arabia objected to the declaration on religious grounds, specifically objecting to Article 18, which specifies the freedom to change and practice the religion of one's choice. These provisions did not merely contravene specific Saudi laws, which, for example, forbade (and still forbid) the practice of the Christian religion in Saudi Arabia, but they also contravened the tenets of Islam, which does not recognize a right of apostasy. Here, to complete the picture, we have an assertion of third-generation rights and a denial of the universalism of the declaration. Thus, the opening moment of the universal human rights regime sees the emergence of the themes that will make up the politics of human rights over the next sixty years.

Subsequent UN Legislation

Building on the promise of the Universal Declaration, the United Nations took the lead in creating major legally binding international conventions that define rights of specific groups, including women, children, and migrant workers, and that aim to eliminate torture and racial discrimination (see Table 10.2). These conventions provide the intellectual and legal basis for the concept of human security, which we examine later in the chapter.

Enforcement of Human Rights Legislation

A significant number of states, global civil society actors, parliamentarians, lawyers, trade unions, and global social movements have embraced the Universal Declaration of Human Rights, and each promotes these rights and uses them as guidelines in its professional and personal activities. The UN Commission on Human Rights has the power to monitor,

Table 10.2

UN Conventions Following the 1948 Universal Declaration of Human Rights

Convention	Year
International Convention on the Elimination of All Forms of Racial Discrimination (ICERD)	1965
International Covenant on Civil and Political Rights (ICCPR)	1966
International Covenant on Economic, Social, and Cultural Rights (ICESCR)	1966
Optional Protocol to the International Covenant on Civil and Political Rights (ICCPR-OP1)	1966
Convention on the Elimination of All Forms of Discrimination against Women (CEDAW)	1979
Convention against Torture and Other Cruel, Inhuman, or Degrading Treatment or Punishment (CAT)	1984
Convention on the Rights of the Child (CRC)	1989
Second Optional Protocol to the International Covenant on Civil and Political Rights, aiming to abolish the death penalty (ICCPR-OP2)	1989
International Convention on the Protection of the Rights of All Migrant Workers and Members of Their Families (ICRMW)	1990
Optional Protocol to the Convention on the Elimination of Discrimination against Women (OP-CEDAW)	1999
Optional Protocol to the Convention on the Rights of the Child on the Involvement of Children in Armed Conflict (OP-CRC-AC)	2000
Optional Protocol to the Convention on the Rights of the Child on the Sale of Children, Child Prostitution, and Child Pornography (OP-CRC-SC)	2000
Optional Protocol to the Convention against Torture and Other Cruel, Inhuman, or Degrading Treatment or Punishment (OP-CAT)	2002
Optional Protocol to the Convention on the Rights of Persons with Disabilities (OP-CRPD)	2006
International Convention for the Protection of All Persons from Enforced Disappearance (CPED)	2006
Convention on the Rights of Persons with Disabilities (CRPD)	2006
Optional Protocol of the Covenant on Economic, Social and Cultural Rights (ICESCR-OP)	2008

report, and advise, but the United Nations lacks the resources and authority to enforce these rights. Member states may, however, publicly criticize or shame states guilty of violating the rights of their citizens. Some states, such as the social democratic countries of Europe, have placed conditions on aid and trade agreements, demanding that states follow the rights articulated in all UN legal conventions. With the 2005 Responsibility to Protect (R2P) agreement, states have the obligation to prevent abuse and to protect citizens from governments that abuse the rights of their citizens. The 2011 military action against Libya was required under the R2P, in response to the government's repression and violence against its citizens.

Charles Norchi (2004) suggests that those seeking to promote and enforce international human rights legislation face four challenges:

1. The first challenge is the global promotion of human rights standards and policies. More financial and technical support is essential if information on rights is to be disseminated and these same rights enforced.

2. The second major challenge is the application of the established rights and laws to a set of events or actions. Effective enforcement depends on the willingness of nation-states to use tools of statecraft (see Chapter 5) to punish states that violate these rights.

3. A third challenge lies in the debate between those who believe in universal rights and those who believe more in a particularistic view of rights. The United Nations must find a way to be sensitive to cultural interpretations of rights, but it must stop any gross violations of human rights.

4. The fourth challenge is keeping the focus on the norms and values promoted by the UN human rights regime. The United Nations' failure to respond to the genocide in Rwanda and Darfur and the recent veto by China and Russia of UN Security Council resolutions aimed at stopping government violence and repression in Syria suggest that national governments are unlikely to surrender sovereignty to promote universal rights.

What Is Human Security?

human security The security of people, including their physical safety, their economic and social well-being, respect for their dignity, and the protection of their human rights.

Like the doctrines of human rights, the concept of **human security** represents a powerful but controversial attempt (as we will discuss) by sections of the academic and policy community to redefine and broaden the meaning of security. Traditionally, security meant protection of the sovereignty and territorial integrity of states from external military threats. This was the essence of the concept of national security, which dominated security analysis and policy making during the Cold War period. In the 1970s and 1980s, academic literature on security, responding to the Middle East oil crisis and the growing awareness of worldwide environmental degradation, began to describe security in broader, nonmilitary terms. Yet the state remained the object of security, or the entity to be protected.

The concept of human security challenges the state-centric notion of security by focusing on the individual. Human security is about security for the people rather than for states or governments. Hence, it has generated much debate. Critics wonder whether such an approach would widen the boundaries of security studies too much and whether "securitizing" the individual is the best way to address the challenges facing the international community from the forces of globalization. On the other side, advocates of human security find the concept effectively highlights the dangers to human safety and survival posed by poverty, disease, environmental stress, and human rights abuses as well as armed conflict. These disagreements notwithstanding, the concept of human security captures a growing realization that, in an era of rapid globalization, security must encompass a broader range of concerns and challenges than simply defending the state from external military attack.

Origin of the Concept

The origin of the concept of human security can be traced to the publication of the *Human Development Report* of 1994, issued by the UN Development Programme. The report defined the scope of human security to include seven areas:

CASE STUDY : Human Insecurity in Southeast Asia

BACKGROUND

Whether going by the narrow (freedom from fear) or broad (freedom from want) conception, Southeast Asia faces some of the most critical challenges to human security in the world. The region, comprising Vietnam, Laos, Cambodia, Myanmar (Burma), Indonesia, Malaysia, Thailand, the Philippines, Brunei, and Singapore, has witnessed some of the worst violence of the twentieth century.

THE CASE

The Khmer Rouge regime in Cambodia killed about 1.7 million (a quarter of the Cambodian population) during its brutal rule between 1975 and 1979 (Yale University Cambodian Genocide Program). In Indonesia, anticommunist riots in the mid-1960s, which accompanied the transition from President Sukarno to President Suharto, claimed about 400,000 lives (Schwarz 1999, 20). The US war in Vietnam produced 250,000 South Vietnamese, 1.1 million North Vietnamese, and 60,000 American casualties (Olson 1988). Ethnic and separatist movements in East Timor and Aceh have claimed 200,000 and more than 2,000 lives, respectively (Wessel and Wimhofer 2001). And while there are no proper collated figures for ethnic separatism in Myanmar—usually low-scale, random casualties and conflicts—600,000 internally displaced persons from these conflicts have been recorded (US Department of State 2003).

The region has been free of major conflict since the fighting in Cambodia (1979–1991) ended. But internal conflicts in southern Thailand, southern Philippines, and Myanmar pose a serious challenge to human security. Military rule, which accounted for some of the worst human rights violations in the region, continues in Myanmar, has returned in Thailand, and remains a possibility in the Philippines.

OUTCOME

Southeast Asia also faces other threats to human security. Absolute poverty levels have declined, but the prevalence of underweight children under five years of age in Southeast Asia is third highest in the world (28 percent), after sub-Saharan Africa (30 percent) and South Asia (47 percent). In Asia, national HIV-infection levels are highest in Southeast Asia. The outbreaks of highly pathogenic H5N1 avian influenza, which began in Southeast Asia in mid-2003 and have now spread to parts of Europe, are the largest and severest on record.

Southeast Asia has also experienced a range of transnational threats in recent years. These include the Asian economic crisis of 1997, described by the World Bank as "the biggest setback for poverty reduction in East Asia for several decades" (Ching 1999). Other challenges include the recurring haze problem (1997, 2006) from forest fires in Indonesia, the severe acute respiratory syndrome outbreak in 2003, and the Indian Ocean tsunami that devastated coastal areas in Indonesia, Thailand, and other Southeast Asian nations in December 2004 and killed at least 200,000 people in Asia, with Indonesia suffering 128,000 dead and 37,000 missing.

Conceptually, Southeast Asia shows a link between underdevelopment and conflict. Its poorest areas—Indonesia, Cambodia, Myanmar, and the southern regions of Thailand and the Philippines—have been especially prone to conflict. Economic development has led to relative stability in Singapore and Malaysia.

For Discussion

1. Should the countries of Asia be left to work out their own problems without intervention from European or North American states?
2. How does the constructivist perspective help us understand the crisis of insecurity in Asia?
3. To what extent has globalization increased or decreased threats to human security in Asia?

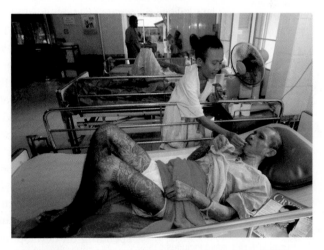

An AIDS hospice in Thailand was the site of a test of anti-HIV drugs in 2009. Should states make such medicines available at reduced costs to all citizens in the world?

- *Economic security*—ensuring basic income for all people, usually from productive and remunerative work or, as the last resort, from some publicly financed safety net.
- *Food security*—ensuring that all people at all times have both physical and economic access to basic food.
- *Health security*—guaranteeing a minimum of protection from diseases and unhealthy lifestyles.
- *Environmental security*—protecting people from the short- and long-term ravages of nature, human threats in nature, and deterioration of the natural environment.
- *Personal security*—protecting people from physical violence, whether from the state or external states, from violent individuals and substate factors, from domestic abuse, or from predatory adults.
- *Community security*—protecting people from the loss of traditional relationships and values and from sectarian and ethnic violence.
- *Political security*—ensuring that people live in a society that honors their basic human rights, and ensuring the freedom of individuals and groups from government attempts to exercise control over ideas and information.

The seven areas appear to describe the basic purpose of every country; and yet, as with other UN programs, the *Human Development Report* has had numerous critics. The primary complaint has been that the report has issued an unfunded mandate: it could be used to admonish countries that did not reach the standards, yet the report provided little or no funding to reach them. As you will see in the next section, this tension between standard setting in human rights and human security and assessing country performance has been a consistent strain since 1945. The leaders of many governments resent what they perceive as interference in the sovereign affairs of their countries.

Human Security and Development

Unlike many other efforts to redefine security, where political scientists played a major role, human security was the handiwork of a group of development economists, such as the late Pakistani economist Mahbub ul Haq, who conceptualized the UN Development Programme's *Human Development Report*. They were increasingly dissatisfied with the orthodox notion of development, which viewed it as a function of economic growth (as we will discuss in depth in Chapter 13). Instead, they proposed a concept of **human development** that focuses on building human capabilities to confront and overcome poverty, illiteracy, diseases, discrimination, restrictions on political freedom, and the threat of violent conflict: "Individual freedoms and rights matter a great deal, but people are restricted in what they can do with that freedom if they are poor, ill, illiterate, discriminated against, threatened by violent conflict or denied a political voice . . ." (UN Development Programme 2011, 18–19).

Closely related to the attempt to create a broader paradigm for development was the growing concern about the negative impact of defense spending on development, or the "guns versus butter" dilemma. As a global study headed by Inga Thorsson of Sweden concluded, "the arms race and development are in a competitive relationship" (Roche 1986, 8). Drawing on this study, a UN-sponsored International Conference on the Relationship Between Disarmament and Development, in 1986 in Paris,

human development The notion that it is possible to improve the lives of people. Basically, it is about increasing the number of choices people have. These may include living a long and healthy life, access to education, and a better standard of living.

Human security includes freedom from fear, freedom from want, and the rule of law. But it also includes education. Here a Syrian child answers a teacher's question at a UN refugee camp in Amman, Jordan. With the civil war continuing in Syria and conflicts in Africa, refugee numbers are increasing worldwide.

sought "to enlarge world understanding that human security demands more resources for development and fewer for arms."

Common Security

The move toward human security was also advanced by the work of several international commissions. They offered a broader view of security that looked beyond the Cold War emphasis on East-West military competition. Foremost among them was the Palme Commission of 1982, which proposed the doctrine of **common security**, emphasizing noncompetitive, cooperative approaches to achieving human security for all. Its report stressed that "in the Third World countries, as in all our countries, security requires economic progress as well as freedom from military fear" (Palme Commission 1982, xii). In 1987, the report of the World Commission on Environment and Development (also known as the Brundtland Commission) highlighted the linkage between environmental degradation and conflict: "The real sources of insecurity encompass unsustainable development, and its effects can become intertwined with traditional forms of conflict in a manner that can extend and deepen the latter" (Brundtland et al. 1987, 230).

> **common security** At times called "cooperative security," it stresses noncompetitive approaches and cooperative approaches through which states—both friends and foes—can achieve security. The belief that no one is secure until all people are secure from threats of war.

Along with attempts to broaden the notion of security to include nonmilitary threats, there was a growing emphasis on the individual as the central object of security. The Palme Commission's notion of common security became the conceptual basis of the Conference on Security and Cooperation in Europe (CSCE). The CSCE made East-West security cooperation conditional on the improvement of the human rights situation in the former Soviet bloc. The North-South Roundtable on the "Economics of Peace," held in Costa Rica in 1990, called for a shift from "an almost exclusive concern with military security . . . to a broader concern for overall security of individuals from social violence, economic distress and environmental degradation" (Jolly and Ray 2006, 3).

WHAT'S YOUR WORLDVIEW

Are the elements of human security rights or privileges? On what evidence and theoretical perspective do you base your argument?

History of Humanitarian Activism and Intervention

As the concepts of human rights and human security have developed, many opinion leaders and politicians in democratic societies have become increasingly aware that the state must take action in the face of challenges to human lives and dignity. In effect, many politicians have come to believe that the state should do more than defend borders and that cooperative and purposeful international action might be necessary to safeguard people.

One reason human security has become a more salient issue in recent decades is that civil wars and intrastate conflicts are more frequent. These have entailed huge losses of life, ethnic cleansing, displacement of people within and across borders, and disease outbreaks. Traditional national security approaches have not been sufficiently sensitive toward conflicts that arise

The world's newest state, South Sudan, is in an internal conflict as rival tribal leaders fight for control of the government. The US ambassador to the UN, Samantha Power, considered by many to be a "humanitarian hawk," listens to the UN Security Council debate that resulted in an increase of peacekeeping troops in South Sudan from 7,000 to 12,500. Power is a strong advocate for humanitarian intervention.

over cultural, ethnic, and religious differences, as happened in Eastern Europe, Africa, and Central Asia in the post–Cold War era (Tow and Trood 2000).

Another reason for greater humanitarian awareness is the spread of democratization (see Map 10.1), which has been accompanied by more emphasis on human rights and **humanitarian intervention**. Proponents of interventions take the position that the international community is justified in intervening in the internal affairs of states accused of gross violation of human rights. This has led to the realization that while the concept of national security has not been rendered irrelevant, it no longer sufficiently accounts for the kinds of danger that threaten societies, states, and the international community.

The notion of human security has also been brought front and center by crises induced by accelerating globalization. For example, the widespread poverty, unemployment, and social dislocation caused by the Asian financial crisis of 1997 underscored people's vulnerability to the effects of economic globalization (Acharya 2004). This vulnerability played a major role in the 2010–2011 **Arab Spring** uprisings. These protests and revolutionary uprisings began in Tunisia in 2010 and spread across Egypt, Libya, Syria, Yemen, Bahrain, Saudi Arabia, and Jordan in 2011. At the heart of these protests was a desire for more democratic and transparent political systems and more open and equitable economic systems. The inspiration for the first Arab Spring event was the actions of a 26-year-old Tunisian fruit and vegetable vendor, Mohamed Bouazizi, who set himself on fire after his cart was seized by police because he had no permit to sell goods. His act of desperation inspired other citizens across the Arab world to demand the end of authoritarian rule and to seek greater access to resources and wealth now held by very few in their countries. This message of protest spread quickly throughout the Middle East and around the world as cell phone cameras captured the images of protest, many of which were shared on the Internet. During the recent global economic recession, international aid agencies saw a sharp decline in donations for countries and individuals, thus undermining their ability to meet basic needs.

Intervention and Nonintervention in the 1990s

It has become common to describe the immediate post–Cold War period as something of a golden era for humanitarian activism and intervention. Thomas Weiss (2004, 136) argues that "the notion that human beings matter more than sovereignty radiated brightly, albeit briefly, across the international political horizon of the 1990s." There is no doubt that, during the 1990s, states began to contemplate intervention to protect imperiled strangers in distant lands. This was symbolized for many by NATO's intervention to halt Serb atrocities in Kosovo in March 1999 and the Australian-led intervention to end mass atrocities in East Timor. But the 1990s also saw the world stand aside during the genocides in Rwanda and Srebrenica. To make sense of these developments, let's focus on international interventions in northern Iraq, Somalia, Rwanda, and Kosovo and divide our discussion into three parts: the place of humanitarian impulses in decisions to intervene; the legality and legitimacy of the interventions; and the effectiveness of these military interventions.

In the cases of northern Iraq in April 1991 and Somalia in December 1992, domestic public opinion played an important role in pressuring policy makers into using force for humanitarian purposes. In the face of a massive refugee crisis caused by Saddam Hussein's oppression of the Kurds in the aftermath of the 1991 Gulf War, US, British, French, and Dutch military forces intervened to create protected "safe havens" for the Kurdish people. Similarly, the US military intervention in Somalia

humanitarian intervention The use of military force by external actors to end a threat to people within a sovereign state.

Arab Spring Protests and revolutionary uprisings that began in Tunisia in 2010 and spread across Egypt, Libya, Syria, Yemen, Bahrain, Saudi Arabia, and Jordan in 2011. At their core was a desire for more democratic and transparent political systems and more open and equitable economic systems.

WHAT'S YOUR WORLDVIEW

Why is the idea of humanitarian intervention so controversial? Why are states so unwilling to intervene to save people in danger?

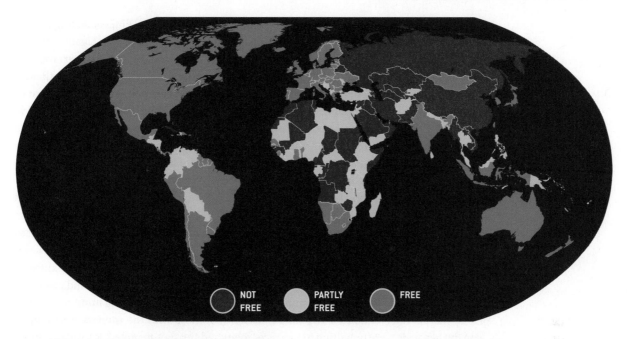

Map 10.1 Democracy in the World 2013.

This map from Freedom House represents a specifically American view of democracy. In many countries, democracy is only tenuously established, and human rights abuses continue. Some of the newly democratic countries in Africa have slipped back to being one-party states, and in other parts of the world, there has been clear evidence of rigged elections, as in Afghanistan in 2009. The majority of the world's countries now support the International Covenant on Civil and Political Rights (ICCPR), adopted by the United Nations in 1966, which sets out a range of rights, including freedom of conscience, freedom from torture and slavery, and the right to demonstrate peaceably. *Source: Freedom in the World 2013: Democratic Breakthroughs in the Balance; Freedom House Report (pp. 14-18) http://www.freedomhouse.org/sites/default/files/FIW%202013%20Booklet.pdf.*

in December 1992 was a response to sentiments of compassion on the part of US citizens. This sense of solidarity disappeared, however, once the United States began sustaining casualties.

The fact that the White House pulled the plug on its Somali intervention after the loss of eighteen US Rangers in a firefight in October 1993 indicates how capricious public opinion is. Television pictures of starving and dying Somalis had persuaded the outgoing Bush administration to launch a humanitarian rescue mission, but once the US public saw dead Americans dragged through the streets of Mogadishu, the Clinton administration announced a timetable for withdrawal. What the Somalia case demonstrates is that the "CNN effect" is a double-edged sword: it can pressure governments into humanitarian intervention yet with equal speed produce public disillusionment and calls for withdrawal. These cases also suggest that even if there are no vital national interests at stake, liberal states might launch humanitarian rescue missions if sufficient public pressure is mobilized. Certainly, there is no evidence in either of these cases to support the realist claim that states cloak power-political motives behind the guise of humanitarianism.

By contrast, the French intervention in Rwanda in July 1994 seems to be an example of abuse. The French government emphasized the strictly humanitarian character of the operation, but this interpretation lacks credibility given the evidence that it was covertly pursuing national self-interest. France had propped up the one-party Hutu state for twenty years, even providing troops when the Rwandan Patriotic Front (RPF), consisting largely of members of the rival Tutsi population and operating out of neighboring Uganda, threatened to overrun the country in 1990 and 1993. French President François Mitterrand was reportedly anxious to restore waning French influence in Africa and was fearful that an RPF victory in French-speaking Rwanda would bring the country under the influence of Anglophones. France therefore did not intervene until the latter stages of the genocide against the Tutsis, which was ended primarily by the RPF's military victory. Thus, it seems that French behavior accords with the realist premise that states will risk their soldiers only in defense of the national interest. French leaders may have been partly motivated by humanitarian sentiments, but this seems to be a case of a state abusing the concept of humanitarian intervention because the primary purpose of the intervention was to protect French national interests.

The moral question raised by French intervention is why international society failed to intervene when the genocide began in early April 1994. French intervention may have saved some lives, but it came far too late to halt the genocide. Some 800,000 people were killed in a mere hundred days. The failure of international society to stop the genocide indicates that state leaders remain gripped by the mind-set of national interests trumping human interests. There was no intervention for the simple reason that those with the military capability to stop the genocide were unwilling to sacrifice troops and treasure to protect Rwandans. International solidarity in the face of genocide was limited to moral outrage and the provision of humanitarian aid.

If the French intervention in Rwanda can be criticized for being too little too late, NATO's intervention in Kosovo in 1999 was criticized for being too much too soon. At the beginning of the war, NATO said it was intervening to prevent a humanitarian catastrophe. To do this, NATO aircraft were given two objectives: reduce Serbia's military capacity and coerce Milosevic into accepting the Rambouillet settlement, with the emphasis initially placed on the former. Three arguments were adduced to support NATO's claim that the resort to force was justifiable. First, it was argued that Serbian actions in Kosovo had created a humanitarian emergency and breached a whole range of international legal commitments. Second, NATO governments argued that the Serbs were committing crimes against humanity, possibly including genocide. Third, it was contended that the Milosevic regime's use of force against the Kosovar Albanians challenged global norms of common humanity.

Closer analysis of the justifications articulated by Western leaders suggests that while humanitarianism may have provided the primary impulse for action, it was by no means the exclusive impulse, and the complexity of the motives of the interveners colored the character of the intervention. Indeed, NATO was propelled into action by a mixture of humanitarian concern and self-interest gathered around three sets of issues. The first might be called the "Srebrenica syndrome"—a fear that, left unchecked, Milosevic's henchmen would replicate the carnage of Bosnia. The second is related directly to self-interest and was a concern that protracted conflict in the southern Balkans would create a massive refugee crisis in Europe. Finally, NATO governments were worried that if they failed to contain the crisis, it would spread and engulf several neighboring states, especially Macedonia, Albania, and Bulgaria (Bellamy 2002, 3). This suggests that humanitarian intervention might be prompted by mixed motives. It only becomes a problem if the nonhumanitarian motives undermine the chances of achieving the humanitarian purposes.

WHAT'S YOUR WORLDVIEW

Economic, social, and cultural rights were very controversial during the Cold War and remain so today. Why do you think these proposed rights remain so controversial? Do they challenge the power and influence of certain economic and political interests?

Universalism Challenged

Paradoxically, the success of the global human rights regime caused a growing backlash to the development of international norms of behavior. If taken seriously and at face value, human rights laws after 1945 would create a situation where all states would be obliged to conform to a quite rigid template that dictated most aspects of their political, social, and economic structures and policies. And so, from 1945, opponents of both the human rights and the human security regimes objected that (1) the norms were an unwarranted intrusion in the affairs of sovereign states and (2) these norms also sought to overturn existing assumptions about the role of the state and its jurisdiction.

The Cambodian genocide lasted from 1975 to 1979, and during this period 1.7 million people (21% of Cambodia's population) lost their lives. The Khmer Rouge regime led by Pol Pot operated one of the most repressive regimes in the history of humankind. In this photo, Cambodian villagers line up for the trial of two Khmer Rouge leaders at the October 2013 combined UN/Cambodian tribunal in Phnom Penh.

Conventional defenders of human rights and human security argue that universalism would be a good thing; the spread of best practice in these matters is in the interest of all people. However, others disagree. Does post-1945 law constitute best practice? The feminist critique of universal human rights is particularly appropriate here. The universal documents all, in varying degrees, privilege a patriarchal view of the family as the basic unit of society. Even such documents as the Convention on the Elimination of All Forms of Discrimination Against Women (CEDAW) of 1979 do no more than extend to women the standard liberal package of rights, and modern feminists debate whether this constitutes a genuine advance (Peters and Wolper 1995).

More fundamentally, is the very idea of "best practice" sound? We have already met one objection to the idea in the Saudi abstention of 1948. The argument is simple: universalism is destructive not only to undesirable differences between societies but also to desirable and desired differences. The human rights movement stresses the *common* humanity of the peoples of the world, but for many, the qualities that distinguish us from one another are as important as the characteristics that unify us. For example, the Declaration of Principles of Indigenous Rights adopted in Panama in 1984 by a nongovernmental group, the World Council of Indigenous Peoples, lays out positions that are designed to preserve the traditions, customs, institutions, and practices of indigenous peoples (many of which, it need hardly be said, contradict contemporary liberal norms). As with feminist critiques, the argument here is that the present international human rights regime rests too heavily on the experiences of one part of humanity, in this case, Western Europe, Canada, and the United States. Of course, in practice, the cultural critique and the feminist critique may lead in different directions.

This philosophical point took on a political form in the 1990s. In the immediate post–Cold War world, and especially after the election of US president Bill Clinton in 1992, there was some talk of the United States adopting active policies of democracy promotion. A number of East Asian governments and intellectuals asserted in response the notion that there were specifically "Asian values" that required defending from this development. The argument was that human rights boil down to no more than a set of particular social choices that need not be considered binding by those whose values (and hence, social choices) are differently formed—for example, by Islam or Confucianism rather than by an

GLOBAL PERSPECTIVE   Asian Values

That Western states, intergovernmental organizations, and NGOs have sometimes taken it upon themselves to promote human rights has always been resented as hypocritical in the non-Western world, where the imperialist record of the West over the last four centuries has not been forgotten. In the 1990s, this resentment led a number of the leaders of the quasi-authoritarian newly industrializing nations of Southeast Asia to assert the existence of Asian values that could be counterpoised to the (allegedly) Western values associated with the international human rights regime. In this, they seemed to confirm the forthcoming "clash of civilizations" forecast by Huntington (1996).

Such thinking was partially reflected in the Bangkok Declaration of 1993, made by Asian ministers in the run-up to the Vienna Conference of that year (for texts, see Tang 1994). Western notions of human rights were seen as excessively individualistic, as opposed to Asian societies' stress on the family, and insufficiently supportive of (if not downright hostile to) religion. Further, some regarded the West as morally decadent because of the growth of gay rights and the relative success of the women's movement in combating gender discrimination. Some have argued that such positions are simply intended to legitimate authoritarian rule, although it should be noted that "Asian values" can perform this task only if the argument strikes a chord with ordinary people.

More to the point, are the conservative positions expressed by proponents of Asian values Asian in any genuine sense? Many Western conservatives and fundamentalists share their critique of the West, while progressive Asian human rights activists are critical. Notions such as "the West" or "Asia" are unacceptably essentialist. All cultures and civilizations contain

Human rights activist Ka Hsaw Wa (left), an ethnic Karen from Myanmar, has led the struggle for minority national rights and environmentalism within that country.

different and often conflicting tendencies; the world of Islam or of "Confucian capitalism" is no more monolithic than is Christianity or Western secularism. The Asian values argument petered out at the end of the 1990s, but the problems it illustrated remain.

For Discussion

1. Is this really a debate between Asian and Western values, or is it a debate between universal views on rights versus more limited views on rights? Why?

2. Huntington's "clash of civilizations" is dismissed as a new realist argument for global intervention and maintaining a strong military to counter future enemies like China. What is wrong with this argument? Can conflict be avoided?

3. Will the world ever come to agreement on a universal view of rights that applies to all? Why or why not?

increasingly secularized Christianity. The wording of the Vienna Declaration on Human Rights of 1993, which refers to the need to bear in mind "the significance of national and regional particularities and various historical, cultural and religious backgrounds" when considering human rights, partially reflects this viewpoint—and has been criticized for this by some human rights activists.

Returning to the history of rights, it is here that the distinction between rights grounded in natural law and rights grounded in a contract becomes crucial. As noted earlier, it is only if rights are grounded in some account of human progress and reason that they may be regarded as genuinely universal in scope. But is this position, as its adherents insist, free of cultural bias, a set of ideas that all rational beings must accept? It seems not, at least insofar as many apparently rational Muslims, Hindus, Buddhists, atheists, utilitarians, and so on clearly do not accept its doctrines. It seems that either the standards derived from natural law (or a similar doctrine) are cast in such general terms that virtually any continuing social system will exemplify them, or if the standards are cast more specifically, they are not in fact universally desired.

Of course, we are under no obligation to accept all critiques of universalism at face value. Human rights may have first emerged in the West, but this does not in itself make rights thinking Western. Perhaps an apparently principled rejection of universalism is, in fact, no more than a rationalization of tyranny. How do we know that the inhabitants of Saudi Arabia, say, prefer not to live in a democratic system with Western liberal rights, as their government asserts? There is an obvious dilemma here: if we insist that we will only accept democratically validated regimes, we will be imposing an alien test of legitimacy on these societies. Yet what other form of validation is available?

In any event, the body of legal acts for the protection of universal human rights applies, does it not, even if rights are essentially convenient fictions? Again, defenders of difference will argue that international law is itself a Western, universalist notion, and they rightly note that the Western record of adherence to universal norms does not justify any claim to moral superiority. They point to the many crimes of the age of imperialism as well as to contemporary issues such as the treatment of asylum seekers and refugees and, of course, the byproducts of the global war on terror such as torture and imprisonment without trial.

There is no neutral language for discussing human rights. Whatever way the question is posed reflects a particular viewpoint, and this is no accident. It is built into the nature of the discourse. Is there any way the notion of universal rights can be saved from its critics? Two modern approaches seem fruitful. Even if we find it difficult to specify human *rights*, it may still be possible to talk of human *wrongs*. Similarly, some have argued that it is easier to specify what is *unjust* than what is *just* (see Booth 1999). To use Michael Walzer's terminology (1994), there may be no thick moral code that is universally acceptable, to which all local codes conform, but there may be a thin code that at least can be used to delegitimize some actions. Thus, for example, the Genocide Convention of 1948 seems a plausible example of a piece of international legislation that outlaws an obvious wrong, and while some local variations in the rights associated with gender may be unavoidable, it is still possible to say that practices that severely restrict human capabilities, such as female genital mutilation, are simply wrong. Any code that did not condemn such suffering would be unworthy of respect.

This may not take us as far as some would wish. Essential to this approach is the notion that there are some practices that many would condemn but that must be tolerated, but it may be the most appropriate response to contemporary pluralism. An alternative approach involves recognizing that human rights are based on a particular culture—Richard Rorty (1993) calls this the "human rights culture"—and it requires defending them in these terms rather than by reference to some cross-cultural code. This approach would involve abandoning the idea that human rights exist. Instead, it involves proselytizing on behalf of the sort of culture in which rights are deemed to exist. The essential point is that human life is safer, pleasanter, and more dignified when rights are acknowledged than when they are not.

Humanitarian Dimensions

Both human rights and human security have become part of an international discourse about proper norms of behavior and the best methods to promote these norms. The disagreements that exist today tend to be questions about the responsibilities of governments to live up to these standards. In this section, we discuss some dimensions of this discourse, with particular emphasis on political and economic rights and security, human rights and human security during times of conflict, rights to and security of natural resources, and women's rights.

Political and Economic Rights and Security

"No one shall be subjected to torture or to cruel, inhuman or degrading treatment or punishment" (UN Declaration, Article 5, Covenant on Civil and Political Rights, Article 7, Convention on Torture, etc.). This is an immunity that is now well established, but what in practice does this mean for someone faced with the prospect of such treatment? If the person is fortunate enough to live in a country governed by the rule of law, domestic courts may uphold his or her immunity, and the international side of things will come into play only on the margins. Thus, a European who is dissatisfied with treatment at home may be able to take a legal dispute over a particular practice beyond his or her national courts to the European Commission on Human Rights and the European Court of Human Rights. In non-European countries governed by the rule of law, no such direct remedy is available, but the notion of universal rights at least reinforces the rhetorical case for rights that are established elsewhere.

The more interesting case emerges if potential victims do not live in such a law-governed society—that is, if their government and courts are the problem and not the source of a possible solution. What assistance should they expect from the international community? What consequences will flow from their government's failure to live up to its obligations? The problem is that even in cases where violations are quite blatant, it may be difficult to see what other states are able to do, even supposing they are willing to act—which cannot be taken for granted because states rarely if ever act in terms of human rights considerations.

Thus, during the Cold War, the West regularly issued verbal condemnations of human rights violations by the Soviet Union and its associates but rarely acted on these condemnations. The power of the Soviet Union made direct intervention imprudent, and even relatively minor sanctions would be adopted only if the general state of East-West relations suggested this would be appropriate. Similar considerations apply today to relations between Western countries and China. Conversely, violations by countries associated with the West were routinely overlooked or, in some cases, even justified; the global war on terror provides contemporary examples. With the ending of the Cold War, it seemed possible that a more evenhanded approach to human rights violations might emerge, and indeed, more active policies have been pursued in some cases, but expectations of major changes in attitude have not been met. In 1997, for example, the incoming Labour government in Britain declared its determination to place human rights at the heart of its

The Chinese government is not afraid to censor the media and arrest citizens who defy it. Press freedom does not exist in China. Here a policeman arrests a supporter of the Southern Weekly newspaper in Guangzhou, China. China also limits access to the Internet and other social media.

foreign policy. Perhaps predictably, the actual policy of the government was frequently seen to be as determined by political and commercial considerations as in the past, and this was true even before the impact of 9/11 and the war on terror are taken into consideration (K. E. Smith and Light 2001).

All told, it seems unlikely that individuals ill-treated by nonconstitutional regimes will find any real support from the international community unless their persecutors are weak, of no strategic significance, and commercially unimportant. Even then, it is unlikely that effective action will be taken unless one additional factor is present—namely, the force of public opinion. This is the one positive factor that may goad states into action: the growth of humanitarian nongovernmental organizations (NGOs) has produced a context in which the force of public opinion can sometimes make itself felt, not necessarily in the oppressing regime but in the policy-formation processes of the potential providers of aid.

WHAT'S YOUR WORLDVIEW

With the war on terrorism and the rise of new security challenges, one must ask if states are prepared to respond. In this era of globalization, can states deliver on their promise to provide security for their citizens and still maintain certain rights and freedoms?

The situation with respect to second-generation rights is more complicated. Consider, for example, "the right of everyone to an adequate standard of living for himself and his family, including adequate food, clothing and housing, and to the continuous improvement of living conditions" (Covenant on Economic, Social and Cultural Rights, Article 11.1) or the "right of everyone to be free from hunger" (Article 11.2). It has been argued by numerous cosmopolitan writers that such rights are, or should be, central. For example, Henry Shue (1996) argues that only if such basic rights are met can any other rights be claimed, and Thomas Pogge (2002) sees the relief of world poverty as a central task for the human rights regime.

The covenant makes the realization of these rights an obligation on its signatories, but this is arguably a different kind of obligation from the obligation to refrain from, for example, "cruel or degrading" punishments. In the latter case, as with other basically political rights, the remedy is clearly in the hands of national governments. The way to end torture is, simply, for states to stop torturing. The right not to be tortured is associated with a duty not to torture. The right to be free from hunger, on the other hand, is not a matter of a duty on the part of one's own and other states not to pursue policies that lead to starvation. It also involves a duty to act to "ensure an equitable distribution of world food supplies in relation to need" (Covenant on Economic, Social and Cultural Rights, Article 11.2[b]). The distinction here is sometimes seen as that between "negative" and "positive" rights, although this is not entirely satisfactory, because negative (political) rights often require positive action if they are to be protected effectively. In any event, there are problems with the notion of economic rights.

First, it is by no means clear that, even assuming goodwill, these social and economic goals could always be met, and to think in terms of having a right to something that could not be achieved is to misuse language. In such circumstances, a right simply means "a generally desirable state of affairs," and this weakening of the concept may have the effect of undermining more precise claims to rights that actually can be achieved (e.g., the right not to be tortured).

Second, some states may seek to use economic and social rights more directly to undermine political rights. Thus, dictatorial regimes in poor countries quite frequently justify the curtailment of political rights in the name of promoting economic growth or economic equality. In fact, there is no reason to accept the general validity of this argument—Amartya Sen argues cogently that development and freedom go together (Sen 1999)—but it will still be made and not always in bad faith.

Finally, if it is accepted that all states have a positive duty to promote economic well-being and freedom from hunger everywhere, then the consequences go beyond the requirement of the rich to share with the poor, revolutionary though such a requirement would be. Virtually all national social and economic policies become a matter for international regulation. Clearly, rich states would have a duty to make economic and social policy with a view to its consequences on the poor, but so would poor states. The poor's right to assistance creates a duty on the rich to assist, but this in turn creates a right of the rich to insist that the poor have a duty not to worsen their plight—for example, by failing to restrict population growth or by inappropriate economic policies. Aid programs promoted by the Commonwealth and World Bank, and the structural-adjustment programs of the International Monetary Fund, regularly include conditions of this kind. They are, however, widely resented because they contradict another widely supported economic and social right: "All peoples have the right of self-determination. By virtue of that right they freely determine their political status and freely pursue their economic, social and cultural development" (Covenant on Economic, Social and Cultural Rights, Article 1.1). Even when applied in a well-meaning and consistent way, external pressures to change policy are rarely popular, even with those they are intended to benefit.

On the other hand, it is certainly true that people suffering from brutal poverty and severe malnourishment are unlikely to be able to exercise any rights at all unless their condition is attended to, and it may be true, as Pogge argues, that the transfers required to raise living standards to an acceptable level across the world are sufficiently modest that they would not raise the problems we have outlined. Still, most economic and social rights are best seen as collectively agreed-on aspirations rather than as rights as the term has conventionally been used.

Human Rights and Human Security During Conflict

Why the continued importance of national security over human rights and human security? For developing countries, state sovereignty and territorial integrity take precedence over security of the individual. Many countries in the developing world are artificial nation-states whose boundaries were drawn arbitrarily by the colonial powers in the nineteenth century without regard for the ethnic composition or historical linkages among peoples. State responses to ethnic separatist movements (now conflated with terrorism), which are partly rooted in people's rejection of colonial-imposed boundaries, have been accompanied by the most egregious violations of human security by governments. Moreover, many third world states, as well as China, remain under authoritarian rule. Human security is stymied by the lack of political space for alternatives to state ideologies and by restrictions on civil liberties imposed by authoritarian regimes to ensure their own survival.

In the developed as well as the developing world, one of the most powerful challenges to human rights and human security has come from the war on terror led by the United States in response to the 9/11 attacks. These attacks revived the traditional emphasis of states on national security (Suhrke 2004, 365). Although terrorists target innocent civilians and thus threaten human security, governments have used the war on terror to restrict and violate civil liberties. The US decision to put Saddam Hussein on trial in an Iraqi court rather than the International Criminal Court (ICC) illustrated the continued US defiance of a key policy instrument of human security, even though it focused on the more Western-oriented conception of "freedom from fear." The US questioning of the applicability of the Geneva Conventions, and the abandoning of its commitments on the issue of torture in the context of war in Iraq, further undermined the agenda of human security. So did Russia's flouting of a wide range of its international commitments—including the laws of war, Conference on Security and Co-operation in Europe (CSCE) and Organization for Security and Co-operation in Europe (OSCE) commitments, and international and regional conventions on torture—in the context of its war in Chechnya.

A pioneering report released by the Human Security Center at the University of British Columbia (2005) points to several significant trends in armed conflicts around the world (Figure 10.1). What explains the overall downward trend in armed conflicts? The report lists several factors: growing democratization (the underlying assumption here being that democracies tend to be better at peaceful resolution of conflicts); rising economic interdependence (which increases the costs of conflict); the declining economic utility of war, owing to the fact that resources can be more easily bought in the international marketplace than acquired through force; the growth in the number of international institutions that can mediate in conflicts; the impact of international norms against violence such as human sacrifice, witch burning, slavery, dueling, war crimes, and genocide; the end of colonialism; and the end of the Cold War. A specific reason identified by the report is the dramatic increase in the UN's role: its work in areas such as preventive diplomacy and peacemaking activities, its postconflict peacebuilding, the willingness of the UN Security Council to use military action to enforce peace agreements, the deterrent effects of war crime trials by the ICC and other tribunals, and the greater resort to reconciliation and addressing the root causes of conflict (see Chapter 6 for more on the ICC and UN peacekeeping operations). The 80 percent decline in the most deadly civil conflicts since the early 1990s, argued the report, is due to the dramatic growth of international efforts at preventive diplomacy, peacemaking, and peacebuilding (University of British Columbia 2005, pt. V).

Yet, the optimism created by the report did not last long. The more recent 2009–10 Human Security Report found a 25% increase in armed conflicts between 2003 to 2008. (See Figure 10.2) A large percentage of these conflicts—a quarter of those that started between 2004 and 2008—were related to "Islamist political violence." These increases were partly due to "minor conflicts" with few casualties. While the "war on terror" played an important part in the increasing number and the deadliness of conflicts, viewed from a longer-term perspective, the level of conflict in the Islamic world is lower than two

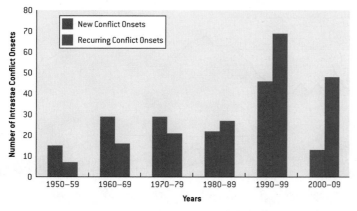

Figure 10.1 New versus Recurring Intrastate Conflicts, 1950–2009.

Source: UCDP/HSRP Dataset.

decades earlier. And in terms of casualty levels, the average annual battle-death toll per conflict was less than 1000 in the new millennium compared to the 1950s. Yet there remains the possibility of violence associated with the "Arab Spring" and its aftermath, which, although low for now, could escalate due to the ongoing strife in Syria and instability in transitional societies.

And there are some horrific costs associated with these conflicts. For example, deaths directly or indirectly attributed to the conflict in the Democratic Republic of the Congo since 1998 have surpassed casualties sustained by Britain in World Wars I and II combined. The conflict in Sudan's Darfur region displaced nearly 2 million people (UN Development Programme 2005, 12). In Iraq, a team of American and Iraqi epidemiologists estimated that Iraq's mortality rate more than doubled following the US invasion: from 5.5 deaths per 1,000 people in the year before the invasion to 13.3 deaths per 1,000 people per year in the postinvasion period. Violence continued even after the war officially ended in December 2011. As of April 2012, an estimated 116,184 Iraqi civilians had been killed since the US invasion in March 2003 (iraqbodycount.org).

The share of civilian casualties in armed conflict has increased since World War II. Civilians accounted for 10 percent of the victims during World War I and 50 percent of the victims during World War II. They constitute between 80 and 85 percent of the victims of more recent wars. Many of these victims are children, women, the sick, and the elderly (*Gendering Human Security* 2001, 18). Although death tolls from organized campaigns against civilians have declined in recent years, the number of such campaigns increased by 55 percent between 1989 and 2005 (University of British Columbia 2006, 3).

International terrorist incidents and related fatalities increased worldwide between 2002 and 2005. Most of the increases were associated with the war in Iraq, where the number of fatalities grew from about 1,700 in 2004 to approximately 3,400 in 2005 (National Counterterrorism Center 2005). Excluding Iraq, however, terrorist action killed fewer people worldwide in 2005—1,500 as opposed to 3,000 in 2004 (National Counterterrorism Center 2005).

Furthermore, some of the most serious issues of human security in armed conflicts still need to be overcome, such as child soldiers and landmines. According to one study,

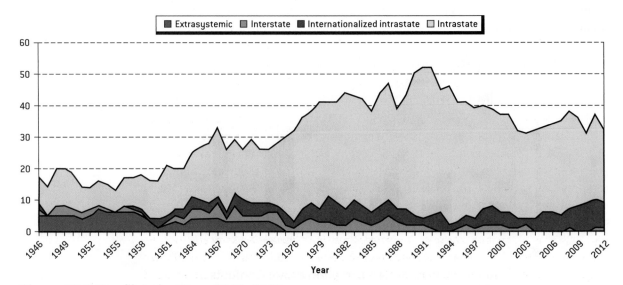

Figure 10.2 Conflicts by Type, 1946–2012.

Source: Journal for Peace Research http://jpr.sagepub.com/content/early/2013/06/28/0022343313494396.full.

75 percent of the armed conflicts today involve child soldiers (University of British Columbia 2005, 35). Landmines and unexploded ordnance cause between 15,000 and 20,000 new casualties each year (United States Campaign to Ban Landmines 2007). Despite the justified optimism generated by the Ottawa Treaty (discussed later), there remain 80 million live mines undetected—someone steps on a landmine every twenty-eight minutes—and 80 percent of those killed or injured by landmines are civilians (Koehler 2007).

WHAT'S YOUR WORLDVIEW

Genocide continues and states have often not responded despite the fact that many states have signed international agreements requiring it. Why do you think states have failed to act effectively?

Finally, the decline in armed conflicts around the world is not necessarily irreversible. Some of the factors contributing to the decline of conflicts, such as democratization and the peace-operations role of the United Nations, can suffer setbacks due to lack of support from major powers and the international community. And there remain serious possible threats to international peace and security that can cause widespread casualties, such as a conflict in the Korean Peninsula and war between China and Taiwan.

Battle deaths are not themselves an adequate indicator of threats to human security posed by armed conflict. Many armed conflicts have indirect consequences on human life and well-being. Wars are a major source of economic disruption, disease, and ecological destruction, which in turn undermine human development and thus create a vicious cycle of conflict and underdevelopment. As the *Human Development Report* (UN Development Programme 2005, 12) puts it: "Conflict undermines nutrition and public health, destroys education systems, devastates livelihoods and retards prospects for economic growth." It found that of the fifty-two countries that are reversing or stagnating in their attempts to reduce child mortality, thirty have experienced conflict since 1990. A British government white paper on international development notes:

> Violent conflict reverses economic growth, causes hunger, destroys roads, schools and clinics, and forces people to flee across borders. Women and girls are particularly vulnerable because they suffer sexual violence and exploitation. And violent conflict and insecurity can spill over into neighboring countries and provide cover for terrorists or organized criminal groups. (Department for International Development 2006, 45)

Wars also damage the environment, as happened with the US use of Agent Orange defoliant during the Vietnam War and Saddam Hussein's burning of Kuwaiti oil wells in the 1990–1991 Gulf War, leading to massive air and land pollution. Similar links can be made between conflict and the outbreak of disease: "[W]ar-exacerbated disease and malnutrition kill far more people than missiles, bombs and bullets" (University of British Columbia 2005, 7). Disease accounts for a significant percentage of the 5.4 million people who have died in the conflict in the Democratic Republic of the Congo (UN Development Programme 2005, 45).

Just as wars and violent conflict have indirect consequences such as economic disruption, ecological damage, and disease (see Table 10.3), levels of poverty and environmental degradation contribute to conflict and hence must be taken into consideration in human security research (as we will discuss in Chapters 13 and 14). One study shows that a country at $250 GDP per capita has an average 15 percent risk of experiencing a civil war in the next five years, while at a GDP per capita of $5,000, the risk of civil war is less than 1 percent (Humphreys and Varshney 2004, 9; Department for International Development 2005, 8). Although no direct link can be established between poverty and terrorism, terrorists often "exploit poverty and exclusion in order to tap into popular discontent—taking advantage of fragile states such as Somalia, or undemocratic regimes such as in Afghanistan in the 1990s, to plan violence" (UN Development Programme 2005, 47).

Table 10.3
Trends in Disease

Those who take a broad definition of human security look at threats to the survival and safety of the individual not only from violent conflict but also from such nonviolent factors as disease, environmental degradation, and natural disasters. Following are some of the key trends in disease.

- The world has seen the appearance of at least thirty new infectious diseases, including avian flu, HIV/AIDS, severe acute respiratory syndrome, hepatitis C, and West Nile virus, in the past three decades. Twenty diseases previously detected have reemerged with new drug-resistant strains. (Rice 2006, 79)
- AIDS is the leading cause of death in Africa and the fourth leading cause of death worldwide. Around 40 million people worldwide are infected with HIV, 95 percent of whom live in developing countries. In 2004, approximately 5 million people were newly infected with the virus. HIV/AIDS killed more than 20 million people worldwide, and 3.1 million people died of AIDS-related causes in 2004. It is estimated that per capita growth in half of the countries in sub-Saharan Africa is falling by 0.5–1.2 percent each year as a direct result of AIDS. By 2010, per capita GDP in some of the hardest-hit countries may drop by 8 percent, and per capita consumption may fall even farther. (The Global Fund to Fight AIDS, Tuberculosis and Malaria, http://www.theglobalfund.org/en/hivaids/)
- Malaria causes about 350–500 million infections in humans and approximately 1–3 million deaths annually (Breman 2001, 1–11); this would translate to about one death every thirty seconds (Greenwood et al. 2005, 1487–1498). The majority, which amounts to 85–90 percent of malaria fatalities, occur in sub-Saharan Africa. The economic impact of malaria has been estimated to cost Africa $12 billion every year. (World Health Organization n.d.)
- Annually, 8 million people become ill with tuberculosis, and 2 million people die from the disease worldwide (Centers for Disease Control 2005). Presently, tuberculosis is the world's greatest infectious killer of women of reproductive age and the leading cause of death among people with HIV/AIDS. (PR Newswire Europe 2002)
- The outbreaks of highly pathogenic H5N1 avian influenza that began in Southeast Asia in mid-2003 and have now spread to parts of Europe are the largest most severest on record. To date, nine Asian countries have reported outbreaks (listed in order of reporting): the Republic of Korea, Vietnam, Japan, Thailand, Cambodia, the Lao People's Democratic Republic, Indonesia, China, and Malaysia. (World Health Organization 2006)

Access to Resources

One component of human security that connects our broader discussions is access to resources. Environmental degradation, which is often linked to poverty, is a common source of conflict (Homer-Dixon 1991, 1994). Analysts have identified competition for scarce resources such as water and arable land as a source of possible conflict between Israel and its Arab neighbors, between India and Pakistan, between Turkey and Syria, and even between countries that share the use of an important waterway, like Egypt and Ethiopia (Rice 2006, 78).

The world's poorer countries, where families often see the need for more children to compensate for a high infant mortality rate and to raise their income potential, account for a significant proportion of the growth in the world's population, which doubled between 1950 and 1998 (Rice 2006, 80). Population growth in turn contributes to resource scarcity and environmental stress, often resulting in conflict. For example, South Asia, one of the poorest and most heavily populated regions of the globe, faces intensified competition and the possibility of conflict over scarce water resources. Specific examples include the

Indo-Pakistan dispute over the Wular Barrage, the Indo-Bangladesh water dispute over the Farakka Barrage, and the Indo-Nepal dispute over the Mahakali River Treaty (Power and Interest News Report 2006).

The potential for political upheaval or war as a consequence of environmental problems is evident in a host of poor regions around the world, including North Africa, the sub-Saharan Sahel region of Africa (including Ethiopia, Sudan, Somalia, Mali, Niger, and Chad), the island nations of the western Pacific Ocean, the Ganges River Basin (principally northeastern India and Bangladesh), and some parts of Central and South America (Petzold-Bradley, Carius, and Vincze 2001). Darfur illustrates the linkages among poverty, environmental degradation, and conflict. Traditional intercommunal conflict in Darfur over scarcity of resources and land deteriorated as a result of desertification and a shortage of rainfall. In the 1970s and 1980s, droughts in northern parts of Darfur sent its nomadic population southward in search of water and herding grounds, bringing it into conflict with the local tribes (Environmental Degradation and Conflict in Darfur 2004).

Natural disasters can also affect the course of conflicts by either exacerbating or mitigating them. The December 2004 Indian Ocean tsunami changed the course of two separatist conflicts: Aceh in Indonesia and Tamil separatism in Sri Lanka. In Aceh, where the government announced a cease-fire to permit relief work, prospects for reconciliation improved. In contrast, the conflict in Sri Lanka, where relief supplies did not reach rebel-held territory, saw an escalation of violence.

Women, Conflict, and Human Security

The relationship between gender and human security has multiple dimensions. The UN Inter-Agency Committee on Women and Gender Equality notes five aspects: (1) violence against women and girls; (2) gender inequalities in control over resources; (3) gender inequalities in power and decision making; (4) women's human rights; and (5) women (and men) as actors, not victims (UN Inter-Agency Committee on Women and Gender Equality 1999, 1). Recent conflicts have shown women as victims of rape, torture, and sexual slavery. For example, between 250,000 and 500,000 women were raped during the 1994 genocide in Rwanda. Such atrocities against women are now recognized as a crime against humanity (Rehn and Sirleaf 2002, 9).

War-affected areas often see a sharp increase in domestic violence directed at women and a growth in the number of women trafficked to become forced laborers or sex workers. Women and children comprise 73 percent of an average population but account for 80 percent of the refugees in the world today and perhaps a larger percentage as internally displaced persons. Another important aspect of the gender dimension of human security is the role of women as actors in conflicts. This involves considering the participation of women in combat. In the Eritrean war of independence, women made up 25 to 30 percent of combatants. A similar proportion of women were fighting with the Tamil Tigers. Women play an even larger role in support functions, such as logistics, staff, and intelligence services, in a conflict. It has been noted that women become targets of rape and sexual violence because they serve as a social and cultural symbol. Hence, violence against them may be undertaken as a deliberate strategy to undermine the social fabric of an opponent. Similarly, securing women's participation in combat may be motivated by a desire, among the parties to a conflict, to increase the legitimacy of their cause. It signifies "a broad social consensus and solidarity, both to their own population and to the outside world" (*Gendering Human Security* 2001, 18).

THEORY IN PRACTICE

Gendered Perspective on Human Rights

THE CHALLENGE

Before the emergence of a global feminist movement, it was conventional for human rights treaties to be cast in language that assumes that the rights bearer is a man and the head of a household. Many feminists argue that this convention reflects more than an old-fashioned turn of phrase. The classic political and civil rights (freedom of speech, association, from arbitrary arrest, etc.) assume that the rights bearer will be living, or would wish to live, a life of active citizenship, but until very recently, such a life was denied to nearly all women in nearly all cultures. Instead of this public life, women were limited to the private sphere and subjected to the arbitrary and capricious power of the male head of the household. It is only very recently in the Western liberal democracies that women have been able to vote, to stand for office, or to own property in their

A global press and the Internet have made local and national decisions the concern of communities across the globe. Indonesian Muslim students protest the French decision to ban Muslim headscarves and other religious clothing in public schools.

own name, and issues such as the criminalization of rape in marriage and the effective prevention of domestic violence against women are still controversial. The situation is even worse in some non-Western polities. It may be that a genuinely gender-neutral account of human rights is possible, but some radical feminists argue that an altogether different kind of thinking is required (see Mackinnon 1993).

OPTIONS

Both cultural critics and feminists argue, convincingly, that the model of a rights bearer inherent in the contemporary international human rights regime is based on the experiences of Western men. Agreement collapses, however, when the implications of this common position are explored. Liberal feminists wish to see the rights of men extended to women, whereas radical feminists wish to promote a new model of what it is to be human that privileges neither men nor women. Most cultural critics, on the other hand, wish to preserve inherited status and power differences based on gender.

APPLICATION

The contradictions here are sharpest when it comes to relations between the world of Islam and the human rights regime, largely because relations between Islam and the West are so fraught on other grounds that all differences are magnified. Radical or traditional Islamists argue for conventional gender roles, support quite severe restrictions on the freedom of women, and promote the compulsory wearing of restrictive clothing such as the niqab or the burqa. Many of these petty restrictions have no basis in the Koran or the sayings of the prophet and can simply be understood as methods of preserving male dominance—although

it should be said that they are often accepted by Muslim women as ways of asserting their identity. More serious for the human rights regime are those verses of the Koran that unambiguously deny gender equality. It is often, and truly, said that the Koran's attitude toward the status of women was in advance of much contemporary seventh-century thought—including Christian and Jewish thought of the age—but it remains the case that, for example, in a sharia court, the evidence of a woman is worth less than that of a man, and sexual intercourse outside marriage is punishable for a woman even in the case of rape. The other Abrahamic religions continue to preserve misogynist vestiges, but mainstream Christian and Jewish theologians have reinterpreted those aspects of their traditions that radically disadvantage women. Given the importance attached to the literal text of the Koran, this reinterpretation will prove more difficult for Muslims, though many Islamic thinkers discuss women's rights. The role of women under Islam will be a continuing problem for the international human rights regime as it attempts to divest itself of its Western Judeo-Christian heritage and adopt a more inclusive framework. It will, of course, be an even bigger problem for women who live in oppressive Muslim regimes.

For Discussion

1. Should local cultural standards outweigh externally derived norms?
2. The rights of women all over the world, including in many OECD countries, are at risk. To what extent is the focus on women in Islamic societies justified?
3. Are certain human rights not universal?

In recent years, there has been a growing awareness of the need to secure the greater participation of women in international peace operations. The UN Department of Peacekeeping Operations noted in a 2000 report:

> Women's presence [in peacekeeping missions] improves access and support for local women; it makes male peacekeepers more reflective and responsible; and it broadens the repertoire of skills and styles available within the mission, often with the effect of reducing conflict and confrontation. Gender mainstreaming is not just fair, it is beneficial. (cited in Rehn and Sirleaf 2002, 63)

In 2000, the United Nations passed Security Council Resolution 1325 mandating a review of the impact of armed conflict on women and the role of women in peace operations and conflict resolution. The review was released in 2002 and entitled *Women, Peace and Security* (United Nations 2002). In his introduction to the report, UN secretary-general Kofi Annan noted that "women still form a minority of those who participate in peace and security negotiations, and receive less attention than men in post-conflict agreements, disarmament and reconstruction" (United Nations 2002, ix). There is still a long way to go before the international community can fully realize the benefits of greater participation by women in UN peace operations and conflict-resolution activities.

Globalization has made it more difficult for leaders of countries to assert that national cultural norms are more important than global standards of behavior. Transnational corporations, the globalized entertainment industry, and the United Nations itself all penetrate national borders and erode traditional values. As we will see in the next section, the international community of countries is actively involved in this process.

The Role of the International Community

Because of the broad and contested nature of the idea of human security, it is difficult to evaluate policies undertaken by the international community that can be specifically regarded as human security measures. But the most important multilateral actions include the ICC, the Antipersonnel Landmines Treaty, and the 2005 Responsibility to Protect document adopted by the United Nations, which (as discussed in Chapter 6) asserted the moral obligations for states to intervene against human rights violations in other states.

The ICC was established on July 1, 2002, with its headquarters in The Hague, Netherlands, although its proceedings may take place anywhere. It is a permanent institution with "the power to exercise its jurisdiction over persons for the most serious crimes of international concern" (Rome Statute, Article 1). These crimes include genocide, crimes against humanity, war crimes, and the crime of aggression, although the court would not exercise its jurisdiction over the crime of aggression until such time as the state parties agree on a definition of the crime and set out the conditions under which it may be prosecuted. The ICC is a "court of last resort." It is "complementary to national criminal jurisdictions," meaning that it can only exercise its jurisdiction when national courts are unwilling or unable to investigate or prosecute such crimes (Rome Statute, Article 1). The court can only prosecute crimes that were committed on or after July 1, 2002, the date its founding treaty entered into force. Since its establishment, the ICC has opened investigations in seven cases in African countries, including five warrants against Joseph Kony and four others in the Lord's Resistance Army in Uganda, as well

The United Nations High Commissioner for Refugees special envoy, Angelina Jolie, speaks to refugees from the Syrian civil war at a military camp in Jordan. This UN agency reported in 2013 that most of the refugees in the world had fled from five war-affected countries: Afghanistan, Somalia, Iraq, Syria, and Sudan.

as situations in the Democratic Republic of the Congo, Darfur, the Central African Republic, Kenya, and Libya. In March 2012, it issued its first conviction against Thomas Lubanga from the Democratic Republic of the Congo. The ICC has indicted twenty-eight people and is conducting legal proceedings against twenty-three.

The Convention on the Prohibition of the Use, Stockpiling, Production, and Transfer of Anti-Personnel Mines and on Their Destruction, signed in Ottawa on December 3–4, 1997, bans the development, production, acquisition, stockpiling, transfer, and use of antipersonnel mines (Ottawa Treaty, Article 1, General Obligations, 1997). It also obliges signatories to destroy existing stockpiles. Among the countries that have yet to sign the treaty are the People's Republic of China, the Russian Federation, and the United States.

The surge in UN peacekeeping and peacebuilding operations has contributed to the decline in conflict and enhanced prospects for human security. The number of UN peacekeeping operations increased threefold between the first forty years of the UN's founding and the twenty years since—from thirteen to forty-seven missions (UN Peacekeeping website, n.d.). More recently, a UN Peacebuilding Commission was inaugurated in 2006. Its goal is to assist in postconflict recovery and reconstruction, including institution building and sustainable development, in countries emerging from conflict. The United Nations has also been center stage in promoting the idea of humanitarian intervention, a central policy element of human security. The concept of humanitarian intervention was endorsed by the report of the UN Secretary-General's High-Level Panel on Threats, Challenges and Change, *A More Secure World* (2004, 66, 106), the subsequent report by the secretary-general entitled *In Larger Freedom* (United Nations 2005), and finally, by the UN Summit in September 2005.

United Nations specialized agencies play a crucial role in promoting human security. For example, the UN Development Programme and the World Health Organization (WHO) have been at the forefront of fighting poverty and disease, respectively. Other UN agencies, such as the UN High Commissioner for Refugees (UNHCR), UN Children's Fund (UNICEF), and UN Development Fund for Women (UNIFEM), have played a central role in getting particular issues, such as refugees and the rights of children and women, onto the agenda for discussion and in providing a platform for advocacy and action (MacFarlane and Khong 2006).

Nongovernmental organizations (NGOs) contribute to human security in a number of ways: giving information and early warning about conflicts, providing a channel for relief operations (often being the first to do so in areas of conflict or natural disaster), and supporting government- or UN-sponsored peacebuilding and rehabilitation missions. Nongovernmental organizations also play a central role in promoting sustainable development. A leading NGO with a human security mission is the International Committee of the Red Cross (ICRC). Established in Geneva, it has a unique authority based on the international humanitarian law of the Geneva Conventions to protect the lives and dignity of victims of war and internal violence, including the war wounded, prisoners, refugees, civilians, and other noncombatants, and to provide them with assistance. Other NGOs include Médicins Sans Frontières (Doctors Without Borders; emergency medical assistance), Save the Children (protection of children), and Amnesty International (human rights).

At times, these agencies overlap in the services they provide or the issue for which they advocate. As you will see, this tends to be the case in international relations. However, given the complex nature of international human rights law and the demands of providing for human security, each organization can play a part in helping advance the international agenda.

At the UN Millennium Assembly in 2000, Canadian prime minister Jean Chretien announced that Canada would sponsor an International Commission on Intervention and State Sovereignty (ICISS). The government invited Gareth Evans, a former Australian foreign minister and current head of the International Crisis Group, and Mohamed Sahnoun, a former Algerian diplomat and an experienced UN adviser, to serve as cochairs.

In September 2000, the commission was charged by Foreign Minister Axworthy to find "new ways of reconciling seemingly irreconcilable notions of intervention and state sovereignty" (ICISS 2001, 81). This was a very careful review of the right of humanitarian intervention. The key question the commission explored is whether it is appropriate for states to take coercive military action in another state for the purposes of protecting citizens at risk in that other state.

Many human rights groups supported the 2011 NATO intervention that provided air support and safe skies for opposition rebels in Libya. Bombing raids by NATO were aimed at protecting civilians from Muammar Qaddafi's forces.

The *basic principles* (ICISS 2001, xi) of the report fit nicely with many of the universal goals of religious NGOs.

Basic Principles

A. State sovereignty implies responsibility, and the primary responsibility for the protection of its people lies within the state itself.

B. Where a population is suffering serious harm, as a result of internal war, insurgency, repression or state failure, and the state in question is unwilling or unable to halt or avert it, the principle of nonintervention yields to the international Responsibility to Protect. Elements, or specific responsibilities:

1. **The Responsibility to Prevent**: This means addressing the causes of conflict and other crises that put populations at risk.

2. **The Responsibility to React**: Refers to the necessity to respond to situations that put individuals at risk with appropriate measures, which might include various forms of intervention.

3. **The Responsibility to Rebuild**: After a natural disaster or military intervention, the international community must provide assistance for recovery and reconstruction. In addition, the international community should assist with reconciliation efforts aimed at addressing the causes of conflict and violence.

4. **The Responsibility to Protect (R2P)**: Documents and resulting strategies all emphasize the importance of prevention. Clearly stated, that means addressing fundamental *human security* issues: freedom from fear, freedom from want, and the need for the rule of law to provide for a just and peaceful society.

The 2011 situation in Libya presented the most recent test of the R2P principle. In March 2011, the UN Security Council authorized an intervention to protect the citizens of Libya from attacks by pro-Qaddafi forces. World leaders maybe sought to avoid another 1995 Srebrenica massacre, and once again, NATO used its superior air power and surveillance resources to protect citizens, prevent more conflict, and rebuild Libya as a democratic state.

Conclusion

For more than sixty years, leaders and citizens of countries have worked to develop the paired concepts of human rights and human security. Although governments around the world—including some in Europe and North America, the intellectual homelands of the concepts—from time to time violate the very freedoms they once endorsed, when they ratified the various human rights treaties, it is understood that these are transgressions of longstanding norms of behavior. Certainly, more can be done to promote freedom from fear and freedom from want. The *Human Development Report* of 2005 estimates that the rich nations of the world provide $10 to the military budget for every $1 they spend on aid. For example, the current global spending on HIV/AIDS, "a disease that claims 3 million lives a year, represents three days' worth of military spending" (UN Development Programme 2011, 8).

Perhaps the greatest challenge today in the issue area of human rights and human security is the need to change the ways government officials and citizens see the role of the state. Does it exist solely to defend the country along the lines suggested in the Westphalian model of an independent and sovereign state? Or do we have an obligation as humans to help other humans in need? Until this is resolved, debates about human rights and human security will continue.

WHAT'S YOUR WORLDVIEW ?

The recent intervention in Libya by NATO forces raises questions about who will or should act to protect citizens. Do you think the United Nations should have its own independent military force for humanitarian intervention, peacemaking and even state building? Is this the only way to ensure that something is done about these crimes against humanity?

CONTRIBUTORS TO CHAPTER 10: Amitav Acharya, Alex J. Bellamy, Chris Brown, Nicholas J. Wheeler, and Steven L. Lamy.

REVIEW QUESTIONS

1. What is the relationship between rights and duties?
2. Why is the promotion of human rights so rarely seen as an appropriate foreign policy goal of states?
3. What are the problems involved in assigning rights to peoples as opposed to individuals?
4. In what ways can gender bias be identified in the modern human rights regime?
5. What is the relationship between democracy and human rights? Is it always the case that democracies are more likely to respect human rights than authoritarian regimes?
6. Can the compromising of human rights in the face of the threat of terrorism ever be justified as the lesser of two evils?
7. What is human security? How is it different from the concept of national security?
8. Describe the main difference between the two conceptions of human security: freedom from fear and freedom from want. Are the two understandings irreconcilable?
9. How do you link poverty and health with human security?
10. What are the main areas of progress in the promotion of human security by the international community?
11. What are the obstacles to human security promotion by the international community?
12. Why do we need to give special consideration to the suffering of women in conflict zones?

FURTHER READING

Brownlie, I., and Goodwin-Gill, G. (eds.) (2006), *Basic Instruments on Human Rights*, 5th rev. ed. (Oxford: Clarendon Press). Contains the texts of all the most important treaties and declarations.

Finnis, J. (1980), *Natural Law and Natural Rights* (Oxford: Clarendon Press). The best introduction to modern natural law thinking.

Freeman, M. (2002), *Human Rights: A Multidisciplinary Approach* (Cambridge: Polity Press). Discusses the philosophical problems posed by the idea of rights.

Jones, P. (1994), *Rights* (Basingstoke: Macmillan). This book also discusses the philosophical problems posed by the idea of rights.

Norchi, C. (2004), "Human Rights: A Global Common Interest," in J. Krasno (ed.), *The United Nations. Confronting the Challenges of a Global Society* (Boulder, Col.: Lynne Rienner). An excellent review of all the major challenges faced by the United Nations and other institutions of global governance.

Steiner, H. J., and Alston, P. (2000), *International Human Rights in Context: Law, Politics, Morals: Texts and Materials*, 2nd ed. (Oxford: Clarendon Press). Contains abbreviated texts and a great deal of useful commentary in its 1,500+ pages! It is the single most useful book for the study of international human rights. A third edition was issued in 2007.

International human rights:

Donnelly, J. (2002), *Universal Human Rights in Theory and Practice*, 2nd ed. (Ithaca, N.Y.: Cornell University Press). Another valuable introduction to international human rights.

Smith, K. E., and Light, M. (eds.) (2001), *Ethics and Foreign Policy* (Cambridge: Cambridge University Press). Examines the problems involved in making human rights central to foreign policy.

Second-generation rights:

Pogge, T. (2002), *World Poverty and Human Rights: Cosmopolitan Responsibilities and Reforms* (Cambridge: Polity Press). The most important and influential modern statement in this area.

Shue, H. (1996), *Basic Rights: Subsistence, Affluence and US Foreign Policy*, 2nd rev. ed. (Princeton, N.J.: Princeton University Press). A very influential defense of second-generation rights as genuine rights.

Third-generation rights:

Bauer, J., and Bell, D. A. (eds.) (1999), *The East Asian Challenge for Human Rights* (Cambridge: Cambridge University Press). The best collection of writings on the Asian value debate, covering a wide range of perspectives.

Sen, A. (1999), *Development as Freedom* (Oxford: Oxford University Press). Persuasively disposes of the argument that development requires the curtailment of human rights.

Academic disagreements about human rights:

Huntington, S. (1996), *The Clash of Civilizations and the Remaking of World Order* (New York: Simon & Schuster). A key contribution, much criticized by academics, but which has entered the public consciousness, especially since 9/11.

Peters, J. S., and Wolper, A. (eds.) (1995), *Women's Rights, Human Rights: International Feminist Perspectives* (New York: Routledge). A good collection of feminist views.

Walzer, M. (1994), *Thick and Thin: Moral Argument at Home and Abroad* (Notre Dame, Ind.: University of Notre Dame Press). Argues for a "thin" cross-cultural moral code.

Human rights, the war on terror, and the "torture debate":

Greenberg, K. (ed.) (2006), *The Torture Debate in America* (New York: Cambridge University Press). A collection of essays, mostly by lawyers, focusing on Guantánamo and Abu Graib, as opposed to the more philosophically oriented papers collected in Levinson (ed.) (2004).

Ignatieff, M. (2005), *The Lesser Evil: Political Ethics in an Age of Terror* (Princeton, N.J.: Princeton University Press) and

Ignatieff, M. (2005), *American Exceptionalism and Human Rights* (Princeton, N.J.: Princeton University Press). Both texts offer a more nuanced approach to the problem of the appropriate means to combat terrorism.

Levinson, A. (ed.) (2004), *Torture: A Collection* (New York: Oxford University Press). Contains essays by Michael Walzer, Jean Bethke Elshtain, and Alan Dershowitz.

The most useful journals in the field are *Human Rights Quarterly: A Comparative and International Journal of the Social Sciences, Philosophy and Law* (Baltimore, Md.: Johns Hopkins University Press), *Ethics and International Affairs* (New York: Carnegie Institute), and *The International Journal of Human Rights* (London: Frank Cass).

Human security:

Acharya, A. (2001), "Human Security: East Versus West," *International Journal* 56(3): 442–460. Examines the debate between two conceptions of human security, "freedom from fear" and "freedom from want," with particular reference to Asia.

Commission on Human Security (2003), *Human Security Now: Protecting and Empowering People* (New York: United Nations).

Gough, I. (2004), *Insecurity and Welfare Regimes in Asia, Africa and Latin America: Social Policy in Development Contexts* (Cambridge: Cambridge University Press). A comparative study of social and economic welfare approaches to addressing human security challenges in the developing world.

Haq, M. (1995), *Reflections on Human Development* (Oxford: Oxford University Press). The book by the late Pakistani development economist, who played a pioneering role in the *Human Development Report*, outlines his thinking on human development and human security.

Human Security Report Project (2011), *Human Security Report 2009/2010* (New York: Oxford University Press). The latest study of the causes of peace and the costs of war from the Canadian human security project.

United Nations Development Programme (1995), *Human Development Report 1994* (Oxford: Oxford University Press). The original source of the idea of human security.

INTERNET RESOURCES

Amnesty International
www.amnesty.org
A leading NGO working to protect human rights around the world.

Center for World Indigenous Rights
http://cwis.org/
The political and economic rights of indigenous peoples have gained prominence recently. This is an excellent source of information on this topic.

European Human Rights Centre
http://www.ehrcweb.org/
A clearinghouse for information on human rights.

Genocide Intervention Network
http://www.genocideintervention.net
With student chapters in over 1,000 secondary schools and colleges, this organization seeks to educate citizens about genocide and mass atrocities and hold leaders accountable for their commitments to prevent further violence.

Global Centre for the Responsibility to Protect
http://globalr2p.org
Created in 2007, this organization publishes materials and sponsors program to promote the R2P agreement that was approved at the World Summit in 2005.

Human Rights Watch
www.hrw.org
A US-based NGO that exposes human rights abuses.

International Coalition for the Responsibility to Protect
http://www.responsibilitytoprotect.org/
This is an organization of NGOs from around the world that seek to enhance our understanding of the normative dimensions of R2P and to strengthen the capacity of citizens and states to respond to genocide, ethnic cleansing, and other crimes against humanity.

UN Development Programme
www.undp.org
The primary development organization within the United Nations now focused on the Millennium Development goals.

UN Office of the High Commissioner for Human Rights
http://www.ohchr.org
With offices in New York and Geneva and with over 200 human rights officers around the world, the commissioner is the principal human rights official of the United Nations. This office works with the Human Rights Council and with other UN offices involved in human rights and human security issues.

Carnegie Council: "EIA Interview: Michael Doyle on Nonintervention and the Responsibility to Protect"—Michael W. Doyle
http://www.carnegiecouncil.org/resources/video/data/000303
Michael Doyle discusses where the line is drawn between rhetoric and action. Using Darfur as an example, he applies and analyzes the concept of responsibility to protect.

Carnegie Council: "A Conversation with David A. Hamburg: The Commitment to Prevention"—David A. Hamburg and David C. Speedie
http://www.carnegiecouncil.org/resources/video/data/000224
David Hamburg clearly presents the idea that responsibility to protect need not be approached if the proper steps are taken to prevent genocide.

Carnegie Council: "EIA Interview: Alex Bellamy on the Responsibility to Protect"—Alex J. Bellamy and John Tessitore
http://www.carnegiecouncil.org/resources/video/data/000219
According to Alex Bellamy, the concept of responsibility to protect is increasingly moving toward becoming a social norm, and in the absence of government action, civil society will heed the R2P call.

TED Talk: Zainab Salbi: "Women, Wartime and the Dream of Peace"
http://www.ted.com/talks/lang/eng/zainab_salbi.html
Zainab Salbi discusses the "silence of humanity" in war and brings in her own experiences from living in war-torn Iraq. Salbi is bothered by women's role as victims during war and in the negotiating process thereafter.

For more information, quizzes, case studies and other study tools, please visit us at **www.oup.com/us/lamy**

What Should Be Done? National Interests Versus Human Interests

BACKGROUND

Takastand is a new nation-state that once was part of a large authoritarian empire. It is resource rich and is located in a strategic region that is important to many of the major powers, including China, India, Russia, and the United States. It is a multiethnic state with five major ethnocultural communities. Although it professes to be a democratic state, one political party controls the government. This political party also represents the dominant ethnic community, and it openly discriminates against the other ethnic communities. The police and the military have led secret raids against ethnic minorities, and international human rights organizations have found mass graves. The Takastand government denies any connections to the human rights abuses and blames international criminal networks or fundamentalist religious groups that are attempting to overthrow the government. The government also believes that stability is more important than rights at this stage of the country's development. Furthermore, the government's claim that it is being attacked by fundamentalist Islamic forces backed by Al Qaeda has led to significant security assistance from the US government and its NATO partners.

Most of the opposition groups claim that they stand for individual rights and freedoms and democracy, and they all claim that they will implement a true democracy that protects the rights and freedoms of all citizens. They also claim that they will end the country's dependency on the West and that they will challenge the hegemony of the United States and its allies.

Although this is a very poor country, it has significant energy reserves, but most of the profits end up in the hands of the political and military elites. Close to 85 percent of the wealth is controlled by 13 percent of the population. A number of European governments and NGOs have established effective development programs focusing on the UN's Millennium Development Goals. More women and children in rural areas are now receiving healthcare, food, and education. The government representatives in these regions control the programs and usually demand payments to allow them to continue. Recently, they have arrested NGO workers and local activists who challenged their authority. Four NGO project leaders were arrested, prosecuted before a military court, and sentenced to death.

ASSIGNMENT

This action has prompted an international conference to address the human security problems and the repression in Takastand. The conference is modeled after similar conferences held to decide how to help Rwanda, Iraq, and Afghanistan. Your assignment is to describe how the world should respond. Take a look at other international-assistance conferences and use those models for your work. Is this a military, political, economic, or human rights issue? Then follow these three steps in planning your conference. This can be a group activity.

Step One

What issues should the conference address? Consider economic, political, military, and human rights and security issues.

Step Two

Consider who should be involved. Should this be an action of the United Nations, or should the great powers take care of this crisis? What role should NGOs play in this human security crisis?

Step Three

Answer these questions:

- Is stability in this region more important than human rights? Why or why not?
- Is it more important to provide access to economic opportunities or to provide cultural and political freedoms? Why?
- Should citizens of some countries be forced to give up rights and freedoms so that others may have access to material goods and resources that help them enjoy the good life? Why?

PART FIVE

Global Issues: Political Economy and the Environment

While Part Four looked at questions of war, security, and violence, this final part looks at primarily economic and environmental issues with global impacts. Economic questions are at the core of the debates about globalization; how states and other actors address these questions will determine how millions of people around the world will live. Often neglected, the condition of the environment may determine how and where we live in the near future. This part looks at the crucial issues of trade, finance, poverty, hunger, and environmental challenges such as climate change. First, in Chapter 11, we will discuss *international political economy* and examine the evolving relationship of states to corporations as the latter have internationalized their production sourcing and methods. In Chapter 12, we will see how new *trade tactics and financial instruments* have fueled this process of globalized production. Chapter 13 looks at people who have missed the benefits of economic globalization, as we investigate *poverty, hunger, and economic development*. Chapter 14, on *global environmental problems*, pulls all the other topics together. As you will see, every global issue you have studied has environmental impacts. Unless the world's leaders successfully address all the other issues, we might no longer have clean air to breathe and clean water to drink. Some contributors to this text see opportunities for greater cooperation because of globalization, but others see dangers of increased levels of conflict at the beginning of the twenty-first century. However, all of the contributors agree on one point: by the end of this book, you should have your own well-informed position with regard to this debate.

Over 20,000 Ukrainian activists are protesting in Independence Square in Kiev, Ukraine, in December 2013. They oppose the government's decision to reject a deal to associate with the European Union in favor of a closer cooperation with Russia. After the Russian annexation of Crimea the future integrity and sovereignty of Ukraine is at stake.

11 | International Political Economy

The ideas of economists and political philosophers, both when they are right and when they are wrong, are more powerful than is commonly understood. Indeed, the world is ruled by little else.

—*John Maynard Keynes*

The market itself is a source of power that influences political outcomes. Economic dependence establishes a power relationship that is a fundamental feature of the contemporary world economy.

—*Robert Gilpin*

The notion of a free market unfettered by any sort of government intervention is a chimera. Governments often determine the direction the economy may take. The government of Ukraine abandoned over five years of negotiations with the European Union and decided to move closer to Russia. This was more than an economic choice. It was an existential choice between a post-Soviet system that is corrupt and dysfunctional and a European Union that is built on the rule of law and a respect for both markets and individuals. Note how the leaders of the liberal global economy responded to the recent economic crisis.

As the global economic crisis gained speed in October 2008, the government of Iceland shut down the stock market and seized control of the last major independent bank in the country. Long a member of the Western European financial system yet unable to find credit in the usual markets, the Icelandic government was forced to turn to Russia for a bridge loan to keep itself afloat. By early 2009, the country was bankrupt, and the government leaders resigned in disgrace. Iceland was the most prominent example of the potential downside of globalization. The country supported the free flow of goods, services, and investments. Its lack of regulation led the country's banks to participate in a ten-year debt-fueled binge. Banks expanded aggressively, and citizens borrowed and bought. When the value of their currency fell, they could not pay their debts. Iceland is a member of the Organisation of Economic Co-operation and Development (OECD), the organization of the world's most advanced economies. Yet the government had to turn

Iceland's currency (the króna), shown here, took a pounding in the economic downturn of 2009–2010. In 2012, as the global economic crisis continued, Greece and Italy faced similar challenges to their fi scal and monetary stability, potentially affecting the entire eurozone.

to the International Monetary Fund (IMF) for support to restore fiscal and monetary stability, a tactic that many developing countries resort to in time of emergency. Iceland was not alone; by the end of 2009, Georgia, Ukraine, Hungary, the Seychelles, Pakistan, Latvia, and Belarus had all taken loans from the IMF.

In 2011 and continuing into 2012, both Greece and Italy faced similar economic problems. Journalists called Greece the epicenter of European financial disarray. The governments of both Greece and Italy failed, and leadership changed hands as each government was forced to enact severe austerity measures—challenging the assumption in most social democratic states that citizens' rights include healthcare, education, and pensions. Unfortunately, both Greece and Italy continued to provide extensive programs and failed to collect taxes and support revenue-producing activities that would pay for these programs. The global financial crisis that began in 2008 continued. France and Germany stepped up to design ways to protect the eurozone and to bail out Greece and prevent Italy from a similar fate. They began to discuss ways of creating a real economic government over the seventeen countries that use the euro as their primary currency.

The financial crisis was the result of serious shortcomings in domestic financial regulation and the failure of global cooperation, especially with regard to global financial institutions. Beginning in the late fall of 2008, many politicians and academic specialists argued that it was time for world leaders to reform the international economic institutions that were created after World War II. As you will see in this chapter, much has changed since 1945: there are now more state actors, more global financial actors, and more transnational corporations. The worldwide **economic collapse of 2008–2009** and the ongoing economic crisis it triggered show that globalization has made all of this more difficult to manage, if not control. Open economies grew much faster than closed economies, but they also opened themselves to the spread of financial difficulties.

economic collapse of 2008–2009 The global economic collapse that began in the United States when the housing bubble burst, affecting banks around the world that had created products based on mortgages. Trust in banks evaporated, credit diminished, and global markets plunged downward. The resulting crisis is ongoing.

Introduction

International political economy (IPE) is about the interplay of economics and politics in world affairs. The core question of IPE is: What drives and explains events in the world economy? For some people, this comes down to a battle of "states versus markets." However, this is misleading. The markets of the world economy are not like local street bazaars where all items can be openly and competitively traded and exchanged. Equally, politicians cannot rule the global economy, much as they might like to. World markets—and countries, local firms, and multinational corporations that trade and invest within them—are all shaped by layers of rules, norms, laws, organizations, and even habits. Political scientists call all these features of the system "institutions." International political economy tries to explain what creates and perpetuates institutions and what impact institutions have on the world economy.

Since the 1970s, IPE has continued to advance as a core subject of international relations. As will be discussed in this chapter, globalization (with its causes and effects on states, processes of international cooperation, and institutions) has become a defining feature of international relations. Furthermore, the end of the Cold War curtailed many of the geostrategic aspirations and much of the influence the West had enjoyed. The challenge of integrating the former Eastern Bloc countries into the world system was soon defined primarily as one of economic transformation and integration. At the same time, an explosion of tribal, religious, and ethnic conflict on the edges of Europe (in the former Yugoslavia) as well as in Africa (e.g., in Somalia and the Congo), in Asia (e.g., in Indonesia), and in the Middle East forced analysts to examine more closely the links between **poverty**, economic stagnation, and the indebtedness of countries on the one hand and intrastate conflict on the other (see Chapters 10 and 13). Finally, the end of the Cold War thrust international institutions into the limelight. The United Nations, the International Monetary Fund (IMF), the **World Bank Group**, and the newly created **World Trade Organization (WTO)** all became an important focus of study and attention, providing further grist for the mill of IPE scholars concerned with examining the causes, determinants, and impact of international institutions and cooperation among states in economic affairs.

After reading and discussing this chapter, you will have a clearer understanding of how the global economic system has developed since the end of World War II. You will be able to identify the key economic actors—namely, the global economic institutions that work with national governments and regional institutions to manage the forces of globalization that shape the global economy. Finally, you will have a better understanding of economic globalization and its impact on the quality of life in both rich and poor states.

The Postwar World Economy

The institutions and framework of the world economy have their roots in the planning for a new economic order that took place during the last phase of World War II. In 1944, policy makers from forty-four countries gathered in New Hampshire at the Bretton Woods resort to consider how to resolve two very serious problems. First, they needed to ensure that the **Great Depression** of the 1930s would not happen again; they had to find ways to ensure a stable global monetary system and an open world-trading system. Second, they needed to rebuild the war-torn economies of Europe.

poverty According to the United Nations, poverty is a denial of choices and opportunities, a violation of human dignity. It means lack of basic capacity provided by material possessions or money to participate effectively in society.

World Bank Group A collection of five agencies, the first established in 1945, with head offices in Washington, D.C. The WBG promotes development in medium- and low-income countries with project loans, structural-adjustment programs, and various advisory services.

World Trade Organization (WTO) A permanent institution established in 1995 to replace the provisional GATT. It has greater powers of enforcement and a wider agenda, covering services, intellectual property, and investment issues as well as merchandise trade.

Great Depression The global economic collapse that ensued following the US Wall Street stock market crash in October 1929. Economic shockwaves rippled around a world already densely interconnected by webs of trade and foreign direct investment.

How did the Bretton Woods conference of 1944 set up a political and economic system that clearly benefited the United States and its allies?

At Bretton Woods, three institutions were planned to promote a new world economic order. The International Monetary Fund (IMF) was created to ensure a stable exchange rate and the provision of emergency assistance to countries facing a temporary crisis in their balance of payments. The International Bank for Reconstruction and Development (IBRD; later called the World Bank) was created to facilitate private investment and reconstruction in Europe. The bank was also charged with assisting development in other countries, a mandate that later became the main reason for its existence. Finally, the General Agreement on Tariffs and Trade (GATT) was signed in 1947 and became a forum for negotiations on **trade liberalization**, the removal or reduction of barriers to free trade.

The 1944 plans for the world economy, however, were soon postponed when in 1945 the United States made its priority the containment of the Soviet Union. Fearing the rise of communism in war-ravaged Europe, the United States took a far more direct role than planned in reconstructing Europe and managing the world economy. In 1947, the United States announced the **Marshall Plan**, which directed massive financial aid to Europe and permitted the United States to set conditions on it. Proposed by Secretary of State George Marshall and officially known as the European Recovery Program, it was offered to all European states, including the Soviet Union. These funds played a critical role in European recovery. That same year, the planned gold standard was replaced by the **dollar standard**, which the United States managed directly, backing the dollar with gold. Unsurprisingly, by the time the IMF, the World Bank, and the GATT began to function in the 1950s, they were distinctly Western-bloc organizations that depended heavily on the United States.

United States support for what became known as the **Bretton Woods system** began to change when weaknesses emerged in the US economy. After 1965, the United States widened its costly military involvement in Vietnam and also started to spend more money on public education and urban redevelopment programs at home (President Johnson's Great Society programs), and all this without raising taxes. The damage was dramatic. As prices rose within the US economy, the competitiveness of US goods and services in the world economy dropped. Likewise, confidence in the US dollar plummeted. Firms and countries turned away from the dollar, and the US capacity to back its currency with gold was brought into question. Meanwhile, other countries in the world economy were enhancing their position. European allies were benefiting from the growing and deepening economic integration in Europe. By the late 1960s, the development of the European Economic Community (EEC) provided a springboard for European policy makers to diverge from US positions on such subjects as NATO, military exercises, and support for the gold standard. In Asia, the phenomenal success of **export-led growth** in Japan and in newly industrializing countries such as South Korea and Taiwan created a new challenge to US trade competitiveness and a new agenda for trade negotiations. These countries took advantage of cheap labor to gain control of industries like electronics and textiles, thereby controlling most of the exports to the world.

Facing these pressures, the United States changed the rules of the international monetary system in 1971. The government announced that it would no longer convert dollars to gold at $35 per ounce and that it was imposing a 10 percent surcharge on import duties (to improve its trade balance by curtailing imports, which were flooding into the United States, and to try to stem the outflow of dollars to the rest of the world). These actions broke the Bretton Woods system. This was not the only change in the world economy in the 1970s.

In the 1970s, the period of high growth enjoyed after World War II came to an abrupt end, leaving very high inflation. Further compounding the problem, the first oil crisis in 1973 plunged the world economy

---

trade liberalization The removal or reduction of barriers to free trade such as tariffs or quotas on the trading of specific goods.

Marshall Plan An American program of financial and other economic aid for Europe after World War II. It was intended to combat the spread of Soviet communism by helping rebuild European economies.

dollar standard The use of the US dollar since 1947 as the key currency in the international monetary system.

Bretton Woods system A system of economic and financial accords that created the IMF, the World Bank, and GATT/WTO following World War II. It is named after the hamlet in northern New Hampshire where leaders from forty-four countries met in 1944.

export-led growth An outward-oriented economy that is based on exploiting its own comparative advantages, such as cheap labor or resources, to capture a share of the world market in a given industry.

WHAT'S YOUR WORLDVIEW ?

How far should governments go to control or manage the world economy? Can the market self-regulate and create opportunities for all citizens across the world?

into stagflation (a combination of economic stagnation, or low growth, and high inflation). In the monetary system, the role of the IMF collapsed when the Bretton Woods system broke down in 1971 and the major industrialized countries failed to find a way to coordinate their exchange rate policies within the IMF framework. Instead, the major currencies floated, and industrialized countries began to discuss monetary issues among themselves in groups such as the Group of Seven (comprising the United States, Japan, Germany, the United Kingdom, France, Italy, and Canada), which first met in 1975.

In the trading system, cooperation had steadily grown in negotiations under the auspices of the GATT. However, in the 1970s, the gains that had been made in reducing tariff barriers, especially among industrialized countries, were reversed by an emerging **protectionism**—actions to protect domestic industries from more efficient foreign producers. As each country grappled with stagflation, many introduced new forms of barriers (or "nontariff barriers"), in particular to keep out the new competitive imports from successful developing countries like those experiencing export-driven growth. An egregious example of the new protectionism was the Multifiber Arrangement of 1973, which placed restrictions on all textile and apparel imports from developing countries, blatantly violating the GATT principle of nondiscrimination.

The GATT was an interim agreement signed in 1947 in the expectation that it would be superseded by an international trade organization. A permanent trade organization was not created until 1994; hence, for four decades, the interim GATT continued to exist as an arrangement among "contracting parties," backed up by a very small secretariat based in Geneva and a minuscule budget. In essence, the GATT was a forum for trade negotiations. Numerous rounds of talks culminated in the very successful Kennedy Round of 1962–1967, where breakthroughs were made in the reduction of trade barriers among industrialized countries. However, when protectionism flourished in the 1970s, the GATT proved unable to restrain powerful members such as the United States and European countries from imposing trade barriers (e.g., the Multifiber Arrangement of 1973 restricting textile imports) and abusing the many exceptions and safeguards written into the agreement. The GATT also functioned as a forum for dispute settlement (i.e., upholding trade rules). However, it was both slow and impotent in this regard, constrained by the need for consensus on any decision regarding disputes.

The GATT was replaced by the World Trade Organization (WTO) as a result of agreements forged in the last round of GATT talks, the Uruguay Round (1986–1994). Established on January 1, 1995, the WTO has the following functions: administering WTO trade agreements; providing a forum for trade negotiations; handling trade disputes; monitoring national trade policies; supplying technical assistance and training for developing countries; and cooperating with other international organizations. It is located in Geneva with a secretariat staff of 500.

The new protectionism in industrialized countries further fueled the anger of people in developing countries, who, in the 1970s, launched a concerted campaign in the UN General Assembly for a New International Economic Order (NIEO). Organized as the Group of 77 (G-77), the developing countries were determined to alter the rules of the game, and their strategy for change was bolstered by the success of OPEC oil-producing developing countries in raising oil prices in 1973. The agenda of the NIEO covered trade, aid, investment, the international monetary and financial system (including debt forgiveness), and institutional reform. Developing countries sought better representation in international economic institutions, a fairer trading system, more aid, the regulation of foreign investment, the protection of economic sovereignty, and reforms to ensure a stabler and more equitable financial and monetary system.

protectionism Not an economic policy but a variety of political actions taken to protect domestic industries from more efficient foreign producers. Usually, this means the use of tariffs, nontariff barriers, and subsidies to protect domestic interests.

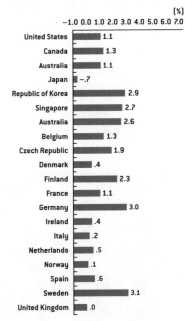

REAL GDP GROWTH.
This chart shows the per capita real GDP growth of selected countries (2010–2011). Does anything about these data surprise you? Based on what you have read in this book and studied in your course, how would you explain the data presented here?

summit diplomacy A direct meeting between heads of government (of the superpowers in particular) to resolve major problems. The summit became a regular mode of contact during the Cold War.

interdependence A condition where states (or peoples) are affected by decisions taken by others. Interdependence can be symmetric (i.e., both sets of actors are affected equally), or it can be asymmetric (i.e., the impact varies between actors).

free market A market ruled by the forces of supply and demand, where all buying and selling is not constrained by government regulations or interventions.

global capital markets Banks, investment companies, insurance companies, trusts, hedge funds, and stock exchanges that transfer funds to industries and other commercial enterprises globally.

A kind of **summit diplomacy** also took place in the 1970s between North (industrialized countries) and South (developing countries). These direct, leader-to-leader negotiations were underpinned by a different kind of thinking and scholarship about IPE. The developing countries' push for reform of the international economic system reflected dependency and Marxist theories of international economic relations that highlighted negative aspects of **interdependence**, a condition where states (or peoples) are affected by others' decisions. Interdependence can be symmetric in that both actors are affected equally, or it can be asymmetric when the impact varies between actors. If political or economic costs of interdependence are high, a state is in a vulnerable position. If costs are low, it is a situation of sensitivity interdependence.

As you remember from Chapter 4, dependency and Marxist theorists sought to identify aspects of the international economy and institutions that impeded the possibilities of development in the South. Their central concern was to answer why so many countries within the world economy remained underdeveloped in spite of the promises of modernization and global growth. The most sympathetic official Northern answer to these concerns was voiced in the Brandt Report in 1980, the findings of a group of high-level policy makers from rich and poor states that had been asked to examine how and why the international community should respond to the challenges of interdependence and development. The Brandt Report urged the wealthy states in the North to increase development assistance and to reduce trade and investment restrictions for poor countries in the South. Closing the gap between rich and poor states was presented as the biggest security challenge facing world leaders.

The NIEO campaign was unsuccessful for several reasons. The UN General Assembly was an obvious institution for developing countries to choose in making their case because, unlike the IMF or World Bank, it offers every country one vote. However, the UN General Assembly had no power to implement the agenda of the developing countries. Furthermore, although many industrialized countries were sympathetic to the developing countries' case in the 1970s, these governments did not act, and by the 1980s a new set of governments with a distinctly less sympathetic **free market** ideology had come to power in the United States, the United Kingdom, and West Germany. According to this ideology, markets should be ruled only by the forces of supply and demand, and buying and selling should not be constrained by government regulations or interventions.

The World Trade Organization and the United Nations work together to address issues that divide the rich and poor states. Here Pascal Lamy, former director general of the WTO, and UN secretary-general Ban Ki-moon meet in 2011 to discuss aid and trade issues.

The 1980s opened with a shift in US economic policy. In 1979, the US Federal Reserve dramatically raised interest rates in an effort to stem inflation by contracting economic activity in the United States. However, the reverberations in the rest of the world economy were immediate and extensive. During the 1960s and 1970s, US and European policies had facilitated the rapid growth of **global capital markets** (institutions that transfer funds to industries globally) and financial flows. In the 1970s, these flows were further buoyed by the investments of oil producers who needed to find outlets for the vast profits made from the oil price rise of 1973. The money found its way to governments in developing countries, which were offered loans at very low prices. The rise in interest rates in 1979 was an abrupt wake-up call to both borrowers and creditors (many of whom were US-based banks), who suddenly realized that many

| CASE STUDY | Microcredit: Empowering Women Through Investment | **11.1** |

In 1976, a Bangladeshi economist, Muhammad Yunus, founded the Grameen Bank. The bank is a lending program that provides its largely female clientele with small loans for business investment. These small loans, which are called "microcredit," are directed toward women because women have a better record for investment and repayment than men. Women are more likely to invest the loans rather than spend them on themselves, and they are more likely to repay. Loan-repayment rates fluctuate between 96 percent and 100 percent. Loans directed toward women are also seen as a method of empowerment that gives women access to resources, economic security, and higher status in the household. Up to 5 percent of borrowers per year rise out of poverty. Borrowers also increase the educational and nutritional standards within their families.

In Bangladesh in 2006, Grameen Bank reported 6.83 million borrowers in 73,609 villages, 97 percent of whom were women. In addition to financing small enterprises, homebuilding, and education, the bank empowers women by fostering entrepreneurialism and encouraging family planning. Borrowers now own 94 percent of the bank, with the other 6 percent owned by the government. The bank earns a profit and, since 1995, has been self-sufficient. The Grameen Bank and its founder were jointly awarded the 2006 Nobel Peace Prize.

Microcredit is widely publicized as a successful model for development *and* the empowerment of women. However, many organizations, including commercial banks, that have tried to replicate the Grameen Bank have failed. This has led to a fierce debate about what makes microcredit effective. The Grameen Bank succeeded not just by carefully managing its loans to ensure that individual women could repay but also because its programs actively addressed reasons for default. Only a few organizations have replicated this.

For Discussion

1. Kiva is a major microcredit organization with chapters on many college campuses. Do some research and find out how it is doing. Why is it succeeding? Where is it succeeding?
2. Another research task: Why have microcredit schemes run by commercial banks failed?
3. Eventually poor societies will need some major industries that employ large numbers of people. Could you say that the microcredit experience might make societies more attractive to outside investors? Why or why not?

of the loans could not be repaid. The IMF was immediately called in to prevent any developing country from defaulting on these loans, since it was feared that such a default would cause a global financial crisis.

The debt crisis meant that the IMF's role in the world economy became largely one of ensuring that indebted countries undertook "structural adjustment" in their economies. Structural adjustment meant immediate measures to reduce inflation, government expenditure, and the role of the government in the economy, including trade liberalization, privatization, and **deregulation**. These "neoliberal" policies were in marked contrast to the Keynesian analysis that had prevailed until the 1980s, during the decades of growth in the world economy. Keynesians (named after economist John Maynard Keynes) believe that governments should play an active and interventionist role in the economy to ensure both growth and equity. By contrast, neoliberalism sought to roll back the state and the role of government, leaving decisions about allocation, production, and distribution in the economy to the market. By the late 1980s, the term **Washington Consensus** was used, sometimes pejoratively, to imply that these policies were mainly a reflection of US interests.

The 1990s brought the end of the Cold War and the challenge of how to integrate Central and Eastern European countries and the former Soviet Union into the global economy. The IMF and World Bank became deeply involved, but the Washington Consensus was not broad enough for the purpose. Both institutions began to embrace a broader and

deregulation The removal of all regulation so that market forces, not government policy, control economic developments.

Washington Consensus The belief of key opinion formers in Washington that global welfare would be maximized by the universal application of neoliberal economic policies, which favor a minimalist state and an enhanced role for the market.

WHAT'S YOUR WORLDVIEW ?

In the face of the 2008–2012 global economic collapse, how well did the leaders of countries coordinate their economic policies? Did these efforts include both rich and poor states?

conditionality When regional or international lending agencies require that recipient national governments accept certain policy conditions to receive a loan or some form of economic assistance.

intellectual property rights Rules that protect the owners of content through copyright, patents, trademarks, and trade secrets. The World Intellectual Property Organization (WIPO) is the forum where states (184 members in 2010) discuss this issue.

Engaging with the
WORLD
G8 and G20 Youth Summits

The **G8 and G20 Youth Summits** are premier international youth conferences that bring together young leaders representing the Group of Eight (G-8) and Group of Twenty (G-20) nations to facilitate discussions of international affairs, promote cross-cultural understanding, and build global friendships. The most recent summits were held in Washington, D.C., in June 2012. Further information on the summits can be found at www.g8-g20 -youth-summits.org.

deeper view of **conditionality** aimed at promoting "good governance" in member countries. This conditionality meant that regional and international lending agencies required recipient national governments to accept certain policy conditions to receive loans and economic assistance. But many thought conditionality had gone too far when, in the wake of the East Asian financial crisis in 1997, the IMF imposed far-reaching and overly draconian conditions on countries such as Korea.

The impact would be felt in subsequent years as the IMF's lending role waned in most emerging market economies. Over this period, the World Bank sought to broaden its appeal through enhanced relations with governments as well as with nongovernmental organizations (NGOs). Its legitimacy seemed less tarnished. At the same time, the newly established World Trade Organization began operations in 1995, opening up a new forum within which a broad range of international issues would be negotiated, including not only traditional trade but also such issues as **intellectual property rights** (which protect content owners), trade-related investment measures, and food-safety standards.

In the first decade of the twenty-first century, a shift in global economic power was occurring. In September 2003, during global trade negotiations in Mexico, a group of twenty countries, including Brazil, South Africa, India, and China, resisted the powerful United States and European Union and refused to engage in trade talks unless some of their terms were heeded. In the IMF in 2006, a shift in voting power was conceded in favor of China, Mexico, Turkey, and Korea, and further shifts were conceded in the wake of the financial crisis. Yet few believed this would be enough to fully engage these countries in the institutions. Several emerging countries—with China in the lead—became more powerful donors in their own right. As world energy consumption grew, so too did the power of countries supplying energy resources. In Venezuela, President Hugo Chavez painted the world in the style made popular in the 1970s, blaming the United States and other countries of the global North for the economic conditions in the global South.

The G-20 is a new global economic actor that may play a major role in future talks about trade and development and economic stability. It is made up of the finance ministers and central bank governors of the European Union and nineteen non-EU countries, both developed and developing: Argentina, Australia, Brazil, Canada, China, France, Germany, India, Indonesia, Italy, Japan, Mexico, Russia, Saudi Arabia, South Africa, the Republic of Korea, Turkey, the United Kingdom, and the United States. The managing director of the IMF, the president of the World Bank, and chairs of some of the critical committees of the IMF and World Bank also participate in G-20 meetings. The G-20 was established in 1999 after the 1997 Asian financial crisis in an effort to stabilize the global financial market. Finance ministers and the members' central bank administrators meet regularly to discuss strategies to promote global financial stability and to promote sustainable growth and development. The member states of the G-20 represent nearly 90 percent of global gross national product (GNO), 80 percent of global trade, and 67 percent of the world's population. The G-20 has successfully created a stronger regulation and policy coordination system and has improved macroeconomic cooperation among G-20 members, but it has yet to prove that it is able to coordinate the economic policies of the major global economies. In a 2011 summit, the members failed to agree on a financial assistance program for European states like Greece and Italy.

Meanwhile, across most industrialized countries, calls for greater efforts to reduce climate-changing emissions became ever stronger. For scholars of international relations,

GLOBAL PERSPECTIVE | The Bretton Woods Institutions and the Global South

For many people in the developing world, the international finance institutions of the Bretton Woods system are yet another form of neocolonial exploitation. Politicians, news media, and ordinary people condemn the oppression of the globalized system based in the capital of the hegemon, the United States. Although the Bretton Woods system has not been the only cause of underdevelopment in the global South, there is some basis for these criticisms.

Both the International Monetary Fund and the International Bank for Reconstruction and Development (IBRD; later known as the World Bank) were established in 1946, after wartime negotiations held at the Bretton Woods resort in New Hampshire, with headquarters (opposite one another) in Washington, D.C. The IMF was created to promote international monetary cooperation and resolve the interwar economic problems, although several of these functions ended when the Bretton Woods system broke down in 1971. The IMF now has a membership of 186 countries, and each contributes a quota of resources to the organization (proportionate to the size of their economy), which also determines their percentage of voting rights and the amount of resources to which they can have automatic access. Since the 1980s, the IMF has become an institution offering financial and technical assistance to developing and transitional economies. The terms on which countries receive assistance include the government having to commit to specific conditions, or policy reforms, called *conditionality* (see www.imf.org).

The World Bank started out as an agency to finance reconstruction in war-torn Europe as well as development in the rest of the world. It has since become the world's largest source of development assistance, providing nearly $16 billion in loans annually to eligible member countries through the IBRD, the International Development Association (IDA), the International Finance Corporation (IFC), and the Multilateral Investment Guarantee Agency (MIGA). As with the IMF, the World Bank requires members to whom it lends to undertake specific reforms within their economy. Most recently, this has included the requirement of borrowing governments to demonstrate their commitment to reducing poverty within their countries. With the exception of the IDA (which is funded by donations), the World Bank's resources come from its issue of bonds in the capital markets. These bonds are backed by guarantees provided by the governments that belong to the institution (see www.worldbank.org).

At the time of their creation, the IMF and the World Bank were not intended to help what we now call the "developing world." In 1944, most of Africa and significant parts of Asia were colonies of European countries. The colonies of Africa and Asia might benefit indirectly from the IMF's exchange rate mechanism, but it was by design a procedure to bring stability to the international economic transactions of the Europeans' homelands. The weighted voting procedure of the IMF was another indication of the lack of status of certain countries in the system. While weighted voting acknowledged the size of the US contribution to the IMF and it gave leadership status as well, it also locked in place the subordinate status for the colonies as they won their independence from Europe. In the 1980s and early 1990s, the IMF's Structural Adjustment Programs (SAP)—which demanded an end to price subsidies for basics like food and cooking oil—were, from the perspective of the global South, an even greater intrusion in the affairs of the nominally sovereign developing countries.

The formal name of the World Bank, the International Bank for Reconstruction and Development, provides a clue to the inherent difficulties that the newly independent former European colonies had with the organization. Reconstruction

Economic prosperity is not spread evenly around the world. When rich states provide subsidies for their farmers, third world farmers are left behind.

Continued

came before Development in the name because the bank was originally founded primarily to deal with the needs of Europeans and reconstruction. With the increasing power of developing countries in the 1960s and 1970s, most visibly in the United Nations with the creation of the UN Conference on Trade and Development (UNCTAD; see Chapter 13) and later the Group of 77, the World Bank created special lending facilities such as IDA, mentioned earlier, to help the global South. However, like the IMF, the World Bank's facilities were still controlled from Washington, D.C., with the decision-making bodies seemingly under the control of the United States. This impression is reinforced by the fact that the

head of the World Bank has always been a citizen of the United States.

For Discussion

1. Is it time to entirely transform rather than merely reform the institutions that were originally a part of the Bretton Woods system?

2. If the current Millennium Development Goals campaign fails, should the global leaders consider an alternative to the current system?

3. We now have the G-20, which includes many countries in the global South. Should the global South have a greater voice in the policies of the World Bank?

the twenty-first century brought serious questions about how international institutions might assist not only in managing new challenges in the global economy but equally in managing a shift in power among the states that make up—and make work—the existing institutions.

Traditional Approaches to IPE: Liberal, Mercantilist, and Marxist

We have learned that in international relations there are contending theories or traditions that offer competing descriptions and explanations of conditions and events. As we try to understand the complexities of the global economy—past, present, and future—we should consider three competing traditions or economic belief systems (see Table 11.1). The liberal tradition dominated most discussion of the international economic system that was created after World War II and is still much used to explain the present global economy. The mercantilist tradition focuses on competition among states, stressing that states must protect their own interests and power to protect their citizens in the competitive international economy. The Marxist or socialist tradition favors a more equitable political economy that ends the exploitation of workers around the world and closes the gap between rich and poor states. These three traditions have a particular moral and analytic slant on global economic relations.

The Liberal Tradition

The liberal tradition is the free market belief system in which the role of voluntary exchange and markets is emphasized as both efficient and morally desirable. The assumption is that free trade and the free movement of capital will ensure that investment flows to where it is most profitable to invest (e.g., into less developed areas where maximal gains might be made). Free trade is crucial for it permits countries to benefit from their comparative advantages. That is, each country can exploit its own natural advantages, resources, and endowments and gain from specialization. The economy is oiled by freely

Table 11.1
Dominant Perspectives on IPE

Liberal	Mercantilist	Marxist
The world economy has the potential to be a seamless global marketplace in which free trade and the free movement of capital shape the policies of governments and economic actors. Order would be achieved by the invisible hand of competition in the global marketplace.	As an arena of interstate competition, the world economy is one in which states seek to maximize their wealth and independence vis-à-vis other states. Order is achieved only where there is a balance of power or hegemony.	The world economy is best described as an arena of capitalist competition in which classes (capitalists and workers) and social groups are in constant conflict. Capitalists (and the states they are based in) are driven by the search for profits, and order is achieved only where they succeed in exacting the submission of all others.

exchangeable currencies and open markets that create a global system of prices, which, like an **invisible hand**, ensures an efficient and equitable distribution of goods and services across the world economy. This view was promoted by Scottish economist Adam Smith and his influential book, *The Wealth of Nations* (1776), which advocated free trade over mercantilism. Order in the global economy is fairly minimal. The optimal role of governments and institutions is to ensure the smooth and relatively unfettered operation of markets. It is assumed that governments face a wide range of choices in the world system and likewise vis-à-vis their own societies and populations. This means governments that fail to pursue "good" economic policies do so because decision makers are either too corrupt or too ignorant of the correct economic choices they might make.

invisible hand The concept from the eighteenth-century writing of Adam Smith that proposed governments leave trade and financial sectors alone.

The Mercantilist Tradition

The mercantilist tradition stands in stark contrast to the liberal tradition. Whereas liberals have a view that all states can benefit from a free market (positive sum), mercantilists share the presumptions of realists in international relations that states exist in a **zero-sum world**. They do not focus on individual policy makers and their policy choices but rather assume that the world economy is an arena of competition among states seeking to maximize relative strength and power. Simply put, the international system is like a jungle in which each state has to do what it can to survive. For this reason, the aim of every state must be to maximize its wealth and independence. States will seek to do this by ensuring their self-sufficiency (sometimes called **autarchy**) in key strategic industries and commodities and by using trade protectionism (tariffs and other limits on exports and imports), subsidies, and selective investments in the domestic economy. Obviously, within this system, some states have more power and capability than others. As we saw in Chapter 3, the most powerful states define the rules and limits of the system through hegemony, alliances, and balances of power. Indeed, stability and order will only be achieved where one state can play the role of hegemon, or is willing and able to create, maintain, and enforce basic rules. Amid this, the economic policies of any one government will always be subservient to its quest to secure the external and internal sovereignty of the state.

zero-sum world A pessimistic view that, in any interaction, another's gains are your losses.

autarchy The mercantilist recommendation that states strive for economic self-sufficiency by using trade protectionism or policies of complete isolation.

The Marxist Tradition

The Marxist tradition also sees the world economy as an arena of competition but not among states. Capitalism is the driving force in the world economy. Using Marx's language, this means world economic relations are best conceived as a class struggle between the oppressor and the oppressed. The oppressors, or capitalists, own the means of production (trade and industry). The oppressed are the working class. The struggle between the two arises because capitalists seek to increase their profits, and this requires them to exploit ever more harshly the working class. This description of class relations within a capitalist system has been applied to international relations in various ways. Lenin, founder of the USSR, believed that imperialism was the highest stage of capitalism. Theorists like Immanuel Wallerstein contend that between the core (industrialized countries) and periphery (developing countries) an unequal exchange occurs. Dependency theorists (who have focused mainly on Latin America) describe the ways classes and groups in the core link to the periphery. Underdevelopment and poverty in so many countries are explained as the result of economic, social, and political structures that have been deeply influenced by international economic relations. The global capitalist order within which these societies have emerged is, after all, a global capitalist order that reflects the interests of those who own the means of production.

> ## WHAT'S YOUR WORLDVIEW ?
>
> *If the present neoliberal system cannot address the inequalities in the system, will states become more mercantilist? Will a new Marxist movement emerge?*

It becomes clear in contrasting these traditions of thinking about international economic relations that each focuses on different actors and driving forces in the world economy and that each has a different conception of what "order" means and what is necessary to achieve it.

Comparing the different traditions also highlights two different levels of analysis (system and national levels): the structure of the international system (be that international capitalism or the configuration of power among states in the system), the nature of a particular government or competition within its institutions, and the role of interest groups and societal forces within a country (see levels of analysis discussions in Chapters 1 and 5). At each of these levels of analysis, we need to ask what drives the actors concerned and how we might therefore explain their preferences, actions, and the outcomes that result. In answering this question, we enter into more methodological preoccupations that today divide the study of IPE.

For neo-Marxists—dependency theorists—the major problem in international relations is **maldevelopment**. This is a qualitative concept introduced by the French in the 1990s intended to capture the stark discrepancies between people's living conditions and their needs—economic, social, cultural, and environmental. Maldevelopment complements the more prevalent quantitative concept of **underdevelopment**, which measures rates of poverty and persons lacking access to healthcare, potable water, food, education, or housing. A global system controlled economically and politically by core states creates and sustains maldevelopment.

Marxists and neo-Marxists share some common beliefs:

- Economic realities shape the behavior of individuals, corporations, and states.
- The world is divided between core (rich) and periphery (poor) states.
- International relations is defined by the interactions between these two types of states.
- Economic elites control the governments in both rich and poor states by using political power to protect their economic interests and to prevent any changes in the global capitalist system.

maldevelopment The failure of states to develop economically and politically because of the nature of the international system and its distribution of power.

underdevelopment The lack, in a state or region within a state, of economic resources and adequate political structures to maintain security, order, and well-being.

THEORY IN PRACTICE

Contending Views of Capitalism

Ever since Deng Xiaoping launched the second revolution in 1978 which introduced free market reforms and opened China to the outside world, China's economy has grown about 10 percent a year. China has quickly become the industrial workshop for the world. It has just overtaken Japan as the world's second largest economy, and some economists predict it will overtake the United States within twenty years. The concern among many is whether China will use its economic wealth and influence to extend its power in a nationalistic or mercantilist way. China is a successful state capitalist system, and because of its economic strength, it was able to avoid most of the economic crisis from 2008 to the present. However, as demand in the United States and Europe declines due to the recession, the Chinese economy may also slow down. There are many in Washington and in European capitals that see China as both an economic and potentially a military or security threat. Many people are asking if the future will be a peaceful one with the great powers, including China and India, working together to find solutions to the global economic crisis, or if instead there will be a new scramble for resources and markets that increases the tensions and conflicts among the major powers. Many free market capitalists have complained about China's monetary policies and its use of subsidies to support certain industries. One reason for the concern is a misunderstanding or lack of knowledge about the differences between the Anglo-American form of capitalism, or what is known as the *Washington Consensus,* with its emphasis on minimal government and free market solutions, and the Asian form of capitalism, or the *Beijing Consensus*, with its emphasis on the economy serving the interests of the state.

James Fallows provides an excellent description of the purpose of economic life in the Anglo-American and Asian models.* The purpose of economic life in the Anglo-American model is to raise the individual consumer's standard of living, whereas the Asian model places a priority on increasing national strength by making the state more independent and self-sufficient. In terms of power, the Asian model seeks to concentrate power to serve the common good, and the Anglo-American model seeks to break up any concentrated power. From this perspective, economic development "means that people have more choice" and a greater number of opportunities to pursue personal wealth. In the Asian capitalist system, the primary goal is to "develop the productive base of the country" by supporting the industries at home and those abroad that are owned by your citizens around the world. This also means using government resources to support efforts at securing both markets and strategic resources essential for economic growth. This state capitalist view suggests that the consumer's welfare and interests are less important than the corporation that is producing goods and services for the welfare of the state. Not surprisingly, then, China is considered an economic superpower by most of the world's leading economists. It has the second-largest national economy and is the world's second-largest exporter.

The Obama administration has continued the policy of pressuring China to address a number of issues, including the value of its currency, its use of subsidies, and its failure to address issues related to the protection of intellectual property rights. Clearly, US political leaders are motivated by the economic recession and their own political aspirations. The US House of Representatives passed a bill that

Female Chinese workers sew clothes to be exported to the United States and Europe at a garment factory in Huaibei City, East China's Anhui province.

Continued

THEORY IN PRACTICE *continued*

would seek trade sanctions against China by a margin of 348 to 79, and President Obama described China as a country that does not play fair in the global economic game because it provides subsidies for industries and steals intellectual property.

The Chinese government generally dismisses international criticism as unwarranted finger pointing. China had a $198 billion trade surplus with the world in 2009, and its exports to the United States outpace imports by a four-to-one margin. Evidence is mounting that China is following a two-pronged strategy to maintain its economic growth. First, it uses the WTO to fight protectionism among its trade partners. China has filed more cases with the WTO's trade tribunals in Geneva than any other country.

Second, China is holding down the value of its currency, and since 2007, it has also suppressed a series of IMF reports that document the undervaluation of its currency.

Historically, every rising power has used the resources of the state

to help key economic players grow. After World War II, Marshall Plan funds combined with other public investments to rebuild European industries and create thriving welfare states. Many nation-states still own or have major control over key industries such as energy, telecommunications, financial services, and manufacturing. So is China the only culprit here, or are we witnessing a shift from Anglo-American liberal capitalism to a state capitalist system? Will the current economic crisis force many states to take over key economic sectors to provide employment, secure key resources, and protect the interests of their citizens?

*James Fallows, *Looking at the Sun. The Rise of the New East Asian Economic and Political System* (New York: Vintage Books, 1995).

Discussion Questions

1. A recent issue of *The Economist* (January 21, 2012) included a

special section on state capitalism called "The Visible Hand," which argues that the future of capitalism may mean more government control of the economy. What do you think about that idea? Should government play a more extensive role in our economic lives?

2. The neoliberal institutions that we expect to manage the global economy (e.g., the IMF) push for less government intervention in the economy. Will these institutions need to change their guidelines or should they be replaced with new institutions based on new global realities?

3. Both China and India are members of the G-20, and their economic and political power is on the rise. Is this the end of Western hegemony? What might a more pluralistic form of global governance look like?

WHAT'S YOUR WORLDVIEW

How would liberals, Marxists, and constructivists explain the 2008 economic crisis? What might they suggest world leaders do to prevent this from happening again?

Marxists and neo-Marxists differ in their views about how capitalism spreads across the globe. "Old school" Marxists (e.g., Marx, Engels, and Lenin) predicted that capitalism would spread to underdeveloped areas of the world via imperialism. They theorized that it would eventually shift centers of production to the periphery, politicizing workers so they would foment revolution and change. Neo-Marxists argue that capitalism intentionally sustains the periphery's dependency as a mechanism to ensure access to critical resources, cheap labor, and markets for goods and services. Structural characteristics of the global capitalist system define roles for center and periphery states. Workers in rich and poor states are exploited, while their leaders in both types of states share the common goal of sustaining the structural exploitation.

Thus, for neo-Marxists, revolutionary forces for change will not emerge from within a single state due to exploitation from within. Forces for change develop as people in dependent states become aware of their position and as the gap between rich and poor grows even larger. Fundamentally, they must realize that the structure of the international capitalist system is the problem. The major assumptions of dependency theorists include the following:

- An international feudal structure exists that is not explained by the existence of a dual economy—agriculture and industrial—because economies in developing states respond to the needs of core states rather than to local needs.
- Poverty and human security problems will not be addressed, because elites in the North and South benefit from the situation.
- Dominant class interests are uniform and global.
- The critical issue is uneven economic development and the predatory nature of globalization.
- The solution to ending war and violence in the international system is ending the exploitation and closing the gap between rich and poor.

New Approaches to IPE

International political economy is divided by the different normative concerns and analytic questions that are highlighted by the traditions we have outlined. The discipline is now subject to a lively methodological debate about how scholars might best explain policies and outcomes (see Table 11.2). In essence, this debate is about whether you can assume what states' (and other actors') preferences and interests are. If you can, then rational choice (or "neoutilitarian") approaches to IPE make sense. However, if you open up the question as to why and how states and other actors come to have particular preferences, then you are pushed toward approaches now often labeled "constructivism" (see Chapter 4).

Political Economy: The Application of Rational Choice to Groups Within the State

In the United States, the study of IPE has become dominated by a "rational choice," or neoutilitarian, approach. This borrows economic concepts to explain politics. Instead of exploring the ideas, personalities, ideologies, or historical traditions that lie behind policies and institutions, rational choice focuses on the incentive structure faced by those making decisions. It is assumed that actors' interests and preferences are known or fixed and that actors can make strategic choices as to how best to promote their interests. The term *rational choice* is useful to describe this approach because it proposes that, even though a particular policy may seem stupid or wrong, it may have been rational. Rational in this sense means that for the actor or group concerned, this was the optimal choice given the specific incentives and institutional constraints and opportunities that existed at the time.

Rational choice has been applied to interest groups and their influence on IPE in what has been called a **political-economy approach**. This approach, which has its roots in explanations of trade policy that focus on interest groups, studies interactions between states or public actors and the market at domestic and international levels. More recent applications have attempted to explain why countries adapt in particular ways to changes in the world economy (see Table 11.2). The analysis proceeds on the assumption that governments and their policies are important but that the policies and preferences of governments reflect the actions of specific interest groups within the economy. These groups may emerge along class or sectoral lines. Indeed, the assumptions of rational choice are applied to explain how particular groups within the economy emerge and what their goals and policy preferences are. Furthermore, rational choice provides a framework for understanding the coalitions into which these groups enter and their interactions with other institutions. For example, in explaining developing-country responses to the debt crisis of the 1980s, a political-economy approach starts out by examining how interest

political-economy approach
The study of the interactions between states or public actors and the market at domestic and international levels.

Table 11.2

Examples of New Approaches to IPE

Institutionalist	Political Economy	Constructivist
Institutionalists regard the world economy as an arena of interstate cooperation. They see the core actors as governments and the institutions to whom they delegate power, and the key driving forces as rational choice at the level of the state motivated by the potential gains from cooperation. For institutionalists, the key condition for order is the existence of international institutions that permit cooperation to continue.	For political economists, the world economy is characterized by competition among vested interests within different kinds of states, and the core actors are interest groups formed within domestic economies. The key driving force is rational choice at the level of groups within the domestic economy responding to changes in the international economy. Political economists are not concerned with theorizing about the conditions necessary for international order.	Constructivists see the world economy as an overarching structure of knowledge, ideas, and institutions that reflects the interests of dominant actors and within which competition takes place. They regard the structure of the system itself as vital in understanding the identities and preferences of the actors. The key driving force of the system is capitalist competition, which is constrained by the need of the powerful to gain the consent of the less powerful. Dominance by one state is an insufficient condition for international order. Hegemony requires control over the structures of knowledge and ideas as well.

economic shock An event that produces a significant change within an economy despite occurring outside it. Economic shocks are unpredictable and typically impact supply or demand throughout the markets.

groups are affected by **economic shocks**, which are unpredictable, external events such as high interest rates, sudden rises in commodity prices, and devaluation of currencies. By demonstrating that the power of some interests (e.g., those working in the export sector) has increased and the power of others (e.g., those working in industries relying on diminishing state subsidies) has diminished, the approach proffers an explanation for radical shifts in government policies.

Institutionalism: The Application of Rational Choice to States

A different application of rational choice lies in the institutionalist approach to IPE. This approach applies the assumptions of rational choice to states in their interaction with other states. Drawing on theories of delegation and agency, it offers an explanation of why institutions exist and for what purposes. The core assumption is that states create international institutions and delegate power to them to maximize utility within the constraints of world markets and world politics. Frequently, this comes down to the need to resolve collective action problems. For example, states realize that they cannot achieve their goals in areas such as trade or the environment unless all other states also embark on a particular course of action. Hence, institutions are created to ensure that there is no defection or free riding, and the collective goal is achieved.

Constructivism

In contrast to rational choice analysis, other approaches to IPE assume that policies within the world economy are affected by historical and sociological factors. Much more attention is paid to the ways actors formulate preferences as well as to the processes by which decisions are made and implemented. Rather than assuming that a state's or decision maker's preferences reflect rational choices within given constraints and opportunities, analysts in a broader tradition of IPE examine the beliefs, roles, traditions, ideologies, and patterns of influence that shape preferences, behavior, and outcomes.

Interests, actions, and behavior in the world economy are conceived as taking place within a structure of ideas, culture, and knowledge. We cannot assume that the preferences of actors within the system reflect objectively definable competing "interests." Rather, the way actors understand their own preferences depends heavily on prevailing beliefs and patterns of thinking in the world economy, many of which are embodied in institutions. The question this poses is: Whose interests and ideas are embodied in the rules and norms of the system?

For some, the answer to the question *in whose interest* lies in **hegemony**, a system regulated by a dominant leader. The dominant power within the system will achieve goals not just through coercion but equally by ensuring the consent of other actors. This means dominant powers will promulgate institutions, ideologies, and ideas, all of which help persuade other actors that their best interests converge with those of the dominant power. For example, constructivists interpret the dominance of neoliberalism since the 1980s as a reflection of US interests in the global economy, successfully projected through structures of knowledge (it became the dominant paradigm in top research universities), through institutions (e.g., the IMF, which became a forceful proponent of neoliberal policy prescriptions), and through broader cultural beliefs and understandings (the very language of free market contrasting with restricted or repressive regimes).

New approaches to IPE highlight a powerful debate about whether we should treat states' interests and preferences as given or fixed. We return to this question in the next section of this chapter. There we will examine why states form institutions and what role such institutions might play in managing globalization. First, though, we need to establish what globalization in the world economy is and what its implications are.

> **WHAT'S YOUR WORLDVIEW ?**
>
> *Is globalization eroding the sovereignty of states? How has it influenced your own way of living?*

hegemony A system regulated by a dominant leader, or political (and/or economic) domination of a region. It also means power and control exercised by a leading state over other states.

Meetings of the WTO attract a range of protesters opposed to what they see as the predatory nature of globalization.

The Globalization Debate in IPE

The nature and impact of globalization are subjects of profound debate within IPE (as within other areas of international relations discussed in this book). The term *globalization* refers to at least four different sets of forces or processes in the world economy (see Table 11.3). Internationalization describes the increase in economic transactions across borders, which has been taking place since the turn of the century but which some argue has undergone a quantitative leap in recent decades. The technological revolution is a second aspect of globalization, identifying the effect of new electronic communication that permits firms and other actors to operate globally with much less regard for location, distance, and borders. One effect of the technological revolution is to speed up deterritorialization, or the smaller influence territorial distances, borders, and places have on the way people collectively identify themselves, act, and seek political voice or recognition. Finally, liberalization describes the policies undertaken by states that have made a new global economy possible. These include both the rules and the institutions created by powerful states to facilitate a new scale of transnational economic activity in certain sectors of the world economy. It also includes the policies of smaller and less powerful states (e.g., Iceland) in the system, which, by liberalizing trade, investment, and production, have integrated into the world economy.

In IPE, several competing claims are made about globalization. For example, some scholars argue that globalization is nothing new, but others posit that globalization is dramatically diminishing the role of the state (see Chapter 1). Still others claim that globalization is exacerbating inequalities and giving rise to a more unjust world. To make sense of these different arguments and the evidence adduced to support them, it is worth thinking about the approaches to IPE covered in previous sections, for they help identify key differences in emphasis that give rise to conflicting interpretations of globalization. For example, skeptics who deny that globalization is transforming world politics tend to focus on the internationalization element of globalization (see Table 11.3). They can then draw on evidence that throws into doubt whether the number of transactions taking place among states has indeed risen (UN Development Programme 1997) and make the argument that there is "nothing new" in the growing interdependence of states. By contrast, liberal enthusiasts of globalization focus on technological innovation and the nonpolitical "objective" forces that are shrinking the world economy. They argue that this is creating a less political, more efficient, more unified world order. Those who focus on deterritorialization highlight that there is also a negative side to globalization. Just as technological innovation permits a more active global civil society, so too does it permit the growth of an uncivil one.

Terrorist networks and transnational crime grow easily and are harder to combat in an era of globalization. This puts an important caveat on a final argument about globalization—one that prioritizes the role powerful states play in shaping the process. Focusing on liberalization, several analysts highlight the role of powerful states in setting the rules of the new globalized international economy and their increasing influence over less powerful states. Yet this has two faces. Powerful states find it relatively easy to set down rules with little or no consultation with less powerful states. This is as true in the global economy as it has been in recent years in the United States' (and selected allies') war against terrorism and invasions of Afghanistan and Iraq. Yet in the latter case, the subsequent challenge of pacifying weakened states through military occupation reveals how difficult it is even for the most powerful states to control other countries.

Table 11.3

Four Aspects of Globalization

1. *Internationalization* describes the increase in transactions among states reflected in flows of trade, investment, and capital (see the argument that these flows have not increased as much as is claimed; UN Development Programme 1997). The processes of internationalization have been facilitated and are shaped by international agreements on trade, investment, and capital as well as by domestic policies permitting the private sector to transact abroad.

2. The *technological revolution* refers to the way modern communications (Internet, satellite communications, high-tech computers), made possible by technological advances, have made distance and location less important factors not just for government (including at local and regional levels) but equally in the calculations of other actors, such as firms' investment decisions or the activities of social movements.

3. *Deterritorialization* is accelerated by the technological revolution and refers to the declining influence of territorial places, distances, and boundaries over the way people collectively identify themselves or seek political recognition. This permits an expansion of global civil society but equally an expansion of global criminal or terrorist networks.

4. *Liberalization* describes government policies that reduce the role of the state in the economy such as through the dismantling of trade tariffs and barriers, the deregulation and opening of the financial sector to foreign investors, and the privatization of state enterprises.

Is Globalization Diminishing the Role of the State in the World Economy?

"A global economy is emerging," claim those who depict a world in which multinational trade, production, investment, and financing move in and out of countries ever more easily. The globalists tell us that, as a result, governments and states are losing their capacity to control economic interactions. This is partly because the quantity and rapidity of flows make it more difficult for governments to regulate trade, investment, or capital. Equally important is the fact that firms and investors can more easily take their business elsewhere. This puts new constraints on governments trying to retain and encourage investment. The argument here is that footloose modern businesses will exit from a country if a government does not pursue liberalizing policies that foster corporate profitability and flexibility. For this reason, governments are under pressure to reduce taxes and to cut back state expenditure on health, education, pensions, and so forth. When it comes to regulating international business, governments are permitting investors themselves to set the rules, and these private actors are doing so though new private international networks and self-regulatory agencies. In sum, states are losing power in a global economic order in which state borders and governments are less influential. This eventuality is, of course, embraced by those interpreting it from a liberal starting point.

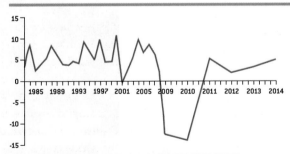

VOLUME OF WORLD MERCHANDISE EXPORTS.
This graph represents the annual percentage change in the volume of world merchandise exports. What do these data tell you about world trade over the last twenty-five years? What patterns do you notice here? What factors may have influenced each of the significant fluctuations?

The Global Skeptics

A variety of skeptics counter the "global economy" view, pointing out flaws in the argument and the evidence that the state is losing power. The proposition that states are under pressure to cut taxes and reduce expenditure is attacked by scholars who examine data of industrialized countries and demonstrate that the evidence does not back up this claim. Nor does the evidence suggest that transnational corporations (TNCs) relocate investment to areas where there are lower wages and lower taxes. Rather, contemporary research into patterns of TNC investment discloses that in the new knowledge-intensive economy, factors such as the availability of skilled and semiskilled labor, good infrastructure, and proximity to market are crucial ingredients to choices of location. The conclusion drawn from this evidence is that the role of states is not eroding. To the contrary, states and government still have a very important and substantial role to play in a successful economy.

New Constraints on States

Although skeptics knock holes in some of the arguments about the erosion of state power in the face of global multinational enterprises, other aspects of globalization do constrain all states. In particular, the fact that billions of dollars can flood in—or out—of a country overnight sets a new constraint on monetary policy and opens up new vulnerabilities in the financial sectors of all countries. Today, governments need to be very careful in managing interest rates and managing or floating exchange rates. In the same way, they need robust domestic banking and financial systems to weather the onslaught or recession of a tidal wave of capital. The punishment for poor policy is instantaneous and devastating. Furthermore, as the Asian financial crisis of 1997 showed, it is not only the culprit country that bears the punishment. The financial crisis in Asia brought to light

When the euro became the new currency in the countries in the Eurozone, old bills were shredded. How will the euro stay strong with economic crises and the addition of more countries from the former Soviet bloc?

the potential vulnerability of all countries to massive inflows and outflows of capital. It also underlined that some states suffer the impact of globalization more than others.

International Institutions in the Globalizing World Economy

We have seen that globalization is increasing interdependence among states. It is also increasing global interconnectedness and the capacity of some states to influence others. The Asian financial crisis exhibited all three of these changes. The countries of Asia had liberalized into global capital markets (with much encouragement from the United States and other industrialized countries) and soon became recipients of large inflows of short-term capital. As soon as confidence in Thailand faltered, reactions were instantaneously transmitted to investors (through the new communications networks). The subsequent debacle of 1997 demonstrated how quickly, easily, and devastatingly a financial crisis in one country can spill over into others.

The management of the Asian financial crisis led some policy makers to call for stronger, more effective international institutions, including a capacity to ensure better information and monitoring, deeper cooperation, and regulation in the world economy. At the same time, however, others argued that the crisis revealed the problems and flaws of existing international institutions and the bias or interests they reflect. These positions echo a larger debate in IPE about the nature and impact of institutions in the world economy. This debate is important in helping us determine what role international institutions might play in managing the new problems and challenges arising from globalization (see Table 11.4).

Competing accounts of institutions echo the differences in approaches to IPE already discussed. Institutionalists (or neoliberal institutionalists; see Chapter 3) tell us that states will create institutions to better achieve gains through policy cooperation and **coordination** (pursuing a common strategy to avoid a mutually undesirable outcome). However, several preconditions are necessary for this to occur. Under certain conditions, institutionalists argue, states will agree to be bound by certain rules, norms, or decisions of **international organizations**. This does not mean the most powerful states in the system will always obey the rules. Rather, institutions affect international politics because they open up new reasons to cooperate, they permit states to define their interests in a more cooperative way, and they foster negotiations among states as well as compliance with mutually agreed rules and standards.

The institutionalist account offers reasons for a certain kind of optimism about the role international institutions will play in managing globalization. Institutions will smooth over many gaps and failures in the operation of markets and serve to ensure that states make genuinely rational and optimizing decisions to cooperate. Globalization will be managed by existing institutions and organizations, and indeed, new institutions will probably also emerge. Globalization managed in this way will ensure that the world economy moves more toward the liberal model and that both strong and weak states benefit. Although there have been many protests about international organizations, these are the result of people misunderstanding the advantages of free trade and free movements of capital in the world economy.

Realists (and structural realists in particular) disagree with institutionalists. Realists reject the idea that institutions emerge primarily as a solution to universal problems or market failures. They argue that international institutions and organizations will always reflect the interests of dominant states within the system. When these dominant

coordination A form of cooperation requiring parties to pursue a common strategy to avoid the mutually undesirable outcome arising from the pursuit of divergent strategies.

international organization Any institution with formal procedures and formal membership from three or more countries. The minimum number of countries is set at three, rather than two, because multilateral relationships have significantly greater complexity than bilateral relationships.

Table 11.4
Debates About Institutions

	Institutionalist (or Neoliberal Institutionalist)	Realist (or Neorealist)	Constructivist
Under what conditions will states create international institutions?	For mutual gains (rationally calculated by states).	Only where relative position vis-à-vis other states is not adversely affected.	Institutions arise as a reflection of the identities and interests of states and groups, which are themselves forged through interaction.
What impact do institutions have on international relations?	Expand the possible gains to be made from cooperation.	Facilitate the coordination of policies and actions but only insofar as this does not alter the balance of power among states.	Reinforce particular patterns of interaction and reflect new ones.
What are the implications for globalization?	Institutions can manage globalization to ensure a transition to a more liberal economy.	Institutions will manage globalization in the interests of dominant and powerful states.	Changing patterns of interaction and discourse will be reflected in institutional responses to globalization.

states wish to coordinate policies with others, they will create institutions. Once created, however, these institutions will not (as the institutionalists argue) transform the way states define and pursue their interests. Institutions will be effective only for as long as they do not diminish the power of dominant states vis-à-vis other states.

Let us consider what this means in practice. Take a state deciding whether to sign a new trade agreement or support the decision of an international organization. The institutionalists argue that policy makers will consider the absolute gains to be made from the agreement, including the potential longer-term gains, such as advancing a stabler and more credible system of rules. The structural realists, by contrast, argue that policy makers will primarily be concerned with relative gains. Rather than asking, "Do we gain from this?" they will ask, "Do we gain more from this than other states?" If other states stand to gain more, then the advantages of signing the agreement are outweighed by the fact that the power of the state will be diminished in relation to other states.

For realists, cooperation and institutions are heavily constrained by underlying calculations about power. Having signed an agreement or created an international organization, a powerful state will not necessarily be bound by it. Indeed, if it gets in the way of the state's interests (defined in realist terms), a powerful state will sweep the institution aside. The implications for globalization and its impact on weak states are rather grim. International institutions, including the IMF, the World Bank, the WTO, the G-20, and

CASE STUDY
The European Economic Crisis and Its Global Consequences
11.2

BACKGROUND
In 1999, seventeen of twenty-seven countries in the European Union adopted the euro as their common currency. The agreement allowed poorer members to borrow money at the same low interest rates as wealthier, more financially solvent members.

THE CASE
In 2011, it became clear that Ireland, Portugal, and Greece were in trouble from debts associated with an extensive public welfare state and less tax income due to reduced economic growth. European institutions were willing to provide bailout funds in return for austerity plans. In June 2011, Greek lawmakers began to reduce government spending and sold off a number of national assets. These actions eased some of the crisis, but the Papandreou government did not survive these austerity plans. It appeared that budget cuts, layoffs, tax increases, and forced asset sales might not be enough to prevent a collapse of the Greek government, leaving the offered bailouts its only resort.

OUTCOME
As of the writing of this book, it is not clear whether the bailouts will work. If they do not, meaning Greece defaults and its government collapses, the rest of Europe (led by Germany and France) will need to act quickly to prevent similar problems in Ireland, Portugal, and Spain. Because there is no powerful central bank in the eurozone, the chance of the crisis spreading is more likely. The cost of borrowing will rise because investors will be fearful of other risks in the European region. Investors will move money quickly to safe areas if they feel the richer countries are not willing to act decisively. German chancellor Angela Merkel stated in November 2011 that Europe faced the most difficult hours since World War II. She argued that more political integration within the European Union was essential for the euro to survive as a common currency.

Meanwhile, the Italian government collapsed at the end of 2011, and its parliament announced new austerity plans. At the same time, Spain voted out its socialist government, which had been in power since 2004, electing a more fiscally conservative government in its place.

If the crisis spreads as feared, the consequences will be felt globally. Investors in the United States will move their investments out of Europe as the slowdown in European markets decreases US exports and hurts the US economy. Exposure to European debt is likely to affect the economies of big global creditors like China, Saudi Arabia, and other petroleum-exporting states.

For Discussion
1. If European leaders fail, how will this affect economies across the world?
2. Some people argue that socialism is the problem. How then do you explain the success of Sweden and Norway?
3. The debt crisis could force some countries to pass legislation that protects their economic interests. Economic nationalism contributed to both World War I and World War II. Could similar conflicts between states happen again? Why or why not?

the European Union, will manage globalization but in the interests of their most powerful members. Institutions will only accommodate the needs and interests of weaker states where in so doing they do not diminish the dominant position of powerful states. From a realist perspective, it follows that antiglobalization protesters are correct to argue that the international institutions do not work for the interests of poor and developing countries. However, the realists are equally certain that such protests will have little impact.

Constructivists reject the idea that institutions reflect the rational calculations of states either within interstate competition (realists) or as part of a calculation of longer-term economic advantage and benefits from cooperation (institutionalists). In fact, what constructivists reject is the idea that states' interests are objectively definable and fixed. Instead, they argue that any one state's interests are affected by its identity as a state and that both its interests and identity are influenced by a social structure of interactions, normative ideas, and beliefs. If we cannot assume that states have a particular identity or interest prior to their interactions, then the institutionalists are wrong to assume that institutions

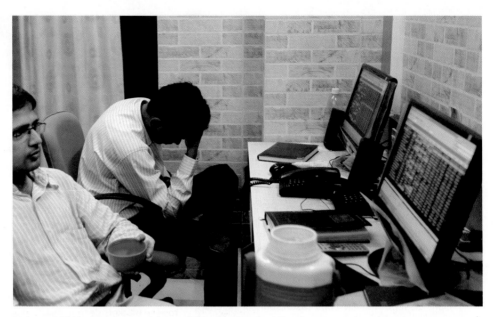

In August 2011, stocks around the world tumbled as the US economy continued to stagnate. Stockbrokers in Bombay react to the US market losses.

emerge as rational responses to the needs of markets, trade, finance, and the like. Equally, the realists are incorrect to assume that institutions can only be reflections of power politics. To quote constructivist Alexander Wendt, "Anarchy is what states make of it" (1992). Identities and interests are more fluid and changing than realists permit. Through their interactions and discourse, states change, and these changes can reflect in institutions.

The constructivist approach examines actors and processes involved in globalization that are neglected in realist and institutionalist accounts and have important ramifications for institutions. For example, the protesters against the WTO, the IMF, and the World Bank can be construed as part of an ongoing dialogue that affects states in several ways. The international attention to these issues places them on the agenda of international meetings and organizations. It also puts pressure on political leaders and encourages interest groups to form within the state. As a result, the beliefs, ideas, and conceptions of interest in international relations change, and this can shift the attention, nature, and functions of international institutions. In this view, globalization is not only a process affecting and managed by states. Several other actors are involved both within and across societies, including international institutions, which play a dynamic role. The governance or management of globalization is shaped by a mixture of interests, beliefs, and values about how the world works and how it ought to be. The existing institutions doubtlessly reflect the interests of powerful states. However, these interests are the products of the way states interact and are subject to reinterpretation and change.

Conclusion

In this chapter, we have covered the basics of the major post–World War II international financial institutions and how they work. The global economic events of 2008–2012 put a major strain on the ability of these institutions to cope with the collapse. Some IPE analysts believe that the very institutions that were intended to bring stability to the system helped cause the recent global recession. Institutions like the IMF and World Bank looked to adapt to a more pluralistic economic system in which economic power is diffused among a number of states and nonstate actors.

The present economic system is no longer controlled by the United States. The 2008–2012 crisis has forced the rich and poor states to come together, reform the present global economic institutions, and create new ones—like the G-20 group of leaders, which first met in November 2008 in Washington, D.C., bringing together the Group of Seven and major emerging economies. When the subprime mortgage crisis struck the US markets in the summer of 2008, the effects were felt worldwide.

In 2011 and 2012, the economic crisis in both Greece and Italy affected the confidence of consumers and investors worldwide. Global stock markets fell over the failure of European leaders to adequately address the economic crisis in the euro zone. The economic future stability of Europe and maybe the world will depend on the ability of the leaders of Germany and France to design an effective bailout program that can be acceptable to the citizens of both Greece and Italy. The citizens of Germany must stand behind their government's efforts to support a plan to save Europe, and citizens of Greece and Italy must also be willing to accept austerity plans and reduce their national debt. World leaders must react and reform the present system or risk further turbulence as new crises emerge. We are facing several potential problems. First, we need to address the growing inequality within and between states; second, we need to address new vulnerabilities and risks unleashed by globalized financial markets; and third, the world must deal with the growing scarcity of critical resources like oil and water. Otherwise, we face a future of resource wars and collapsing economies.

CONTRIBUTORS TO CHAPTER 11: Ngaire Woods and Steven L. Lamy.

REVIEW QUESTIONS

1. In what ways did the Bretton Woods framework for the postwar economy try to avoid the economic problems of the interwar years?
2. What was the breakdown in the Bretton Woods system?
3. Did a loss of US hegemony cause the breakdown of the Bretton Woods system?
4. What is different about the Marxist and mercantilist depictions of power in the international economy?
5. Does rational choice theory explain more about outcomes than actors' preferences?
6. In what way do constructivists invoke structure in their explanation of IPE?
7. Why do skeptics doubt that globalization is transforming IPE?
8. What vulnerabilities faced by states in the globalizing economy did the Asian financial crisis demonstrate? What about the current European economic crisis?
9. How can we explain the different impact globalization has on different states?
10. How and why do institutionalists argue that institutions change the behavior of states?

FURTHER READING

Frieden, J., and Lake, D. A. (eds.) (2000), *International Political Economy: Perspectives on Global Power and Wealth* (New York: St. Martin's Press). Offers very useful editors' introductions to core texts from each approach to international political economy.

Grieco, J. M., and Ikenberry, G. J. (2003), *State Power and World Markets: The International Political Economy* (New York: W. W. Norton). An overarching text with an underlying realist view of the world economy.

Held, D., McGrew, A., Goldblatt, D., and Perrator, J. (1999), *Global Transformations: Politics, Economics and Culture* (Cambridge: Polity Press). A useful resource book on the empirical evidence of globalization in all aspects of international relations.

Helleiner, E. (1994), *States and the Reemergence of Global Finance: From Bretton Woods to the 1990s* (Ithaca, N.Y.: Cornell University Press). Explains how the policies of states have shaped the emergence of the international financial system.

Katzenstein, P., Keohane, R., and Krasner, S. (1998), "International Organization and the State of World Politics," *International Organization* 52(4): 645–685. Reviews key developments in the study of international relations and international political economy.

Oatley, T., and Silver, M. (2003), *International Political Economy: Interests and Institutions in the Global Economy* (Harlow: Pearson). An example of the public or rational choice approach to international political economy.

Palan, R. (ed.) (2000), *Global Political Economy: Contemporary Theories* (London: Routledge). A sampling of European approaches and theories of international political economy.

Rodrik, D. (1999), *The New Global Economy and Developing Countries: Making Openness Work* (Washington, D.C.: Overseas Development Council). A critical analysis of the advantages and disadvantages of globalization for developing countries.

Stiglitz, J. E. (2010), *Freefall: America, Free Markets, and the Sinking of the World Economy* (New York: W. W. Norton). A view of the current US-initiated economic crisis from a Nobel laureate.

Woods, N. (2006), *The Globalizers: The IMF, the World Bank, and Their Borrowers* (Ithaca, N.Y.: Cornell University Press). An overview on the roles, evolution, and politics of the IMF and World Bank and their relations with developing countries.

INTERNET RESOURCES

Gapminder
www.gapminder.org
An NGO that tracks the gap between rich and poor countries and people around the world.

International Monetary Fund
www.imf.org
Part of the Bretton Woods system, this multilateral organization helps manage the global economy.

The Group of Twenty
http://www.g20.org/
The economic forum of the 20 leading national economies. The group gained prominence during the 2008–2010 global recession.

World Bank
www.worldbank.org
The International Bank for Recovery and Development, or World Bank, is the most important multilateral international lending organization. It provides funding for both large-scale infrastructure and smaller-scale human development programs.

World Trade Organization
http://www.wto.org
The prime multilateral organization that sets the "rules of the game" in international trade.

Carnegie Council: "How the Economy Works: Confidence, Crashes and Self-Fulfilling Prophecies"—Roger Farmer
http://www.carnegiecouncil.org/resources/video/data/000318
Roger Farmer discusses the three key economic events in the last century: the Great Depression, stagflation in the 1970s, and the "Great Recession." He goes on to discuss economic philosophies.

Carnegie Council: "The End of the Free Market: Who Wins the War Between States and Corporations?"—Ian Bremmer
http://www.carnegiecouncil.org/resources/video/data/000329
Consumer, capital, and labor markets are the core drivers of economic development today according to Ian Bremmer. He spells out an end to the free market economy and the further rise of corporations as the dominant economic actor at the expense of states.

Carnegie Council: "Reform of the International Monetary and Financial System"—Joseph E. Stiglitz, Bert Koenders, and José Antonio Ocampo
http://www.carnegiecouncil.org/resources/video/data/000265
Nobel laureate Joseph Stiglitz along with panel members Bert Koenders and José Ocampo point to international trade and financial service practices that must be reformed to prevent future global economic crises.

For more information, quizzes, case studies and other study tools, please visit us at **www.oup.com/us/lamy**

THINKING ABOUT GLOBAL POLITICS

Globalization: Productive, Predatory, or Inconsequential?

INTRODUCTION

Globalization has become a buzzword that many pundits and scholars use to describe anything and everything happening in the world today. All of the authors in this text share several definitions, and these suggest that globalization is more than just an economic process. But what makes this era of globalization different from previous eras? Is it a positive, negative, or marginal process? How do the various processes of globalization shape issues and events in the political, economic, social, and cultural worlds? This exercise will explore some of these questions.

DISCUSSION

1. Find a definition of globalization that makes the most sense to you. What are the different dimensions of globalization? What does *globalization from above and below* mean?
2. Globalization is said to cause *denationalization or delocalization*. What does that mean?
3. Is globalization a recent process? What makes this era different from previous periods of world trade and interdependence? Were the periods of colonialism and imperialism early phases of globalization?
4. What factors push globalization, making it faster, wider, and deeper?

5. Is the process of globalization taking power away from the state, or does it actually enhance the power of some states and weaken others? How?

FOLLOW-UP EXERCISE

What do we expect a state to do? In theory, we expect a state to provide services and resources in three areas:

1. *defining activities*, which include supporting a means of exchange or marketplace, providing a system of law and order, and protecting the boundaries of the state;
2. *accumulation-of-wealth activities*, such as building infrastructure; and
3. *redistribution activities*, such as providing healthcare and education.

Professor Manuel Castells (2005) has written that globalization has led to four crises within states: an *efficiency crisis*, a *legitimacy crisis*, an *identity crisis*, and an *equity crisis*. Is this just an academic claim, or are countries really suffering in these areas? Find at least two countries where one, several, or all of these crises are having a major impact on a state's capacity to provide for its citizens in the three basic areas listed. More precisely, how does globalization influence a state's ability to provide defining activities, accumulation-of-wealth activities, and redistribution activities?

Trade is the oldest and most important economic nexus among nations. Indeed, trade along with war has been central to the evolution of international relations.

—*Robert Gilpin*

There can be different brands of free-market vanilla and you can adjust your society to it by going faster or slower. But, in the end, if you want higher standards of living in a world without walls, the free market is the only ideological alternative left. One road. Different speeds. But one road.

—*Thomas L. Friedman*

How did it happen? The global economy was cruising along in the fast lane. Stock prices seemed to have no ceiling with each day bringing a new all-time high. The annual bonuses that CEOs of multinational corporations and bond traders of Wall Street gave themselves were more than the GDPs of most developing countries. Then, although the danger was there to see for some time, subprime mortgages in the United States managed to spark a worldwide economic collapse in 2008. Some economists had warned that the "ownership society" of the Bush administration could cause an economic catastrophe. We soon saw that the policy of encouraging people who barely met the income guidelines for mortgages to purchase houses with flexible-rate loans would lead to foreclosure and bankruptcy. These bad mortgages had become an aspect of the new pattern of global investments for the most part unfettered by government regulation. Nobel Prize–winning economist Joseph Stiglitz stated in 2010 that one of the legacies of this crisis will be a new debate on which kind of economic system "is most likely to deliver the kind of economic system likely to deliver the greatest benefit." Communism is out of the debate, but what about Asian capitalism, with its emphasis on an economy that enriches the state, or the Nordic social democratic strategy that is creating economic stability and growth in Sweden? Time will tell whether the future of capitalism will include more or less government intervention in the market and whether states will continue to provide their citizens with a wide variety of social services.

But the economic collapse of 2008–2009 was more than bad personal finances and massive government bailouts for banks

Stock markets across the world are interconnected. On this day in January 2014, Japanese stock markets sank after a sell-off of stocks in the US. The interdependence of global economies means that one state's economic security may be dependent on economic security and stability around the world.

375

and corporations. Indeed, in early 2009, Dennis Blair, the new director of national intelligence for the United States, warned members of the Senate that the global economic crisis was the most serious security challenge facing the United States and the world. Blair stated that 25 percent of the countries in the world have experienced low-level instability that is attributed to unemployment and poor economic conditions. Economic refugees might topple weak governments, and failed states might never get off the bottom. Even wealthy states have been adversely affected by the global economic crisis; after all, working and effective global trade and financial systems are also critical elements of global security.

Introduction

The globalization of world politics involves, among other things, a globalization of economics. As we discussed in previous chapters, politics and economics are inseparable within social relations. Economics does not explain everything, but no account of world politics (and hence, no analysis of globalization as a key issue of contemporary world history) is adequate if it does not explore the economic dimension.

Like the Bretton Woods system, which we discussed in the previous chapter, the global trade and finance systems developed in reaction to the events that followed World War I. The freewheeling capitalism of the Roaring Twenties, many people believed, helped cause the Great Depression. In the United States, for example, overproduction and underconsumption, buying stocks on margin, the corrupt investment strategies known as Ponzi schemes (made famous again by the recent actions of Bernie Madoff), and land speculation were all parts of the problems inherent when governments did not regulate business activity. Once the Great Depression struck in 1929, international trade measures such as increased tariffs exacerbated the preexisting domestic market distortions.

International trade, however, did not lend itself to solutions like the IMF and World Bank of the Bretton Woods system. John Maynard Keynes, Harry Dexter White, and the other economists and political leaders who met in New Hampshire in July 1944 planned a third part of the system, the International Trade Organization (ITO). Unfortunately, largely because of opposition in the US Senate, the Havana Charter of the ITO never entered into force. In its place, the GATT secretariat—which was intended to oversee trade on a temporary basis—took on the task of organizing global trade negotiations.

The United States is stuck in an economic slump that is as bad as the 1929 depression, and as we discussed in the previous chapter, the United States is not alone. Europe is struggling to prevent national debt issues from becoming a major banking crisis, and China and other major emerging economies are now feeling the effects of the economic crisis as stagnant economies in Europe and the United States weaken the demand for exports. Many experts are concerned that the United States and Europe may face a long period of slow growth, high unemployment, and deflation. Historically, this is what Japan experienced when its own real estate and stock bubble burst in the 1990s. It is critical that regional and global institutions act together to address these issues.

In this chapter, you will learn about the global players and their roles in global trade and the financial system. You will also develop a thorough understanding of the nature of the global trading system, the financial and banking system, and the global economy. You will develop a more sophisticated understanding of the complexity of the global economy and the challenges faced by any national leader who attempts to respond alone to these challenges.

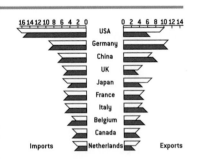

THE MAIN TRADING NATIONS.
The white bars show the imports and exports of the top ten trading nations as a percentage of world trade. The blue bars show each country's trade manufactured also as a percentage of world trade. What patterns do you see in this graph? What do these patterns suggest about global trade?

Global Trade and Finance Actors

Countless discussions of globalization have brought its economic aspects front and center. For example, the late Milton Friedman, a Nobel Prize–winning economist, remarked that it has become possible "to produce a product anywhere, using resources from anywhere, by a company located anywhere, to be sold anywhere" (cited in Naisbitt 1994, 19). A senior researcher with American Express has described the global financial integration of recent decades as marking "the end of geography" (O'Brien 1992). Global governance bodies like the Bank for International Settlements (BIS), the Group of Eight (G-8), the International Monetary Fund (IMF), the Organisation for Economic Co-operation and Development (OECD), the UN Conference on Trade and Development (UNCTAD), the World Bank Group (WBG), and the World Trade Organization (WTO) have all put economic globalization high on their agendas (see Table 12.1). Usually, these official circles have endorsed and encouraged the trend, as have most national governments. Meanwhile, many social movements have focused their critiques of globalization on economic aspects of the process. Their analyses have depicted contemporary globalization of trade and finance as a major cause of higher unemployment, a general decline in working standards, increased inequality, greater poverty for some (see Chapter 13), recurrent financial crises, and large-scale environmental degradation (see Chapter 14).

In their different ways, all of these assessments agree that economic globalization is a key development of contemporary history. True, the scale and impact of the trend are often exaggerated. However, it is just as wrong to argue, as some skeptics have done, that claims about a new globalizing economy rest on nothing but hype and myth. Instead, as in the case of most historical developments, economic globalization involves an intricate interplay of changes and continuities. Certainly, the economic crisis that began in 2008 shows how interconnected and globalized the world's economy has become.

A Globalizing Economy

One key reason for disagreements over the extent and significance of economic globalization relates to the contrasting definitions that different analysts have applied to notions of what it means to be global. What, more precisely, is "global" about the global economy? The following paragraphs distinguish three contrasting ways the globalization of trade and finance has been broadly conceived—namely, in terms of (1) the crossing of borders, (2) the opening of borders, and (3) the transcendence of borders. Although the three conceptions overlap to some extent, they involve important differences of emphasis. Most arguments concerning economic globalization have pitted skeptics, who adopt the first perspective, against enthusiasts, who apply the second. However, the third conception of globality offers a more distinctive and revealing approach. Later sections of this chapter therefore develop that alternative notion in relation to trade and finance.

Cross-Border Transactions

Skepticism about the significance of contemporary economic globalization has often arisen when analysts have conceived the process in terms of increased cross-border movements of people, goods, money, investments, messages, and ideas. From this perspective, globalization is seen as equivalent to internationalization. No significant distinction is drawn between global companies and international companies, between global

WHAT'S YOUR WORLDVIEW

Why do these disputes about the character of globalization matter? In your own life, is globalization a positive or negative process?

Table 12.1

Major Public Global Governance Agencies for Trade and Finance

BIS—Bank for International Settlements. Established in 1930 with headquarters in Basel. Membership (2010) of fifty-six shareholding central banks, although many other public financial institutions also use BIS facilities. Promotes cooperation among central banks and provides various services for global financial operations. For example, the Basel Committee on Banking Supervision, formed through the BIS in 1974, has spearheaded efforts at multilateral regulation of global banking. (www.bis.org)

G-8—Group of Eight. Established in 1975 as the G-5 (France, Germany, Japan, the United Kingdom, and the United States); subsequently expanded as the G-7 to include Canada and Italy and, since 1998, as the G-8 to include the Russian Federation. The G-8 conducts semiformal collaboration on world economic problems. Government leaders meet in annual G-8 summits, while finance ministers and/or their leading officials periodically hold other consultations.

G-20—Established in 1999, this group is made up of finance ministers and central bank governors of nineteen countries and the European Union. Members include Argentina, Australia, Brazil, Canada, China, France, Germany, India, Indonesia, Italy, Japan, Mexico, Russia, Saudi Arabia, South Africa, South Korea, Turkey, the United Kingdom, and the United States. This is an informal forum that was created after the financial crisis in the mid-1990s. The members discuss national policies, plans for international cooperation, and ideas for reforming institutions that manage the global economy. (http://www.g20.org)

GATT—General Agreement on Tariffs and Trade. Established in 1947 with offices in Geneva. Membership had reached 122 states when it was absorbed into the WTO in 1995. The GATT coordinated eight rounds of multilateral negotiations to reduce state restrictions on cross-border merchandise trade. (www.wto.org)

IMF—International Monetary Fund. Established in 1945 with headquarters in Washington, D.C. Membership (2009) of 185 states. The IMF monitors short-term cross-border payments and foreign exchange positions. When a country develops chronic imbalances in its external accounts, the IMF supports corrective policy reforms, often called "structural-adjustment programs." Since 1978, the IMF has undertaken comprehensive surveillance both of the economic performance of individual member states and of the world economy as a whole. The IMF also provides extensive technical assistance. In recent years, the fund has pursued various initiatives to promote efficiency and stability in global financial markets. (www.imf.org)

IOSCO—International Organization of Securities Commissions. Established in 1983 with headquarters in Montreal; secretariat now in Madrid. Membership (2010) of 193 official securities regulators as well as (nonvoting) trade associations and other agencies. The IOSCO aims to promote high standards of regulation in stock and bond markets, to establish effective surveillance of transborder securities transactions, and to foster collaboration between securities markets in the detection and punishment of offenses. (www.iosco.org)

OECD—Organisation for Economic Co-operation and Development. Founded in 1962 with headquarters in Paris. Membership (2010) of thirty-one states with advanced industrial economies and further relationships with some seventy other states. Provides a forum for multilateral intergovernmental consultations on almost all policy issues except military affairs. The OECD measures have especially addressed environmental questions, taxation, and transborder corporations. At regular intervals, the OECD secretariat produces an assessment of the macroeconomic performance of each member, including suggestions for policy changes. (www.oecd.org)

UNCTAD—United Nations Conference on Trade and Development. Established in 1964 with offices in Geneva. Membership (2010) of 193 states. The UNCTAD monitors the effects of world trade and investment on economic development, especially in the South. It provided a key forum in the 1970s for discussions of a New International Economic Order. (www.unctad.org)

WBG—World Bank Group. A collection of five agencies, the first established in 1945, with head offices in Washington, D.C. The WBG promotes development in medium- and low-income countries with project loans, structural-adjustment programs, and various advisory services. (www.worldbank.org)

WTO—World Trade Organization. Established in 1995 with headquarters in Geneva. Membership (2010) of 153 states. The WTO is a permanent institution to replace the provisional GATT. It has a wider agenda covering services, intellectual property, and investment issues as well as merchandise trade. The WTO also has greater powers of enforcement through its Dispute Settlement Mechanism. The organization's Trade Policy Review Body conducts surveillance of members' commercial measures. (www.wto.org)

trade and international trade, between global money and international money, or between global finance and international finance.

When conceived in this way, economic globalization is nothing particularly new. Commerce between different territorial-political units has transpired for centuries and in some cases even millennia. Ancient Babylon and the Roman Empire knew forms of long-distance lending and trade, for example. Shipments between Arabia and China via South and Southeast Asia occurred with fair regularity more than 1,000 years ago. Certain coins circulated widely around maritime Southeast Asia in a prototypical "international monetary regime" of the tenth century. Long-distance monies of the premodern Mediterranean world included the Byzantine solidus from the fifth century onward and the Muslim dinar from the eighth to the

General Electric's chairman visits their turbine factory in Brazil. Investment, finance, production, and trade are all global.

thirteenth centuries. Banks based in Italian city-states maintained (temporary) offices along long-distance trade routes as early as the twelfth century. The Hanseatic League in the fourteenth century and companies based in Amsterdam, Copenhagen, London, and Paris in the seventeenth century operated overseas trading posts. The first brokerage houses with cross-border operations appeared in the eighteenth century with Amsterdam-based Hope & Co. and London-based Barings.

Indeed, on certain (though far from all) measures, cross-border economic activity reached similar levels in the late nineteenth century as it did 100 years later. Relative to world population of the time, the magnitude of permanent migration was in fact considerably greater than today. When measured in relation to world output, cross-border investment in production facilities stood at roughly the same level on the eve of World War I as it did in the early 1990s. International markets in loans and securities also flourished during the heyday of the gold-sterling standard between 1870 and 1914. Under this regime, the British pound, fixed to a certain value in gold, served as a global currency and thereby greatly facilitated cross-border payments. Again citing proportional (rather than aggregate) statistics, several researchers (e.g., Zevin 1992) have argued that these years witnessed larger capital flows between countries than in the late twentieth century. Meanwhile, the volume of international trade grew at some 3.4 percent per annum in the period 1870–1913 until its value was equivalent to 33 percent of world output (Barraclough 1984, 256; Hirst and Thompson 1999, 21). By this particular calculation, cross-border trade was greater at the beginning than at the end of the twentieth century.

For the skeptics, then, the contemporary globalizing economy is nothing new. In their eyes, recent decades have merely experienced a phase of increased cross-border trade and finance, much as occurred 100 years earlier. Moreover, they note, just as growth of international interdependence in the late nineteenth century was substantially reversed with a forty-year wave of protectionism after 1914, so economic globalization of the present day may prove to be temporary. Governments can block cross-border flows if they wish, say the skeptics of globalization, and national interest may dictate that states once more tighten restrictions on international trade, travel, foreign exchange, and capital movements. Contemporary economic globalization gives little evidence, say these doubters, of an impending demise of the state, a weakening of national loyalties, and an end of war. Thus, for example, skeptics

Engaging with the
WORLD
WTO Secretariat

The WTO Secretariat maintains a limited internship program for postgraduate university students wishing to gain practical experience and deeper knowledge of the multilateral trading system. Only a limited number of such internship posts are available. Intake to the program is on a continuing basis, with no specific recruitment period. Assignments are intended to enhance interns' knowledge and understanding of the WTO and of trade policy more generally. To learn more, visit http://www.wto.org.

regularly point out that most so-called global companies (1) still conduct the majority of their business in their country of origin, (2) retain strong national character and allegiances, and (3) remain heavily dependent on states for the success of their enterprises.

Open-Border Transactions

In contrast to the skeptics, enthusiasts for contemporary globalization of trade and finance generally define these developments as part of the long-term evolution toward a global society. In this second conception, globalization entails not an extension of internationalization but the progressive removal of official restrictions on transfers of resources between countries. In the resultant world of open borders, global companies replace international companies, global trade replaces international trade, global money replaces international money, and global finance replaces international finance. This process results in markets that are much larger than regional arrangements like the European Union (EU) and the North American Free Trade Association (NAFTA). From this perspective, globalization is a function of liberalization—that is, the degree to which products, communications, financial instruments, fixed assets, and people can circulate throughout the world economy free from state-imposed controls. Whereas skeptics generally back up their arguments of historical repetition with proportional data, globalists usually substantiate their claims of historical change with aggregate statistics, many of which do indeed appear quite staggering (see Table 12.2).

Globalists regard the forty-year interlude of protectionism (ca. 1910–1950) as a temporary detour from a longer historical trend toward the construction of a single integrated world economy. In their eyes, the tightening of border controls in the first half of the twentieth century was a major cause of economic depressions, authoritarian regimes, and international conflicts such as the world wars. In contrast, the emergent open world economy (so runs the globalist promise) will yield prosperity, liberty, democracy, and peace for all humanity. From this perspective, which is often termed *neoliberalism*, contemporary economic globalization continues the universalizing project of modernity launched several centuries ago.

Recent history has indeed witnessed considerable opening of borders in the world economy. For one thing, a succession of interstate accords through the General Agreement on Tariffs and Trade (GATT) has, since 1948, in a series of negotiations called "rounds," brought major reductions in customs duties, quotas, and other measures that previously inhibited cross-border movements of merchandise. Average tariffs on manufactures in countries of the North fell from more than 40 percent in the 1930s to less than 4 percent by 1999. Following the Uruguay Round of multilateral trade negotiations (1986–1994), the GATT was subsumed within the new World Trade Organization. This successor agency has greater competences both to enforce existing trade agreements and to pursue new avenues of liberalization—for example, with respect to shipping, telecommunications, and investment flows. Meanwhile, regional frameworks like the European Union and NAFTA have (to varying degrees) removed official restrictions on trade between participating countries. Encouraged by such liberalization, cross-border trade expanded between 1950 and 1994 at an annual rate of just over 6 percent, thus almost twice as fast as in the late nineteenth century. Total international trade multiplied fourteen-fold in real terms over this period, and expansion of trade in manufactures was even greater, with a twenty-six-fold increase (World Trade Organization 1995).

Borders have also opened considerably to money flows since 1950. As discussed in the previous chapter, the gold-dollar standard became fully operational through the IMF in 1959. Under this regime, major currencies—and especially the US dollar—could circulate

Table 12.2
Some Indicators of Contemporary Economic Globalization ($ Billion)

Measure (Worldwide Figures)	Earlier Level	Recent Level
Foreign direct investment	$68 (1960)	$1.3 trillion (2012)
Exports	$629 (1960)	$10,159 (2005)
Official foreign exchange reserves	$100 (1970)	$5,028 (2006)
Daily turnover on foreign exchange markets	$100 (1979)	$1,880 (2004)
Bank deposits by nonresidents	$20 (1964)	$7,876 (1995)
Cross-border loan announcements	$9 (1972)	$1,465 (2000)
Cross-border bond issues	$1 (1960)	$1,157 (1999)
Euroequity* issues	Initiated 1984	$50 (1995)
Cross-border share dealing	$10 (1980)	$120 (1994)
Daily turnover of financial derivatives contracts	Small before 1980	$1,162 (1995)

Sources: BIS, IMF, OECD, UNCTAD, WTO.

* When a company's shares are made available internationally rather than just where the company has its home base (*Financial Times*).

world wide (though not in communist-ruled countries) and be converted to local monies at an official **fixed exchange rate**. The gold-dollar standard thereby broadly re-created the situation that prevailed under the gold-sterling standard in the late nineteenth century. Contrary to many expectations, the US government's termination of dollar-gold convertibility on demand in 1971 did not trigger new restrictions on cross-border payments. Instead, a regime of **floating exchange rates** developed—de facto from 1973 and formalized through the IMF in 1976. Moreover, from the mid-1970s onward, most states with developed economies reduced or eliminated restrictions on the import and export of national currencies. In these circumstances, the average volume of daily transactions on the world's wholesale foreign exchange markets burgeoned from $15 billion in 1973 to $1,900 billion in 2004.

Alongside the liberalization of trade and money movements between countries, recent decades have also witnessed the widespread opening of borders to investment flows. These movements involve both direct investments (i.e., fixed assets like research facilities and factories) and portfolio investments (i.e., liquid assets like loans, bonds, and stocks). One result is that the 2008 global economic implosion began with the sale of securities of unwise mortgages made in the United States.

Apart from a spate of expropriations in the South during the 1970s (many of them subsequently reversed), states have generally welcomed **foreign direct investment (FDI)** into their jurisdictions in contemporary history. Indeed, many governments have actively lured externally based business by lowering corporate tax rates, reducing restrictions on the repatriation of profits, relaxing labor and environmental standards, and so on. Since 1960, there has been a proliferation of what are variously called international, multinational, transnational, or global corporations (hence, the frequently encountered abbreviations MNC

fixed exchange rate The price a currency will earn in a hard currency. Here a government is committed to keep it at a specific value.

floating exchange rate The market decides what the actual value of a currency is compared to other currencies.

foreign direct investment (FDI) The capital speculation by citizens or organizations of one country into markets or industries in another country.

and TNC). The number of such companies grew from 3,500 in 1960 to 64,000 in 2005. The aggregate stock of FDI worldwide increased in tandem from $68 billion in 1960 to $10,672 billion in 2005 compared with only $14 billion in 1914 (UN Conference on Trade and Development 1996, ix, 4; 2006b). In this world of more open borders, various globalists have described MNCs as "footloose" and "stateless." This is a process that Cynthia Enloe calls "the globetrotting sneaker."

Substantial liberalization has also occurred since the 1970s with respect to cross-border portfolio investments, which provided another cause of the 2008 economic recession and the continuing global crisis. For example, many a state now permits nonresidents to hold bank accounts within its jurisdiction. Other **deregulation** has removed legal restrictions on ownership and trading of stocks and bonds by nonresident investors. Further legislation has reduced controls on participation in a country's financial markets by externally based banks, brokers, and fund managers. As a result of such deregulation (e.g., the repeal of the Glass-Steagall Act in 1999), financial institutions from all over the world have converged on global cities like Hong Kong, New York, Paris, and Tokyo. Levels of cross-border banking and securities business have risen markedly since the 1960s in tandem with such liberalization, as several statistics in Table 12.2 indicate. It is important to note that corresponding indicators for the period between 1870 and 1914 come nowhere close to these current aggregate figures.

In sum, legal obstructions to economic transactions between countries have greatly diminished worldwide in contemporary history. At the same time, cross-border flows of merchandise, services, money, and investments have reached unprecedented levels, at least in aggregate terms. To this extent, enthusiasts for globalization as liberalization can argue against the skeptics that borders have opened more than ever. That said, significant official restrictions on cross-border economic activity persist. They include countless trade restrictions and continuing **capital controls** in many countries. While states have on the whole welcomed FDI, there is as yet no multilateral regime to liberalize investment flows comparable to the GATT/WTO with respect to trade or the IMF with respect to money. (Negotiations for a Multilateral Agreement on Investment were abandoned at the end of 1998, although states have concluded hundreds of liberalizing bilateral investment treaties.) In addition, many governments have loosened visa and travel restrictions in recent times, but **immigration controls** are on the whole as tight as ever. Indeed, many have recently been reinforced. To this extent, skeptics have grounds to affirm that international borders remain very much in place and can be opened or closed as states choose.

Transborder Transactions

As mentioned earlier, most debates concerning economic globalization have unfolded between skeptics, who regard the current situation as a limited and reversible expansion of cross-border transactions, and globalists, who see an inexorable trend toward an open world economy. However, these two most common positions do not exhaust the possible interpretations. Indeed, neither of these conventional perspectives requires a distinct concept of globalization. Both views resurrect arguments that were elaborated using other vocabulary long before the word *globalization* entered widespread circulation in the 1990s. In a third conception, human lives are increasingly played out in the world as a single place. In this usage, globalization refers to a transformation of geography that occurs when a host of social conditions become less tied to territorial spaces.

Along these lines, in a globalizing economy, patterns of production, exchange, and consumption become increasingly delinked from a geography of territorial distances and

deregulation The removal of all regulation so that market forces, not government policy, control economic developments.

capital controls The monetary policy device that a government uses to regulate the flows into and out of a country's capital account (i.e., the flows of investment-oriented money into and out of a country or currency).

immigration controls A government's control of the number of people who may work, study, or relocate to its country. It may include quotas for certain national groups for immigration.

GLOBAL PERSPECTIVE — NAFTA and Mexico

Most people in the United States had not heard of the North American Free Trade Agreement (NAFTA) prior to the 1992 presidential election campaign. In the first televised presidential debate, independent candidate H. Ross Perot skewered then-president George H. W. Bush, asserting that the NAFTA—the terms of which were largely unknown in the United States—would result in what Perot called "a giant sucking sound" as American jobs went south to Mexico. As expected, the three candidates said little about what the deal would mean for Mexico. With the agreement more than fifteen years old, what has the NAFTA done for Mexico?

According to statistics found on the website of the Office of the United States Trade Representative (USTR), by 2003, all sectors of the Mexican economy had benefited from the country's membership in the NAFTA. For example, exports of Mexican-grown agricultural products to the United States increased 103 percent

Former President Clinton advocated for NAFTA and its terms have helped some economic sectors in the three countries and harmed others.

from 1993 to 2000. Overall farm production increased by over 50 percent during the same period, with changes of 25 percent in pork production, 27 percent in fruit production, and a stunning 80 percent increase in poultry production.

In higher-wage industrial manufacture jobs, similar changes swept most sectors by 2003. In export-oriented industries, according to the USTR, the NAFTA is responsible for more than 3.5 million new jobs, and these jobs on average pay 37 percent more than non-export-linked manufacturing employment. (http://www.ustr.gov/Document_Library/Fact_Sheets/2003/NAFTA_at_10_Myth_-_NAFTA_Was_a_Failure_for_Mexico.html)

Statistics, as Mark Twain famously said, can lie. Put somewhat more diplomatically, statistics are but one perspective on a complex economic situation. As noted in Chapters 8 and 9 of this book, government-compiled economic figures tell only part of the story. Ignored in government data are those sectors of an economy in which payment for a job completed might be in the form of a basket of fruit or a chicken. Or if people are paid in cash and do not report this payment on their income tax forms, the transaction escapes government notice. This is often the case in developing countries with what is disparagingly called "women's work."

There are several signs that the NAFTA is not working for most Mexicans if people in the United States are willing to look beyond official data. When US college students on spring break descend on Cancún and Puerto Vallarta, they could, if they stopped to think, recognize the limited extent of the NAFTA's success. Jobs in support of the tourist industry are low paid, low status, and high stress. Cleaning up after tourists from El Norte, as the United States is called, is unrewarding at best.

Another sign of the very focused character of NAFTA's success for Mexico can be seen in the thousands of young Mexicans, primarily males, who risk arrest and death by trekking across the Sonoran Desert to gain illegal entry into the United States. Once here, these "illegal immigrants," as US opponents of the current immigration policies call them, compete for low-wage jobs. They can be seen in neighborhoods throughout the southwestern states, waiting to be hired as day laborers. Immigration also became a part of the November 2010 elections in the United States, where, for example, the Republican candidate for governor in California had

Continued

GLOBAL PERSPECTIVE — NAFTA and Mexico *continued*

to explain why she had hired an "undocumented" and therefore "illegal" immigrant as a domestic helper.

The irony of the economic recession that began in 2008 is seen in a surprising statistic: the US Border Patrol is intercepting fewer people trying to gain illegal entry into the country. With few jobs in El Norte, why risk death in the desert, abuse at the hands of human traffickers, or arrest in the United States? Better, perhaps, to stay in Mexico and hope that the NAFTA will bring you a job.

For Discussion

1. In what ways is NAFTA about free trade but not fair trade?
2. Should the United States reform its immigration laws to permit workers to seek employment regardless of their citizenship? Why or why not?
3. Does the United States have a responsibility to improve working conditions in Mexico? Why or why not?

---

transborder Economic, political, social, or cultural activities crossing or extending across a border.

supraterratoriality Social, economic, cultural, and political connections that transcend territorial geography.

territorial borders. *Global* economic activity—for industries and people linked to it—extends across widely dispersed terrestrial locations at the same time and moves between locations scattered across the planet, often in effectively no time. Although the patterns of *international* economic interdependence are strongly influenced by territorial distances and national divisions, patterns of *global* trade and finance often have little correspondence to distance and state boundaries. With air travel, satellite links, the Internet, telecommunications, transnational organizations, global consciousness (i.e., a mind-set that conceives of the planet as a single place), and more, much contemporary economic activity transcends borders. In this third sense, globalization involves the growth of a **transborder** (as opposed to cross-border or open-border) economy.

This rise of **supraterritoriality** (transcendence of territorial geography) is evidenced by, among other things, more transactions between countries. However, the geographic character of these global movements is different from the territorial framework that has traditionally defined international interdependence. This qualitative shift means that contemporary statistics on international trade, money, and investment can only be crudely compared with figures relating to earlier times. Moreover, economic statistics ignore or do not count activities that are not modern but are nonetheless vital in some societies. These can include such items as a woman gathering firewood to cook the evening meal in a traditional society or a grandparent providing unpaid childcare in present-day New York City. Hence, the issue is not so much the amount of trade between countries but the way much of this commerce forms part of transborder production processes and global marketing networks. The problem is not only the quantity of money that moves between countries but also the instantaneity with which most funds are transferred. The question is not simply the number of international securities deals as much as the emergence of stock and bond issues that involve participants from multiple countries at the same time. In short, if one accepts this third conception of globalization, then both the skeptics and the enthusiasts are largely missing the crucial point of historical change.

WHAT'S YOUR WORLDVIEW ?

It may be comforting to travel around the world and find Nike shops, Xerox machines, and Starbucks—but what are the costs to local businesses? What is lost economically and culturally? Do you think this form of global homogenization is good or bad?

Global Trade

The distinctiveness of transborder, supraterritorial economic relations will become clearer with illustrations. Examples of global trade are given in this section. Others regarding global finance are discussed in the next section. In each case, their significance relates mainly to contemporary history (although the phenomena in question made some earlier appearances).

The rules of the global trading system are to a great extent only those the countries themselves put on the firms that operate within their borders. Most of the world's trade takes place within the framework of the World Trade Organization (see Figure 12.1); however, as the organization's press office indicates, it is a multilateral discussion forum, not a global trade system. Member states of the WTO agree, among other things, to lower tariffs and to eliminate nontariff barriers to trade, but it is left to the member states to enforce the agreements. Following the concept of international regime that you read about in Chapter 3, the principle that guides the WTO is that multilateral free trade pacts are better than bilateral deals. Another key principle is **most favored nation status**, whereby member states pledge not to discriminate against their trading partners.

Of course, disputes occur in the world's trading system, often to serve a domestic political purpose. For example, the United States and the European Union from time to time have disagreements about bovine growth hormone in beef products grown in the United States, and the United States has had a long-running dispute with China over trade-related aspects of intellectual property rights (TRIPS). To address such disagreements, the WTO has a dispute-resolution panel that keeps the process at the multilateral level so that members will not take unilateral action that could undermine the WTO's goals. Frequently, however, once a country begins the Dispute Settlement Body (DSB) process, both parties settle the dispute before it reaches the full panel. From the creation of the WTO in 1995 to July 2005, members filed 332 unfair-trade complaints, but less than a third reached the DSB panel stage. Because of the risk of retaliation, members prefer to utilize the good offices, reconciliation, and mediation services of the secretary-general, as provided for in Article 5 of the WTO covenant.

Transborder Production

Transborder production arises when a single process is spread across widely dispersed locations both within and between countries. Global coordination links research centers, design units, procurement offices, material-processing installations, fabrication plants, finishing points, assembly lines, quality-control operations, advertising and marketing divisions, data-processing offices, after-sales services, and so on.

Transborder production can be contrasted with territorially centered production. In the latter instance, all stages of a given production process—from initial research to after-sales service—occur within the same local or national unit. In global production, however, the stages are dispersed across different and often widely scattered countries. Each of the various links in the transborder chain specializes in one or several functions, thereby creating economies of scale or exploiting cost differentials between locations. Through **global sourcing**, the company draws materials, components, machinery, finance, and services from anywhere in the world. Territorial distance and borders figure only secondarily, if at all, in determining the sites. Indeed, a firm may relocate certain stages of production several times in short succession in search of profit maximization.

What have been described as global factories were unknown before the 1940s. They did not gain major prominence until the 1960s, and most have spread since the 1970s. Transborder production has developed primarily in the manufacture of textiles, garments, motor vehicles, leather goods, sports articles, toys, optical products, consumer electronics, semiconductors, airplanes, and construction equipment. As you can see, there is little that is not produced transnationally (see Chapter 1).

most favored nation status The status granted to most trading partners that says trade rules with that country will be the same as those given to their most favored trading partner.

global sourcing Obtaining goods and services across geopolitical boundaries. Usually, the goal is to find the least expensive labor and raw material costs and the lowest taxes and tariffs.

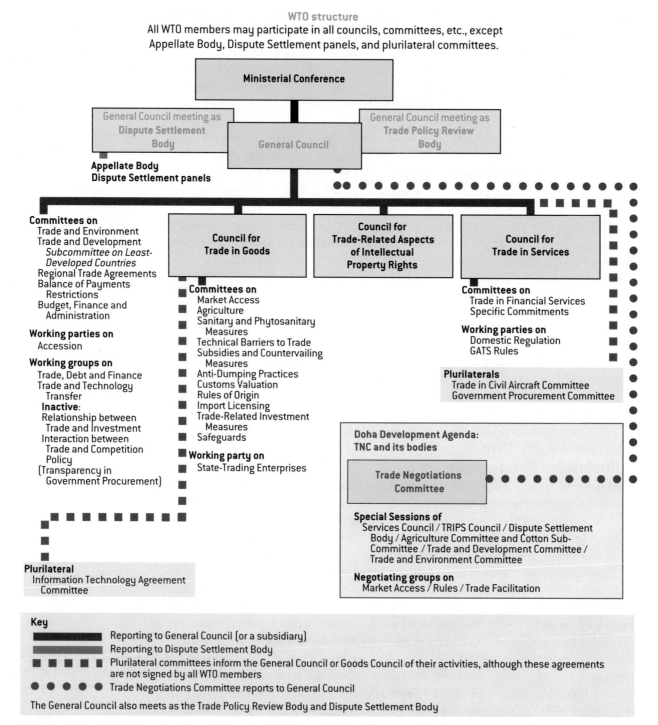

Figure 12.1 The Organizational Chart of the World Trade Organization.

With the growth of global production, a large proportion of purportedly international transfers of goods and services have entailed **intrafirm trade** within transborder companies. When the intermediate inputs and finished goods pass from one country to another, they are officially counted as "international" commerce; yet they primarily involve movements within a global company rather than between national economies. Conventional statistics do not measure intrafirm transfers, but estimates of the share of such exchanges in total cross-border trade have ranged from 25 to more than 40 percent.

Much (though far from all) transborder production has taken advantage of what are variously called special economic zones (SEZs), export processing zones (EPZs), or free production zones (FPZs). Within these enclaves, the ruling national or provincial government exempts assembly plants and other facilities for transborder production from the usual import and export duties. The authorities may also grant other tax reductions, subsidies, and waivers of certain labor and environmental regulations. The first such zone was established in 1954 in Ireland, but most were created after 1970, mainly in Asia, the Caribbean, and the maquiladora areas along the Mexican frontier with the United States. Several thousand EPZs are now in place across more than 100 countries. One distinguishing trait of these manufacturing centers is their frequent heavy reliance on female labor.

intrafirm trade The international trade from one branch of a TNC to an affiliate of the same company in a different country.

Transborder Products

Much of the output of both transborder and country-based production has acquired a planet-spanning market in the contemporary globalizing economy. Hence, a considerable proportion of international trade now involves the distribution and sale of **global goods**, often under a transworld brand name. Consumers dispersed across many corners of the planet purchase the same articles at the same time. The country location of a potential customer for, say, a Xerox photocopier, a Snow Patrol CD, or Kellogg's Corn Flakes is of secondary importance. Design, packaging, and advertising determine the market far more than territorial distances and borders.

global goods Products that are made for a global market and are available across the world.

Like other aspects of globalization, supraterritorial markets have a longer history than many contemporary observers appreciate. For example, Campbell Soup and Heinz began to become household names at widely dispersed locations across the world in the mid-1880s following the introduction of automatic canning. From the outset, Henry Ford regarded his first automobile, the Model T, as a world car. Coca-Cola was bottled in twenty-seven countries and sold in seventy-eight by 1929 (Pendergrast 1993, 174). On the whole, however, the numbers of goods, customers, and countries involved in these earlier global markets were relatively small.

In contrast, global goods pervade the contemporary world economy. They encompass a host of packaged foods, bottled beverages, tobacco products, designer clothes, household articles, music recordings, audiovisual productions, printed publications, interactive communications, office and hospital equipment, armaments, transport vehicles, and travel services (see Tables 12.3 and 12.4). In all of these sectors and more, global products inject a touch of the familiar almost wherever on Earth a person might visit. The countless examples include Nescafé (sold in 200 varieties worldwide), Heineken beer

How much do you depend on Google? In China, it would be Baidu—modeled after Google but adapted to the Chinese market.

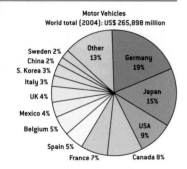

Motor Vehicles
World total (2004): US$ 265,898 million

Sweden 2%
China 2%
S. Korea 3%
Italy 3%
UK 4%
Mexico 4%
Belgium 5%
Spain 5%
France 7%
Other 13%
Germany 19%
Japan 15%
USA 9%
Canada 8%

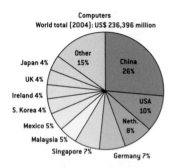

Computers
World total (2004): US$ 236,396 million

Japan 4%
UK 4%
Ireland 4%
S. Korea 4%
Mexico 5%
Malaysia 5%
Singapore 7%
Germany 7%
Other 15%
China 26%
USA 10%
Neth. 8%

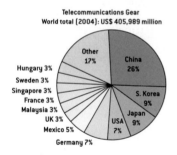

Telecommunications Gear
World total (2004): US$ 405,989 million

Hungary 3%
Sweden 3%
Singapore 3%
France 3%
Malaysia 3%
UK 3%
Mexico 5%
Germany 7%
Other 17%
China 26%
S. Korea 9%
Japan 9%
USA 7%

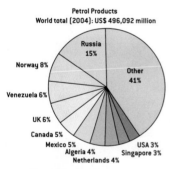

Petrol Products
World total (2004): US$ 496,092 million

Norway 8%
Venezuela 6%
UK 6%
Canada 5%
Mexico 5%
Algeria 4%
Netherlands 4%
Russia 15%
Other 41%
USA 3%
Singapore 3%

MAJOR EXPORTS.

These charts show a snapshot of the leading manufactured items and their exporters. What do these charts reveal about the nature of distribution and sale of global goods?

Table 12.3

Your Global Morning as a College Student

With an 8 a.m. class, you rely on a good working alarm clock this semester. You also rely on a global production and distribution system.

Your alarm clock is a product of the Sony Corporation, a Japanese-based multinational corporation. The clock was assembled in a Sony plant in Brazil from components produced in Japan, Mexico, and Germany. It was shipped to the United States in a Greek-owned ship manufactured in Sweden, licensed in Liberia, and staffed by a Portuguese crew.

Not much to wear to class because you have not had time to wash anything for a few weeks.

Now you are wearing the international. Your shorts were made in Japan from cotton exported to Japan from the United States. Your socks were made in Vietnam using wool grown in Australia.

Just enough time to stop at the dining hall for some breakfast.

Your stomach is full of the international. The bacon was brought to you by the UPS Corporation, a multinational shipping company. The pig your bacon came from consumed more grain than the majority of humans eat each year. The bread you ate was Wonder Bread, a product of International Telephone and Telegraph, another multinational company. The technology that heated your bread to make toast is a product from another multinational, General Electric. The butter that you put on your toast contains dried milk imported from Germany. Finally, the coffee is a product of the Nestlé Corporation, a Swiss multinational.

Wondering how the Red Sox did last night and whether the US team won its qualifying round for the World Cup, you take a look at the local newspaper.

Now you are reading the international. Much of the news on the front page that you skimmed is about events outside the United States and the role the United States plays as a global leader. The newspaper received much of its news from the British Broadcasting Corporation, Agence France-Presse, the Associated Press, and Reuters, all transnational information agencies. The major sports story today is about the World Cup and the various international athletes.

(quaffed in over 170 countries), Kiwi shoe polish (applied in almost 200 countries), Nokia mobile phones (used in more than 130 countries), Thomas Cook tourist offices (available in 140 countries), American International Group insurance policies (offered in more than 130 countries), television programs by Globo of Brazil (distributed in 128 countries), and the *Financial Times* newspaper (printed in 19 cities across the globe). Covering smokers in 170 lands, Marlboro Country is a distinctly global place.

Today, many shops are mainly stocked with transborder articles. Moreover, since the 1970s, a number of retail chains have gone global. Examples include Italy-based Benetton, Japan-based 7-Eleven, Sweden-based IKEA, UK-based Body Shop, and US-based Toys "R" Us. Owing largely to the various megabrands and transborder stores, shopping centers of the twenty-first century are in good part global emporia. Unfortunately for many of these globalized corner stores, the economic recession that began in 2008 has caused a global fire sale of products.

Table 12.4

An Example of a Global Product: Your IBM ThinkPad X31

Memory: Ten manufacturers worldwide, the largest in Korea

Case and keyboard: Made in Thailand

Wireless card: Intel, made in Malaysia

Battery: Made in Asia (various locations in the region possible)

Display screen: Two major screen makers are Samsung and LG Philips in South Korea

Graphics controller chip: ATI, made in Canada, or TMSC, made in Taiwan

Microprocessor: Intel, made in the United States

Hard drive: Made in Thailand

Assembly: Mexico

Did IBM officials consider US national security interests when they sold their personal computer business to the Chinese corporation Lenovo? Should US leaders be concerned or is the nature of the global economy?

Other supraterritorial markets have developed since the 1990s through **electronic commerce**. Today's global consumer can—equipped with a credit card and telephone, television, or Internet link—shop across the planet from home. Mail-order outlets and telesales units have undergone exponential growth, while e-commerce on the World Wide Web has expanded hugely.

Through transborder production and transworld products, global trade has become an integral part of everyday life for a notable proportion of the world's firms and consumers (see Tables 12.3, 12.4, and the Case Study on the iPod from Chapter 1). Indeed, these developments could help explain why the recessions of contemporary history have not, in spite of frequently expressed fears of "trade wars," provoked a wave of protectionism. In previous prolonged periods of commercial instability and economic hardship (e.g., during the 1870s–1890s and 1920s–1930s), most states responded by imposing major protectionist restrictions on cross-border trade. Reactions to the recession that began in 2008 have been more complicated (see Milner 1988). Although many territorial interests have pressed for protectionism, global commercial interests have generally resisted it. Thus, many transborder companies actively promoted the Uruguay Round and have, on the whole, vigorously supported the WTO.

Global Finance

Finance has attracted some of the greatest attention in contemporary debates on globalization, especially following a string of crises in Latin America (1994–1995), Asia (1997–1998), Russia (1998), Brazil (1999), Argentina (2001–2002), and the ongoing globalized collapse that began in 2008. The rise of supraterritoriality has affected both the forms money takes and the ways it is deployed in banking, securities, derivatives, and (although not detailed here) insurance markets. As international cross-border activities, such dealings have quite a long history. However, as commerce that unfolds through telephone and computer networks that make the world a single place, global finance has experienced its greatest growth since the 1980s.

electronic commerce
The buying and selling of products and services over the telephone or Internet. Amazon and eBay are examples of leaders in this area of commerce.

WHAT'S YOUR WORLDVIEW

With all these transnational institutions and policies, is it possible for any state or even a group of states to manage the global economy? Who should be charged with protecting average people and their savings accounts?

Global Money

The development of global production and the growth of global markets have each encouraged—and been facilitated by—the spread of global monies. It was noted earlier that the fixed and later floating exchange regimes operated through the IMF have allowed a number of national currencies to enter transworld use. As familiar "bureau de change" signs indicate, today, retail outlets in scores of countries deal in multiple currencies on demand.

No national denomination has been more global in this context than the US dollar. About as many dollars circulate outside as inside the United States. Indeed, in certain financial crises, this global money has displaced the locally issued currency in the everyday life of a national economy. Such "dollarization" has occurred in parts of Latin America and Eastern Europe. Since the 1970s, the German mark (now superseded by the euro), Japanese yen, Swiss franc, and other major currencies have also acquired a substantial global character. Hence, huge stocks of notionally "national" money are now used in countless transactions that never touch the home soil.

Foreign exchange dealing has become a thoroughly supraterritorial business. This round-the-clock, round-the-world market has no central meeting place. Many of the deals have nothing directly to do with the countries where the currencies involved are initially issued or eventually spent. The trading itself has also taken place without distance. Transactions are generally concluded over the telephone and confirmed by telex or e-mail between buyers and sellers across whatever distance. Meanwhile, shifts in exchange rates are flashed instantaneously and simultaneously on video monitors across the main dealing rooms worldwide.

Transborder money also takes other forms besides certain national currencies. Gold has already circulated across the planet for several centuries, although it moves cumbersomely through territorial space rather than instantly through telecommunication lines. A newer and more fully supraterritorial denomination is the **Special Drawing Right (SDR)**, issued through the IMF since 1969. Special Drawing Rights reside only in computer memories and not in wallets for everyday transactions.

Meanwhile, other supraterritorial money has entered daily use in plastic form. For example, many bank cards can extract local currency from automated teller machines (ATMs) worldwide. In addition, several types of smart card (e.g., Mondex, a part of the MasterCard network) can simultaneously hold multiple currencies as digital cash on a microchip. Certain credit cards like Visa and MasterCard are accepted at millions of venues the world over to make purchases in whatever local denomination.

In sum, contemporary globalization has—through the spread of transborder currencies, distinctly supraterritorial denominations, digital purses, and global credit and debit cards—significantly altered the shape of money. No longer is money restricted to the national, state, or territorial form that prevailed from the nineteenth to the middle of the twentieth century.

Special Drawing Right (SDR) Members of the IMF have the right to borrow this asset from the organization up to the amount that the country has invested in the IMF. The SDR is based on the value of a "basket" of the world's leading currencies: British pound, euro, Japanese yen, and US dollar.

Globalized banking lets you conduct your business nearly anywhere, including Istanbul, Turkey.

Global Banking

Globalization has touched banking mainly in terms of (1) the growth of transborder deposits, (2) the advent of transborder bank lending, (3) the expansion of transborder branch networks, and (4) the emergence of instantaneous transworld interbank fund transfers.

So-called eurocurrency deposits are bank assets denominated in a national money different from the official currency in the country where the funds are held. For instance, euroyen are Japanese yen deposited in, say, Canada. Eurocurrency accounts first appeared in the 1950s but mainly expanded after 1970, especially with the flood of petrodollars that followed major rises of oil prices in 1973–1974 and 1979–1980. Eurocurrencies are supraterritorial; they do not attach neatly to any country's money supply, nor are they systematically regulated by the national central bank that issued them.

Globalization has also entered the lending side of banking. Credit creation from eurocurrency deposits first occurred in 1957, when American dollars were borrowed through the British office of a Soviet bank. However, euroloans mainly proliferated after 1973 following the petrodollar deluge. Today, it is common for a loan to be issued in one country and denominated in the currency of a second country (or perhaps a basket of currencies of several countries) for a borrower in a third country by a bank or syndicate of banks in a fourth or additional countries.

Global banking takes place not only at age-old sites of world finance like London, New York, Tokyo, and Zurich but also through multiple **offshore finance centers**. Much like EPZs in relation to manufacturing, offshore financial arrangements offer investors low levels of taxation and regulation. Although a few offshore finance centers, including Luxembourg and Jersey (a dependency of the United Kingdom that is part of the Channel Islands), predate World War II, most have emerged since 1960 and are now found in over forty jurisdictions. For example, less than thirty years after passing relevant legislation in 1967, the Cayman Islands hosted more than 500 offshore banks with total deposits of $442 billion (S. Roberts 1994; Bank for International Settlements 1996, 7).

The supraterritorial character of much contemporary banking also lies in the instantaneity of interbank fund transfers. Electronic messages have largely replaced territorial transfers by check or draft—and cost far less. The largest conduit for such movements is the Society for Worldwide Interbank Financial Telecommunications (SWIFT). Launched in 1977, SWIFT interconnected more than 8,300 financial institutions in 208 countries by 2009, carrying an average of 12.3 million payments per day.

offshore finance centers
The extraterritorial banks that investors use for a range of reasons, including the desire to avoid domestic taxes, regulations, and law enforcement agencies.

Global Securities

Globalization has altered not only banking but also the shape of securities markets. First, some of the bonds and stocks themselves have become relatively detached from territorial space. Second, many investor portfolios have acquired a transborder character. Third, electronic interlinkage of trading sites has created conditions of anywhere/anytime securities dealing. Each of these factors contributed to the 2008 economic collapse; subprime US home mortgages were sold in European markets and traded twenty-four hours a day seven days a week. When the housing market collapsed in the United States and more people failed to pay their mortgages, the mortgage bundles purchased by banks around the world lost their value. The US crisis became a global crisis. This mortgage crisis certainly contributed to the current crisis, which is more about sovereign debt and the lack of available credit from banks trying to recover from the previous crisis.

In regard to the first point, contemporary globalization has seen the emergence of several major securities instruments with a transborder character. These bonds and equities can involve issuers, currencies, brokers, and exchanges across multiple countries at the same time. For example, a so-called eurobond is denominated in a currency that is alien to a substantial proportion of the parties involved: the borrower who issues it, the underwriters who distribute it, the investors who hold it, or the exchange(s) that

---

CASE STUDY : Southern Debt in Global Finance

The global character of much contemporary finance is well illustrated by the struggles that many middle- and low-income countries have had with large transborder debts. The problems developed in the 1970s, when the surge in oil prices generated huge export earnings of so-called petrodollars, which were largely placed in bank deposits. The banks in turn needed to lend the money, but demand for loans in the OECD countries was low at the time owing to recession. So instead, large bank loans went to countries of the South (in some cases, partly to help pay for the increased cost of oil imports). Often, the lenders were insufficiently careful in extending these credits, and often, the borrowers were reckless in spending the money. Starting with Mexico in August 1982, a string of borrowing governments in the South defaulted on their transborder loans.

The initial response to this situation of unsustainable debts was to implement short-term emergency rescue packages for each country as it ran into crisis. Payments were rescheduled, and additional loans were provided to cover unpaid interest charges. This piecemeal approach only tended to make things worse. From 1987 onward, a series of comprehensive plans for third world debt relief were promoted. During the following decade, unsustainable commercial bank loans were gradually written off or converted into long-term bonds. Many bilateral loans from Northern governments to Southern borrowers were also canceled. However, in the mid-1990s, major problems persisted in regard to debts owed by low-income countries to multilateral

lenders such as the IMF and the World Bank. A much-touted Highly Indebted Poor Countries (HIPC) initiative, launched in 1996 and recast in 1999, has brought slow and limited returns. In 2005, the G-8 Summit in Gleneagles agreed to write off the debts of eighteen HIPCs to the multilateral agencies.

Throughout these twenty years, programs of debt relief for low-income countries have received major support from global citizen campaigns. Activists formed a first Debt Crisis Network in the mid-1980s. Regional coalitions such as the European Network on Debt and Development emerged in the early 1990s. These efforts coalesced and broadened in the global Jubilee 2000 campaign of the late 1990s, which, among other things, assembled 70,000 people in a "human chain" around the G-8 Summit in Birmingham, UK, in 1998. Most commentators agree that these global citizen mobilizations significantly increased, improved, and accelerated programs of debt relief.

For Discussion

1. Why was it considered so important to pay off the debts of developing countries? Would a similar system work to help Greece today?
2. How much do you think colonialism and the Cold War contributed to the debt in developing countries?
3. The Jubilee movement was a transnational social movement that had some success. Why do you think we have not seen a similar movement supporting the Millennium Development Goals?

---

equity A number of equal portions in the nominal capital of a company; the shareholder thereby owns part of the enterprise; also called "stock" or "share."

list it. This transborder financial instrument is thereby different from a foreign bond, which is handled in one country for an external borrower. Cross-border bonds of the latter type have existed for several hundred years, but eurobonds first appeared in 1963. In that year, the state highway authority in Italy issued bonds denominated in US dollars through managers in Belgium, Britain, Germany, and the Netherlands, with subsequent quotation on the London Stock Exchange.

On a similar pattern, a euroequity issue involves a transborder syndicate of brokers selling a new share release for simultaneous listing on stock exchanges in several countries. This supraterritorial process contrasts with an international offer, where a company based in one country issues **equity** in a second country. Like foreign bonds, international share quotations have existed almost as long as stock markets themselves. However, the first transborder equity issue occurred in 1984, when 15 percent of a privatization of British Telecommunications was offered on exchanges in Japan, North America, and Switzerland concurrently with the majority share release in the United Kingdom. Transworld placements of new shares have occurred less frequently than eurobond issues. However, it has become quite common for major transborder firms to list their equity on different stock exchanges across several time zones, particularly in Asia, Europe, and North America.

Not only various securities instruments but also many investor portfolios have acquired a transborder character in the context of contemporary financial globalization. Thus, for example, an investor in one country may leave assets with a fund manager in a second country who in turn places those sums on markets in a collection of third countries. Thus, even when individual securities have a territorial character, they can be combined in a supraterritorial investment package. Indeed, a number of pension funds, insurance companies, and unit trusts have created explicitly designated "global funds" whose component securities are drawn from multiple corners of the world. Many transborder institutional investors have furthermore registered offshore for tax and other cost advantages. For example, the Africa Emerging Markets Fund has its investments in Africa, its listing in Ireland, and its management office in the United States. As of 1995, Luxembourg hosted some $350 billion in offshore investment funds, largely outside the regulatory reach of the managers' home governments.

Finally, securities markets have gone global through the growing supraterritorial character of many exchanges since the 1970s. The open-outcry trading floors of old have largely given way to electronic transactions by telephone and computer networks. These telecommunications provide the infrastructure for distanceless deals (called "remote trading") in which the brokers can, in principle, be located anywhere on Earth. Most major investment banks (Daiwa Securities, Dresdner Kleinwort, Fidelity, etc.) now coordinate offices across several time zones in round-the-clock, round-the-world trading of bonds and shares. The first computerized order-routing system became operational in 1976, connecting brokers across the United States instantly to the trading floor of the New York Stock Exchange. Similar developments have, since 1996, begun to link brokers anywhere in the European Union directly to its main exchanges. For its part, the wholly computer-based National Association of Securities Dealers Automated Quotations system (NASDAQ) has, since its launch in 1971, had no central meeting place at all. This transborder cyberspatial network has become the world's largest stock market, listing around 3,200 companies with a combined market capitalization of over $4.1 trillion and annual trading of 580 billion shares as of 2011. Meanwhile, beginning with the Toronto and American stock exchanges in 1985, a number of securities markets have established electronic links to enable transborder dealing between them. This extensive growth of supraterritoriality in the securities markets helps explain why, for example, the Wall Street crash of October 1987 triggered transworld reverberations within hours.

Much like global banking, transborder securities trading is mainly conducted through computerized clearing systems. The equivalents of SWIFT are the Euroclear network, established in 1968, and Cedel (now renamed Clearstream), launched in 1971. Euroclear alone handled a turnover of over €350 trillion (euros) in 2005.

Global Derivatives

A fourth area of finance suffused with globalization—and a major villain in the drama of the 2008–2009 economic collapse—is the derivatives industry. A derivative product is a contract, the value of which depends on (hence, is "derived" from) the price of some underlying asset (e.g., a raw material or an equity) or a particular reference rate (e.g., an interest level or stock market index). Derivatives connected to tangible assets like raw minerals and land date from the middle of the nineteenth century, and derivatives based on financial indicators have proliferated since their introduction in 1972.

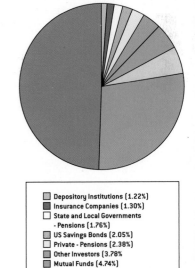

- ☐ Depository Institutions (1.22%)
- ■ Insurance Companies (1.30%)
- ☐ State and Local Governments
  - Pensions (1.76%)
- ☐ US Savings Bonds (2.05%)
- ☐ Private - Pensions (2.38%)
- ■ Other Investors (3.78%
- ■ Mutual Funds (4.74%)
- ☐ State and Local Governments (5.50%)
- ☐ Foreign and International (27.90%)
- ■ Federal Reserve and
  Intragovernmental Holdings (49.37%)

ESTIMATED OWNERSHIP OF ALL US TREASURY SECURITIES.
What two groups own the most US Treasury securities?

futures Derivatives that oblige a buyer and seller to complete a transaction at a predetermined time in the future at a price agreed on today. Futures are also known as "forwards."

options Derivatives that give parties a right (without obligation) to buy or sell at a specific price for a stipulated period of time up to the contract's expiry date.

Derivatives contracts take two principal forms. The first type, called **futures** or "forwards," oblige a buyer and seller to complete a transaction at a predetermined time in the future at a price agreed on today. The second main type, called **options**, give parties a right (without obligation) to buy or sell at a specified price for a stipulated period of time up to the contract's expiry date. Other kinds of derivatives include swaps, warrants, and further—seemingly ever more obscure—financial instruments.

Additional technical details and the various rationales relating to derivatives need not detain us here. It suffices for present purposes to emphasize the magnitude of this financial industry and its near total lack of government regulation prior to 2009. Public derivatives exchanges have proliferated worldwide since 1982 along with even larger over-the-counter (OTC) markets. By 1995, the volume of trading on world derivatives markets totaled some $1.2 trillion per day. The notional value of outstanding OTC financial derivatives contracts alone reached $370 trillion in mid-2006 (Bank for International Settlements 1996, 27; 2006).

Like banking and securities, much derivatives business has become relatively distanceless and borderless. For example, a number of the contracts relate to supraterritorial indicators, such as the world price of copper or the interest rate on euro–Swiss franc deposits. In addition, much derivatives trading is undertaken through global securities houses and transworld telecommunications links. A number of derivatives instruments are traded simultaneously on several exchanges in a round-the-world, round-the-clock market. For example, contracts related to three-month eurodollar interest rates have been traded concurrently on Euronext.liffe (a pan-European derivatives exchange), the New York Futures Exchange (NYFE), the Sydney Futures Exchange (SFE), and the Singapore Exchange (SGX).

Owing to these tight global interconnections, major losses in the derivatives markets can have immediate worldwide repercussions. For example, deficits of $1.3 billion accumulated by Singapore-based futures trader Nick Leeson triggered a transborder collapse of the venerable Barings investment bank in 1995. A succession of similarly huge losses in other quarters caused some analysts to worry that global derivatives trading could undermine the world financial system as a whole, although the sector remained largely unregulated in Europe and the United States.

Continuity and Change in Economic Globalization

Having now reviewed the development of a supraterritorial dimension in the contemporary world economy (summarized chronologically in Table 12.5) and emphasized its significance, we need to recognize continuities alongside these changes. One can appreciate the importance of globalization without slipping into globalism. In the following sections, we will discuss four factors of continuity: the unevenness of globalization, which we call irregular incidence; the enduring importance of territoriality; the role of the state in an era of globalization; and the persistence of nationalism and cultural diversity.

Irregular Incidence

Globalization has not been experienced everywhere and by everyone to the same extent. In general, transborder trade and finance have developed furthest (1) in East Asia, North America, and Western Europe, (2) in urban areas relative to rural districts, and (3) in wealthier and professional circles. On the other hand, few people and places are today completely untouched by economic globalization.

Supraterritorial trade and finance have transpired disproportionately in what we are calling the North and then most especially in its cities. For instance, although McDonald's fast food is dished up in 30,000 establishments across 119 countries, the vast majority of these meals are consumed in a handful of those lands. In contrast to currencies issued in the North, the national denominations of countries in Africa have had scarcely any mutual convertibility. Thus far, three-quarters and more of foreign direct investment, credit card transactions, stock market capitalization, derivatives trade, and transborder loans flowed within the North.

This marginalization of the South is far from complete, however. For instance, certain products originating in the South have figured significantly in global markets (e.g., wines from Chile and South Africa and package holidays in the Caribbean). Electronic banking has even reached parts of rural China. A number of offshore finance centers and large sums of transborder bank debt are found in the South. Global portfolios have figured strongly in the development of new securities markets in major cities of Africa, Asia, Eastern Europe, and Latin America since the mid-1980s. The Singapore Exchange (SGX) and the São Paulo–based Bolsa de Mercadorias & Futuros (BM&F) have played a part in the burgeoning derivatives markets of recent decades.

Indeed, involvement in global trade and finance is often as much a function of class as of the North-South divide. The vast majority of the world's population—including many in the North—have lacked the means to purchase most global products. Likewise, placing investments in global financial markets depends on wealth, the distribution of which does not always follow a North–South pattern. For example, substantial petrodollars have been owned by elites in the oil-exporting countries of Africa, Latin America, and the Middle East.

Space limitations do not permit full elaboration of the point here, but transborder markets and investments can be shown to have contributed significantly to growing wealth gaps within countries as well as between North and South (Scholte 2005, chap. 10). For example, the global mobility of capital, in particular to low-wage production sites and offshore finance centers, has encouraged many countries, including the United States, to reduce upper tax brackets and to downgrade some social welfare provisions. Such steps have contributed to growing inequality across much of the contemporary world. Increasingly, poverty has become connected as much to supraterritorial class, gender, and race structures as to country of domicile (see Chapter 4).

> **WHAT'S YOUR WORLDVIEW**
>
> *Who has been left out of this global or transnational economy? Can these states and their citizens be brought into the system?*

The Persistence of Territory

Yet the transcendence of territorial space in the contemporary world economy must not be overestimated. True, evidence presented earlier in this chapter suggests that distance and borders have often lost the determining influence on economic geography that they once had. However, this is not to say that the nation-state has lost all significance in the contemporary organization of production, exchange, and consumption.

On the contrary, after several decades of accelerated globalization, a great deal of commercial activity is still linked to a specific country and has only a secondary supraterritorial dimension. For example, although transborder manufacturing through global factories has affected a significant proportion of certain industries, most processes have remained within one country. Even many globally distributed products (Boeing jets, Ceylon teas) are prepared within a single country.

Many types of money, too, have remained restricted to a national or local domain. Likewise, the great bulk of retail banking has stayed territorial, as clients deal with their local

Table 12.5

Some Key Events in Global Trade and Finance

1929	Institution of the first offshore finance arrangements (in Luxembourg)	1971	Establishment of the first wholly electronic stock exchange (NASDAQ)
1944	Bretton Woods Conference drafts constitutions of the IMF and the World Bank	1972	Launch of markets in financial derivatives, starting with currency futures
1954	Establishment of the first export processing zone (in Ireland)	1973	Quadrupling of oil prices floods euromarkets with petrodollars
1954	Launch of the "Marlboro cowboy" as a global commercial icon	1974	Formation of Basel Committee on Banking Supervision following the collapse of two banks heavily involved in foreign exchange dealing
1955	First McDonald's restaurant opens (operating in 119 countries fifty years later)	1974	US government relaxes foreign exchange controls (other states follow in later years)
1957	Issuance of the first eurocurrency loan	1976	IMF meeting in Jamaica formalizes the regime of floating exchange rates
1959	Gold-dollar standard enters into full operation	1977	Inauguration of the SWIFT system of electronic interbank fund transfers worldwide
1963	Issuance of the first eurobond	1982	Mexico's threatened default on global loans triggers third world debt crisis
1965	Start of the maquiladora program in Mexico	1983	Formation of the International Organization of Securities Commissions
1968	Launch of Euroclear computerizes transworld settlement of securities deals	1984	First transborder equity issue (by British Telecommunications)
1969	Introduction of the Special Drawing Right	1985	First transborder electronic link between stock exchanges
1987	Stock market crash on Wall Street reverberates worldwide within hours	2003	Doha Development Round of multilateral trade talks stalls, and bilateral trade agreements increase

continued

branch offices. In spite of substantial growth since the 1980s, transborder share dealing remains a small fraction of total equity trading. Moreover, a large majority of turnover on most stock exchanges continues to involve shares of firms headquartered in the same country.

Most global commercial activity has not been wholly detached from territorial geography. For example, local circumstances have strongly influenced corporate decisions regarding the location of transborder production facilities. In the foreign exchange markets, dealers have mainly been clustered in half a dozen cities, even if their transactions are largely cyberspatial and can have immediate consequences anywhere in the world. It remains rare for a transborder company to issue a large proportion of its stock outside its country of origin.

Hence, the importance of globalization is that it has ended the monopoly of territoriality in defining the spatial character of the world economy. The trend has by no means eliminated

Table 12.5 (*continued*)
Some Key Events in Global Trade and Finance

1994	Conclusion of the Uruguay Round of the GATT	**2007–2009**	Growing concerns over subprime mortgages in the United States; the US government nationalizes insurance giant AIG, General Motors, and several key banks; Italian carmaker Fiat buys controlling share of US firm Chrysler
1995	Inauguration of the World Trade Organization	**2009–2010**	European sovereign debt crisis, in which Greece, Ireland, and Portugal fail to refinance their debts, resulting in a €750 billion rescue package aimed at ensuring financial stability across Europe and establishing the European Financial Stability Facility
1995	Leeson affair highlights the volatility of global derivatives markets	**2011**	Anti-Counterfeiting Trade Agreement (ACTA), a groundbreaking initiative to strengthen the international legal framework enforcing intellectual property rights, combating piracy and commercial-scale counterfeiting, is signed by eight negotiating partners: United States, Australia, Canada, Korea, Japan, New Zealand, Morocco, and Singapore
1997–2002	Crises in Asia, Russia, Brazil, and Argentina raise concerns about underregulated global finance; in 1999, US Glass-Steagall Act repealed	**2013**	World Trade Organization Bali Agreement: a deal to boost global trade is approved by the World Trade Organization's 159 member economies for the first time in nearly two decades, keeping alive the possibility of a broader agreement to create a level playing field for rich and poor countries; at the center of the agreement are measures to ease barriers to trade by simplifying customs procedures and making them more transparent EU countries pledge new financial support to help developing countries implement the WTO Trade Facilitation Agreement, which will simplify, harmonize, and modernize international border procedures

Source: ACTA: http://www.ustr.gov/acta

territoriality. The global dimension of contemporary world commerce has grown alongside, and in complex relations with, its territorial aspects. Globalization has been reconfiguring economic, social, and political geography (alongside concurrent processes of regionalization and localization) rather than obliterating territory.

The Survival of the State

Similarly, globalization has repositioned the (territorial) state rather than signaled its demise. The expansion of transborder trade and finance has made claims of Westphalian sovereign statehood obsolete, but the significance of states themselves remains. Through both unilateral decisions and multilaterally coordinated policies, states have done much to facilitate economic globalization and influence its course.

THEORY IN PRACTICE

What Course to Follow Out of the 2008 Global Recession?

THE CHALLENGE

The debates about international relations theories that you studied in Chapter 3 may have struck you as somewhat sterile. But if you were a political leader seeking a way to bring your country out of the economic recession that began in 2008, you would probably have a clear idea of what the theories mean for the policies you were considering. Although as of this writing in 2014 there is one socialist in the Senate, US political leaders tend to follow one of two dominant models: realism or liberalism.

OPTIONS

The realist perspective on international relations stresses the need to defend the state and its interests. In the past, the recommendations of realism tended to sound like mercantilism, popular in the seventeenth and eighteenth centuries. Countries should seek self-sufficiency, a condition called *autarchy*, and keep as much gold and silver within national

control as possible. In modern times, realists might not call it mercantilism, but their protectionist recommendations can sound like that doctrine—for example, increase tariff barriers to protect domestic industries, buy products made domestically, and stop outsourcing jobs to other countries.

Liberal international relations theories make a very different set of recommendations, many of which are embodied in the WTO. For adherents of this perspective, the way out of an economic recession is by increasing foreign trade, by making trade as free as possible. This means reducing or eliminating tariffs and nontariff barriers and encouraging the process of global sourcing of goods and services. The result of such outward-looking policies would ideally be what economists call "comparative advantage." This is a complex idea that asserts if a country produces and sells what it can make most efficiently, it will be able to buy the other products it needs with the profits from its own production.

APPLICATION

For our hypothetical political leader, the choice is not as simple as it seems. In democratic political systems, politicians must stand for reelection, and they must account for their decisions. In some ways, the realist perspective is the easiest to defend. The politician has promised to defend American jobs and pursued policies that could do that. If the recession is made worse by these protectionist ideas, at least the politician can claim to have tried.

Working against the protectionist counsels of realism is the more than sixty years of effective trade practices, first in the GATT and then after 1995 in the WTO. Therefore, a politician seeking reelection has the historical record to fall back on when debating with a realism-inspired opponent. Beginning in 1947 with twenty-three countries, the eight rounds of trade talks worked to reduce global restrictions on trade in goods and services. Of course, no politician would want to tell a worker it is good that the factory closed its doors and the jobs went to another country where production costs are lower. In good economic times, this is perhaps not necessary; during an economic recession, there is often no choice.

For Discussion

1. How would economic policy recommendations from a feminist perspective differ from those of a realist perspective?
2. When a crisis such as the global recession hits, it is easy to blame politicians. Is that fair? To what extent are citizens responsible for the 2008 economic meltdown?
3. Is autarchy possible in a globalized economy? What about mercantilism?

India's Tata Group acquired Jaguar Land Rover in 2008. The global economic meltdown hurt the auto industry all around the world.

As already mentioned, states have encouraged the globalization of commerce through various policies of liberalization and the creation of special economic zones and offshore finance centers. At the same time, some governments in the developing world have also slowed globalization within their jurisdiction by retaining certain restrictions on transborder activity. However, most states have sooner or later responded to strong pressures to liberalize. In any case, governments have often lacked effective means to fully enforce their territorially bound controls on globally mobile capital. Only with respect to immigration restrictions have states largely sustained their borders against economic globalization, and even then, substantial traffic in unregistered migrants occurs.

> **WHAT'S YOUR WORLDVIEW**
>
> *Has globalization undermined the ability of states to provide what we call "defining activities" of the state: protecting borders, providing a system of law and order, and maintaining a productive economic system?*

Yet states are by no means powerless in the face of economic globalization. Even the common claim that global finance lies beyond the state requires qualification. After all, governments and central banks continue to exert a major influence on money supplies and interest rates, even if they no longer monopolize money creation and they lack tight control over the euromarkets. Likewise, particularly through cooperative action, states can significantly shift exchange rates, even if they have lost the capacity to fix the conversion ratios and are sometimes overridden by currency dealers. We have seen examples of both kinds of behavior as political leaders have tried to halt the current economic crisis. Governments have also pursued collective regulation of transborder banking to some effect via the Basel Committee on Banking Supervision, set up through the BIS in 1974. The survival of offshore finance centers, too, depends to a considerable extent on the goodwill of governments, both the host regime and external authorities. Recent years have seen increased intergovernmental consultations, particularly through the OECD (see Table 12.6), to obtain tighter official oversight of offshore finance. Similarly, national regulators of securities markets have collaborated since 1984 through the International Organization of Securities Commissions (IOSCO).

In short, there is little sign that global commerce and the state are antithetical. On the contrary, the two have shown considerable mutual dependency. States have provided much of the regulatory framework for global trade and finance, albeit sharing these competences with other regulatory agencies. Sadly, despite the potential for collective action, none of the measures countries undertook could stop the pace of the economic collapse in late 2008.

The Continuance of Nationalism and Cultural Diversity

Much evidence also confounds the common presumption that economic globalization is effecting cultural homogenization and a rise of cosmopolitan orientations over national **identities**. Identities are social and thus always formed in relationship to others. Constructivists generally hold that identities shape interests; we cannot know what we want unless we know who we are. But because identities are social and produced through interactions, identities can change. The growth of transborder production, the proliferation of global products, the multiplication of supraterritorial monies, and the expansion of transworld financial flows have shown little sign of heralding an end of cultural difference in the world economy.

True, global trade and finance are moved by much more than national loyalty. Consumers have repeatedly ignored exhortations to buy American and the like in favor of global products. This is one reason US automakers Chrysler, Ford, and General Motors had to beg for cash bailouts from the federal government in 2008–2009. Shareholders and managers have rarely put national sentiments ahead of the profit margin. For example, global media magnate Rupert Murdoch happily traded Australian for US citizenship in 1985 when it suited his

identity The understanding of the self in relationship to an "other." Identities are social and thus always formed in relationship to others. Constructivists generally hold that identities shape interests; we cannot know what we want unless we know who we are. But because identities are social and produced through interactions, identities can change.

Table 12.6
OECD Indicators of Social Justice

	Overall Social Justice Rating	Overall Poverty Prevention Rating	Access to Education	Labor Market Inclusion	Social Cohesion and Nondiscrimination	Health	Intergenerational Justice	Income Inequality
Iceland	8.73	9.07	9.33	9.02	7.66	8.53	7.18	0.301
Norway	8.31	8.87	6.93	8.78	9.22	7.30	8.53	0.250
Denmark	8.20	9.16	7.43	7.88	8.28	7.53	8.10	0.248
Sweden	8.18	8.43	7.86	7.48	8.92	7.87	9.00	0.259
Finland	8.06	8.53	8.22	7.51	8.33	7.17	8.01	0.259
Netherlands	7.72	8.88	6.35	7.95	8.08	7.08	6.82	0.294
Switzerland	7.44	7.39	5.99	8.52	7.62	8.03	7.55	0.303
Luxembourg	7.27	8.35	5.27	7.13	7.98	7.89	7.01	0.288
Canada	7.26	7.00	7.15	7.90	7.83	7.63	6.06	0.324
France	7.25	8.66	6.29	6.27	6.56	7.67	7.17	0.293
Czech Republic	7.17	9.18	6.55	6.22	6.77	5.84	5.97	0.256
New Zealand	7.14	6.27	6.51	8.12	8.21	8.18	6.98	0.330
Austria	7.13	8.49	5.39	7.50	6.09	6.87	7.11	0.261
Germany	7.03	8.12	5.53	7.13	7.12	6.63	6.87	0.295
Britain	6.79	6.92	5.56	7.43	7.44	6.77	6.95	0.345
Belgium	6.73	7.56	6.32	5.79	7.29	7.05	6.10	0.259
Hungary	6.41	9.14	4.77	4.79	6.48	5.08	6.04	0.272
Ireland	6.41	7.51	4.43	5.99	7.64	7.00	6.06	0.293
Italy	6.29	6.78	6.68	5.60	5.42	7.45	5.12	0.337
Poland	6.17	7.15	6.79	5.14	6.01	5.04	5.33	0.305
Australia	6.14	4.24	5.32	8.13	7.80	7.68	6.29	0.336

Japan	6.00	5.21	5.53	7.66	5.39	7.66	4.95	0.329
Portugal	5.97	5.77	5.89	6.53	6.29	5.66	5.60	0.253
Slovakia	5.96	8.33	4.93	4.36	5.73	5.04	5.24	0.257
South Korea	5.89	4.26	5.83	8.15	5.28	7.18	5.72	0.315
Spain	5.83	5.20	7.23	4.42	6.30	7.35	5.77	0.317
United States	5.70	3.85	5.80	7.34	7.01	6.23	5.95	0.378
Greece	5.37	6.24	4.38	5.29	5.57	6.61	3.47	0.307
Chile	5.20	3.30	6.20	7.24	3.62	5.65	5.92	0.494
Mexico	4.75	2.11	6.81	7.68	3.38	3.51	5.34	0.476
Turkey	4.19	4.26	3.67	4.86	3.22	3.79	5.05	0.409

Note: **Poverty Prevention** measured according to three indicators: (1) Poverty Rate: the percentage of persons with disposable income below 50% of the national median; (2) Child Poverty: the percentage of children 17 years old and younger in households with disposable income below 50% of the national median; (3) Senior Citizen Poverty: the percentage of citizens 65 or older in households with a disposable income below 50% of the national median. **Access to Education** measured according to three indicators: (1) Education Policy: policy achievements in delivering high-quality, equitable education and training; (2) Socioeconomic Background and Student Performance: Product of the strength and slope of the socioeconomic gradient; (3) Preprimary Education: Public expenditure on preprimary education as a percentage of GDP. **Labor Market Inclusion** measured according to eight indicators: (1) Employment Rate: Percentage of persons of working age (15–64 years) who are in employment; (2) Older Employment: Employment rate among the older labor force (55–64 years); (3) Foreign-Born-to-Native Employment: Ratio of foreign-born to native employment rate for the 15–64 population; (4) Employment Rates by Gender Women/Men: Ratio of female to male employment (25–64 years); (5) Unemployment Rate: Standardized unemployment rate (percentage of civilian labor force); (6) Long-Term Unemployment; (7) Youth Unemployment; (8) Low-Skilled Unemployment Ratio. **Social Cohesion and Nondiscrimination** measured according to five indicators: (1) Social Inclusion Policy: Policy performance in terms of strengthening social cohesion and inclusion; (2) Gini-coefficient: Income distribution; (3) Nondiscrimination Policy: Policy performance regarding nondiscrimination; (4) Income Inequalities (Women/Men): Percentage of estimated average female income to male earned income; (5) Integration Policy: Policy performance regarding the integration of migrants into society. **Health** measured according to four indicators: (1) Health Policy: Policy achievements in providing high-quality inclusive and cost-efficient healthcare; (2) Infant Mortality: Deaths per 1,000 live births; (3) Healthy Life Expectancy: Average number of years that a person can expect to live in "full health" by taking into account years lived in less than full health due to disease and/or injury; (4) Perceived Health in Relation to Income Levels: Ratio of percentage of persons in the lowest income group with self-reported health status ">= good" to percentage of persons in the highest income group with self-reported health status ">= good." **Intergenerational Justice** measured according to six indicators: (1) Family Policy: Policy performance in allowing for the compatibility of family and career/work; (2) Pension Policy: Policy performance in providing pensions that prevent poverty, are intergenerationally just, and fiscally sustainable; (3) Environmental Policy: Policy performance in the sustainable treatment and use of natural resources and the environment; (4) CO_2 Emissions: CO_2 emissions per unit of GDP at PPP; (5) Research and Development: Gross public expenditure on R&D as a percentage of GDP; (6) National Debt Level: Gross general government financial liabilities as a percentage of GDP.

Source: Social Justice in the OECD—How Do the Member States Compare? (Sustainable Governance Indicators 2011), p. 48 [http://www.sgi-network.org/pdf/SGI11_Social_Justice_OECD.pdf].

A construction worker stands on a scaffold at a new building in the northern Greek port city of Thessaloniki. In November 2013 an OECD report predicted that the Greek economy would shrink further in the next year, and the European Union may need to step in once again.

commercial purposes. Foreign exchange dealers readily desert their national currency to reap financial gain.

However, in other respects, national identities and solidarities have survived—and sometimes thrived—in the contemporary globalizing economy. Most transborder companies have retained a readily recognized national affiliation. Most firms involved in global trade and finance have kept a mononational board of directors, and the operations of many of these enterprises continue to reflect a national style of business practice connected with the country of origin. Different national conventions have persisted in global finance as well. For instance, since equities have traditionally held a smaller place in German finance, globalization in that country has mainly involved banks and the bond markets. Cultural diversity has also persisted in transborder marketing. Local peculiarities have often affected the way a global product is sold and used in different places. Advertising has often been adjusted to local tastes to be more effective.

In sum, then, like globalization in general, its economic dimension has not had universal scope. Nor has the rise of global trade and finance marked the end of territorial space, the demise of the state, or full-scale cultural homogenization. However, recognition of these qualifications does not entail a rejection of notions of globalization on the lines of the skeptics noted earlier.

Conclusion

We began this chapter by asking, "How did it happen?" Prior to the summer of 2008, the world's economy seemed to be gaining wealth. Aside from the historic high price for petroleum products, most economic sectors showed no sign of distress. Yet the seeds of the economic recession that began in 2008 were already planted. As you read in this chapter, the complex relationship of trade in goods and financial instruments was seemingly doomed to fail. Too much of the money was invested in arcane instruments like derivatives and mortgages served up as secure investments. The globalized trade and finance sectors were largely unregulated by host countries. Governments tried financial methods that worked in past recessions and economic crises. Slowly, many of these reforms and interventions—both new and old—have worked to arrest the economic crisis and to help many countries stabilize their banking industries and their financial markets. The US economy is slowly recovering, but partisan political disputes and the rising cost of healthcare and social security, without an increase in taxes and other revenues, may trigger another economic crisis in the United States that will create economic instability around the world. Europe's debt crisis is far from over and might result in slow growth in the rest of the world. In addition, several of the emerging economic leaders, such as India, China, and Brazil, are not growing as fast as they were before the crisis. The worst of the financial crisis might be past, but the pain of loss is still being felt in rich and poor states across the world.

CONTRIBUTORS TO CHAPTER 12: Steven L. Lamy

REVIEW QUESTIONS

1. What are the three main conceptions of economic globalization?
2. To what extent is economic globalization new to contemporary history?
3. How does transborder production differ from territorial production?
4. What are some of the reasons that the economic crisis has gone global?
5. The G-20 may emerge as a major economic actor. What can its member states do about the global economic crisis?
6. How has globalization of trade and finance affected state capacities for economic regulation?
7. How have global products altered ideas of cultural diversity?
8. To what extent can it be said that global capital carries no national flag?
9. Assess the relationship between globalization and income inequality.
10. In what ways might global commerce be reshaped to promote greater distributive justice?

FURTHER READING

Dunning, J. H. (ed.) (2004), *Making Globalization Good: Moral Challenges of Global Capitalism* (Oxford: Oxford University Press). Essays exploring ways to make global markets environmentally sustainable and socially equitable.

Held, D. et al. (1999), *Global Transformations: Politics, Economics and Culture* (Cambridge: Polity Press). Excellent text on indicators and repercussions of economic globalization.

Hirst, P., and Thompson, G. (1999), *Globalization in Question: The International Economy and the Possibilities of Governance*, 2nd ed. (Cambridge: Polity Press). A critique of globalist presumptions that economic globalization is new, irreversible, and wholly beyond state control.

Hocking, B., and McGuire, S. (eds.) (2004), *Trade Politics*, 2nd ed. (London: Routledge). Covers the main issues of, and perspectives on, global trade.

O'Brien, R., and Williams, M. (2004), *Global Political Economy: Evolution and Dynamics* (Basingstoke: Palgrave Macmillan). A thorough overview of the history and current challenges of global production and exchange.

Peterson, V. S., and Runyan, A. S. (1999), *Global Gender Issues*, 2nd ed. (Boulder, Col.: Westview Press). A critical examination of the impacts of globalization on, inter alia, women's employment and the feminization of poverty.

Porter, T. (2005), *Globalization and Finance* (Cambridge: Polity Press). A thorough analysis of global finance and its governance.

Scholte, J. A. (2005), *Globalization: A Critical Introduction*, 2nd ed. (Basingstoke: Palgrave Macmillan). Elaborates the arguments presented in this chapter, including the implications of economic globalization for human security, social justice, and democracy.

Stiglitz, J. E. (2010), *Freefall: America, Free Markets, and the Sinking of the World Economy* (New York: W. W. Norton). Thorough review of the economic crisis in the United States and its global implications.

Stubbs, R., and Underhill, G. R. D. (eds.) (2006), *Political Economy and the Changing Global Order*, 3rd ed. (Basingstoke: Palgrave). A textbook in international political economy with much concerning global trade and finance.

UN Development Programme (1990–), *Human Development Report* (New York: Oxford University Press). This annual publication of the UN Development Program includes much on the welfare consequences of economic globalization. See especially the 1999 edition.

Video Suggestion

Too Big Too Fail. This film explores the start of the global financial crisis from the US perspective.

INTERNET RESOURCES

Bank for International Settlements
www.bis.org
The organization that encourages cooperation between national central banks.

European Union
http://europa.eu/
The website of the European Union provides a treasure chest of information about the organization.

Gapminder
www.gapminder.org
An NGO that tracks the gap between rich and poor countries and people around the world.

Organisation of Economic Co-operation and Development
www.oecd.org
The organization of the world's leading national economies.

Public Citizen NAFTA Page
http://www.citizen.org/trade/nafta/
The website of a US NGO that provides information about a range of topics.

UN Conference on Trade and Development
www.unctad.org
The forum for developing countries within the UN structure.

Carnegie Council: "A Call for Judgment: Sensible Finance for a Dynamic Economy"—Amar Bhidé
http://www.carnegiecouncil.org/resources/video/data/000354
With the current economic conditions in mind, Amar Bhidé explores the keys to economic growth and, perhaps most important, new regulations that should be placed on global banking institutions.

Carnegie Council: "Common Wealth: Economics for a Crowded Planet"—Jeffrey D. Sachs
http://www.carnegiecouncil.org/resources/video/data/000223
Economist Jeffrey Sachs discusses the global financial crisis, specifically monetary policy and financial market operations, and the changes states should make during this time of fiscal upheaval.

For more information, quizzes, case studies and other study tools, please visit us at **www.oup.com/us/lamy**

The Possibilities of Cooperation: The Global Commons Challenge

INTRODUCTION
In a world of finite resources, restraint and cooperation on the part of individuals and nation-states may be the only means of maintaining and promoting the delicate balance and unity of the world's ecosystem. This activity will enable you to judge the value of cooperation in serving human needs and the validity of unrestrained self-interest in an interdependent world.

SCENARIO I:
THE PROBLEM OF THE COMMONS I
Once there was a small pasture held in common by a village of cattle herders. Being rational beings, free, and shrewd, they each sought to maximize their gains from pasturing their animals on the commons. Currently, each herder has two animals grazing on the commons.

One day, herder Smith began to think about increasing the number of animals he had grazing on the commons from two to three. Should he?

Discussion Questions I
1. What does the problem of the commons have to do with you?
2. Are you ever confronted with problems similar to the ones faced by Smith? If so, what considerations do you make?
3. Is your community, nation-state, or world faced with problems similar to the one faced by the village?
4. What is the difference between self or national interest and human interest? Give examples.
5. What is the purpose of understanding the problem of the commons?

SCENARIO II:
THE PROBLEM OF THE COMMONS II
Once there was a small planet, the fate of which was held in common by a number of large and small nation-states. Being rational, free, and shrewd, the peoples of these nation-states sought to maximize their gains by utilizing the resources of the small planet to further each of their own particular ends. The people of one particular nation-state, consisting of 5 percent of the planet's population, use 27 percent of the natural resources of the small planet. Should they continue this level of use? (Note that the original "global commons" story is attributed to G. Hardin. This one is adapted.)

Discussion Questions II
1. What are some possible arguments for and against the country presented in this scenario using a disproportionately high percentage of resources?
2. As a citizen of the country presented in this scenario, how would you respond to the demands to reduce, share, or conserve resources?
3. If you lived in one of the other countries, what type of world redistribution strategy would you support?
4. Is it possible to create a more equitable international system? Why or why not?

MULTILATERALISM, COOPERATION, AND BURDEN SHARING
For the instructor: This part of the activity may require some library research. In small groups, assign each member a research task. One student should find an international issue where nation-states still act unilaterally with minimal cooperation. A second student should find information about a policy area where states engage in limited cooperation but do not give up significant sovereignty. A third student should find evidence where nation-states collaborate by sharing resources, expertise, and some decision making. A fourth research task should be allocated to one who will find examples where nation-states share decision-making authority and actually transfer authority to a regional or international institution.

For students: As you conduct your research, look for answers to the following questions:

1. What are the benefits of cooperation in these areas?
2. Why do you think states are willing to cooperate in some policy areas but not in others?
3. In the policy areas your group identified, is cooperation beneficial?
4. Do you think cooperation changes citizens' images of the international system?
5. Do you think continued cooperation will change the attitudes of leaders in the system?

In the next class session, review your notes with your colleagues in your work group. Your instructor will ask each group to share its findings and its responses to the assigned questions. The end result should be an interesting and useful record of cooperative multilateralism and unilateralism in international relations.

13 | Poverty, Development, and Hunger

Wherever there is great property there is great inequality. For one very rich man there must be at least five hundred poor, and the affluence of the few supposes the indigence of the many.

—Adam Smith

All societies used to be poor. Most are now lifting out of it; why are others stuck? The answer is traps. Poverty is not intrinsically a trap, otherwise we would all still be poor. Think, for a moment, of development as chutes and ladders. In the modern world of globalization there are some fabulous ladders; most societies are using them. But there are also some chutes, and some societies hit them. The countries at the bottom are an unlucky minority, but they are stuck.

—Paul Collier

As we saw in Chapter 7 and will explore further in this chapter, advocacy campaigns linked to celebrities like Kanye West, Radiohead, U2, Angelina Jolie, Panjabi MC, 50 Cent, Madonna, and George Clooney have come to play an important part in shaping the range of choices that politicians make about eliminating poverty, building economic development, and ending hunger worldwide.

Since 1945, we have witnessed not only increasing individual advocacy but unprecedented official development policies and impressive global economic growth. Yet global polarization is increasing, with the economic gap growing between rich and poor states and people. As we have seen in other issue areas in this book, people who work in the academic discipline of international relations have had different ways of thinking about this gap.

- Traditionally, realists have concentrated on issues relating to war and have seen security and development economics as separate issue areas.
- Mainstream realist and liberal scholars have largely neglected the challenges that global underdevelopment presents to human well-being.
- Dependency theorists have been interested in persistent and deepening inequality and relations between North and South, but for decades, they received little attention in the discipline.

The thirty-ninth G-8 summit was held in Northern Ireland in June 2013, and a variety of charities in the United Kingdom launched the IF campaign to pressure the G-8 countries to increase funding for development and hunger projects. Each of these paper flowers represents the millions of children who die each year from malnutrition. Are you part of an organization that seeks to make such a difference in the world?

- During the 1990s, debate flourished, and several subfields developed that touched on matters of poverty, development, and hunger, albeit tangentially (e.g., global environmental politics, gender, international political economy).
- The contributions of a range of theorists and scholars in the 1990s significantly raised the concerns of the majority of humanity and states: postcolonial theorists, Marxist theorists (Hardt and Negri), scholars adopting a human security approach (Nef, Thomas), and the few concerned directly with development (Saurin, Weber).

Now in the twenty-first century, the discipline is better placed to engage with the interrelated issues of poverty, development, and hunger by influencing the diplomatic world, where interest in these issues is growing, spurred on by fears of terrorist threats and recognition of the uneven impact of globalization (Thomas and Wilkin 2004).

Introduction

Despite the trend toward increased activism, poverty, hunger, and disease remain widespread, and women and girls continue to comprise the majority of the world's poorest people. Since the 1980s and 1990s, the worldwide promotion of neoliberal economic policies (the so-called **Washington Consensus**) by **global governance** institutions has been accompanied by increasing inequalities within and among states. During this period, the Second World countries of the former Eastern bloc have been incorporated into the third world grouping of states, and millions of people previously cushioned by their governments have been thrown into poverty. As a result, the developing world is characterized by rising social inequalities, and, within the third world countries, the adverse impact of globalization has been felt acutely. Countries have been forced to adopt free market policies as a condition of debt rescheduling and in the hope of attracting new investment to spur development. The global picture is very mixed, with other factors such as gender, class, race, and ethnicity contributing to local outcomes (Buvinic 1997, 39).

More recently, the enormity of the current challenges was recognized by the United Nations in 2000 with the acceptance of the Millennium Development Goals (www.undp.org).

These set time-limited, quantifiable targets across eight areas, including poverty, health, gender, education, environment, and development. The first goal was the eradication of extreme poverty and hunger, with the target of halving the proportion of people living on less than $1 a day by 2015.

The attempts of the majority of governments, international nongovernmental organizations (INGOs), and nongovernmental organizations (NGOs) since 1945 to address global hunger and poverty can be categorized into two very broad types depending on the explanations they provide for the existence of these problems and the respective solutions they prescribe. These can be identified as the dominant mainstream, or orthodox, approach, which provides and values a particular body of developmental knowledge, and a critical alternative approach, which incorporates other more marginalized understandings of the development challenge and process (see Table 13.1). Most of

Washington Consensus The belief of key opinion formers in Washington that global welfare would be maximized by the universal application of neoliberal economic policies that favor a minimalist state and an enhanced role for the market.

global governance The regulation and coordination of transnational issue areas by nation-states, international and regional organizations, and private agencies through the establishment of international regimes. These regimes may focus on problem solving or the simple enforcement of rules and regulations.

The global poor are short of food for all or part of the year. Some eat only one meal a day. Demonstrators at the UN headquarters in New York urge world governments in 2007 to meet the Millennium Development Goal to reduce hunger by 50 percent by 2015.

Table 13.1

Mainstream and Alternative Conceptions of Poverty, Development, and Hunger

	Poverty	Development	Hunger
Mainstream approach	Unfulfilled material needs	Linear path—traditional to modern	Not enough food to go around
Critical alternative approach	Unfulfilled material and nonmaterial needs	Diverse paths, locally driven	There is enough food; the problem is distribution and entitlement

this chapter will be devoted to an examination of the differences between the mainstream/orthodox approach and the critical alternative approach in view of the three related topics of poverty, development, and hunger, with particular emphasis placed on development. The chapter concludes with an assessment of whether the desperate conditions in which so many of the world's citizens find themselves today are likely to improve. Again, two contrasting approaches are outlined.

After reading and discussing this chapter, you will have a better sense of the factors that cause poverty and the status of efforts aimed at addressing global poverty. You will know about the global institutions that are dedicated to addressing the problems of development. You will also have an understanding of the global strategy called the Millennium Development Goals, which is aimed at ending poverty and addressing other elements of global security. The information in this chapter will help you understand the persistence of poverty and the difficulties of trying to address its devastating effects.

Poverty

Different conceptions of poverty underpin the mainstream and alternative views of development. There is basic agreement on the material aspects of poverty, such as lack of food, clean water, and sanitation, but disagreement on the importance of nonmaterial aspects. Also, key differences emerge in regard to how material needs should be met and, hence, about the goal of development.

Most governments, international organizations (e.g., the IMF and World Bank), and citizens in the West, and many elsewhere, adhere to the orthodox conception of **poverty**, which refers to a situation where people do not have the money to buy adequate food or satisfy other basic needs and are often classified as un- or underemployed.

Since 1945, this mainstream understanding of poverty based on money has arisen as a result of the globalization of Western culture and the attendant expansion of the market. Thus, a community that provides for itself outside monetized cash transactions and wage labor, such as a hunter-gatherer group, is regarded as poor. This meaning of poverty has been almost universalized. Poverty is seen as an economic condition dependent on cash transactions in the marketplace for its eradication. These transactions in turn depend on development defined as economic growth. The same economic yardstick is used to measure all societies and to judge if they merit development assistance.

Poverty has widely been regarded as characterizing the third world, and it has a gendered face that realist and liberal perspectives often ignore. By the mid-1990s, an approach had developed whereby it was seen as incumbent on the developed countries to help the

poverty In the orthodox view, a situation suffered by people who do not have the *money to buy food* and satisfy other basic *material needs*. In the alternative view, a situation suffered by people who are not able to meet their *material and nonmaterial needs* through their own effort.

third world eradicate poverty. As studies show that women and children are most severely impacted by the consequences of poverty, development economists are paying more attention to female poverty and women's roles in economic development. The solution advocated to overcome global poverty is the further integration of the global economy (C. Thomas 2000) and of women into this process (Pearson 2000; H. Weber 2002). Increasingly, however, as globalization has intensified, poverty defined in such economic terms has come to characterize significant sectors of the population in advanced developed countries such as the United States (see Bello 1994).

But for some, poverty cannot be measured in terms of cash. Critical alternative views of poverty place the emphasis not only on money but on spiritual values, community ties, and the availability of common resources. In traditional subsistence methods, a common strategy for **survival** is provision for oneself and one's family via **community**-regulated access to common water, land, and fodder. The work of the UN Development Programme (UNDP) since the early 1990s is significant here for distinguishing between income poverty (a material condition) and human poverty (encompassing human dignity, opportunity, and choices).

The issue of poverty and the challenge of poverty alleviation moved up the global political agenda at the close of the twentieth century, as evidenced in the UN's first Millennium Development Goals, cited earlier in this chapter. World Bank figures for the 1990s showed a global improvement in reducing the number of people living on less than $1 a day (its orthodox measurement of extreme poverty), but the picture was uneven: in sub-Saharan Africa, the situation deteriorated, and elsewhere, such as the Russian Federation, the Commonwealth of Independent States, Latin America and the Caribbean, and some non-oil-producing Middle Eastern states, the picture remains bleak. In 2005, the World Bank stated that almost half the world—more than 3 billion people—lived below the new poverty line, $2.50 a day, and at least 80 percent of the world's population lived on less than $10 a day. On a positive note, the world will meet the Millennium Development Goal (MDG) target of halving global poverty. The proportion of poor people living on less than $1.25 a day fell from 43% in 1990 to 20.6 % in 2010. Most of the global improvement resulted from trends in China and India, but even there, extensive pockets of poverty remain.

Development

Having considered the orthodox and critical alternative views of poverty, we now turn to an examination of the important topic of development. This examination will be conducted in three main parts. The first part starts by examining the orthodox view of development and then proceeds to an assessment of its effect on postwar development in the third world. The second part examines the critical alternative view of development and its application to subjects such as empowerment and democracy. In the third part, we consider the ways the orthodox approach to development has responded to some of the criticisms made of it by the critical alternative approach.

When we consider the topic of **development**, it is important to realize that all conceptions of development necessarily reflect a particular set of social and political values. Since World War II, the dominant understanding—favored by the majority of governments and multilateral lending agencies—has been **modernization theory**, a theory that considers development synonymous with economic growth within the context of a free market international economy. Economic growth is identified as necessary for combating poverty, defined as the inability of people to meet their basic material needs through cash transactions. This

---

survival In this context, it is the survival of the person by the provision of adequate food, clean water, clothing, shelter, medical care, and protection from violence and crime.

community A human association in which members share common symbols and wish to cooperate to realize common objectives.

WHAT'S YOUR WORLDVIEW ?

The poorest 1.4 billion are living below the $1.25 global poverty line and over 1 billion are going hungry. Why is it so hard to get the world to care? Could you make choices that might help the bottom billion?

development In the orthodox view, top-down; reliance on "expert knowledge," usually Western and definitely external; large capital investments in large projects; advanced technology; expansion of the private sphere. In the alternative view, bottom-up; participatory; reliance on appropriate (often local) knowledge and technology; small investments in small-scale projects; protection of the commons.

modernization theory A theory that considers development synonymous with economic growth within the context of a free market international economy.

is seen in the influential reports of the World Bank, where countries are categorized according to their income. Countries that have lower national incomes per capita are regarded as less developed than those with higher incomes, and they are perceived as being in need of increased integration into the global marketplace.

As the wave of decolonization swept the world in the 1960s and early 1970s, an alternative view of development has emerged from a few governments, UN agencies, grassroots movements, NGOs, and some academics. Their concerns have centered broadly on entitlement and distribution. Poverty is identified as the inability to provide for the material needs of oneself and one's family by subsistence or cash transactions and by the absence of an environment conducive to human well-being broadly conceived in spiritual and community terms. These voices of opposition are growing significantly louder as ideas polarize following the apparent universal triumph of economic liberalism at the end of the Cold War. The language of opposition is changing to incorporate matters of democracy such as political empowerment, participation, meaningful self-determination for the majority, protection of the commons, and an emphasis on growth that benefits the poor. The fundamental differences between the orthodox and the alternative views of development can be seen in Table 13.2, supplemented by Case Study 13.1, which illustrates the impact of ideas about development from the contemporary coffee-producing sector. In the following two sections, we will examine how the orthodox view of development has been applied at a global level and assess what measure of success it has achieved.

Post-1945 International Economic Liberalism and the Orthodox Development Model

During World War II, there was a strong belief among the Allied powers that the protectionist trade policies of the 1930s had contributed significantly to the outbreak of the war. As we learned in Chapters 11 and 12, even before World War II had ended, the United States and the United Kingdom drew the plans for the creation of a stable postwar international order, with the United Nations (UN), its affiliates the International Monetary Fund (IMF) and the World Bank Group, plus the General Agreement on Tariffs and Trade (GATT) providing the institutional bases. The latter three provided the foundations of a liberal international economic order based on the pursuit of free trade but allowing an appropriate role for state intervention in the market in support of national security and national and global stability (Rapley 1996). This has been called **embedded liberalism**. Because the decision-making procedures of these international economic institutions favored a small group of developed Western states, their relationship with the United Nations, which in the General Assembly has more democratic procedures, has not always been an easy one.

In the early postwar years, reconstruction of previously developed states took priority over assisting developing states. This reconstruction process really took off in the context of the Cold War, with the transfer of huge sums of money from the United States to Europe in the form of bilateral aid from the Marshall Plan of 1947. In the 1950s and 1960s, as decolonization progressed and developing countries gained power in the UN General Assembly, the focus of the World Bank and the UN system generally shifted to the perceived needs of developing countries. The United States was heavily involved as the most important funder of the World Bank and the United Nations and also in a bilateral capacity.

There was a widespread belief in the developed Western countries, among the managers of the major multilateral institutions, and throughout the UN system that third world states were economically backward and needed to be "developed." Western-educated elites in those countries believed this process would require intervention in their economies.

embedded liberalism A liberal international economic order based on the pursuit of free trade but allowing an appropriate role for state intervention in the market in support of national security and national and global stability.

Table 13.2
Development: A Contested Concept

The Orthodox View

Poverty: A situation suffered by people who do not have the *money to buy food* and satisfy other *basic material needs*.

Purpose: Transformation of traditional subsistence economies defined as "backward" into industrial, commodified economies defined as "modern." Production of surplus. Individuals sell their labor for money, rather than producing to meet their family's needs.

Core ideas and assumptions: The possibility of unlimited economic growth in a free market system. Economies would reach a "takeoff" point, and thereafter, wealth would trickle down to those at the bottom. Superiority of the Western model and knowledge. Belief that the process would ultimately benefit everyone. Domination, exploitation of nature.

Measurement: Economic growth; gross domestic product (GDP) per capita; industrialization, including of agriculture.

Process: Top-down; reliance on "expert knowledge," usually Western and definitely external; large capital investments in large projects; advanced technology; expansion of the private sphere.

The Alternative View

Poverty: A situation suffered by people who are not able to meet their *material and nonmaterial needs* through their own effort.

Purpose: Creation of human well-being through sustainable societies in social, cultural, political, and economic terms.

Core ideas and assumptions: Sufficiency. The inherent value of nature, cultural diversity, and the community-controlled commons (water, land, air, forest). Human activity in balance with nature. Self-reliance. Democratic inclusion, participation: for example, a voice for marginalized groups such as women and indigenous groups. Local control.

Measurement: Fulfillment of basic material and nonmaterial human needs of everyone; condition of the natural environment; political empowerment of marginalized.

Process: Bottom-up; participatory; reliance on appropriate (often local) knowledge and technology; small investments in small-scale projects; protection of the commons.

In the context of independence movements, the development imperative came to be shared by many citizens in the third world. The underlying assumption was that the Western lifestyle and mode of economic organization were superior and should be universally aspired to.

The Cold War provided a context in which there was a competition between the West and the Eastern bloc to win markets in the third world. The United States believed that the path of liberal economic growth would result in development and that development would result in a global capitalist system, which favors the United States. The USSR, by contrast, attempted to sell its centralized economic system as the most rapid means for the newly independent states to achieve industrialization and development. Unfortunately for the Soviet government, because of its own food-supply and consumer-goods production problems, the country's material foreign assistance was usually limited to military equipment.

The majority of third world states were born into and accepted a place within the Western, capitalist orbit, primarily because of preexisting economic ties with their former colonial occupiers, but a few, either by choice or lack of options, ended up in the socialist camp. Yet in the early postwar and postcolonial decades, all newly independent states favored an important role for the state in development.

CASE STUDY : Ideas and Development in the Contemporary Coffee-Producing Sector

13.1

Contemporary debate on the coffee sector provides a graphic example of competing ideas and values concerning development, and it has relevance far beyond coffee. The impact of commodity price volatility and a long-term decline in terms of trade of primary products has profound effects on the livelihoods of millions of rural householders in the poorest countries. In the case of coffee, about 25 million small farmers in more than fifty countries depend directly on coffee production. During the 1980s, export production increased in poor countries, fueled significantly by policy advice from the World Bank and International Monetary Fund (IMF) that hard-currency earnings had to be boosted through increased commodity exports to pay off spiraling third world debt. Over-supply since the early 1980s has resulted in a decline of about 70 percent in nominal coffee prices, with prices reaching a thirty-year low in 2001. The impact on livelihoods of smallholder peasant farmers and plantation workers has been devastating. At the eleventh World Coffee Conference in Salvador da Bahia in September 2005, twelve groups representing peasant farmers and workers launched an alternative approach to coffee production in the Salvador Declaration:

Fair trade NGOs seek to get a fair price for producers of tea, coffee, cocoa, and other food products grown in the developing world.

> For a truly sustainable coffee sector, all who take part in coffee production must share its wealth: small-scale producers, permanent and seasonal rural workers, industry and retail workers. Many say that the solutions to the crisis are only associated with methods of production, including increased investment in substitutes for local coffee varieties, use of toxic fertilisers and pesticides, and mechanization—all aimed at greater productivity. This vision . . . allows for the consolidation of production and marketing by a small group of companies that do not practise social responsibility but make decisions that impact millions of people while they reap the lion's share of the benefits of the trade. This vision is not sustainable . . .

Real sustainability of the coffee sector should not be viewed through an economic lens alone but must include ethical and political perspectives.

From an ethical perspective, the citizenship rights of people who participate in wealth generation must be guaranteed. Those rights are: stability of prices; recognition of efforts to protect the rural landscape and biological diversity by improving cultivation, harvest, and post harvesting practices; and recognition of the basic rights of rural workers, including the fundamental rights of association and collective bargaining, particularly for seasonal rural workers . . .

From a political perspective, . . . governments [must] agree to and implement public policies that guarantee the rights of coffee producers and rural workers. It should be possible to develop a sustainable model based on food security and sovereignty.

In conclusion, we expect the World Coffee Conference to acknowledge . . . the issue of sustainability from the perspective of all actors involved in the coffee chain and sanction space for direct representation by small-scale farmers and rural workers organisations . . . (and) seek to establish the basis for fair trade between nations.

Oxfam 2006, pp. 11–12.

For Discussion

1. Do ethics matter in most economic development stories? Why or why not?
2. Are you willing to pay more for a cup of coffee if you know the coffee farmers were paid a fair wage? Why or why not?
3. How do we all benefit if those producing valuable commodities are paid well and live in stable and free countries?
4. Sustainable development means considering the needs of future generations when we make choices today. Why is it so hard to develop this foresight?

liberalization Government policies that reduce the role of the state in the economy, such as the dismantling of trade tariffs and barriers, the deregulation and opening of the financial sector to foreign investors, and the privatization of state enterprises.

post–Washington Consensus A slightly modified version of the Washington Consensus promoting economic growth through trade liberalization coupled with pro-poor growth and poverty-reduction policies.

With the ending of the Cold War and the collapse of the Eastern bloc after 1989, this neoliberal economic and political philosophy came to dominate development thinking across the globe. The championing of unadulterated liberal economic values played an important role in accelerating the globalization process, representing an important ideological shift. The embedded liberalism of the early postwar decades gave way to the neoclassical economic policies that favored a minimalist state and an enhanced role for the market: the Washington Consensus. The belief was that global welfare would be maximized by the **liberalization** of trade, finance, and investment and by the restructuring of national economies to provide an enabling environment for capital. Such policies would also ideally ensure the repayment of debt. The former Eastern bloc countries were now seen to be in transition from centrally planned to market economies, and throughout the third world, the role of government was reduced and the market given the role of major engine of growth and associated development. This approach was presented as common sense, with the attendant idea that "There Is No Alternative," or TINA (C. Thomas 2000). It informed the strategies of the IMF and World Bank, and, importantly, through the Uruguay Round of trade discussions carried out under the auspices of GATT, it shaped the World Trade Organization (WTO).

By the end of the 1990s, the G-7 (later the G-8, when Russia joined in 1996) and associated international financial institutions were championing a slightly modified version of the neoliberal economic orthodoxy, labeled the **post–Washington Consensus**, which stressed growth benefiting the poor and poverty reduction based on institutional strength, continued domestic policy reform, and growth through trade liberalization. Henceforth, locally owned national poverty-reduction strategy (PRS) papers would be the focus for funding (Cammack 2002). These papers quickly became the litmus test for funding from an increasingly integrated lineup of global financial institutions and donors.

WHAT'S YOUR WORLDVIEW

Some writers have suggested that the Cold War was about whose rule book would govern the world—the Soviet view of socialism or the US brand of capitalism. Capitalism won, but it does not seem to be working for many who live in the developing world. How would you try to explain this situation to the majority of the world's poor? If there is only one economic option—capitalism—how do you sell it to those who are disadvantaged?

regional diversity Each region of the world has experienced economic development differently based on traditions, culture, historical development, and even geographic location.

The Post-1945 International Economic Order: Results

There has been an explosive widening of the gap between the rich and the poor since 1945 compared with previous history. Nevertheless, there have been major gains for developing countries since 1945 as measured by the orthodox criteria of economic growth, GDP per capita, and industrialization. The rates of total and per capita growth for developing countries in the period 1960–2004 are shown in Tables 13.3 and 13.4. A striking feature of both is the marked **regional diversity**. The East Asian experience has been generally positive throughout this period, but not so for Africa. China has been strong since the early 1980s, and India has fared better since the late 1980s.

In the 1990s, the picture was far from positive. The UNDP reports "no fewer than 100 countries—all developing or in transition—have experienced serious economic decline over the past three decades. As a result, per capita income in these 100 countries is lower than it was 10, 20, even 30 years ago" (UN Development Programme 1998, 37). Moreover, the 1990s saw twenty-one countries experience decade-long declines in social and economic indicators compared with only four in the 1980s (UN Development Programme 2003). Financial crises spread across the globe and indicated marked reversals in Mexico, the East Asian states, Brazil, and Russia. The African continent looked increasingly excluded from any economic benefits of globalization, and thirty-three countries there ended the 1990s more heavily indebted than they had been two decades earlier (Easterly 2002). By the end of the century, not a single former second or third world country had joined the ranks of the first world in a solid sense. Significant growth occurred in a handful of countries, such as China, India, and Mexico—the new globalizers—but the benefits were not well distributed within those countries. Despite significant improvements in global social indicators like adult literacy, access to safe water, and infant mortality rates, global deprivation continues. This is illustrated vividly in Figure 13.1.

Having outlined the broad development achievements and failures of the postwar international economic order, we will now evaluate these from two different development perspectives: a mainstream orthodox view and a critical alternative view.

Economic Development: Orthodox and Alternative Evaluations

The orthodox liberal assessment of the past sixty years of development suggests states that have integrated most deeply into the global economy through trade liberalization have grown the fastest, and it praises these "new globalizers." It acknowledges that neoliberal economic policy has resulted in greater inequalities within and between states but regards inequality positively as a spur to competition and the entrepreneurial spirit.

It was clear at least from the late 1970s that "trickle-down" (the idea that overall economic growth as measured by increases in the GDP would automatically bring benefits for the poorer classes) had not worked. Despite impressive rates of growth in GDP per capita enjoyed by some developing countries, this success was not reflected in their societies at large, and while a minority became substantially wealthier, the mass of the population saw no significant change. For some bankers in multilateral organizations and conservative politicians in rich countries, the even greater polarization in wealth evident in recent decades is not regarded as a problem as long as the social and political discontent the inequality creates is not so extensive as to potentially derail implementation of the liberalization project itself. This discontent will be alleviated by the development of national poverty-reduction strategies (PRSs), which it is claimed put countries and their peoples in the driver's seat of development policy, thus empowering the local community and ensuring a better distribution of benefits.

Advocates of a critical alternative approach emphasize the pattern of distribution of gains within global society and within individual states rather than growth. They believe that the economic liberalism that underpins the process of globalization has resulted, and continues to result, in growing economic differentiation between and within countries and that this is problematic. Moreover, they note that this trend has been evident over the very period when key global actors have been committed to promoting development worldwide and, indeed, when there were fairly continuous world economic growth rates and positive rates of GDP growth per capita (Brown and Kane 1995; see Tables 13.3 and 13.4).

The increasing gap between rich and poor was regarded as inevitable and undesirable by dependency theorists such as Andre Gunder Frank (1967). Writing in the 1960s and 1970s, these theorists stressed how the periphery, or third world, was actively underdeveloped by activities that promoted the growth in wealth of the core Western countries and of elites in the periphery (see Case Study 13.2).

At the beginning of the twenty-first century, however, exponents of a critical alternative—in contrast to their orthodox colleagues—question the value of national PRSs, arguing that while a new focus on issues such as health and education is important, the more fundamental issue of possible links between Washington Consensus policies and poverty creation is ignored.

Goals and Targets	Africa		Asia				Oceania	Latin America & the Caribbean	Caucasus & Central Asia
	Northern	Sub-Saharan	Eastern	South-Eastern	Southern	Western			

GOAL 1 | Eradicate extreme poverty and hunger

Reduce extreme poverty by half	low poverty	very high poverty	moderate poverty*	moderate poverty	very high poverty	low poverty	very high poverty	low poverty	low poverty
Productive and decent employment	large deficit in decent work	very large deficit in decent work	large deficit in decent work	large deficit in decent work	very large deficit in decent work	large deficit in decent work	very large deficit in decent work	moderate deficit in decent work	moderate deficit in decent work
Reduce hunger by half	low hunger	very high hunger	moderate hunger	moderate hunger	high hunger	moderate hunger	moderate hunger	moderate hunger	moderate hunger

GOAL 2 | Achieve universal primary education

Universal primary schooling	high enrolment	moderate enrolment	high enrolment	high enrolment	high enrolment	high enrolment	—	high enrolment	high enrolment

GOAL 3 | Promote gender equality and empower women

Equal girls' enrolment in primary school	close to parity	close to parity	close to parity	parity	parity	close to parity	close to parity	parity	parity
Women's share of paid employment	low share	medium share	high share	medium share	low share	low share	medium share	high share	high share
Women's equal representation in national parliaments	low representation	moderate representation	moderate representation	low representation	low representation	low representation	very low representation	moderate representation	low representation

GOAL 4 | Reduce child mortality

Reduce mortality of under-five-year-olds by two thirds	low mortality	high mortality	low mortality	low mortality	moderate mortality	low mortality	moderate mortality	low mortality	moderate mortality

GOAL 5 | Improve maternal health

Reduce maternal mortality by three quarters	low mortality	very high mortality	low mortality	moderate mortality	high mortality	low mortality	high mortality	low mortality	low mortality
Access to reproductive health	moderate access	low access	high access	moderate access	moderate access	moderate access	low access	high access	moderate access

GOAL 6 | Combat HIV/AIDS, malaria and other diseases

Halt and begin to reverse the spread of HIV/AIDS	low incidence	high incidence	low incidence	low incidence	low incidence	low incidence	low incidence	low incidence	intermediate incidence
Halt and reverse the spread of tuberculosis	low mortality	moderate mortality	low mortality	moderate mortality	moderate mortality	low mortality	high mortality	low mortality	moderate mortality

GOAL 7 | Ensure environmental sustainability

Halve proportion of population without improved drinking water	high coverage	low coverage	high coverage	moderate coverage	high coverage	high coverage	low coverage	high coverage	moderate coverage
Halve proportion of population without sanitation	high coverage	very low coverage	low coverage	low coverage	very low coverage	moderate coverage	very low coverage	moderate coverage	high coverage
Improve the lives of slum-dwellers	moderate proportion of slum-dwellers	very high proportion of slum-dwellers	moderate proportion of slum-dwellers	high proportion of slum-dwellers	high proportion of slum-dwellers	moderate proportion of slum-dwellers	moderate proportion of slum-dwellers	moderate proportion of slum-dwellers	—

GOAL 8 | Develop a global partnership for development

Internet users	high usage	moderate usage	high usage	high usage	moderate usage	high usage	low usage	high usage	high usage

The progress chart operates on two levels. The words in each box indicate the present degree of compliance with the target. The colours show progress towards the target according to the legend below:

▇ Target already met or expected to be met by 2015.

▇ No progress or deterioration.

▇ Progress insufficient to reach the target if prevailing trends persist.

▇ Missing or insufficient data.

* Poverty progress for Eastern Asia is assessed based on China's data only.

For the regional groupings and country data, see *mdgs.un.org*. Country experiences in each region may differ significantly from the regional average. Due to new data and revised methodologies, this Progress Chart is not comparable with previous versions.

Sources: United Nations, based on data and estimates provided by: Food and Agriculture Organization of the United Nations; Inter-Parliamentary Union; International Labour Organization; International Telecommunication Union; UNAIDS; UNESCO; UN-Habitat; UNICEF; UN Population Division; World Bank; World Health Organization – based on statistics available as of June 2013.

Compiled by Statistics Division, Department of Economic and Social Affairs, United Nations.

Figure 13.1 2013 Progress Chart for UN Millennium Development Goals.

Table 13.3

GDP Growth in Selected Developing Countries and Regions, 1970–2010

(average annual percentage change)

Region/country	1970–1975	1975–1980	1980–1985	1985–1990	1990–1995	1995–2000	2000–2005	2005–2010
Africa	4.4	3.8	2.2	2.6	1.1	3.4	5.3	4.8
Sub-Saharan Africa	3.9	1.9	1.7	3.2	1.5	3.7	6.7	6.0
Latin America	6.6	5.1	0.5	1.8	3.6	2.8	2.6	3.9
East Asia	6.8	7.6	7.1	8.2	8.8	4.9	7.5	8.7
China	5.1	5.1	11.0	7.8	12.9	8.5	9.8	11.2
First-Tier NIEs (newly industrialized economies)	8.3	9.0	7.1	9.1	7.3	4.2	4.4	4.2
South Asia	2.3	3.6	5.3	5.9	5.0	5.3	6.6	7.2
India	2.4	3.0	5.3	6.6	5.3	5.8	7.0	8.3
Developing Countries	6.4	5.1	2.9	5.4	5.4	4.1	5.4	6.3

Source: http://unctadstat.unctad.org/TableViewer/tableView.aspx

Table 13.4

Per Capita GDP Growth in Selected Developing Countries and Regions, 1970–2010

(average annual percentage change)

Region/country	1970–1975	1975–1980	1980–1985	1985–1990	1990–1995	1995–2000	2000–2005	2005–2010
Africa	1.6	0.9	0.7	−0.2	−1.5	1.0	2.9	2.4
Sub-Saharan Africa	1.1	−1.0	−1.2	0.2	−1.3	1.1	4.0	4.0
Latin America	4.0	2.7	−1.6	−0.2	1.9	1.2	1.3	2.7
East Asia	4.4	5.9	5.4	6.4	7.5	3.8	6.9	8.1
China	2.8	4.6	9.5	6.1	11.7	7.5	9.1	9.1
First-Tier NIEs (newly industrialized economies)	6.1	7.1	5.5	8.0	6.1	3.2	3.9	3.6
South Asia	0.0	1.4	2.9	3.6	2.8	3.3	4.8	5.7
India	0.1	0.9	3.1	4.4	3.3	4.0	5.3	6.7
Developing Countries	3.9	2.9	0.7	2.2	3.5	2.4	3.9	4.8

Source: http://unctadstat.unctad.org/TableViewer/tableView.aspx

THEORY IN PRACTICE

The Terms of Development

THE CHALLENGE

Can any theory of international relations explain the problems of economic underdevelopment? International relations specialists even have trouble deciding what to call the countries of the world once held in European colonial bondage. *Third world* made sense at one time. The term originated with Alfred Sauvy, a French demographer, who in 1952 compared the economic and political conditions of European colonies with those endured by the Third Estate in France prior to the revolution. The typology was a simple one: first world countries had capitalist free market economies, second world countries in the Soviet bloc and China had centrally planned economies, and third world countries lacked industrial bases and provided raw materials for export. With the end of the Cold War, this tripartite typology made less sense.

OPTIONS

Until 1989, "third world" provided a less demeaning alternative to terms often found in the political science literature on Africa, Asia, Oceania, and Latin America: *underdeveloped* or *less developed country* (LDC), sometimes called *least developed country* (also LDC). A brief look at a map reveals another problem. The *global South* is another term often used to indicate the former European colonies in Africa, Asia, and Latin America; the other side of this dyad is the *global North*, meant to describe the former colonial occupiers. But not all countries in the global South are poor, and not all countries that were once colonial occupiers—Portugal and Spain, for instance—are rich. Instead, there are pockets of wealth and poverty in both the South and the North.

APPLICATION

There is another problem for theorists. What do we mean by the term *development* itself? The term might mean industrial output and its related exchange of goods and services. If that is the case, then the term implies that industrialization is a proper goal. The problem of global climate change suggests that industrialization, as it has been practiced, is not a good thing (see Chapter 10). Moreover, the term, according to some gender theorists, only considers transactions that can be counted or that rely on an amount calculated in a currency. This method of accounting can overlook transactions that take place in a barter market or economic activities traditionally done by women: raising crops for household consumption, cutting firewood, caring for children. In a capitalist economy, in Western Europe or the United States, such activities could have a dollar amount attached. For example, the US tax code gives a deduction for the cost of child care.

The realist perspective looks at the problems of economic and political underdevelopment, using the standard definitions found in scholarly books, with an almost Calvinist sensibility: countries are poor because they are poor. Since international politics is a constant struggle for power in conditions of anarchy, then some countries must lose in that struggle. This perspective can help explain the series of internal and transborder wars in central Africa since the late 1980s. Short on their own resources, the neighbors of the Congo tried to destabilize that country to gain access to mineral wealth.

Radical perspectives like Marxism once offered hope for a restructured global system. However, whatever comfort the doctrine once promised, the demise of the Soviet Union ended it. What was left was a theory that outlined the causes and results of political and economic

Residents play table tennis at the Santa Marta slum in Rio de Janeiro, Brazil. Police and government officials are rooting out gangs and bringing services to these favelas to make the city safer for the 2014 World Cup and the 2016 Olympics.

Continued

exploitation but proposed an apparently bankrupt solution.

For analysts in the liberal tradition, the policy prescription does not offer much hope either. This tradition tends to recommend that the former colonies integrate themselves into the global economy, perhaps by planting a cash crop for export or by utilizing untapped resources. As we have seen in this

chapter, however, countries that borrow money from international financial institutions can get caught in a debt trap if the price for the export commodity declines. This can leave the country economically worse off.

Unfortunately, no matter what they are called—the third world, the global South, the LDCs—for many countries, poverty and hunger prevail.

For Discussion

1. Instead of disagreeing about terminology, should leaders work on comprehensive plans to help the poor of the world?
2. Are there alternative views of development that might challenge the orthodox position?
3. What does a state-centric focus (on states as the primary actor in global politics) overlook?

The orthodox and alternative evaluations are based on different values, and they are measuring different things. Glyn Roberts's words are pertinent: "GNP growth statistics might mean a good deal to an economist or to a maharajah, but they do not tell us a thing about the quality of life in a Third World fishing village" (1984, 6).

A Critical Alternative View of Development

Since the early 1970s, there have been numerous efforts to stimulate debate about development and to highlight its contested nature. Critical alternative ideas have been put forward that we can synthesize into an alternative approach. These have originated with various NGOs, grassroots development organizations, individuals, UN organizations, and private foundations. The Nobel Prize committee recognized the alternative approach when in 2006 it gave the Peace Prize to Muhammad Yunus and the microcredit loan institution, Grameen Bank, which he founded (see Case Study 11.1). Disparate **social movements** not directly related to the development agenda have contributed to the flourishing of the alternative viewpoints—for example, the women's movement, the peace movement, movements for democracy, and green movements (C. Thomas 2000). Noteworthy was the publication in 1975 by the Dag Hammarskjöld Foundation of *What Now? Another Development?* This alternative conception of development (see Ekins 1992, 99) argued that the process of development should be

- need-oriented (material and nonmaterial);
- endogenous (coming from within a society);
- self-reliant (in terms of human, natural, and cultural resources);
- ecologically sound; and
- based on structural transformations (of economy, society, gender, and power relations).

Since then, various NGOs, such as the World Development Movement, have campaigned for a form of development that takes aspects of this alternative approach on board. Grassroots movements have often grown up around specific issues, such as dams (Narmada in India) or access to common resources (the rubber tappers of the Brazilian Amazon; the Chipko movement, which began as a women's movement to secure trees in the Himalayas). Such campaigns received a great impetus in the 1980s with the growth of the green movement worldwide. The two-year preparatory process before the UN Conference on Environment and Development (UNCED) in Rio, in June 1992, gave indigenous groups, women, children, and

social movement People with a diffuse sense of collective identity, solidarity, and common purpose that usually leads to collective political behavior. The concept covers all the different NGOs and networks plus all their members and all the other individuals who share the common value(s). Thus, the women's movement and the environmental movement are much more than the specific NGOs that provide leadership and focus on the desire for social change.

CASE STUDY | Haiti: Poverty and Hunger — 13.2

With its per capita income of $556, Haiti is the poorest country in the Western Hemisphere. Two-thirds of the people live in rural areas; four-fifths are poor. Nearly half the population consumes less than 75 percent of the recommended intake of food energy. Rice is a major staple of the diet and mainly produced by small farmers. Twenty percent of the people depend on rice cultivation for their livelihoods, and the sector has a major economic spin-off, with thousands of agricultural laborers, traders, and millers earning their living from it.

In recent years, Haiti has undergone rapid trade liberalization, and it is now one of the most open economies in the world. Liberalization of the rice market started in the 1980s, but the final stroke came in 1994–1995 when, under pressure from the international community (notably, the IMF and the United States), the tariff on rice was cut from 35 percent to 3 percent.

Rice producers reported that prices fell by 50 percent during 1986–1987, after the first wave of liberalization. In 1995, local production fell by 27 percent. Rice imports increased by thirty times between 1985 and 1999 as a result of the market slump. Food aid in rice surged from zero in 1994 to 16,000 metric tons in 1999. Most rice imports are of subsidized US rice.

These trends have severely undermined the livelihoods of more than 50,000 rice-farming families and led to a rural exodus. Cheap imports initially benefited poor consumers, but in recent years, these benefits have vanished. The FAO says that overall malnutrition has increased since the start of the trade liberalization, affecting 48 percent of the population in 1979–1981 and 62 percent in 1996–1998. Even before the recent devastating earthquake, almost half of Haiti's food needs were met by imports.

Globally, around 170 million people are suffering from diseases and dangerous health conditions due to inadequate consumption of food. Malnutrition is the underlying cause of 2.6 million children dying each year. This translates to 300 child deaths every hour. And Haiti is just one country where children suffer today. Half of the deaths will occur in Africa, caused by rising food prices, political instability, and the lack of technological infrastructure essential for increasing the quality and quantity of food. Haiti's problem is a global one.

Source: Oxfam 2003, p. 10.

For Discussion

1. Haiti is a fragile state and dependent on external assistance to survive. As such, what should the OAS or the United Nations be doing to help it to become more self-reliant?
2. Is liberalization for some states the wrong way to organize an economy? Would more state intervention help to control prices and production?
3. How could the United States help here, and does it have a responsibility to do so?

other previously voiceless groups a chance to express their views. This momentum has continued, and it has become the norm to hold alternative NGO forums parallel to all major UN conferences. In addition, the World Social Forum meets annually.

Democracy, Empowerment, and Development

Democracy is at the heart of the alternative conception of development. Grassroots movements are playing an important role in challenging entrenched structures of power in formal democratic societies. In the face of increasing globalization, with the further erosion of local community control over daily life and the further extension of the power of the market and **transnational corporations**, people are standing up for their rights as they define them. They are making a case for local control and local empowerment as the heart of development. They are protecting what they identify as the immediate source of their survival—water, forest, and land. They are rejecting the dominant agenda of private and public (government-controlled) spheres and setting an alternative one. Examples include the Chiapas uprising in Mexico and Indian peasant protests against foreign-owned seed factories. Protests at the annual meetings of the WTO and protests of the IMF and World Bank have become routine since the

transnational corporation A company or business that has affiliates in different countries.

late 1990s and are indicative of an increasingly widespread discontent with the process of globalization and the distribution of its benefits.

Such protests symbolize the struggle for substantive democracy that communities across the world are working for. In this context, development is about facilitating a community's participation and lead role in deciding what sort of development is appropriate for it; it is not about assuming the desirability of the Western model and its associated values. This alternative conception of development therefore values diversity above universality and is based on a different conception of rights.

For some commentators, national PRSs offer the opportunity—albeit as yet unrealized—for greater community participation in development policy making in the South. If all parties operate in the spirit that was intended, the PRS process could enhance representation and voice for states and peoples in the South, and it offers the best hope available for expanding national ownership of economic policy.

A new antiglobalization movement in Europe, "Blockupy," confronts a police barricade in front of the European Central Bank in Frankfurt, Germany, in May 2013. This new alliance of activists is critical of economic globalization and the neoliberal institutions that support and promote it.

Now that we have looked at the critical alternative view of development, we will look at the way the orthodox view has attempted to respond to the criticisms of the alternative view.

The Orthodoxy Incorporates Criticisms

In the mainstream debate, the focus has shifted from growth to sustainable development. The concept was championed in the late 1980s by the influential Brundtland Commission (officially entitled the World Commission on Environment and Development; see Brundtland et al. 1987) and supported in the 1990s by a series of UN global conferences. Central to the concept of **sustainable development** is the idea that the pursuit of development by the present generation should not be at the expense of future generations. Similarly, when faced with critical NGO voices, the World Bank eventually in 1994 came up with its Operational Policy 4.20 on gender. The latter aimed to "reduce gender disparities and enhance women particularly in the economic development of their countries by integrating gender considerations in its country assistance programs" (www.worldbank.org).

Most recently, incorporating the language of poverty reduction into World Bank and IMF policies includes words like "growth with equity" and "pro-poor growth," which some would argue are nothing more than buzzwords because they underlie macroeconomic policy that remains unchanged. An examination of the contribution of the development orthodoxy to increasing global inequality is not on the agenda. The gendered outcomes of macroeconomic policies are largely ignored.

Despite promises of new funding at the UN Monterrey Conference on Financing for Development in 2002, new transfers of finance from developed to developing countries have been slow in coming; meanwhile, most expected new promises to be made by the G-8 during their summit in 2009. In addition to new finance, that summit saw commitments to write off $40 billion of debt owed by the heavily indebted poor countries (HIPCs). However, the commitment was not implemented with immediate effect and didn't cover all needy countries. The North-South agenda has changed little in the years since the Rio Summit, when sustainable development hit the headlines.

sustainable development
The development that meets the needs of the present without compromising the ability of future generations to meet their own needs.

GLOBAL PERSPECTIVE | Life in Zimbabwe: Poverty, Hunger, Development, and Politics

BACKGROUND

It is possible the average person in Zimbabwe was not aware of the global economic downturn of 2009. If people in the southern African country did know about the collapse of banks and, according to the IMF, the loss of perhaps 51 million jobs worldwide, this knowledge would not have changed their lives very much. With a 2008 per capita GDP of $200 already, things could not have gotten much worse.

THE CASE

The previous year had seen an array of problems that few developing countries had seen recently. First, a series of bad harvests had pushed more people than usual to rely on food aid provided mainly by foreign aid agencies, such as the UN's World Food Program, and some EU countries. In power since 1980, President Robert Mugabe's government had banned aid from Britain because the former colonial power had sought to have Zimbabwe suspended from the Commonwealth, an organization of now-independent former British colonies. Critics of Mugabe's government blame the famine not just on low rainfall but, even more, on the badly planned land reform effort that took land away from the most prosperous farmers and gave it to landless Zimbabweans. Although the Mugabe government called the reform program "Zimbabwe for Zimbabweans," it was not only people of European descent who lost land but also people who were not members of President Mugabe's ethnic group. Resistance to land reform led to riots, as government paramilitary units forced people from their farms and into illegal squatter camps.

The famine exacerbated preexisting economic problems. Zimbabwe had little to offer for export earnings beyond the agricultural sector, which provided more than 400,000 jobs. When the land reform began, unemployment increased, as did the inflation rate, because the government printed more money to cover its operating expenses. The US CIA *World Factbook* estimates that prior to the currency reform of January 2009, Zimbabwe's annual inflation rate was 11.2 million percent (https://www.cia-.gov/library/publications/the-world-factbook/geos/zi.html#Econ). This internal economic debacle coincided with the rapid price rise for a barrel of oil. Like many other developing countries, Zimbabwe

In Zimbabwe, a corrupt and inept government tried to reduce prices on basic commodities and left markets with nothing.

does not have domestic sources of petroleum products and must import what it needs. In 2014, Robert Mugabe is back in charge for his thirty-fifth year, and economic experts suggest that his policies will be as destructive as ever. Those with resources are likely to leave or be looking for an exit.

Many analysts of African affairs say that bad harvests, bad weather, and high oil prices are not to blame for Zimbabwe's troubles. Rather, they assert, President Mugabe himself is to blame for the current situation. Left alone by Great Britain and other countries, the president established his personalist regime that favored his family and other members of his ethnic group and intimidated other ethnic groups in Zimbabwean society. If a person wanted to advance in the country, the person had to be a member of Mugabe's political party, Zimbabwe African National Union–Popular Front (ZANU–PF). Like other parties in the country but unlike political parties in most liberal democracies, it is linked to an ethnic group, but membership in the party was not guaranteed. Parliamentary elections in March 2008 sparked another crisis. When the Movement for Democratic Change (MDC) won more seats than ZANU–PF and Mugabe came in second to MDC's leader Morgan Tsvangirai in the presidential election, people knew that trouble was ahead. Mugabe's supporters began to violently harass MDC members, an action that caused Tsvangirai to withdraw from the race. (The current government of national unity is a coalition of ZANU–PF and the MDC, and it was formed in February 2009.)

Continued

OUTCOME

Given this string of unfortunate internal events, an average Zimbabwean can be forgiven if the failure of banks in Iceland, New York, and London is not a cause for great alarm. If workers at Macy's, Home Depot, or Merrill Lynch lose their jobs, this is not news for a resident of Harare. The subprime mortgage crisis in the United States must sound otherworldly to a person who lives in a galvanized metal shack in a shantytown on the outskirts of Bulawayo.

For Discussion

1. In times of global economic stress, should states with developed economies increase their assistance to states like Zimbabwe?
2. To what extent are Zimbabwe's problems the result of European colonization?
3. Do states have an obligation to help other states even if those states are led by authoritarian leaders?

It is important to note that some parts of the UN family have been genuinely responsive to criticisms of mainstream development. The UN Development Programme is noteworthy for its advocacy of the measurement of development based on life expectancy, adult literacy, and average local purchasing power—the Human Development Index (HDI). The HDI results in a very different assessment of countries' achievements than does the traditional measurement of development based on per capita GDP (A. Thomas et al. 1994, 22). For example, China, Sri Lanka, Poland, and Cuba fare much better under HDI assessments than they do under more orthodox assessments, whereas Saudi Arabia and Kuwait fare much worse.

An Appraisal of the Responses of the Orthodox Approach to Its Critics

During 2000, a series of official + 5 miniconferences were held, such as Rio + 5, Copenhagen + 5, and Beijing + 5, to assess progress in specific areas since the major UN conferences five years earlier. The assessments suggested that the international community had fallen short in its efforts to operationalize conference action plans and to mainstream these concerns in global politics.

Voices of criticism are growing in number and range. Even among supporters of the mainstream approach, voices of disquiet are heard, as increasingly the maldistribution of the benefits of economic liberalism are seen to have been a threat to local, national, regional, and even global order. Moreover, the social protest that accompanies economic globalization is regarded by some as a potential obstacle to the neoliberal project. Thus, supporters of globalization are keen to temper its most unpopular effects by modification of neoliberal policies. Small but nevertheless important changes are taking place. For example, the World Bank has guidelines on the treatment of indigenous peoples, resettlement, the environmental impact of its projects, gender, and disclosure of information. It is implementing social safety nets when pursuing structural-adjustment policies, and it is promoting microcredit as a way to empower women. With the IMF, it developed an HIPC initiative to reduce the debt burden of the poorest states. What is important, however, is whether these guidelines and concerns really inform policy and whether these new policies and facilities result in practical outcomes that have an impact on the fundamental causes of poverty.

The bank has admitted that such changes have been incorporated largely due to the efforts of NGOs, which have monitored its work closely and undertaken vigorous international campaigns to change its general operational processes and the way it funds projects. These campaigns continue. The Bretton Woods Campaign, Fifty Years Is Enough, Jubilee 2000,

Engaging with the

W●RLD

InterAction Internships

If you are looking for experience in NGO coordination, development, and humanitarianism, check out InterAction's openings for interns in the Office of the President, Humanitarian Affairs, IT, Annual Forum, and Policy and Communications. Visit http://www.interaction .org/interaction-internship -program.

and, most recently, the Make Poverty History campaign have been particularly significant in calling for open, transparent, and accountable decision making by global economic institutions, for local involvement in project planning and implementation, and for debt write-off. The U2 Singer Bono and his One Campaign have been very active in advocating change and have supportive all efforts to end poverty. In addition to the NGO pressure for change, pressure is building within the institutional champions of the neoliberal development orthodoxy.

There is a tremendously long way to go in terms of gaining credence for the core values of the alternative model of development in the corridors of power nationally and internationally. Nevertheless, the alternative view, marginal though it is, has had some noteworthy successes in modifying orthodox development. These may be significant for those whose destinies have until now been largely determined by the attempted universal application of a selective set of local, essentially Western, values.

Hunger

In addressing the topic of global hunger, it is necessary to face the paradox that while "the production of food to meet the needs of a burgeoning population has been one of the outstanding global achievements of the post-war period" (International Commission on Peace and Food 1994, 104, 106), there were nevertheless in 2006 around 852 million malnourished people in around eighty countries, and at least 40,000 die every day from hunger-related causes. The current depth of hunger across different world regions is shown in Map 13.1. Famines may be exceptional phenomena, but hunger is ongoing. Why?

The Orthodox, Nature-Focused Explanation of Hunger

The orthodox explanation of hunger, first mapped out in its essentials by Thomas Robert Malthus in his *Essay on the Principle of Population* in 1798, focuses on the relationship between human population growth and the food supply. It asserts that population growth naturally outstrips the growth in food production so that a decrease in the per capita availability of food is inevitable. Eventually, a point is reached at which starvation, or some other disaster, drastically reduces the human population to a level that can be sustained by the available food supply. This approach therefore places great stress on human overpopulation as the cause of the problem and seeks ways to reduce the fertility of the human race

In parts of the developing world such as the Congo, more than 50 percent of the population is malnourished.

or, rather, that part of the human race which seems to reproduce faster than the rest—the poor of the third world. Recent supporters of this approach, such as Paul Ehrlich and Dennis and Donella Meadows (1972), argue that there are natural limits to population growth—principally that of the carrying capacity of the land—and that when these limits are exceeded, disaster is inevitable.

The available data on the growth of the global human population indicate that it has quintupled since the early 1800s and is expected to grow from 6 billion in 1999 to 10 billion in 2050. More than 50 percent of this increase is expected to occur in seven countries: Bangladesh, Brazil, China, India, Indonesia, Nigeria, and Pakistan. Figure 13.2 provides data on world population growth from 1800, with projections through 2050, and shows that the rate of world population growth is set to increase over the coming

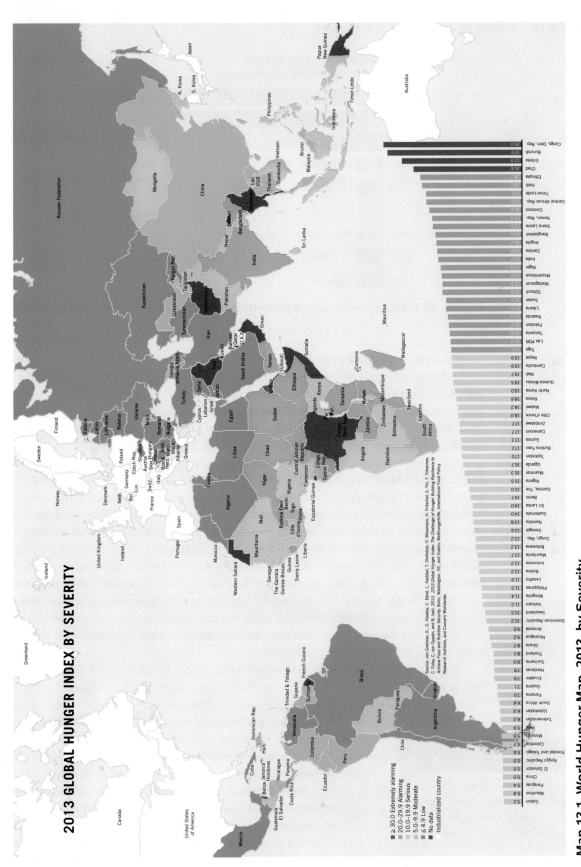

2013 GLOBAL HUNGER INDEX BY SEVERITY

Legend
- ≥ 30.0 Extremely alarming
- 20.0–29.9 Alarming
- 10.0–19.9 Serious
- 5.0–9.9 Moderate
- ≤ 4.9 Low
- No data
- Industrialized country

Source: von Grebmer, K. D. Headey, C. Béné, L. Haddad, T. Olofinbiyi, D. Wiesmann, H. Fritschel, S. Yin, Y. Yohannes, C. Foley, C. von Oppeln, and B. Iseli. 2013. *2013 Global Hunger Index: The Challenge of Hunger: Building Resilience to Achieve Food and Nutrition Security.* Bonn, Washington, DC, and Dublin: Welthungerhilfe, International Food Policy Research Institute, and Concern Worldwide.

Bar chart values (Global Hunger Index)

Congo, Dem. Rep.	39.0
Burundi	37.9
Eritrea	35.0
Chad	30.6
Ethiopia	28.7
Haiti	28.3
Timor-Leste	27.4
Central African Rep.	27.0
Comoros	26.2
Yemen, Rep.	25.8
Sierra Leone	25.2
Bangladesh	24.5
Angola	24.7
Zambia	24.1
India	21.3
Niger	21.0
Mozambique	20.5
Madagascar	22.6
Djibouti	22.6
Sudan	21.5
Liberia	21.0
Rwanda	21.0
Pakistan	20.7
Tanzania	20.6
Lao PDR	20.3
Togo	20.1
Nepal	19.9
Cambodia	19.9
Mali	19.7
Guinea-Bissau	19.6
North Korea	19.0
Kenya	18.6
Malawi	18.2
Côte d'Ivoire	18.0
Zimbabwe	17.7
Cameroon	17.3
Guinea	17.2
Burkina Faso	17.0
Tajikistan	16.7
Uganda	16.3
Myanmar	15.5
Nigeria	15.0
Gambia, The	14.7
Benin	14.0
Sri Lanka	14.0
Guatemala	13.8
Namibia	13.6
Senegal	13.2
Congo, Rep.	13.2
Botswana	12.7
Mauritania	12.2
Indonesia	12.2
Bolivia	11.9
Lesotho	11.5
Philippines	11.4
Mongolia	11.2
Vietnam	10.5
Swaziland	10.2
Dominican Republic	9.5
Armenia	9.2
Nicaragua	8.7
Ghana	8.1
Thailand	8.0
Suriname	7.9
Honduras	7.9
Ecuador	7.1
Guyana	7.0
Panama	6.4
South Africa	6.3
Uzbekistan	6.2
Turkmenistan	5.9
Peru	5.9
Morocco	5.7
Colombia	5.6
Trinidad and Tobago	5.5
Kyrgyz Republic	5.5
El Salvador	5.5
China	5.4
Paraguay	5.4
Mauritius	5.2
Gabon	

Map 13.1 World Hunger Map, 2013, by Severity.

What patterns of hunger do you see around the world? What responsibilities might industrial nation-states have toward helping less developed nation-states?

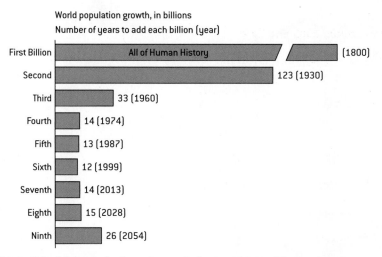

Figure 13.2 World Population Growth from 1800 with Projections to 2050.

decades. Table 13.5 focuses on the most populous countries—almost all of which are located in the third world—and only eleven of them account for over half of the world's population. Figures like these have convinced many adherents of the orthodox approach to hunger that it is essential for third world countries to adhere to strict family-planning policies that one way or another limit their population growth rates. Indeed, in the case of the World Bank, most women-related efforts until very recently were in the area of family planning.

The Entitlement, Society-Focused Explanation of Hunger

Critics of the orthodox approach to hunger and its associated implications argue that it is too simplistic in its analysis and ignores the vital factor of food distribution. They point out that it fails to account for the paradox we observed at the beginning of this discussion on hunger: despite the enormous increase in food production per capita that has occurred over the post-war period (largely due to the development of high-yielding seeds and industrial agricultural techniques), little impact has been made on the huge numbers of people in the world who experience chronic hunger. For example, the UN Food and Agriculture Organization (FAO) estimates that although there is enough grain alone to provide everyone in the world with 3,600 calories a day (i.e., 1,200 more than the UN's recommended minimum daily intake), there are still over 800 million hungry people.

Furthermore, critics note that the third world, where the majority of malnourished people are found, produces much of the world's food, whereas those who consume most of it are in the Western world. Meat consumption tends to rise with household wealth, and a third of the world's grain is used to fatten animals. A worrying recent trend is the use of corn grown in the United States to produce green fuel, thus reducing what is available to feed the hungry people overseas. Such evidence leads opponents of the orthodox approach to argue that we need to look much more closely at the social, political, and economic factors that determine how food is distributed and why access to food is achieved by some and denied to others.

A convincing alternative to the orthodox explanation of hunger was set forward in Amartya Sen's pioneering book, *Poverty and Famines: An Essay on Entitlement and Deprivation* (1981). From the results of his empirical

WHAT'S YOUR WORLDVIEW?

The One Campaign and NGOs like Oxfam have worked hard to end global poverty and hunger, so why do poverty and hunger persist? What appear to be the root causes? The best solutions?

Table 13.5
World Population, 2003 and 2050

Most Populous Countries, 2003			Most Populous Countries, 2050		
Rank	Country	Population (millions)	Rank	Country	Population (millions)
1	China	1,289	1	India	1,628
2	India	1,069	2	China	1,394
3	United States	292	3	United States	422
4	Indonesia	220	4	Pakistan	349
5	Brazil	176	5	Indonesia	316
6	Pakistan	149	6	Nigeria	307
7	Bangladesh	147	7	Bangladesh	255
8	Russia	146	8	Brazil	221
9	Nigeria	134	9	Congo, Dem. Rep. of	181
10	Japan	128	10	Ethiopia	173

research work on the causes of famines, Sen concluded that hunger is due to people not having enough to eat rather than there not being enough to eat. He discovered that famines have frequently occurred when there has been no significant reduction in the level of per capita food availability and, furthermore, that some famines have occurred during years of peak food availability. For example, the Bangladesh famine of 1974 occurred in a year of peak food availability, yet because floods wiped out the normal employment opportunities of rural laborers, the latter were left with no money to purchase the food that was readily available, and many of them starved.

Therefore, what determines whether people starve or eat is not so much the amount of food available to them but whether or not they can establish an entitlement to that food. For example, if there is plenty of food available in the stores, but a family does not have the money to purchase that food and does not have the means of growing their own food, then they are likely to starve. With the globalization of the market and the associated curtailing of subsistence agriculture, the predominant method of establishing an entitlement to food has become that of the exercise of purchasing power, and consequently, those without purchasing power will go hungry amid a world of plenty (Sen 1981, 1983).

Sen's focus on entitlement enables him to identify two groups who are particularly at risk of losing their access to

In parts of the developing world such as Kenya, enough food is available. However, the increased global demand for biofuels has started to push farmers to grow crops like corn that they can sell in that emerging market for a higher price.

food: landless rural laborers, such as in South Asia and Latin America, and pastoralists, such as in sub-Saharan Africa. The landless rural laborers are especially at risk because no arrangements are in place to protect their access to food. In the traditional peasant economy, there is some **security** of land ownership, and therefore, rural laborers have the possibility of growing their own food. However, this possibility is lost in the early stages of the transition to capitalist agriculture, when the laborers are obliged to sell their land and join the wage-based economy. Unlike in the developed countries of the West, no social security arrangements are in place to ensure that their access to food is maintained. In this context, it is important to note that the IMF/World Bank austerity policies of the 1980s ensured that any welfare arrangements previously enjoyed by vulnerable groups in developing countries were largely removed; therefore, these policies directly contributed to a higher risk of hunger in the third world.

Building on the work of Sen, researcher Susan George in *The Hunger Machine* (Bennett and George 1987, 1–10) details how different groups of people experience unequal levels of access to food. She identifies six factors that are important in determining who goes hungry:

1. The North-South divide between developed and developing countries
2. National policies on how wealth is shared
3. The rural-urban bias
4. Social class
5. Gender
6. Age

One could add to the list two other very important, and often neglected, factors determining hunger: race and disability. Consequently, a person is more likely to experience hunger if he or she is disabled rather than able-bodied, black rather than white, a child rather than an adult, poor rather than wealthy, a rural dweller rather than a town dweller, and an inhabitant of a developing country rather than an inhabitant of a developed country.

Globalization and Hunger

It is possible to explain the contemporary occurrence of hunger by reference to the process of globalization. Globalization means that events occurring in one part of the globe can affect, and can be affected by, events occurring in other, distant parts of the globe. Often, as individuals, we remain unaware of our role in this process and its ramifications. When we drink a cup of tea or coffee or eat imported fruit and vegetables, in the developed countries, we tend not to reflect on the changes experienced at the site of production of these cash crops in the developing world. However, it is possible to look at the effect of the establishment of a global system of food production as opposed to a local, national, or regional system. This has been done by David Goodman and Michael Redclift in their book *Refashioning Nature: Food, Ecology and Culture* (1991), and the closing part of this discussion on hunger is based largely on their findings.

Since 1945, a global food regime has been established, and now in the twenty-first century, we are witnessing an increasingly global organization of food provision and of access to food with transnational corporations playing the major role. Local subsistence producers, who traditionally have produced to meet the needs of their family and community, may now be involved in cash-crop production for a distant market. Alternatively, they may have left the land and become involved in the process of industrialization. The most important actor in the development and expansion of this global food regime has been the United

security To be secure is to be safe from harm and to be assured of safety. In this case, it is the safety of self-reliance.

Engaging with the
WORLD
Blue Kitabu

Blue Kitabu sponsors summer fellows to work on a number of projects in areas such as sustainability and education, primarily in sub-Saharan Africa. This organization works with communities and community leaders to build educational infrastructure, needed business and markets, materials, and teacher training for the most vulnerable populations. Visit http://www.bluekitabu.org.

States, which, at the end of World War II, was producing large food surpluses. These surpluses became cheap food exports and initially were welcomed by the war-ravaged countries of Europe. They were also welcomed by many developing countries, for the model of development prevalent then depended on the creation of a pool of cheap wage labor to serve the industrialization process. Hence, to encourage people off the land and away from subsistence production, the incentive to produce for oneself and one's family had to be removed. Cheap imported food provided this incentive, while the resulting low prices paid for domestic subsistence crops made them unattractive to grow; indeed, for those who continued to produce for the local market, such as in Sudan, the consequence has been the production of food at a loss (Bennett and George 1987, 78). Not surprisingly, therefore, in the developing world, the production of subsistence crops for local consumption drastically declined in the postwar period.

The postwar, US-dominated, global food regime has therefore had a number of unforeseen consequences. First, the domestic production of food staples in developing countries was disrupted. Second, consumer preferences in the importing countries changed in line with the cheap imports, and export markets for American-produced food were created. Effectively, a dependency on food aid was created (Goodman and Redclift 1991, 123). Third, there has been a stress on cash-crop production. The result has been the drive toward export-oriented, large-scale, intensively mechanized agriculture in the South. Technical progress resulted in the green revolution, with massively increased yields produced from high-yield seeds and industrialized agricultural practices. This has in some respects been an important achievement. However, the cost has been millions of peasants thrown off the land because their labor was no longer required; the greater concentration of land was in a smaller number of hands; and there was environmental damage from pesticides, fertilizers, and inappropriate irrigation techniques.

Since the early 1980s, the reform of national economies via structural-adjustment policies has further undermined the national organization of agriculture and given a further boost to the activities of agribusiness. The aggressive pursuit of unilateralist trade policies by the United States, such as the invocation of free trade to legitimize opening the Korean agricultural market, has added to this. Global trade liberalization since the early 1980s, and especially the Uruguay Round's Agreement on Agriculture (the original text of which was drafted by the multinational Cargill's vice president Dan Amstutz; Oxfam 2003, 23), is further eroding local food security and throwing peasant producers and their families off the land. The Haitian example portrayed in Case Study 13.2 is repeated across the developing world; for example, the crisis facing Niger in 2005–2006 has been called a "free market famine" (Mousseau and Mittal 2006, 1). This has fueled resentment in the South about the global rules governing agriculture. For example, in India, disputes over intellectual property rights in regard to high-yielding crop seeds have resulted in violent protest by peasant farmers at foreign-owned seed factories. In the North, NGOs have campaigned against the double standards operated by their governments in expecting Southern countries to liberalize their food markets while the Northern countries continue to heavily subsidize and protect their own.

In many parts of the world, farmers use hand tools, not tractors, to cultivate their crops.

Conclusion

In this chapter, we have seen how poverty, development, and hunger are more than merely domestic political issues. Academic theories of international relations tended to ignore these problems until the mid-1980s, when the third world debt crisis threatened to undermine key parts of the global financial system. Political leaders in the rich countries of the North—and in many cases, the South—acted the way realism predicted: to protect the interests of their own states. For the areas of human rights and human security, a very different situation exists. In the next chapter, we will see that, without a clearly defined challenge to their interests, countries are less likely to act to promote human rights.

CONTRIBUTORS TO CHAPTER 13: Caroline Thomas and Steven L. Lamy.

REVIEW QUESTIONS

1. What does poverty mean?
2. Explain the orthodox approach to development and outline the criteria by which it measures development.
3. Assess the critical alternative model of development.
4. How effectively has the orthodox model of development neutralized the critical alternative view?
5. Compare and contrast the orthodox and alternative explanations of hunger.
6. What are the pros and cons of the global food regime established since World War II?
7. Account for the growing gap between rich and poor states and people after fifty years of official development policies.
8. Use a gendered lens to explore the nature of poverty.
9. Is the recent World Bank focus on poverty reduction evidence of a change of direction by the bank?
10. Which development pathway—the traditional or the alternative—do you regard as more likely to contribute to global peace in the twenty-first century?
11. Are national poverty-reduction strategies contributing to national ownership of development policies in the third world?

FURTHER READING

Adams, N. B. (1993), *Worlds Apart: The North–South Divide and the International System* (London: Zed). Presents a broad economic and political history of the North–South divide and focuses on the role of the international economic system. This book provides an effective introduction to the politics of North–South economic relations over the past half-century.

Collier, P. (2007), *The Bottom Billion. Why the Poorest Countries Are Failing and What Can Be Done About It* (New York: Oxford University Press). A thoughtful discussion of the reasons for poverty and ways to end it.

Dreze, J., Sen, A., and Hussain, A. (eds.) (1995), *The Political Economy of Hunger* (Oxford: Clarendon Press). An excellent collection on the political economy of hunger.

Kiely, R. (2006), *The New Political Economy of Development: Globalization, Imperialism and Hegemony* (Basingstoke: Palgrave Macmillan). An important text that examines development in a historical and political-economic context. This is a book for ambitious students who want to take their understanding of development to a deeper level.

Rahnema, M., with Bawtree, V. (eds.) (1997), *The Post-Development Reader* (Dhaka: University Press, and London: Zed). Challenges the reader to think critically about the nature of development and assumptions about meanings. This is an extremely stimulating interdisciplinary reader.

Rapley, J. (1996), *Understanding Development* (Boulder, Col.: Lynne Rienner). Analyzes the theory and practice of development in the third world since World War II in a straightforward, succinct manner. It provides the reader with a firm grasp of changing development policies at the international level and their take-up over time in different states.

Sen, A. (1981), *Poverty and Famines* (Oxford: Clarendon Press). Provides a groundbreaking analysis of the causes of hunger that incorporates detailed studies of a number of famines and convincingly challenges the orthodox view.

Singer, P. (2009), *The Life You Can Save* (New York: Random House). How can we save a child from a life of poverty? What can be done to create a culture of giving?

Thomas, C. (2000), *Global Governance, Development and Human Security* (London: Pluto). Examines the global development policies pursued by global governance institutions, especially the IMF and the World Bank, in the 1980s and 1990s. It assesses the impact of these policies on human security and analyzes different paths toward the achievement of human security for the twenty-first century.

Wiesmann, D. (2006), *Global Hunger Index 2006: A Basis for Cross-Country Comparisons*, Issue Brief 47 (Washington, D.C.: International Food Policy Research Institute). The Global Hunger Index (GHI), published by the International Food Policy Research Institute, was developed in 2006 to increase attention on the hunger problem and to mobilize the political will to address it.

INTERNET RESOURCES

Commission for Global Governance
www.cgg.ch
An NGO that advocates expanded nonstate authority in world affairs.

Foundation for Sustainable Development
www.fsdinternational.org
An NGO that promotes community development projects.

Oxfam International
www.oxfam.org
Perhaps the most famous antipoverty NGO with projects and programs globally.

UN Conference on Trade and Development
www.unctad.org
Created in 1964 as a caucus within the UN structure to provide a voice for the newly independent countries in UN deliberations about economic development. It offers a means to build consensus regarding the often contentious debates about development. The UNCTAD also provides technical assistance and is a clearinghouse for data collection and analysis.

World Food Programme
www.wfp.org
The UN agency that coordinates international famine relief and hunger efforts around the world. In an average year, the organization provides 3.7 tons of food.

Carnegie Council: "Dead Aid: Why Aid Is Not Working and How There Is a Better Way for Africa"—Dambisa Moyo
http://www.carnegiecouncil.org/resources/video/data/000234
Despite receiving over $1 trillion in aid over the last half-century, Africa's problems seem to worsen rather than improve. Zambian native Dambisa Moyo says that the financial aid approach is the wrong one for Africa.

Carnegie Council: "The Life You Can Save: Acting Now to End World Poverty"—Peter Singer
http://www.carnegiecouncil.org/resources/video/data/000231
Working through NGOs and other channels, Peter Singer says that a mere contribution of 1 percent from many Americans would ensure success in achieving the Millennium Development Goals.

Carnegie Council: "Fair Trade for All: How Trade Can Promote Development"—Joseph E. Stiglitz
http://www.carnegiecouncil.org/resources/video/data/000007
According to Joseph Stiglitz, trade—the very backbone of our capitalist society—is also a tool that can be employed to uplift less developed countries.

Ted Talk: Gordon Brown: "Wiring a Web for Global Good"
http://www.ted.com/talks/lang/eng/gordon_brown.html
Former British Prime Minister Gordon Brown enthusiastically discusses changing global ethics and the necessity for state leaders worldwide to create global institutions that represent fairness and stability.

Ted Talk: "Paul Collier on the 'Bottom Billion'"
http://www.ted.com/talks/lang/eng/paul_collier_shares_4_ways_to_help_the_bottom_billion.html
Paul Collier says we need to get serious about providing hope for the bottom billion and to do so we should look at times when the "rich world" wanted to develop floundering states.

For more information, quizzes, case studies and other study tools, please visit us at **www.oup.com/us/lamy**

Development Assistance as Foreign Policy Statecraft

EXPECTATIONS

You will be asked to evaluate contending arguments for aid (official development assistance, or ODA) and then make a case supporting ODA and a case against ODA for developing states.

PROCEDURE

Step One

Participants will be divided into three groups and asked to evaluate proposals requesting development assistance with a specific worldview in mind. The groups and their designated worldview are:

1. Western Security Organization: realists who have a competitive view of international relations
2. European Social Democrats: liberal internationalists favoring multilateral cooperation
3. World Federalists: modern-day utopians or radical liberals who seek to create a world government based on human-centric values and world law

Step Two

Your task is to make recommendations on how much and what kind of aid or development assistance should be allocated. You may recommend the following:

A. Project Aid: funds for specific activities such as the construction of roads and irrigation systems.
B. Program Aid: funds that are loaned to correct problems in a country's capital flow. The funds are used to correct balance-of-payment problems or to enable the country to increase its supply of capital either in the form of savings or foreign currency.
C. Technical Assistance: this includes experts and advisers, training or educational programs, and the supply of equipment for projects.
D. Food Aid: food, medicine, and equipment sent to countries to feed the starving or increase the available stocks of food.
E. Specific Aid: to deal with emergency situations (e.g., drought relief, natural disasters).
F. Military Assistance: to maintain order and make certain the country is stable and the government is not at risk because of extreme poverty or radical movements.

Step Three

You must decide on ODA allocations for the following countries:

Country 1 has requested $100 million in aid from the developed donor countries. The country is governed by a weak democratic system. A Marxist party is strong but holds few government positions. The party currently in power was always pro–United States and now is an active participant in US-led multilateral activities. The economy depends heavily on the export of one crop and one mineral. There is little industry. The aid money will be used to improve and extend the road system, improve the dock and port facilities in the country's only port city, and fund agricultural extension projects.

Country 2 has requested $50 million in aid. The country is governed by a socialist party and has strong ties with Europe's more social democratic states. The president of the country often participates in meetings of heads of state of nonaligned nations, and the country's leaders are very active in multilateral organizations. This country has a diversified economy that exports agricultural products, some minerals, and light manufactured goods. The requested aid will be used to improve the national university, send students abroad for advanced college degrees in business management and science, import farm machinery, and purchase high-tech equipment to develop manufacturing in computers and technology related to the environment.

Country 3 has requested $150 million in aid. The country is totally dependent on outside support. It has suffered from a severe drought, and three tribal groups continue to challenge the military government. The country's only resources are uranium and an abundance of cheap labor. Most aid has ended up in the hands of the elites and has not been used to improve the quality of life of most of the population. Recently, the leaders have begun to discuss a possible alliance with Syria and Iran. The aid will be used to develop a comprehensive education system, develop facilities in rural areas, and build a national highway and rail system.

Based on the assumptions of your group's worldview:

1. Rank the three countries in terms of aid priority.
2. Select an appropriate program (e.g., military assistance and drought relief for Country X).
3. Be prepared to defend your choices. Each group will have an opportunity to decide on its priorities and then present them. Each group should also be prepared to critically review the allocations made by the other groups.

Step Four

As you debate your group's position on these requests, consider the following questions. You may want to ask the other groups to justify their positions by responding to these questions. As you finish the exercise, these three questions may provide a useful debriefing or evaluation of your debate.

1. What is the strongest argument for giving or not giving some form of aid to each country?
2. What assumptions about each country and the international system defined your allocation priorities?
3. Discuss the relative strengths and weaknesses of bilateral and multilateral aid programs. Would you agree with the statement which suggests that the complexity of world development problems requires multilateral responses?

14 | Environmental Issues

Today, the pressure humanity puts on the planet, its Ecological Footprint, is 50 percent greater than the planet's ability to withstand this pressure. It now takes the Earth one year and six months to regenerate what we use in a single year. This global ecological overshoot is depleting the natural capital on which all of life depends.

—Global Footprint Network

The "control of nature" is a phrase conceived in arrogance, born of the Neanderthal age of biology and philosophy, when it was supposed that nature exists for the convenience of man.

—Rachel Carson

In 2011, *Newsweek* magazine stated that "weather panic" is the new normal. As global temperatures rise, climate scientists predict side effects such as droughts, flooding, and ferocious storms. No one is certain of the direct link, but CO_2 emissions are rising by record amounts. Without a doubt, the world's environmental problems have only gotten worse since 1987, when the Brundtland Commission released its UN-sponsored report on the global environment, *Our Common Future.*

Despite leadership from past politicians such as Nobel Prize–winner Al Gore and despite strong grassroots efforts by citizens in some industrial countries to "Reduce, Reuse, and Recycle"—to "Think Globally, Act Locally"—why are other international leaders and many other citizens unwilling to change their lifestyles to respond to urgent challenges like climate change, air and water pollution, and resource scarcity? Why is it so hard to reach agreement when the scientific reports clearly confirm the severity of environmental degradation across the globe? Why are some leaders of political and economic organizations rejecting climate science? Although there are no easy answers to these global problems, such questions can at least be understood more clearly with a careful examination of the facts, along with some perspective afforded us by considering the history and theory of international cooperation involving environmental issues.

The Black Marble, or the Earth, our very fragile home at night. This is an image of Asia and Australia with some of the brighter lights revealing the wildfires in Western Australia. Lights in uninhabited areas include images of fishing boats, gas flaring, lightning, oil drilling, and mining operations.

Introduction

Although humankind as a whole now appears to be living well above Earth's carrying capacity, the **ecological footprints** of individual states vary to an extraordinary extent. See, for example, Map 14.1, an unusual map where the size of countries is proportionate to their carbon emissions. Indeed, if everyone were to enjoy the current lifestyle of the developed countries, more than three additional planets would be required.

This situation is rendered all the more unsustainable by the process of globalization, even though the precise relationship between environmental degradation and the overuse of resources, on the one hand, and globalization, on the other, is complex and sometimes contradictory. Globalization has stimulated the relocation of industry to the global South, caused urbanization as people move away from rural areas, and contributed to ever-rising levels of consumption, along with associated emissions of effluents and waste gases. While often generating greater income for poorer countries exporting basic goods to developed-country markets, ever-freer trade can also have adverse environmental consequences by disrupting local **ecologies** (communities of plants and animals), cultural habits, and livelihoods.

However, some analysts believe there is little evidence that globalization has stimulated a "race to the bottom" in environmental standards, and some even argue that growing levels of affluence have brought about local environmental improvements, just as birth rates tend to fall as populations become wealthier. Economists claim that globalization's opening up of markets can increase efficiency and reduce pollution provided that the environmental and social damage associated with production of a good is properly factored into its market price. Similarly, as we will see in this chapter, globalization has promoted the sharing of knowledge and the influential presence of nongovernmental organizations (NGOs) in global environmental politics. Whatever the ecological balance sheet of globalization, the resources on which human beings depend for survival, such as fresh water, a clean atmosphere, and a stable climate, are now under serious threat.

Global problems may need global solutions and pose a fundamental requirement for **global environmental governance**. Yet the history of environmental cooperation demonstrates that local or regional action remains a vital aspect of responses to many problems. One of the defining characteristics of environmental politics is the awareness of such interconnections and of the need to "Think Globally—Act Locally." Nongovernmental organizations have been very active in this respect, as we saw in Chapter 7.

Despite the global dimensions of environmental change, an effective response still must depend on a fragmented international political system of more than 190 sovereign states. Global environmental governance consequently involves bringing to bear interstate relations, international law, and transnational organizations in addressing shared environmental problems. Using the term *governance*—as distinct from *government*—implies that regulation and control need to be exercised in the absence of a central government, delivering the kinds of service that a world government would provide if it were to exist. In this chapter, we will briefly explore essential concepts employed in regime analysis, which is commonly applied in the study of international governance.

ecological footprint A measure that demonstrates the load placed on Earth's carrying capacity by individuals or nations. It does this by estimating the area of productive land and water system required to sustain a population at its specified standard of living.

ecologies The communities of plants and animals that supply raw materials for all living things.

global environmental governance The performance of global environmental regulative functions, often in the absence of a central government authority. It usually refers to the structure of international agreements and organizations but can also involve governance by the private sector or NGOs.

One of the last frontiers is the Arctic, and demonstrations against drilling are likely to increase. Here, in 2013, Greenpeace leads a campaign in London against the Shell Oil Company. Shell is one of the firms drilling in the Arctic.

Total CO₂ emissions

from fossil-fuel burning, cement production and gas flaring

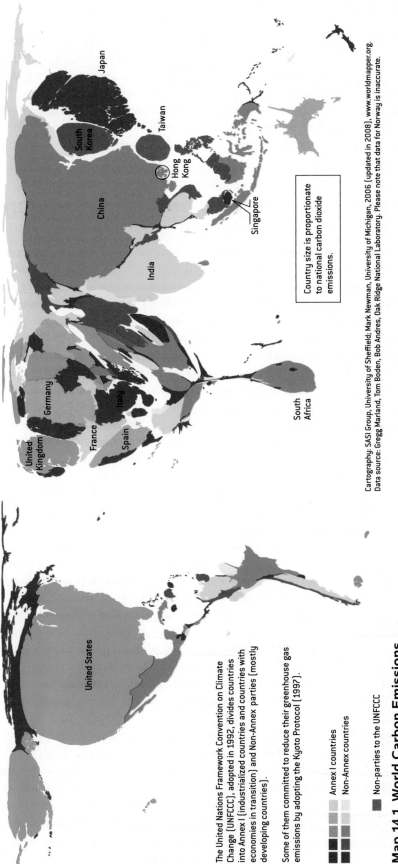

Japan

South Korea

Taiwan

Hong Kong

China

Singapore

India

Germany

United Kingdom

France

Italy

Spain

South Africa

Country size is proportionate to national carbon dioxide emissions.

United States

Cartography: SASI Group, University of Sheffield; Mark Newman, University of Michigan, 2006 (updated in 2008), www.worldmapper.org. Data source: Gregg Marland, Tom Boden, Bob Andres, Oak Ridge National Laboratory. Please note that data for Norway is inaccurate.

The United Nations Framework Convention on Climate Change (UNFCCC), adopted in 1992, divides countries into Annex I (industrialized countries and countries with economies in transition) and Non-Annex parties (mostly developing countries).

Some of them committed to reduce their greenhouse gas emissions by adopting the Kyoto Protocol (1997).

Annex I countries

Non-Annex countries

Non-parties to the UNFCCC

Map 14.1 World Carbon Emissions.

What patterns of CO₂ emission do you see around the world? Does a nation's responsibility toward ending global climate change increase if its CO₂ emission is higher? Which laws govern the global emissions of CO₂? How can they be enforced?

After reading and discussing this chapter, you will have a better understanding of the complexity and range of global environmental issues. You will be familiar with institutions managing environmental policy areas, as well as the various treaties and cooperative efforts aimed at promoting sustainable development and responding to environmental degradation, including pollution and climate change. You will also have a sense of how individuals from each theoretical perspective see each issue. Remember, theories are like lenses: we do not react to an objective reality but to our image of reality, which reflects our beliefs about world politics.

Environmental Issues on the International Agenda: A Brief History

Before the era of globalization, there were two traditional environmental concerns: conservation of natural resources and damage caused by pollution (see Table 14.1). Pollution, like wildlife, does not respect international boundaries, and action to mitigate or avert environmental harm sometimes had to involve more than one state. Early international agreements were designed to conserve specific resources, such as fisheries (1867 convention between France and Great Britain) or fur seals (1891, 1892, 1911 conventions between Great Britain, the United States, and Russia). In 1935, with the Trail Smelter case, leaders of countries recognized that reducing transboundary pollution required joint effort and could be accomplished peacefully. In this landmark case, pollutants from a mineral smelter in Canada drifted south to contaminate portions of the US state of Washington. The resulting treaty between the two countries asserted the legal principle that countries are liable for damage that their citizens cause in another country. There were also numerous, mostly unsuccessful, attempts to regulate exploitation of maritime resources lying beyond national jurisdiction, including several multilateral fisheries commissions. The development of the 1946 International Convention for the Regulation of Whaling (and its International Whaling Commission [IWC]) marked an interesting move away from the goal of the late nineteenth-century fur seal conventions, which entailed conserving an industry by regulating catches, toward the preservation of the great whales by declaring an international moratorium on whaling. This shift still generates bitter confrontation between NGOs, most IWC members, and the small number of nations—Japan, Norway, and Iceland—that wish to resume commercial whaling and still kill what they call "research whales."

After World War II, global economic recovery brought with it evidence of damaging pollution of the atmosphere, of watercourses, and of the sea, notably the Mediterranean, leading to international agreements in the 1950s and 1960s covering such matters as discharges from oil tankers. This worthy activity was, though, not the stuff of great power politics. Such "apolitical" matters were the domain of new UN **specialized agencies**, like the Food and Agriculture Organization (FAO), but were hardly central to diplomacy at the UN General Assembly in New York.

However, the salience of environmental issues grew in the 1960s, and in 1968, the UN General Assembly accepted a Swedish proposal for what became the 1972 UN Conference on the Human Environment "to focus governments' attention and public opinion on the importance and urgency of the question." The Stockholm Conference led to the creation of the UN Environment Programme and the establishment of environment departments by many governments. Yet it was already clear that for the countries of the South, constituting the majority in the UN General Assembly, environmental questions could not be separated from their demands for development, aid, and the restructuring of international economic relations.

specialized agencies
International institutions that have a special relationship with the central system of the United Nations but are constitutionally independent, having their own assessed budgets, executive heads and committees, and assemblies of the representatives of all state members.

Table 14.1
Chronology of Environmental Issues and Actions

1938	Trail Smelter case
1946	International Convention for the Regulation of Whaling
1955	UK Clean Air Act to combat "smog" in British cities
1958	International Convention for the Prevention of Pollution of the Sea by Oil
1959	Antarctic Treaty
1962	Rachel Carson publishes *Silent Spring*
1967	*Torrey Canyon* oil tanker disaster
1969	Greenpeace founded
1971	At the Founex meeting in Switzerland, Southern experts formulate a link between environment and development
1972	United Nations Conference on the Human Environment (UNCHE) in Stockholm United States creates Environmental Protection Agency First Earth Day Establishment of the UN Environment Programme (UNEP)
1973	MARPOL Convention on oil pollution from ships Convention on International Trade in Endangered Species (CITES)
1979	Convention on Long-Range Transboundary Air Pollution (LRTAP)
1980	Convention on the Conservation of Antarctic Marine Living Resources
1982	United Nations Law of the Sea Convention (enters into force in 1994)
1984	Bhopal chemical plant disaster
1985	Vienna Convention for the Protection of the Ozone Layer Antarctic ozone hole confirmed
1986	Chernobyl nuclear disaster
1987	Brundtland Commission Report Montreal Protocol on Substances That Deplete the Ozone Layer
1988	Establishment of the Intergovernmental Panel on Climate Change (IPCC)
1989	Basel Convention on the Control of Transboundary Movements of Hazardous Wastes and Their Disposal
1991	Madrid Protocol (to the Antarctic Treaty) on Environmental Protection
1992	United Nations Conference on Environment and Development (UNCED) held at Rio de Janeiro Publication of the Rio Declaration and Agenda 21 United Nations Framework Convention on Climate Change (UNFCCC) and Convention on Biological Diversity (CBD) both signed Establishment of the Commission on Sustainable Development (CSD)

Continued

Table 14.1 (*continued*)

Chronology of Environmental Issues and Actions

1995	World Trade Organization (WTO) founded
1997	Kyoto Protocol to the UNFCCC
1998	Rotterdam Convention on Hazardous Chemicals and Pesticides
	Aarhus Convention on Access to Information, Public Participation in Decision-Making, and Access to Justice in Environmental Matters
2000	Cartagena Protocol on Biosafety
	Millennium Development Goals set out
2001	US president Bush revokes signature of the Kyoto Protocol
2002	World Summit on Sustainable Development (WSSD), Johannesburg
	Johannesburg Plan of Implementation
2005	Entry into force of the Kyoto Protocol and introduction of the first international emissions-trading system by the European Union
2006	International discussions commence on the climate-change regime after 2012
2007	Fourth Assessment Report of the IPCC
2008	First Commitment Period of Kyoto begins
2009	Copenhagen Accord UNFCCC (Cop 15)
2010	Cancún Conference (COP 16)
	BP oil spill in the Gulf of Mexico
2011	The Fukushima Daiichi nuclear disaster a failure at the Fukushima Nuclear Plant in Japan
	Durban Platform on climate change agreed on
2012	Rio +20 UN Environmental Conference
2015	Paris, New climate change agreement scheduled for signing

sustainable development
Development that meets the needs of the present without compromising the ability of future generations to meet their own needs.

This was the political context surrounding the emergence of the concept of **sustainable development** (i.e., that meets the needs of the present without compromising future ability to meet needs). Before this concept was formulated by the Brundtland Commission in 1987, however, the environment had been pushed to the periphery of the international agenda by the global economic downturn of the 1970s and then the onset of the second Cold War.

Environmental degradation continued nonetheless. Awareness of new forms of transnational pollution, such as sulfur dioxide ("acid") rain, joined existing concerns over point-source pollution (when the pollutant comes from a definite source), followed by a dawning scientific realization that some environmental problems—the thinning of the stratospheric ozone layer and the possibility of climate change—were truly global in scale. The attendant popular concern over such issues and the relaxation of East-West tension created the opportunity for a second great UN conference for which the connection between environment and development had been explicitly drawn through the Brundtland

Commission's notion of sustainable development. Although this conference was subject to many subsequent interpretations, its political essence is an accommodation of the environmental concerns of developed states and the development demands of the South, without which there could have been no Earth Summit and no Rio process.

The 1992 UN Conference on Environment and Development, or Earth Summit, was the largest international conference so far held. It raised the profile of the environment as an international issue while concluding several significant documents and agreements, such as Agenda 21 and international conventions on climate change and the preservation of biodiversity. The event's underlying politics were captured in its title; it was a conference on "environment and development," where the most serious arguments concerned aid pledges to finance the environmental improvements under discussion. A process was created at the United Nations to review the implementation of the Rio agreements, including meetings of the new Commission on Sustainable Development (CSD) and a special session of the UN General Assembly in 1997.

On the UN Conference on Environment and Development's tenth anniversary in 2002, the World Summit on Sustainable Development (WSSD) was held in Johannesburg. The change of wording indicated how conceptions of environment and development had shifted since the 1970s. Now discussion was embedded in recognition of the importance of globalization and of the dire state of the African continent. Poverty eradication was clearly emphasized along with practical progress in providing clean water, sanitation, and agricultural improvements. One controversial element was the role to be played in such provision by private–public sector partnerships.

The UN conferences marked the stages by which the environment entered the international political mainstream, but they also reflected underlying changes in the scope and perception of environmental problems. As scientific understanding expanded, it was becoming common, by the 1980s, to speak in terms of global environmental change, as most graphically represented by the discovery of the ozone hole and the creeping realization that human activities might be dangerously altering the global climate itself.

Alongside environmental degradation and advances in scientific knowledge, the international politics of the environment has responded to the issue-attention cycle in developed countries, peaking at certain moments and then declining. The causes are complex, and during the 1960s, they reflected the countercultural and radical movements of the time along with wider public reactions to a series of trends and events. The most influential of these was publication of Rachel Carson's book *Silent Spring* (1962), which powerfully conjoined the conservationist and antipollution agendas by bringing to light the damage inflicted on bird life by industrial pesticides like DDT. Well-publicized environmental disasters, such as the 1959 mercury poisoning at Minamata in Japan and the 1967 wreck of the *Torrey Canyon* oil tanker close to beaches in southwestern England, fed public concern. The failure of established political parties to effectively respond to these issues encouraged the birth of several new high-profile NGOs—Friends of the Earth, Greenpeace, and the World Wildlife Fund for Nature—alongside more established pressure groups such as the US Sierra Club and the British Royal Society for the Protection of Birds. The interest in international environmental action and, indeed, most of the NGOs exerting pressure to this end were an almost exclusively developed-world phenomenon.

Public attention then receded, and until the end of the second Cold War, it coincided with a new concern over global environmental problems, which provided the political impetus for

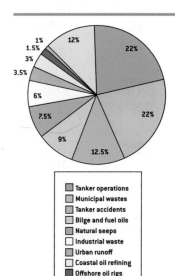

- Tanker operations
- Municipal wastes
- Tanker accidents
- Bilge and fuel oils
- Natural seeps
- Industrial waste
- Urban runoff
- Coastal oil refining
- Offshore oil rigs
- River runoffs
- Other

SOURCES OF MARINE POLLUTION.
What do you notice about the top five sources of pollution in this chart? Based on these data and what you have read in this chapter so far, what do you think world governments can do about transboundary pollution? (Note: These data do not include the British Petroleum oil spill in the Gulf of Mexico in 2010.)

UN secretary-general Ban Ki-moon and Danish prime minister Helle Thorning-Schmidt meet in Copenhagen at a Global Green Growth Forum in 2011 to discuss ways to update and continue the expiring Kyoto Protocol.

the 1992 Earth Summit. Interest waned again during the ensuing decade, although by 2005–2006 public alarm over the impact of climate change again propelled environmental issues up the political agenda. The demand was, of course, for international action and governance, but what exactly did this mean?

In 2011, the world experienced a number of devastating natural catastrophes, including floods, droughts, and tornadoes in the United States, droughts in China and Russia, and floods in Colombia, Pakistan, Australia, and Brazil. Geologists and other scientists, in seeking natural explanations of these crises, look to the history of Earth, which they divide into two periods. The Holocene period, or the first 10,000 years of Earth, is considered a period of weather and temperature stability. This is when humans began building civilizations. In the current geologic era, the Anthropocene, the world has been remade by human behavior. The biggest change is the emission of CO_2, which traps heat near the planet and creates more energy in the atmosphere. Climate scientists predict that rising temperatures will have serious side effects, such as deeper droughts, more floods, more moisture in the air, and potentially more serious storms like hurricanes and tornadoes. These conditions are what some now call a period of *weather panic* or global *weather weirding*. According to

Farmers in Madagascar, like many in the developing world, have used slash and burn techniques to clear forests. The 2010 Cancún climate change meetings created a green fund to pay for the restoration of forests like this one.

insurance experts, 2010 was the warmest year on record to date, and the more heat, the more problems with the weather. Oxfam reported that the number of natural disasters increased from 133 a year in the 1980s to more than 350 a year now. Skeptics argue that there have always been periods of weird weather and extreme events, but scientists argue that these events are becoming severer and more frequent. The scientific community has asked world political leaders to make hard choices and support action in response.

Although the annual international climate conference (UN Framework Convention on Climate Change Conference of Parties) at the end of 2009 failed to achieve a new comprehensive agreement to replace or extend the **Kyoto Protocol** (which set targets for reducing environmentally harmful gas emissions), it did result in the Copenhagen Accord. Many observers were disappointed, but the accord included a list of national pledges on greenhouse gas reductions (and a pledge for China and India to make improvements in energy efficiency rather than reductions). There was also a recognition of the need to keep temperature rises below 2 degrees centigrade, to set up a climate fund to assist developing countries, and to work on halting deforestation. These arrangements were formalized at the meeting in Cancun, Mexico, in 2010 and further developed at the meeting in Durban, South Africa, in 2011. They did not amount to a renewal of the Kyoto Protocol or a new comprehensive climate agreement, but the governments meeting at Durban did commit themselves to producing such an agreement by 2015.

> **Kyoto Protocol** A global environmental treaty passed in 1997 that set binding targets for thirty-seven industrialized countries and the European community for reducing greenhouse-gas emissions.

The Environment and International Relations Theory

Academics who study the international relations of the environment try to understand the circumstances under which potentially effective international cooperation can occur. The later discussion of climate change shows that this question remains important (see the Climate Change section in this chapter as well as the Case Study). Most scholars have used the concept of regime. Note, for instance, how the defining characteristics of regimes—principles, norms, rules, and decision-making procedures—can be applied to the environmental cases mentioned in this chapter. Those who try to explain the record of environmental regimes tend to adopt a liberal-institutionalist stance, stressing as a key motivating factor the joint gains arising from cooperative solutions to the problem of providing public goods such as a clean atmosphere (see Chapters 3 and 4). One significant addition to the regime literature made by scholars of environmental politics points out the importance of scientific knowledge and the roles of NGOs in this area. Whereas orthodox regime approaches assume that behavior is based on the pursuit of power or interest, analysts of international environmental cooperation have noted the independent role played by changes in knowledge (particularly, scientific understanding). This cognitive approach appears in studies of the ways that transnationally organized groups of scientists and policy makers—often referred to as *epistemic communities*—have influenced the development of environmental regimes.

Liberal-institutionalist analysis of regime creation may still be the predominant approach to global environmental change, but it is not the only one. It makes the important, but often unspoken, assumption that the problem to solve is how to obtain global governance in a fragmented system of sovereign states. Marxist writers would reject this formulation (see Chapter 4). For them, the **state system** is part of the problem rather than the solution, and the proper object of study is the way global capitalism reproduces relationships that are profoundly damaging to the environment. The global spread of neoliberal policies accelerates those features of globalization—consumerism, the relocation of production to the South, and the thoughtless squandering of resources—driving the global

> **state system** The regular patterns of interaction between states but without implying any shared values between them. This is distinguished from the view of a "society" of states.

ecological crisis (see Chapter 12). Proponents of this view also highlight the incapacity of the state to do anything other than assist such processes. It follows that the international cooperation efforts described here at worst legitimize this state of affairs and at best provide some marginal improvements to the devastation wrought by global capitalism. For example, they would point to how free market concepts are now routinely embedded in discussions of sustainable development and how the WTO rules tend to subordinate attempts to provide environmental regulation of GMOs. This argument is part of a broader debate among political theorists concerning whether the state can ever be "greened." The opposing view would be that within any time frame that is relevant to coping with a threat as large and immediate as climate change, state and international cooperation remain the only plausible mechanisms for providing the necessary global governance, and we simply need to do the best we can with existing state and international organizational structures.

With the end of the Cold War, some realist international relations specialists began to apply their ideas about anarchy and war to the study of environmental politics. As a result, they contended that conflict, not cooperation, shaped the issue, and they sought proof of this hypothesis. Largely ignoring the many examples of cooperation, like the Antarctic Treaty system (see Table 14.2), they argued that environmental change contributes to the incidence of both internal conflict and interstate war, even though the causal connections are complex and involve many factors. It is already evident that **desertification** (the extreme deterioration of land due to loss of vegetation and soil moisture) and the degradation of other vital resources are intimately bound up with cycles of poverty, destitution, and war in Africa. But these factors can also be attributed to the effects of European colonization of the continent. However, if we consider such predicted consequences of climate change as mass migrations of populations across international boundaries and acute scarcity of water and other resources, the outlines of potential future conflicts come into sharper focus.

Thus, the more immediate *and* persistent consequence of warfare may be the destruction of **ecosystems** (systems of organisms sharing a habitat) that such conflict causes. For example, during World War I, artillery shelling devastated farmland along the trench lines in northern France and Belgium, creating eerie moonscapes for years after the war. Similarly, in Vietnam, the detrimental environmental effects of US weapons, including the use of the herbicide Agent Orange (a form of the carcinogenic compound dioxin) and the carpet bombing of wide swaths of jungle and rice paddies, remain visible today. More recently,

desertification The extreme deterioration of land in arid and dry subhumid areas due to loss of vegetation and soil moisture; it results chiefly from human activities and is influenced by climatic variations. This condition is principally caused by overgrazing, overdrafting of groundwater, and diversion of water from rivers for human consumption and industrial use; all of these processes are fundamentally driven by overpopulation.

ecosystem A system of interdependent living organisms that share the same habitat, functioning together with all of the physical factors of the environment.

Table 14.2
The Antarctic Treaty Regime

1959	Antarctic Treaty
1972	Convention for the Conservation of Antarctic Seals
1980	Convention on the Conservation of Antarctic Marine Living Resources (CCAMLR)
1988	Convention on the Regulation of Antarctic Mineral Resource Activities (CRAMRA)
1991	Protocol on Environmental Protection to the Antarctic Treaty (Madrid Protocol)

GLOBAL PERSPECTIVE

The "Doomsday" Seed Vault

BACKGROUND

One day in February 2008, like a scene out of a postapocalyptic science fiction movie, more than 200 invited guests hunkered inside puffy parkas at the official opening of the Svalbard Global Seed Vault. The luminaries included Wangari Maathai, Nobel Prize winner for her work in reforestation in Africa, the European Commission president, and several heads of government. Unfortunately dubbed in news media the "Doomsday Vault," the facility is located on an island over 600 miles north of Norway and not far from the North Pole. There, at the end of a 400-foot tunnel carved into a mountain and isolated from the outside by a series of air locks, governments will be able to store as many as 2 billion seeds representing almost 4.5 million species of food plants. It is intended to be the storehouse of last resort for the world's plants.

THE CASE

The seed vault is the idea of an NGO based in Rome, Italy, called the Global Crop Diversity Trust. An affiliate of the Food and Agriculture Organization, the trust will administer the facility, which cost more than $9 million. The vault is one response to fears about the long-term effects global warming might have on biodiversity and crop output. It will be a repository for samples of food seeds in the event that a temperature increase will cause plant extinctions. One sign that the host Norwegian government—which covered the entire cost of construction—and Global Crop Diversity Trust believe the threat of global warming is very real is the location of the tunnel. It is far above the current high tide mark and also well above where mean high tide will be if the Arctic, Antarctic, and Greenland ice sheets all melt.

Billing itself as "A Foundation for Food Security," the Global Crop Diversity Trust gives grants in support of food-plant research and to maintain gene banks in accordance with the goals of the 1983 International Treaty on Plant Genetic Resources for Food and Agriculture and the 1993 Biodiversity Convention. In addition, the trust seeks to maintain vital food products eaten in the developing world such as bananas, sorghum, barley, cassava, lentils, and several varieties of beans.

The entry corridor to the Global Seed Vault on Svalbard Island, Norway.

There seems to be little not to like about the Svalbard Global Seed Vault, aside from the eminent threat of highly negative effects of global warming. However, the Global Crop Diversity Trust website (www.croptrust.org) FAQ section provides some hints about one possible controversy. The site carefully asserts that it is national governments that will deposit seeds and that each government will retain ownership of its seeds. A look at the donors section of the website suggests an explanation for this statement of seed ownership. There among a list of donors, such as EU governments, USAID, the Rockefeller Foundation, and the Bill and Melinda Gates Foundation, are the names of two giants of the agribusiness chemical industry: DuPont and Syngenta AG. Many environmentalists remember what Syngenta AG posts on its corporate-history web page: prior to changing its name Syngenta AG in 2001, the chemical firm was known by several names, including Ciba. It was Ciba employees, says the corporate website, who invented both DDT and 2, 4-D (http://www.syngenta.com/en/about_syngenta/companyhistory.html). The former (DDT) was the villain in Rachel Carson's *Silent Spring;* the latter (2, 4-D) is better known as a component of Agent Orange, an herbicide that US forces sprayed in uncounted millions of gallons on Vietnam during the 1960s and early 1970s.

Continued

GLOBAL PERSPECTIVE | The "Doomsday" Seed Vault *continued*

OUTCOME

As we have seen so far in this book, perspective matters when seeking to understand international politics. Some environmental activists resent the fact that agribusiness seems to be trying to exploit global warming by supporting the Global Crop Diversity Trust, especially because the chemical industry bears some of the guilt for causing the greenhouse-gas problem in the first place. However, as Syngenta AG's website indicates, the company is trying to do its best to save biodiversity. Which side is correct? The answer may be buried under a mountain in the permafrost zone at the end of a tunnel 600 miles from the North Pole.

For Discussion

1. If the goal of the Global Seed Vault is good, does it matter who the donors are?
2. Should the concept of national sovereignty extend to control of the world's seeds?
3. Our reliance on technology and plants resistant to all sorts of natural enemies has increased our vulnerability. Does it make sense for us to return to more natural or organic ways of agriculture?

ecotopian Someone who believes in protecting and preserving the environment and promotes progressive political goals that promote environmental sustainability, social justice and economic well-being.

deep ecology Often identified with the Norwegian philosopher Arne Naess, the core belief is that the living environment has a right to live and flourish. The "deep" refers to the need to think deeply about the impact of human life on the environment.

ecocentric Having a nature- or ecology-centered rather than a human-centered set of values.

tank-training exercises in the Mojave Desert of California have increased erosion of the fragile landscape. During both Gulf Wars, fires set at oil wells sent carcinogenic materials aloft to be carried downwind, where people who breathed the air became sick. In addition, the depleted-uranium antitank bullets fired during those wars put radioactive material into the air and soil. Even the less obvious effects of warfare can have unforeseen, negative impacts. A recent lawsuit filed in the US federal court has charged that US Navy sonar-training exercises can hurt the hearing of migrating whales, causing them to become disoriented.

Left out of most discussions about international relations theory and the environment is the **ecotopian** perspective. The **deep ecology** movement, or the **ecocentric** view, represents a radical or transformational perspective. Deep ecologists are purists rejecting the idea of inherent human superiority and giving equal moral weight to all elements of nature. Many of these utopians who seek system transformation have called for an alliance between red (socialist) and green (environmentalist) organizations to address the two overarching political issues of our time: human inequality and environmental destruction.

Deep ecologists lack faith in capitalist systems that are technologically dependent, prone to move toward large centralized corporate control, and protected by undemocratic, elitist political institutions. Strongly opposed to materialism and consumerism, they argue that our throw-away, shop-till-you-drop consumer culture should be replaced by an emphasis on meeting basic human needs. Otherwise, they fear, the environment will be devastated. Ecological and natural laws should help shape morality in human affairs, and the costs of environmental degradation must be considered when policy choices are made. Following their recommendations would certainly require a significant transformation in our political and economic thinking and in our policy priorities.

Clearly, the environmental degradation caused by wars and the instruments of war is impossible to dismiss yet even more difficult to address; by its very nature, warfare is a breakdown of international cooperation. However, when states are not at war and cooperation *is* a viable option, what does it look like and how does it function? Now that we have explored some of the theories surrounding international environmental cooperation, in the next section we will further discuss global mechanisms—or how states and transnational actors attempt to solve environmental issues through formal agreements and cooperative actions.

Regime Theory and the Montreal Protocol

THE CHALLENGE

Academic advocates of international regime theory discussed in this chapter contend that four factors—context, knowledge, interest, and power—can explain why and when countries decide to create a formal commitment in a given issue area. The same four factors also help explain what kinds of restraints countries permit on their behaviors. The evolution of international cooperation to protect the ozone layer provides an excellent case to test this hypothesis. In brief, if there are significant disagreements about the scientific evidence and one or more countries want to limit cooperation, then it is unlikely that other countries will be able to establish an effective international regime.

OPTIONS

The consequences of the thinning of the stratospheric ozone layer include excessive exposure to UVB radiation, resulting in increased rates of skin cancer for human beings and damage to immune systems. Stratospheric ozone depletion arose from a previously unsuspected source—artificial chemicals containing fluorine, chlorine, and bromine that were involved in chemical reaction with ozone molecules at high altitudes. Most significant were the CFCs (chlorofluorocarbons), which had been developed in the 1920s as "safe" inert industrial gases and which had been blithely produced and used over the next fifty years for a variety of purposes from refrigeration to air conditioning and as propellants for hair spray. Despite growing scientific knowledge, there was no universal agreement on the dangers posed by these chemicals, and production and use continued—except, significantly, where the US Congress decided to ban some nonessential uses. This meant that the US chemical industry found itself under a costly obligation

to find alternatives. Until a US-based chemical company developed an alternative to the harmful CFC compound, US diplomats blocked serious discussions at the international level. As evidence on the problem began to mount, UNEP acted to convene an international conference in Vienna. It produced a relatively weak "framework convention"—the 1985 Vienna Convention for the Protection of the Ozone Layer—agreeing that international action might be required and that the parties should continue to communicate and to develop and exchange scientific findings. These findings proved to be very persuasive, particularly with the added public impetus provided by the dramatic discovery of the Antarctic ozone hole.

APPLICATION

Within two years, the Montreal Protocol was negotiated. Some analysts point to a change in US negotiating stance as the reason for the rapid passage of the protocol. Why did this change occur? An American chemical giant found a replacement compound for the ozone-depleting CFCs, seemingly confirming part of the regime-creation hypothesis. In the Montreal Protocol, parties agreed to a regime under which the production and trading of CFCs and other ozone-depleting substances would be progressively phased out. The developed countries achieved this for CFCs by 1996, and Meetings of the Parties have continued to work on the elimination of other substances since that time. There was some initial resistance from European chemical producers, but the US side had a real incentive to ensure international agreement because otherwise its chemical industry would remain at a commercial disadvantage. The other problem faced by the negotiators involved the developing countries, which themselves were manufacturing CFC products. As the

Indian delegate stated, it was the developed countries' mess and their responsibility to clear it up! Why should developing countries be forced to change over to higher-cost CFC alternatives? There were two responses. The first was an article in the protocol giving the developing countries a period of grace. The second was a fund, set up in 1990, to finance the provision of alternative non-CFC technologies for the developing world.

Illegal production and smuggling of CFCs were evident in the 1990s. This tested the monitoring and compliance systems of the protocol (which included a possible use of trade sanctions against offenders). Nonetheless, the regime has generally proved to be effective and has continually widened its scope of activities to deal with further classes of ozone-depleting chemicals. The damage to the ozone layer will not be repaired until the latter part of the twenty-first century, given the long atmospheric lifetimes of the chemicals involved. However, human behavior has been significantly altered to the extent that the scientific subsidiary body of the Montreal Protocol has been able to report a measurable reduction in the atmospheric concentration of CFCs. Therefore, it seems that the context, knowledge, interest, and power hypothesis is correct.

For Discussion

1. How might the alternative theories we have studied explain the case of CFCs and regime creation?

2. Can you think of examples in which a leader in one environmental issue is a laggard on another?

3. Given the apparent pace of climate change in the polar regions, is the regime-creation process too slow to solve Earth's problems?

The Functions of International Environmental Cooperation

Because environmental issues, such as pollution control, often involve more than one country—or region or hemisphere—states must establish international governance regimes to regulate these transboundary environmental problems and sustain the global commons. Yet these regimes encompass more than formal agreements between states, although such agreements are very important. Moreover, there are other functions and consequences of international cooperation beyond regime formation, which we will learn about in the following sections.

Transboundary Trade and Pollution Control

When animals, fish, water, or pollution cross national frontiers, the need for international cooperation arises. The regulation of transboundary environmental problems is a long-established function of international cooperation reflected in hundreds of multilateral, regional, and bilateral agreements providing for joint efforts to manage resources and control pollution.

An important example is provided by the 1979 Convention on Long-Range Transboundary Air Pollution (LRTAP) and its various protocols. They responded to the growing problem of acidification and so-called acid rain by providing mechanisms to study atmospheric pollution problems in Europe and North America and securing commitments by the states involved to control and reduce their emissions. Another set of multilateral environmental agreements (MEAs) regulates the transboundary movement of hazardous wastes and chemicals in the interest of protecting human health and the environment. These agreements require that when hazardous chemicals and pesticides are traded, the government from whose territory the exports originate shall obtain the "prior informed consent" of the importing country (see Table 14.3).

Controlling, taxing, and even promoting trade have always been some of the more important functions of the state, and trade restrictions can also be used as an instrument for nature conservation. The 1973 Convention on International Trade in Endangered Species (CITES) does this by attempting to monitor, control, or prohibit international trade in species (or products derived from them) whose continued survival might be put at risk by the effects of such trade. Species at risk are "listed" in three appendixes to the convention; some 600 animal and 300 plant species currently receive the highest level of protection (a trade ban) through listing in Appendix I, although decisions on the "up-listing" and "down-listing" of species are sometimes controversial, as in the case of the African elephant or the northern spotted owl, bald eagle, and gray wolf in the United States.

The use of trade penalties and restrictions by MEAs has been a thorny issue whenever the objective of environmental protection has come into conflict with the rules of the GATT/WTO trade regime (see Chapters 7 and 11).

The red panda (*Ailurus fulgens*) is listed on the CITES endangered list because of commercial logging in its habitat of Nepal and northern Myanmar.

Table 14.3
Some Environmental Treaties with Weight in International Environmental Law

	Atmospheric Pollution
1985	Convention on Long-Range Transboundary Air Pollution
1988	Protocol on the Reduction of Sulfur Emissions or Their Transboundary Fluxes
1988	Protocol Concerning the Control of Emissions of Nitrogen Oxides
	Stratospheric Ozone Layer
1985	Vienna Convention for the Protection of the Ozone Layer
1987	Montreal Protocol on Substances That Deplete the Ozone Layer
	Hazardous Wastes
1989	Basel Convention on the Control of Transboundary Movements of Hazardous Wastes and Their Disposal
1991	Bamako Convention on the Ban of the Import into Africa and the Control of Transboundary Movement and Management Within Africa of Hazardous Wastes
	Marine Pollution
1969	International Convention on Civil Liability for Oil Pollution Damage
1971	Brussels Convention Relating to Civil Liability in the Field of Maritime Carriage of Nuclear Material
1973–1978	International Convention for the Prevention of Pollution from Ships (MARPOL)
1992	London Convention on the Prevention of Marine Pollution by Dumping Wastes and Other Matter
	Wildlife
1971	Ramsar Convention on Wetlands of International Importance Especially as Waterfowl Habitat
1973	International Convention for the Regulation of Whaling
1973	Convention on International Trade in Endangered Species (CITES)
1979	Bonn Convention on the Conservation of Migratory Species of Wild Animals

Such a problem arose when the international community attempted to address the controversial question of the new biotechnology and genetically modified organisms (GMOs). There was much resistance to the claims of (primarily American) biotechnology corporations that had made huge investments in developing GMO seed, pharmaceuticals, and food products and who argued that these innovations had positive environmental and development potential (through reducing pesticide use and increasing crop yields). European publics, supermarkets, and some developing countries were very wary of GMO technologies on safety and other grounds, which led to pressure for controls on their transboundary movement and to negotiation of the Biosafety Protocol to the Convention on Biological Diversity (CBD) that had been agreed at Rio in 1992. The resulting Cartagena Protocol was signed in 2000 and establishes an advanced informed agreement procedure between governments to be applied when GMOs are transferred across frontiers for ultimate release into the environment. The criteria to guide decisions on blocking imports reflected a precautionary approach rather than insistence on conclusive scientific evidence of harmfulness. Much of the argument in negotiating the Cartagena Protocol concerned the relationship of these new environmental rules to the requirements of the trade regime and arose from the concern of the United States and other potential GMO exporters that the protocol would permit a disguised form of trade protectionism. Whether the WTO trade rules should take precedence over the emerging biosafety rules was debated at length, until the parties agreed to avoid the issue by providing that the two sets of rules should be mutually supportive.

Norm Creation

The development of international environmental law and associated norms of acceptable behavior has been both rapid and innovative over the last thirty years. Some of the norms mentioned earlier are in the form of quite technical policy concepts that have been widely disseminated and adopted as a result of international discussion. The precautionary principle has gained increasing but not uncritical currency (see Table 14.4 for other international environmental laws that affect norm creation). Originally coined by German policy makers, the precautionary principle states that where there is a likelihood of environmental damage, banning an activity should not require full and definitive scientific proof. As we saw in the earlier example of GMOs, the latter has tended to be the requirement in trade law. The norm of "prior informed consent" has also been promoted alongside that of "the polluter pays." In the longer term, one of the key effects of the climate-change regime (dealt with in detail later) may be the dissemination of new approaches to pollution control, such as emissions trading and joint implementation.

The UN Earth Summits were important in establishing environmental norms. The 1972 Stockholm Conference produced its Principle 21, which combines sovereignty over national resources with state responsibility for external pollution. This should not be confused with Agenda 21 issued by the 1992 Rio Earth Summit. Agenda 21 was a complex forty-chapter document of some 400 pages that took two years for members of the United Nations to negotiate in UNCED's Preparatory Committee. Agenda 21 was frequently derided, not least because of its nonbinding character, but this internationally agreed compendium of environmental "best practice" subsequently had a wide impact and remains a point of reference. For example, many local authorities have produced their own local Agenda 21s. Under the Aarhus Convention (1998), North American and European governments agreed to guarantee to their publics a number of environmental rights, including the right to obtain environmental information held by governments, to participate in policy decisions, and to have access to judicial processes.

Aid and Capacity Building

Although not a specific norm of the type dealt with earlier, sustainable development provides a normative framework built on an underlying deal between developed and

Table 14.4

Principles of International Environmental Law That Affect Norm Creation

State Responsibility to Protect Environment
Preventive Action
Good Neighborliness
Sustainable Development
Precautionary Principle
Polluter Pays
Common, Differentiated Responsibility

developing worlds. Frequent North-South arguments since Rio about the levels of aid and **technology transfer** that would allow developing countries to achieve sustainable development have ended in many disappointments and unfulfilled pledges. In 1991, the UN Environment Programme, UN Development Programme, and the World Bank created the Global Environmental Facility (GEF) as an international mechanism specifically for funding environmental projects in developing countries. In 2003–2006, it attracted donations of around $3 billion. Most environmental conventions now aim at **capacity building** through arrangements for the transfer of funds, technology, and expertise because most of their member states lack the resources to participate fully in international agreements. The stratospheric-ozone and climate-change regimes aim to build capacity and could not exist in their current form without providing for this function.

Scientific Understanding

International environmental cooperation relies on shared scientific understanding, as evidenced by the form of some important contemporary environmental regimes. An initial framework convention will signal concern and establish mechanisms for developing and sharing new scientific data, thereby providing the basis for taking action in a control protocol. Generating and sharing scientific information have long been functions of international cooperation in public bodies such as the World Meteorological Organization (WMO) and myriad academic organizations such as the International Council for the Exploration of the Seas (ICES) and the International Union for the Conservation of Nature (IUCN). Disseminating scientific information on an international basis makes sense, but it needs funding from governments because, except in areas like pharmaceutical research, the private sector has no incentive to do the work. International environmental regimes usually have standing scientific committees and subsidiary bodies to support their work. Perhaps the greatest international effort to generate new and authoritative scientific knowledge has been in the area of **climate change** through the Intergovernmental Panel on Climate Change (IPCC).

WHAT'S YOUR WORLDVIEW

The international community seems to understand environmental challenges, but most states seem reluctant to give up sovereignty to solve any global commons problem. Why?

technology transfer The process of sharing skills, knowledge, technologies, methods of manufacturing, and facilities among governments and private actors (e.g., corporations) to ensure that scientific and technological developments are accessible to a wider range of users for application in new products, processes, materials, or services.

capacity building The provision of funds and technical training to allow developing countries to participate in global environmental governance.

climate change A change in the statistical distribution of weather over periods that range from decades to millions of years. It can be a change in the average weather or a change in the distribution of weather events.

Set up in 1988 under the auspices of the WMO and UN Environmental Programme, the IPCC brings together the majority of the world's climate-change scientists in three working groups: on climate science, impacts, and economic and social dimensions. They have produced assessment reports in 1990, 1995, 2001, and 2007, which are regarded as the authoritative scientific statements on climate change. The reports are carefully and cautiously drafted with the involvement of government representatives and represent a consensus view.

The Fourth Assessment Report, published in February 2007, concluded that "warming of the climate system is unequivocal, as is now evident from observations of increases in global average air and ocean temperatures, widespread melting of snow and ice and rising global sea level" (IPCC 2007, 4). Most of the temperature increase "is *very likely* due to the observed increase in anthropogenic greenhouse gas concentrations" (IPCC 2007, 8; original italics). The use of words is significant here, for the IPCC defines *very likely* as more than 90 percent certain. This represents a change from the previous report, which had only estimated that human activity was *likely*, or more than 66 percent certain, to be responsible for temperature increases.

The IPCC agreed in 2008 to prepare a Fifth Assessment Report. This report (AR5, scheduled for completion in 2014) focuses on assessing the socioeconomic aspects of climate change and the implications for sustainable development policies and risk-management efforts across the world.

> ## WHAT'S YOUR WORLDVIEW ?
>
> Which is more important: economic development or environmental protection? Is it possible to achieve both goals? Can we achieve sustainable development?

Governing the Commons

global commons The areas and resources not under national sovereignty that belong to no single country and are the responsibility of the entire world. The oceans beyond the 200-mile limit, outer space, and Antarctica are global commons areas.

The **global commons** are usually understood as areas and resources not under sovereign jurisdiction—that is, not owned by anybody. The high seas and the deep ocean floor come within this category (beyond the two hundred nautical mile exclusive economic zone that states could claim under the 1992 UN Convention on the Law of the Sea), as does Antarctica (based on the 1959 Antarctic Treaty). Outer space is another highly important commons area, with use vital to modern telecommunications, broadcasting, navigation, and surveillance. Finally, there is the global atmosphere.

The global commons have an environmental dimension not only as resources but also as a kind of garbage dump for waste products from cities and industry. The fish and whale stocks of the high seas have been relentlessly overexploited to the point where some species have been wiped out and long-term protein sources for human beings are imperiled. The ocean environment has been polluted by land-based effluent and oil and other discharges from ships. It has been a struggle to maintain the unique wilderness of the Antarctic in the face of increasing pressure from human beings, and even outer space now faces an environmental problem in the form of increasing orbital debris left by decades of satellite launches. Similarly, the global atmosphere has been degraded in a number of highly threatening ways, through damage to the stratospheric ozone layer and, most important, by the enhanced **greenhouse effect** now firmly associated with changes to Earth's climate. This is often characterized as a "tragedy of the commons." Where there is unrestricted access to a resource owned by no one, there will be an incentive for individuals to grab as much as they can, and if the resource is finite, there will come a time when it is ruined by overexploitation as the short-term interests of individual users overwhelm the longer-run collective interest in sustaining the resource.

greenhouse effect The trapping of the sun's warmth in Earth's lower atmosphere due to gases that act like the glass of a greenhouse.

Environmental Regimes

Within the jurisdiction of governments, it may be possible to solve the problem by turning the commons into private property or nationalizing them, but for the global commons, such a solution is, by definition, unavailable. Therefore, the function of international cooperation in this context is the very necessary one of providing a substitute for world government to ensure that global commons are not misused and subject to tragic collapse. Regimes have been created that have enjoyed varying degrees of effectiveness. Many of the functions that have been discussed can be found in these global commons regimes, but their central contribution is a framework of rules to ensure mutual agreement between users about acceptable standards of behavior and levels of exploitation consistent with sustaining commons ecology.

A river of trash: in many developing countries, finding enough water is not the problem; common practices like dumping garbage create major health hazards and make rivers impassable, as shown in this photo from Jakarta, Indonesia, in 2011.

Enforcement poses difficult challenges due to the incentives for users to "free ride" by taking more than a fair share or refusing to be bound by the collective arrangements. Free riding can potentially destroy regimes because other parties will then see no reason to restrain themselves either. In local commons regimes, inquisitive neighbors might deter rule breaking, and a similar role at the international level can be performed by NGOs. However, it is very difficult to enforce compliance by sovereign states; this is a fundamental difficulty for international law and hardly unique to environmental regimes. Mechanisms have been developed to cope with the problem, but how effective they and the environmental regimes to which they apply can be is hard to judge; this involves determining the extent to which governments are in legal and technical compliance with their international obligations. Moreover, it also involves estimating the extent to which state behavior has been changed as a result of the international regime concerned. Naturally, the ultimate and most demanding test of the effectiveness of global commons regimes is whether or not the resources or ecologies concerned are sustained or even improved.

In South Sudan in 2010, a local official points to open pools of chemical liquids, byproducts of oil production that pollute farms and waterways.

Some of the first and least-successful global commons regimes were the various fisheries commissions for the Atlantic and elsewhere, which sought agreement on limiting catches to preserve stocks. Pollution from ships has been controlled by MARPOL (the 1973 international marine environmental convention—short for "marine pollution"), and there is a patchwork of other treaties to manage such issues as the dumping of radioactive waste at sea. For the Antarctic, a remarkably well-developed set of rules designed to preserve the ecological integrity of this last great wilderness has been devised within the framework of the 1959 treaty.

WHAT'S YOUR WORLDVIEW

International relations describes a world of nation-states and sovereignty. How would you convince these states to give up or share sovereignty to address common problems like pollution or climate change?

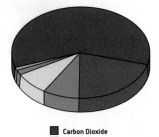

Carbon Dioxide
Ozone
Methane
Nitrous Oxide
CFC 12
CFC 11

THE PROPORTIONS OF GREENHOUSE GASES.

This chart combines the potency and volume of major heat-absorbing gases in the atmosphere. Since the Industrial Revolution, carbon dioxide concentrations have grown exponentially from 280 parts per million to 400 ppm in 2013. If nothing is done to curb intensive fossil fuel emissions, what will happen to the average global temperature? What effects might that have?

The Antarctic regime is a rather exclusive club: the treaty's "Consultative Parties" include the states that had originally claimed sovereignty over parts of the area, and new members of the club must demonstrate their involvement in scientific research on the frozen continent. There is a comprehensive agreement on conserving the marine ecosystem around the continent, and in the late 1980s, preparations for regulated mineral mining were defeated and replaced by a new 1988 Protocol on Environmental Protection, which included a fifty-year mining ban. The success, with only a minimal level of formal organization, of a restricted group of countries in governing this crucial laboratory for understanding global environmental change demonstrates what can be achieved by international action.

Antarctic science was crucial to the discovery of a problem that resulted in what is perhaps the best example of effective international action to govern the commons. In 1985, a British Antarctic Survey balloon provided definitive evidence of serious thinning of the stratospheric ozone layer. A diminishing ozone layer is a global problem par excellence because the ozone layer protects Earth and its inhabitants from the damaging effects of the sun's ultra violet radiation. A framework convention was signed in 1985, followed in 1987 by its Montreal Protocol imposing international controls over ozone-depleting chemicals. The further evolution of the ozone-layer regime offers the paramount example of how international cooperation can achieve an effective solution to a global environmental problem. The problem's causes were isolated, international support was mobilized, and compensatory action was taken to ensure that developing countries participated. A set of rules and procedures were developed that proved to be effective, at least in reducing the concentration of the offending chemicals in the atmosphere, if not yet fully restoring the stratospheric ozone layer.

Climate Change

Unlike the ozone-layer problem, which was clearly the result of damage caused when people used chlorofluorocarbons (CFCs) in industry, air conditioning, and personal products like hair spray, climate change and the enhanced greenhouse effect had long been debated among scientists. Only in the late 1980s did sufficient international scientific and political consensus emerge to stimulate action—a clear case of the development and influence of an epistemic community. There were still serious disagreements, however, over the likelihood that human-induced changes in mean temperatures were altering the global climate system.

Naturally occurring greenhouse gases in the atmosphere insulate Earth's surface by trapping solar radiation. Before the Industrial Revolution, carbon dioxide concentrations in the atmosphere were around 280 parts per million. They have since grown exponentially. In 2007 they were measured at 379 ppm, by 2013 they had reached 400 ppm. This rising concentration was due to burning fossil fuels and reductions in some of the "sinks" for carbon dioxide, notably forests. Methane emissions have also risen with the growth of agriculture (Intergovernmental Panel on Climate Change 2007, 11).

The best predictions of the IPCC are that if nothing is done to curb intensive fossil fuel emissions, there will be a likely rise in mean temperatures on the order of 4.3–11.5 degrees Fahrenheit (2.4–6.4 degrees Celsius) by 2099. The exact consequences of this are difficult to predict on the basis of current climate modeling, but sea level rises and turbulent weather are generally expected. In 2010 it was internationally agreed that to avoid climate catastrophe, it would be necessary to hold temperature increases below 3.6 degrees Fahrenheit (2 degrees Celsius) by keeping atmospheric CO_2 concentrations below 550 ppm. In the first decade of the twenty-first century, unusual weather patterns, storm events, and the melting of polar ice sheets have added a dimension of public concern to the fears expressed by the scientific community.

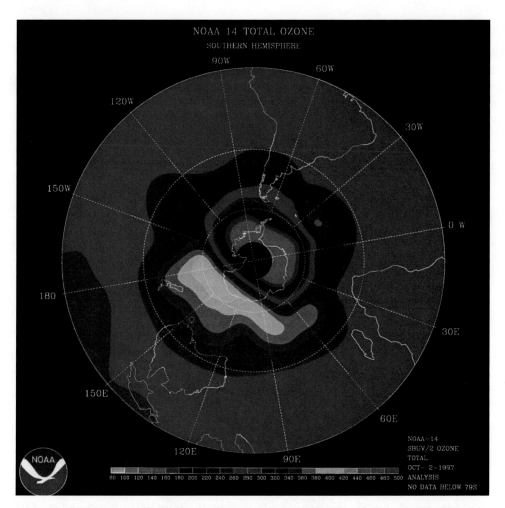

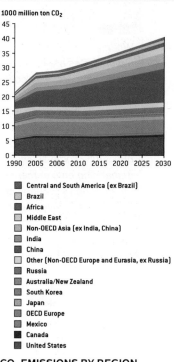

- Central and South America (ex Brazil)
- Brazil
- Africa
- Middle East
- Non-OECD Asia (ex India, China)
- India
- China
- Other (Non-OECD Europe and Eurasia, ex Russia)
- Russia
- Australia/New Zealand
- South Korea
- Japan
- OECD Europe
- Mexico
- Canada
- United States

CO_2 EMISSIONS BY REGION.
Global CO_2 emissions increased from 15.3 billion tons in 1970 to 22.5 billion tons in 1990; by 2012, emissions had increased to 33 billion tons. What are governments doing to reverse this trend? What impediments do they face in implementing their plans?

International agreements have reduced the amount of ozone-depleting gases that industries release, but the gases remain a cause of atmospheric damage, as this NASA satellite image shows.

As a common problem, climate change is on a quite different scale from anything that the international system has previously encountered. Climate change is really not a normal international environmental problem; it threatens huge changes in living conditions and challenges existing patterns of energy use and security. There is almost no dimension of international relations that it does not actually or potentially affect, and it has already become the subject of "high politics," discussed at G-8 summits and in high-level meetings between political leaders. Indeed, the UK foreign secretary stated in 2006 that climate change and climate security must now be a priority for foreign policy. Although recognizing the importance of this issue for the health of the planet and all living creatures, national leaders are still attempting to negotiate a comprehensive climate agreement.

One way of examining the dimensions of the problem and the steps taken at the international level to respond to the threat is to make a comparison to the stratospheric-ozone problem discussed in the previous section. There are, of course, some similarities. Chlorofluorocarbons are in themselves greenhouse gases, and the international legal texts on climate change make it clear that controlling them is the responsibility of the Montreal Protocol. The experience with stratospheric ozone and other recent conventions has clearly influenced efforts to build a climate-change regime. At the very start of climate discussions, the same approach was adopted: a framework convention followed by protocols.

WHAT'S YOUR WORLDVIEW ?

When it comes to environmental issues, some nation-states are incrementalists and others are postponers. Few political leaders fail to recognize the current environmental challenges. Some want to work slowly toward environmental policy action, whereas others want to postpone any action. They are all pushed by some activists who are zealots demanding environmental action. With these different goals among actors, do you think collective action is possible?

The UN Framework Convention on Climate Change (UNFCCC) was signed at the Rio Earth Summit in 1992. It envisaged the reduction of greenhouse-gas emissions and their removal by carbon sequestration, a process through which carbon-based gases are injected into the ground or into peat bogs. The signatories hoped that including a commitment from the developed nations to cut their emissions back to 1990 levels by 2000 could make a start. In a US election year, this proved to be impossible, and the parties had to be content with a non-binding declaration that an attempt would be made. There was a binding commitment, however, for parties to draw up national inventories of sources and sinks. As this included the developing nations, many of whom were ill equipped to fulfill this obligation, there was also funding for capacity building. Most important, the convention locked the signatories into holding a continuing series of annual Conferences of Parties (CoPs) to consider possible actions and review the adequacy of existing commitments, supported by regular meetings of the subsidiary scientific and implementation bodies. By the CoP in Kyoto in 1997, the parties agreed on a "control" measure—the Kyoto Protocol involving emissions reductions by developed countries facilitated by "flexibility mechanisms."

The problem faced by the framers of the Kyoto Protocol was vastly more complex and demanding than that which their counterparts at Montreal had confronted so successfully in 1987. Instead of controlling a single set of industrial gases for which substitutes were available, reducing greenhouse-gas emissions would involve energy, transport, and agriculture—the fundamentals of life in modern societies. This challenges the whole idea of sustainable development. Whether this must involve real sacrifices in living standards and impossible political choices is a tough question for governments, although there are potential economic benefits from cutting emissions through the development of alternative-energy technologies. Politicians in Europe have taken the lead in trying to reduce greenhouse-gas emissions. Unfortunately, for most of the 1990s and the first decade of the new millennium, United States politicians—representing one of the worst greenhouse-gas-offending countries by several indicators—were reluctant to make the necessary adjustments.

The Kyoto Protocol to the Climate Convention entered into force in 2005. It committed developed countries to make an average 5.2 percent cut in their greenhouse-gas emissions from a 1990 baseline. Within this range, different national targets were negotiated: for example 8 percent for the European Union, 6 percent for Japan, and 7 percent for the US. (The US eventually refused to participate on the grounds that its economic competitors, China and India, were not required to make similar cuts). These targets were to be achieved by the first commitment period—2008–2012. To provide flexible ways of achieving these targets, three mechanisms were also agreed on.

First there was **emissions trading**, where rights to emit carbon could be bought and sold. The EU established its own emissions trading system and carbon markets began to grow up elsewhere. Second and third were two offset mechanisms, **Joint Implementation** and the **Clean Development Mechanism** (CDM). They allow countries to meet their own national targets by investing in carbon reduction projects elsewhere in the world. The CDM has been very extensively used, especially in China. It was hoped that there would be a renewal of the Kyoto Protocol covering all the developed countries and lasting from 2013 to 2020, in the event only a limited second phase was achieved, covering only 15% of global emissions and without commitments from the US and Japan.

Even with what appeared to be a flexible framework and some useful mechanisms built into the Kyoto Protocol, there was much disagreement and international posturing. Another reason for dissent was that, despite a quite unprecedented international scientific effort in support of the IPCC to establish the causes and consequences of warming, there was not the kind of scientific consensus that had promoted agreement on CFCs—at least not in 1997. At the time, there was disagreement over the significance of human activities and over projections of future change (which has since narrowed dramatically). And there were those who had an economic interest in denying or misrepresenting the science, including fossil fuel interests and producers such as Saudi Arabia. At the other end of the spectrum, the Alliance of Small Island States, some of whose members' territory would disappear under projected sea level rises, were desperately concerned that these projections be taken seriously.

At a landfill in California in 2009, methane gas created by garbage is converted to liquid natural gas for use as fuel. Have you ever wondered where your trash goes?

There is a further problem in that, even though the effects of climate change are not fully understood, there is enough evidence for some nations to calculate that there might be benefits to them from climatic alterations. Regions of Russia, for example, might become more temperate with rises in mean temperature, and more suitable for agricultural production (although one could equally well argue the extremely damaging effects of melting permafrost in Siberia). In North America, variations in rainfall patterns have already begun to disrupt agriculture that relies on irrigation. Snowfall patterns in the major mountain ranges are changing, and some species of frogs and insects—especially honeybees necessary for crop pollination—are slowly disappearing. One generalization that can be made with certainty is that the developing nations, with limited infrastructure and major populations located at sea level, are most vulnerable. In recognition of this and on the understanding that a certain level of warming is now inevitable, international attention has begun to shift toward the problem of adaptation to the effects of climate change as well as mitigation of its causes. Once again, the comparative simplicity of the stratospheric-ozone problem is evident; the effects of ozone depletion were spread across the globe and affected North Europeans as well as those living in the Southern Hemisphere.

At the heart of the international politics of climate change as a global environmental problem is the structural divide between North and South (see Chapters 6 and 12). For the Montreal Protocol, there was a solution available at an acceptable price delivered through the Multilateral Ozone Fund. Once again, climate change is different. One of the most significant principles set out in the UN Framework Convention on Climate Change was that of common but differentiated responsibilities. That is to say, although climate change was the common concern of all, it had been produced as a consequence of the development of the old industrialized nations, and it was their responsibility to take the lead in cutting emissions.

What is happening to the bees? A bee works on collecting nectar from a fruit tree. Bee experts say conditions that create a honeybee die-off include mild winters and unseasonably warm early spring weather, which creates conditions for an explosion in the mite populations that kill off many colonies.

CASE STUDY | Common but Differentiated Responsibilities?

A key principle of the climate-change regime, written into the 1992 UNFCCC, was the notion of "common but differentiated responsibilities." This, in effect, meant that although all nations had to accept responsibility for the world's changing climate, it was developed nations that were immediately responsible because they had benefited from the industrialization generally regarded as the source of the excess carbon dioxide emissions (refer to Map 14.1).

Consider the relationship between national carbon dioxide emissions and share of global population. The United States emits around 25 percent of the global total but has only 4.5 percent of the global population. The Chinese figures are 14 percent and over 20 percent of the world's population, while the thirty-five least developed nations emit less than 1 percent and account for more than 10 percent of the world's population.

Accordingly, the developed countries were listed in Annex I of the convention, and it was agreed that they, rather than developing countries, would have to lead the way in making emissions reductions.

This approach was followed in the Kyoto Protocol, where only developed-country parties are committed to make reductions. Even before the protocol was agreed, the US Senate passed the Byrd-Hagel Resolution making it clear that it would not ratify any agreement where developing nations, who were now economic competitors of the United States, did not also need to make emissions reductions.

However, in 2004, the International Energy Agency published projections that underlined how globalization was radically changing the pattern of energy-related carbon dioxide emissions; it estimated that emissions would rise by 62 percent by 2030 but, most significantly, that at some point in the 2020s, developing-world emissions would overtake those of the developed OECD countries.

It therefore became clear that to have any chance of success, the future climate-change regime would have to include emissions reductions by countries such as China and India but that they in turn would not even consider reductions if the United States remained outside the Kyoto system.

The fundamental question is thus: *On what basis should countries be asked to reduce their emissions*?

The most radical and equitable answer might be to give each individual a fixed carbon allowance, probably allowing rich people to maintain something of their lifestyle by buying the allowances of the poor. A more likely alternative is to find ways of creating and then raising a global carbon price so that alternatives to fossil fuel become economically attractive. Which approach would you support? Why? What alternatives can you imagine?

For Discussion

1. Why is climate change such a politically charged issue?
2. Developing states want a chance to develop like the rich countries of the global North. What is the argument against their development? Should they care about the environment?
3. Economic interests and environmental concerns are often in conflict. As states develop, do they have a responsibility to prevent further environmental degradation?

Global industrial growth has caused an increased demand for power generation, often through the burning of fossil fuels that produce greenhouse gases.

The Kyoto Protocol, in its first phase, accomplished relatively little and much more greenhouse gas reduction occurred under the Montreal protocol in the same period, for chlorofluorocarbons are also powerful greenhouse gases. It became increasingly clear that, given the fact that by 2005 developing countries were responsible for the majority of current emissions and that in 2007 China overtook the US as the primary emitter, an effective climate agreement would have to include all the Parties to the Convention. This continues to be very difficult to achieve because of the legitimate claims to development and climate justice made by Southern countries and, of course, because many of the emissions from a country like China have been displaced by the globalization of production from Europe and America. It is also true that developed countries, suffering from the world economic crisis of 2008, were not prepared to take risks with their economies. In 2007 it was agreed to have two negotiation tracks, one on the future of Kyoto and the other on the future of the Convention. The US was prepared to participate in the latter because it avoided Kyoto 'targets and timetables.' It was hoped that a new comprehensive agreement could be reached at Copenhagen in 2009.

Copenhagen was a high profile event, attended by the new US President Obama and other world leaders. They failed to produce a new legally binding and comprehensive agreement. Instead, the US and the BASIC countries (a coalition of large emerging economies including Brazil, China, India and South Africa) struck a deal known as the Copenhagen Accord. This has tended to set the course of negotiations through to the agreement on the 'Durban Platform' in 2011. The key assumptions are that a new agreement, unlike Kyoto, will be 'bottom up'—that is countries will offer their 'contributions' to emissions reductions that they regard as appropriate. All countries will participate, which breaks down the strict divide between developed and developing countries, but the CBDR principle will remain so that contributions can be 'differentiated'. How strictly contributions will be assessed and how far they will be legally binding, remains to be seen. These issues are scheduled to be resolved in Paris in 2015, for an agreement that will enter into force in 2020. It is clear that the contributions offered at the moment will not be sufficient to put the world on a pathway that avoids breaching the 2 degree Celsius threshold. There will have to be much greater ambition amongst the major emitters before 2015, if the task is not to become much more costly and difficult to achieve in future decades.

> ## WHAT'S YOUR WORLDVIEW
>
> *The political culture of some countries emphasizes individual rights and responsibilities, yet protecting the environment asks us to live collectively and consider the other. Is it possible or even necessary to change the individualistic perspective?*

In 2007, the Nobel Prize committee recognized the IPCC and former vice president Al Gore for their work on the causes and ramifications of global warming.

Conclusion

In this chapter, we have seen that cooperation to protect the global environment, though sometimes difficult to achieve, is possible. The determinants of successful cooperation can be found in international-regime theory, beginning with the acceptance of proper norms of behavior because the costs of not cooperating are potentially too great. Indeed, the environmental issues we are faced with today—global climate change, desertification, and other environmental degradation—can become severer and less manageable for future generations, as we have seen in our own brief history of the twentieth and early twenty-first century. Solving these issues now requires new perspectives and unprecedented cooperation on a global scale.

CONTRIBUTORS TO CHAPTER 14: John Vogler and Steven L. Lamy.

REVIEW QUESTIONS

1. What are the possible connections, both negative and positive, between globalization and environmental change?

2. Why did environmental issues appear on the international agenda, and what were the key turning points?

3. Summarize the consequences of the 1972 UN Conference on the Human Environment and the 1992 UN Conference on Environment and Development.

4. How would you interpret the meaning of sustainable development?

5. How can regime concepts be applied to the study of international environmental cooperation?

6. Can international trade and environmental protection ever be compatible?

7. Why did the framework convention/control protocol prove useful in the cases of stratospheric ozone depletion and climate change?

8. How does the tragedy of the commons story help illustrate the need for governance of the global commons?

9. Describe the free rider problem in relation to the climate-change regime.

10. Consider the possible security implications of the climate predictions made by the Intergovernmental Panel on Climate Change.

FURTHER READING

Barnett, J. (2001), *The Meaning of Environmental Security: Ecological Politics and Policy in the New Security Era* (London: Zed Books). This lively and critical book is for readers who wish to explore the growing connections between environmental and security issues.

Barry, J., and Eckersley, R. (eds.) (2005), *The State and the Global Ecological Crisis* (Cambridge, Mass.: MIT Press). A provocative set of essays on the continuing relevance of the state, long forsaken by green activists but still the fundamental unit of global environmental governance.

Birnie, P., and Boyle, A. (2002), *International Law and the Environment* (Oxford: Oxford University Press). An invaluable source of detailed information on formal aspects of international environmental cooperation.

Brenton, T. (1994), *The Greening of Machiavelli: The Evolution of International Environmental Politics* (London: Earthscan). A diplomatic participant's account of the international politics of the environment up to and including the Rio Earth Summit.

Dauvergne, P. (ed.) (2005), *Handbook of Global Environmental Politics* (Cheltenham: Edward Elgar). This very extensive collection of thirty essays covering state governance and security, capitalism, trade and corporations, civil societies, knowledge, and ethics will provide the reader with a more in-depth view of current concerns and controversies in the field.

DeSombre, E. (2006), *Global Environmental Institutions* (Abingdon: Routledge). Provides a concise introduction within a series on global governance.

Dessler, A. E., and Parson, E. A. (2006), *The Science and Politics of Global Climate Change: A Guide to the Debate* (Cambridge: Cambridge University Press). As the title promises, this book presents the essentials of the debate about climate change in an unbiased manner.

Dryzek, J. (1997), *The Politics of the Earth: Environmental Discourses* (Oxford: Oxford University Press). Still extremely useful as a guide to thinking through the different approaches that are applied to the problems of environmental politics and sustainable development.

Elliott, L. (2004), *The Global Politics of the Environment* (Basingstoke: Palgrave). This comprehensive text provides detailed and wide-ranging coverage of the field and of the key international agreements.

Gleick, P. H. (1993), "Water and Conflict: Fresh Water Resources and International Security," *International Security* 18(1): 79–112. An important article by one of the academic pioneers of the connections between environmental degradation and security risks.

Gleick, P. H. (November 2003), "Global Freshwater Resources: Soft-Path Solutions for the Twenty-First Century," *Science:* 1524–1528. After many years of researching the possibility of war over scarce resources like water, the author offers suggestions to avoid such crises.

Lipschutz, R. D. (2004), *Global Environmental Politics: Power, Perspectives, and Practice* (Washington, D.C.: CQ Press). Makes innovative and critical connections between global environmental politics and a broad array of relevant political thought and practice.

McKibben, B. (2010), *Eaarth. Making a Life on a Tough New Planet* (New York: Times Books). A leading environmentalist who warned us about global warming now calls for a fundamental change in our way of life.

Paterson, M. (2001), *Understanding Global Environmental Politics: Domination, Accumulation, Resistance* (Basingstoke: Palgrave). As the title suggests, this book provides an alternative critical view of global environmental politics, investigating such problems as the political economy of car use.

Vogler, J. (2000), *The Global Commons: Environmental and Technological Governance* (Chichester: John Wiley). Uses regime analysis to compare and account for the various international arrangements for the ocean, Antarctic, space, and atmospheric commons.

Video Suggestion

Film: *The Age of Stupid*. Looking back from the year 2055, one man tries to understand how citizens of the world allowed their planet to decay and collapse when they had everything but the will power to change its course.

INTERNET RESOURCES

Center for International Earth Science Information Network
www.ciesin.org/TG/PI/TRADE/tradhmpg.html
Information on trade regimes and the environment.

European Environment Agency
www.eea.eu.int
The European Union's supranational agency for monitoring the environment.

The Global Footprint Network
http://www.footprintnetwork.org
A research organization aimed at influencing policy and providing empirical data that measure our human footprint and its impact on the environment.

International Institute for Sustainable Development
www.iisd.ca
Works to promote environmentally sound development practices.

Convention on Biological Diversity
www.biodiv.org
An important and reliable source of information on the topic.

UN Environment Programme
www.unep.org
Coordinates efforts in this area.

UN Framework Convention on Climate Change Secretariat
www.unfccc.de
An important and reliable source of information on the topic.

World Wildlife Fund
www.panda.org
An NGO working to protect species around the world.

Carnegie Council: "*The Plundered Planet: Why We Must—and How We Can—Manage Nature for Global Prosperity*"—Paul Collier

http://www.carnegiecouncil.org/resources/video/
data/000320

Working from his book *The Plundered Planet*, Paul Collier explores the recent rush of governments to lay claim to natural assets and how we need to look past the economic method of intergenerational utilitarianism when dealing with the environment.

Carnegie Council: "Sustainable Societies" —Sartaz Ahmed, Larry Burns, Joan Krevlin, and Thomas Stewart

http://www.carnegiecouncil.org/resources/video/
data/000348

In this panel discussion, key industry experts explore ideas and future plans for sustainable growth.

Carnegie Council: "Climate Change and New Security Issues"—H. E. Dr. Olafur Ragnar Grimsson, President of Iceland

http://www.carnegiecouncil.org/resources/video/data/000048

The president of Iceland discusses how his state is meeting its own energy needs through hydrothermal or geothermal power and is writing the book on how a state should go green.

Ted Talk: Al Gore's New Thinking on the Climate Crisis

http://www.ted.com/talks/lang/eng/al_gore_s_new
_thinking_on_the_climate_crisis.html

Former US Vice President Al Gore discusses new evidence suggesting that key climate-change indicators may be worse than previously expected.

For more information, quizzes, case studies and other study tools, please visit us at **www.oup.com/us/lamy**

THINKING ABOUT GLOBAL POLITICS

The Environment: Images and Options

INTRODUCTION

This exercise asks students to evaluate different and contending images of the future. These images of the future consider environmental, political, economic, and sociocultural factors.

Reluctantly, many citizens are now coming to the realization that there are real environmental costs associated with humankind's goal to achieve the good life. Citizens and leaders alike are also now recognizing the potential challenges posed by continuing policies that abuse the delicate ecological balance. These challenges to economic and political security and the good life are explored in this exercise.

PROCEDURE

Before beginning to explore the four alternative futures, students should read and review journal articles or texts that explore environmental problems associated with the contending images. Here are some suggested readings:

The World Commission on Environment and Development, *Our Common Future* (New York: Oxford University Press, 1987).

Barry Hughes, *World Futures: A Critical Analysis of Alternatives* (Baltimore: Johns Hopkins University Press, 1985).

Robert Woyach, "Global Resources and Growth," in S. Lamy (ed.), *Contemporary International Issues* (Boulder, Col.: Lynne Rienner, 1988).

Second, review the different elements of the four possible futures. What are the fundamental similarities and differences among these images? Consider which future you

Continued

THINKING ABOUT GLOBAL POLITICS *continued*

feel would be most beneficial to you and your family. Would this future create a world society in which all people could benefit? Why or why not? Which future would result in the following conditions?

1. full employment
2. less air pollution
3. more time for recreational activities
4. less government
5. greater equality
6. more citizen participation
7. exploration and use of alternative energy sources
8. a world economy that encourages equitable and balanced growth
9. a reduction of waste and overconsumption
10. less spending on military
11. more economic opportunities
12. increased conflict

Debriefing Questions

1. What image of the future is challenged by a more balanced ecological view?
2. Do these images of the future correspond in any way with the different theories in Chapter 3?
3. Why are environmental issues becoming so significant in international politics?
4. Is a sustainable development strategy a possibility for the future?

Note: Sustainable development is usually defined as a process of development that meets the needs of the present without compromising the ability of future generations to meet their own needs.

The Four Possible Futures

	Future One	Future Two	Future Three	Future Four
	A society that provides the necessities for all while encouraging equal opportunities for self-development.	A free enterprise society in which major economic growth provides economic benefits for all.	A society in which people recognize the limits to uncontrolled growth; people limit personal wealth, build communities that are in harmony with nature, and encourage reduction of waste.	A society in which independent people are given opportunities to develop themselves without harming the environment.
Society	As well as being individuals, most people live in social groups. People need support from one another to grow and be happy.	People benefit most when there is equal opportunity for all people to seek their own best interest. Government must not tell them what to do or what not to do.	People must cooperate, not compete. They must blend their own self-interest into that of the greater good.	Well-informed individuals can exercise freedom of choice to satisfy their own interest. This will contribute to creative problem solving and increased well-being for all.

Continued

THINKING ABOUT GLOBAL POLITICS *continued*

The Four Possible Futures *continued*

	Future One	**Future Two**	**Future Three**	**Future Four**
Environment	The world around us is to be used. New inventions will make some resources (e.g., the sun and wind) useful before or after others (coal and gas) are used up.	The land and sea around us are full of riches. They should be used to the fullest in making us happy and prosperous.	It is important to preserve the balance between ourselves and the land and sea around us. They belong both to us and to those who come after us.	By inventing new ways of using our resources, we can prosper without harming our natural riches.
Government	Central government should be strong and guarantee a job for all with equal pay for equal work. It must also allow people to develop private businesses.	Central government should play a very limited role in our lives. Its main jobs are to keep peace at home and protect us from attack.	Attention should be turned away from central government and toward local community government. Local government aids social and natural harmony.	Central government should give some support to its citizens. It should provide education and information and protect our natural resources.
Economics	Maximum effort will be made to cut our dependency on foreign resources. The government will pay for basic human services such as healthcare and education.	Large-scale industry can best use the natural resources of our land and oceans. They are most fit to lead development and make the most money in a world eager to buy our goods.	Local economies promote doing more with less in the design of all systems and question the ever-growing demand for consumer goods. Industries favor reuse or recycling of materials.	New industries with advanced equipment and the invention of new technologies should be encouraged. All new industries must be responsible for using our resources with care.

Glossary

absolute gains The notion that all states seek to have more power and influence in the system to secure their national interests. Offensive neorealists are also concerned with increasing power relative to other states. One must have enough power to secure interests and more power than any other state in the system—friend or foe.

adaptation strategies Changes in foreign policy behavior in reaction to changes in the international system or international events and adjusting national goals to conform to the effects of events external to that state.

African Union (AU) Created in 2002 and consisting of fifty-four member states, this union was formed as a successor to the Organization of African Unity. It maintains fourteen goals primarily centered in African unity and security, human rights, peace security and stability, economy, sustainable development, and equality. The AU's Assembly acts as a center for multilateral decision making, and the African Union often acts as an immediate bridging intervention and peacekeeping force until UN peacekeeping forces respond.

Al Qaeda Most commonly associated with Osama bin Laden, "The Base" (its meaning in Arabic) is a religious-based group whose fighters swear an oath of fealty to the leadership that succeeded bin Laden.

Americanization The spread of American values, practices, popular culture, and way of life.

anarchic system A realist description of the international system that suggests there is no common power or central governing structure.

anarchy A system operating in the absence of any central government. It does not imply chaos but the absence of political authority.

appeasement A policy of making concessions to a territorially acquisitive state in the hope that settlement of more modest claims will assuage that state's expansionist appetites.

Arab Spring Protests and revolutionary uprisings that began in Tunisia in 2010 and spread across Egypt, Libya, Syria, Yemen, Bahrain, Saudi Arabia, and Jordan in 2011. At their core was a desire for more democratic and transparent political systems and more open and equitable economic systems.

armistice A cease-fire agreement between enemies in wartime. In the case of World War I, the armistice began at 11 a.m. on November 11, 1918.

arms embargo Similar to economic sanctions, an arms embargo stops the flow of arms from one country to another.

arms race A central concept in realist thought. As states build up their military to address real or perceived threats to their national security, they may create insecurity in other states. These states in turn develop their military capacities and thus begin an arms race. This never-ending pursuit of security creates the condition we know as a security dilemma.

Association of Southeast Asian Nations (ASEAN) A geopolitical and economic organization of several countries located in Southeast Asia. Initially formed as a display of solidarity against communism, it has since redefined its aims and broadened to include the acceleration of economic growth and the promotion of regional peace.

asymmetric conflicts In symmetrical warfare, armies with comparable weapons, tactics, and organizational structures do battle. Wars are fought on near-equal terms. When stakes are high and those actors in conflict are not equal in terms of weapons and technology, the weaker side adopts asymmetrical tactics. These include guerrilla warfare, roadside bombs, attacks on civilians, and other terrorist tactics.

autarchy The mercantilist recommendation that states strive for economic self-sufficiency by using trade protectionism or policies of complete isolation.

balance of power In the international system, a state of affairs in which there is parity and stability among competing forces, and no one state is sufficiently strong to dominate all the others.

bipolar An international political order in which two states dominate all others. It is often used to describe the nature of the international system when the two superpowers, the Soviet Union and the United States, were dominant powers during the Cold War.

blitzkrieg The German term for "lightning war." This was an offensive strategy that used the combination of mechanized forces—especially tanks—and aircraft as mobile artillery to exploit breaches in an enemy's front line.

Bretton Woods system A system of economic and financial accords that created the International Monetary Fund, the World Bank, and GATT/WTO following World War II. It is named after the hamlet in northern New Hampshire where leaders from forty-four countries met in 1944.

capacity building The provision of funds and technical training to allow developing countries to participate in global environmental governance.

capital controls The monetary policy device that a government uses to regulate the flows into and out of a country's capital account (i.e., the flows of investment-oriented money into and out of a country or currency).

capitalism A system of production in which human labor and its products are commodities that are bought and sold in the marketplace.

charter rights Civil liberties guaranteed in a written document such as a constitution.

civic nationalism The idea that an association of people can identify themselves as belonging to the nation and have equal and shared political rights and allegiance to similar political procedures.

civil society The totality of all individuals and groups in a society who are not acting as participants in any government institutions or acting in the interests of commercial companies.

clandestine or sleeper cell Usually, a group of people sent by an intelligence organization or terrorist network that remains dormant in a target country until activated by a message to carry out a mission, which could include prearranged attacks.

class A social group that in Marxism is identified by its relationship with the means of production and the distribution of societal resources. Thus, we have the bourgeoisie, or the owners or upper classes, and the proletariat, or the workers.

classical realism The belief that it is fundamentally the nature of people and the state to act in a way that places interests over ideologies. The drive for power and the will to dominate are held to be fundamental aspects of human nature.

climate change A change in the statistical distribution of weather over periods that range from decades to millions of years. It can be a change in the average weather or a change in the distribution of weather events.

coercive diplomacy The use of diplomatic and military methods that force a state to concede to another state. These methods may include the threat of force and the mobilization of the military to gradually "turn the screw" but exclude the actual use of force. The implication is that war is the next step if diplomacy fails.

Cold War The period from 1946 to 1991 defined by ideological conflict and rivalry between the United States and the Soviet Union. This was a global struggle for the hearts and minds of citizens around the world that was characterized by political conflict, military competition, proxy wars, and economic competition.

collective security An arrangement where "each state in the system accepts that the security of one is the concern of all, and agrees to join in a collective response to aggression" (Roberts and Kingsbury 1993, 30).

common security At times called "cooperative security," it stresses noncompetitive approaches and cooperative approaches through which states—both friends and foes—can achieve security. The belief that no one is secure until all people are secure from threats of war.

community A human association in which members share common symbols and wish to cooperate to realize common objectives.

comparative advantage A theory developed by David Ricardo stating that two countries will both gain from trade if, in the absence of trade, they have different relative costs for producing the same goods. Even if one country is more efficient in the production of all goods than the other (absolute advantage), both countries will still gain by trading with each other as long as they have different relative efficiencies.

Concert of Europe An informal institution created in 1815 by the five great powers of Europe (Austria, Britain, France, Prussia, and Russia), whereby they agreed on controlling revolutionary forces, managing the balance of power, and accepting interventions to keep current leaders in power. This system kept the peace in Europe from 1815 until World War I.

conditionality When regional or international lending agencies require that recipient national governments accept certain policy conditions to receive a loan or some form of economic assistance.

Congress of Berlin A meeting of the European states that had an interest in colonizing Africa. The Berlin conference redrew the existing political map of Africa with a goal to avoid conflict between the European governments in Africa.

Congress of Vienna A meeting of major European leaders (1814–1815) that redrew the political map of Europe after the Napoleonic Wars. The congress was an attempt to restore a conservative political order in the continent.

constructivism An approach asserting that ideas construct or shape how we view the world; concerned with the relationship between agents and structures and the notion that ideas define and can transform global politics.

containment An American political strategy for resisting perceived Soviet expansion first publicly espoused by an American diplomat, George Kennan, in 1947 and aimed at limiting Soviet expansion in Europe.

coordination A form of cooperation requiring parties to pursue a common strategy to avoid the mutually undesirable outcome arising from the pursuit of divergent strategies.

cosmopolitan culture A pattern of relations within which people share the same goals and aspirations, generally to improve that culture for all members.

cosmopolitan democracy A condition in which international organizations, transnational corporations, and global markets are accountable to the peoples of the world.

critical theory Theories that are critical of the status quo and reject the idea that things can be fixed under the present system. These theories challenge core assumptions of the dominant paradigm and argue for transformation and not just reform.

deep ecology Often identified with the Norwegian philosopher, Arne Naess, the core belief is that the living environment has a right to live and flourish. The deep refers to the need to think deeply about the impact of human life on the environment.

defensive realism A structural theory of realism that views states as security maximizers—more concerned with absolute power as opposed to relative power. According to this view, it is unwise for states to try to maximize their share of power and seek hegemony.

democratic deficit Leaders have created many policy-making institutions at the global, regional, and national levels with policy-making power led by individuals who are appointed and not elected. Thus, policy decisions are not subject to review by citizens.

democratic peace thesis A central plank of liberal-internationalist thought, the democratic peace thesis makes two claims: first, liberal polities exhibit restraint in their relations with other liberal polities (the so-called separate peace), but second, they are imprudent in relations with authoritarian states. The validity of the democratic peace thesis has been fiercely debated in the international relations literature.

dependency theory A school of thought that offers explanations for economic development and underdevelopment. Dependency theorists emphasize that social and economic development is conditioned by external forces—namely, the domination of underdeveloped states by more powerful countries.

deregulation The removal of all regulation so that market forces, not government policy, control economic developments.

desertification The extreme deterioration of land in arid and dry subhumid areas due to loss of vegetation and soil moisture; it results chiefly from human activities and is influenced by climatic variations. This condition is principally caused by overgrazing, overdrafting of groundwater, and diversion of water from rivers for human consumption and industrial use; all of these processes are fundamentally driven by overpopulation.

détente The relaxation of tension between East and West; Soviet-American détente lasted from the late 1960s to the late 1970s and was characterized by negotiations and nuclear arms control agreements.

deterrence The threat or use of force to prevent an actor from doing something the actor would otherwise do.

development In the orthodox view, top-down; reliance on "expert knowledge," usually Western and definitely external; large capital investments in large projects; advanced technology; expansion of the private sphere. In the alternative view, bottom-up; participatory; reliance on appropriate (often local) knowledge and technology; small investments in small-scale projects; protection of the commons.

diplomacy The process by which international actors communicate as they seek to resolve conflicts without going to war and find solutions to complex global problems.

doctrine A stated principle of government policy, mainly in foreign or military affairs, or the set of beliefs held and taught by an individual or political group.

dollar standard The use of the US dollar since 1947 as the key currency in the international monetary system.

ecocentric Having a nature or ecologically centered rather than a human centered set of values.

ecological footprint A measure that demonstrates the load placed on Earth's carrying capacity by individuals or nations. It does this by estimating the area of productive land and water system required to sustain a population at its specified standard of living.

ecologies The communities of plants and animals that supply raw materials for all living things.

economic base For Marxists, the substructure of the society is the relationship between owners and workers. Capitalists own the means of production and control technology and resources. The workers are employed by the capitalists, and they are alienated, exploited, and estranged from their work and their society.

economic collapse of 2008 The global economic collapse that began in the United States when the housing bubble burst, affecting banks around the world that had created products based on mortgages. Trust in banks evaporated, credit diminished, and global markets plunged downward. The resulting crisis is ongoing.

economic sanctions A tool of statecraft that seeks to get a state to behave by coercion of a monetary kind—for example, freezing banking assets, cutting aid programs, or banning trade.

economic shock An event that produces a significant change within an economy despite occurring outside it. Economic shocks are unpredictable and typically impact supply or demand throughout the markets.

ecosystem A system of interdependent living organisms that share the same habitat, functioning together with all of the physical factors of the environment.

ecotopian Someone who believes in protecting and preserving the environment and promotes progressive political goals that promote environmental sustainability, social justice and economic well-being.

electronic commerce The buying and selling of products and services over the telephone or Internet. Amazon and ebay are examples of leaders in this area of commerce.

elite nationalism The use of nationalist ideology to encourage unity within an existing state. This is often a tactic that state-strengthening nationalists use.

embedded liberalism A liberal international economic order based on the pursuit of free trade but allowing an appropriate role for state intervention in the market in support of national security and national and global stability.

empire A distinct type of political entity, which may or may not be a state, possessing both a home territory and foreign territories. This may include conquered nations and colonies.

Enlightenment A movement associated with rationalist thinkers of the eighteenth century. Key ideas (which some would argue remain mottoes for our age) include secularism, progress, reason, science, knowledge, and freedom. The motto of the Enlightenment is "*Sapere aude!*" (Have courage to know!) (Kant 1991, 54).

epistemic community A network of professionals with expertise in an issue area that is recognized by policy makers as relevant to their work and critically important for formulating and implementing policy.

equity A number of equal portions in the nominal capital of a company; the shareholder thereby owns part of the enterprise; also called "stock" or "share."

ethic of responsibility For realists, it represents the limits of ethics in international politics; it involves the weighing up of consequences and the realization that positive outcomes may result from amoral actions.

ethics Ethical studies in international relations and foreign policy include the identification, illumination, and application of relevant moral norms to the conduct of foreign policy and assessing the moral architecture of the international system.

enthnonationalism A strain of nationalism marked by the desire of an ethnic community to have absolute authority over its own political, economic, and social affairs. Loyalty and identity shift from the state to an ethnic community that seeks to create its own state. It is often indicated that the interests of this particular ethnic group are not served by the nation/political situation it currently exists within.

European Union (EU) The union formally created in 1992 following the signing of the Maastricht Treaty. However, the origins of the European Union can be traced back to 1951 and the creation of the European Coal and Steel Community, followed in 1957 with a broader customs union (the Treaty of Rome, 1958). Originally a grouping of six countries in 1957, "Europe" grew by adding new members in 1973, 1981, and 1986. Since the fall of the planned economies in Eastern Europe in 1989, Europe has grown and now includes twenty-eight member states.

exceptionalism The belief that a country has a unique set of domestic and foreign policy traditions. An implication is that other countries should embrace the same set of policies.

export-led growth An outward-oriented economy that is based on exploiting its own comparative advantages, such as cheap labor or resources, to capture a share of the world market in a given industry.

failed or collapsed state A state that fails to provide basic services and provide for its citizens. Such a state cannot protect its boundaries, provide a system of law and order, or maintain a functioning marketplace and means of exchange.

feminist theory A theory critical of the biases of the discipline. Many feminists focus their research on the areas where women are excluded from the analysis of major international issues and concerns.

fixed exchange rate The price a currency will earn in a hard currency. Here a government is committed to keep it at a specific value.

floating exchange rate The market decides what the actual value of a currency is compared to other currencies.

foreign direct investment (FDI) The capital speculation by citizens or organizations of one country into markets or industries in another country.

foreign policy The articulation of national interests and the means chosen to secure those interests, both material and ideational, in the international arena.

foreign policy style Often shaped by a state's political culture, history, and traditions, this describes how a country deals with other states and how it approaches any decision-making situation. For example, does it act unilaterally or multilaterally? Does it seek consensus on an agreement or does it go with majority rule?

foreign policy tradition A tradition that includes national beliefs about how the world works and a list of national interests and priorities based on these beliefs. It also refers to past actions or significant historical events that act as analogs and give guidance to leaders about what strategy would best secure their national interests.

foundation A type of nonstate actor that is established as a charitable trust or a nonprofit INGO with the purpose of making grants to other institutions or to individuals.

Fourteen Points President Woodrow Wilson's vision of international society, first articulated in January 1918, included the principle of self-determination, the conduct of diplomacy on an open (not secret) basis, and the establishment of an association of nation-states to provide guarantees of independence and territorial integrity (League of Nations).

fragile state A state that has not yet failed but whose leaders lack the will or capacity to perform core state functions.

free market A market ruled by the forces of supply and demand, where all buying and selling is not constrained by government regulations or interventions.

free trade An essential element of capitalism that argues for no barriers or minimal barriers to the exchange of goods, services, and investments among states.

functionalism An idea formulated by early proponents of European integration that suggests cooperation should begin with efforts aimed at resolving specific regional or transnational problems. It is assumed that resolution of these problems will lead to cooperation, or spillover, in other policy areas.

futures Derivatives that oblige a buyer and seller to complete a transaction at a predetermined time in the future at a price agreed on today. Futures are also known as "forwards."

game theory A branch of mathematics that explores strategic interaction.

genocide The deliberate and systematic extermination of an ethnic, national, tribal, or religious group.

glasnost A policy of greater openness pursued by Soviet leader Mikhail Gorbachev from 1985, involving more toleration of internal dissent and criticism.

global capital markets Banks, investment companies, insurance companies, trusts, hedge funds, and stock exchanges that transfer funds to industries and other commercial enterprises globally.

global commons The areas and resources not under national sovereignty that belong to no single country and are the responsibility of the entire world. The oceans beyond the 200-mile limit, outer space, and Antarctica are global commons areas.

global environmental governance The performance of global environmental regulative functions, often in the absence of a central government authority. It usually refers to the structure of international agreements and organizations but can also involve governance by the private sector or NGOs.

global goods Products that are made for a global market and are available across the world.

global governance The regulation and coordination of transnational issue areas by nation-states, international and regional organizations, and private agencies through the establishment of international regimes. These regimes may focus on problem solving or the simple enforcement of rules and regulations.

globalization A historical process involving a fundamental shift or transformation in the spatial scale of human social organization that links distant communities and expands the reach of power relations across regions and continents.

global politics The politics of global social relations in which the pursuit of power, interests, order, and justice transcends regions and continents.

global polity The collective structures and processes by which "interests are articulated and aggregated, decisions are made, values allocated and policies conducted through international or transnational political processes" (Ougaard 2004, 5).

global sourcing Obtaining goods and services across geopolitical boundaries. Usually, the goal is to find the least expensive labor and raw material costs and the lowest taxes and tariffs.

government The people and agencies that have the power and legitimate authority to determine who gets what, when, where, and how within a given territory.

Great Depression The global economic collapse that ensued following the US Wall Street stock market crash in October 1929. Economic shockwaves rippled around a world already densely interconnected by webs of trade and foreign direct investment.

great power A state that has the political, economic, and military resources to shape the world beyond its borders. In most cases, such a state has the will and capacity to define the rules of the international system.

greenhouse effect The trapping of the sun's warmth in Earth's lower atmosphere due to gases that act like the glass of a greenhouse.

gross domestic product (GDP) The sum of all economic activity that takes place within a country.

guerrilla wars Conflicts or insurgencies that involve irregular forces. Fighters in these wars use unconventional methods of warfare, such as sabotage, ambushes, roadside bombs, and sniping.

hard power The material threats and inducements leaders employ to achieve the goals of their state.

hegemony A system regulated by a dominant leader, or political (and/or economic) domination of a region. It also means power and control exercised by a leading state over other states.

Holocaust The attempts by the Nazis to murder the Jewish population of Europe. Some 6 million Jewish people were killed in concentration camps, along with a further million that included Soviet prisoners, Roma, Poles, communists, homosexuals, and the physically or mentally disabled.

horizontal proliferation An increase in the number of actors who possess nuclear weapons.

human development The notion that it is possible to improve the lives of people. Basically, it is about increasing the number of choices people have. These may include living a long and healthy life, access to education, and a better standard of living.

humanitarian intervention The use of military force by external actors to end a threat to people within a sovereign state.

human rights The inalienable rights such as life, liberty, and the pursuit of happiness that one is entitled to because one is human.

human security The security of people, including their physical safety, their economic and social well-being, respect for their dignity, and the protection of their human rights.

hyperpower The situation of the United States after the Cold War ended. With the Soviet Union's military might greatly diminished and China having primarily only regional power-projecting capability, the United States was unchallenged in the world.

idealism Referred to by realists as *utopianism* since it underestimates the logic of power politics and the constraints this imposes on political action. Idealism as a substantive theory of international relations is generally associated with the claim that it is possible to create a world of peace based on the rule of law.

ideational/ideal interest The psychological, moral, and ethical goals of a state as it sets foreign and domestic policy.

identity The understanding of the self in relationship to an "other." Identities are social and thus always formed in relationship to others. Constructivists generally hold that identities shape interests; we cannot know what we want unless we know who we are. But because identities are social and produced through interactions, identities can change.

immigration controls A government's control of the number of people who may work, study, or relocate to its country. It may include quotas for certain national groups for immigration.

imperialism The practice of foreign conquest and rule in the context of global relations of hierarchy and subordination. It can lead to the establishment of an empire.

improvised explosive device (IED) Usually, a homemade device or a crude booby trap, designed to cause death or injury, that can be made of a variety of explosive materials.

integration A process of ever-closer union between states in a regional or international context. The process often begins with cooperation to solve technical problems.

intellectual property rights Rules that protect the owners of content through copyright, patents, trademarks, and trade secrets. The World Intellectual Property Organization (WIPO) is the forum where states (184 members in 2010) discuss this issue.

intercontinental ballistic missiles (ICBMs) Weapons system the United States and Soviet Union developed to threaten each other with destruction. The thirty- to forty-minute flight times of the missiles created a situation that is sometimes called "mutually assured destruction" (MAD) or "the balance of terror."

interdependence A condition where states (or peoples) are affected by decisions taken by others. Interdependence can be symmetric (i.e., both sets of actors are affected equally), or it can be asymmetric (i.e., the impact varies between actors). If political or economic costs of interdependence are high, a state is in a vulnerable position. If costs are low, it is a situation of sensitivity interdependence.

intergovernmental organization (IGO) An organization whose members are states, such as the United Nations, NATO, the European Union, the World Trade Organization, the International Monetary Fund, and the Arctic Council.

International Court of Justice (ICJ) The main judicial organ of the United Nations consisting of fifteen judges elected jointly by the General Assembly and Security Council. The ICJ handles disputes between states, not individuals and states, and although a state does not have to participate in a case, if it elects to do so it must obey the decision.

International Covenant on Civil and Political Rights (1966) A covenant set forth by the UN General Assembly that proclaims the "recognition of the inherent dignity and of the inalienable rights of all members of the human family as the foundation of freedom, justice and peace in the world" (ICCPR Preamble). Requires committing parties to respect the civil and political rights of individuals, including the right to life, freedom of religion, freedom of speech, freedom of assembly, electoral rights, and rights to due process and a fair trial.

International Criminal Court (ICC) The first permanent, treaty-based, international criminal court, established to help end impunity for the perpetrators of the most serious crimes of concern to the international community. The ICC is governed by the Rome Statute and an independent international organization.

international institutions Complexes of norms, rules, and practices that prescribe behavioral roles, constrain activity, and shape expectations.

international law The formal rules of conduct that states acknowledge or contract between themselves.

International Monetary Fund (IMF) Established in 1945 with its headquarters in Washington, D.C., the IMF is an organization of 188 countries (as of 2012) working to foster global monetary cooperation, secure financial stability, facilitate international trade, promote high employment and sustainable economic growth, and reduce poverty around the world. Most recently, the IMF has provided financial resources and pursued various programs to promote efficiency and stability in global financial markets and to prevent the financial collapse of Greece.

international nongovernmental organization (INGO) A formal nongovernmental organization with members from at least three countries.

international order The normative and the institutional pattern in the relationship between states. The elements of this may be thought to include such things as sovereignty, the forms of diplomacy, international law, the role of the great powers, and the codes circumscribing the use of force. It is a shared value and condition of stability and predictability in the relations of states.

international organization Any institution with formal procedures and formal membership from three or more countries. The minimum number of countries is set at three, rather than two, because multilateral relationships have significantly greater complexity than bilateral relationships.

international relations The study of the interactions of states (countries) and other actors in the international system. Departments of international relations include concentrations in international security, political economy, foreign policy, human rights, global governance, and environmental issues.

interparadigm debate The debate between the main theoretical approaches in the field of global politics: realism, liberalism, and sometimes Marxism. Some analysts present this debate as one between neorealism and neoliberalism. Critics argue that this is no real debate because the theoretical approaches share many assumptions.

intervention The direct involvement within a state by an outside actor to achieve an outcome preferred by the intervening agency without the consent of the host state.

intrafirm trade The international trade from one branch of a TNC to an affiliate of the same company in a different country.

intransigent foreign policy A foreign policy that challenges the rules established by the great powers or rule-making states.

invisible hand The concept from the eighteenth-century writing of Adam Smith that proposed governments leave trade and financial sectors alone.

jihad In Arabic, *jihad* means "struggle." Jihad can refer to a purely internal struggle to be a better Muslim or a struggle to make society more closely align with the teachings of the Koran.

Kyoto Protocol A global environmental treaty passed in 1997 that set binding targets for thirty-seven industrialized countries and the European community for reducing greenhouse-gas emissions.

League of Nations The first permanent collective international security organization aimed at preventing future wars and resolving global problems. The League failed due to the unwillingness of the United States to join and the inability of its members to commit to a real international community.

legitimacy An authority that is respected and recognized by those it rules and by other rulers or leaders of other states. The source of legitimacy can be laws or a constitution and the support of the society.

levels of analysis Analysts of global politics may examine factors at various levels—such as individual, domestic, systemic, and global—to explain actions and events. Each level provides possible explanations on a different scale.

liberal account of rights The belief that humans have inherent rights that the state has a responsibility to protect.

liberal democracy A government that champions freedom of the individual, constitutional civil and political rights, and laissez-faire economic arrangements.

liberal feminism A position that advocates equal rights for women but also supports a more progressive policy agenda, including social justice, peace, economic well-being, and ecological balance.

liberal internationalism A perspective that seeks to transform international relations to emphasize peace, individual freedom, and prosperity and to replicate domestic models of liberal democracy at the international level.

liberalism A theoretical approach that argues for human rights, parliamentary democracy, and free trade—while also maintaining that all such goals must begin *within a state*.

liberalism of privilege The perspective that developed democratic states have a responsibility to spread liberal values for the benefit of all peoples of the earth.

liberalization Government policies that reduce the role of the state in the economy, such as the dismantling of trade tariffs and barriers, the deregulation and opening of the financial sector to foreign investors, and the privatization of state enterprises.

maldevelopment The failure of states to develop economically and politically because of the nature of the international system and its distribution of power.

market democracies See *liberal democracies.*

Marshall Plan An American program of financial and other economic aid for Europe after World War II. It was intended to combat the spread of Soviet communism by helping rebuild European economies.

Marxist theory A theory critical of the status quo, or dominant capitalist paradigm. It is a critique of the capitalist political economy from the view of the revolutionary proletariat, or workers. Marxists' ideal is a stateless and classless society.

mass nationalism The use of nationalist ideology to encourage separation from an existing state. This is a tactic often employed with secessionist nationalism.

material Things we can see, measure, consume, and use, such as military forces, oil, and currency.

material interest The physical goals of state officials as they set foreign and domestic policy.

materialism In this context, it is the spreading of a global consumer culture and popular-culture artifacts like music, books, and movies. Christopher Lasch called this the "ceaseless translation of luxuries into necessities." These elements are seen as undermining traditional cultural values and norms.

material structure An arrangement based on economic, political, and military resources.

middle powers These states, because of their position and past roles in international affairs, have very distinctive interests in world order. Middle powers are activists in international and regional forums, and they are confirmed multilateralists in most issue areas. Most middle powers see themselves as global problem solvers, mediators, and moderators in international disputes (Holbraad 1984; Wood 1998).

military-industrial complex The power and influence of the defense industries and their special relationship with the military. Both have tremendous influence over elected officials.

modernization theory A theory that considers development synonymous with economic growth within the context of a free market international economy.

modern state A political unit within which citizens identify with the state and see the state as legitimate. This state has a monopoly over the use of force and is able to provide citizens with key services.

monopoly capitalism A term introduced by Lenin suggesting that competitive capitalism had been replaced by large corporations that control the market in specific sectors.

most favored nation status The status granted to most trading partners that says trade rules with that country will be the same as those given to their most favored trading partner.

multilateralism The process by which states work together to solve a common problem.

multinational corporation or enterprise (MNC/MNE) A business or firm with administration, production, distribution, and marketing located in countries around the world. Such a business moves money, goods, services, and technology around the world depending on where the firm can make the most profit.

Munich Agreement of 1938 An agreement negotiated after a conference held in Munich between Germany and the United Kingdom and other major powers of Europe along with Czechoslovakia. It permitted the Nazi German annexation of Czechoslovakia's Sudetenland, an area along the Czech border that was inhabited primarily by ethnic Germans.

North Atlantic Treaty Organization (NATO) The organization established by treaty in April 1949 comprising twelve (later sixteen) countries from Western Europe and North America. The most important aspect of the NATO alliance was the American commitment to the defense of Western Europe. Today, NATO has twenty-eight member states.

nation A community of people who share a common sense of identity, which may be derived from language, culture, or ethnicity; this community may be a minority within a single country or live in more than one country.

national interest The material and ideational goals of a nation-state.

nationalism The *idea* that the world is divided into nations that provide the overriding focus of political identity and loyalty, which in turn should be the basis for defining the population of states. Nationalism also can refer to this idea in the form of a strong sense of identity (*sentiment*) or organizations and movements seeking to realize this idea (*politics*).

national liberation A doctrine promoted by the Soviet Union and other nationalist groups that encouraged anticolonial or anti-Western insurgencies in the developing world.

national security A fundamental value in the foreign policy of states secured by a variety of tools of statecraft including military actions, diplomacy, economic resources, and international agreements and alliances. It also depends on a stable and productive domestic society.

national self-determination The right or desire of distinct national groups to become states and to rule themselves.

nation-state A political community in which the state claims legitimacy on the grounds that it represents all citizens, including those who may identify as a separate community or nation.

natural law The idea that humans have an essential nature, which dictates that certain kinds of human goods are always and everywhere desired; because of this, there are common moral standards that govern all human relations, and these common standards can be discerned by the application of reason to human affairs.

neoclassical realism A version of realism that combines both structural factors such as the distribution of power and unit-level factors such as the interests of states.

neoliberalism Theory shaped by the ideas of commercial, republican, sociological, and institutional liberalism. Neoliberals see the international system as anarchic but believe relations can be managed by the establishment of international regimes and institutions. Neoliberals think actors with common interests will try to maximize absolute gains.

new terrorists (see *postmodern terrorists*)

new wars Wars of identity between different ethnic communities or nations, and wars that are caused by the collapse of states or the fragmentation of multiethnic states. Most of these new wars are internal or civil wars.

new world order The post–Cold War rhetoric of President George Herbert Walker Bush, who called for a new world order based on neoliberal values of democracy, capitalism, and the rule of law. After periods of turmoil or war, the victors often call for a new world order based on their values, beliefs, and interests.

niche diplomacy Every state has its national interests and its areas of comparative advantage over other international actors. This is its area of expertise and where it has the greatest interest. Hence, this is where the state concentrates its foreign policy resources.

noncompliance The failure of states or other actors to abide by treaties or rules supported by international regimes.

nongovernmental actor Any participant in global politics that is neither acting in the name of government nor created and served by government.

nongovernmental organization (NGO) An organization, usually a grass-roots one, with policy goals but not governmental in makeup. An NGO is any group of people relating to each other regularly in some formal manner and engaging in collective action, provided the activities are noncommercial and nonviolent and are not on behalf of a government.

nonnuclear weapons state (NNWS) A state that is party to the Treaty on the Nonproliferation of Nuclear Weapons, meaning that it does not possess nuclear weapons.

nonpolar An international system in which power is not concentrated in a few states but is diffused among a variety of state and nonstate actors.

nonstate actor Any participant in global politics that is not a state. Examples include nongovernmental organizations (NGOs), intergovernmental organizations (IGOs), global crime syndicates, terrorist networks, and multinational corporations (MNCs).

nonintervention The principle that external powers should not intervene in the domestic affairs of sovereign states.

normative orientation In foreign policy, promoting certain norms and values and being prescriptive in one's foreign policy goals.

normative theory The systematic analyses of the ethical, moral, and political principles that either govern or ought to govern the organization or conduct of global politics. The belief that theories should be concerned with what ought to be rather than merely diagnosing what is.

norms These specify general standards of behavior and identify the rights and obligations of states. Together, norms and principles define the essential character of a regime, and these cannot be changed without transforming the nature of the regime.

nuclear deterrence Explicit, credible threats to use nuclear weapons in retaliation to deter an adversary from attacking with nuclear weapons.

nuclear terrorism The use of or threat to use nuclear weapons or nuclear materials to achieve the goals of rogue states or revolutionary or radical organizations.

nuclear weapon state (NWS) A state that is party to the non-proliferation treaty and has tested a nuclear weapon or other nuclear explosive device before January 1, 1967.

offensive realism A structural theory of realism that views states as power maximizers.

offshore finance centers The extraterritorial banks that investors use for a range of reasons, including the desire to avoid domestic taxes, regulations, and law enforcement agencies.

oligarchs A term from ancient Greece to describe members of a small group that controls a state.

options Derivatives that give parties a right (without obligation) to buy or sell at a specific price for a stipulated period of time up to the contract's expiry date.

Organization of African Unity (OAU) A regional organization founded in 1963 as a way to foster solidarity among African countries, promote African independence, and throw off the vestiges of colonial rule. The Organization of African Unity had a policy of noninterference in member states, and it had no means for intervening in conflicts; as a result, this organization could be only a passive bystander in many violent conflicts.

Organization of American States (OAS) A regional international organization composed of thirty-five member states. It is the world's oldest regional organization, founded in 1890 as the International Union of American Republics and changing its name to Organization of American States in 1948. The goals of this organization are to create "an order of peace and justice, to promote their solidarity, to strengthen their collaboration, and to defend their sovereignty, their territorial integrity, and their independence."

Ostpolitik The West German government's "Eastern Policy" of the mid- to late 1960s, designed to develop relations between West Germany and members of the Warsaw Pact.

paradigm A model or example. In the case of international relations theory, the term is a rough synonym for "academic perspective." A paradigm provides the essential basis for a theory, describing what is real and significant in a given area so that we can select appropriate research questions.

paradox A seemingly absurd or self-contradictory statement that, when investigated or explained, may prove to be well founded or true.

patriarchy A persistent societywide structure within which gender relations are defined by male dominance and female subordination.

peace dividend The misplaced belief that the end of the Cold War would bring about a fundamental change in international relations and provide funds for domestic programs or even result in a reduction in taxes.

peace enforcement Designed to bring hostile parties to agreement and may occur without the consent of the parties.

peacekeeping The interposition of third-party military personnel to keep warring parties apart.

peacemaking Active diplomatic efforts to seek a resolution to an international dispute that has already escalated.

Peace of Utrecht (1713) The agreement that ended the War of the Spanish Succession and helped to consolidate the link between sovereign authority and territorial boundaries in Europe. This treaty refined the territorial scope of sovereign rights of states.

Peace of Westphalia (1648) Ended the Thirty Years' War and was crucial in delimiting the political rights and authority of European monarchs.

perestroika Gorbachev's policy of restructuring, pursued in tandem with glasnost and intended to modernize the Soviet political and economic system.

pluralism A political theory holding that political power and influence in society do not belong just to the citizens nor only to elite groups in various sectors of society but are distributed among a wide number of groups in the society. It can also mean a recognition of ethnic, racial, and cultural diversity.

political-economy approach The study of the interactions between states or public actors and the market at domestic and international levels.

positivism The position arguing that we can explain the social world as effectively as natural and physical scientists explain phenomena.

postcolonial feminism A position that works at the intersection of class, race, and gender on a global scale. It especially analyzes the gendered effects of transnational culture and the unequal division of labor in the global political economy.

postconflict peace building Activities launched after a conflict has ended that seek to end the condition that caused the conflict.

postmodern feminism A position that criticizes the basic distinction between sex and gender that earlier feminist theories found so useful in thinking about the roles of men and women in global politics and in analyzing the gendered concepts of global politics itself. This distinction between sex and gender was useful because it allowed feminists to argue that the position of women and men in the world was not natural but highly contingent and dependent on the meaning given to biological differences.

postmodernity An international system where domestic and international affairs are intertwined, national borders are permeable, and states have rejected the use of force for resolving conflict. The European Union is an example of the evolution of the state-centric system (Cooper 2003).

postmodern or new terrorists Groups and individuals subscribing to millennial and apocalyptic ideologies and system-level goals. Most value destruction for its own sake, unlike most terrorists in the past, who had specific goals, usually tied to a territory.

postmodern state A political unit within which citizens are less nationalistic and more cosmopolitan in their outlook on both domestic and foreign policy. Policy-making authority for this kind of state is shared with a variety of actors at the local, national, regional, and international levels.

post–Washington Consensus A slightly modified version of the Washington Consensus promoting economic growth through trade liberalization coupled with pro-poor growth and poverty-reduction policies.

poverty According to the United Nations, poverty is a denial of choices and opportunities, a violation of human dignity. It means lack of basic capacity provided by material possessions or money to participate effectively in society.

power This is a contested concept. Joseph Nye (2011) states that power is the capacity to do things and, in social and political situations, to affect others to get the outcome one wants. Sources of power include material or tangible resources and control over meaning or ideas.

preemptive war A war with another country that is itself clearly about to attack.

premodern state A state within which the primary identity of citizens or subjects is to national, religious, or ethnic communities. People think of themselves as members of the subnational group first rather than the state.

preventive diplomacy Measures that states take to keep a disagreement from escalating.

preventive war A war to eliminate a perceived threat from another country, often started prior to the escalation of a crisis or before the enemy is itself prepared to attack.

problem-solving theory Realism and liberalism are problem-solving theories that address issues and questions within the dominant paradigm or the present system. How can we fix capitalism? How can we make a society more democratic? These are problem-solving questions that assume nothing is wrong with the core elements of the system.

promotive foreign policy A foreign policy that promotes the values and interests of a state and seeks to create an international system based on these values.

protectionism A variety of political actions taken to protect domestic industries against foreign producers. Usually, this means the use of tariffs, nontariff barriers, and subsidies to protect domestic interests.

Protestant Reformation A social and political movement begun in 1517 in reaction to the widespread perception that the Catholic Church had become corrupt and had lost its moral compass.

public diplomacy The use of media, the Internet, and other cultural outlets to communicate the message of a state.

radical liberalism The utopian side of liberalism best exemplified by the academic community called the World Order Models Project (WOMP). These scholars advocate a world in which states promote values like social justice, economic well-being, peace, and ecological balance. The scholars see the liberal order as predatory and clearly in need of transformation.

rapprochement The reestablishment of more friendly relations between the People's Republic of China and the United States in the early 1970s.

realism The theoretical approach that analyzes all international relations as the relation of states engaged in the pursuit of power. Realists see the international system as anarchic, or without a common power, and they believe conflict is endemic in the international system.

realpolitik First used to describe the foreign policy of Bismarck in Prussia, it describes the practice of diplomacy based on the assessment of power, territory, and material interests, with little concern for ethical realities.

reciprocity A form of statecraft that employs a retaliatory strategy, cooperating only if others do likewise.

regime A set of implicit or explicit principles, norms, rules, and decision-making procedures around which actors' expectations converge in a given area of international relations. Often simply defined as a governing arrangement in a regional or global policy area.

regional diversity Each region of the world has experienced economic development differently based on traditions, culture, historical development, and even geographic location.

relative gains One of the factors that realists argue constrain the willingness of states to cooperate. States are less concerned about whether everyone benefits (absolute gains) and more concerned about whether someone may benefit more than someone else.

Responsibility to Protect (R2P) The 2001 final report of the International Commission on Intervention and State Sovereignty; this report and subsequent UN documents (2005 and 2006) state that the international community has the responsibility to (1) prevent mass atrocities with economic, political, and social measures; (2) react to current crises by diplomatic engagement, more coercive actions, and military intervention as a last resort; (3) protect citizens who are victims of war or abuses; (4) rebuild by bringing security and justice to the victim population; and (5) prevent future problems by finding the root causes of crises.

revolution in military affairs (RMA) The effect generated by the marriage of advanced communications and information processing with state-of-the-art weapons and delivery systems. It is a means of overcoming the uncertainty and confusion that are part of any battle in war.

risk culture A pattern of relations within which people share the same perils.

secessionist nationalism The use of nationalist ideology to create a new state, often by seceding from an existing multiethnic state.

security The measures taken by states to ensure the safety of their citizens, the protection of their way of life, and the survival of their nation-state. Security can also mean the ownership of property that gives an individual the ability to secure the enjoyment or enforcement of a right or a basic human need.

security community A regional group of countries that have the same guiding philosophic ideals—usually liberal-democratic principles, norms, and ethics—and tend to have the same style of political systems.

security dilemma In an anarchic international system, one with no common central power, when one state seeks to improve its security it creates insecurity in other states.

self-help In realist theory, in an anarchical environment, states cannot assume other states will come to their defense even if they are allies. Each state must take care of itself.

September 11, 2001 The day Islamic terrorists in the United States hijacked four passenger jets, crashing two into the World Trade Center in New York, one into the Pentagon, and one into a field in Pennsylvania; also known as 9/11.

sex and gender Sex is biological difference, born male or female; the sex act; sexual difference. Gender is what it means to be male or female in a particular place or time; the social construction of sexual difference.

sharia law Traditional Islamic law of the Koran ("al Qur'an") and the "Sunna," which are the interpretations of the life of the Prophet Muhammad.

skyjacking The takeover of a commercial airplane for the purpose of taking hostages and using these hostages to bargain for a particular political or economic goal.

social democracy A system of government in which the state may regulate the economy in a number of ways and through a variety of instruments. It may use budgetary and fiscal policies to provide private corporations with incentives to be responsive to the people. In an ideal social democratic society, government uses its political power to ensure that no one in that society is unfairly advantaged or disadvantaged.

socialist/Marxist feminism Because of its insistence on the role of material and primarily economic forces in determining the lives of women, this approach is also sometimes known as *materialist feminism* (Hennessy and Ingraham 1997). For Marxist feminism, the cause of women's inequality is found in the capitalist system; overthrowing capitalism is the necessary route for the achievement of the equal treatment of women (Sargent 1981).

social movement A mode of collective action that challenges ways of life, thinking, dominant norms, and moral codes; seeks answers to global problems; and promotes reform or transformation in political and economic institutions.

social structure An arrangement based on ideas, norms, values, and shared beliefs. According to constructivists, the social domain does not exist in nature but is constructed through processes of interaction and the sharing of meaning.

society of states An association of sovereign states based on their common interests, values, and norms.

soft power A concept developed by Joseph Nye to describe the influence and authority deriving from the attraction that a country's political, social, and economic ideas, beliefs, and practices have for people living in other countries.

specialized agencies International institutions that have a special relationship with the central system of the United Nations but are constitutionally independent, having their own assessed budgets, executive heads and committees, and assemblies of the representatives of all state members.

social movement People with a diffuse sense of collective identity, solidarity, and common purpose that usually leads to collective political behavior. The concept covers all the different NGOs and networks plus all their members and all the other individuals who share the common value(s). Thus, the women's movement and the environmental movement are much more than the specific NGOs that provide leadership and focus on the desire for social change.

sovereign equality The idea that all countries have the same rights, including the right of noninterference in their internal affairs.

sovereignty The condition of a state having control and authority over its own territory and being free from any higher legal authority. It is related to, but distinct from, the condition of a government being free from any external political constraints.

Special Drawing Right (SDR) Members of the International Monetary Fund (IMF) have the right to borrow this asset from the organization up to the amount that the country has invested in the IMF. The SDR is based on the value of a "basket" of the world's leading currencies: British pound, euro, Japanese yen, and US dollar.

standards of civilization A nineteenth-century, European discourse about which values and norms made a country civilized or barbaric and uncivilized. The conclusion was that civilized countries should colonize barbaric regions for the latter's benefit.

standard operating procedures (SOPs) The prepared-response patterns that organizations create to react to general categories of events, crises, and actions.

standpoint feminism Drawing on socialist-feminist interpretations of structure, standpoint feminism began to identify how the subordination of women, as a particular class, by virtue of their sex rather than economic standing (although the two are seen as related), possessed a unique perspective—or standpoint—on global politics as a result of their subordination.

state A legal territorial entity composed of a stable population and a government; it possesses a monopoly over the legitimate use of force; its sovereignty is recognized by other states in the international system.

statecraft The methods and tools that national leaders use to achieve the national interests of a state.

state sovereignty The concept that all countries are equal under international law and that they are protected from outside interference; this is the basis on which the United Nations and other international and regional organizations operate.

state-strengthening nationalism The use of nationalist ideology to bolster or reform a government or seek to regain territory at the expense of other states.

state system The regular patterns of interaction between states but without implying any shared values between them. This is distinguished from the view of a "society" of states.

Strategic Arms Reductions Treaty (START) Negotiations between the United States and Soviet Union over limiting nuclear arsenals began in 1982 and progressed at a very slow pace over eight years. The eventual treaty in 1991 broke new ground because it called for a reduction of nuclear arms rather than just a limit on the growth of these weapons.

Strategic Defense Initiative (SDI) A controversial strategic policy advocated by the Reagan administration and nuclear physicists such as Edward Teller, who helped create the hydrogen bomb. The plan, which is often derisively nicknamed "Star Wars," called for a defensive missile shield that would make Soviet offensive missiles ineffective by destroying them in flight.

structural realism (neorealism) A theory of realism that maintains the international system and the condition of anarchy or no common power push states and individuals to act in a way that places interests over ideologies. This condition creates a self-help system. The international system is seen as a structure acting on the state with individuals below the level of the state acting as agency on the state as a whole.

summit diplomacy A direct meeting between heads of government (of the superpowers in particular) to resolve major problems. The summit became a regular mode of contact during the Cold War.

superpower A state with a dominant position in the international system. It has the will and the means to influence the actions of other states in favor of its own interests, and it projects its power on a global scale to secure its national interests.

superstructure The government or political structure that is controlled by those who own the means of production.

supranational global organization An authoritative international organization that operates above the nation-state.

supraterratoriality Social, economic, cultural, and political connections that transcend territorial geography.

survival In this context, it is the survival of the person by the provision of adequate food, clean water, clothing, shelter, medical care, and protection from violence and crime.

sustainable development Development that meets the needs of the present without compromising the ability of future generations to meet their own needs.

tactics The conduct and management of military capabilities in or near the battle area.

technology transfer The process of sharing skills, knowledge, technologies, methods of manufacturing, and facilities among governments and private actors (e.g., corporations) to ensure that scientific and technological developments are accessible to a wider range of users for application in new products, processes, materials, or services.

terrorism The use of violence by nonstate groups or, in some cases, states to inspire fear by attacking civilians and/or symbolic targets and eliminating opposition groups. This is done for purposes such as drawing widespread attention to a grievance, provoking a severe response, or wearing down an opponent's moral resolve to effect political change.

theocracy A state based on religion.

theory A proposed explanation of an event or behavior of an actor in the real world. Definitions range from "an unproven assumption" to "a working hypothesis that proposes an explanation for an action or behavior." In international relations, we have intuitive theories, empirical theories, and normative theories.

think tank (or research institute) A body of experts providing advice and ideas on specific political or economic problems.

third-tier states Sometimes called the "less-developed states" or the "premodern states." These countries fail to provide the basics, such as border protection, law and order, and maintenance of a functioning economy.

Thirty Years' War (1618–1648) The last of the great wars in Europe fought nominally for religion.

trade liberalization The removal or reduction of barriers to free trade such as tariffs or quotas on the trading of specific goods.

transborder Economic, political, social, or cultural activities crossing or extending across a border.

transnational actor Any nonstate or nongovernmental actor, such as a multinational corporation or one country's religious humanitarian organization, that has dealings with any actor from another country or with an international organization.

transnational advocacy network (TAN) A network of activists—often, a coalition of NGOs—distinguishable largely by the centrality of principled ideas or values in motivating its formation.

transnational corporation A company or business that has affiliates in different countries.

transnational relations Interactions across national boundaries when at least one actor is a nonstate actor (as defined by Robert Keohane and Joseph Nye).

transnational terrorist networks Terrorists use existing global or transnational economic, transportation, and communication systems to manage and maintain terrorist organizations around the world. These networks facilitate the movement of followers and material to global locations.

Treaty of Versailles, 1919 Formally ended World War I (1914–1918).

trench warfare Warfare in which armies dug elaborate defensive fortifications in the ground, as both sides did in World War I. Because of the power of weapons like machine guns and rapid-fire cannons, trenches often gave the advantage in battle to the defenders.

Truman Doctrine A statement made by US President Harry Truman in March 1947 that it "must be the policy of the United States to support free people who are resisting attempted subjugation by armed minorities or by outside pressures." Intended to persuade Congress to support limited aid to Turkey and Greece, the doctrine came to underpin the policy of containment and American economic and political support for its allies.

Trusteeship Council Upon creation of the United Nations, this council was established to provide international supervision for eleven trust territories administered by seven member states in an effort to prepare them for self-government or independence. By 1994, all trust territories had attained self-government or independence, and the council now meets on an ad hoc basis.

underdevelopment The lack, in a state or region within a state, of economic resources and adequate political structures to maintain security, order, and well-being.

United Nations Founded in 1945 following World War II, it is an international organization composed of 193 member states dedicated to addressing issues related to peace and security, development, human rights, humanitarian affairs, and international law.

United Nations Charter (1945) The legal regime that created the United Nations as the world's only supranational organization. The charter defines the structure of the United Nations, the powers of its constitutive agencies, and the rights and obligations of sovereign states party to the charter. Among other things, the charter is the key legal document limiting the use of force to instances of self-defense and collective peace enforcement endorsed by the UN Security Council.

United Nations Economic and Social Council (ECOSOC) This council is intended to coordinate the economic and social work of the United Nations and the UN family organizations. The ECOSOC has a direct link to civil society through communications with nongovernmental organizations (NGOs).

United Nations General Assembly Often referred to as a "parliament of nations," it is composed of all member states, which meet to consider the world's most pressing problems. Each state has one vote, and a two-thirds majority in the General Assembly is required for decisions on key issues. Decisions reached by the General Assembly only have the status of recommendations and are not binding.

United Nations Secretariat The Secretariat carries out the administrative work of the United Nations as directed by the General Assembly, Security Council, and other organs. The Secretariat is led by the secretary-general, who provides overall administrative guidance.

United Nations Security Council The council made up of five permanent member states (sometimes called the P-5)—namely, Great Britain, China, France, Russia, and the United States—and ten nonpermanent members. The P-5 all have a veto power over all Security Council decisions.

Universal Declaration of Human Rights The principal normative document on human rights, adopted by the UN General Assembly in 1948 and accepted as authoritative by most states and other international actors. It asserts that all humans beings are inherently entitled to a certain set of universal rights, and it proposes "a common standard of achievement for all people and all nations" (UDHR Preamble).

venture philanthropy The practice of supporting philanthropists or social entrepreneurs by providing them with networking and leveraging opportunities.

vertical proliferation An increase in the number of nuclear weapons a state possesses and in other technologies used for delivery of weapons. Recently, concerns were raised about the production of tactical nuclear weapons like bunker busters that could be used to destroy caves and underground facilities in Afghanistan.

veto power The right of the five permanent members of the Security Council (United States, Russia, China, France, and Great Britain) to forbid any action by the United Nations.

virtual jihad academy The use of the Internet to plan, promote, and propagate both physical attacks and cyberattacks as well as train and educate future followers or jihadists.

Warsaw Pact An agreement of mutual defense and military aid signed in May 1955 in response to West Germany's rearmament and entry into NATO. It comprised the USSR and seven communist states (though Albania withdrew support in 1961). The pact was officially dissolved in July 1991.

Washington Consensus The belief of key opinion formers in Washington that global welfare would be maximized by the universal application of neoliberal economic policies that favor a minimalist state and an enhanced role for the market.

weapons of mass destruction A category defined by the United Nations in 1948 to include "atomic explosive weapons, radioactive material weapons, lethal chemical and biological weapons, and any weapons developed in the future which have characteristics comparable in destructive effects to those of the atomic bomb or other weapons mentioned above."

widening school of international security Sometimes called the Copenhagen school, these are authors who extend the definition of security to include economic, political, societal, and environmental policy areas.

World Bank Group A collection of five agencies, the first established in 1945, with head offices in Washington, D.C. The WBG promotes development in medium- and low-income countries with project loans, structural-adjustment programs, and various advisory services.

world order A wider category of order than the international. It takes as its units of order, not states, but individual human beings, and assesses the degree of order on the basis of the delivery of certain kinds of goods (be they security, human rights, basic needs, or justice) for humanity as a whole.

world-system theory A theory emphasizing that world systems, and not individuals or states, should be the basic unit of analysis. Thus, the political and economic structure of the world shapes global politics. "World system" refers to the international division of labor, which divides the world into core countries, semiperiphery countries, and periphery countries. The foreign policies of these states are shaped by their position in the global system.

World Trade Organization (WTO) A permanent institution established in 1995 to replace the provisional GATT. It has greater powers of enforcement and a wider agenda, covering services, intellectual property, and investment issues as well as merchandise trade.

zero-sum world A pessimistic view that, in any interaction, another's gains are your losses.

References

Acharya, A. (2004), "A Holistic Paradigm," *Security Dialogue* 35: 355–356.

Acharya, A. (2007), *Promoting Human Security: Ethical, Normative and Educational Frameworks in South East Asia* (Paris: United Nations Scientific, Cultural and Educational Organization).

Addams, J. (1922), *Peace and Bread in Time of War*. With introduction by Katherine Joslin. Urbana: University of Illinois Press, 2002. Reprint.

Adler, E. (1992), "The Emergence of Cooperation: National Epistemic Communities and the International Evolution of the Idea of Nuclear Arms Control," *International Organization* 46: 101–145.

Allison, G. (2000), "The Impact of Globalization on National and International Security." In J. S. Nye and J. D. Donahue (eds.), *Governance in a Globalizing World*, 72–85 (Washington, D.C.: Brookings Institution).

Andrew, H. (2002), "Norms and Ethics in International Relations." In W. Carlnaes, T. Risse and B. Simmons (editors), *Handbook of International Relations* (Thousand Oaks, C.A.: Sage).

Anheier, H., Glasius, M. and Kaldor, M. (editors), (2004), Global Civil Society Yearbook 2004 (London: Sage).

Armstrong, D. (1993), *Revolution and World Order: The Revolutionary State in International Society* (Oxford: Clarendon Press).

Aron, R. (1966), *The Century of Total War* (Garden City, N.Y.).

Axworthy, L. (2003), *Navigating a New World* (Toronto: Alfred A. Knopf Canada).

Bacevich, A. (2008), "Introduction." In R. Niebuhr, *The Irony of American History* (Chicago: University of Chicago Press).

Bakker, E. (2006), *Jihadi Terrorists in Europe, Their Characteristics and the Circumstances in Which They Joined the Jihad: An Exploratory Study* (Clingendael: Netherlands Institute of International Relations).

Bank for International Settlements (1996), *International Banking and Financial Market Developments* (Basel: Bank for International Settlements).

Bank for International Settlements (2006), Semiannual OTC Derivatives Statistics at End-June 2006. www.bis.org/statistics (accessed June 25, 2007).

Barnett, M. (2011), "Social Constructivism." In Baylis, Smith, and Owens, *The Globalization of World Politics* (Oxford, UK: OUP).

Barraclough, G. (ed.) (1984), *The Times Atlas of World History* (London: Times Books).

Beitz, C. (1979), *Political Theory and International Relations* (Princeton, N.J.: Princeton University Press).

Bellamy, A. J. (2002), *Kosovo and International Society* (Basingstoke, UK: Palgrave).

Bello, W. (1994), *Dark Victory: The United States, Structural Adjustment and Global Poverty* (London: Pluto Press).

Bennett, J., and George, S. (1987). *The Hunger Machine* (Cambridge: Polity Press).

Bethell, L. (1970), *The Abolition of the Brazilian Slave Trade: Britain, Brazil and the Slave Trade Question 1807–1869* (Cambridge: Cambridge University Press).

Bloom, M. (2005), *Dying to Win: The Allure of Suicide Terror* (New York: Columbia University Press).

Booth, K. (1999), "Three Tyrannies." In T. Dunne and N. J. Wheeler (eds.), *Human Rights in Global Politics* (Cambridge: Cambridge University Press).

Booth, K. (ed.) (2004), *Critical Security Studies in World Politics* (Boulder, Col.: Lynne Rienner).

Booth, K., and Dunne, T. (1999), "Learning Beyond Frontiers." In T. Dunne and N. J. Wheeler (eds.), *Human Rights in Global Politics*, 303–328 (Cambridge: Cambridge University Press).

Braun, L. (1987), *Selected Writings on Feminism and Socialism* (Bloomington: Indiana University Press).

Breman, J. G. (2001), "The Ears of the Hippopotamus: Manifestations, Determinants, and Estimates of the Malaria Burden." *American Journal of Tropical Medicine and Hygiene* 64(1/2): 1–11. http://www.ajtmh.org/cgi/reprint/64/1_suppl/1-c (accessed June 25, 2007).

Brewer, A. (1990), *Marxist Theories of Imperialism: A Critical Survey*, 2nd ed. (London: Routledge).

Brittan, A. (1989), *Masculinity and Power* (Oxford: Basil Blackwell).

Brocklehurst, H. (2007), "Children and War." In A. Collins (ed.), *Contemporary Security Studies*, 367–382 (Oxford: Oxford University Press).

Brodie, B. (ed.) (1946), *The Absolute Weapon: Atomic Power and World Order* (New York: Harcourt Brace).

Brown, D. (2006), "Study Claims Iraq's 'Excess' Death Toll Has Reached 655,000." *Washington Post*, October 11, A12.

Brown, L. R., and Kane, H. (1995), *Full House: Reassessing the Earth's Population Carrying Capacity* (London: Earthscan).

Brundtland, G. H., et al. (1987), *Our Common Future: Report of the World Commission on Environment and Development* (The Brundtland Report) (Oxford: Oxford University Press).

Bull, H. (1977), *The Anarchical Society: A Study of Order in World Politics* (London: Macmillan).

Buvinic, M. (1997), "Women in Poverty: A New Global Underclass." *Foreign Policy*: 38–53.

Buzan, B. (1991), *People, State & Fear: An Agenda for International Security Studies in the Post-Cold War Era* (second edition), (Hertfordshire: Harvester Wheatsheaf). First published in 1983.

Cammack, P. (2002), "The Mother of All Governments: The World Bank's Matrix for Global Governance." In R. Wilkinson and S. Hughes (eds.), *Global Governance: Critical Perspectives* (London: Routledge).

Carver, T. (1996), *Gender Is Not a Synonym for Women* (Boulder, Col.: Lynne Rienner).

Castells, M. (2005), "Global Governance and Global Politics," *PS* 38(1): 9–16.

Centers for Disease Control (2005), Fact Sheet: Tuberculosis in the United States, March 17. http://www.cdc.gov/tb/pubs/TBfactsheets.htm (accessed June 25, 2007).

Chalk, P. (1996), *West European Terrorism and Counter-Terrorism: The Evolving Dynamic* (New York: St. Martin's Press).

Charles Norchi (2004) "Human Rights: A Global Common Interest" in Jean Krasno, ed., *The United Nations: Confronting the Challenges of a Global Society* (Lynne Rienner Publishers).

Ching, F. (1999), "Social Impact of the Regional Financial Crisis." In Linda Y. C. Lim, F. Ching, and Bernardo M. Villegas (eds.), *The Asian Economic Crisis: Policy Choices, Social Consequences and the Philippine Case* (New York: Asia Society). http://www.asiasociety.org/publications/update_crisis_ching.html (accessed June 25, 2007).

Christensen, T., Jørgensen, K. E., and Wiener, A. (eds.) (2001), *The Social Construction of Europe* (London: Sage).

Clark, I. (1980), *Reform and Resistance in the International Order* (Cambridge: Cambridge University Press).

Clark, I. (1989), *The Hierarchy of States: Reform and Resistance in the International Order* (Cambridge: Cambridge University Press).

Coglianese, C. (2000), "Globalization and the Design of International Institutions." In J. S. Nye and J. D. Donahue (eds.), *Governance in a Globalizing World*, 297–318 (Washington, D.C.: Brookings Institution Press).

Cohn, C. (1987), "Sex and Death in the Rational World of Defense Intellectuals," *Signs* 12(4): 687–718.

Connell, R. W. (1995), *Masculinities* (London: Routledge).

Cooper, A., Higgott, R., and Nossal, K. R. (1993), *Relocating Middle Powers* (Vancouver: University of British Columbia Press).

Cooper, R. (2000), *The Breaking of Nations: Order and Chaos in the 21st Century* (New York: Atlantic Monthly Press).

Cox, R. (1981), "Social Forces, States and World Orders: Beyond International Relations Theory," *Millennium Journal of International Studies* 10(2): 126–155.

Cox, R. (1989), "Middlepowermanship, Japan, and the Future World Order," *International Journal* 44(4): 823–862.

Crenshaw, M. (ed.) (1983), *Terrorism, Legitimacy, and Power* (Middletown, Conn.: Wesleyan University Press).

Cronin, A. K. (2002–2003), "Behind the Curve: Globalization and International Terrorism," *International Security* 27(3): 30–58.

Davis, Z. S., and Frankel, B. (eds.) (1993), *The Proliferation Puzzle: Why Nuclear Weapons Spread and What Results* (London: Frank Cass).

Department for International Development (2005), *Fighting Poverty to Build a Safer World* (London: HMSO). http://www.dfid.gov.uk/pubs/files/securityforall.pdf (accessed June 25, 2007).

Department for International Development (2006), *Eliminating World Poverty: Making Governance Work for the Poor*, Cm 6876 (London: HMSO).

http://www.dfid.gov.uk/pubs/files/whitepaper2006/wp2006section3.pdf, (accessed June 25, 2007).

Doyle, M. W. (1986), "Liberalism and World Politics," *American Political Science Review* 80(4): 1151–1169.

Doyle, M. W. (1995) "On Democratic Peace," *International Security* 19(4): 164–184.

Doyle, M. (1995a), "Liberalism and World Politics Revisited." In Charles W. Kegley (ed.) *Controversies in International Relations Theory: Realism and the Neoliberal Challenge*, 83–105 (N.Y.: St. Martins Press).

Doyle, M. (1995b), "On Democratic Peace" *International Security*, 19(4): 164–84.

Doyle, M. W. (1997), *Ways of War and Peace: Realism, Liberalism, and Socialism* (New York: W. W. Norton).

Easterly, W. (2002), "How Did Heavily Indebted Poor Countries Become Heavily Indebted? Reviewing Two Decades of Debt Relief," *World Development* 30(10): 1677–1696.

Ekins, P. (1992), *A New World Order: Grassroots Movements for Global Change* (London: Routledge).

Elshtain, J. B. (1987), *Women and War* (New York: Basic Books).

Elshtain, J. B. and Tobias, S. (eds.) (1990), *Women, Militarism, and War: Essays in History, Politics, and Social Theory* (Totowa, N.J.: Rowman & Littlefield).

Enloe, C. (1989), *Bananas, Beaches and Bases: Making Feminist Sense of International Politics* (London: Pandora Books).

Enloe, C. (1993), *The Morning After: Sexual Politics at the End of the Cold War* (Berkeley: University of California Press).

Enloe, C. (2000), *Maneuvers: The International Politics of Militarizing Women's Lives* (Berkeley: University of California Press).

Environmental Degradation and Conflict in Darfur: A Workshop Organized by the University of Peace of the United Nations and the Peace Research Institute, University of Khartoum, Khartoum, December 15–16 2004.

Falk, R. (1995a), "Liberalism at the Global Level: The Last of the Independent Commissions," *Millennium Special Issue: The Globalization of Liberalism?* 24(3): 563–576.

Falk, R. (1995b), *On Humane Governance: Toward a New Global Politics* (Cambridge: Polity Press).

Fanon, F. (1990), *The Wretched of the Earth* (Harmondsworth: Penguin).

Fausto-Sterling, A. (1992), *Myths of Gender: Biological Theories About Women and Men* (New York: Basic Books).

Fausto-Sterling, A. (2000), *Sexing the Body: Gender Politics and the Construction of Sexuality* (New York: Basic Books).

Finnemore, M. (1996a), "Norms, Culture, and World Politics: Insights from Sociology's Institutionalism," *International Organization* 50(2): 325–347.

Finnemore, M. (1996b), *National Interests in International Society* (Ithaca, N.Y.: Cornell University Press).

Finnemore, M., and Sikkink, K. (October 1998), "International Norm Dynamics and Political Change," *International Organization* 52: 887–918.

Finnis, J. (1980), *Natural Law and Natural Rights* (Oxford: Clarendon Press).

Forsythe, D. P. (1988), "The United Nations and Human Rights." In L. S. Finkelstein (ed.), *Politics in the United Nations System* (Durham, N.C., and London: Duke University Press).

Fox-Keller, E. (1985), *Reflections on Gender and Science* (New Haven, Conn.: Yale University Press).

Frank, A. G. (1967), *Capitalism and Underdevelopment in Latin America* (New York: Monthly Review Press).

Friedman, J., (ed.) (2003), *Globalization, the State and Violence* (Oxford: AltaMira Press).

Friedman, T. (2005), *The World is Flat: A Brief History of the 21st Century* (New York: Farrar, Straus, Giroux).

Fukuyama, F. (1989), "The End of History," *The National Interest* 16(Summer): 3–18.

Gaddis, J. L. (2004), *Surprise, Security and the American Experience* (Cambridge, Mass.: Harvard University Press).

Gardner, G. T. (1994), *Nuclear Nonproliferation: A Primer* (London and Boulder, Col.: Lynne Rienner).

Gendering Human Security: From Marginalisation to the Integration of Women in Peace-Building (Oslo: Norwegian Institute of International Affairs and Fafo Forum on Gender Relations in Post-Conflict Transitions, 2001). http://www.fafo.no/pub/rapp/352/352.pdf (accessed June 25, 2007).

George, A. (1991), *Forceful Persuasion* (Washington, D.C.: USIP).

Giddens, A. (2000), *Runaway World: How Globalization is Shaping Our Lives* (London: Routledge).

Gioseffi, D. (ed.) (2003), *Women on War: An International Anthology of Women's Writings from Antiquity to the Present*, 2nd ed. (New York: Feminist Press at the City University of New York).

Glendon, M. A. (2002), *A World Made New: Eleanor Roosevelt and the Universal Declaration of Human Rights* (New York: Random House).

Goldstein, J., and Keohane R. (eds.) (1993), *Ideas and Foreign Policy: Beliefs, Institutions, and Political Change* (Ithaca, N.Y.: Cornell University press).

Gong, G. W. (1984), *The Standard of "Civilization" in International Society* (Oxford: Clarendon Press).

Goodman, D., and Redclift, M. (1991), *Refashioning Nature: Food, Ecology and Culture* (London: Routledge).

Gottlieb, R. S. (ed.) (1989), *An Anthology of Western Marxism: From Lukacs and Gramsci to Socialist-Feminism* (Oxford: Oxford University Press).

Gowa, J. (1983), *Closing the Cold Window: Domestic Politics and the End of Bretton Woods* (Ithaca, N.Y.: Cornell University Press).

Grace, C. S. (1994), *Nuclear Weapons: Principles, Effects and Survivability* (London: Brassey's).

Gray, C. S. (1996a), "The Second Nuclear Age: Insecurity, Proliferation, and the Control of Arms." In W. Murray (ed.), *The Brassey's Mershon American Defense Annual, 1995–1996: The United States and The Emerging Strategic Environment*, 135–154 (Washington, D.C.: Brassey's).

Gray, C. S. (1999b), "Clausewitz Rules, OK? The Future Is the Past—with GPS," *Review of International Studies* 25: 161–182.

Green, D. (1995), *Silent Revolution: The Rise of Market Economics in Latin America* (London: Latin America Bureau).

Greenwood, B. M., Bojang, K., Whitty, C. J., and Targett, G. A. (2005), "Malaria," *The Lancet* 365(9469): 1487–1498.

Gunaratna, R. (2002), *Inside Al Qaeda: Global Network of Terror* (New York: Columbia University Press).

Haass, R. (2008), "The Age of Nonpolarity," *Foreign Affairs* 87(3): 44–56.

Haraway, D. (1989), *Primate Visions: Gender, Race, and Nature in the World of Modern Science* (New York: Routledge).

Haraway, D. (1991), *Symians, Cyborgs and Women: The Re-Invention of Nature* (New York: Routledge).

Harrington, M. (1989), *Socialism Past and Future* (New York: Arcade Publishing).

Hartsock, N. (1998), *The Feminist Standpoint Revisited and Other Essays* (Boulder, Col.: Westview Press).

Hebron, L. and Stack, J. F. (2011), *Globalization* (Boston, M.A.: Longman).

Held, D. (1993), "Democracy: From City-States to a Cosmopolitan Order? In D. Held (ed.), *Prospects for Democracy: North, South, East, West*, 13–52 (Cambridge: Polity Press).

Held, D. (1995), *Democracy and the Global Order: From the Modern State to Cosmopolitan Governance* (Cambridge: Polity Press).

Held, D., and McGrew, A. (2002), *Globalization/Anti-Globalization* (Cambridge: Polity Press; 2nd ed., 2007).

Henderson J., Jackson, K., and Kennaway, R. (eds.) (1980), *Beyond New Zealand: The Foreign Policy of a Small State* (Auckland, N.Z.: Methuen).

Hennessy, R., and Ingraham, C. (eds.) (1997), *Materialist Feminism: A Reader in Class, Difference, and Women's Lives* (London: Routledge).

Hettne, B. (1999), "Globalization and the New Regionalism: The Second Great Transformation." In B. Hettne, A. Intoai, and O. Sunkel (eds.), *Globalism and the New Regionalism* (Basingstoke: Macmillan).

Higgins, R. (1994), *Problems and Process: International Law and How We Use It* (Oxford: Oxford University Press).

Hill, C. (2003), *The Changing Politics of Foreign Policy* (Houndmills, Basingstoke: Palgrave Macmillan).

Hirst, P., and Thompson, G. (1999), *Globalization in Question: The International Economy and the Possibilities of Governance* (Cambridge: Polity Press).

Holbraad, C. (1984), *Middle Powers in International Politics* (London: Macmillan).

Holsti, K. (1991), *Peace and War: Armed Conflicts and International Order 1648–1989* (Cambridge: Cambridge University Press).

Homer-Dixon, T. (1991), "On the Threshold: Environmental Changes as Causes of Acute Conflict," *International Security* 16: 76–116.

Homer-Dixon, T. (1994), "Environmental Scarcities and Violent Conflict: Evidence from Cases," *International Security* 19(1): 5–40.

Hudson, V. (2007), *Foreign Policy Analysis. Classic and Contemporary Theory* (Lanham, MD: Rowman and Littlefield).

Human Security Report Project. *Human Security Report 2012: Sexual Violence, Education, and War: Beyond the Mainstream Narrative* (Vancouver, Human Security Press, 2012).

Humphreys, M., and Varshney, A. (2004), "Violent Conflict and the Millennium Development: Goals: Diagnosis and Recommendations," CGSD Working Paper No. 19 (New York: Center on Globalization and Sustainable Development, The Earth Institute at Columbia University). http://www.earthinstitute.columbia.edu/cgsd/documents/humphreys_conflict_and_MDG.pdf (accessed June 25, 2007).

Huntington, S. (1993), "The Clash of Civilizations," *Foreign Affairs* 72(3): 22–169.

Huntington, S. (1996), *The Clash of Civilizations and the Remaking of the World Order* (New York: Simon & Schuster).

Hurrell, A. and Woods, N. (1995), "Globalization and Inequality," *Millennium*, 24(3): 447–70.

Hymans, J. E. (2006). *The Psychology of Nuclear Proliferation* (Cambridge: Cambridge University Press).

Ikenberry, G. J. (1999), "Liberal Hegemony and the Future of American Post-War Order." In T. V. Paul and J. A. Hall (eds.), *International Order and the Future of World Politics*, 123–145 (Cambridge: Cambridge University Press).

Ingebritsen, C., Neumann, I., Gstohl, S., and Beyer, J. (2006), *Small States in International Relations* (Seattle: University of Washington Press).

Intergovernmental Panel on Climate Change (IPCC) (2007), *Climate Change 2007: The Physical Science BASIS*, Contribution of Working Group 1 to the Fourth Assessment Report of the Intergovernmental Panel on Climate Change. www.ipcc.ch.

International Commissionon Intervention and Sovereignty (2001), *The Responsibility to Protect* (Ottawa, Canada: International Development Research Centre).

International Commission on Peace and Food (ICPF) (1994), *Uncommon Opportunities: An Agenda for Peace and Equitable Development* (London: Zed).

Jolly, R., and Ray, D. B. (2006), *National Human Development Reports and the Human Security Framework: A Review of Analysis and Experience* (Brighton: Institute of Development Studies).

Junaid, S. (2005), *Terrorism and Global Power Systems* (Oxford: Oxford University Press).

Kant, I. (1991), *Political Writings*, Hans Reiss (ed.) (Cambridge: Cambridge University Press).

Karp, A. (1995), *Ballistic Missile Proliferation: The Politics and Technics* (Oxford: Oxford University Press for Stockholm International Peace Research Institute).

Keck, M., and Sikkink, K. (1998), *Activists Beyond Borders: Transnational Advocacy Networks in International Politics* (Ithaca, N.Y.: Cornell University Press).

Keohane, R. (1984), *After Hegemony: Cooperation and Discord in the World Political Economy* (Princeton, N.J.: Princeton University Press).

Keohane, R. (ed.) (1989a), *International Institutions and State Power: Essays in International Relations Theory* (Boulder, Col.: Westview Press).

Keohane, R. (1989b), "Theory of World Politics: Structural Realism and Beyond." In R. Keohane (ed.), *International Institutions and State Power: Essays in International Relations Theory* (Boulder, Col.: Westview Press).

Keohane, R. (2002a), "The Globalization of Informal Violence, Theories of World Politics, and the 'Liberalism of Fear.'" In R. Keohane (ed.), *Power and Governance in a Partially Globalized World*, 272–287 (London: Routledge).

Keohane, R. (2002b), "The Public Delegitimation of Terrorism and Coalitional Politics." In K. Booth and T. Dunne (eds.), *Worlds in Collision: Terror and the Future of Global Order*, 141–151 (London: Palgrave Macmillan).

Keohane, R., and Nye, J. (eds.) (1972), *Transnational Relations and World Politics* (Cambridge, Mass.: Harvard University Press).

Kinsella, H. M. (2003), "For a Careful Reading: The Conservativism of Gender Constructivism," *International Studies Review* 5: 294–297.

Kinsella, H. M. (2005a), "Discourses of Difference: Civilians, Combatants, and Compliance with the Laws of War," *Review of International Studies* (Special Issue): 163–185.

Kinsella, H. M. (2005b), "Securing the Civilian: Sex and Gender and Laws of War." In M. Barnett and R. Duvall (eds.), *Power in Global Governance*, 249–272 (Cambridge: Cambridge University Press).

Kinsella, H. M. (2006), "Gendering Grotius: Sex and Sex Difference in the Laws of War," *Political Theory* 34(2): 161–191.

Kirkpatrick, J. (1979), "Dictatorships and Double Standards," *Commentary* 68(5): 34–45.

Kissinger, H. A. (1977), *American Foreign Policy*, 3rd ed. (New York: W. W. Norton).

Knutsen, T. (1997), *A History of International Relations* (Manchester, UK: Manchester University Press).

Koehler, S. (February 7, 2007), "Professor Explains Continuous Threat from Land Mines," *Ozarks Local News*. http://www.banminesusa.org (accessed June 25, 2007).

Krause, K., and Williams, M. C. (eds.) (1997), *Critical Security Studies: Concepts and Cases* (London: UCL Press).

Laqueur, W. (1996), "Post-Modern Terrorism," *Foreign Affairs* 75(5): 24–37.

Lavoy, P. (1995), "The Strategic Consequences of Nuclear Proliferation: A Review Essay," *Security Studies* 4(4): 695–753.

Leventhal, P., and Alexander, Y. (eds.) (1987), *Preventing Nuclear Terrorism* (Lexington, Mass., and Toronto: Lexington Books).

Lind, W. S. and Colleagues (1989, 23), The Changing Face of War: Into the Fourth Generation William S. Lind, Colonel Keith Nightengale (USA), Captain John F. Schmitt (USMC), Colonel Joseph W. Sutton (USA), and Lieutenant Colonel Gary I. Wilson (USMCR). *Marine Corps Gazette*. October 1989, 22–26.

Little, R. (1996), "The Growing Relevance of Pluralism?" In S. Smith, K. Booth, and M. Zalewski (eds.), *International Theory: Positivism and Beyond*, 66–86 (Cambridge: Cambridge University Press).

Longino, H. E. (1990), *Science as Social Knowledge: Values and Objectivity in Scientific Inquiry* (Princeton, N.J.: Princeton University Press).

Luard, E. (ed.) (1992), *Basic Texts in International Relations* (London: Macmillan).

MacFarlane, N., and Khong Yuen Foong (2006), *Human Security and the UN: A Critical History* (Bloomington: Indiana University Press).

Mackinnon, C. (1993), "Crimes of War, Crimes of Peace." In S. Shute and S. Hurley (eds.), *On Human Rights* (New York: Basic Books).

Marx, K. (1888), "Theses on Feuerbach." In *Selected Works*, K. Marx and F. Engels, 28–30 (London: Lawrence and Wishart, 1968).

Marx, K., and Engels, F. (1848), *The Communist Manifesto*, intr. by E. Hobsbawm (London: Verso, 1998).

Marx, K. (1992), *Capital*, student ed. C. J. Arthur (ed.) (London: Lawrence & Wishart). First published 1867.

Mathews, J. (1997), "Power Shift," *Foreign Affairs* 76(1): 50–66.

Mead, W. R. (2001), *Special Providence: American Foreign Policy and How It Changed the World* (New York: Alfred A. Knopf).

Meadows, D. H., Meadows, D. L., and Randers, J. (1972), *The Limits to Growth* (London: Earth Island).

Mearsheimer, J. (1994–1995), "The False Promise of International Institutions," *International Security* 19(3): 5–49.

Mearsheimer, J. (2001), *The Tragedy of Great Power Politics* (New York: W. W. Norton).

Metz, S. (2004), *Armed Conflict in the 21st Century: The Information Revolution and Post Modern Warfare* (Honolulu, Haw.: University Press of the Pacific).

Meyer, S. M. (1984), *The Dynamics of Nuclear Proliferation* (Chicago: University of Chicago Press).

Milner, H. V. (1988), *Resisting Protectionism: Global Industries and the Politics of International Trade* (Princeton, N.J.: Princeton University Press).

Mingst, K. (2004), *Essentials of International Relations* (New York: W. W. Norton).

Mitrany, D. (1943), *A Working Peace System* (London: RIIA).

Morgenthau, H. J. ([1948] 1955, 1962, 1978), *Politics Among Nations: The Struggle for Power and Peace*, 2nd ed. (New York: Alfred A. Knopf).

Morgenthau, H. J. (1952), *American Foreign Policy: A Critical Examination* (also published as *In Defence of the National Interest*) (London: Methuen).

Morgenthau, H. J. (1960), *Politics Among Nations* (New York: Alfred A. Knopf).

Morgenthau, H. J. (1985), *Politics Among Nations*, 6th ed. (New York: McGraw-Hill).

Mousseau, F., and Mittal, A. (October 26, 2006), Free Market Famine: Foreign Policy in Focus Commentary. www.fpif.org/pdf/gac/0610famine.pdf (accessed June 25, 2007).

Muldoon, J. (2004), *The Architecture of Global Governance: An Introduction to the Study of International Organizations* (Boulder, CO: Westview Press).

Naisbitt, J. (1994), *Global Paradox: The Bigger the World-Economy, the More Powerful Its Smallest Players* (London: Brealey).

Nardin, T. (1983.), *Law, Morality and the Relations of States* (Princeton, N.J.: Princeton University Press).

National Counter Terrorism Center (2005), NCTC Fact Sheet and Observations Related to 2005 Terrorist Incidents. www.NCTC.gov (accessed June 25, 2007).

National Security Strategy (2001, 2002). *National Security Strategy of the United States of America* (Washington, D.C.: US Government Printing Office).

Norchi, C. (2004), "Human Rights: A Global Common Interest." In Jean Krasno, ed., *The United Nations: Confronting the Challenges of a Global Society* (Lynne Rienner Publishers).

Nussbaum, M. (1996), *For Love of Country: Debating the Limits of Patriotism* (Boston: Beacon Press).

Nye, J. S. (2004), *Soft Power* (New York: Public Affairs).

O'Brien, R. (1992), *Global Financial Integration: The End of Geography* (London: Pinter).

Office of the Director of National Intelligence (2005), Letter from Al-Zawahiri to Al-Zarqawi, October 11.

Ogilvie-White, T. (1996), "Is There a Theory of Nuclear Proliferation?" *The Nonproliferation Review* 4(1): 43–60.

Ogilvie-White, T., and Simpson, J. (2003), "The NPT and Its Prepcom Session: A Regime in Need of Intensive Care," *The Nonproliferation Review* 10(1): 40–58.

Olson, J. S. (ed.) (1988), *Dictionary of the Vietnam War* (New York: Greenwood Press).

Onwudiwe, I. D. (2001), *The Globalization of Terror* (Burlington, Vt.: Ashgate).

Ougaard, M. (2004), *Political Globalization—State, Power and Social Forces* (London: Palgrave).

Owens, P. (2007), *Between War and Politics: International Relations and the Thought of Hannah Arendt* (Oxford: Oxford University Press).

Oxfam (2003). "Boxing Match in Agricultural Trade," Briefing Paper No. 32. www.oxfam.org (accessed June 25, 2007).

Oxfam (2006), Grounds for Change: Creating a Voice for Small Farmers and Farm Workers with Next International Coffee Agreement. http://www .oxfam.org/en/policy/briefingnotes/bn0604_coffee _groundsforchange (accessed June 25, 2007).

Palme Commission (1982), *Common Security: A Programme for Disarmament. The Report of the Palme Commission* (London: Pan Books).

Panofsky, W. K. H. (1998), "Dismantling the Concept of 'Weapons of Mass Destruction,'" *Arms Control Today* 28(3): 3–8.

Pape, R. (2006), *Dying to Win: The Strategic Logic of Suicide Terrorism* (New York: Random House).

Pastor, R. (1999), *A Century's Journey: How the Great Powers Shape the World* (New York: Basic Books).

Pearson, R. (2000), "Rethinking Gender Matters in Development." In T. Allen and A. Thomas (eds.), *Poverty and Development into the Twenty-First Century*, 383–402 (Oxford: Oxford University Press).

Pendergrast, M. (1993), *For God, Country and Coca-Cola: The Unauthorized History of the Great American Soft Drink and the Company That Makes It* (London: Weidenfeld & Nicolson).

Peters, J. S., and Wolper, A. (eds.) (1995), *Women's Rights, Human Rights: International Feminist Perspectives* (New York: Routledge).

Petzold-Bradley, E., Carius, A., and Vincze, A. (eds.) (2001), *Responding to Environmental Conflicts: Implications for Theory and Practice* (Dordrecht, the Netherlands: Kluwer Academic).

Pogge, T. (2002), *World Poverty and Human Rights: Cosmopolitan Responsibilities and Reforms* (Cambridge: Polity Press).

Power and Interest News Report (2006), "Asia's Coming Water Wars," August 22. http://www.pinr.com (accessed June 25, 2007).

Price, R. (1998), "Reversing the Gun Sights: Transnational Civil Society Targets Land Mines," *International Organization* 52(3): 613–644.

Price, R., and Tannenwald, N. (1996), "Norms and Deterrence: The Nuclear and Chemical Weapons Taboos." In P. J. Katzenstein (ed.), *The Culture of National Security: Norms and Identity in World Politics*, 114–152 (New York: Columbia University Press).

Pugh, M. (2001), "Peacekeeping and Humanitarian Intervention." In B. White, R. Little, and M. Smith (eds.), *Issues in World Politics*, 2nd ed. (London: Palgrave).

Rabasa, A., Chalk, P., et al. (2006), *Beyond al-Qaeda: Part 2, The Outer Rings of the Terrorist Universe* (Santa Monica, Cal.: RAND).

Rapley, J. (1996,) *Understanding Development* (Boulder, Col.: Lynne Rienner).

Rehn, E., and Sirleaf, E. J. (2002), Women, War, Peace: The Independent Experts' Assessment on the Impact of Armed Conflict on Women and Women's Role in Peace-Building. http://www.unifem.org/resources/ item_detail.php?ProductID=17 (accessed June 25, 2007).

Reus-Smit, C. (1999), *The Moral Purpose of the State* (Princeton, N.J.: Princeton University Press).

Reus-Smit, C. (2001a), "The Strange Death of Liberal International Theory," *European Journal of International Law* 12(3): 573–593.

Rhodes, E. (2003), "The Imperial Logic of Bush's Liberal Agenda," *Survival* 45: 131–154.

Rice, S. (2006), "The Threat of Global Poverty," *The National Interest* 83: 76–82.

Richardson, J. L. (1997), "Contending Liberalisms: Past and Present," *European Journal of International Relations* 3(1): 5–33.

Rischard, J. F. (2002), *High Noon: Twenty Global Problems, Twenty Years to Solve Them* (New York: Basic Books).

Roberts, A. (1996), "The United Nations: Variants of Collective Security." In N. Woods (ed.), *Explaining International Relations Since 1945*, 309–336 (Oxford: Oxford University Press).

Roberts, A., and Kingsbury, B. (1993), "Introduction: The UN's Roles in International Society Since 1945." In A. Roberts and B. Kingsbury (eds.), *United Nations, Divided World* (Oxford: Clarendon Press).

Roberts, G. (1984), *Questioning Development* (London: Returned Volunteer Action).

Roberts, S. (1994), "Fictitious Capital, Fictitious Spaces: The Geography of Offshore Financial Flows." In S. Corbridge et al. (eds.), *Money, Power and Space* (Oxford: Blackwell).

Roche, D. (1986), "Balance Out of Kilter in Arms/Society Needs," *Financial Post,* January 18, 8.

Rodrik, D. (1999), *The New Global Economy and Developing Countries: Making Openness Work* (Washington, D.C.: Overseas Development Council, 148).

Rorty, R. (1993), "Sentimentality and Human Rights." In S. Shute and S. Hurley (eds.), *On Human Rights* (New York: Basic Books).

Rosamond, B. (2000), *Theories of European Integration* (Basingstoke: Macmillan).

Rose, G. (1998), "Neoclassical Realism and Theories of Foreign Policy," *World Politics* 51(1): 144–172.

Rosenau, J. (1981), *The Study of Political Adaptation* (London: Pinter Publishers).

Sagan, S. D., and Waltz, K. N. (1995), *The Spread of Nuclear Weapons: A Debate* (New York and London: W. W. Norton; 2nd ed., 2003).

Sageman, M. (2004), *Understanding Terror Networks* (Philadelphia: University of Pennsylvania Press).

Sargent, L. (ed.) (1981), *Women and Revolution: A Discussion of the Unhappy Marriage of Marxism and Feminism* (Boston: South End).

Scholte, J. A. (2005), *Globalization: A Critical Introduction* (Basingstoke, UK: Macmillan; 2nd ed., 2005).

Schwarz, A. (1999), *A Nation in Waiting: Indonesia's Search for Stability* (Sydney: Allen & Unwin).

Schweller, R. L. (1996), "Neo-Realism's Status-Quo Bias: What Security Dilemma?" *Security Studies* 5: 90–121.

Schweller, R. L. (1998), *Deadly Imbalances: Tripolarity and Hitler's Strategy of World Conquest* (New York: Columbia University Press).

Seidler, V. (1989), *Rediscovering Masculinity: Reason, Language and Sexuality* (London: Routledge).

Sen, A. (1981), *Poverty and Famines* (Oxford: Clarendon Press).

Sen, A. (1983), "The Food Problem: Theory and Policy." In A. Gauhar (ed.), *South–South Strategy* (London: Zed).

Sen, A. (1999), *Development as Freedom* (Oxford: Oxford University Press).

Shue, H. (1996), *Basic Rights*, 2nd ed. (Princeton, N.J.: Princeton University Press).

Simon Fraser University, Human Security Research Group (2011), "Human Security Report 2009–2010", Retrieved from: http:// www.hsrgroup.org/human-security-reports/20092010/text.aspx

Smith, K. E., and Light, M. (eds.) (2001), *Ethics and Foreign Policy* (Cambridge: Cambridge University Press).

Smith, M. J. (1986), *Realist Thought from Weber to Kissinger* (Baton Rouge: Louisiana State University Press).

Smith, M. J. (2002), "On Thin Ice: First Steps for the Ballistic Missile Code of Conduct," *Arms Control Today* 32(6): 9–13.

Smith, S. (1999), "The Increasing Insecurity of Security Studies: Conceptualising Security in the Last Twenty Years," *Contemporary Security Policy* 20(3).

Spivak, G. C. (1988), "Can the Subaltern Speak?" In C. Nelson and L. Grossberg (eds.), *Marxism and the Interpretation of Culture* (Basingstoke: Macmillan).

Steans, J. (1998), *Gender and International Relations: An Introduction* (Cambridge: Polity Press).

Suganami, H. (1989), *The Domestic Analogy and World Order Proposals* (Cambridge: Cambridge University Press).

Suhrke, A. (2004), "A Stalled Initiative," *Security Dialogue* 35(3): 365.

Tang, J. H. (ed.) (1994), *Human Rights and International Relations in the Asia-Pacific Region* (London: Pinter).

Thomas, A., et al. (1994), *Third World Atlas*, 2nd ed. (Milton Keynes: Open University Press).

Thomas, C. (2000), *Global Governance, Development and Human Security* (London: Pluto).

Thomas, C., and Wilkin, P. (2004), "Still Waiting After All These Years: The Third World on the Periphery of International Relations," *British Journal of Politics and International Relations* 6: 223–240.

Thucydides ([1954] 1972), *The Peloponnesian War*, R. Warner (trans.) (London: Penguin).

Tickner, J. A. (1992), *Gender in International Relations: Feminist Perspectives on Achieving Global Security* (New York: Columbia University Press).

Tow, W. T., and Trood, R. (2000), "Linkages Between Traditional Security and Human Security." In W. T. Tow, R. Thakur, and In-Taek Hyun (eds.), *Asia's Emerging Regional Order* (New York: United Nations University Press).

UN Conference on Trade and Development, Division on Transnational Corporations and Investment (1996), *Transnational Corporations and World Development* (London: International Thomson Business Press).

UN Conference on Trade and Development (2006a), *Trade and Development Report* (Geneva: United Nations Conference on Trade and Development).

UN Conference on Trade and Development (2006b), *World Investment Report 2006* (Geneva: United Nations Conference on Trade and Development).

UN Development Programme (1994), *United Nations Human Development Report* (New York: Oxford University Press).

UN Development Programme (1997), *United Nations Human Development Report 1997* (New York: United Nations Development Programme).

UN Development Programme (1998), *United Nations Human Development Report 1998* (Oxford: Oxford University Press).

UN Development Programme (2003), *United Nations Human Development Report* (New York: United Nations Development Programme).

UN Development Programme (2005), *Human Development Report 2005: International Cooperation at a Crossroads* (New York: United Nations Development Programme).

United Nations (2002), *Women, Peace and Security: Study Submitted by the Secretary-General Pursuant to Security Council Resolution 1325 (2000)* (New York: United Nations). http://www.un.org/womenwatch/feature/wps/ (accessed June 25, 2007).

United Nations (2004), *A More Secure World.* UN Secretary-General's High-Level Panel on Threats, Challenges and Change. http://www.un.org/secureworld

United Nations (March 2005), *In Larger Freedom: Towards Development, Security and Human Rights for All: Report of the Secretary-General.*

United Nations Inter-Agency Committee on Women and Gender Equality (December 7–8, 1999), *Final Communiqué, Women's Empowerment in the Context of Human Security* (Bangkok, Thailand: ESCAP). http://www.un.org/womenwatch/ianwge/collaboration/finalcomm1999.htm (accessed June 25, 2007).

University of British Columbia, Human Security Center (2005), *Human Security Report 2005: War and Peace in the 21st Century* (New York: Oxford University Press).

University of British Columbia, Human Security Center (2006), *The Human Security Brief 2006.* http://www.humansecuritybrief.info/ (accessed June 25, 2007).

Uppsala Conflict Data Program (UCDP), *Uppsala University, Uppsala, Sweden/ Human Security Report Project, School for International Studies,* Simon Fraser University, Vancouver, Canada.

US Department of State (March 31, 2003), *Country Reports on Human Rights Practices, Burma.* http://www.state.gov/g/drl/rls/hrrpt/2002/18237.htm (accessed June 25, 2007).

Vincent, R. J. (1974), *Nonintervention and International Order* (Princeton, N.J.: Princeton University Press).

von Grebmer, K., Headey, D., Olofinbiyi, T., . . . and Haddad, L. (2013). "2013 Global Hunger Index—The Challenge of Hunger: Building Resilience to Achieve Food and Nutrition Security. "Global Hunger Index Scores by Severity" map." Bonn, Germany: Welthungerhilfe; Washington, DC: International Food Policy Research Institute; Dublin, Ireland: Concern Worldwide.

Wallerstein, I. (1979), *The Capitalist World-Economy* (Cambridge: Cambridge University Press).

Walt, S. (2002), "The Enduring Relevance of the Realist Tradition." In I. Katznelson and H. V. Milner (eds.), *Political Science: The State of the Discipline* (New York: W. W. Norton).

Waltz, K. (1959), *Man, the State and War* (New York: Columbia University Press).

Waltz, K. (1979), *Theory of International Politics* (Reading, Mass.: Addison-Wesley).

Waltz, K. (1989), "The Origins of War in Neorealist Theory." In R. I. Rotberg and T. K. Rabb (eds.), *The Origin and Prevention of Major Wars*, 39–52 (Cambridge: Cambridge University Press).

Walzer, M. (1977), *Just and Unjust Wars: A Moral Argument with Historical Illustration* (Harmondsworth: Penguin and New York: Basic Books).

Walzer, M. (1994), *Thick and Thin: Moral Argument at Home and Abroad* (Notre Dame, Ind.: University of Notre Dame Press).

Walzer, M. (1995), "The Politics of Rescue," *Dissent* (Winter): 35–40.

Weaver, O., Buzan, B., Kelstrup, M., and Lemaitre, P. (1993), *Identity, Migration and the New Security Agenda in Europe* (London: Pinter).

Weber, H. (2002), "Global Governance and Poverty Reduction." In S. Hughes and R. Wilkinson (eds.), *Global Governance: Critical Perspectives* (London: Palgrave).

Weber, M. (1949), *The Methodology of the Social Sciences*, E. Shils and H. Finch (eds.) (New York: Free Press).

Weiss, T. G. (2004), "The Sunset of Humanitarian Intervention? The Responsibility to Protect in a Unipolar Era," *Security Dialogue* 35(2): 135–153.

Wendt, A. (1992), "Anarchy Is What States Make of It: The Social Construction of Power Politics," *International Organisation* 46(2): 391–425.

Wendt, A. (1995), "Constructing International Politics," *International Security* 20(1).

Wendt, A. (1999), *Social Theory of International Politics* (Cambridge: Cambridge University Press).

Wessel, I., and Wimhofer, G. (eds.) (2001), *Violence in Indonesia* (Hamburg: Abera-Verl).

Weston, B. H., Falk, R., and D'Amato, A. (1990), *Basic Documents in International Law*, 2nd ed. (St. Paul, Minn.: West Publishing).

Wheeler, N. J., and Booth, K. (1992), "The Security Dilemma." In J. Baylis and N. J. Rengger (eds.), *Dilemmas of World Politics: International Issues in a Changing World* (Oxford: Oxford University Press).

Wiener, A., and Diez, T. (eds.) (2004), *European Integration Theory* (Oxford: Oxford University Press).

Wilkinson, P. (2003), "Implications of the Attacks of 9/11 for the Future of Terrorism." In M. Buckley and R. Fawn (eds.), *Global Responses to Terrorism* (London: Routledge).

Wood, B. (1998), *The Middle Powers and the General Interest* (Ottawa: North-South Institute).

World Health Organization (n.d.), Roll Back Malaria: The Economic Costs of Malaria (Geneva: WHO). http://www.rbm.who.int/cmc_upload/0/000/015/363/RBMInfosheet_10.htm (accessed June 25, 2007).

World Health Organization (February 2006), Avian Influenza ("Bird Flu")—Fact Sheet. www.who.int/mediacentre/factsheets/avian_influenza/en/ (accessed June 25, 2007).

World Trade Organization (1995), *International Trade: Trends and Statistics* (Geneva: WTO).

Wright, R. (1986), *Sacred Rage: The Wrath of Militant Islam* (New York: Simon & Schuster).

Yale University Cambodian Genocide Program. http://www.yale.edu/cgp

Zakaria, F. (1998), *From Wealth to Power: The Unusual Origins of America's World Role* (Princeton, N.J.: Princeton University Press).

Zalewski, M. (1993), "Feminist Standpoint Theory Meets International Relations Theory: A Feminist Version of David and Goliath," *Fletcher Forum of World Affairs* 17(2).

Zalewski, M., and Parpart, J. (eds.) (1998), *The "Man" Question in International Relations* (Boulder, Col.: Westview Press).

Zevin, R. (1992), "Are World Financial Markets More Open? If So, Why and with What Effects?" In T. Banuri and J. B. Schor (eds.), *Financial Openness and National Autonomy: Opportunities and Constraints* (Oxford: Clarendon Press).

Credits

Mark Baker; p. 453: Nurcholis / Rex Features via AP Images; p. 453: MCT via Getty Images; p. 455: AP Photo/NOAA; p. 457: AP Photo/ Marcio Jose Sanchez; p. 457: AP Photo/Wichita Falls Times Record News, Torin Halsey; p. 458: AP Photo/Aris Messinis; p. 459: AP Photo/John McConnico

FIGURE CREDITS

Chapter 2
p. 45: © Natural Resources Defense Council; p. 56: *Vital Signs 2006–2007*, The Worldwatch Institute

Chapter 4
p. 120: Inter-Parliamentary Union

Chapter 5
p. 136: Pew Global Attitudes Project, a project of the Pew Research Center; p. 157: CIA World Factbook

Chapter 6
p. 181: © United Nations; p. 183: "The United Nations System" © United Nations Department of Public Information, 2007.

Chapter 7
p. 219: Union of International Associations; p. 232: 2012 *Global Go To Think Tanks Report and Policy Advic. FINAL UNITED NATIONS UNIVERSITY EDITION, JANUARY 28, 2013. Think Tanks and Civil Societies Program* © *2012, University of Pennsylvania, International Relations Program*

Chapter 8
p. 256: U.S. Congressional Research Service, "Conventional Arms Transfers to Developing Nations, 1999–2006," September 26, 2007, RL34187, Richard F. Grimmett; p. 258: Gizmodo World Conflict Map 2012, *The Atlas of War and Peace*, and Globalmajority. org; p. 261: U.S. Congressional Research Service, "Conventional Arms Transfers to Developing Nations, 2001–2008," September 4, 2009, R40796, Richard F. Grimmett

Chapter 9
p. 287: Office of the Director of National Intelligence, National Counterterrorism Center, "2008 Report on Terrorism," 30 April 2009; p. 295: Office of the Director of National Intelligence, National Counterterrorism Center, "2008 Report on Terrorism," 30 April 2009

Chapter 10
p. 331: Human Security Report Project. Human Security Report 2012: Sexual Violence, Education, and War: Beyond the Mainstream Narrative. Vancouver, Human Security Press, 2012; p. 332: Themnér, Lotta & Peter Wallensteen, 2013. "Armed Conflict, 1946–2012." *Journal of Peace Research* 50(4).

Chapter 11
p. 351: Per capita Real GDP Growth Rates of Main Countries from "On Globalization and the World Economy in 2010 - Prospects and Policy Implications to Japan - The Report of the Globalization Working Group in the Economic Outlook Committee," the

Economic Council, Japan; p.365: Word Trade in 2009/ http.www.abh-ace.org/impor_en/info-center/trade-statistics/ comments-mf/2009/12-months-wto-com_en.pdf/Volume of world merchandise exports, 1965-2009 (Annual % change)/Word Trade Organisation-March 2010

Chapter 12
p. 376: Copyright Philip's; p. 386: WTO Structure / http://www .wto.org/english/thewto_e/whatis_e/tif_e/org2_e.htm; p. 388: Copyright Philip's; p. 393: *Treasury Bulletin* (June 2010), Financial Management Service, U.S. Department of the Treasury

Chapter 13
p. 416: United Nations, based on data and estimates provided by: Food and Agriculture Organization of the United Nations; Inter-Parliamentary Union; International Labour Organization; International Telecommunication Union; UNAIDS; UNESCO; UN-Habitat; UNICEF; UN Population Division; World Bank; World Health Organization – based on statistics available as of June 2013. Compiled by Statistics Division, Department of Economic and Social Affairs, United Nations; p. 426: First and second billion: Population Reference Bureau. Third through ninth billion: United Nations, World Population Prospects: The 1998 Revision (medium scenario). See www.prb.org.

Chapter 14
p. 441: Copyright Philip's; p. 454: Copyright Philip's; p. 455: Netherland's Environmental Assessment Agency

MAP CREDITS

Frontmatter
xxviii–xxix: Cartography © Philip's; xxx: Cartography © Philip's; xxxi: Cartography © Philip's; xxxii: Cartography © Philip's; xxxiii: Cartography © Philip's; xxxiv: Cartography © Philip's; xxxv: Cartography © Philip's

Chapter 2
p. 32: Cartography © Philip's; p. 36: Cartography © Philip's; p, 38: Cartography © Philip's

Chapter 10
p. 323: Freedom in the World 2013: Democratic Breakthroughs in the Balance. Selected Data from Freedom House's Annual Survey of Political Rights and Civil Liberties. Freedom House: http:// www.freedomhouse.org/sites/default/files/FIW%202013%20 Booklet.pdf

Chapter 13
p. 425: von Grember et al. (2013). Reprinted with permission from the International Food Policy Research Institute

Chapter 14
p. 437: Cartography: SASI Group, University of Sheffield; Mark Newman, University of Michigan, 2006 (updated 2008), www .worldmapper.org / Data source: Gregg Marland, Tom Boden, Bob Andres, Oak Ridge National Laboratory. Please note that data for Norway is inaccurate.

Index